CRIMINAL INVESTIGATION

CRIMINAL INVESTIGATION

FOURTH EDITION

Bruce L. Berg
Department of Criminal Justice
California State University, Long Beach

McGraw-Hill
Higher Education

Boston   Burr Ridge, IL   Dubuque, IA   New York   San Francisco   St. Louis
Bangkok   Bogotá   Caracas   Kuala Lumpur   Lisbon   London   Madrid   Mexico City
Milan   Montreal   New Delhi   Santiago   Seoul   Singapore   Sydney   Taipei   Toronto

McGraw-Hill
Higher Education

Published by McGraw-Hill, an imprint of The McGraw-Hill Companies, Inc., 1221 Avenue of the Americas, New York, NY 10020. Copyright © 2008. All rights reserved. No part of this publication may be reproduced or distributed in any form or by any means, or stored in a database or retrieval system, without the prior written consent of The McGraw-Hill Companies, Inc., including, but not limited to, in any network or other electronic storage or transmission, or broadcast for distance learning.

♲ This book is printed on acid-free paper.

3 4 5 6 7 8 9 0 QPD/QPD 0 9

ISBN: 978-0-07-340124-9
MHID: 0-07-340124-2

Editor in Chief: *Emily Barrosse*
Publisher: *Frank Mortimer*
Senior Sponsoring Editor: *Katie Stevens*
Marketing Manager: *Lori DeShazo*
Developmental Editor: *Craig Leonard*
Editorial Coordinator: *Teresa Treacy*
Associate Production Editor: *Alison Meier*
Text Designer: *Kay Lieberherr*
Cover Designer: *Preston Thomas*
Art Editor: *Ayelet Arbel*
Illustrators: *Dartmouth Publishing, Inc. and Ayelet Arbel*
Photo Research: *Brian J. Pecko*
Production Supervisor: *Randy Hurst*
Composition: *11/13 Garamond by Aptara, Inc.*
Printing: *PMS 147, 45# New Era Matte Recycled, Quebecor World*

Cover: © Douglas Keister/Corbis

Credits: The credits section for this book begins on page 517 and is considered an extension of the copyright page.

Library of Congress Cataloging-in-Publication Data

Berg, Bruce L. (Bruce Lawrence), 1954–
    Criminal investigation / Bruce Berg.—4th ed.
        p. cm.
    Includes bibliographical references and index.
    ISBN 13: 978-0-07-340124-9; ISBN 10: 0-07-340124-2 (alk. paper)
    1. Criminal investigation. I. Title.
HV8073.B435 2007
363.25—dc22

                                    2007010569

The Internet addresses listed in the text were accurate at the time of publication. The inclusion of a Web site does not indicate an endorsement by the authors or McGraw-Hill, and McGraw-Hill does not guarantee the accuracy of the information presented at these sites.

BRIEF CONTENTS

CONTENTS

PART TWO   Gathering and Organizing Information

PART THREE   Crimes against People

PART FOUR   Crimes against Property

PART FIVE   Enterprise Crimes

PART SIX   Terrorism and Cyber Predators

PREFACE

Crime continues to be a serious problem in society, and advances in technology have created new criminal opportunities and new challenges for law enforcement. Those involved in the investigation of crime play a critical role in both combating crime and protecting citizens. *Criminal Investigation, Fourth Edition*, integrates modern instruments of investigation with practical elements of crime detection and investigation. Along with traditional topics involved in criminal investigation, this edition features updated and expanded coverage of timely and important topics such as terrorism and homeland security, cyber criminals, identity theft, white-collar crimes, identification and use of physical evidence, digitized fingerprints, DNA analysis, report writing, interviewing and interrogations, and much more.

Thanks to television programs such as *CSI* and its spin-offs, many people confuse crime scene investigation, forensics, and criminal investigation. A growing number of students enter criminal justice and criminology programs thinking they will become crime scene investigators just like the ones they see on television. They are surprised to learn that CSIs are chiefly civilians, do not carry guns or badges, do not analyze physical evidence (although they do collect evidence), do not apprehend or interrogate suspects or witnesses, nor do they have any arrest powers—you've got to love television! Criminal investigators, on the other hand, actually are involved in all of these activities to some extent.

Opportunities in investigation have changed since the terrorist attacks of September 11, 2001. New areas of federal law enforcement have opened up, and different approaches to investigation have been taken at the local level. *Criminal Investigation* does explore a number of changes at the federal level but remains focused mainly on criminal investigation at the local level. The book is intended as a practical, down-to-earth, nuts-and-bolts examination of various contemporary aspects of criminal investigation, with special attention placed on helping students better understand the legal aspects of collecting and processing evidence to ensure that their work will stand up in court.

ORGANIZATION OF THE TEXT

For maximum flexibility, the content is divided into twenty-two chapters, separated into six sections, that can easily be customized for quarter or semester courses. Part 1 provides a general orientation to investigation. These chapters introduce the student to the broad field of investigation, the basics of establishing whether a crime has been committed, and the use of inductive and deductive reasoning (Chapter 1); preliminary and secondary investigations (Chapter 2); preservation of the crime scene, various patterns of search, and sketching and photographing the scene, with a new discussion on the use of **digital photography** (Chapter 3); the nature of physical evidence, including an **updated and expanded discussion on DNA** and the use of blood-typing, as well as consideration of various other types of physical evidence and trace evidence, and the value of evidence when presented in court (Chapter 4); and identification of criminal patterns and *modus operandi,* an examination of psychological profiling, and a new section on **geographic profiling,** a recent computer-augmented strategy being used with increasing success (Chapter 5). Court decisions are offered and discussed when relevant to various topics throughout the text.

Part 2 describes various activities undertaken by criminal investigators. These involve conducting interviews and interrogations, including an exploration of cognitive interviewing and the **Reid method of behavioral analysis** interviews, and a review of various types of witnesses (Chapter 6); locating, developing, and using fingerprints, automated fingerprint indexing systems, and a new discussion on **biometric automated toolsets,** which are portable digitized fingerprint devices being tested in Iraq to identify terrorists in the field (Chapter 7); descriptions of how to conduct surveillance, including various types of surveillance and technological advances in surveillance, with a new section on **facial recognition systems** and procedures for tracing and locating people (Chapter 8); and writing various common investigative reports and their value, characteristics of good report writing, and mechanical elements of standard police reports (Chapter 9).

Part 3 describes the major categories of crimes against people. These include robbery (Chapter 10), assault (Chapter 11), sexual assault and rape (Chapter 12), kidnapping and extortion (Chapter 13) and homicide (Chapter 14). Each chapter discusses the *corpus delicti* (necessary elements) of the crime. Chapter 10 considers various categories of robbery including a new consideration of **automated teller robberies,** discussion of types of robbers, and various response approaches to robberies in progress. Chapter 11 details the categories of assault and has expanded discussions on **stalking** and **intrafamily violence.** Chapter 12 offers an expanded discussion on **sexual crime classifications,** a new description of **rape-murder categories,** a new discussion and **differentiation between child molesters and pedophiles,** and a section on interviewing child victims of sex crimes. Chapter 13 considers kidnapping and development of the Lindbergh Act. Descriptions also include the various stages in a kidnapping and procedures for undertaking a kidnapping investigation. Chapter 13 further explores extortion and hostage taking and the rules guiding hostage negotiations. Chapter 14 discusses various categories of homicide, both illegal and justifiable. The chapter also offers a new section on **murder and *corpus delicti,*** explaining how a murder suspect may be brought to trial even in the absence of a body. Various modes and motives for homicide are discussed as well as methods for estimating the time of death; there is also a new discussion on the **body farm.**

Part 4 examines major categories of crimes against property. These include burglary (Chapter 15), larceny-theft (Chapter 16), motor vehicle theft (Chapter 17), and arson and bombing investigations (Chapter 18). Chapter 15 outlines various categories of burglars and modes of accomplishing burglaries. A new section is offered on **victims of burglary,** and various modes of safe burglaries are described. Chapter 16 considers categories of larceny, including exploration of grand and petty theft and shoplifting. As well, Chapter 16 considers fraud and flim-flam and offers a newly expanded discussion on **counterfeiting.** The section on **telemarketing and mail fraud** has been expanded, and a new section on **identity theft** has been added. Chapter 17 explores the crimes associated with motor vehicle theft, including consideration of different types of motor vehicle thefts, descriptions of how to investigate motor vehicle thefts, and techniques to prevent motor vehicle thefts. Chapter 18 delves into the crimes of arson and bombing, providing a new discussion on **fire classifications** and descriptions of how to investigate arsons. The section on bombs and bombings has been significantly expanded to include discussions on **investigating bombs and bombings,**

methods for disposing of unexploded bombs, investigating an exploded bomb, and a new section on **suicide bombings.**

Part 5 examines enterprise crimes, including organized crime (Chapter 19), white-collar crimes (Chapter 20), and narcotics and dangerous drugs (Chapter 21). Chapter 19 outlines what organized crime is and describes a number of significant **organized criminal groups,** all of which have been expanded and extensively updated. Chapter 20 explores the difference between white-collar crime in general and occupational crimes in particular. The chapter examines a number of categories of white-collar crimes including updated sections on **embezzlement and employee thefts, insider trading,** and a new section on **computers and cyber crime,** which addresses how to **investigate computer crimes,** and the **latent nature of electronic evidence.** Chapter 21 discusses the sinister world of narcotics investigation, explaining **what narcotics are.** Descriptions of various types of narcotics have been expanded for this edition. The examination of hallucinogens now includes new sections on **nutmeg and mace, kava, and ecstasy (MDMA).**

Part 6 focuses on two serious contemporary problems confronting law enforcement: terrorism and cyber predators. The third edition of *Criminal Investigation* had the distinction of being the first criminal investigation text to include a chapter on terrorism. In this edition, this chapter has been completely revamped and updated **to reflect the changes in government agencies and investigative approaches** since the September 11, 2001, terrorist attacks. The chapter also examines the frightening world of **cyber terrorism** and **cyber predators,** including **child pornography on the Internet** and **child sexual tourism.**

This edition of *Criminal Investigation* contains hundreds of new references to ensure substantive documentation and timely relevance to the process of criminal investigation. Critical Thinking Exercises and Investigative Skill Builders, many of which have been updated, can be found at the end of each chapter.

FEATURES

Focus on Technology

Focus on Technology highlights a variety of technologies available to criminal investigators. These technologies range from computerized criminal investigation systems to crime scene sketching software, and from reflective ultraviolet photography to trace explosives detectors. This feature appears in each chapter, providing a practical introduction to the wide range of technologies available to help investigators do their jobs.

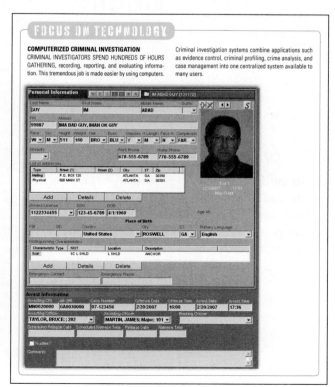

Career Focus

Career Focus presents useful information about employment opportunities for criminal investigators. Included are such careers as police detective, corporate investigator, and foreign service special agent.

CAREER FOCUS

POLICE DETECTIVE

WHEN PEOPLE HEAR THE TERM *CRIMINAL INVESTIGATOR*, they generally think of a police detective. Detectives are almost always plainclothes investigators who gather facts and collect evidence in criminal cases. In large police departments, detectives are organized into specialized units such as the homicide division, the narcotics division, or the arson division.

Detectives do some of their work at a desk and some out in the field in a variety of environments. They may be assigned as many as two or three cases a day, and having thirty cases to handle at one time is not unusual. Schedules for detectives often are irregular, and overtime as well as working at night and on the weekend may be necessary.

To become a police detective, one must first have experience as a police officer. Hiring requirements for police officers vary, but most departments require at least a high school diploma. In almost all large cities, the hiring of police officers follows local civil service regulations. In some departments, a college degree may be necessary for some or all police positions. After gaining three- to five-years' experience in the department and demonstrating the skills necessary for detective work, a police officer may be promoted to a position as a detective. In some police departments, candidates must first take a qualifying exam. There is usually a training program for new detectives that may last from a few weeks to several months.

Students interested in becoming detectives should take a diverse course load that includes English, U.S. history, government, business law, psychology, sociology, chemistry, and physics. Also important are courses in journalism, a foreign language, using a computer, and keyboarding. Salaries for police detectives range from about $27,500 to nearly $45,000, depending on location. With experience the salary increases considerably.

FYI

FYI (For Your Information) provides interesting sidelights related to the chapter content.

FYI Tests on physical evidence discovered at the crime scene are usually conducted in a crime laboratory. Some tests, however, must be conducted in the field. For example, a special test can determine whether blood has been cleaned from a floor. When a chemical known as *luminol* is sprayed on the floor, even minute traces of blood will fluoresce, or light up, when viewed under ultraviolet light.

Statistics

Statistics presents useful data showing trends, developments, and changes.

STATISTICS In 2002 about 25 percent of convicted property and drug offenders had committed their crimes to get money for drugs, compared to 5 percent of violent and public order offenders. More than 68 percent of local jail inmates were found to be dependent on drugs or alcohol or abusing them according to this same survey of men and women held in local jails (Karlberg & James, 2005).

History

History focuses on people and events and provides an interesting backdrop to the study of the chapter concepts.

HISTORY

DURING THE EARLY MORNING HOURS OF MARCH 13, 1964, Catherine Genovese—whose friends called her Kitty—was returning home from her job as the manager of Ev's Eleventh Hour Club, a bar in Hollis, New York. As she approached her apartment in the upscale neighborhood of Kew Garden's Queens, New York, she was attacked and stabbed by an assailant. She screamed as she was stabbed, "Oh, my God, he stabbed me! Please help me! Please help me!" Lights came on in several neighbors' windows, and a man's voice cried out "Leave her alone." The assailant ran and hid, only to return in a few minutes to stab Kitty again. There were more screams, more lights, and Kitty's assailant fled a second time. Kitty managed to stagger to her doorway, bleeding profusely from her knife wounds. The assailant returned for a third time and completed his attack. When he was done, Kitty Genovese had been fatally stabbed. Throughout the attack, which by some accounts lasted nearly 15 minutes, only one individual of what police later reported were as many as 38 witnesses ever called the police. Witnesses would later explain their reluctance to call the authorities for a variety of reasons, including not wanting to speak with police because they simply didn't want to get involved, because they had warrants out against them, or because they assumed someone had already called the police (Rosenthal, 1999; Wainwright, 1964).

CRITICAL THINKING AND INVESTIGATIVE SKILL-BUILDING EXERCISES

At the end of every chapter, **real-world critical thinking** and workplace **skill-building** exercises offer opportunities to connect knowledge and skills to the workplace.

CRITICAL THINKING EXERCISE

Read the following description of a hypothetical case involving the robbery of a motel and decide what data you would include in the *modus operandi* part of a report. Prepare a written report using the subdivisions in the section titled "The *Modus Operandi* Parts of a Report." Compare your *modus operandi* report with others in the class and resolve any discrepancies that may exist.

Facts

On July 8, 2006, at 12:30 a.m., John Gomer, the night clerk, was working behind the registration desk inside the front entrance of the Shining Star Motel. The motel is located one mile outside of town on State Route 286. A tall man walked in. John noticed that he was rather good-looking except for a small scar over his left eyebrow. The man asked John, "Do you have a room for two, for one night?" John nodded yes and placed a registration card on the counter. As he did so, the man drew a black 9-millimeter pistol from his pocket. The man pointed the gun at John and said, "Turn around and don't look at me. If you keep quiet and cooperate, we won't have any trouble." The man reached around to John's eyeglasses and removed them, placing them on the desk. He ordered John to go into a back room, where he bound John's hands and feet with duct tape and covered his eyes with a red bandana. The man also placed a red bandana with a knot in the middle in John's mouth as a gag. The man removed John's

INVESTIGATIVE SKILL BUILDERS

Serving Clients

You have just driven into a strip mall parking lot and stopped your car near the grocery store entrance. It is 12:30 p.m. This lot has been the site of a number of reports of items stolen from parked cars. The M.O. report indicated that the thefts occurred between 12:00 p.m. and 2:00 p.m. on weekdays. Although the thefts have been strung out over about 4 weeks, they have occurred only once or twice a week. The items taken have been only loose things left on the seats of unlocked vehicles. Items have included stuffed animals, toys, and expensive fountain pens. Many of the vehicles have had radios, telephones, and CB radios installed in them, but those items were left untouched.

Your eye catches the image of a small boy moving swiftly between cars. As your eyes meet his, he quickly moves a bag he is holding behind him and starts to move off. You call to him to stop as you get out of your car. The boy is about 7 or 8 years old and is holding his bag behind him to keep it out of your view.

You ask the boy who he is and where his parents are, thinking that a small child such as this should not be in the lot all alone. He tells you his name is Bobby, his father is dead, and his mother is unemployed for several months. You ask the boy if you can see what he has in his bag, and he obligingly brings the bag into your view. Inside are

---

Critical Thinking Exercises

Critical Thinking Exercises require students to analyze a situation and make a choice, develop a hypothesis, reach a conclusion, or propose a solution.

Investigative Skill Builders

Investigative Skill Builders help students develop investigative skills that can be used on the job. They include such skills as acquiring and evaluating information, participating as a member of a team, allocating time, and teaching others.

Integrity/Honesty exercises confront students with ethical situations involving clients or fellow officers that can arise in the workplace; they must make a decision or propose a course of action for each situation.

RESOURCES FOR THE STUDENT

Study Guide

The Study Guide is a learning aid that provides independent study and reinforcement of the chapter concepts. The Study Guide contains study outlines, key terms review, concept review, and application exercises. The study guide can be found at www.mhhe.com/berg4.

Online Learning Center Website

A unique, book-specific website is available to students at no additional charge. The website features additional exercises, quizzes, and links to relevant websites, as well as flashcards that can be used to master vocabulary and an interactive glossary. Check it out at www.mhhe.com/berg4.

RESOURCES FOR THE INSTRUCTOR

Instructor's Manual

The Instructor's Manual contains a variety of resources to assist both new and experienced instructors. Included are chapter outlines, chapter summaries, discussion questions, teaching suggestions, and answers to the end-of-chapter exercises. The Instructor's Manual is available for download at www.mhhe.com/berg4.

PowerPoint Lecture Presentation

Complete chapter-by-chapter slide shows feature text, art, photos, and tables. The PowerPoint presentation is available for download at www.mhhe.com/berg4.

Computerized Test Bank

This easy-to-use computerized testing program is compatible with both Windows and Macintosh computers; it contains multiple-choice, true/false, and short answer questions for each chapter.

ACKNOWLEDGMENTS

I gratefully acknowledge the contributions of the following individuals who helped in the development of this textbook.

J. Michael Aaron
Forensic Specialist, Camden, NJ

Carl R. Butcher
Missouri Western State College, St. Joseph, MO

Brenda Collins
Ohio State Highway Patrol, Columbus, OH

Tim Elliget
Newark Police Forensic Services, Newark, OH

Alan L. Hart
Northwestern Michigan College, Traverse City, Michigan

James C. Helmkamp
National White Collar Crime Center, Richmond, VA

Dawn Herkenham
Forensic Science Systems Unit FBI Laboratory, Washington, DC

C. Wayne Johnston
Arkansas State University, State University, AR

Roger Kahn
Ohio Bureau of Criminal Identification & Investigation, London, OH

John I. Kostanoski
State University of New York, Farmingdale, NY

George L. Lawless
South Plains College, Levelland, TX

Mona M. McKinniss
U.S. Postal Inspection Service, Columbus, OH

Sarah Nordin
Solano Community College, Suisun City, CA

Joyce Riggs
FBI Bomb Data Center, Washington, DC

Tim Sweeney
National Law Enforcement Telecommunications Systems, Inc., Phoenix, AZ

Clarence Terrill
Harford Community College, Bel Air, MD

ABOUT THE AUTHOR

Bruce L. Berg is professor of criminal justice at California State University, Long Beach where he has served as department chair, graduate adviser, and director of interdisciplinary studies. Previously he was a professor of criminology at Indiana University of Pennsylvania and a faculty member in the Department of Sociology at the University of Massachusetts, Boston Harbor Campus. He also served as the internship director and faculty member at Florida State University's School of Criminology. Dr. Berg received his PhD in sociology from Syracuse University. He has published more than three dozen articles, essays, and book chapters in the areas of policing, deviance, elder abuse, criminology, and research methods. He is the author of *Qualitative Research Methods for the Social Sciences, Law Enforcement: An Introduction to Policing in Society,* and coauthor of *Research Methods for the Social Sciences: Applications and Practice.* Dr. Berg has been an active member of the American Society of Criminology and the Academy of Criminal Justice Sciences since 1983. He has presented numerous papers and workshops at meetings of these associations and served on several committees. Dr. Berg has repeatedly traveled to China to observe police training there.

Basic Grounding and Overview

CHAPTER OBJECTIVES

After completing this chapter, you will be able to:

1 Identify and define the nature of crime.
2 Name the sources of criminal law in the United States.
3 Explain the distinction between *felonies* and *misdemeanors.*
4 Summarize the objectives of criminal investigation.
5 Understand the nature of inductive and deductive reasoning in criminal investigations.

When people hear the term *criminal investigation* today, most immediately think of testing DNA samples, locating suspects by examining watermarks on pages torn from some odd paper stock, matching a bullet to a particular gun, and various pieces of high-tech equipment. Some may think of Lt. Horatio Cain, Gil Grissom, or perhaps even Special Agent Leroy Jethro Gibbs—all fictional characters on crime scene investigative television shows. For most people these highly fictionalized depictions of crime scene investigations *are* criminal investigation.

Perhaps almost as beguiling are recent, highly celebrated criminal cases that were highlighted in the news media. One such case was the Scott Peterson murder case, which began on December 24, 2003, with the disappearance of Scott Peterson's pregnant wife, Laci, and concluded on March 16, 2005, when Scott Peterson was found guilty of murdering Laci Peterson and their unborn child and was sentenced to death. At trial the prosecution reported on forensic tests that had been conducted on the bodies of the victims, the boat of the defendant, and various household articles including a knife. In many ways this case resembled the plot of one of the criminal investigative television shows so many Americans enjoy (Ablow, 2005; Crier, 2005).

Another celebrated case involved television actor Robert Blake, who in 2001 was arrested and charged with the murder of his wife, Bonny Lee Bakley. Bonny was shot once in the head while waiting in the car for Robert Blake to return; he had gone back to the restaurant where they had just dined to retrieve his handgun, which he had removed during diner and left at their table. Blake explained to the police that he carried a gun because his wife—who had a checkered and criminal past—feared for her life. Following nearly a year while Blake was incarcerated awaiting a bail hearing, and a trial that rivaled both television and Peterson's for various elements of forensic showmanship on the part of the prosecutor's office, Robert Blake was acquitted of his wife's murder. Ironically, Blake was acquitted on March 16, 2005—the very day Scott Peterson was sentenced to death.

What, then, you well may ask, is criminal investigation? The short answer is that **criminal investigation** is the lawful search for people and things to reconstruct the circumstances of an illegal act, identify a suspect, or determine the guilty party to pursue—and, of course, to aid in the state's prosecution of the offender once he or she is apprehended. The longer answer will be described throughout this book. Criminal investigation has the following primary objectives:

- Respond to emergencies at the scene of the crime.
- Determine whether a crime has been committed, and, if so, what crime.
- Establish crime scene priorities.
- Identify suspects.
- Gather and preserve evidence.
- Recover stolen property.
- Assist in prosecution and conviction of the defendant or defendants.

Crime will be the focus of much of the discussion throughout this book, so before continuing further, it would seem reasonable to consider what a crime is.

WHAT IS A CRIME?

Whenever you read the newspaper, listen to the radio, or watch the news on television, you are confronted with crime—shootings on city streets or on school campuses, robberies of convenience stores, beatings of spouses and children, prostitution, automobile thefts, and the list goes on and on. But what exactly is crime?

A **crime** in a broad sense is any behavior that violates a politically sanctioned statute, ordinance, or law. In a more narrow sense, a crime is a violation of criminal

criminal investigation The lawful search for people and things to reconstruct the circumstances of an illegal act, apprehend or determine the guilty party, and aid in the state's prosecution of the offender.

crime An offense against the public at large, proclaimed in a law and punishable by a governing body.

law, which is a branch of law that deals with the commission of crimes and their punishments. George Rush (2004, p. 86) defines a crime as follows:

- An act committed or omitted in violation of law forbidding or
- Commanding it, for which the possible penalties upon
- Conviction for an adult include incarceration.

Rush's definition does not tell us what behaviors are forbidden or commanded, what constitutes a violation of the law, who is responsible for investigating and locating information about these behaviors, or who is responsible for prosecuting these errant behaviors. Edwin Sutherland and Donald Cressey (1974), in their classical description of crime, suggest the following four primary factors in classifying a behavior as a crime:

- The behavior is offensive to some political authority.
- The behavior is specifically defined both in terms of the offense and the punishment.
- The prohibition is uniformly applied to all.
- The remedy contains penal sanctions enforced by the state.

To summarize Sutherland and Cressey's orientation, crime is an offense against the public at large, proclaimed in a law, and punishable by an official governing body. The body of law that defines criminal behavior and prescribes the punishment to be imposed for such behavior is **criminal law.** The purpose of criminal law is to prevent harm to society.

criminal law The body of law that for the purpose of preventing harm to society defines what behavior is criminal and prescribes the punishment to be imposed for such behavior.

Development of Criminal Law

At one time most people considered crime a private matter. When one person wronged another, the injured party sought compensation or relief in the form of revenge. Unfortunately, this sometimes resulted in bloody feuds between individuals and their entire families. Worse still, the conflict could result from a misunderstanding or mistake by the injured party!

In time, societies evolved into nation-states, and the customs and traditions that had guided individual behavior were replaced with written law. The state, or the government, became the representative of the public at large. Thus the government became the *plaintiff,* the party that accuses a person of a crime. Usually, the government is referred to as the **prosecutor.** The person who is accused of a crime is called the **defendant.**

Public sentiment may change about which behaviors should be illegal. For example, until recently, in most jurisdictions of the United States it was not legally possible for a husband to rape his wife, and in 1996 Arizona and California passed laws making

prosecutor Name given to the government as the party that accuses a person of a crime.

defendant In criminal law, the person who is accused of a crime.

HISTORY

THE FIRST WRITTEN LAWS (circa 3000 BC) were found on clay tablets among the ruins of Ur, one of the city-states of Sumeria (now southeastern Iraq). The laws tried to free poor people from abuse by the rich, and everybody from abuse by the priests. One law forbade the high priest to go into the garden of a poor mother and take wood or fruit from her to pay taxes. Others cut burial fees and forbade the clergy and high officials to share among themselves the cattle that were sacrificed to the gods.

it lawful for people with certain medical conditions to smoke marijuana. No act or behavior can be considered criminal unless it is prohibited by the law of the place where it is committed, and the law provides for the punishment of the offenders. Let's look at the sources of laws that define what conduct is criminal and that prescribe the punishment to be imposed for such conduct.

Sources of Criminal Law in the United States

Each crime must have an exact definition. Crimes are defined in several different bodies of law that govern behavior in the United States. These bodies of law include the following:

- Common law
- Statutory law
- Case law
- Administrative law

Common Law   One of the earliest sources of definitions of crimes is the common law. The early American colonists came from England, and they adopted the law of England as the law of their new land. In the early days of English history, the kings had tried to centralize the English government and establish a court system. Judges traveled in circuits around the countryside, deciding cases based on custom and tradition. They settled disputes in as consistent a manner as possible. The judges maintained this consistency by relying on previous legal decisions whenever they faced a similar set of circumstances. Every effort was made to share the law "in common" with everyone else throughout the country. This body of decisions became known as the **common law.**

common law   Principles and rules of action based on usage and custom in ancient England and incorporated into colonial American laws and subsequent state statutes.

statutory law   The body of laws passed by legislative bodies, including the U.S. Congress, state legislatures, and local governing bodies.

penal code   A collection of state statutes that define criminal offenses and specify corresponding fines and punishments.

Statutory Law   Most crimes are defined by **statutory law.** This is the body of laws passed by legislative bodies, including the U.S. Congress, state legislatures, and local governing bodies. On the federal and state levels, these laws are known as *statutes;* on the local level, they may be known as city *ordinances* or town *bylaws.* In many states, the legislature has standardized common law definitions of such crimes as murder, burglary, arson, and rape by defining them in statutes. Other states have created a separate **penal code,** a collection of statutes that define criminal offenses and specify corresponding fines and punishments. See Figure 1.1 for some examples of state criminal statutes.

The distinction between federal and state criminal laws is very important. The U.S. Constitution created a national government with limited powers, and one of the limitations is of police power. The federal government has no general police power; it can create criminal statutes only for those areas over which the federal government has jurisdiction. For example, Congress can create laws against counterfeiting because the federal government has the power to coin money. Some federal jurisdiction overlaps with state criminal laws. For example, both the federal government and state governments have statutes that outlaw the manufacture, sale, and use of certain drugs.

On the state level, criminal liability is defined quite specifically. Crimes are considered serious transgressions against the public safety, and conviction of a crime can result in imprisonment or death. Although the criminal statutes of the states generally resemble one another, the exact definitions and penalties may differ from jurisdiction to jurisdiction. The exact charges also may differ; for example, petty larceny in one state may be grand larceny in another.

FIGURE 1.1 Examples of State Criminal Statutes

California State Penal Code Section 211: Robbery

211. Robbery is the felonious taking of personal property in the possession of another, from his person or immediate presence, and against their will, accompanied by means of force or fear.
212. The fear mentioned in Section 211 may be either:
    1. The fear of an unlawful injury to the person or property of the person robbed, or of any relative of his or member of his family; or,
    2. The fear of an immediate and unlawful injury to the person or property of anyone in the company of the person robbed at the time of the robbery.

New York State Penal Code Section 160.00: Robbery

Sec. 160.00 Robbery; defined.

Robbery is forcible stealing. A person forcibly steals property and commits robbery when, in the course of committing a larceny, he uses or threatens the immediate use of physical force upon another person for the purpose of:

1. Preventing or overcoming resistance to the taking of the property or to the retention thereof immediately after the taking; or
2. Compelling the owner of such property or another person to deliver up the property or to engage in other conduct which aids in the commission of the larceny.

Case Law

Case Law The rules of law announced in court decisions also provide a source for definitions of crime. **Case law** includes the sum total of reported judicial cases that interpret previous decisions, statutes, regulations, and constitutional provisions. Each interpretation becomes part of the law on the subject and serves as a **precedent.** That is, the decision furnishes an example or authority for deciding subsequent cases in which identical or similar facts are presented.

case law The sum total of all reported cases that interpret previous decisions, statutes, regulations, and constitutional provisions that then become part of a nation's or a state's common law.

precedent A decision in a court case that furnishes an example or authority for deciding subsequent cases in which identical or similar facts are presented.

STATISTICS Most criminal law—more than 80 percent, in fact—is made by state legislatures. Unlike the federal government, state governments have inherent police power, which allows them to pass statutes to protect the public health, safety, welfare, and morals.

Administrative Law Legislators and judges cannot do all that is needed to protect the public good. To broaden the power of the law, legislators set up administrative agencies to create rules, regulate and supervise, and render decisions in such areas as communications, labor relations, and working conditions. The decrees and decisions of these agencies are known as **administrative law** and can include criminal penalties for violations. One such example is the regulation dealing with mailing obscene material.

administrative law The body of law created by administrative agencies in the form of rules, regulations, orders, and decisions, sometimes with criminal penalties for violations.

Classification of Crimes

Crimes can be classified in a number of ways. One way to classify crimes is according to the severity of the criminal behavior. The more serious the crime, the more stringent the punishment. Generally, a **felony** is a relatively serious offense punishable by death

felony A relatively serious criminal offense punishable by death or by imprisonment for more than a year in a state or federal prison.

misdemeanor A less serious crime that is generally punishable by a prison sentence of not more than one year in a county or city jail.

or by imprisonment for more than a year in a state or federal prison. Some felonies are also punishable by a fine. Felony crimes include murder, rape, and assault. A **misdemeanor** is a less serious crime that is generally punishable by a prison sentence of not more than one year in a county or city jail. Disorderly conduct is an example of a misdemeanor. Because crimes may be defined differently in various bodies of law and from one jurisdiction to another, it is important that criminal investigators be familiar with their area's criminal laws.

> **FYI** Some states assign varying degrees of severity to each class of crimes. For example, the most serious felonies might be labeled first-degree felonies, whereas the least serious felonies might be labeled fourth- or fifth-degree felonies. In some states the number of times an individual has committed a particular offense determines the degree of the offense. Some states also have a separate category for their least serious offenses. These vary, but two of the most common are petty offenses and minor misdemeanors.

Now that you know a little bit about the meaning of crime and the various bodies of law that are typically associated with criminal behaviors, we have come full circle to our earlier question: What is this thing called criminal investigation?

WHAT IS CRIMINAL INVESTIGATION?

Criminal investigation is a scientific and systematic series of activities designed to use various pieces of information and evidence to explain the events surrounding a crime, identify a suspect, and link that suspect to a particular crime or series of crimes. In this process, police and detectives use items such as weapons, fingerprints, blood, fibers, and other traces found at the scene of a crime, computer technology, and a number of scientific and academic disciplines, along with logical reasoning, to solve the crime. Throughout the course of the criminal investigation, certain legal guidelines prevail to ensure that the investigating officers have operated lawfully and have not infringed on the rights of an individual who may only be accused of a crime.

Rights of the Accused

substantive law The body of law that creates, defines, and regulates rights and defines crime and its penalties.

procedural law The body of law that prescribes the manner or method by which rights and responsibilities may be exercised and enforced.

due process of law The rights of people suspected of or charged with crimes, prescribed by the U.S. Constitution, state constitutions, and federal and state statutes.

Our previous discussion of criminal law has dealt with **substantive law,** the body of law that creates, defines, and regulates rights and defines crime and its penalties. **Procedural law,** on the other hand, governs the ways in which substantive laws are administered. For the criminal investigator, procedural law covers such subjects as the way suspects can legally be arrested, searched, and interrogated. Procedural law is concerned with **due process of law,** the rights of people suspected of or charged with crimes. Most of the procedural, or due process, rights of criminal suspects in the United States are found in the Bill of Rights, the first ten amendments to the United States Constitution (Figure 1.2). These ten amendments were added to the U.S. Constitution soon after it was adopted because many felt the Constitution did not adequately protect the people's rights. Other due process rights are found in state constitutions and federal and state statutes. Criminal investigators must know and apply all relevant due process procedures for their particular jurisdictions.

FIGURE 1.2 A Summary of the Bill of Rights

Guarantees of Basic Citizens' Rights

First Amendment: freedom of religion, speech, press, assembly, and of the right to petition the government

Protection against Arbitrary Police and Court Action

Fourth Amendment: prohibits unreasonable searches and seizures

Fifth Amendment: requires grand jury indictment for serious crimes, bans double jeopardy, prohibits having to testify against oneself, and guarantees no loss of life, liberty, or property without due process of law

Sixth Amendment: guarantees right to speedy, public, impartial trial in criminal cases, with counsel and right to cross-examine witnesses

Seventh Amendment: guarantees right to jury trial in civil suits

Eighth Amendment: prohibits excessive bail or fines and cruel and unusual punishment

Protection of States' Rights and Other Rights

Ninth Amendment: affirms that rights not listed in other amendments are not necessarily denied

Tenth Amendment: states that powers not delegated to the national government or denied to the states are reserved to the states

Military Protection and Rights

Second Amendment: guarantees the right to organize state militias and to bear arms

Third Amendment: prohibits the quartering of soldiers in homes in peacetime

---

REQUISITES OF A SUCCESSFUL CRIMINAL INVESTIGATOR

A criminal investigator must have many attributes. Some of these special qualities are listed in Figure 1.3. One of the most important is the ability to make reasoned connections between the information and evidence gathered from the crime scene and witnesses and a possible suspect in the crime. These connections may be made through either deductive or inductive reasoning.

Deductive Reasoning

Suppose an investigator notices a kitchen knife extending from the back of the victim and also sees a pool of blood beneath the victim. The investigator deduces that the weapon used in the death of the victim was a knife. Moreover, because the knife is stuck in the back of the victim, the investigator further deduces that it was a murder. The investigator is using **deductive reasoning;** that is, he or she begins with a general explanation of the crime and then tests that formulation against specific available information (Atkinson, 2005). In the preceding example, the officer saw the knife in the victim's back, and knowing that if one stabs a large knife into the back of another, it is likely to cause death, the officer then could deduce that the victim was killed by stabbing. Because the knife was found in the middle of the victim's back, the officer could assume it was unlikely to be suicide and, hence, deduce it was murder.

deductive reasoning
Drawing conclusions from logically related events or observations.

FIGURE 1.3 Characteristics of a Successful Criminal Investigator

- Curiosity, habitual inquisitiveness
- Observation, using all five senses
- Suspicion and refusal to take anything for granted
- Memory, ability to recall facts and past events
- Ordinary intelligence and common sense
- An unbiased mind
- Avoidance of inaccurate conclusions
- Patience, understanding, and courtesy
- Ability to play a role
- Ability to gain and hold confidence
- Persistence and endless capacity for work
- Knowledge of the essential elements of a crime
- Interest in sociology and psychology
- Ability to recognize criminal activity or operations
- Resourcefulness
- Ability to make friends and secure the cooperation of others
- Tact, self-control, and dignity
- Knowledge of investigative techniques
- Interest in the job and pride of accomplishment
- Loyalty

Inductive Reasoning

inductive reasoning
Making inferences from apparently separate observations or pieces of evidence.

Inductive reasoning moves from examining apparently separate pieces of evidence to drawing an inference or building an explanation of the crime based on a logical connection between these separate elements. Suppose, for example, an investigator finds a victim lying in a pool of blood, and this victim has numerous cuts from what might have been a sharp cutting object. The investigator could, using inductive reasoning (moving from separate pieces of evidence to a generalized inference), infer that the victim died as a result of the wounds inflicted by a knife—despite the fact that no knife may have been found at the crime scene. However, such an inference is only what the officer thinks may have happened based on the available and observable facts at his or her disposal at the time. A more complete analysis of the wounds and types of cuts inflicted on the victim's body and additional information and evidence may lead to a different conclusion. For instance, it could be that the wounds were too superficial to cause death and, upon closer inspection, a bullet fired into the base of the victim's skull was the actual cause of death.

Drawing Conclusions

Whether investigators use deductive or inductive reasoning, any conclusion drawn by a criminal investigator should be based on careful reasoning and systematic collection of information and evidence. It is especially important that investigators remain objective and avoid preconceived notions about possible crimes or explanations of apparent criminal behavior.

Inductions are not always proof of a crime. For example, upon entering a corner grocery store after receiving a possible-robbery-in-progress broadcast, an officer might observe an unconscious man on the floor next to a small package of groceries; the man is bleeding from an apparent gunshot wound. Inductively, the officer might assume

CAREER FOCUS

POLICE DETECTIVE

WHEN PEOPLE HEAR THE TERM *CRIMINAL INVESTIGATOR*, they generally think of a police detective. Detectives are almost always plainclothes investigators who gather facts and collect evidence in criminal cases. In large police departments, detectives are organized into specialized units such as the homicide division, the narcotics division, or the arson division.

Detectives do some of their work at a desk and some out in the field in a variety of environments. They may be assigned as many as two or three cases a day, and having thirty cases to handle at one time is not unusual. Schedules for detectives often are irregular, and overtime as well as working at night and on the weekend may be necessary.

To become a police detective, one must first have experience as a police officer. Hiring requirements for police officers vary, but most departments require at least a high school diploma. In almost all large cities, the hiring of police officers follows local civil service regulations. In some departments, a college degree may be necessary for some or all police positions. After gaining three- to five-years' experience in the department and demonstrating the skills necessary for detective work, a police officer may be promoted to a position as a detective. In some police departments, candidates must first take a qualifying exam. There is usually a training program for new detectives that may last from a few weeks to several months.

Students interested in becoming detectives should take a diverse course load that includes English, U.S. history, government, business law, psychology, sociology, chemistry, and physics. Also important are courses in journalism, a foreign language, using a computer, and keyboarding. Salaries for police detectives range from about $27,500 to nearly $45,000, depending on location. With experience the salary increases considerably.

that the man is a customer who fell victim to the robbery attempt. A moment later, a woman wielding a handgun comes from the backroom crying. After disarming her, the officer might learn that she is the proprietor and that she accidentally shot the customer who is lying on the floor while attempting to shoot the escaping robber. In short, although both induction and deduction are important reasoning skills, investigators must carefully check the facts of every situation before drawing conclusions.

Case Study

A California Highway Patrol officer heard over the radio that a fellow officer was chasing a white and blue late-model Cadillac on the interstate. The information indicated that the speeding car had run off the road and into the center divider during the chase. The officer who had heard the radio bulletin saw the suspect Cadillac coming his way, traveling erratically. He followed the car and clocked it on radar at speeds well over the legal limit as it crossed over several lanes of traffic. The officer forced the vehicle to pull over. From his patrol car, the officer observed that the vehicle had Illinois license plates that were old and bent. A check of the license plate number revealed that there was no warrant out for it.

The officer *induced* that the driver was drunk. Because the driver exhibited symptoms of intoxication while driving and when questioned, the officer administered a series of sobriety tests. The driver performed poorly on the tests, leading the officer to *deduce* that the driver was in fact driving under the influence of an intoxicating beverage.

Even after arresting the man for driving under the influence (DUI), the officer continued to feel the driver was concealing something and induced that there might

The ability to reason based on observation and facts is important to investigators.

be more wrong with the situation than met the eye. He checked the vehicle identification number (VIN) and noticed that it was not securely attached to the car as it should be—itself a violation of the law.

The officer opened the hood of the Cadillac and wrote down the engine identification number. This number is cross-referenced with the VIN. A check with the FBI's National Crime Information Center (NCIC) in Washington, D.C., revealed that the car had been stolen and the VIN replaced with another but that the thieves had neglected to replace the engine identification number. A female passenger in the car refused to provide any identification and was placed under arrest, along with the driver, for possession of a stolen vehicle.

The driver told the officer that he had some gold bullion and rare coins in a case in the backseat of the car. He indicated that he did not wish to leave this case in the car unattended. With the suspect's permission, the officer opened the case and indeed found gold bullion. However, the officer also found 8 ounces of cocaine, a number of blank Illinois drivers' licenses, several blank Social Security cards, and other sets of identification. Bank books, safe-deposit keys, and registrations for additional automobiles were also found.

A subsequent FBI fingerprint check revealed that the driver was not the person he claimed to be. He was, in fact, a felon with a record dating back to age 16. He was now 42 years old. His record showed the following arrests: murder of a police officer, assault on a police officer, grand theft, auto theft, smuggling, and possession of narcotics.

As the result of what had begun as a rather routine drunk-driving arrest, officers uncovered a major auto theft ring in Los Angeles and Chicago. The power of inductive and deductive reasoning, combined with careful observation and persistence, produced a successful police investigation.

FOCUS ON TECHNOLOGY

COMPUTERIZED CRIMINAL INVESTIGATION

CRIMINAL INVESTIGATORS SPEND HUNDREDS OF HOURS GATHERING, recording, reporting, and evaluating information. This tremendous job is made easier by using computers.

Criminal investigation systems combine applications such as evidence control, criminal profiling, crime analysis, and case management into one centralized system available to many users.

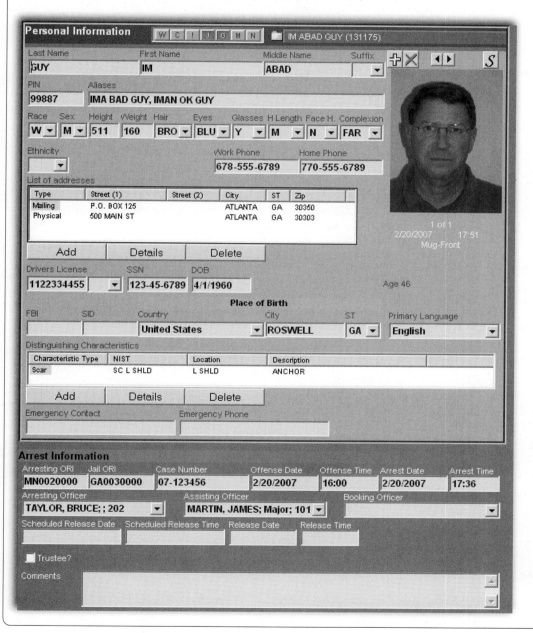

SUMMARY

Learning Objective 1

Crime is a behavior that is offensive to some political authority and for which both the offense and the punishment have been specifically defined. The prohibition against the behavior is uniformly applied to all, and the remedy contains penal sanctions enforced by punishments administered by the state.

Learning Objective 2

Criminal law is the body of law that, for the purpose of preventing harm to society, defines what behavior is criminal and prescribes the punishment to be imposed for such behavior. The sources of criminal law are common law, statutory law, case law, and administrative law.

Learning Objective 3

Crimes can be classified by the severity of the criminal behavior and by the punishment for the behavior. A felony is a serious crime, such as murder, robbery, or arson, that is punishable by imprisonment or death. A misdemeanor is a less serious crime that is generally punishable by a fine or by imprisonment for less than one year.

Learning Objective 4

The objectives of criminal investigation include the following: deal with emergencies; determine whether a crime has been committed and, if so, what crime; establish crime scene priorities; identify suspects; apprehend the suspects; gather and preserve evidence; recover stolen property; and assist in prosecution and conviction of the defendant or defendants.

Learning Objective 5

It is important for an investigator to be able to make reasoned connections between the information and evidence gathered from the crime scene and witnesses and a possible suspect in the crime. These connections may be made through either deductive or inductive reasoning. Inductive reasoning moves from apparently separate observations to drawing a general inference. Deductive reasoning reaches a conclusion based on related observable facts.

KEY TERMS

criminal investigation 2

crime 2

criminal law 3

prosecutor 3

defendant 3

common law 4

statutory law 4

penal code 4

case law 5

precedent 5

administrative law 5

felony 5

misdemeanor 6

substantive law 6

procedural law 6

due process of law 6

deductive reasoning 7

inductive reasoning 8

QUESTIONS FOR REVIEW

Learning Objective 1

1. Define *crime, criminal law, prosecutor,* and *defendant.*

2. What are four primary factors in determining what constitutes a crime?

3. Does public sentiment influence what constitutes a crime? Explain.

Learning Objective 2

4. What are the sources of criminal law in the United States?

5. How did English common law become part of the laws in most U.S. states?

6. Which source of criminal law contains the most definitions of crimes? Explain why.

7. What is meant by the term *precedent* in case law?

Learning Objective 3

8. How can one distinguish between a *misdemeanor* and a *felony*?

9. Is rape a felony or a misdemeanor?

Learning Objective 4

10. What are the primary objectives in any criminal investigation?

Learning Objective 5

11. How do inductive reasoning and deductive reasoning differ?

12. Why must an investigator not rely solely on inductive or deductive reasoning?

CRITICAL THINKING EXERCISE

Using the hypothetical facts that follow, test your ability to make inductive inferences and deductive conclusions. Carefully read the facts of the case, and then list what you can reasonably infer or safely deduce from the information provided.

Facts

You have been called to the scene of what appears to be a double homicide. Upon arriving, you receive the following information from the uniformed officer already on the scene:

There are two victims—a man and a woman—both white. The woman is approximately 25 years old, 5 feet 6 inches tall, and 120 pounds. She has blond hair just past her shoulders and is wearing makeup that appears to be smeared. The man is also about 25 years old. He is about 5 feet 11 inches tall and weighs about 175 pounds. His hair is short and light brown. A man walking his dog found the victims on the porch of the house.

The keys to the house are in the door, but the door is locked. Neither victim has any identification. There is a large brown purse open on the ground, with the contents emptied onto the ground. The man's wallet has not been found. Neither victim is wearing any jewelry although each victim has a light trace of a line on the ring finger of the left hand. The man is fully clothed, but the woman is naked from the waist down. The man's body has twelve wounds that appear to be stab wounds, and there are several cuts on his hands and forearms. The woman's neck is bruised, and she has a single stab wound just under her sternum, or breastbone.

After an autopsy and a laboratory examination, the following information is provided:

The man had three deep stab wounds to the chest, any of which could have been fatal. Each of these wounds was 6 inches deep and had severed one or more arteries. In addition, he had nine shallow stab wounds, varying in depth from 1 inch to 2 inches, none in lethal locations. The wounds had been made by a single-edged cutting instrument, such as a single-edged knife.

The woman's neck showed signs of fingers imprinted in her bruises. She died from asphyxiation, caused by a crushed windpipe. The single stab wound was 6 inches deep but was inflicted after death. The wound was pointed at both ends of the entry, making it consistent with a double-edged cutting instrument, such as a bayonet or a double-edged knife. There was semen in the woman's vagina. Laboratory tests of the semen revealed three separate blood types, including one matching the dead man's blood type.

INVESTIGATIVE SKILL BUILDERS

Acquiring and Evaluating Information

You and your partner answer a radio call to investigate a house burglary. When you arrive, you take a look around the house while your partner talks to the victim. You check ground-level windows and doors. At the back door, you find that the glass pane nearest the door lock has been broken. You look on the floor, but there are very few glass shards there. You look through the door's window and see a pile of broken glass lying on the ground outside the house.

As you continue looking around the house, you note that all the windows in the house are securely locked. In the living room a large area rug has been rolled back, and a floor safe under it is open. You peer into the safe and see that it is empty. There are several empty jewelry boxes, from rings and bracelets or necklaces, lying around the opening of the safe.

As you reenter the room where your partner is speaking with the homeowner, the victim asks your partner when he should contact his insurance company about the burglary. You observe that the victim seems very calm about the entire situation. At no time does the victim ask whether you or your partner think the burglar will be caught.

1. What might you deduce from the broken pane of glass in the back door?
2. What might you induce about the burglary itself?
3. What kinds of questions might you ask the victim at this point in the investigation?

Integrity/Honesty

You make a routine traffic stop of a woman driving at excessive speed. You obtain her driver's license and begin writing her a ticket. She begins to cry. She tells you it is her third speeding offense and not only will she probably lose her license but her husband will beat her. She begs you not to write the ticket. What action will you take in this situation?

Problem Solving

You have been called to a backyard pool. When you arrive, you see a woman in a bathing suit lying motionless on her back. Emergency medical service (EMS) personnel motion to you. As you near the woman, they inform you that she has drowned. They also say that she has a large bump on the side of her head.

A man is sitting at a metal patio table about 6 feet from the body. He is wearing casual clothing and sneakers. He is reserved and seems calm. You speak with him and learn that he is the woman's husband and was inside the house when he heard his wife call for help. He tells you, "By the time I got out back, it was too late. She was already dead." He explains that he left his wife's body in the pool and called the EMS, who pulled his wife's body from the water after they arrived.

1. What can you induce about the man's story?
2. What kinds of questions are you going to ask the husband?

The Preliminary Investigation

INITIAL RESPONSE

The major activities commonly associated with the investigation of a crime are shown in Figure 2.1. These can serve as a guideline for a general overview and discussion of the investigative process.

Whenever a crime is committed there are three potential outcomes. First, the crime may go undetected. For example, in a well-planned art theft where a forgery is used to replace some real work of art, the deception may remain undetected. Second, the

FIGURE 2.1   Major Activities Associated with a Criminal Investigation

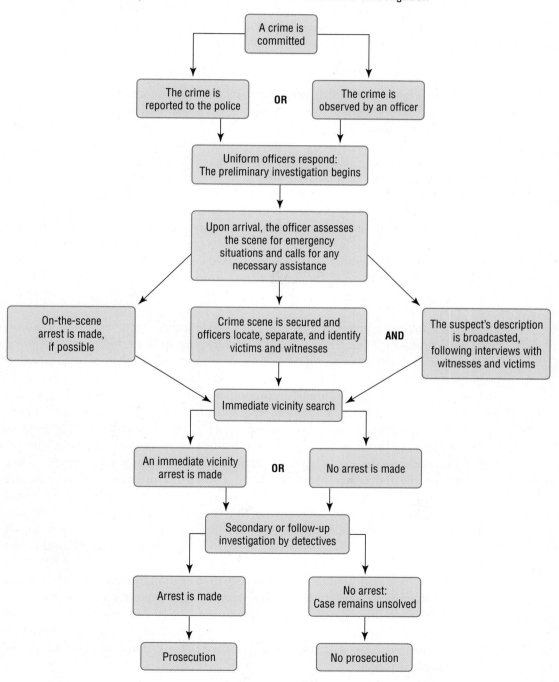

crime may be observed or discovered by a private citizen and reported to the police. For example, the missing artwork is reported to the police when the proprietor discovers the forgery hanging in his gallery. Third, the crime may be detected or observed by the police. For example, a patrol officer might see someone carrying a painting from the rear of the gallery late one night and investigate what he or she has observed. Alternatively, the officer might be acting on information received from an informant or on some other type of tip.

Regardless of the outcome, a crime can only become part of an investigation once it has been reported to, or been detected by, the police. The bulk of the initial investigative activities undertaken at the crime scene will fall on the shoulders of the uniform police patrol and forms what is referred to as the initial response and the preliminary investigation (Brown, 2003; Greenwood et al., 1975).

PRELIMINARY INVESTIGATION

preliminary investigation
Fact-gathering activities that take place at the scene of a crime immediately after the crime has been reported to or discovered by police officers.

The fact-gathering activities that take place at the scene of a crime immediately after the crime has been reported to or discovered by police officers are all part of the **preliminary investigation.** The bulk of the preliminary investigative activities are undertaken by the uniformed patrol of the police agency because they are the individuals most likely to respond to a call for assistance (Berg, 1999; Ogle, 2007).

Sometimes a call to the police requires immediate action to save a life or to apprehend an offender still at the crime scene. It may be a call for a robbery in progress, an assault, a riot, a domestic disturbance, or a prowler. These sorts of crimes are ongoing or very recent criminal events, and there is a very good chance of apprehending a suspect at the scene or in the near vicinity. Other types of crimes, such as prostitution, illegal gambling, automobile theft, passing bad checks, various forms of fraud, and burglaries detected following someone's return from a vacation, may not require an immediate response from police. These crimes can be handled at a somewhat lower priority level.

When responding police officers arrive at a crime scene, they often find a situation filled with confusion. The scene at a bank robbery may include frightened or injured customers and employees. At an assault or rape scene, a number of well-meaning people may be watching or comforting the victim. After a burglary, family members may feel unsafe in their own home. In any of these situations, the responding officer must remain calm and take charge and very quickly assess whether additional police personnel or medical assistance are required (Peak, 2006).

A preliminary investigation may be the prelude to an in-depth investigation. In larger departments, detectives typically carry out the in-depth investigation. They also conduct the follow-up investigation, apprehend the offender, and prepare the case for court. In smaller departments, the responding officer is more often responsible for both the preliminary investigation and the follow-up investigation. The roles and responsibilities of uniformed officers and detectives, therefore, are not always distinguishable. Much will depend on the size of the agency that undertakes the preliminary investigation.

The initial information from the preliminary investigation, regardless of who collects it, provides the foundation for the eventual criminal case against a suspect. Failure to carefully collect, accurately record, and skillfully process all the available information will leave the follow-up investigation without the benefit of all the existing evidence. It may necessitate repeating much of the preliminary investigation and may lead to the loss of valuable evidence.

STATISTICS A study of police fast-response times in Florida, Illinois, New York, and California showed that only 2.9 percent of all responses resulted in immediate suspect apprehension. A major reason this rate is so low is that only 25 percent of the calls received concerned crimes in progress, those for which a fast response is critical (Spelman & Brown, 1981).

The partnership of patrol officers and detectives might be compared to that of a baseball team. If the players do not support their pitcher in the field and at bat, they cannot win the ball game. Likewise, if errors of omission or commission are made in handling the investigation, the case may be lost in court.

PROCESSING THE CRIME SCENE

The scene of the crime is the focus of the preliminary investigation. When done correctly, crime scene processing is a *slow, methodical, systematic,* and *orderly* process that involves *protocols* and a processing *methodology.* Many textbook authors, including this one, hesitate to expose students to the *checklist approach* for something as important as criminal investigation. Using a checklist is not wrong or a bad idea, but an investigator following a checklist too closely may never learn to think independently of that list. Consequently, the investigator is limited to simply going through the motions as detailed on the checklist. Crime scenes differ from one situation to the next and may require various sorts of inductive and deductive reasoning. As a result, they cannot be standardized to a single checklist (Gardner, 2005). All that having been said, a checklist such as the one shown in Figure 2.2 provides the inexperienced investigator with a list of processing activities and elements necessary for the basic primary investigation.

Deal with Emergency Situations

When approaching a crime scene, the responding officer should be cautious, scan the entire area to thoroughly assess the scene, and note any possible secondary crime scenes. Be aware of any persons or vehicles in the vicinity that may be related to the crime (National Institute of Justice [NIJ], 2000). The first responsibility of any law enforcement officer is to protect and preserve the personal safety of the public. When arriving at the scene of a criminal call, the responding officer should quickly determine whether anyone is injured or needs medical treatment and should summon the necessary health professionals.

Determine Whether a Crime Has Been Committed

Officers usually determine whether a crime has been committed and what that crime is as soon as possible after arriving on the scene. Doing so requires visual inspection of the area and interviewing any victims and witnesses. Such activities provide the responding officer with information about whether the situation involves a criminal act. Furthermore, the officer can determine if additional assistance is required.

Establish Crime Scene Priorities

When the responding officer arrives, he or she must decide on a plan of action. Sometimes this is dictated by the flow of observed events. If the crime scene involves an emergency, such as a hit-and-run accident or a shooting, there may be injured persons

FIGURE 2.2   Crime Scene Investigation Checklist

Victim

1. Identify and treat the victim, or obtain proper medical care as needed.
2. Interview the victim if he or she is able to speak.
3. Get a description of the offender.
4. Broadcast a general description of the event and the offender's description.

Evidence

1. Determine what types of evidence are present. Are there any specific needs such as special technical assistance, photography, care in preservation and securing of items, or casting?
2. What elements of real or direct evidence have been found? List and detail each item.
3. What elements of circumstantial evidence are present or identified from interviews?

Witnesses

1. Obtain and confirm the identity of each witness.
2. Separate all witnesses.
3. Conduct a separate interview with each witness.
4. Determine relationships of witnesses with the victim, the offender, and other witnesses.
5. Determine where witnesses were positioned during the incident and what they were doing.
6. Obtain a description from them of the offender.

Method of Operation

1. Indicate how the crime was committed.
2. Indicate the time the crime occurred.
3. Indicate where the crime occurred.
4. Were any weapons used? If so, what weapons?
5. Who was involved in the incident? Indicate all parties.
6. Was anyone injured? If so, indicate the nature and extent of the injuries.
7. How did the offender arrive at and leave the scene?
8. Check with headquarters concerning similar types of crimes occurring recently.

Property Involved

1. Was any property taken? If so, what property?
2. Was any property damaged? If so, what was it, and to what extent was it damaged?
3. What is the value of the property taken or damaged?
4. Are there any identifying marks on any of the items taken?
5. Were any weapons taken?

---

who need immediate medical attention. In another situation, an officer may arrive and come under fire from unknown assailants. This, of course, would change the officer's plan of action.

A general protocol on crime scene investigation, processing, and analysis that serves as a guideline for most plans of action at the crime scene can be found in many textbooks and handbooks (see, for example, FBI, 2004; NIJ, 2000). This protocol involves five basic steps:

- Interview
- Examine
- Photograph
- Sketch
- Process

These steps are discussed and developed throughout this book.

Quick thinking and good judgment are essential for responding officers. Sometimes decisions are simple, and there is sufficient time to consider options. Frequently, however, crime scene conditions require split-second decisions. If an officer arrives at the scene of a crime, sees a person shoot another person, and then sees the shooter run away, should the officer tend to the injured party or take chase and try to apprehend the shooter? Typically, one would expect the officer to try to save the wounded person's life. The responding officer may have to take a **dying declaration,** a statement given by the victim in anticipation of death. However, if the officer believes nothing can be done to save the wounded person's life (or sees the victim is not breathing), pursuing the assailant is the better alternative (FBI, 2004). After killing one person, the assailant poses a serious threat of injuring or killing others.

dying declaration A statement given by a victim at a crime scene, in anticipation of death. It is admissible as evidence in court.

Identify a Suspect

Officers responding to a call may see a suspect fleeing the scene and give chase. Or the victim and eyewitnesses, if any, may provide descriptions of the perpetrator during interviews. Officers, familiar with crime patterns in the area, may recognize the perpetrator's *modus operandi* (method of operation) and identify the suspect in the crime. Officers should be mindful to examine how the crime was committed and how the perpetrator came to and fled the scene. If the suspect has fled the scene, officers should request a broadcast of the description of the suspect, his or her vehicle, if any, and the direction of flight as soon as such information has been secured.

Descriptions are intended to set one person apart from another to make identification and eventual apprehension of the suspect easier. Every characteristic or feature added to a description eliminates suspects, thereby reducing the broad field in which the search is to be made. For instance, if the officer establishes that the suspect was an Asian man, men of other racial groups can be eliminated from the search. It is important to remember, however, that witnesses sometimes exaggerate their descriptions. An average-sized man sometimes looks much taller when holding a gun aimed at a victim. Looking up at a criminal who has knocked you down may alter your perception on height and weight. A person's state of mind during the course of a crime may affect his or her ability to describe a suspect. Furthermore, most people have lied about their own weight for so many years that they are not very good at accurately estimating the weight of others.

To overcome these problems, investigators typically use comparison descriptions. A **comparison description** allows the witness to look at a person whose height is known and note the similarities and differences between that person and the suspect. For example, the officer might ask a witness if the suspect was as tall as he or she, or taller. The officer will know his or her own height, so learning that the subject was about that height or was taller or shorter provides a reference point for the comparison. Ruled-edged measuring devices have been hung along the doorjambs in some convenience stores and banks, enabling clerks and tellers to see approximately how tall a person is as he or she passes through the doorway.

comparison description A physical description in which a victim or witness notes similarities and differences between the suspect and another person, whose characteristics are known.

In many cases, the witness has seen the suspect only briefly—and under distressing circumstances. The average witness will not be able to recall all of the characteristics in detail. However, with proper interviewing and the use of comparisons, an experienced investigator should be able to draw out a fairly detailed description of the suspect. When there are many witnesses, a **composite description** should be compiled from all the interviews. In other words, if descriptions of the height of a suspect are given by eight witnesses as 5 ft 8 in., 5 ft 8 in., 5 ft 9 in., 5 ft 9 in., 5 ft 10 in.,

composite description A description obtained by compiling separate, slightly varying descriptions into a whole.

FOCUS ON TECHNOLOGY

COMMUNICATIONS/VIDEO SYSTEMS (*Left*)

WHEN EVERY SECOND COUNTS, communications control consoles make it possible for dispatchers to relay critical information to field officers and investigators. (*Right*) A video camera is situated next to the rearview mirror in this patrol car. A video monitor shows all the action. The videotape supports the officer's observations and report.

5 ft 9 in., 5 ft 11 in., and 5 ft 10 in., respectively the composite for the suspect's height averages to an approximate range of 5 ft 8 in. to 5 ft 11 in.

At a minimum, the description of a suspect should include the following: race; approximate age; height; weight; build; complexion; color of hair; hairline and hairstyle; speech characteristics; basic shape of ears, eyes, nose, and mouth; dental features, such as overbite, underbite, or missing or discolored teeth; facial hair; and chin and head shape. An investigator should seek out any peculiarities or features witnesses recall about a suspect. Any single unusual feature, such as a tattoo, scar, or blemish, may eliminate hundreds of suspects. In addition, officers should obtain descriptions of the suspect's clothing. Was the suspect wearing a baseball cap or another kind of hat? What color were the suspect's shirt, pants, and shoes? Did witnesses notice any items of jewelry, such as a watch, pin, necklace, or ring?

Apprehend the Suspect

Apprehending suspects is best accomplished when officers act immediately and an arrest is made at the scene of the crime. Unfortunately, this is not typically the case. In fact, with an exception for murders (62.6 percent) and aggravated assault (55.6 percent), all other crimes cleared by an arrest represent less than half of those crimes committed. Less than 25 percent of all property crimes such as burglary, larceny, and auto theft are cleared by an arrest (Uniform Crime Report [UCR], 2005, p. 264). The proportion of arrests that actual take place at the scene of the crime is appreciably smaller. When there is a silent alarm, coincidental observance by officers, or a very fast response, police may arrive on the scene while suspects are still present and can be taken into custody.

HISTORY

IN MARCH 1963 ERNESTO MIRANDA, a 25-year-old mentally impaired man, was arrested for the kidnapping and rape of an 18-year-old woman. Miranda was arrested in his home and taken to a police station, where the victim identified him in a line-up. What followed was an intensive 2-hour interrogation. During this process, Miranda was not told that he could remain silent or have a lawyer present. Miranda confessed, was convicted, and then appealed. In *Miranda v. Arizona* (1966) the Supreme Court reversed the conviction. The court ruled that suspects must be informed of their rights before police question them. Unless they are so informed, their statements may not be used in court. Ernesto Miranda was later retried (under an assumed name) for the same offenses of kidnapping and rape. His original confession was not used, but he was convicted on the basis of other evidence gathered by the police. After serving time in prison, Miranda was released on parole. He was killed in 1972 in a skid row card game in Phoenix, Arizona.

When suspects are taken into custody, they are typically *Mirandized,* or given a **Miranda warning** informing them of their constitutional rights. **Custody** is loosely defined as a situation in which an officer has deprived a suspect of liberty and the suspect feels he or she is not free to leave. As a matter of practice, an officer will advise a suspect of his or her rights whenever the individual has been taken into custody (Berg, 1999; Roberg, 2005). A common rule of thumb police officers follow is to *Mirandize* whenever the conversation with a suspect changes from an interview or simple questioning to an interrogation. If a suspect is arrested, the *Miranda* warning is routinely given prior to interrogation.

In other cases, a suspect may flee just as the officers arrive. Under such circumstances, the police may pursue the fleeing suspect. If the suspect leaves the officer's jurisdiction while being pursued, the chase may continue and is called a **hot pursuit.** If the suspect has already fled when the officer arrives, the officer should quickly relay descriptive information to other police units.

Gather and Preserve Evidence

The crime scene should be secured and protected against interference by unauthorized people. It should remain secured until the investigators have examined it for evidence and have released it. Securing the crime scene may require covering suspected items with paper, boxes, or plastic to ensure they are not moved by wind or damaged or contaminated by falling rain or snow. It may also require setting up barricades, taping off the area, or stationing officers to guard against entry into the area (Gardner, 2005).

The **chain of command** at the crime scene is very important, especially given that a crime scene can often be filled with chaos because of onlookers, the media, various witnesses and victims, emergency medical teams, and so forth. Most police agencies expect that the initial responding patrol officer will remain in charge until a sergeant (or officer of higher rank) arrives on the scene (Weston & Lushbaugh, 2006). The sergeant remains in command until a detective or an officer of higher rank relives him or her. At the scene of a minor crime, the sergeant may relinquish command simply by calling in to advise the dispatcher that he or she has turned over command to the superior officer or detective. At the scene of a more serious crime, the sergeant will

Miranda warning   A cautionary statement to suspects in police custody, advising them of their rights to remain silent and to have an attorney present during interrogation.

custody   Loss of the liberty to leave the presence of a law enforcement officer, regardless of whether one has been told specifically, "You are under arrest."

hot pursuit   Crossing jurisdictional lines during an ongoing chase of a suspect.

chain of command   A supervisory hierarchy; levels of personnel from the top to the bottom providing span of control and regulated communications channels.

remain in command until investigating detectives have arrived. The sergeant will then both turn over command and provide the detectives with a briefing on which officers are present on the scene; what has already been unearthed regarding evidence, descriptions, and events; and a general status report. For these serious crimes, the sergeant will likely remain on the scene to command the uniformed patrol officers (Gardner, 2005; Weston & Lushbaugh, 2006).

As suggested in the protocol, two important aspects to crime scene investigation are photographing and sketching the crime scene. This should be accomplished before physical evidence is actually collected. In some cases, a search for latent fingerprints is made, and casts of footprints, tracks, and tool impressions are taken when these are present. Generally speaking, an item should be considered a piece of evidence if it fits any one of the following categories:

- It has the potential to offer clues to the suspect's identity (fingerprints, footprints, hair, skin scrapings, and so forth).
- It tends to suggest the manner or method in which the crime was committed (weapons, documents, tools, or other instrumentation).
- It is not usually found at the location. Out-of-place items may have been left or moved by the suspect.

When gathering and preserving evidence, officers should never touch anything with their naked hands or move anything before it has been recorded (photographed and sketched) and cataloged. The goal of investigators is to protect all of the evidence and make sure that no one touches, moves, or removes it. After securing the crime scene, investigators can request technical assistance in gathering evidence. Officers and investigators must maintain an irrefutable **chain of custody** for all evidence found, documenting its possession from the time it is discovered until it is produced in court. Procedures for gathering and preserving evidence are more fully described in Chapters 3 and 4.

chain of custody Proof of the possession of evidence from the moment it is found until the moment it is offered in evidence at court.

RECORDING THE CRIME SCENE

Among the many activities undertaken at the crime scene, one of the most important is note taking. There are several reasons for the critical importance of taking notes in a criminal investigation, particularly at the preliminary stage of the investigation. First, taking notes requires investigators to commit their observations to writing. Second, it enables them to keep a detailed chronological record of everything they see and do. It is not unusual for some seemingly unimportant item in the investigator's notes to become a pivotal point in the prosecution of the suspect. Third, carefully prepared records can also provide a mechanism for jogging an investigator's memory when he or she testifies in court (Davis, 2004).

Field notes should be neat, legible, and comprehensive. Notes that are sloppy or incomplete or have mixed-up chronology can be misinterpreted later or lead to inaccurate descriptions in court. Be as specific as possible in taking notes in the field. For example, avoid saying that a weapon was found "near" a victim. Instead, specify the distance from the victim that the weapon was found. Also indicate the time that an item of evidence was discovered. Notes should be complete enough for someone reading them 25 years in the future to have a clear idea of what was found and done by investigators at the crime scene.

Whether notes are from a preliminary or follow-up investigation, complete and accurate notes are critically important. They should be taken on every call, or contact,

CAREER FOCUS

REGULATORY AGENCY INVESTIGATOR

MANY STATES, COUNTIES, AND CITIES have criminal investigators who are not assigned to the state, municipal, or sheriff's department. Rather, they are employed by public agencies with specialized regulatory responsibilities with police power. The names and functions of these agencies vary among states and localities but can include such agencies as alcoholic beverage license and control, gambling and wagering commission, bureau of taxation and finance, environmental conservation, and industrial safety commission. As employees of such agencies, investigators ensure that the role of the agency is carried out according to the guidelines established by the state, county, or municipality.

The work may involve investigating and apprehending persons suspected of criminal activities as agency employees, as persons doing business with the agency, or as individuals over whom the agency has licensing or regulatory control. For example, an investigator working for the state inspector general's office may investigate the possibility of fraud, waste, and abuse at a financially troubled state university and recommend that school officials face criminal charges. Like other investigators, agency investigators gather information about suspects, study records, set up surveillance, conduct court-ordered wiretaps, execute search warrants, participate in raids, and operate as undercover agents.

Education requirements vary depending on the location and specific nature of an agency's role. Some positions may require a college degree and related experience in addition to passing a civil service examination. Training requirements and use of firearms vary with each agency.

made by an officer while conducting an investigation. Each contact should then be followed by an appropriate report. Not only are these reports important for possible use at trial, but they enable the department head to render accurate accounts of officers' time to the city manager, mayor, city council, or board of supervisors.

When creating field notes, officers are often guided by questions concerning *who, what, when, where, how,* and *why.* Answers to these questions, along with other elements of evidence and physical identification, are key pieces of information for later reports. Figure 2.3 shows how these questions might be formulated into a set of guidelines to assist a preliminary investigation.

FIGURE 2.3 Guidelines for Writing Field Notes

Who were the people involved (names, ages, residences, businesses, telephone numbers, descriptions)? Who did what to or with whom? Who saw or heard anything of importance? Who handled the evidence? Who discovered the crime? Who had custody of the property last?

What happened? What crime was committed? What time did it occur? What weapon was used? What is the suspect's method of operation? What was the reason for the crime? What was taken? What vehicle, if any, was involved?

When did the crime occur (time of day)? When was the crime discovered? When were the police notified? When was the victim last seen? When was the property last seen?

Where did the crime occur? Where was the victim at the time? Where were the witnesses? Where was the suspect first seen? Where was the suspect last seen? From where was the property taken?

How was the crime committed? How did the suspect get to the scene? How did the suspect leave or make a getaway? How many people were involved? How much money or property was taken?

Why was the crime committed (what events preceded the offense)? Why did so much time elapse before the police were notified? Why was this particular victim attacked? Why was the criminal act committed in this particular way?

FIGURE 2.4 Sample field notes

03-07-06

Case # 12345

Time: 1200 hours

Burglary - at 5 Klamath, Irvine, CA.

Victim - Jane Jones

Tel. # 555-1234

Victim Jones states she returned home from shopping at 1100 hours.

States she found her front door open - but she says she is certain it was closed & locked when she left (no sign of forced entry).

Window may have been jimmied

Victim Jones states the following items are missing:

1 - Panasonic Stackable Stereo
- serial # unknown
- smoke gray & black in color
- small chip on left corner (front) of phono dust cover
- value: $465

2 - G.E. Color Television
- wood grain color
- serial # unknown
- no special identifying marks
- value: $249

Specificity is important in creating field notes (see Figure 2.4). Be careful not to accept vague comments such as "He was young" or "He was old," or even "He was tall" or "He was short." Clarify these comments by asking, "Approximately how old would you say the suspect was?" or "Approximately how tall was the suspect?" When property has been taken, descriptive data should include the quantity and kind of articles taken, the trade name, a physical description, serial numbers, personal identifying marks, any damage, the age, the condition, and the current estimated market value. It is a good idea never to leave the scene of a crime or end an interview until you are satisfied that you have accumulated all available information. For police notes, the operative maxim is "More is better."

Field notes are the major frame of reference and raw source from which operational reports are prepared. The demands of a case often require field notes to be taken down out of order or by several people, and unavoidable interruptions and sequence problems

It is imperative to maintain a written record of all phases of investigation, including preliminary and follow-up procedures. These notes will be the basis for all reports and may be entered as evidence.

may occur. To overcome these sorts of problems, many officers rely on a loose-leaf notebook, recording each interview on a separate sheet of paper. A loose-leaf binder allows the investigator to sort pertinent notes together while maintaining chronology. Notes can be organized and reorganized as necessary to prepare operational reports.

Recently, some officers have begun using microcassette recorders to tape-record their field notes. If you choose this route, make a written transcription of your field recordings as quickly as possible to ensure their accuracy. Remember, in most jurisdictions, an officer's field notes—whether written or recorded—can be subpoenaed during a criminal court case. Inaccurate field notes can lose a criminal conviction in the same way that accurate ones might win the case.

For example, on March 3, 1991, Rodney King failed to stop when signaled to do so by a police car traveling behind him. In fact, King increased his speed and tried to elude the police car chasing him. After a prolonged chase at speeds estimated at 100 mph, King did finally come to a halt. Police physically removed Rodney King from his vehicle and delivered 56 baton strikes and 6 kicks to King in a period of approximately 2 minutes; producing 11 skull fractures, brain damage, and kidney damage. Initially unaware that the incident had been videotaped, the officers involved filed inaccurate reports, not mentioning the fact that Rodney King was left with head wounds. As many will recall from the extensive news coverage of this event, this inaccurate police reporting was the catalyst for a number of challenges to the truthfulness and accuracy of the police reports that were written about this incident. As a consequence, four police officers were indicted, and ultimately two of these officers were convicted and sentenced to 30 months in prison. These events also have been credited with having precipitated 6 days of riots in Los Angeles, where 54 people were killed, 2,383 were injured, and 13,212 were arrested (Lepore, 2004).

As should be fairly obvious from this incident, keeping detailed, accurate field notes and police reports is critically important. While it is unlikely that having had accurate notes would have significantly changed the eventual outcome for the two officers convicted of violating Rodney King's civil rights, it is possible that having had accurate notes could have led to disciplinary action being taken against the officers involved. Such disciplinary action might have stemmed the riots that resulted largely as a consequence of the police department taking no actions against the offending officers.

Ideally, once operational reports are complete, field notes or copies of them should be placed in the file of the case to which they relate. Many officers retain copies of their field notes. Notes made at the time of the investigation can be used later to refresh the officer's memory in court. Defense counsels have the right to cross-examine an officer on his or her testimony. Field notes, therefore, should be neat, legible, accurate, and written in an understandable fashion. A number of police agencies across the country employ technical writers to train their officers on how to keep accurate and literate field notes (Biggs, 2003). Writing has become so important that a *virtual* cottage industry of writing software specifically for police officers has been developed during the past decade (see, for example, software shown on PoliceOne.com at http://www.policeone.com/police-technology/software/report-writing/).

THE LEGAL SIGNIFICANCE OF EVIDENCE

Responding officers are typically responsible for certain aspects of the preliminary investigation. For example, an officer arriving on the scene of an incident must immediately determine what has happened and whether anyone is injured. The officer must assess whether a crime has been committed and, if so, what type of crime. Should the initial allegations prove unfounded or the acts represent noncriminal behavior, the matter can be closed with the first report. If, on the other hand, the officer's findings indicate that a criminal law has been violated, then proof of the *corpus delicti* of the particular offense must be established. **Corpus delicti,** which is Latin for "body of the crime," consists of the material facts showing that a crime has been committed. It includes all of the physical elements that, taken together, demonstrate that a crime has been committed.

> **corpus delicti** All the material facts showing that a crime has been committed; Latin for "body of the crime."

To sustain a conviction, it is necessary to establish that the elements of a crime, as defined in criminal law, have occurred. These elements must be demonstrated. Misunderstandings about *corpus delicti* are common; the term does not, however, necessarily refer to a dead body (Perkins, 1962). For example, in a murder a "dead body" is neither necessary nor sufficient to establish the *corpus delicti*. Rather, it is evidence that the death occurred as a result of some criminal act that represents the *corpus delicti* of murder. Testimony that a defendant pushed someone off a bridge into a raging river can establish the *corpus delicti* of murder even if the body is never recovered. Conversely, the body of a young woman found dead in a forest would not in itself establish the *corpus delicti* for murder absent proof of some criminal act having caused her death (Morris, 1959; Perkins, 1962). Many murder convictions are obtained each year even though the body of the alleged victim is never found. Similarly, there is a *corpus delicti* for burglary, robbery, tax evasion, and, indeed, for every criminal offense. At each crime scene, investigators must know and keep in mind the requirements to prove that a crime has been committed. They must try to find evidence that meets these requirements.

> **prima facie evidence** Evidence good and sufficient on its surface to establish a given fact or chain of facts, if not rebutted or contradicted, to be proof of the fact; Latin for "on the surface."

Sometimes the *corpus delicti* of a crime can be established on the basis of *prima facie* **evidence.** That is, the evidence is good and sufficient on its face to establish a given fact. Suppose an officer stops a motorist who is driving in an erratic fashion. Noting the driver's slurred speech after having observed the irregular driving pattern, the officer decides to administer a field sobriety test. Failure of this test is taken to mean that the driver's blood alcohol is at least 0.1 percent, evidence of intoxication in that state. The officer can now arrest the driver for driving under the influence of alcohol, basing the arrest on *prima facie* evidence. In some states, such as Pennsylvania, drivers who refuse to take a breath or blood analysis for alcohol have their license revoked whether they are guilty or not. In effect, refusing to submit to the test constitutes *prima facie* evidence of guilt.

Had the officer in the preceding example used only the driving pattern and the slurred speech to determine that the driver was intoxicated, the officer would have been relying on circumstantial evidence. **Circumstantial evidence** is evidence of associated facts from which one can logically deduce that facts are proven indirectly. Circumstantial evidence is not always as useful as some other forms of evidence. For example, the driver's erratic driving pattern and slurred speech might be the result of fatigue and a speech impediment rather than alcohol. In many cases, however, any or all of these elements of a crime can be proven by circumstantial evidence. By using deductive reasoning (see Chapter 1), the investigator can conclude from a series of known elements that a crime has occurred.

> **circumstantial evidence** Evidence of other facts from which deductions can be drawn to show indirectly the facts to be proven.

Rules of Evidence

When a suspect is apprehended at the crime scene or shortly thereafter, the evidence collected by the officer in the primary investigation becomes the basis of the charges the state then brings against the defendant. Every criminal investigator must have a working knowledge of the **rules of evidence** to ensure that the evidence collected during the investigation will be admissible in court.

> **rules of evidence** Rules of court that govern the admissibility of evidence at trials and hearings.

FYI A system of rules and procedures for presenting evidence in U.S. courts has developed over the past 200 years. Originally derived from the English legal system, these rules of evidence have been significantly amended through federal and state court decisions and legislative actions. Today, the Uniform Rules of Evidence, the Federal Rules of Evidence, and state rules, such as the Maine Rules of Evidence and the California Evidence Code, set the standards of admissibility against which evidence will be judged.

Admissibility is the essence of the rules of evidence. Virtually anything may be admitted in court as evidence provided there is no rule that prohibits its admissibility. Rules concerning the limitation or exclusion of evidence in a court case center on a doctrine known as the **exclusionary rule.** According to this rule, when evidence has been obtained in violation of the rights guaranteed by the U.S. Constitution, that evidence must be excluded at trial. The exclusionary rule is grounded in the Fourth Amendment and is intended to protect citizens from illegal searches and seizures. In practice, it means that police officers and investigators must abide by certain guidelines when searching for and seizing material that may be used as evidence in a court of law.

> **exclusionary rule** The rule that evidence obtained in violation of constitutional guarantees against unlawful search and seizure cannot be used at trial.

Three tests—relevancy, materiality, and competency—govern a judge's ruling on admissibility of evidence. **Relevancy** is the application of evidence in determining the truth or falsity of the issue being tried. Relevant evidence relates to, or bears directly on, the point or fact at issue, from which inferences can be drawn. Evidence is relevant when it has any tendency in reason to make the fact that it is offered to prove or disprove either more or less probable (Emanuel, 2004).

> **relevancy** The applicability of evidence in determining the truth or falsity of the issue being tried; a requirement for admissibility in court.

materiality   The importance of evidence in influencing the court's opinion because of its connection with the issue; a requirement for admissibility in court.

competency   The quality of evidence, or its fitness to be presented, to assist in determining questions of fact; a requirement for admissibility in court; also used to describe a witness as legally fit and qualified to give testimony.

Even if the evidence is relevant, it may be denied admissibility if it is such an insignificant point that it will not affect the outcome of the case. **Materiality** is the importance of the evidence in influencing the court's opinion on an issue. In other words, is the evidence important enough for the court to take time to hear?

Finally, evidence must pass the test of competency. **Competency** is the quality of a piece of evidence or of a person offering evidence. If the credibility of a piece of evidence or of an individual offering evidence is faulty, the value of the evidence diminishes, and it may be ruled inadmissible.

Types of Evidence

There are four traditional types of evidence: real, demonstrative, documentary, and testimonial. Some rules of evidence apply to all four types, and some rules apply only to some or one of them. Let's briefly review these types of evidence.

Real Evidence   Real evidence is some item or thing the existence or characteristics of which are relevant and material. Usually this item or thing was directly involved in some event in the crime. For example, a signed contract, where there is a dispute between parties, is real evidence both to prove its terms and that it was executed by the two parties who signatures appear on it. If it is a handwritten document, and the writing appears faltering or as if written by an unsteady hand, it may be relevant to show that the writer was under duress at the time of its execution, and hence, the document might not be admissible (Best, 2004; Mueller & Kirkpatrick, 2004). The bloody knife, shown to be the murder weapon in a homicide, a broken automobile headlight in a hit-and-run accident, skin scrapings found under the nails of a rape victim—all may be seen as real evidence.

Demonstrative Evidence   Demonstrative evidence, as the name implies, demonstrates or illustrates the testimony of a witness. Demonstrative evidence is admissible when, with accuracy sufficient for the purpose for which this evidence is being used, it fairly and accurately reflects the witness's testimony and is otherwise unobjectionable (Best, 2004; Mueller & Kirkpatrick, 2004). Typical examples of demonstrative evidence include photographs, maps, diagrams of the scene of an accident, charts, animations, computer simulations, and the like. Because its purpose is to illustrate testimony, and not to represent testimony in itself, the witness whose testimony is being illustrated must authenticate demonstrative evidence. Typically, this is done by the witness identifying salient features of the exhibit and testify that it fairly and accurately reflects what he or she saw or heard on a particular occasion. For example, an officer might identify a photograph of a crime scene by indicating that the image accurately reflects his or her memory of the scene at the time the criminal investigation unit took the photograph.

Police officers and investigators must know the guidelines for admissibility of evidence in court.

Documentary Evidence   Documentary evidence is often a kind of real evidence and, as the name implies, involves documents used as evidence. For example, letters may be offered as proof of threats contained in love letters sent by a stalker to a victim. When a document is used as evidence, it is authenticated the same way as any other real evidence—by having a witness who identifies it. In the letter example, the stalking victim would identify the letters as those she received from the defendant. It should be noted that some documents, such as certified copies of public records, official documents, newspaper articles, periodicals, and other published or commercial documents, to some extent or another are typically viewed as self-authenticating.

Testimonial Evidence   Testimonial evidence, or what is sometimes referred to as "eyewitness" evidence, is the most basic form of evidence and the only kind that does not usually require another form of evidence as a prerequisite for its admissibility. Testimonial evidence, literally, is offered as what the witness heard or saw relevant to the questions at hand concerning the crime (Emanuel, 2004; Yeschke, 2002). This must, however, be information heard or seen by the witness firsthand, and not information told to the witness by a third party, which would constitute hearsay, not firsthand information.

Suppose, for example, that prosecutors in a case involving a series of letter bombs (explosive devices delivered in letters or mailed packages) want to introduce various materials found in the suspect bomber's home—items that could be used to construct bombs. To have these items ruled admissible, the prosecution must demonstrate the relevancy of the materials to the case. In other words, a link between the specific types of bomb-making materials found in the suspect's home and those used in the letter bombs needs to be shown. Certainly, items such as wire, packaging materials, timers, and detonators are material to a case brought against a suspected letter bomber. Officers and forensic scientists with ample training can demonstrate the competency of the evidence by explaining the relationship between the various materials found at the home and the construction of bombs. If there are drawings or sketches of the bombs found at the suspect bomber's home, these documents may be entered as evidence once their authenticity has been accomplished through testimony by competent forensic scientists or trained officers.

SUMMARY

Learning Objective 1

The information gathered in the preliminary investigation provides the foundation for the eventual court case against a criminal suspect. This information must be carefully collected, accurately recorded, and skillfully processed.

Learning Objective 2

During the preliminary investigation, investigators should fulfill these responsibilities: deal with emergency situations, determine whether a crime has been committed, establish crime scene priorities, identify a suspect, apprehend the suspect, and gather and preserve evidence.

Learning Objective 3

Maintaining clear, literate, and accurate field notes during all phases of an investigation is absolutely essential to preparing a good report and a solid case against a defendant. Field notes are the source from which operational reports are prepared.

Learning Objective 4

Corpus delicti, which is Latin for "body of the crime," consists of the material facts showing that a crime has been committed. It includes all the physical elements that demonstrate that a crime has been committed. To sustain a conviction, the elements of a crime, as defined in criminal law, have to be established and demonstrated.

Learning Objective 5

Evidence collected at a crime scene may be of two types: *prima facie* evidence, which is good and sufficient on its face to establish a given fact, and circumstantial evidence, which is indirect evidence or associated facts from which conclusions can be drawn.

Learning Objective 6

Evidence collected at a crime scene must pass three tests of admissibility in court: relevancy (Is it proper to apply it to determining the truth or falsity of the issue being tried?), materiality (Is it important enough to influence the court?), and competency (Is the quality of the evidence or the witness explaining it free of faults?). Evidence also must be gathered without violating a person's constitutional rights against unlawful search and seizure.

KEY TERMS

preliminary investigation **18**

dying declaration **21**

comparison description **21**

composite description **21**

Miranda warning **23**

custody **23**

hot pursuit **23**

chain of command **23**

chain of custody **24**

corpus delicti **28**

prima facie evidence **28**

circumstantial evidence **29**

rules of evidence **29**

exclusionary rule **29**

relevancy **29**

materiality **30**

competency **30**

QUESTIONS FOR REVIEW

Learning Objective 1

1. What is a preliminary investigation?

Learning Objective 2

2. Define *dying declaration, comparison description, composite description, hot pursuit,* and *chain of custody.*

3. Enumerate the investigative responsibilities at a crime scene.

4. Why must an officer secure a crime scene upon arrival?

5. What method could you use to help a victim or a witness provide as accurate a description as possible of a suspect?

6. When are suspects generally given a *Miranda* warning, and what is it?

Learning Objective 3

7. List the six basic questions that an investigator's field notes should answer about a crime.

Learning Objective 4

8. What is the meaning and importance of the term *corpus delicti?*

Learning Objective 5

9. With which type of evidence—*prima facie* or circumstantial—would an investigator be most apt to use deductive reasoning?

Learning Objective 6

10. What is meant by the exclusionary rule? Why is it significant for criminal investigators?

11. Identify three tests that a judge might apply to evidence gathered at a crime scene to determine its admissibility in court.

CRITICAL THINKING EXERCISE

You are a police officer dispatched by radio to assist Officer Murray, already on the scene and checking out a suspicious person in a supermarket parking lot. As you turn your cruiser into the parking lot, you hear two gunshots and see Officer Murray fall to the ground as the car he was standing near speeds away with wheels squealing. What actions will you take? Explain your answer.

INVESTIGATIVE SKILL BUILDERS

Acquiring and Evaluating Information

Go around the room and count off by ones and twos. The instructor then flips a coin to determine whether the ones or the twos will be the investigators; the other group will be witnesses. The instructor leaves the room for about 15 minutes. Working in pairs, the investigators interview the witnesses to obtain a description of the suspect—your instructor. Try to include information about the following characteristics: race; approximate age; height; weight; build; complexion; color of hair; hairline and hairstyle; type of speech; the basic shape of ears, eyes, nose, and mouth; dental features, such as overbite, underbite, or missing or discolored teeth; chin and head shape; facial hair; unusual eyebrows; and scars, blemishes, or tattoos. Also include clothing descriptions. Investigators should record the descriptions as field notes. When your instructor returns, read aloud the descriptions to compare their accuracy.

Integrity/Honesty

You are the first to arrive at the crime scene. After looking around and acquiring the necessary information about victims and witnesses, you begin to secure the scene. While doing so, you unconsciously light a cigarette. When you finish smoking, you casually drop the butt on the ground within the crime scene. Later you notice that one of the forensic technicians has found, bagged, and tagged your cigarette butt. Will you tell the detective leading the crime scene investigation that it is your cigarette butt? Explain.

Problem Solving

You and your partner arrive on the scene of an armed robbery of a convenience store. It is not clear whether the suspect has fled. There are five people in the store.

1. What do you do upon arriving at the scene?

2. Should you assume the suspect has fled and treat the people as victims?

3. What precautions might you take to protect yourself, your partner, and the victims?

Preserving the Crime Scene

CHAPTER OBJECTIVES

After completing this chapter, you will be able to:

1 Discuss the role of evidence in criminal investigation.
2 List the eight basic steps for gathering and preserving evidence at a crime scene.
3 Identify what investigators consider the location of a crime scene.
4 Explain the importance of photography in preserving a crime scene.
5 Tell how crime scene sketches complement still photography, and list the five methods used to prepare sketches.
6 Give the five search patterns from which investigators may choose when conducting a search.
7 Understand the importance of securing and preserving evidence found at a crime scene.

EVIDENCE AND THE CRIME SCENE

A criminal investigation must be concerned with both people and things. Together they constitute the field of physical evidence for an investigation and comprise the ingredients that, when combined, may produce a solution to a crime. Utilizing both human testimony and physical evidence, a prosecuting attorney will bring a case against a defendant. The prosecuting attorney can muster a strong case only if the investigators have done their job thoroughly. This means that they have effectively sought and collected *usable* evidence. **Evidence,** in criminal investigation, is any item that helps to establish the facts of a related criminal case. Evidence may be found at the scene of the crime or on the victim or be taken from the suspect or the suspect's environment. How that evidence is protected, collected, secured, and transported will affect its later usefulness when introduced in a criminal court case.

Forensic science has become a household word as the popularity of crime scene investigation television programs have blossomed. But what exactly is forensic science? Saferstein (2003) broadly defines forensic science as the application of science to law and includes the application of the knowledge of science and technology for determining the evidential value of the crime scene and related evidence.

Criminalists, or **forensic specialists,** are people specifically trained to collect evidence and to make scientific tests and assessments of various types of physical evidence. In some jurisdictions investigators can call on these trained technicians to aid in the search for evidence, and they are often referred to as crime scene investigators (CSI). During most preliminary investigations, however, the responding officer or investigator must take on the role of the forensic specialist. A review of the literature (Gardner, 2005; Giard, 2007; Vince, 2005) suggests that an investigator must consider eight basic procedures during the crime scene investigation to gather and preserve evidence:

1. Recognize or discover relevant physical evidence.
2. Examine evidence to determine that it can be tested or compared in a crime laboratory.
3. Collect evidence with care and diligence, according to standard procedures, and in a lawful manner.
4. Carefully handle, package, and label evidence to avoid damage, loss, contamination, or questionable links in the chain of custody.
5. Carefully record how, where, and by whom evidence was located to ensure that evidence has not been tampered with or altered.
6. Carefully transport evidence to a laboratory, maintaining the proper chain of custody and security.
7. Maintain the integrity of the chain of custody from the crime lab to the court after tests have been completed.
8. Present or explain evidence in a court proceeding, substantiate the find if necessary, and document the chain of custody.

To be effective in gathering evidence at a crime scene, an investigator must know what qualifies or is significant as physical evidence in a particular crime; how to properly collect, preserve, and transport the evidence; and what the crime lab can do with it. The crime laboratory is only as good as the investigator. If the investigator fails to locate adequate evidence, there is little a crime laboratory can do. Generally speaking, the investigator has there main sources for evidence: (1) the scene of the crime, (2) the victim, if any, and (3) the suspect and his or her environment (Gardner, 2005; Worrall, 2005).

evidence Any item that helps to establish the facts of a related criminal case. It may be found at the scene of the crime or on the victim or taken from the suspect or the suspect's environment.

forensic science The application of science to law, and the use of science and technology to determine the value of evidence.

criminalist (or forensic specialist) A person specifically trained to collect evidence and to make scientific tests and assessments of various types of physical evidence.

FYI Tests on physical evidence discovered at the crime scene are usually conducted in a crime laboratory. Some tests, however, must be conducted in the field. For example, a special test can determine whether blood has been cleaned from a floor. When a chemical known as *luminol* is sprayed on the floor, even minute traces of blood will fluoresce, or light up, when viewed under ultraviolet light.

Among the decisions an investigator must make during the preliminary investigation is what constitutes the crime scene. The boundaries must be established so that the entire crime scene can be effectively preserved. The crime scene can be understood to include all areas in which the criminal, any possible victim, and any eyewitnesses moved during the time the crime was committed. Typically, one might expect this to include a fairly stable, limited area. In some crimes, however, the crime scene may actually comprise several different sites. For instance, say that a young girl was abducted from her bedroom one evening. She was then transported by car to a cabin in the woods and sexually assaulted. Following the assault, the abductor shot her to death and carried the body into the woods, where he buried it in a shallow grave. In this example, each location—the bedroom, the car, the cabin, and the area around the grave—is part of the crime scene. The boundaries of a given part of the crime scene, however, are well defined physically and must be preserved.

The ultimate success or failure of a criminal investigation depends on the thoroughness exercised at the crime scene in preserving, collecting, and recording all available information. Very often the position of an article in a room, in a lot, or in a building will convey to the trained eye the events preceding the crime. It is important, therefore, to repeat the rule that nothing at a crime scene should be touched, moved, or altered in any way until it has been identified, photographed, sketched, measured, and recorded. Among the first ways of recording a crime scene is by taking pictures.

PICTORIAL DOCUMENTATION OF THE CRIME SCENE

One of the investigator's most important jobs at the crime scene is to create an accurate, objective visual record before any item or objects are moved or removed as possible elements of evidence. Photographs of the scene of a serious criminal act should be taken as soon as possible after preliminary investigation priorities have been taken care of, before note taking, sketching, or the search of additional evidence begins (Robinson, 2006; Staggs, 1997).

Photographing the Crime Scene

The role of photographs in a criminal investigation is to present a logical story visually. Nothing in the crime scene should be disturbed before photographs are taken. The pictures should illustrate the original, uncontaminated condition of the crime scene. The objective of photographing the crime scene is to visually preserve the scene as it was when found by the investigators, and presumably as left by the perpetrator; to record the location and position of items of evidence; and to document and record the points of view of principals and potential witnesses. In

A measuring device helps to depict the size of the object.

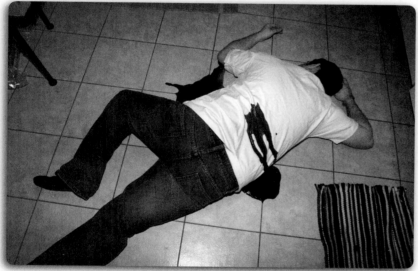

The progression of photographs from different distances helps to reconstruct the crime that was committed.

addition, photographs document the spatial relationship of various items located in and about the crime scene (Ogle, 2004).

Crime scene photographs, properly executed, help to ensure a thorough investigation and subsequent prosecution. A series of poorly planned and poorly taken pictures may result in a weak, ineffectual prosecution. When photographing a crime scene, follow the axiom "More is better." That is, if there is a question whether some object or aspect of the scene should be photographed, it should be. Later, if it becomes apparent that some seemingly innocuous part of the scene was indeed important, but not photographed, it may be too late to photographically preserve it (Ogle, 2004).

Camera Choices

Many departments have moved from 35 mm cameras to digital and even video recording devices (Gardner, 2005). Both black and white and colored film may be used at the crime scene, and high-speed films are especially useful for capturing pictures even in low-light conditions (Weston & Lushbaugh, 2006). Traditionally, however, a single lens reflex (SLR) camera has been selected to photograph crime scenes. The SLR camera typically is compact and comes in a variety of formats, from manually focusing units to fully automatic units complete with automatic focusing, flash, and winding (Ogle, 2004). Lenses are available in a wide assortment of long-range and close-up (macro) choices. Zoom lenses can be of particular value in crime scene photography. A zoom lens with the range of 35–70 mm with a macro capability, along with a long-range zoom lens in the range of 8–200 mm, is typically adequate for most types of pictures taken at a crime scene.

Digital cameras have a number of advantages when used in crime scene photography: they require no chemical processing, can be displayed on the camera immediately, and can be transferred to a computer and stored in an electronic database (Smith, 2003). Because digital photos are very easy to alter, however, until recently they had little value as evidence in court. Today digital crime scene photographs are becoming accepted in most courts across the nation. In fact, the prosecutors in the bombing trial of Timothy McVeigh used digital photographs when presenting their case. Nonetheless, the possible misuse of digital photographs is a reality, and proper procedures are necessary to protect the integrity of these images (Ogle, 2004). Careful logs and storage of these digital images in a database are critical for maintaining the authenticity of photos.

megapixels Refers to picture image resolution. A mega equals 1 million. Pixels are the smallest unit of brightness and color; more pixels means sharper, clearer, and better images.

For crime scene investigation, the digital camera should have four or more megapixels, close-up capabilities, and a flash attachment. **Megapixels** refer to *image resolution*. A pixel is the smallest unit of brightness and color in an image. The more pixels you have, the sharper, clearer, and better picture you can produce. (Mega means one million, so four megapixels equals four million pixels.) The more pixels, the more detail that can be captured. This is important when photographing small items of evidence. Also, the difference in megapixels is important when making prints for court. Two megapixels gives a good 5 × 7-inch print. Three megapixels gives a good 8 × 10-inch print. Four megapixels gives a good 11 × 14-inch print. Five megapixels gives a good 16 × 20-inch print.

Video cameras also provide an easy and inexpensive way to document crime scenes, and they provide jurors with a more realistic sense of the crime scene than still pictures of an accident, room, or area. The zoom on video cameras is more often digital rather than optical, and the pictures have slightly less clarity than fixed photographs, and to some extent even digital images. Videos are, in general, a good briefing tool for police officers who have not visited the crime scene and can be an additional aid for the prosecutor in presenting a criminal case. They are not a substitute, however, for either photographs or sketches of the crime scene.

Photo Organization

To adequately present the crime scene visually, the photographs must form an organized sequence and show all relevant locations and objects. One guideline for taking crime scene photographs is to progress from the general to the specific. This involves using three major types of vantage points: long-range, mid-range, and close-up. What constitutes a long-range, mid-range, or close-up photograph is somewhat relative. For instance, a long-range photograph of an apartment complex may be an aerial view of the entire area. A long-range photograph of a room may be a view from the doorway to the room. The actual vantage points will depend on the immediate area where the crime was committed and the kind of location involved.

A separate series of photographs should be taken for each distance. For instance, in a homicide investigation the photographer might snap the following: *long-range* photographs of the overall scene, to show the murder scene as a person would view it from a standing position in the doorway and from different corners of the room, including the victim and all the objects in the room; *mid-range* photographs from different angles about 8 or 10 feet from the victim, omitting some of the objects shown in the long-range views; *close-up* photographs, taken from about 5 feet or less from the victim, showing wounds on the victim's body, an arm, leg, or torso, or objects close to the victim's body such as a gun, empty cartridges, and blood patterns.

Sometimes it may be necessary to include a measurement scale in photographs of objects at a crime scene. This helps those viewing the photographs to understand the size and distance relationships depicted. Whenever practical, depending on the subject matter of the photograph, a measuring device should appear in the photograph along with the crime scene object. It is critical to note, however, that judges sometimes demand to see crime scene photographs without the clutter of extraneous scaling devices. Therefore, always remember to photograph subject matter at the crime scene as it is originally found. Then repeat the photograph with a scaling or identification marker.

The first photograph on every roll of film shot at the crime scene should be a title card (Figure 3.1) indicating the crime location, date, case identifier, photographer, and roll number. All subsequent photographs taken at the crime scene should be identified by number and entered in the photo log.

SKETCHING THE CRIME SCENE

Why, you might ask, should the crime scene be sketched if it has already been photographed or videotaped? Sketches are useful in questioning witnesses and suspects and when writing investigative reports. Sketches are also excellent companions to photographs. Where photographs provide exacting details, sketches offer accurate information about the placement of objects, and they show relationships and distances between things. Sketches can be used to refresh an investigator's memory; to reflect the relationship of objects to the surrounding area; to help the prosecutor, judge, and jury understanding the conditions at the crime scene; and to supplement photographs of the scene (Fisher, 2004). See Figure 3.2 for a completed sketch of a homicide scene. Note how the sketch preparer depicted the locations of the victim, the gun cartridge cases, and the footprints.

Geberth (2006) suggests that for a sketch or diagram to be legally admissible in court, it must meet the following requirements:

- It must be part of a qualified person's testimony.
- It must recall the situation that the preparer saw.
- It must express the place or scene correctly.

FIGURE 3.1 Photo Title Card and Photo Log

PHOTOGRAPHIC LOG

LOCATION: _Master Bedroom_

DATE: _03-17-07_

CASE IDENTIFIER: _B-2345_

PREPARER/ASSISTANTS: _Sgt. Dwyer_
Off. Torres

CAMERA: _#12_

TYPE OF FILM
AND RATING: _Kodak/400/24_

REMARKS: _Roll #1_

PHOTO #	DESCRIPTION OF PHOTOGRAPHIC SUBJECT	USE OF SCALE	MISCELLANEOUS COMMENTS	SKETCH (IF APPLICABLE)
1.	Long shot - room (rt corner angle)		All photos from left side of victim	
2.	Mid shot - victim			LOCATION: _Master Bedroom_
3.	Mid shot - head			DATE: 03-17-07
4.	Close shot - wound (entrance)			CASE IDENTIFIER: _B-2345_
5.	Mid shot - wound			PHOTOGRAPHER: _Off. Torres_
6.	Mid shot - left hand & gun			ROLL NUMBER: _1 of 1_
7.	Close shot - gun			
8.	Long shot - room (lft corner angle)		All photos from right side of victim	
9.	Close shot - body			
10.	Close shot - head			
11.	Close shot - wound (exit)			
12.	Mid shot - note			
13.	Close shot - note			
14.	Mid shot - head			
15.	Long shot - room (from door)		All photos from victim's feet	
16.	Mid shot - body (from door)			
17.	Mid shot - head (from door)			
18.	Close shot - head			
19.	Close shot - wound (entrance)			
20.	Mid shot - left hand & gun			
21.	Mid shot - body			
22.	Long shot - room (rt corner angle)		From right side of victim	
23.	Long shot - room (lft corner angle)		From right side of victim	
24.	Close shot - head		From right side of victim	

Preparing the Sketch

A crime scene sketch complements the notes and photographs taken during the crime scene investigation. The purpose of the sketch is to present accurate information, not necessarily to be artistic (Genge, 2002). A simple line drawing with accurate measurements is sufficient. Some outdoor measurements may be paced off, estimated, or obtained by using the odometer of a car. However, in a final sketch for a report, precise measurements and accurate reproduction of the crime scene are essential (Lee, Palmbach, & Miller, 2001).

Initially, the sketch preparer should take a general look around the scene and decide which details to include in the sketch. Next, the investigator must decide what scale to use. In general, try to use the largest scale possible. To determine what scale to use, divide the longest measurement at the scene by the longest measurement of the sketching paper to be used. Most reports and records are kept on 81/2 × 11-inch paper. Thus if the longest measurement at the scene is 100 feet, let 1 inch equal 10 feet so that the drawing will fit comfortably within the 11-inch length of the paper. Graph paper also makes it easier to draw objects while maintaining scale.

All sketches should include a compass or an orienting compass arrow indicating north; a legend or key to explain letters, numbers, or symbols used; and an indication of the scale used (Figure 3.2).

FIGURE 3.2 Crime Scene Sketch

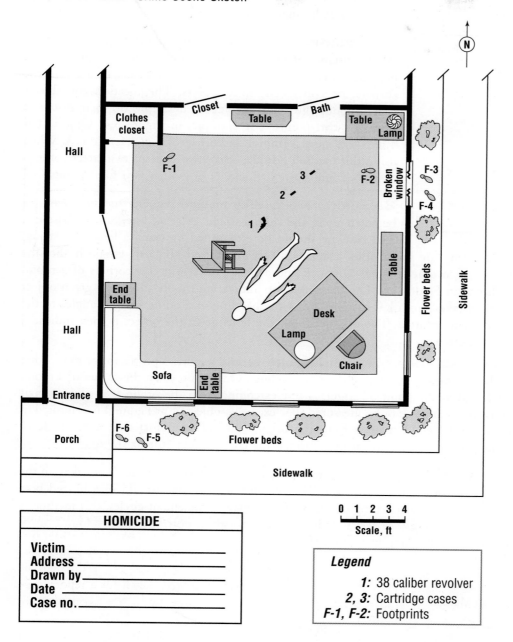

HOMICIDE

Victim _____
Address _____
Drawn by_____
Date _____
Case no._____

0 1 2 3 4
Scale, ft

Legend
1: 38 caliber revolver
2, 3: Cartridge cases
F-1, F-2: Footprints

Sketching Methods

Several different methods can be used to prepare crime sketches. These methods all establish the location of evidence and other objects as observed at the crime scene. The typical crime scene sketch is presented as a bird's-eye view of the scene. Only horizontal surfaces are apparent, and only evidence located on these horizontal surfaces is included in the sketch (Gardner, 2005).

Rectangular Coordinates The **rectangular-coordinates method** requires two reference lines at right angles to each other. It is often used to locate objects in a room, as depicted in Figure 3.3. Two walls of the room serve as the lines. Distances

rectangular-coordinates method A sketching method that involves measuring the distance of an object from two fixed lines at right angles to each other. It is often used to locate an object in a room.

FIGURE 3.3
Rectangular Coordinates Method

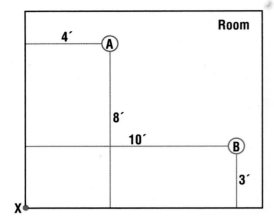

triangulation method
A sketching method that requires measuring the distance of an object along a straight line from two widely separated, fixed reference points.

baseline method   A sketching method that takes measurements along and from a single reference line, called a baseline, which can be established by using a length of string, a chalk line, or some convenient means.

are measured from the objects to the walls along lines perpendicular (at right angles) to the walls.

Triangulation   The **triangulation method** requires measuring the distance of an object from two fixed reference points. This procedure may be used either inside or outside. In a room, the corners are convenient fixed points. The locations of objects strewn about the room are recorded simply by their distances from the two points. For example, in Figure 3.4, Object *A* is 4 feet (1.2 meters) from *Y* and 8 feet (2.4 meters) from *X*. When using this method outside, select two trees or two street corners, a mailbox and a fire hydrant, or any other two fixed points.

Baseline   The **baseline method** requires measurements to be taken along and from a single reference line, called a baseline. The baseline should be established by using a length of string, a chalk line, or some other convenient means. Often you can establish the line between two objects, such as a rock and a tree, or between two corners of a room, as shown in Figure 3.5. The measurements indicating the location of a given object are then taken from left to right along the baseline to a point at right angles to the object being plotted. The distance from the baseline to the object is then indicated on the sketch.

Compass Point   The **compass point method** requires a protractor or some other method of measuring angles between two lines. One point, often the corner of a room, is selected as the point of origin. A line extending from the origin is used as an axis from which angles can be measured. For example, object *A* in Figure 3.6 is located at a point 10 feet (3 meters) from the origin (the corner point) and at an angle of 20 degrees from the vertical line through the corner point (the axis).

Cross Projection   In the **cross projection method** the crime scene takes on the appearance of a box opened out. The ceiling opens up like the lid of a hinged box, with the four walls opening outward. In some law enforcement circles, this method is also called an *exploded sketch*. It is an effective way to portray evidence found on or in the walls or ceiling of a room (Figure 3.7).

FIGURE 3.4   Triangulation Method

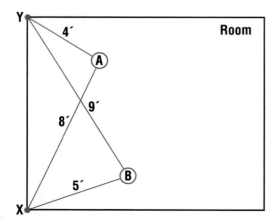

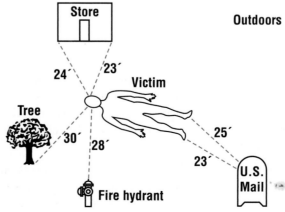

FIGURE 3.5 Baseline Method

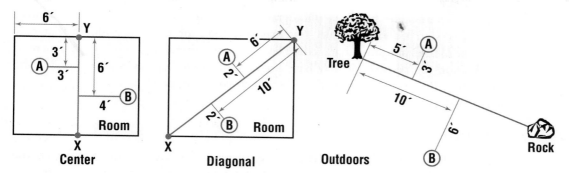

Center | Diagonal | Outdoors

Equipment for Sketches

As in other aspects of crime scene investigation, officers should do advance preparation to have the right equipment available to draw crime scene sketches. The following are some items an investigator should carry to create sketches at the scene:

- A supply of pencils (medium or hard lead)
- Graph paper and blank paper
- A clipboard or other solid portable drawing surface
- A metal tape measure of at least 50 feet
- A folding ruler, such as the standard 6-foot folding ruler used by carpenters, for short measurements
- A 12- or 15-inch ruler for drawing straight lines, drawing to scale, or making very short measurements
- A reliable compass or some other means of finding north
- A protractor for drawing and measuring angles

FIGURE 3.6
Compass Point Method

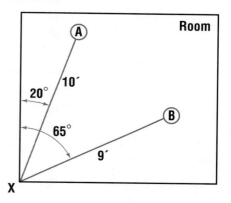

FIGURE 3.7 Cross Projection Method

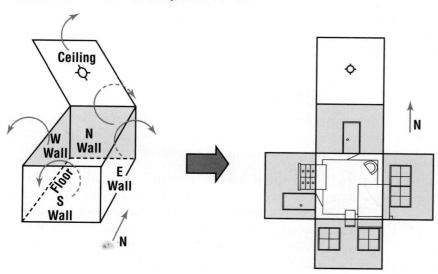

compass point method
A sketching method that requires a protractor or some method of measuring angles between two lines. One point is selected as the origin, and a line extended from the origin becomes an axis from which angles can be measured.

cross projection method
A sketching method in which the ceiling appears to open up like the lid of a hinged box, with the four walls opening outward. Measurements are then indicated from a point on the floor to the wall.

DISCOVERING AND RECOGNIZING EVIDENCE

After the crime scene has been photographed and sketched, you can begin a search. When you search a crime scene, systematically look for physical evidence that may prove useful in establishing that a crime has been committed, determining what method of operation the perpetrator may have used, eliminating suspects, and identifying the perpetrator. Reasoning and experience will help you determine the value and relevance of the evidence you find.

Equipment for Searches

In many departments, patrol officers take a prepared evidence-gathering kit to the crime scene. Particularly in smaller departments where much of the crime scene security and evidence gathering will be undertaken by patrol officers, patrol cars should be equipped with an assortment of items included on this list suggested by the Technical Working Group on Crime Scene Investigation (NIJ, 2004):

Latex gloves	Compass
Camera, film	String
Rope	Knife
Evidence tags	Steel tape measure
Assorted containers	Ruler
Assorted envelopes	Pens
Pill boxes	Indelible marker
Magnifier	Paper
Test tubes	Fingerprint kit
Plastic bags	Shovel
Bottles	Flashlight, batteries
Cellophane tape	Probing rod
Ax	Wire
Saw	First-aid kit
Wrecking bar	Metal detector
Chalk, chalk line	

spiral search pattern A search pattern typically used in outdoor areas and normally launched by a single person. He or she begins at the outermost corner and walks in a decreasing spiral toward a central point.

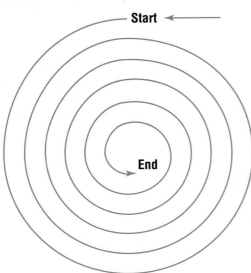

FIGURE 3.8 Spiral Search Pattern

In larger departments the crime scene investigation team (usually composed of civilian technicians) likely will be called out, and they will arrive with the necessary equipment to collect, label, and secure evidence found at the crime scene.

Search Patterns

Depending on the location or the type of crime, the investigator may choose one of the following five basic patterns for searching a crime scene: spiral, strip, grid, zone, or pie patterns.

Spiral The **spiral search pattern** is typically used in an outdoor crime scene and is launched by a single investigator. He or she begins at the outermost corner and walks in a decreasing spiral toward a central point (Figure 3.8). Following the spiral from the outermost edge to the center provides a detailed search. This pattern should not be undertaken in reverse. That is, you should never begin at a central point and

COMPUTER-AIDED CRIME SCENE SKETCHING

SOPHISTICATED SOFTWARE makes it possible for investigators to generate professional crime scene drawings as well as reconstructions of motor vehicle accidents. In some cases this involves the use of a computer-aided drafting and design program (CADD). By using CADD, technicians can create extremely accurate sketches that can easily be projected on large screens for courtroom presentations. Some CADD programs come complete with symbol libraries, enabling the technician to select and place various items in the sketch that were observed at the crime scene.

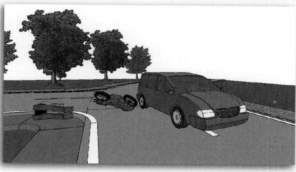

spiral outward; in entering the central area to begin, you are likely to trample or destroy evidence.

Strip The **strip search pattern,** like the spiral, is typically used outdoors, but it may be used in large open indoor areas, such as a warehouse or factory, or even in smaller areas, such as a room. Strip searches may be undertaken by a single officer or several officers. This search pattern involves imagining a series of lanes dividing up the entire space to be searched, as depicted in Figure 3.9. The searchers move up and down each lane, continuing until the area has been completely searched. When more than one person is searching and one person finds evidence, all the other searchers should freeze until the evidence has been properly collected. Then they can resume the search from the points where they stopped.

Grid The **grid search pattern** begins like a strip search. However, after completing the search by horizontal lanes, the searchers double back at right angles to the original strip search, as shown in Figure 3.10. In effect, the searchers are conducting another strip search, perpendicular to the first. The grid search pattern is both more time-consuming and more thorough. Often, simply looking at the same area from two different angles yields evidence that would be missed in a simple strip search.

strip search pattern A search pattern in which the space to be searched is divided into a series of lanes. One or more searchers proceed up and down the lane, continuing until the area has been completely searched.

grid search pattern A search pattern that consists of two strip searches, the second perpendicular to the first. It allows the area to be viewed from two angles.

FIGURE 3.9 Strip Search Pattern

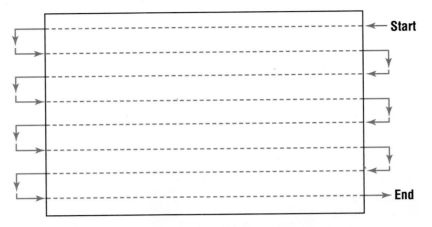

FIGURE 3.10 Grid Search Pattern

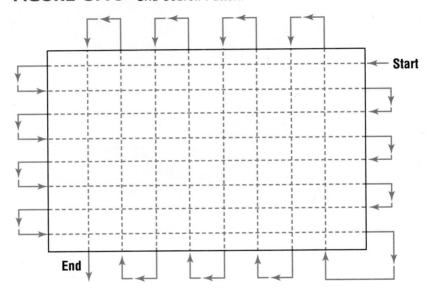

zone search pattern A search pattern in which the area is divided into four quadrants, each of which is then examined with one of the other patterns.

pie (or wheel) search pattern A search pattern in which the area is divided into pie-shaped sections, usually six in number. Each section is then searched, usually by a variation of the strip search.

Zone In a **zone search pattern** the investigator creates two imaginary axes, which divide the area into four quadrants (Figure 3.11). Each quadrant can then be examined with one of the previously described patterns. When the area is particularly large, a zone search pattern is sometimes used to create four smaller and more manageable search areas.

Pie or Wheel The **pie search pattern,** like the zone pattern, involves dividing the search area into smaller sections. In the pie pattern, the sections are pie slices, or sections of a wheel, usually six in number, as depicted in Figure 3.12. Each slice of the pie is then searched with a variation of the strip search.

The strip and grid search patterns are most commonly used by investigators. When search areas are very open or large, the spiral, zone, or pie patterns prove productive. The preferred method of searching varies with the crime, the type of evidence sought, and the purpose of the search. Guards should be posted at doors, gates, and other entryways while a search is being conducted.

When searching your assigned section, be alert for areas that appear to have been recently disturbed. Watch for indications of tampering, such as loose moldings, detached light fixtures, uncovered air ducts, splintered floorboards, new nails or screws, and patches in plaster or cement. Also be alert to new paint, fresh stains, soil disturbances, new grass or sod, broken twigs, freshly turned soil, and recent scratch marks on window frames or walls. Unusual arrangements, dust disturbances, outlines from missing wall hangings, and tool marks should all be examined. Also look for special hiding places, such as hidden compartments, false bottoms, hollowed-out objects, and stuffed toys. Obvious places, such as furniture, beds, vacuum cleaners, ice trays, food boxes, and other containers, should not be overlooked.

FIGURE 3.11 Zone Search Pattern

Zone A	Zone B
Zone C	Zone D

COLLECTING AND MARKING EVIDENCE

We have already discussed the importance of legal search and seizure when identifying and collecting evidence. We also know that the evidence presented in court must be material, relevant, and competent. In addition, the court will want answers to the following questions about evidence collected at the crime scene:

- Who found it?
- What did it look like?
- When was it found?
- Where was it found, and what is its relation to other objects at the scene?
- Where was it held from its collection to its presentation in court?

To answer these questions, complete logs and notes of all evidence found during a search must be maintained.

Investigators should handle all evidence carefully and should wear latex gloves to ensure that they leave no accidental fingerprints and to protect themselves from toxic materials and infectious disease. Small items of evidence generally can be lifted and placed directly into a test tube, small bottle, or plastic bag. Large items can be placed in boxes or bags. A fairly common evidence container in use today is a 9 × 12-inch manila envelope.

FIGURE 3.12
Pie, or Wheel, Search Pattern

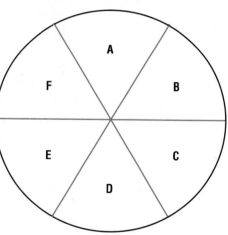

The investigator who finds the evidence should place his or her personal identifying mark on it. The mark should be permanent and capable of positive identification. In addition, this mark should not be placed on any area that might need to be examined in the lab. A knife can be used to mark hard objects; a pen can be used on absorbent materials. Evidence that cannot be physically marked, such as bird shot or liquids, should be placed in an appropriate container. This receptacle should then be sealed and identified with a label or property tag indicating the title of the case, the officer's name or initials, the date, the time, the specific location where it was found, and the case number, if available. It is preferable to have another investigator present at the time the evidence is found, and the name of this investigator also should be recorded on the evidence log.

HISTORY

ONE OF THE FIRST CRIME LABORATORIES WAS SET UP IN 1910 IN LYONS, FRANCE, by a doctor named Edmond Locard. Locard helped develop scientific methods for investigating crimes. The first crime laboratory in the United States was established in Los Angeles in 1923. Today the United States has almost 300 crime laboratories. Some crime laboratories examine only one type of evidence. The FBI crime laboratory, organized in 1932, is one of the best known in the world.

standard of comparison

A model, measure, or object with which evidence is compared to determine whether both came from the same source.

Some kinds of evidence are more valuable than others. For example, evidence in its original, unaltered state is more valuable than evidence that has been damaged. Also, some types of evidence, such as fingerprints, require a standard of comparison. A **standard of comparison** is a model, measure, or object with which evidence is compared to determine whether both came from the same source. A fingerprint found at a crime scene must be matched with a known print to be of value. A shard of glass found on a suspect's clothing could be compared with glass collected from a broken window at a burglary to provide evidence of the suspect's participation in the crime. Specimens of blood, hair, fibers, soil, bullets, paper, cloth, paint, and so forth must be collected in sufficient quantity to make comparison possible.

As mentioned at the beginning of the chapter, how evidence is protected, collected, secured, and transported affects its value. As an investigator, it is your job to ensure that evidence does not lose its value through improper collection, handling, packaging, or identification.

SUMMARY

Learning Objective 1

Evidence in a criminal investigation is any item that helps to establish the facts of a related criminal case. How evidence is protected, collected, secured, and transported affects its later usefulness when introduced in a criminal court case.

Learning Objective 2

Basic steps in gathering and preserving evidence during a criminal investigation include recognizing and examining relevant physical evidence; carefully collecting, handling, and recording evidence and transporting it to a crime lab; maintaining the security of evidence from the lab to the courtroom; and presenting or explaining evidence in court.

Learning Objective 3

The crime scene includes all areas in which the criminal, any victim, and any eyewitnesses moved during the time the crime was committed. It generally encompasses a limited area, but in some instances it may include several sites.

Learning Objective 4

Photography in criminal investigation involves the pictorial documentation of the crime scene and objects at the crime scene before anything is touched. Crime scene photographs are generally taken from long-range, mid-range, and close-up vantage points. In some police agencies, videotaping is used as an adjunct to still photography.

Learning Objective 5

Crime scene sketches are companions to still photographs because they provide accurate information about the placement of objects at the scene and show the actual relationships and distances between things. When preparing sketches, investigators may use one of the following methods: rectangular coordinates, triangulation, baseline, compass point, and cross projection.

Learning Objective 6

Investigators may search for evidence at a crime scene by using the spiral, strip, grid, zone, or pie (or wheel) search pattern. The strip and grid search patterns are most commonly used by investigators.

Learning Objective 7

A complete accounting of evidence found at a crime scene should include who found or collected it, where and how it was transferred for safekeeping, and how it has been protected and stored since its collection.

KEY TERMS

evidence **35**

forensic science **35**

criminalist or forensic
  specialist **35**

megapixels **38**

rectangular-coordinates
  method **41**

triangulation method **42**

baseline method **42**

compass point method **43**

cross projection method **43**

spiral search pattern **44**

strip search pattern **45**

grid search pattern **45**

zone search pattern **46**

pie, or wheel, search
  pattern **46**

standard of comparison **48**

QUESTIONS FOR REVIEW

Learning Objective 1

1. Define *evidence* and *criminalist.*
2. Name three main sources of evidence.
3. What affects the usefulness of evidence when it is introduced in court?

Learning Objective 2

4. Which of the eight basic steps in gathering and preserving evidence in a criminal investigation is the most important from a forensic specialist's point of view?

Learning Objective 3

5. If a rape was committed in the park, but the victim's unconscious body was found two blocks away behind a grocery store, which is the crime scene?

Learning Objective 4

6. Why should a crime scene be photographed before anything in it is touched or moved?

7. List the three distances from which crime scene photographs should be taken.

Learning Objective 5

8. What purpose does a sketch serve in a criminal investigation?

9. Why must the elements of a crime scene sketch be drawn to scale?

10. Which sketching method is useful for showing items in the walls? For measuring the distance of an object from two fixed lines? For measuring along a straight line from two widely separated reference points?

Learning Objective 6

11. In which search pattern do searchers complete one pattern and then double back at right angles across the area being examined? In which pattern does a searcher move in decreasing concentric circles?

12. Why must you never begin a spiral search pattern from the innermost point and move outward?

Learning Objective 7

13. Define *standard of comparison.*

14. Why is a chain of custody for evidence important to a criminal investigation?

CRITICAL THINKING EXERCISE

Divide into five groups, one for each of the five sketching methods described in the chapter. Individually prepare a sketch of your classroom, or another room or area that your instructor may designate, using the sketching method assigned to your group. The members of the group may discuss the sketching method and may help one another as appropriate. When your sketch is complete, compare it with the other sketches and analyze how you might improve your sketch.

INVESTIGATIVE SKILL BUILDERS

Allocating Resources

You have been assigned to lead a team investigating a homicide in a twelve-unit apartment building. When you arrive, the uniformed officer tells you that, besides the murder victim, there are no other injured victims.

1. What tasks do you need to perform, and in what sequence?

2. What area(s) will you secure as the crime scene?

3. What do you think are the priorities?

4. Estimate how many officers you will need to secure the crime scene and conduct the preliminary investigation.

Integrity/Honesty

You are the first to arrive on the scene of a violent crime. When the sergeant arrives, he asks you to take photos, and another officer, one more senior than yourself, is assigned to assist you, by writing up the photo log as you take the pictures. While you are calling out the type of shot (mid-range head, and so forth), you notice that the assisting officer is smoking a cigarette, and drops the butt on the ground. You also notice that she is lighting up another cigarette.

1. Do you ask the officer to pick up the butt she dropped?

2. Do you ask the officer not to smoke in the crime scene?

3. Do you report the officer's actions to your sergeant?

4 Physical Evidence

CHAPTER OBJECTIVES

After completing this chapter, you will be able to:

1 Explain the role of the crime laboratory in criminal investigation.
2 Relate the correct procedures for collecting various kinds of physical evidence.
3 Understand the importance and application of DNA profiling.
4 Discuss the nature and importance of blood and semen evidence.
5 Explain how hair and fiber evidence may be used to identify suspects.
6 Describe the importance of glass and paint evidence.
7 Explain the importance of firearm evidence in criminal investigation.
8 Describe how to collect comparison specimens of document evidence.

LOS ANGELES POLICE DEPARTMENT

CRIMINALISTICS LABORATORY
SCENE PROCESSING UNIT

CA 52018

THE CRIME LABORATORY

Crime laboratories provide scientific forensic support to policing agencies at various governmental levels (county, state, and federal). Crime laboratories work closely with criminal investigators and other police personnel in an effort to determine whether a crime has actually been committed, who may or may not have committed it, and—sometimes—how the crime was committed. Crime labs use physical evidence collected by investigators or CSI technicians from the crime scene, victims, and suspects to scientifically consider answers to these questions. Scientific examination of physical evidence plays a vital role in the successful prosecution of criminals and in clearing people who are innocent.

There are about 350 crime laboratories in the United States, and most (around 80 percent) are affiliated with a police agency. The remaining labs are in the private sector. Unlike television portrayals, not every police-affiliated crime lab has the capacity to scientifically examine DNA or to undertake gas chromatography (identification of a chemical mixture's component compounds by passing it through a system that retards each compound to a varying degree). Most can examine and identify fingerprints and conduct a number of other important scientific tests (for example, assess whether a white powder collected at a crime scene is baking soda or cocaine). In fact, only about 120 laboratories in the United States are equipped to undertake DNA analysis (Steadman, 2002).

The examinations undertaken by crime laboratories can be described in two words: *identify* and *compare*. A reddish stain in the trunk of a murder suspect's car is identified as human blood and compared with the victim's; the hair found on the shirt of the victim is compared with one obtained from the suspect and found to match his DNA. Such examinations and comparisons assist in convicting the guilty; however, these same examinations can also ensure protection and exoneration for the innocent.

A crime lab is often actually a large group of laboratories under one roof. Each laboratory specializes in its own area or branch of science, such as pathology, toxicology, ondontology, or ballistics. Each laboratory, likewise, has its own specialized equipment, ranging from scanning electron microscopes to emission spectrographs, to atomic absorption spectrometers, to equipment for thin-layer chromatography and electrophoresis.

DNA Profiling

One of the most important advances in crime lab technologies is **DNA profiling** (Williams & Johnson, 2005). Today crime laboratories are capable of matching suspects with even minuscule amounts of biological evidence from a crime scene (Butler & Becker, 2001). DNA (deoxyribonucleic acid) is a molecule present in all life forms. It determines an organism's traits, and the way those traits are passed on from generation to generation. It is different for each person, except for identical twins. Forensic scientists can get information about the identity of biological evidence by conducting sophisticated laboratory tests on the DNA. The process begins when DNA is extracted from comparison samples collected from victims and suspects. The scientist analyzes these DNA samples and compares them to determine whether they could have had a common origin. The final result is a genetic DNA profile, which can be used to strongly link a suspect to a crime scene, a victim, a weapon or turn attention away from a suspect.

DNA profiling has very quickly become a vital criminal investigative procedure. In spite of its early use, chiefly in paternity cases, and the various controversies and challenges by some defense attorneys, the use and admissibility of DNA evidence in

DNA profiling A process where DNA is extracted from biological evidence samples collected at a crime scene and compared with samples taken from the victim and suspects. The DNA samples are analyzed and compared to determine whether they have a common origin.

ALTHOUGH THE FIRST CRIME LAB IN THE UNITED STATES was set up in Los Angeles in 1923, one of the best known early forensic laboratories was set up by Chicago police in 1929. That year, in the St. Valentine's Day Massacre, four gangsters dressed as police officers gunned down seven rival Chicago gangsters after standing them up against a brick wall (Helmer & Bilek, 2004). Colonel Calvin Goddard, an independent forensic consultant, came to Chicago, and with physical evidence collected at the scene of the killings, including photographs and various diagrams, he reconstructed the slaying of the seven mobsters. Goddard later published his report in the first issue of the *American Journal of Police Science* (Goddard, 1930).

courtrooms has become routine. The question remains, however, What exactly does a criminal investigator need to know about DNA matches?

Each molecule of DNA is composed of a long spiral structure that has been likened to a twisted ladder (the double helix). The two parallel "handrails" of the ladder are held together by a series of rungs. Each rung on this twisted ladder consists of a **base pair,** two of four varieties of nucleic acid. The sequence of these rungs or base pairs constitutes the genetic coding of DNA.

DNA in humans can be found in every cell that contains a nucleus, with the exception of red blood cells. The nucleus of cells (except sperm and egg cells) contains the full complement of an individual's DNA, sometime referred to as the **genome.** The genome is identical in every cell of that individual. The genome is composed of approximately 3 billion base pairs, among which only about 3 million or so differ from one person to the next, and from which various traits in people are affected. The base pairs that vary, however, represent a virtually incalculable variety of possible combinations. Individual differences within a particular segment of a DNA sequence are referred to as **alleles.**

When typing DNA, the investigator identifies and isolates discrete fragments of these alleles in the specimen and compares one specimen to another (Butler, 2005). If identical fragments appear in both samples, they are called a match. In its simplest form, each specimen is sliced into fragments and tagged with a radioactive probe so it will expose X-ray film. The resulting pattern of stripes that appears on the film has come to be called **DNA fingerprinting,** and it is this series of line patterns that are compared.

As technology has advanced, new variations and applications of this basic version of DNA fingerprinting have emerged, and the terms *DNA typing* or *profiling* have been applied to the forensic comparison of DNA specimens. This early method of DNA typing is called *restricted fragment length polymorphism* (RFLP) *analysis* and is detailed in Figure 4.1.

Frequently, the sample specimen obtained by the CSI or the investigator contains only a very small amount of DNA, making it unsuitable for effective RFLP analysis. In these cases, *polymerase chain reaction* (PCR) *analysis* may be used (see Figure 4.1). Through this procedure, the small amounts of DNA are replicated to generate sufficient quantities of the material to be analyzed (Fierro, 1993; Rudin & Iman, 2001). Each cycle can double the quantity of DNA. This technique has enabled DNA laboratories to develop DNA profiles from even minuscule samples of biological material found on a victim or at the scene of a crime.

base pair Two of four varieties of nucleic acid found on each rung of the DNA ladder.

genome The full complement of an individual's DNA.

alleles Individual differences in base pairs in a DNA sequence.

DNA fingerprinting In its simplest form, this involves taking a specimen, slicing it into fragments, radiating these fragments, and exposing them to X-ray film. The resulting line patterns on the film are the DNA fingerprints.

FIGURE 4.1 How DNA Profiling Is Performed

DNA, deoxyribonucleic acid, is the material that carries the genetic pattern that makes each person unique. Scientists in the laboratory can map DNA patterns in samples of skin, blood, semen, or other body tissues or fluids. The DNA patterns can then be analyzed and compared.

There are two main DNA testing procedures used in criminal forensics.

1 Samples are taken of tissue or body fluids at crime scenes. Comparison samples are taken from victims and suspects.

RFLP (Restriction Fragment Length Polymorphism)

2 In the laboratory, DNA genetic material is extracted from the samples and mixed with enzymes to cut the DNA into fragments.

3 The DNA fragments are put in a special gel and exposed to an electrical charge to sort the fragments by size.

4 Genetic tracers are used to search out and lock onto specific fragments of the DNA.

5 The tracers reveal a pattern. Each evidence sample will have a pattern that can be compared with the sample from the victim and the sample from the suspect.

PCR (Polymerase Chain Reaction)

2 In the laboratory, DNA is extracted from the samples.

3 Part of the DNA molecule is amplified in a test tube to produce billions of copies of that part.

4 The amplified DNA is analyzed.

5 The analysis of the evidence sample can be compared with the analysis of the sample from the victim and the sample from the suspect.

Comparing the patterns in the samples results in a DNA profile representing distinctive features of the samples that may or may not match.

Crime evidence	Suspect	Victim
Match		

Crime evidence	Suspect	Victim
No match		

Because each cycle doubles the quantity of DNA, the original specimen can be replicated several million times within a relatively short time. By examining several different locations, or *loci,* where variations occur, the technician is able to produce a profile of the DNA (Saferstein, 2003). The Federal Bureau of Investigation (FBI) has identified 13 **short tandem repeat (STR) loci** to serve as a standard battery of core loci, each of which contains a short sequence of DNA (two to five base pairs long). The likelihood that any two people (with the exception of twins) would have the same 13-loci DNA profile is calculated as approximately 1 in 1 billion—or more. The 13 core loci identified by the FBI are used in their Combined DNA Index System (CODIS).

CODIS is a computer network used by forensic laboratories throughout the nation to compare samples of DNA recovered at a crime scene or on a victim with an FBI database of DNA profile samples obtained from offenders convicted of particular crimes. CODIS combines computer and DNA technologies to create a fast and effective tool for locating potential suspects—provided the suspect is in the database. The

short tandem repeat (STR) loci A standard battery of 13 core loci, each containing a short sequence of DNA, that differ among individuals and can be used for identification.

CODIS A computer network combining a database of several indexes of DNA profiles obtained from criminal offenders, crime scenes, and unidentified persons.

convicted offender index
Contains DNA profiles of individuals convicted of felony sex offenses and other violent crimes.

forensic index Contains DNA profiles created from various crime scene evidence.

current version of CODIS employs two major indexes. The **convicted offender index** contains the DNA profiles of individuals convicted of felony sex offenses and other violent crimes. Each state has different *qualifying offenses* for which an individual found guilty must submit a biological sample. Second, is the **forensic index,** which contains DNA profiles created from various crime scene evidence samples. In addition to these two main indexes, CODIS also includes a missing persons index, composed of an unidentified persons index, and a reference index. The unidentified persons index contains DNA profiles from recovered remains including bone, teeth, and hair. The reference index includes DNA profiles from related individuals of missing persons so that they can be periodically compared to the unidentified persons index.

Mitochondrial DNA (mtDNA) analysis is another variation on technological advances in DNA profiling. As indicated previously, RFLP and PCR analysis require DNA extracted from the nucleus of a cell. However, biological evidence may be obtained from cells lacking a nucleus such as hair shafts, bones, and teeth (Saferstein, 1993). Under such circumstances, mtDNA analysis may be able to obtain a viable DNA profile for comparison because cells also possess a unique mitochrondrial form of DNA.

FYI CODIS is designed to permit individual forensic laboratories to maintain control over their own data but also to access and share their data with other laboratories and policing agencies. There are three different levels of CODIS sharing: local, state, and national. All three indexes (the forensic, offender, and missing persons indexes) may exist at each level.

Typically, the Local DNA Index System, or LDIS, is installed at crime laboratories affiliated with a local or state police agency. At the local level, DNA examiners use CODIS software in their labs, and examiners may also transfer unknown subject profiles into the local forensic index, where they are searched against other unknown subject profiles.

Each state participating in the CODIS program has a single State DNA Index System (SDIS). The SDIS database typically is operated by the agency responsible for implementing the state's convicted offender statute. At the state level, interlaboratory searching can also occur. That is, the DNA profiles submitted by different laboratories within a given state are compared against all other profiles submitted to that state's database. Forensic profiles developed at local laboratories are also searched against the (federal) convicted offender index. The state custodian can share these data with the rest of the CODIS community by forwarding it to the national database (NDIS) controlled by the FBI. The NDIS provides a mechanism for forensic crime laboratories located throughout the United States to share and exchange DNA profiles.

Submitting Evidence to the Lab

Evidence transmitted to the laboratory for examination should be accompanied by certain information if the laboratory is to make a useful and complete comparison. Administrative data—such as the nature of the offense, the date it was collected, its location, the names of the victim and suspect, and the case number—should be provided. Also included should be a summary of the case, including the crime scene report, and a list of articles of evidence submitted and the examinations requested. Finally, the information submitted should include the urgency of the request, the

A crime scene fingerprint lab in a typical municipal police agency.

person to whom the evidence should be returned, and the person to whom the report should be directed.

The physical evidence that crime labs analyze can be anything. Glass, paint, soil, bullets, blood, handwriting, paper, capsules, and knives are only a few examples. In size, physical evidence may range from a battleship to a grain of pollen, from an apartment building to a sample of air. Let's look as some of the common types of evidence investigators may encounter at crime scenes. For your convenience, a condensed physical evidence collection guide appears at the end of this chapter (see Figure 4.7).

BLOOD AS EVIDENCE

Blood is among the most common forms of evidence found at the scene of serious and violent crimes. Blood may be found in trace amounts, puddles, spatters, smears, or droplets. It is useful as evidence whether it is wet or dry. Blood may appear on the floor, walls, ceiling, articles of clothing, furniture, and objects used in the course of the crime or in an attempt to conceal it. Dried spills or drops of blood are referred to as **bloodstains.** Blood samples may also be collected from suspects and victims for examination and comparison. Blood evidence can help narrow the group of suspects, support the identification of a suspect, and even guide the reconstruction of a crime.

Before an investigator at a crime scene begins documenting and collecting blood evidence, he or she should consider the value of this evidence and how it fits in the overall events associated with the crime. There are three common applications of blood evidence:

1. Finding blood with the victim's genetic markers (ABO blood type, DNA profile, and so forth) on the suspect, on something in the suspect's possession, or on something associated with the suspect (such as the suspect's fingerprints).

bloodstains Dried spills or drops of blood at the crime scene.

2. Finding blood with the suspect's genetic markers on the victim, on something in the victim's possession, or on something associated with the victim.

3. Investigative information determined from blood spatter or blood location (the nature of the attack, velocity and direction of impact, and so forth).

Generally, blood evidence is more informative in cases where a suspect and victim are in fairly close contact or proximity to one another. For example, if a suspect stabs or beats a victim, there could be an exchange of blood between the victim and the suspect. If a suspect shoots a victim from across a room, it is less likely that an exchange of blood will occur—although *backspatter* (blood splattered back toward the assailant) and other blood traces could assist the investigator in reconstructing the events (James & Eckert, 1998).

Crime scene investigation should always be undertaken in a slow and methodical manner to effectively collect and preserve evidence. The only time that an investigator should make rapid decisions concerning evidence is when the evidence is in danger of being destroyed or compromised. This is particularly true when collecting and handling blood. Although blood is an excellent form of evidence because of its ability to distinguish among individuals, blood can be a serious health hazard regardless of whether it is wet or dry. Handling hepatitis- or HIV-contaminated blood samples increases one's risk of contracting one or the other of these serious diseases. Everyone at crime scenes, autopsies, and in the lab should wear latex, vinyl, or rubber gloves for protection. Also, when working around other human specimens, such as stool, urine, saliva, semen, or vaginal secretions, investigators should exercise extreme caution. Most police agencies have written guidelines for correctly and safely handling biological specimens, and these guidelines should be scrupulously followed. If you have questions regarding proper handling of specimens, consult your local department of health or a qualified health professional.

Blood is an easily visible fluid, and it is difficult to remove from many fabrics and carpeting. Persons who commit crimes sometimes try to remove the incriminating crimson fluid from weapons and other objects. Forensic technology has advanced to a point, however, where even minute traces of blood may be discerned by the use of any of a number of **reagents**—substances used to detect or test for the presence of blood. Each of these tests is extremely sensitive, and each has certain advantages and disadvantages. For example, although the reagent luminol can detect even very minute traces of blood not visible to the naked eye, it must be used in total darkness. Benzedine, on the other hand, is used only in a controlled laboratory setting because it can cause cancer.

reagents   Chemicals used to detect or test for the presence of blood or other substances.

Value in Cases

The following are cases in which bloodstains would be of value as evidence.

Assault and Murder   Blood may be found on both victim and suspect. Clothing, weapons involved, and fingernail scrapings are also common sources of blood evidence. Rags, handkerchiefs, hats, towels, tissues, toilet paper, rugs, or other materials that the perpetrator may have used to wipe off hands or the weapon are potential sources of bloodstains. Additional potential sources include sink traps, floor cracks, carpet and padding, and crevices in tiles or flooring. If the offense occurred outdoors, vegetation or soil from the crime scene may contain traces of blood.

> **FYI** It is important to have a lab test confirm that a substance found at a crime scene is blood—and human blood at that. Occasionally, an apparently bloodstained knife sent to the crime laboratory for testing turns out to have only rust stains or traces of animal or fish blood. Under certain circumstances, rust stains have an appearance similar to bloodstains and may sometimes even give a weak positive reaction when tested in the field with certain screening agents.

Burglary Broken windows and doorframes, or walls with bloodstains on them, may reveal evidence of injury to a burglar. Similarly, droplets of blood on floors or flooring may provide useful blood evidence in a burglary.

Hit-and-Run Accidents Points of impact and the undercarriage of the vehicle are common areas where suspicious bloodstains may be located. Similarly, there may be blood smears on fenders, headlights, or other parts of the vehicle.

Rape The clothing and especially the undergarments of both the victim and the suspect may be stained with blood, as may bedding, upholstery, and carpeting. If the crime was committed outdoors, soil in the vicinity of the attack may also reveal blood traces.

What Bloodstains Can Reveal

The location and appearance of blood drops, splashes, or spatter can sometimes provide information about how a crime occurred (James & Eckert, 1998; James & Nordby, 2005). Spatters of blood may permit determination of the direction of the falling drops that produced them. The shape of blood spots may permit an estimate of the velocity, the impact angle, the distance fallen from the source of the spatter, or all three (James & Nordby, 2005). Figure 4.2 illustrates various bloodspatter shapes and their possible utility. The diameter of a blood spot is useful only for the first 5 or 6 feet from the impact. Distances beyond 6 feet show little reliable change in the spatter pattern. The degree of spatter from a single drop depends more on the type of surface on which it falls than on the distance it falls. The coarser the surface, the more likely it is that the drop will rupture and spatter rather than land as a round drop.

Conclusions about velocity and impact should not be drawn from a very small bloodstain. Very fine specks of blood may actually represent castoffs, satellites of larger drops of blood. However, when these smaller castoffs appear in great numbers, they may have been caused by an impact. The smaller the diameter of the droplets, the higher the velocity of the impact.

Spatters can indicate the position of a victim and the perpetrator at the time an attack took place. For example, considerable backspatter on walls, furnishings, or objects behind the victim is likely from a gunshot wound. Small, independent spatters usually have a uniform taper in the shape of a teardrop. In these cases, the tail of the teardrop always points away from the direction of impact. Small castoffs resemble tadpoles and tend to be longer and narrower than the teardrop shape of independent droplets. The sharper end of these stains always points back toward the direction of their impact.

Blood provides fairly uniform patterns, regardless of the age or gender of the victim. Additionally, since blood spattered from a body is at a constant temperature and is normally exposed to environmental conditions for only a short time, atmospheric temperature, pressure, and humidity have little discernible effect on blood's behavior.

FIGURE 4.2 The Significance of the Shape of Blood Stains

a

Blood dropped vertically from a height of 50 inches (1.3 meters) onto a flat surface shows a radiating, or bursting, effect. The stain is 1 inch (2.5 centimeters) in diameter.

b

The same amount of blood as in *a*, but dropped vertically onto a flat surface from a height of 8 inches (20 centimeters), makes a smaller stain (3/4 inch [about 2 centimeters]) with a wavy edge.

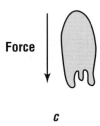

Force

c

Oval stain has spattering showing two or three spikes (splashes). Broad portions of the splashes indicate the point at which the blood first struck obliquely on a flat surface and thus show the direction from which it came.

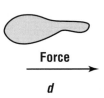

Force

d

Stain shows two oval spots like an exclamation mark and indicates a left-to-right direction of blood drop.

Blood-Typing

blood-typing Method of classifying blood into four major groups: A, B, AB, and O. Another factor, called *Rh factor,* also helps determine a person's blood type, which is positive or negative for the Rh factor.

Blood-typing evidence is useful for eliminating suspects as well as for incriminating them. **Blood-typing** classifies certain aspects of the blood into different categories. There are four major blood groups, A, B, AB, and O. A person's blood type depends on the presence or absence of certain substances, called *antigens,* in blood (Figure 4.3). Another factor, called the *Rh factor,* also helps determine a person's blood type. Most people are positive for this factor (Rh-positive); that is, their blood plasma contains the Rh+ antigen. Rh− refers to someone who does not have Rh antigens in his or her blood plasma.

Using the just described classifications, tests can determine whether a particular blood sample could have come from a specific person. Blood type and Rh factor cannot positively link a suspect to a crime scene, but they can positively rule out a suspect. For example, let's say a sample of blood found at the crime scene of a murder is A negative. A test of the victim's blood proves the victim was B positive. This result shows that the victim is not the source of the blood and that any suspect in this murder will likely have A negative blood (assuming there were no bystanders or injured witnesses).

FIGURE 4.3 ABO Blood Grouping System

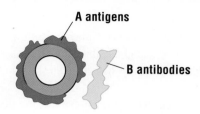

A antigens

B antibodies

Blood Group A
A antigens appear on the surface of the red blood cell and B antibodies float in the blood plasma.

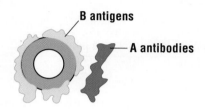

B antigens

A antibodies

Blood Group B
B antigens appear on the surface of the red blood cell and A antibodies float in the blood plasma.

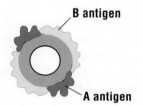

B antigen

A antigen

Blood Group AB
Both A and B antigens appear on the surface of the red blood cell and there are no A or B antibodies in the blood plasma.

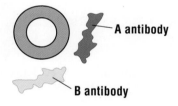

A antibody

B antibody

Blood Group O
Neither A nor B antigens appear on the surface of the red blood cell and <u>both</u> A and B antibodies float in the blood plasma.

If a suspect with A negative blood type were apprehended, DNA analysis could then be used to positively link the suspect to the murder scene.

Possible Examination Results

Laboratory examination of blood evidence can answer three main questions:

1. Is the substance blood? If not, what is it?
2. Is the substance human blood? If not, from what animal did it come?
3. If it is human blood, to what blood group does it belong? (Josefi, 1995)

SEMEN AS EVIDENCE

Always handle semen stain areas as carefully as possible. Rough treatment will break up any spermatozoa present so that a positive identification may be impossible. Submit all articles for semen stain examination to the laboratory immediately. Do not neglect to submit all swabs, smears, and stains removed from the victim during examination by a physician.

HISTORY

IN 1901 KARL LANDSTEINER FOUND that when the blood of one human being was transfused with that of another human being, differences in their blood might well be the cause of shock, jaundice, and the blood disorder hemoglobinuria, which had resulted in earlier blood transfusions.

Landsteiner classified human blood into A, B, and O groups and demonstrated that transfusions between humans of a single blood group did not result in the destruction of new blood cells and that this catastrophe occurred only when a person was transfused with the blood of a person belonging to a different group. A fourth main blood type, AB, was found in 1902 by A. Decastrello and A. Sturli (Landsteiner, 1947; Saferstein, 2003).

It should be noted that *semen* and *sperm,* although frequently used as synonyms in common lay parlance, actually are not the same thing. Semen is the grayish-white fluid produced by the testes and ejaculated during orgasm. The fluid's odor has been likened to a mild Clorox or chlorine smell; when dried, it appears almost translucent and starchlike. Sperm are the tadpole-shaped cells that are contained in and swim through semen on their reproductive journey to fertilize the female egg. It is important to understand this distinction as the tests to search for each are quite different. For example, assume a rapist who is sterile has left semen traces in the underwear of his victim; no sperm will be present. DNA is derived from sperm, not from semen, so trace amounts of semen, in the absence of sperm, would yield no DNA information.

Value in Cases

The victims of certain types of crimes are the most important sources of evidence when considering semen and sperm.

Death The victim's body and clothing, as well as bedding, towels, and other articles at the scene, may be sources of such stains. Other possible sources of such evidence are suspects and items in their surrounding environments, such as clothing, bedding, and their automobiles.

Rape and Other Sex Offenses Semen and sperm are often, although by no means always, found as physical evidence in sex offenses. Through DNA typing, it is possible to match semen stains (containing sperm) with a person's blood sample or, in some cases, other biological specimens such as saliva, skin, or similar materials (Saferstein, 2002).

FYI DNA is a 3-foot-long molecule that is tightly wound inside the 46 chromosomes in each cell of the body. Half of the chromosomes are contributed by the male's sperm and half by the female's egg. Every cell derived from that fertilized egg will have identical DNA.

Possible Examination Results

Here are three main questions that laboratory examination of semen stains may answer:

1. Does the stain contain human semen?
2. Can the blood group (A, B, O, AB) of the stain be determined? If so, what is it?
3. If a blood specimen from the suspect is available, does it match the DNA present in the semen sample?

HAIR AS EVIDENCE

Hair is a valuable, though sometimes overlooked, means of personal identification. Human hair grows from follicles in the skin at a rate of about 1/2 inch a month, although this varies. Unlike body fluids and skin, human hair generally retains its structural features for a very long time. It is an ideal source of information about an individual and can be used to identify both the sex and the race of a person (Moenssen, Inbau, & Starrs, 1986).

Although hair cannot absolutely identify a particular individual, as a fingerprint can, scientific examination can fairly conclusively rule out a strand's having come from a particular individual. Sometimes eliminating a suspect is as important as identifying one. Furthermore, certain drugs and chemicals remain in hair for many months. Thus, a 2-inch length of hair taken from a suspect could offer important information about substances that the suspect has ingested during the past 2 years.

Value in Cases

There are several types of cases in which collecting hair samples should be a regular part of the investigator's routine.

Assault   At a crime scene, hair from the victim, the suspect, or both may be found. Clothing, weapons—even spent bullets—and the surrounding environment are common locations for finding hair and other biological specimens. Individual strands, clumps, or tufts of hair may be grasped in the hand of a victim. Microscopic examination of a hair may suggest whether it has fallen out or has been forcibly pulled out (Josefi, 1995; Saferstein, 2003).

Rape   Investigators should direct particular attention toward locating and examining hair of all types. Samples of pubic hair, along with vaginal smears for semen and sperm, should be taken when rape is believed to have occurred. Pubic hair may be found on the undergarments of the victim and the suspect as well as on bedding, clothing, furnishings, or auto upholstery. Microscopic examination of hairs can aid in determining whether *consent* was given or *nonconsensual force* was used to engage in intercourse (Saferstein, 2003). Proof of lack of consent is a key element in successfully prosecuting a rape case.

Hit-and-Run   The points of impact and the undercarriage of the suspect vehicle may carry hair evidence. When a vehicle strikes a person, hairs and fibers often become embedded in areas of fresh damage. Torn fenders, loose chrome, and bug-deflectors are all possible places to search for hair evidence. If hair is firmly attached to a removable part of the vehicle, remove the part from the vehicle, if possible, rather than the hair from the part.

Death   As a matter of routine, many agencies collect a sample of about 20 strands of hair from the deceased in all cases of sudden or unusual death.

Possible Examination Results

From a laboratory examination of hair samples, the following questions may be answered:

1. Is the hair sample human or animal?
2. If human, from which part of the body did it originate?
3. If animal, what type of animal was it (dog, cat, deer, wolf)?
4. Are there any indications of the characteristics of the individual from whom it came?
5. Could the hair have come from a particular person? If so, what is the probability that it did come from that person?
6. Did the hair fall out naturally, was it pulled out, or was it cut by a sharp instrument?
7. Are there any foreign substances adhering to the hair such as dye, blood, or grease?

FIBERS AS EVIDENCE

Fibers are present in crime scenes more frequently than any other type of microscopic evidence, but investigators often overlook this evidence because of its extremely small size. Articles of clothing, and even torn fragments, easily visible to the naked eye are often collected as evidence in a variety of types of criminal cases. Fibers, however, are more difficult to locate. Good investigators know how and where to look for such evidence. Fibers are often transferred from one person's clothing to another's or may be impressed in a bullet that has penetrated a particular garment, fabric, or furnishing (Robertson, 1992). Fibers may even be found under the fingernails of a victim, at various points of entry in break-ins, or on various parts of a suspect's or victim's body.

adhesive-tape technique
A method of collecting microscopic evidence in which transparent tape is used to cover an area to which physical evidence such as fibers may be present. When the tape is pulled off, the evidence adheres to the sticky surface of the tape.

naturally occurring fibers
Derived from various vegetative and animal sources and used in manufacturing cords, ropes, linens, and clothing.

manufactured fibers
Comprised of two subgroups: regenerated and synthetic fibers. Regenerated fibers are made from natural materials processed from the cellulose in cotton and wood pulp. Synthetic fibers are produced entirely from chemicals.

If fiber evidence is suspected but not visible—for example, on a windowsill, a car bumper, or an article of clothing—use the **adhesive-tape technique** to collect the evidence. Cover the area to which fibers may have adhered with ordinary transparent tape. When you pull the tape off, any fibers that were present will adhere to the sticky surface of the tape. Attach the tape, sticky side down, to a clean, smooth, nonabsorbent surface (glass, plastic, or similar material). Be careful not to contaminate the tape with fibers from your own clothing. Even if it looks as if there are no fibers clinging to the tape, microscopic examination of the tape may reveal the presence of a number of fibers.

Fibers can be classified into two major groups: naturally occurring and manufactured. **Naturally occurring fibers** derive from various sorts of vegetative and animal fiber sources including (but not limited to) jute (used in sacking and cords), sisal (used in cords and ropes), hemp (used in cords and linens), and cotton, silk, and wool (used in assorted clothing products). **Manufactured fibers** have taken center stage in the production of fabrics. There are two subgroupings of manufactured fibers: regenerated fibers and synthetic fibers. *Regenerated fibers* are made from natural materials by processing these materials to form a fiber structure. This process is referred to as cellulosics when regenerated fibers are derived from the cellulose in cotton and wood pulp. Rayon and acetate are two common regenerated fibers. *Synthetic fibers* encompass a wide variety of products made entirely from chemicals. Synthetic fibers are usually stronger than either natural or regenerated fibers. Synthetic fibers and regenerated acetate fiber are thermoplastic, which is to say they are softened by heat. Consequently, manufacturers are able to shape these fibers at high temperatures, adding such features as pleats and creases. An important identifying characteristic of synthetic fibers is that they will melt if touched with a heat source such as a match or too hot an iron. Common forms of synthetic fibers include nylon (polyamide), polyester, acrylic, and olefin.

Fiber Analysis

The forensic benefit of fibers found at a crime scene rests on the criminalist's ability to trace their origins and compare known fiber samples with those found at the crime scene, on a victim, or on or about a suspect. Fibers can be better sources of evidence and information than hairs found at a crime scene because fibers are more distinguishable than human hair. Microscopic examination can determine the uniformity of thickness of strands, the actual number of microscopic fibers in every strand, color or dye origins, lengthwise striations, and the direction of fiber twists (Robertson, 1992; Saferstein, 2003).

Value in Cases

Fiber evidence can be a corroborative aid in establishing the facts in a number of cases.

Assault This crime usually involves personal contact of some sort; as a result, clothing fibers may be transferred between victim and suspect. Weapons and fingernail cuttings can also be important sources of fiber evidence.

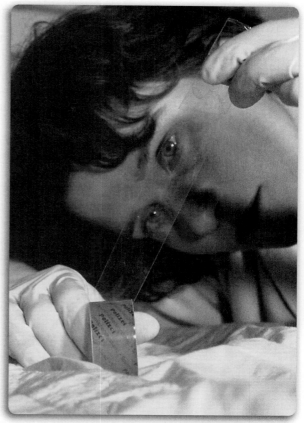

The adhesive-tape technique is useful for collecting fibers for microscopic examination.

Burglary Clothing fibers can almost always be found at the point of entry—a window, skylight, or other opening. Snags of fibers also may be found on rough surfaces such as door frames or textured walls.

Death As in assault, traces of fibers may be transferred between the victim and the assailant. Fiber evidence may also be found at various points of entry.

Rape The nature of this and other sexual crimes frequently results in the transfer of fibers between the clothing of the victim and the clothing of the suspect. Fibers may also be found on other articles such as bedding, automobile seat covers, or furniture. Weapons used in the assault and scrapings from under the victim's fingernails may also yield fiber evidence.

Possible Examination Results

From a laboratory examination of fibers, the following questions may be answered:

1. What type of fiber is the sample?
2. Is the same type of fiber present in samples of the victim's and suspect's clothing?
3. Does the sample exactly match when compared with a standard sample taken from the victim's or the suspect's clothing?
4. Is it the exact shade of color as the standard?
5. Are there any points of similarity?

GLASS AS EVIDENCE

Glass fragments can be extremely useful as evidence. First of all, many different formulas are used to manufacture glass, and the variations in density, refractive index, and light dispersion give glass a very high value as evidence. Second, very tiny shards of glass sometimes adhere to a suspect's shoes, clothing, hair, or skin. Criminals frequently are unaware that they are carrying small glass particles or have left glass residue at the crime scene. Furthermore, most criminals do not realize how important even microscopic fragments of glass can be in an investigation (Brewster et al., 1985). Larger pieces of glass can be examined for fingerprints, or they may be fit back together to indicate how the glass was broken (Caddy, 2001; Scientific Working Group for Material Analysis [SWGMAT]; 2005a). An investigator may need to decide whether a pane of glass was broken from the inside or the outside, or whether it was struck by a bullet or a rock. Glass from a broken pane frequently can tell an important story about the events leading to its having been broken.

It is important for investigators to understand the ways in which glass reacts to force. They can then use this information to understand patterns of glass fractures to determine facts about the crime and the crime scene. Whenever an object is thrown through a pane of glass, two types of fractures usually result. Together, these fractures form a pattern that resembles a spider's web. **Radial fractures** are cracks that start at the center of the point where the object struck the glass and radiate outward, creating a slightly star-shaped pattern. **Concentric fractures** form irregular, but concentric, circular crack patterns in the glass around the point of impact (SWGMAT, 2005b). Figure 4.4 illustrates these two fracture patterns. By examining the fracture patterns on a pane of glass, it is possible to determine which of two shots fired at close proximity occurred first. By studying the radial and concentric fractures, the investigator can see which stops the fracture lines of the other.

If you look at the edge of a piece of broken glass, you see a series of curved lines that form right angles with one side of the glass and curve obliquely toward the other, forming a shell- or cone-shaped pattern. This is a **conchoidal fracture,** and it can provide information about the direction of the force that broke the glass. As glass breaks, it breaks first on the side opposite the force applied to it (SWGMAT, 2005a). Thus, when a bullet breaks a window, it blasts out a cone-shaped hole (a Hertzian cone) on the opposite side of the glass from the shooter (and initial impact of the bullet).

radial fractures Cracks that start at the center of the point of impact where an object strikes a pane of glass and radiate outward, creating a slightly star-shaped pattern.

concentric fractures Irregular, but concentric circular crack patterns in the broken glass around the point of impact.

conchoidal fractures Provides information about the direction of the force that broke the glass because glass breaks first on the side opposite to the force applied to it.

FIGURE 4.4 Glass Fractures from a Bullet

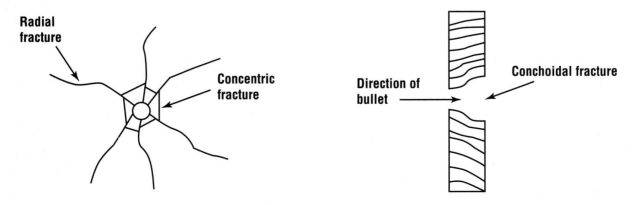

Radial fracture

Concentric fracture

Direction of bullet

Conchoidal fracture

Value in Cases

Physical examination of glass may assist in determining the facts of a case in many different crime situations.

Burglary Burglars often break a window or door to quickly escape the crime scene. Any person standing close to glass when it is broken invariably picks up fragments on his or her clothing. In cases where windows have been broken, the clothing of burglary suspects will often carry microscopic glass fragments.

Hit-and-Run In a hit-and-run accident, a headlight is often broken. Less common, but also possible, is a broken windshield. The scene of the accident, the vehicle, and the clothing of the victim can all be sources of glass fragments.

Possible Examination Results

From a laboratory examination of glass, the following questions may be answered:

1. If a window was struck by a blunt instrument, such as a rock, stick, or fist, from which side was it struck?
2. If a window was struck by a bullet, from which side was it fired?
3. If two or more bullets were fired, is it possible to determine the sequence of firing?
4. Can the composition of the window glass be matched to known comparison specimens?
5. Can the refractive index of the glass sample be used to match the sample with known comparison specimens?

PAINT AS EVIDENCE

Paint can occur as physical evidence in three different forms: (1) chips or flakes, as may be found adhering to clothing; (2) smears, from either fresh paint or old "chalking" paint; and (3) intact finishes, on objects such as tools or automobiles at the crime scene.

Value in Cases

Paint evidence may be found in a variety of crimes but is most often present in the following cases.

Burglary Paint fragments, often microscopic, may be found on the clothing of a suspect, on the tools used to commit a burglary, or in a vehicle.

Hit-and-Run The clothing of the victim, upon microscopic examination, will often yield minute paint fragments resulting from impact with the vehicle. In collisions between vehicles, a considerable amount of paint will invariably be interchanged.

Possible Examination Results

From a laboratory examination of paint, the following questions may be answered:

1. Can the flakes of paint be fit together along a common fracture to provide a conclusive identification of the paint's source?
2. Can the source of the paint be identified with a high degree of probability if both the sample and the comparison specimen contain identical layers or components?
3. Is it possible to establish the color, year, and make of an American-made or imported vehicle from a paint chip?

FIREARMS/AMMUNITION AS EVIDENCE

Firearms evidence is common at many crime scenes and can include revolvers, pistols, rifles, shotguns, loaded cartridges, misfired cartridges, casings, bullets, powder residues, shot pellets, and even wads from muzzle-loaded black powder weapons and some older shotguns (Ogle, 2004). Many of these items may offer additional clues to the identity of the shooter because they may reveal a fingerprint or have blood, hair, or fibers adhering to them.

Investigators should become familiar with different types of firearms. They should develop sufficient familiarity that they can immediately distinguish between a pistol and a revolver or a rifle and a shotgun. They should learn which weapons must be loaded with a single shot, which use a rotating cylinder, which feed cartridges semi-automatically, and which have automatic actions.

Investigators should also know how many cartridges different types of firearms can hold and what caliber of cartridge each requires.

When investigators locate a firearm at a crime scene, they should use caution in securing and handling this weapon. Unlike the technique used on many television police programs, it is a very bad idea to use a pencil or pen shoved into the barrel of the weapon to pick it up. Doing this can damage potentially useful gunpowder residue evidence or scratch the inside of the barrel, negatively affecting ballistic tests (DePresca, 1997).

One important question that may be asked about crimes involving firearms is, "Was a particular bullet fired from a specific gun?" Some firearms, such as most shotguns, have a smooth interior the full length of the barrel, or **bore,** of the weapon. In contrast, most pistols and rifles have *grooves* or ridges that run the length of the bore. The high sides of the solid sections formed between the grooves are called *lands* (see Figure 4.5). Bullets are composed of a material softer and just slightly larger than the diameter of the bore. As the bullet speeds through the barrel of the gun, it picks up marks, or **striations,** peculiar to that gun. These markings, in turn, enable lab technicians to match a bullet to a particular weapon.

To assess whether a particular weapon fired a specific bullet, it is necessary to compare the recovered bullet with one test-fired through the suspect weapon. If the recovered bullet is in poor shape or severely fragmented, it will be impossible to make an adequate comparison. Similarly, if the bore has been severely damaged by corrosion, tampering, or mechanical alterations, it may not be possible to positively identify a comparison bullet fired through the weapon.

bore   The opening in the barrel of a gun or rifle.

striations   Marks and lines or scratches on the sides of a bullet made as the bullet passes through the rifled bore of a weapon.

FIGURE 4.5   Rifled Barrel Features

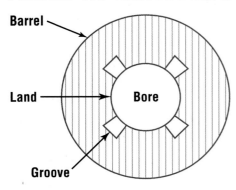

FOCUS ON TECHNOLOGY

CRIME LAB TECHNOLOGIES

(*Top Left*) Microscopic examination of characteristics of vegetation to determine if it is marijuana. (*Top Right*) Testing for presence of semen on underwear using ultraviolet light and filter. (*Bottom Left*) Thin-layer chromatography testing to determine the presence of cocaine. (*Bottom Right*) Analyzing blood sample from shoe to determine blood type.

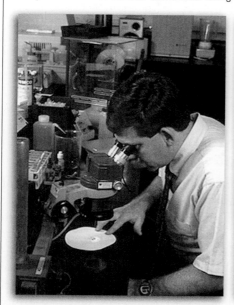

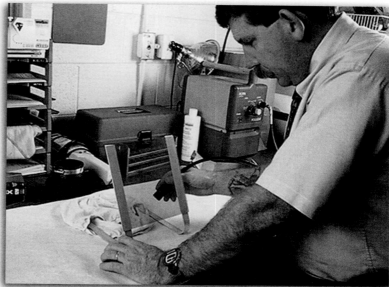

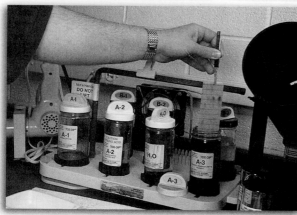

A physician should remove evidence bullets or pellets from the body of an injured or deceased person. The doctor should be instructed, however, to take special care—using rubber-tipped forceps, for example—in recovering the bullet so as not to damage the delicate markings essential for laboratory identification and comparison. Similarly, when pellets are removed, care should be taken to avoid damaging them. Investigators should never place evidence bullets loose in their pockets along with hard metal objects such as keys or coins.

Additional Information from Bullets and Cartridges

Shell casings may have partial fingerprints on them, and their gunpowder residue can sometimes provide a link to the weapon that fired it.

cartridge   The casing that holds the bullet (projectile), gunpowder, and primer together as a single unit.

Bullets recovered at a crime scene or from the body of a victim are seldom in pristine condition (unlike the perfect bullets television investigators always seem to pry out of walls using pocket knives). Fired bullets typically experience some degree of damage or fragmentation. However, this fragmenting and misshaping of the bullet may also collect minute traces of blood, bone, hair, or fiber evidence. Care should be taken to assure that such evidence is not damaged or lost by mishandling the recovered bullet fragments.

Cartridges are the casings that hold the bullet and the gunpowder in a bullet, and cartridge casings are frequently found at the scene of shootings. Furthermore, these casings may have a number of different useful pieces of identifying evidence on them. For example, the back or sides of the cartridge casing may have a fingerprint made when the shooter loaded it into the gun or the gun's magazine. There may be a firing pin impression on the base of the cartridge casing created when the gun's hammer struck the primer held in that cartridge's base during firing of the weapon. Marks also may be left on the cartridge by the gun when it ejected the cartridge after it was fired, as is the case when using semiautomatic and automatic weapons. Similar to comparisons made between a found bullet and a test-fired bullet, one can test the markings created by the gun's ejection mechanism and the firing pin by test firing a round and comparing it to the found cartridge casing (Hatcher, 1998).

Value in Cases

Crimes against persons, such as aggravated assaults and homicides, are often sources of firearms evidence. Any stolen, found, or confiscated weapons should be submitted to the laboratory for test firing and for comparison with evidence in pending cases. Never clean guns before submitting them to the crime lab. Fibers, hairs, or other microscopic evidence may have adhered to the gun and may be matched with similar material in the suspect's pocket.

Possible Examination Results

From a laboratory examination of firearms, the following questions can be answered:

1. From what type or make of firearm was the fatal bullet fired?
2. Was the fatal bullet fired from the suspect's gun?
3. Was the discharged cartridge case fired from the suspect's gun?
4. Were two or more bullets fired from the same gun?
5. Were two or more cartridge cases fired from the same gun?
6. What was the gauge of the shotgun used?
7. What size shot was used?
8. What was the composition of the shot used (lead or steel)?
9. How far from the victim was the gun held?
10. Is there any foreign material attached to the bullet that would indicate its path or flight?
11. Was this gun carried in the suspect's pocket?
12. What were the serial numbers that might have been ground off this gun?
13. Has the gun ever been used to commit an offense, not yet solved, in which bullets or cartridges were previously submitted?
14. Are there any identifiable fingerprints on either the weapon or the cartridges or shells?

Investigators should become familiar with the types of firearms so that they can quickly identify them.

DRUGS AS EVIDENCE

Criminals are often high on drugs or alcohol when they commit crimes or when they are arrested (Bennett & Halloway, 2005; Goldstein, 1992; Greenfeld, 1998). Drugs may be found concealed in objects or on individuals, and occasionally in balloons inside of individuals, or lying in plain sight. Drug identification kits can be used in the field to make a preliminary analysis of substances found at the crime scene or on suspects. Full analysis of suspicious substances must be undertaken at a laboratory. Chapter 21 discusses the recognition and investigation of controlled drugs and narcotics in greater detail.

Value in Cases

Following are some cases in which drugs may be of value as evidence.

Assault Since assaults generally involve aggressive or violent contact between the victim and the assailant, it is possible that vials or packages of drugs may be lost or dropped during the struggle. Handle any small envelopes, bottles, vials, or plastic bags found at the scene very carefully because they may contain important evidence and may also hold fingerprint evidence.

Death As a matter of routine, always look around a homicide crime scene to see if there is any evidence of drugs. Drugs may have been used by either the victim or the suspect or may have been a contributing factor in the homicide—either as the murder weapon or as the subject of the dispute leading to the death.

Illegal Drug Laboratories Use caution when searching an illegal drug lab, and handle all material found there with care. Until analyzed, all substances found in such crime scenes should be considered highly toxic and dangerous.

Possible Examination Results

From a laboratory examination of drug substances, the following determinations can be made:

1. Confirm *corpus delicti*. Laboratory analysis can establish what the powder or other substance found at the crime scene actually is. In many cases, such analysis is necessary to determine that an illegal act has occurred.
2. Identify designer drugs. So-called *designer drugs* involve modifications of controlled substances that alter the chemical structure to the point where it may no longer be identified as an illegal and regulated substance. Nonetheless, the modified drug may still possess all of the original drug's effects on the mind or behavior.
3. Quantify the amounts of illegal drugs. Tests can determine the total weight and quantitative analysis of the illegal drugs. The quantity of a particular drug may alter the specific charge brought against a suspect (personal consumption, distribution, or manufacturing).

DOCUMENTS AS EVIDENCE

When considering documents, investigators are generally concerned with comparisons. Handwriting or typefaces may be compared with other written or printed materials to establish their identity (Baucher, 2005). Documents can also be checked for latent fingerprints. Further, documents may contain watermarks or special imprints that can help an investigator identify a distribution or manufacturing source. Always maintain a document, throughout the investigation, in the condition in which it was found. Never handle documents with ungloved hands or subject them to dirt or unnecessary heat, light, or moisture. Documents should not be torn, folded, or placed under papers one may be writing on.

Value in Cases

A document is anything on which a mark has been made to convey some message. Any form of document may be useful to investigators in establishing whether a crime has been committed.

Identity Theft During the past decade, a virtual epidemic of identity thefts (using the identity of another to fraudulently gain money, credit, or property) has swept the nation. Identity thefts frequently require the criminal to create or misuse an assortment of documents including checks, credit card applications and forms, mortgage applications, drivers' licenses, birth certificates, and an array of other documents.

These various documents may provide leads to the identity or whereabouts of the perpetrator.

Suicide   A suicide note or letter left by a suicide victim, once authenticated, may explain the reason the person took his or her life. If not authenticated, the same document may provide a clue to the person who actually killed the victim and tried to make it look like a suicide.

Forgeries   Copying or simulating a signature on checks or credit card slips is an enormous crime problem. Examination of a document may determine whether the forger simulated the signature, copied it, or had no knowledge of the way the genuine signature looked.

Cases in Which Documents Are Questioned   Documents can play an important role in may types of offenses. An anonymous letter could be important in the investigation of a kidnapping. The handwriting on a hotel registration card might lead to the conclusion that a burglary suspect was in the vicinity on the night of a break-in, and irregular or faint lines on a Social Security card might be determined to derive from the card having been altered and photocopied.

Comparison Specimens of Documents

Document evidence can be useful in answering such crime scene questions as, "Is this the deceased's writing on this suicide note?" or "Is this the victim's or the suspect's signature on this check?" It is important for investigators to know what kinds of documents to examine and how best to obtain comparison specimens. The *Handbook of Forensic Science* (Josefi, 1995, pp. 25–28) lists fourteen types of documents and writing implements that might be examined: (1) handwriting (script), (2) hand printing or lettering, (3) forgeries, (4) typewriting, (5) photocopies, (6) mechanical impressions (from printers, check writers, rubber stamps, embossers, and seals), (7) altered or obliterated writing, (8) carbon paper, (9) writing instruments (pencils, pens, crayons, and markers), (10) burned or charred paper, (11) typewriters (brand identification from typewriting), (12) printers (brand identification from printout), (13) facsimile machines (brand name identification from sample), and (14) paper (watermark and safety paper identification).

When an investigator has a suspect under investigation and wants to collect samples of his or her handwriting to compare with the document evidence, the investigator should use the following technique. If the case involves suspected forged checks, obtain blank check forms of the same size as the checks in question. Then have the suspect write, at your direction, the material appearing on the worthless check. The suspect should not be assisted with regard to form, spelling, or punctuation. Also, the suspect should use the same type of writing instrument as was used in the fraudulent check. The suspect should not be permitted to see the check in question. At least six samples—and preferably more—should be obtained from the suspect. Each specimen should be taken from the suspect as it is completed. In addition to writing on the blank checks, the investigator should seek to obtain genuine standards of the subject's writing from other sources, such as letters, legal documents, or employment records.

FYI   In some documents it may be apparent to the naked eye that there has been an alteration or obliteration of a statement or a signature. This is sometimes determined and deciphered by the document examiner, or the examiner may determine that there is an ink differentiation. In addition to a naked-eye or low-magnification visual examination of the questioned material, an examination may also incorporate the use of selective color filters or color filter combinations. More in-depth examinations of the questioned document using selective portions of the light spectrum can be accomplished either photographically or by use of a process generically known as video spectral comparison (VSC). The Video Spectral Comparator 2000 is among the newer technological weapons in the FBI laboratory's tool chest, and it enables technicians to more effectively analyze questioned documents. The VSC2000 is an imaging device that allows an examiner to analyze inks, visualize hidden security features, and reveal alterations on a document (Mokrzycki, 1999).

Typewriter Comparison Specimens

As with any mechanical device, the repeated use of a typewriter will result in wear and damage to the machine's movable parts. These wear points and damages occur in a fairly random and irregular fashion, creating individualized characteristics on different typewriters (Saferstein, 2003). These may include variations in vertical or horizontal alignment of characters, or differences between character spacing. As well, there may be changes in the typeface itself resulting from wear or dirt collecting in the typeface.

To make a comparison, the investigator should type the specimen on paper similar to that of the questioned document. If there is doubt about the type of paper that was used, standard typewriter paper can be used. Type the questioned text word for word three times. If the document is very long, specimens of the first page or two will suffice. On separate sheets of paper, also type some common letter groups (Figure 4.6) as well as three complete impressions of the typewriter typeface, made by individually striking all the keys in each row. Remove the typewriter ribbon, and submit the ribbon and the typing specimens to the lab for examination.

Computer Printer Comparison Specimens

The lowered cost and ease of use of personal computers over the past decade or so has resulted in widespread use of business and home personal computation and printing devices. These changes have created new problems for law enforcement in a number of regards, including document examination. Early printer devices used a daisy-wheel technology, similar to that of a typewriter. The wheel contained a metal typeface that spun and struck the paper through a cloth or film ribbon, leaving an impression on the paper. The printed output could look only like the various characters contained on the spinning daisy wheel. The next generation of printers used a dot matrix system of printing. Pinlike points pressed against a ribbon created letters from a series of pinpoint marks. This type of printer allowed greater variety in character size and font choice. Next came the laser and laser jet technology, which most modern printers continue to use. Unlike their predecessor printers, modern laser and laser jet printers do not use ribbons. Instead, they used carbon powder or toner, which

FIGURE 4.6   Common Letter Groups for Typewriter Comparison Specimens

ing, act, at, ed, it, ar, in, ten, es, ies, eis, est, art, ord, que, quo, che, chi, men, man, ain, tion, the, thi, er, ion, ent, ry, pe, pi, pos, poi, te, ta, po, pie, ew, we, wa, wo, tr, oy, king, rot, rat, rut, boy, ad, aid, af, go, age, bad, dab, able, fall, fix, just, sta, sti, gun, ill, igo, get, gone, hun, hut, hob, had, his, ape, sh, fu, lu, roc, run, muk, ac, ck, ek, cu, he, bid, bex.

is distributed on the page to form letters, lines, and complex graphics. These printers offer a wide variety of fonts styles and font sizes. Many printers possess the ability to print in full color and to produce photo-quality digital photographic reproductions.

Despite the changes that have occurred in printing technologies, modern printers, like their earlier typewriter predecessors, develop individualized flaws in the way they imprint characters. Some of these flaws are endemic to certain brands of printers and thereby permit identification of particular brands. Other individualized characteristics may permit an examiner to match a questioned document to a particular printer. Sometimes these flaws are visible to the naked eye, and other times microscopic examination is required to reveal comparable characteristics in letter configurations.

Possible Examination Results

From a laboratory examination of documents, the following determinations can be made:

1. Was a particular document written by a particular individual?
2. Is a particular writing forged?
3. What was the make, model, and approximate age of the typewriter or printer used?
4. Was a particular typewriter used to type a particular document?
5. Was a particular check protector used to make a particular imprint?
6. What was the content of an erased, obliterated, altered, or written-over writing, typing, or printing?
7. What differences, if any, are there between inks in one or several documents?
8. Which stroke was written last when two strokes of writing cross one another?
9. Did two pieces of paper come from the same source?
10. Do uneven edges of torn paper match, proving that several pieces originally formed the whole document?
11. Do the perforated edges of a check, receipt, or stamp match the corresponding checkbook, receipt book, or sheet or book of stamps?
12. Will the creases and folds in the document aid in determining where it has been—for example, in a particular billfold?
13. What is the context of writing or printing on burned or charred paper?

FLAMMABLES AS EVIDENCE

Most forensic scientists are in agreement that gas chromatography is the most effective way to detect and characterize flammable residues (Saferstein, 2003). Furthermore, most arsons are started using petroleum distillates such as gasoline or kerosene, and both of these liquids are composed of complex hydrocarbons (a compound consisting only of carbon and hydrogen). The gas chromatograph is able to separate the hydrocarbon components and produce chromatographic patterns consistent with a particular petroleum product. When collecting arson evidence, collect residue in airtight containers to prevent samples from further evaporation or damage. In some instances, it may be possible to seal the original container of a suspect accelerant found at the scene of the crime.

Value in Cases

When investigating cases in which flammables are involved, the investigator generally wants to determine the source of the flame and what was ignited.

Arson   Flammable liquids may be suspected as the cause of a fire either because of the nature of the fire or because of the absence of a natural cause. The most common liquids encountered are gasoline, kerosene, and paint thinner. Less frequently encountered are isopropyl (rubbing) alcohol, charcoal lighter, and a variety of petroleum-based products.

Theft   The siphoning of gasoline from automobiles and the theft of petroleum products from storage locations are examples of cases in which flammables may be significant physical evidence.

Possible Examination Results

From a laboratory examination of flammables, the following determinations can be made:

1. Confirm *corpus delicti.* The laboratory can isolate the flammable liquid from the fire debris and determine whether it is gasoline, kerosene, or a more exotic flammable. Such examination can furnish evidence from which the jury may infer that the fire was intentionally set.
2. Connect flammables with a source available to the suspect. If the liquid has not evaporated appreciably (for example, if it is present in a can left at the scene or is well soaked into an unburned material), the laboratory can compare it with material available to the suspect. The liquid might come from a drum of paint thinner in the suspect's garage or may be gasoline from a service station.

CORROSIVES AS EVIDENCE

Liquids such as acids and alkalies require special handling and containers. Consult and follow the advice of a laboratory expert before handling, preparing, or transporting any such liquids.

EXPLOSIVES AS EVIDENCE

When dangerous explosives are involved, immediately clear the area for a reasonable distance. Notify the crime laboratory. Do not try to disarm, move, or transport explosive materials unless directed to do so by explosives experts.

FIGURE 4.7 Condensed Physical Evidence Collection Guide

Evidence Specimen	Identification/Packaging	Notebook Record
Ammunition Fired bullets	Scratch identifying mark on base of bullet with knife or scriber; otherwise, mark on tip or nose. Wrap each bullet separately in soft tissue or cotton. Pack tightly in small container; seal and label with case identifying data. If more than one bullet, use item number to designate. (If embedded in material such as wood or plaster, cut out and send that portion.) Package and seal in larger, substantial container and transmit to lab.	Record date, time, case number, recovery location, type of identifying mark, location of mark, witness to recovery, and disposition. Sketch recovery area and show relationship to other evidence at scene.
Fired metallic cartridge cases	Scratch mark on inside of open end, or identify on outside near top, with initials and date. Handle evidence and packaging as suggested above for fired bullets.	Same as above.
Loaded metallic cartridges	Scratch identifying mark or initials and date on side of case near top. Note number, location, and manufacturer's designation (e.g., Rem-UMC, .38 S&W). Mark boxes of ammunition on side with ink or indelible marker. Wrap and package as indicated for cartridge cases and bullets.	Same as above.
Loaded shotgun shells	Place initials and date on side of shell in ink or indelible pencil. Wrap shells separately, and package as noted for fired bullets.	Same as above.
Fired shotgun shells	Same as above.	Same as above.
Shot pellets	Place collected pellets in cotton or tissue, and package as for fired bullets. On outside of container indicate nature of contents, date and place obtained, name of officer, and case identifying data.	Notes should include date, time, location and method of recovery, witness to recovery, method of packaging, and disposition. Make small sketch of recovery area.
Shot wads	Place date and initials on wad with pen or indelible marker. Put in glass vial, small envelope, or pill box. Seal; label with identifying case data. Package and transmit as for fired bullets.	Notes similar to above.
Empty cartridge cases	Scratch mark on *inside* of open end, never on closed end. If found in revolver, note chamber location of each.	Same as for fired bullets.
Blood Liquid	Have drawn by authorized person, collecting at least 5 cc in a sterile container. Place identifying data on adhesive tape affixed to outside of sterile test tube containing specimen. Seal and deliver to laboratory as soon as possible. If delay is involved, refrigerate but do not freeze. (Do not use preservative except when requesting DNA analysis.) Seal and label in more substantial container to submit to lab.	Include date, name of victim or suspect, case identification, identity of doctor who obtained specimen, location where obtained, and disposition.

FIGURE 4.7 (*Continued*)

Evidence Specimen	Identification/Packaging	Notebook Record
Liquid recovered at crime scene	Place identifying data on adhesive tape attached to sterile glass test tube containing specimen. Seal and transmit as above.	Record date, time, recovery location, name of victim or suspect, method of collecting and identifying specimen, disposition, and case number. Sketch recovery area, indicating measurements.
Bloodstains On small objects	Place initials and date on object, away from stain area. Package entire object in container large enough that stain will not rub against surfaces. Seal package and label it with identifying case data. Forward to lab.	Same as above.
On large, immovable objects	Note size, shape, and location of blood spots. Photograph or videotape. Then cut out portion around stain and remove intact. Place initials and date on material away from stain. Place in container, seal, and label with identifying case data. If stain portion cannot be cut out, scrape or chip each specimen into a clean glass vial, plastic pillbox, or clean sheet of paper. Use a clean instrument for each scraping. Seal and label appropriately. Package in more substantial container to transmit to lab.	Same as above.
On clothing and other textile materials	Submit the entire article. Mark each item directly on the material, away from stain area. Attach an identifying tag. Never package a wet article; allow it to air dry. Do not fold or crumple garments. Place on clean sheets of paper and wrap separately. Place in larger container, seal, and forward to the lab.	Include date obtained, kind of article, location of recovery, type and place of stain, method of identification, and disposition.
In soil	Place identifying data on adhesive tape affixed to glass jar containing the soil specimen. Seal jar and deliver to laboratory.	Record date, appearance of stain, location, amount, relationship to fixed objects, and disposition. Make sketch, including measurements.
Clothing	Mark identification directly on clothing items in an inconspicuous place. Wrap each item separately, seal, and label with identifying case data. Date and initial.	Record date, case identification, type of article, place of recovery, method of identification, disposition, and case number.
Corrosive materials (acids, alkalies)	Consult crime laboratory for advice.	
Documents Requiring handwriting examination	Mark on reverse side in lower right or left corner. Place in manila envelope, taking care not to crease. Seal, and label with identifying case data, indicating which writing is in question. In suspected forgeries, submit examples of genuine writing.	Include date and title of case, type of document, identity of person furnishing item or place where obtained, and disposition.

FIGURE 4.7 (*Continued*)

Evidence Specimen	Identification/Packaging	Notebook Record
Requiring other examinations (erasures, ink, typewriters, printers)	Same as above.	Same as above.
Charred or burned paper	Place charred material on top of loose cotton and then in a cardboard container. Seal, mark "Fragile," and deliver to laboratory. Show date, case identification data, and initials of officer.	Same as above.
Drugs Powders, capsules, pills, tablets, cigarettes	Retain in container or carefully collect loose drugs and place in appropriate container. Place date, initials, and case number on container. Leave drugs in container and place in special sealing envelope. Identify envelope with pertinent case data.	Record date, place of recovery, suspect's name, method of marking, witness to recovery, and disposition. Make sketch of recovery area. If more than one item, use an item number sequence.
Liquids	Mark and date each bottle. Seal cap tightly and place in evidence envelope. Label appropriately.	Same as above.
Explosives	Clear the area for a reasonable distance, and notify the crime lab. Do not try to disarm, move, or transport explosive materials.	
Fibers Visible or firmly attached	Photograph and videotape, and draw a diagram of position and amount. Carefully remove and place in small pillbox, glass vial, or other tightly capped container. Label, seal, and transmit to lab. If fibers are small, use adhesive-tape technique. Label, seal, and transmit to the lab.	Record date, place of recovery, suspect's name, method of marking, witness to recovery, and disposition. Make sketch of recovery area. If more than one item, use an item number sequence.
Visible, not firmly attached	Same as above.	Same as above.
Not visible, but suspected	Use adhesive-tape technique, sealing and labeling as above.	Same as above.
Transferred to victim's or suspect's clothing	Keep all items separate when placing in containers. Mark outside stained area with ink or indelible marker. Label as "Fibers possibly transferred to victim/suspect."	Same as above.
Transferred to other fibrous materials	Same as above.	Same as above.
Fingernail cuttings or scrapings	Cuttings are preferred from both suspect and victim. If scrapings are taken, use a clean instrument for each person. Place cuttings or scrapings from each hand or foot in separate pillbox, glass vial, or other tightly closing container. Label, seal, and transmit as above.	Same as above.

FIGURE 4.7 (*Continued*)

Evidence Specimen	Identification/Packaging	Notebook Record
Firearms Handguns	Scratch identifying mark on frame, side of barrel, cylinder, or other part of gun not readily removed. Attach a reinforced tag to trigger guard. On tag, record make, type, model, case identification data, officer's identity, and date. Place weapon in polyethylene bag, plastic pouch, or manilla evidence envelope. Seal container and label appropriately. If gun is to be unloaded, record the position of the fired and unfired cartridges in the gun's cylinder. Deliver in person. If sent to lab, first unload, then lace with twine into holes punched into box. Place in larger container, wrap, seal, label, and ship.	Include make, type, caliber, barrel length, color, and all numbers showing on weapon. Also record date, time, method of identification, witness to recovery, and disposition of weapon. Draw small sketch of recovery area and relationships to other items of evidence. Include measurements.
Rifles/shotguns	Scratch identifying mark on an inconspicuous part of barrel or other major component of weapon. Attach a reinforced tag to trigger guard containing identifying data: make, model, caliber, serial number, place of recovery, officer's initials, and date. Package as for handguns. Deliver in person. If gun is to be unloaded, identify position of ammunition in gun and clip using a numerical figure to represent each round. If sent to lab, follow directions for handguns. Dismantle for easier shipment.	Same as above.
Shot or powder burns	Cautiously remove clothing to avoid dislodging loose particles. Mark outside burn area with ink or indelible marker. Do not fold or cut garment. Place between clean sheets of paper, then between pieces of heavy cardboard, and tape firmly in place. Label, wrap in substantial container, and send to lab. If burn is on unclothed part of body, photograph and videotape before and after cleaning, and forward visuals to lab.	Same as above.
Flammables Liquid in containers	Close top of container and seal with tape, taking care not to destroy fingerprints. Cork uncapped containers or transfer portion of liquid to clean container. Affix identifying tag, including item number and description of liquid, and transmit to lab. Be sure to request quick analysis.	Record location where liquid was found; date it was obtained; the collector's name, position, and badge or serial number; and case identification.
Distributed at scene	*Soil:* Collect at least 1 gallon of most likely soil in clean 1-gallon paint can or canning jar; seal securely; transmit. *Upholstery:* Collect fabric and stuffing; handle as above. *Flooring/Carpeting:* Cut out section and seal as above, or wrap material in plastic sheeting and deliver to lab. *Rags:* Place in airtight containers and handle as above.	Same as above.

FIGURE 4.7 *(Continued)*

Evidence Specimen	Identification/Packaging	Notebook Record
Glass	Preserve as for glass fragments (even though fragments do not retain identifiable traces of liquid) for possible connection to suspect.	Same as above.
Clothing	Quickly obtain samples if suspicious odor is detected on suspect, as flammables quickly dissipate. Handle same as for "Flammables, distributed at scene."	Same as above.
Comparison specimens	Collect as soon as possible and seal securely. Do not mix suspected liquids found at the scene. If possible, find out date of delivery. Handle as above for all categories.	Same as above.
Glass fragments Microscopic	Wrap all articles separately, attaching an identifying tag. Possible sources of fragments should be packed in smallest container possible to avoid loss. Do not pack with cotton or protective material. May be fastened to bottom of container with cellophane tape. Seal completely so that no particles can escape.	Record date, place of recovery, suspect's name, method of marking, witness to recovery, and disposition. Make sketch of recovery area. If more than one item, use an item number sequence.
Large, visible	If matching of edges is a possibility, embed thin, protuding edges in clay, putty, or similar substance. Carefully package in larger, substantial container, and label, seal, and transmit as above. If submitted to determine direction of impact, record which side was on outside and which was on inside.	Same as above.
Comparison specimens	Take samples at least the size of a quarter to accompany other glass evidence submitted. Take from area near point of impact. Keep comparison and evidence samples separate. Package and transmit as above.	Same as above.
Hair Visible and firmly attached	Leave intact on object. Draw diagram showing position and amount of hair. Label and pack so hairs will not be dislodged. If object is immovable, carefully remove hairs and place in pillbox, glass vial, or clean folded white paper. Label and seal as for fibers.	Record date, place of recovery, suspect's name, method of marking, witness to recovery, and disposition. Make sketch of recovery area. If more than one item, use an item number sequence.
Visible, not firmly attached	Collect and handle as above.	Same as above.
Presence suspected	Wrap articles separately in clean paper. Never mix articles from the suspect and the victim. Place wrapped article in larger container, and label, seal, and transmit as for clothing.	Same as above.
Comparison specimens	Pull samples from several areas, obtaining at least several dozen hairs, or run clean comb through hair. Collect and handle as above.	Same as above.

FIGURE 4.7 (*Continued*)

Evidence Specimen	Identification/Packaging	Notebook Record
Paint On clothing	Wrap all articles separately, attaching an identifying tag. Mark, label, seal, and transmit as for clothing.	Notes should be similar to those made for glass fragments.
On small, portable objects	Submit entire object, wrapping carefully or placing in clean paper bag, ensuring that area with paint smear is protected. Handle as above.	Notes similar to above.
On large, nonportable objects	Scrape paint fragments off with clean instruments. Record exact location, amount, nature, color, and surface. Keep samples from different locations separate. Handle as for fibers or hair.	Same as above.
As liquid or wet smears	Place liquid samples in widemouthed tins, glass bottles, or jars. Let wet smears air dry completely before preparing for shipment. Handle as for blood.	Same as above.
Comparison specimens	Take samples from area near apparent damage. Put paint samples from each location near point of impact in an individual container. Flake specimen down to the bare surface. Handle as for fibers.	Same as above.
Semen stains On clothing and other textiles	Collect and handle as for bloodstains on clothing.	Record date, time, title of case, type of material, recovery area, and method of collection and identification. Sketch location where obtained.
On small portable items	Submit all objects, such as paper, wood, and sanitary protection products, with stain intact. Mark, identify, and label completely. Package separately in breathable container such as a paper bag. Ensure that stained areas do not rub against any other surface. Seal and package in a more substantial container and forward to lab.	Same as above.
On large, immovable objects	Note size, shape, and location of stains. Cut around entire stain and remove it intact, including portion of unstained area. Place specimen in clean box or bag and handle as above.	Same as above.
On victim or suspect	Have examining professional transfer stain from legs or thighs onto filter paper and clip or pull hairs that may be stained. If applicable, have vaginal smears obtained, and have fluid in vaginal tract preserved. Place soaked-off stains in clean, breathable containers after air drying. Preserve fluid in tightly capped vial. Handle hairs as above. Transport slides in cardboard holders.	Same as above.

Note: In each case involving the recovery of evidence, and whenever necessary, obtain adequate standards of material from the crime scene for later comparison with similar materials found on the person, clothing, shoes, car, tools, and so forth of a suspect who may be apprehended on the day of the crime or later.

SUMMARY

Learning Objective 1

Scientific examinations conducted in crime laboratories on specimens collected by criminal investigators can help determine whether a crime has been committed, who may have committed it, and how the crime was committed.

Learning Objective 2

Knowing the correct procedures for collecting, preserving, and transmitting physical evidence is essential to the work of every criminal investigator.

Learning Objective 3

Deoxyribonucleic acid (DNA) is an organic substance found in the molecules of human cells. These molecules carry genetic information and establish each person as separate and distinct. Analysis of DNA from blood, semen, hair, saliva, urine, or tissue can be used to match victims or suspects with a crime scene and to positively identify an individual.

Learning Objective 4

Blood is the most common form of evidence found at crime scenes and may assist in identifying a suspect through blood typing or DNA analysis. How blood evidence is distributed at a crime scene may also help investigators re-create portions of the crime scene. Semen, like blood, may assist in identifying a suspect through DNA analysis of samples taken from the victim or the crime scene and specimens obtained from a suspect.

Learning Objective 5

Hair is often a valuable means of personal identification. It retains its structural features for a very long time and can be used to identify both the sex and race of a person. Fibers are actually more distinguishable than hair because microscopic analysis can determine the characteristics of each strand and link it to a specific garment.

Learning Objective 6

Physical examination of glass fragments can help in determining how the glass was broken, what direction the force came from, and whether the glass matches comparison specimens. Paint evidence generally appears in three forms—chips or flakes, smears, and intact finishes on objects—which the crime lab will try to match to known comparison specimens.

Learning Objective 7

Firearm evidence can include a variety of weapons as well as many types of ammunition. It is important for investigators to be able to distinguish among the various types of firearms and to known the kinds of ammunition each uses. In addition to their value as evidence, firearms may also carry additional physical evidence, such as fingerprints, blood, or hair.

Learning Objective 8

A range of documents and writing instruments can be examined to compare handwriting, typefaces, and other written and printed materials to establish their identity. Samples of a suspect's writing should be obtained from personal and legal documents or in a controlled setting using paper and writing instruments similar to the document in question.

. . . .

KEY TERMS

DNA profiling 53	convicted offender index 56	manufactured fibers 64
base pair 54	forensic index 56	radial fractures 66
genome 54	bloodstains 57	concentric fractures 66
alleles 54	reagents 58	conchoidal fractures 66
DNA fingerprinting 54	blood-typing 60	bore 68
short tandem repeat (STR)	adhesive-tape technique 64	striations 68
loci 55	naturally occurring fibers 64	cartridge 70
CODIS 55		

. . . .

QUESTIONS FOR REVIEW

Learning Objective 1

1. What should an investigator know about collecting, identifying, and managing physical evidence for laboratory examination?
2. What should accompany physical evidence transmitted to the crime lab?

Learning Objective 2

3. Why should an investigator know the correct procedures for collecting, identifying, and transmitting evidence?

Learning Objective 3

4. What is DNA, and why is it important to criminal investigation?

Learning Objective 4

5. How can knowing a suspect's blood type assist in some criminal investigations?
6. What information can a blood spatter tell the investigator?
7. In what types of cases can semen stain evidence be of value?

Learning Objective 5

8. In what types of cases should investigators routinely collect head and body hair samples from victims?
9. Why might finding fibers at a crime scene be a better source of information than finding a suspect's hair?

Learning Objective 6

10. What type of glass fracture appears as a shell or cone? As a series of circular cracks around the point of impact? As cracks that form a star-shaped pattern?
11. What can broken glass suggest about a crime scene?
12. Why must paint samples be chipped from the surface rather than scraped?
13. What is the evidentiary value of glass and paint evidence?

Learning Objective 7

14. Why should investigators develop a familiarity with firearms and ammunition?

Learning Objective 8

15. How might a computer-printed document be matched with the printer that originally produced the document?

. . . .

CRITICAL THINKING EXERCISE

Read the following case facts, and write a report in which you answer the questions that follow them. Then participate in a class discussion in which you compare your responses with those of others in the class.

Case Facts

At exactly 9:00 p.m. a man entered a neighborhood grocery store and grabbed a shopping cart. The lone store clerk observed him proceeding up and down the store aisles, selecting items. When the man entered, there were three other customers in the store. At one point the man in question was observed at the magazine rack near the front of the store, leisurely flipping through a copy of *Field and Stream.*

A few minutes later the man approached the checkout counter with several items in his cart. At that point he was the only customer remaining in the store. As the store clerk began to ring up the items from the man's cart, the man drew a blue, short-barrel revolver from beneath his green Miami Hurricanes sweatshirt. He leaned far over the counter and demanded, "Give me all the bills! Make it snappy or I'll blow your head off!"

At first the clerk pretended to comply, but after moving several of the bills from the register into a paper bag, the clerk lunged at the man. There was a scuffle, and the man struck the clerk's head with the barrel of the gun several times, causing a deep, bleeding laceration. The impact of the third blow caused the gun to discharge. A bullet grazed the forehead of the clerk and became embedded in the side wall of the store, just above the milk coolers. The man seemed genuinely surprised by the gun's discharge, and he let it slip from his hand. It fell behind the counter and bounced behind a pile of paper bags on a shelf. The clerk took a solid swing at the man and punched him in the nose. Blood spattered from the man's nose, and he shouted profanities at the clerk as he turned and ran from the store.

As the man fled the store, he ran toward the door with both hands in front of him. He pressed both hands against the glass door and flung it open with such force that it whipped back on its hinges and crashed into the doorstop. By this time the clerk had come from behind the counter. Though still bleeding himself, he managed to watch through the open doorway as the man ran across the street. The clerk noticed that the man was holding his face with his right hand. In his haste the man ran into the front corner of a parked car directly across from the store and barely stopped himself by deflecting the fender with his right hand. He ran up the street about 15 feet farther, jumped into a waiting red Toyota Tercel, and zoomed off. With blood trickling into his eyes, the clerk could make out only that it was a Massachusetts license plate with the first three letters "TUC."

When the investigators arrived, they found the clerk and the shopping cart waiting. The cart contained a copy of *Field and Stream,* a can of Edge shaving cream, a loaf of Wonder bread, a flashlight, two D batteries, and a bag of cheese doodles.

The suspect was described to the investigators as a white male in his early 20s, 5 ft 9 in. to 5 ft 10 in., who weighed approximately 180 pounds and had short dirty-blond hair. He was wearing white, high-top Nike sneakers, blue jeans, and a green sweatshirt with the Miami Hurricanes logo on it.

1. What areas would you search for evidence?

2. How would you search for the evidence?

3. What types of evidence would you look for?

4. How would you collect the evidence?

5. How would you package, identify, and transport each piece of evidence?

6. What type of analysis would you request from the crime laboratory for each piece of evidence?

INVESTIGATIVE SKILL BUILDERS

Applying Technology to the Task

You have arrived at the scene of a gang-related execution of two teenagers, one male and one female. The female is completely naked and lying on her back. She is about 16 years old, has long brown hair, is about 5 ft 3 in. tall, and weighs about 110 pounds. The male is lying face down about 3 feet from her. His hands and feet have been bound with duct tape. He, too, is about 16 years old. He has short, dark brown hair, is about 5 ft 8 in. tall, and weighs about 135 pounds. His head is resting in a small pool of blood that appears to be coming from a wound on his left temple. The female's mouth is filled with what appears to be a pair of panties. There are bruises on the inner portion of her thighs and near her vagina. There is also what may be dried semen on her pubic hair and on her stomach. Like the male, she has what appears to be a single gunshot wound to the left temple.

1. What items of evidence will you collect?

2. What types of tests or analysis will you request from the crime laboratory?

3. Who will you want to interview?

Integrity/Honesty

You are on a drug raid. By the time you and your backup team enter the home of the known drug dealer, he has already flushed the evidence, about a pound of uncut cocaine, down the toilet. The suspect is laughing at you and your team and saying, "Hey, man, look around—you got nothing. You guys are nothing! You can't arrest me. You got nothing." After a thorough search for evidence, you find no drugs.

1. Should you begin carrying small amounts of cocaine or heroin to plant on known drug dealers in the future, in case they also effectively destroy the actual evidence?

2. Should you arrest the suspect and take him to headquarters, just to create an inconvenience for him because he was so arrogant?

3. Could you run cellophane tape over his hands and have the crime laboratory test for any microscopic evidence of cocaine?

Criminal Patterns

After completing this chapter, you will be able to:

1 Discuss the nature and meaning of *modus operandi*.
2 Discuss how deductions may arise from *modus operandi*.
3 Examine how *modus operandi* can assist in identifying and apprehending a suspect or repressing crime.
4 Explore the *modus operandi* parts of a report.
5 Understand how to report *modus operandi* data.
6 Consider psychological profiling and its relationship to *modus operandi*.
7 Explain what is meant by geographic profiling.

CRIME PATTERNS AND HUMAN BEHAVIOR

Human beings are largely creatures of habit and comfort and are, to some extent, predictable in their behavior. If this were not the case, sociologists, psychologists, and criminologists could never undertake research or suggest any theories or explanations about criminal behavior. This is not to suggest that everything humans do can be predetermined with absolute mathematical accuracy. It does suggest, however, that many criminals commit crimes for specific reasons, select definite targets, and take particular repetitive types of actions. In other words, most criminal behavior is not the result of random acts, and certain types of criminals engage in certain kinds of criminal behavior for similar reasons, or **motives.** Many criminals are consistent in their methods of crime commission. Some even have *trademarks* or *signatures* that distinguish them from other perpetrators of the same sort of crimes. In general, the methods and procedures used by a criminal during the commission of a crime are called the *modus operandi* or M.O. Recognizing an offender's M.O. can assist in identifying a suspect and perhaps even in apprehending him or her.

motive A wrongdoer's reason(s) for committing a crime.

MODUS OPERANDI

modus operandi (M.O.) The method of operation that a criminal uses to commit a crime; Latin term for "mode of operation."

Modus operandi is a Latin term for mode, or method, of operation. In police work it describes the activities used by a criminal in committing a crime (Gaines & Kappeler, 2003). It was once believed that every criminal followed a particular M.O. and would rarely, if ever, change the type of crime committed or the method of committing it. For example, in the 1970s it was a relatively simple matter for New York police officers to recognize the work of David Berkowitz, the "Son of Sam," also called the ".44-Caliber Killer." All of Berkowitz's victims were young females, with the single exception of a long-haired male that police believed Berkowitz mistook for a woman. All were shot with the same type of weapon, at close range, and at night (Calohan & Jareo, 2001). Yet it was not solely on the basis of his M.O. that Berkowitz was eventually captured. His capture resulted from an unpaid parking ticket he received on the night of one of his murders.

Modus operandi data can assist in more subtle ways. For instance, a neighborhood suffers a wave of burglaries, each committed between 10:00 a.m. and noon and all involving entry through a sliding glass door. It could be inferred that the same person committed all of these burglaries. If only jewelry and stereos are taken in these burglaries, the likelihood that the same party or parties committed all the burglaries increases. Now, let us say the burglaries suddenly stop in this community, and burglaries with similar methods of entry, times of commission, and items of theft occur in a nearby neighborhood. One could now deduce that the burglar has moved on to this new location. The likelihood that the burglaries in these two communities are unrelated is quite small.

Inferences drawn from the M.O. are not certainties, but they can greatly assist investigators in their pursuit of criminals. In reality, some criminals do commit several different types of crimes and may even intentionally change the type of crime they commit or their methods (Chaiken & Chaiken, 1982).

Deductions from *Modus Operandi* Data

The M.O. file is an orderly method of recording and coding information designed to reveal habits, traits, or practices of criminal suspects. The trained analyst, as well as the investigator, should be able to see beyond the physical aspects of the way a crime was committed to determine why it was done in a specific manner. Leads regarding M.O. should be weighed according to the degree of probability they will lead to a suspect. Here are some deductions that may result from a review of M.O. data:

- A theft by stealth rather than by violence or fraud may indicate either that the criminal is physically nonaggressive and lacks confidence in his or her powers of persuasion or that the theft was more easily accomplished by stealth.

- A theft by stealth may mean the thief is known to the victim or intends to remain in the community and might be recognized later should contact be made with the victim during the crime.

- Well-planned crimes generally eliminate the emotionally unstable as suspects.

- A certain type of premises might be selected, not only because of the type of business conducted but also because the criminal is familiar with the victim's habits and manner of conducting business.

- A burglary of a residence may suggest a criminal with knowledge of the activities of persons who frequent that area at a certain time (the victim, neighbors, police, and so on) and with knowledge of the probable whereabouts of the people living in the residence.

- Burglaries where more vandalism than theft occurs usually indicate amateur juvenile burglars rather than adult professionals. Crimes committed in areas frequented only by people working or living in that vicinity usually indicate a local criminal.

- The occupation or previous experience of the criminal may be indicated by the tools selected for the crime as well as by the skill with which they are employed.

- The point of entry (window, rear door, skylight, and so on) may have been chosen because of observation of a burglar alarm system outside the premises.

- Prior "casing" of the victimized target may have been needed because of conditions at the location or precautionary measures taken by the owner or manager.

- A suspect with physical disabilities may be eliminated if the type of crime calls for an agile person, unless evidence of a more physically fit accomplice is developed.

Uses of *Modus Operandi* Data

One segment of a suspect's M.O. can have greater value than another for purposes of identification, apprehension, or repression. Compiling M.O. information furnished

Crimes of opportunity require little or no planning and, therefore, have no consistent M.O.

identification A process in which physical characteristics and qualities are used to definitely know or recognize a person.

apprehension The act of seizing or arresting a criminal offender.

repression The act of suppressing or preventing an action from taking place.

by witnesses in several robberies can aid in the **identification** of a suspect if certain information on physical characteristics—such as facial features, scars, marks, deformities, height, weight, and other data—recurs in descriptions of suspects. Even a nickname or street name (unless used as a decoy) may assist in the identification of a suspect.

The method of operation can assist police in **apprehension** of a suspect by pinpointing certain operational patterns. For a check passer, for instance, the type of business establishment victimized, the locality, the time, the day of the week, the type of purchase made, the dress of the check passer, any conversation, and the identification used permit the police to counterattack by alerting merchants in projected areas, placing stops, and using special check bulletins as well as other aids.

Modus operandi data can indicate a likely time and location for future criminal activity. Therefore, steps can be taken in **repression,** or suppression, of criminal activity, given the M.O. data. For example, in a series of prowler complaints, the M.O. data obtained from the reports of several preliminary investigations showed that the incidents occurred generally between 9:30 p.m. and 11:30 p.m. in a certain seven-block area. A concentrated patrol in that area during those times resulted in a sharp drop-off in prowler calls.

Information obtained from investigative reports can also be applied in other ways. For example, in the interrogation of a suspect, it is possible to clear related cases. Leads are furnished to the investigator to help identify suspects who have used the same M.O. The administrator can use this information in the assignment of personnel and equipment to places where surveillance is needed. Data on M.O. are an excellent means of identifying criminals who move about the state or even the nation.

NATIONAL LAW ENFORCEMENT TELECOMMUNICATIONS SYSTEM

THE NATIONAL LAW ENFORCEMENT TELECOMMUNICA-TIONS SYSTEM (NLETS) is a computer-controlled message switching network linking local, state, and federal agencies together to exchange information. The law enforcement agencies are linked together by means of computers, terminals, and communication lines. Officers can access the network through mobile data terminals linked to a departmental central computer, which is part of a state network tied into NLETS. The system is operational 24 hours per day, 7 days a week.

The *Modus Operandi* Parts of a Report

Much of the *modus operandi* information investigators work with comes from police crime reports. Crime report forms may vary in format between law enforcement agencies, but the *modus operandi* data are generally broken down into ten categories.

1. Time of Attack, or Date and Time Committed The exact time the offense was committed should be reported if it is known. If the time and date are unknown, then the entire period should be noted in reporting: for example, "May 8 or 9, 7:00 p.m. to 5:00 a.m." Many criminals operate between specific hours, and some commit their crimes only on a particular weekday or only on the weekend. Thus the time or day can be an identifying trait.

2. Person Attacked (Type of Victim) This subdivision is used because the criminal often picks people of a particular occupation or class as victims. The information wanted here is the type of person attacked: for example, liquor store owner, bank messenger, jewelry seller, high school student, or doctor. The name of the victim is not used.

3. Property Attacked, or Type of Premises Entered The place in which the offense was committed is described in this section. For example, a liquor store robber may rob only those places situated on corners. Therefore, in a report this type of store location should be listed as "liquor store—corner." Other types of premises attacked should be accurately listed. For example, we might find the descriptions "one-story, six-room, stucco dwelling," "hallway, third floor," "single-family attached corner house," "eight-story office building," or "bank, midblock." For reporting purposes under this section, a street, alley, sidewalk, highway, vacant lot, or field may be considered "property attacked."

4. How Attacked (Point of Entry) This section requires information about how the offense was committed and how it was made possible. The exact type of information is determined by the class of crime committed. For example, in a robbery case, show what induced the victim to hand over the property. The entry for this category might be "beaten," "threatened," "bound and gagged," or

The objective of a crime may be to obtain money, jewelry, weapons, or other items of value.

something similar. In fraudulent check cases, the method of attack might be "forged signature," "forged endorsement," "signed fictitious name and address," or "used counterfeit payroll checks." In burglary cases, the method of attack refers to the place of entry and the manner by which entry was effected. If a safe is burglarized, the investigator should also indicate whether the safe was attacked by drilling, explosives, burning, peeling, punching, pulling, hauling away, or some other means. In sex crimes, the method would be what made the victim submit to the offense—promise of marriage, gifts, threat, and others. In a swindle or confidence game, the method might be introducing a companion to the victim as a prominent person in politics, business, entertainment, or other fields.

5. Means of Attack (Tool or Equipment Used in Committing the Crime)
The instrument used to gain entry should be reported, first by size and then by type: for example, in a burglary case "3/4-inch drill," "hook and line," "glass cutter," "1/2-inch jimmy," or ".38-caliber nickel-plated revolver." The means of attack may also be bodily force. In the body of the report, any marks left by the instrument should be described in detail.

6. Objective of Attack (Why the Crime Was Committed or Attempted)
The objective might be to obtain money, jewelry, furs, stamp or coin collections, narcotics, firearms, cigarettes, or other items, regardless of value. In crimes against the person, the objective of the attack, or reason the crime was committed, may be ransom, revenge, or perpetration of another crime, such as homicide. The objective of the attack in a homicide case might be robbery or rape. In other homicide cases, the objective might be to prevent witnesses from testifying, to secure an estate or inheritance, to gratify sexual desires, or another reason. Identifiable property listed in a report as stolen and later found in possession of a suspect tends to connect that person with the crime.

7. Trademark or Peculiarity   A **trademark** is a personal habit shown by the criminal. Notes in this section might be "ate food during crime," "wore gloves," "lowered window shades," "left note behind," "malicious damage done to property," or "pretended to be a customer." While committing a robbery, for example, some criminals say very little and are cool in their operations; others appear excited and talk more than necessary. Some criminals perform sadistic or perverted acts that establish their trademark. They might, as an example, cut off genitals before killing victims. Generally speaking, the more unusual the trademark is, the greater the value it has in identifying the offender. However, any crime will disclose to the diligent investigator some individual characteristic that will assist in identification of a suspect. The trademark behavior may occur before, during, or after commission of the crime.

8. What Suspect Said   Quote verbatim, if possible. In the investigation and reporting of crimes such as robbery, con games, check forgeries, and others in which the victim conversed with the criminal, pay particular attention to what the suspect said and did, as well as to the physical description. The suspect may mispronounce a particular word or use a peculiar expression, mannerism, or dialect that will assist in identification. Speech habits seldom change over time and may become more pronounced when the individual is tense. Furthermore, expressions such as "Get your hands up, or I'll blow out your guts," "Reach for God," or "This is a stickup" may unconsciously become a part of the criminal's *modus operandi.*

9. Written Words or Symbols   Certain symbols or words are commonly associated with ritualized crimes and those related to cults. Generally speaking, **cults** are groups of people sharing a system of religious or quasi-religious beliefs. Cults both invent their own rituals and use rituals commonly associated with the occult in general. Consequently, many symbols left at a crime scene may offer a potential means of identifying a specific cult. Symbols such as circles, goats' heads, inverted crosses, hexagrams (six-pointed stars), or pentagrams (five-pointed stars) may direct an investigator to a cult (Figure 5.1).

Recently, law enforcement officials have become aware that street gangs have begun using various symbolic codes scrawled on walls to communicate with one another and to issue warnings to rival gangs. Terms and initials once thought to be simply **tagging,** or writing one's street nickname or initials as a form of graffiti, are now believed to be symbolic gang codes.

10. Transportation Used or Observed   Include vehicle type, year, make, model, color, license or identification number, and unusual features. Descriptive data, such as type of tires, seat covers, emblems, exhaust pipes, spotlights, antennas, and bumper stickers, are helpful in identifying a car or another vehicle, such as a motorcycle or boat.

How to Report *Modus Operandi* Data

Suppose a series of nighttime burglaries occurred in a certain area. The burglar's M.O. was to enter a medical office building through an open or unlocked window from the fire escape. The burglar gained access to the medical and dental offices by using a 2-inch jimmy bar with a V notched in the blade. Money, narcotics, and prescription forms were taken. The burglar left the premises via the fire escape. The M.O. data

trademark   A distinctive characteristic by which a criminal becomes known.

cults   Religious or quasi-religious groups sometimes considered extreme, with followers who sometimes act in an unconventional manner.

tagging   Writing a word, initials, or a symbol on a wall to identify an individual or group such as a gang.

FIGURE 5.1   Common Occult and Satanic Symbols

BEELZEBUB   The Devil; Satan.

MARKOS   Abracadabra.

NATAS   Reversed spelling of Satan.

 Various ways of representing the *Beast* or the *Antichrist,* son of Satan.

 The Cross of Confusion, which questions the existence of Jesus Christ and hence the validity of Christianity.

 An inverted double-bladed axe, the symbol of antijustice.

 Pentagram, representing the four elements of earth controlled by the Spirit.

 Inverted pentagram, the symbol of the occult.

 Hexagram circle, for protection and control of demons.

 Double circles, representing containment and control over evil power.

 Satanic traitor, symbolizing someone who has betrayed the coven. Sometimes used as a warning sign. Sometimes used as a death threat or ritual of revenge.

from one of these burglaries would be recorded in a manner similar to that shown in Figure 5.2 for a home burglary.

The body of the report should contain a complete chronological narrative of all the facts obtained during the investigation, including an explanation of the M.O. factors. Any details that might be connected with the crime should be set forth. Information that is not strictly part of the suspect's method of operation (a physical description or a description of the property stolen) should also be included. *Modus operandi* factors would include such acts as lying in wait, luring the victim, drugging the victim, detouring a vehicle, casing a target, establishing the confidence of victims, or purchasing or

FIGURE 5.2 *Modus Operandi* Parts of a Report

MODUS OPERANDI (SEE INSTRUCTIONS)									
39. DESCRIBE CHARACTERISTICS OF PREMISES AND AREA WHERE OFFENSE OCCURRED *5 Klamath, Irvine, CA. Single family attached home - living room/bedroom*									
40. DESCRIBE BRIEFLY HOW OFFENSE WAS COMMITTED *Window jimmied to gain entrance (front window)* *Stolen property taken through front door (see attached property list)*									
41. DESCRIBE WEAPON, INSTRUMENT, EQUIPMENT, TRICK, DEVICE OR FORCE USED *Possible pry marks left on window frame*									
42. MOTIVE – TYPE OF PROPERTY TAKEN OR OTHER REASON FOR OFFENSE *Color T.V. ; stackable stereo, one gold ring with ruby, one 18k gold 24" necklace*									
43. ESTIMATED LOSS VALUE AND/OR EXTENT OF INJURIES – MINOR, MAJOR *Total value $1150*									
44. WHAT DID SUSPECT/S SAY – NOTE PECULIARITIES *Unknown*									
45. VICTIM'S ACTIVITY JUST PRIOR TO AND/OR DURING OFFENSE *Shopping at local market (appoximately 60 minutes)*									
46. TRADEMARK – OTHER DISTINCTIVE ACTION OF SUSPECT/S *A pair of victim's panties found on bed - may have semen on them*									
47. VEHICLE USED – LICENSE NO. – ID NO. – YEAR – MAKE – MODEL – COLORS (OTHER IDENTIFYING CHARACTERISTICS) *Unknown*									

48. SUSPECT NO. 1 (LAST, FIRST, MIDDLE) *Unknown*	49. RACE – SEX -	50. AGE -	51. HT. -	52. WT. -	53. HAIR -	54. EYES -	55. ID NO. OR DOB -	56. ARRESTED YES ☐ NO ☐

57. ADDRESS, CLOTHING AND OTHER IDENTIFYING MARKS OR CHARACTERISTICS *Specimen of semen taken in evidence*								

58. SUSPECT NO. 2 (LAST, FIRST, MIDDLE) *Unknown*	59. RACE – SEX -	60. AGE -	61. HT. -	62. WT. -	63. HAIR -	64. EYES -	65. ID NO. OR DOB -	66. ARRESTED YES ☐ NO ☐

67. ADDRESS, CLOTHING AND OTHER IDENTIFYING MARKS OR CHARACTERISTICS *N/A*								

REPORTING OFFICERS *George Billing*	RECORDING OFFICER	TYPED BY *GB*	DATE AND TIME *03-07-07*	ROUTED BY *ALB*

acquiring equipment. Other procedures such as developing contacts, gaining employment with ulterior objectives, procuring accomplices, securing a market for disposal of loot, wiping off fingerprints, wearing a mask, and placing a lookout should also be part of a complete report.

Modus operandi files are typically organized into two major categories of information: (1) information pertaining to crimes committed by unidentified offenders and (2) information concerning crimes committed by identified and apprehended offenders. In many police agencies, data that pertain to the *modus operandi* of a reported crime are entered into the department's computer information management system. These M.O. data then are available to investigators to analyze and consider when cases arise with similar characteristics. Often it is not the unique characteristics of a crime that identify the suspect but the common elements that reoccur with each criminal incident.

> ## HISTORY
>
> One of the early instances of psychological profiling was undertaken during World War II by the Office of Strategic Services (OSS), a secret intelligence agency of the United States government that was dissolved after the war ended in 1945. In 1943 one of the projects undertaken by the OSS involved hiring Walter Langer, a psychiatrist, and asking him to produce a profile of Adolf Hitler. Using all of the information known about Hitler, Langer developed what was called a *psychodynamic personality profile*, which, among other things, suggested Hitler had an Oedipal complex and constantly needed to prove his manhood to his mother. As well, Langer suggested that Hitler suffered from coprolagnia (sexual arousal produced by the thought or sight of feces, similar to coprophilia). Langer also predicted that Hitler would commit suicide after being defeated in his war efforts (Langer, 1978).

Legally, the *modus operandi* can be used only as an investigative lead. It can be introduced in court only as evidence to show the common purpose and design of the criminal when a series of crimes have been committed and linked to the defendant. Otherwise, enough evidence, direct or circumstantial, must be obtained to prove a specific case against an arrested person.

PSYCHOLOGICAL PROFILING

As should be evident by this point, one of the main objectives in any criminal investigation is to identify a suspect in the crime. Comparing the manner in which a crime was committed with available *modus operandi* files is one way of identifying a possible suspect. If the crime has particular abnormalities or suggests a pattern without a reason for the crime, investigators may turn to psychological profiling for help in identifying a suspect.

psychological profiling
A method of suspect identification that seeks to identify an individual's mental, emotional, and personality characteristics as manifested in things done or left behind at the crime scene.

Psychological profiling is an investigative technique that has had several names throughout its history and has been practiced on many levels for a very long time. It is a popular theme or subtheme in books, television, and movies. Psychological profiling, or criminal profiling, as it is sometimes called, is commonly associated with law enforcement investigations, and especially with the FBI, although profiling takes place in other areas and in other contexts not limited to criminal justice (Bumgarner 2004; Harris 2002).

Profiling is a method of suspect identification that seeks to identify an individual's mental, emotional, and personality characteristics as manifested in things done or artifacts left behind at the crime scene. It is typically used in crimes of violence, such as homicides, sex crimes, ritualistic crimes, and arsons in which there are no apparent motives or there are a series of crimes. Profiles provide investigators with corroborative evidence in cases with unknown suspects or with clues about likely suspects. Profiles do not, however, immediately lead investigators to a specific offender. Rather, they point to the type of person most likely to commit the crime under investigation and, thereby, may narrow the field of potential suspects.

The process used to create a psychological profile can be characterized by seven basic steps (Douglas & Burgess, 1986):

1. Evaluate the criminal act itself.
2. Analyze evidence from, and conditions at, the crime scene.
3. Consider characteristics and, when available, statements of the victim.

4. Analyze all information from the preliminary reports.
5. Evaluate the medical examiner's autopsy protocol or the physician's physical examination report.
6. Develop a profile of the offender's psychological and personality characteristics.
7. Make investigative suggestions to investigators based on the profile.

As implied by these steps, the basic process of psychological profiling is to try to recognize and interpret evidence found at the scene of the crime as indicating certain aspects of the criminal's personality. Profiles are not all-inclusive and do not even always provide the same type of information. They are based on what may or may not have been left at the scene of the crime. Since the amount of physical evidence left at a crime scene varies from one crime to the next, so too will the detail of the psychological assessments that can be made (Girod, 2004). Typically, psychological profiles try to include the following pieces of information:

- The perpetrator's race.
- His or her gender.
- An age range.
- The likelihood of employment or employability.
- The degree of sexual maturity and ability to function normally.
- Marital status.
- The likelihood that the offender will commit the same crime again.
- The probability that the offender had previously committed a similar crime.
- The possibility of previous arrests.
- The possible state of mind of the offender at the time of the crime (rage, calm rational intent, passion, and so on).

Psychological profiles sometimes provide the only clues in a case and can be very effective tools. They can help develop suspects or eliminate them, thus saving the investigator considerable time. Geberth (1996) and Holmes and Holmes (2002) identify a number of crimes where profiling is frequently used to assist investigators:

- Sadistic torture.
- Serial sex crime (sexual assaults and rapes).
- Homicides involving slashing and cutting.
- Serial arsons.
- Lust and mutilation murders.
- Crimes involving aspects of ritualism or the occult.
- Child sexual abuse including pedophilia.
- Bank robberies.
- Obscene and terrorist letter writing.
- Kidnappings.

The physical evidence left at the crime scene often contributes to the development of a psychological profile of a person who committed the crime. Symptoms of various behavioral patterns may be revealed by the way an individual *acts out* and may be observed in the way the crime was committed or in traces of things left behind. The level of violence or destruction found at the crime scene may reveal

FYI

In 2004, 9,966,877 people were arrested for a crime in the United States. Here is how those arrests broke down by age groups.

Age	Percent	Age	Percent
Under 15	5.1%	40–44	9.2
15–17	15.8	45–49	6.2
18–20	14.1	50–54	3.3
21–24	15.3	55–59	1.5
25–29	13.0	60–64	.07
30–34	10.5	Over 64	.06
35–39	9.8		

Source: FBI, 2005, table 41.

a perpetrator's rage or hatred. Sexual dysfunction may be shown by evidence of a postmortem rape in a murder. The crime may reflect many of the criminal's personality characteristics, in the same way one's style of dress or choice of a particular car make and model reflect one's personality.

Sometimes a potential suspect will emerge from a consideration of the psychological profile and the offender's M.O. At other times the profile may cause investigators to eliminate suspects who have past behaviors fitting the M.O. but not the psychological profile. Profiling is an extremely useful tool, but it is not a panacea. In some less extreme cases, police officers, calling upon their knowledge and experience, may use their own version of profiling. However, this is not really profiling. Officers are able use experience to make forecasts from various *modus operandi* they see repeatedly in the field. However, good profiling requires more than field experience as an officer; it requires a blend of educational and training backgrounds. To be a good profiler, one needs to have knowledge of sociology, psychology, psychiatry, and criminology, and be able to blend the theories of these disciplines with common sense—and, yes, field experience.

GEOGRAPHIC PROFILING

geographic profiling
A computer-assisted investigative method that uses locations of a series of crimes to determine the most likely area where an offender may be found.

Geographic profiling is a fairly recent, computer-augmented investigative methodology that uses the locations of a connected series of crimes to determine the most likely area of an offender's residence, or next likely target. Geographic profiling has been applied in a variety of types of cases including serial murder, rape, arson, robbery, and even bombings. This process was developed at Simon Fraser University and is based on a model that describes offender's *hunting grounds* (Rossmo, 2000; Weiss & Davis, 2004).

Geographic profiling uses a mathematical algorithm based on a psychological theory known as the *least-effort principle.* This principle suggests that an individual will try to adapt to the environment or will try to change the environment to suit his or her needs, whichever is easier. In investigating crime, geographic profiling suggests that criminals tend to commit crimes within a certain comfort zone, an area located near—but not too close—to their own residence (Godwin, 1996; Rossmo, 2000).

Thus geographic profiling begins with the notion that crimes do not occur completely at random; instead, they often have an underlying spatial structure that reflects this principle of least-effort. Crimes tend to occur at locations where the criminal feels familiar with his or her surroundings and where, in terms of profit and risk, the criminal can find suitable victims or targets for crimes. As an offender moves between home, work, and recreational activities, his or her space (comprised of these locations and their connecting paths and access ways) provides the offender with a kind of cognitive map of the area. By inputting a series of coordinates corresponding to events linked to a specific geographic area and a suspected unknown criminal, these programs can map these locations, showing the most probable locations of the center of these events and activities. This, in turn, can direct investigators to the geographic area where it is most likely that the offender resides.

FYI   Geographic information systems (GIS) are various computer programs that use an analytic framework to literally map locations of criminal events, to better understand trends, manage and integrate data, and make predictions of future criminal trends and event locations. The power of a GIS comes from the ability to relate different information in a spatial context and to reach a conclusion about this relationship.

Unlike traditional criminal profiling, geographic profiling does not concern itself with the criminal's age, gender, race, educational level, or even his or her psychological motives for comitting crime. Instead, geographic profiling focuses on locations and times when crimes have occurred. By putting these times and locations together, along with known patterns of similar criminals' behaviors, it is possible to predict the approximate residence of the unknown suspect (Godwin, 2004).

Geographical profiling does not "solve" criminal cases. Rather, the method provides an additional avenue of scientific investigation that, along with other forensic specialties, may provide some help for the investigation of a number of types of criminal cases.

SUMMARY

Learning Objective 1

Modus operandi (M.O.) is a Latin term for "mode or method of operation." In police work it describes the activities of criminals in preparing for and committing a crime.

Learning Objective 2

The M.O. file is an orderly method of recording and coding information designed to reveal habits, traits, or practices of criminal suspects. Consideration of these traits and practices enables investigators to make deductions about the crime and possible suspects.

Learning Objective 3

Modus operandi information compiled from several crimes can aid in the identification of a suspect if physical characteristics recur in descriptions of suspects. *Modus operandi* information can aid in the apprehension of a suspect by pinpointing certain operational patterns. It can also aid in the repression of future crimes by indicating where patrols should be increased.

Learning Objective 4

Modus operandi data are generally broken down into major subdivisions that include time and date of crime, person attacked, property attacked, method of attack, means of attack, objective of attack, trademark, words used, symbols, and transportation used.

Learning Objective 5

The body of the report should contain a complete chronological narrative of all the facts obtained during the investigation, including an explanation of the M.O. factors. Information that is not strictly part of the suspect's M.O. should also be included.

Learning Objective 6

The psychological profiling method of suspect identification seeks to identify an individual's mental, emotional, and personality characteristics as manifested in things done or left behind at the crime scene.

Learning Objective 7

Geographic profiling is a computer-assisted method of mapping seemingly unrelated criminal events and offender activities spatially to make predictions about the residence of the offender.

KEY TERMS

motive 88	repression 90	psychological profiling 96
modus operandi (M.O.) 88	trademark 93	geographic profiling 98
identification 90	cults 93	
apprehension 90	tagging 93	

QUESTIONS FOR REVIEW

Learning Objective 1

1. What is meant by *modus operandi*?
2. In what year did the earliest published material on *modus operandi* appear?

Learning Objective 2

3. What might be deduced about a suspect from a well-planned crime?
4. What type of suspects can be ruled out if the crime involves special equipment that was not skillfully used?

Learning Objective 3

5. How might M.O. assist in the apprehension of a suspect?
6. How might knowing an M.O. assist in repressing crime?

Learning Objective 4

7. Why is the "person attacked (type of victim)" portion of the M.O. report included?

8. How might knowing an M.O. assist in suppressing crime?

Learning Objective 5

9. What should the body of an M.O. report contain?

Learning Objective 6

10. On what does an analyst base a psychological profile?

11. How might a psychological profile assist in the interrogation of a suspect?

Learning Objective 7

12. How does geographic profiling work?

- -

CRITICAL THINKING EXERCISE

Read the following description of a hypothetical case involving the robbery of a motel and decide what data you would include in the *modus operandi* part of a report. Prepare a written report using the subdivisions in the section titled "The *Modus Operandi* Parts of a Report." Compare your *modus operandi* report with others in the class and resolve any discrepancies that may exist.

Facts

On July 8, 2006, at 12:30 a.m., John Gomer, the night clerk, was working behind the registration desk inside the front entrance of the Shining Star Motel. The motel is located one mile outside of town on State Route 286. A tall man walked in. John noticed that he was rather good-looking except for a small scar over his left eyebrow. The man asked John, "Do you have a room for two, for one night?" John nodded yes and placed a registration card on the counter. As he did so, the man drew a black 9-millimeter pistol from his pocket. The man pointed the gun at John and said, "Turn around and don't look at me. If you keep quiet and cooperate, we won't have any trouble." The man reached around to John's eyeglasses and removed them, placing them on the desk. He ordered John to go into a back room, where he bound John's hands and feet with duct tape and covered his eyes with a red bandana. The man also placed a red bandana with a knot in the middle in John's mouth as a gag. The man removed John's watch and wallet and went back into the other room.

John could hear the man moving around in the other room but could hear no one else. Just as the man opened the door to leave, he called to John, "Hey, you! Don't forget to leave the light on for me now, you hear?" The man laughed and left the motel.

When the day manager arrived in the morning, she freed John, who then telephoned the police. John reported the theft of $1,200 from the cash drawer, $200 from his wallet, and his watch, valued at $198.

Investigating Officer Chuck Waters responded to the call and examined the crime scene. He found the cash drawer open and John's cash-depleted wallet on the desk. All of John's credit cards were still there, as were all of his identification cards. In the back room, Officer Waters collected the pieces of gray duct tape and the bandanas used to blindfold and gag John. One of the bandanas had a small circular price tag on it and the store's name. Officer Waters interviewed several of the motel guests, but no one admitted to hearing or seeing anything. Officer Waters completed his incident report.

· ·

INVESTIGATIVE SKILL BUILDERS

Serving Clients

You have just driven into a strip mall parking lot and stopped your car near the grocery store entrance. It is 12:30 p.m. This lot has been the site of a number of reports of items stolen from parked cars. The M.O. report indicated that the thefts occurred between 12:00 p.m. and 2:00 p.m. on weekdays. Although the thefts have been strung out over about 4 weeks, they have occurred only once or twice a week. The items taken have been only loose things left on the seats of unlocked vehicles. Items have included stuffed animals, toys, and expensive fountain pens. Many of the vehicles have had radios, telephones, and CB radios installed in them, but those items were left untouched.

Your eye catches the image of a small boy moving swiftly between cars. As your eyes meet his, he quickly moves a bag he is holding behind him and starts to move off. You call to him to stop as you get out of your car. The boy is about 7 or 8 years old and is holding his bag behind him to keep it out of your view.

You ask the boy who he is and where his parents are, thinking that a small child such as this should not be in the lot all alone. He tells you his name is Bobby, his father is dead, and his mother is shopping in the grocery store. He also tells you he lives with his mother in the projects and that his mother has been unemployed for several months. You ask the boy if you can see what he has in his bag, and he obligingly brings the bag into your view. Inside are several toys and pens and two paperback books. You ask Bobby where he got the items, and he tells you he found them. Bobby is unable to tell you exactly where he found them, and instead simply says "around." You take Bobby by the hand and begin walking back toward your car. As you walk, you notice several parked cars with doors ajar. Again, you ask Bobby where he got the items in his bag. Bobby frowns and begins to cry. He tells you he took the items from the cars but that he is really sorry. You ask him what he was going to do with the things in the bag. He tells you he just wanted to play with them because his mother cannot afford to buy him things to play with. Just then a woman exits the grocery store and comes running over, calling Bobby's name. She asks what the problem is and whether Bobby is all right.

1. What can you deduce from the M.O. of the previous thefts about Bobby's possible involvement?

2. What actions should you take?

Integrity/Honesty

You are off duty and shopping with your spouse and teenage daughter in a grocery store. As you walk around, you realize that this is the store you read about during your last shift. The store has been hit recently by a rash of shoplifting. The M.O. report indicated that the thefts have been discovered at various times during the day and on different days of the week. The connecting element has been finding empty boxes on shelves from products that have been stolen. Many of these products have been beauty products.

Several of your daughter's friends come over and say hello. Your daughter chats a minute with her friends and then rejoins you and your spouse. As you turn the corner of an aisle a few minutes later, you notice your daughter's friends slipping lipsticks and other small cosmetics into their pockets. As they move away, you see empty packaging from cosmetics on the shelf near where the girls stood. What action will you take?

Interviews and Interrogations

CHAPTER OBJECTIVES

After completing this chapter, you will be able to:

1 Identify sources of information available to criminal investigators.
2 Explain the difference between *interviews* and *interrogations*.
3 Describe some useful techniques for interviewing witnesses.
4 Discuss the legal aspects of interrogating a person in police custody.
5 Describe some effective interrogation techniques.
6 Discuss special considerations for interrogating juveniles.
7 Distinguish between *confessions* and *admissions*.

SOURCES OF INFORMATION

Information is the lifeblood of police work. Without adequate information, a police investigation can very quickly come to a shattering standstill. Sometimes information can be obtained from the physical evidence and the crime scene itself. Bloodstains, broken glass, foot- and fingerprints all tell investigators certain things about the criminal and sometimes the way the crime was committed. Investigative reports, *modus operandi* files, geographic profiling, arrest records, and other reports are also important and useful sources of information. In most cases, however, police investigators get the most information and spend most of their time interviewing or interrogating people (Yeschke, 2002).

Distinguishing between interviews and interrogations is important. In its most basic form, an **interview** may be defined as "a conversation with a purpose"; namely, "to gather information" (Berg, 2007, p. 91). To accomplish this purpose, police officers must be able to communicate in a self-aware and effective manner with witnesses, victims, informants, and suspects (Milne & Bull, 1999). An **interrogation,** in contrast, may be defined as questioning persons suspected of being directly or indirectly involved in a crime (Buckley, 2005).

There are both legal and practical reasons to make a distinction between interviewing and interrogation. From a practical standpoint, one typically does not interrogate someone who is not in custody. As is discussed later in this chapter, once individuals have been taken into custody—that is, had their liberty to leave the presence of the officer taken away—information obtained from them cannot be used in court unless they have been advised of their constitutional rights. Interviews, however, do not require that one be either taken into custody or advised of one's rights. Information obtained during the course of an interview and recorded in an officer's field notes is admissible in court if it meets the tests of competency, materiality, and relevance (see Chapter 2).

Sometimes a person being interviewed may say something that causes the officer to believe he or she actually should be a suspect. At this juncture the officer may take the person into custody, advise the person of his or her rights, and continue talking. Technically, the officer is now conducting an interrogation. In other words, what was an interview 5 minutes ago has now become an interrogation. In both cases the officer is seeking information. However, several important changes are likely to have occurred during this shift from interview to interrogation.

interview Questioning to obtain information regarding a person's knowledge about a crime, suspect, or event.

interrogation Questioning to obtain information from persons suspected of being directly or indirectly involved in a crime.

> **FYI** Information about a crime or a confession freely offered during the course of a noncustodial interview is admissible in court as a *voluntary admission of guilt* provided the subject understood that he or she was not in custody at the time of the statement. Voluntary admissions are admissible to serve the public's interest (*Moran v. Burbine,* 1986).

During interviewing, officers' attitudes and demeanor are generally open, friendly, informal, and conversational. The direction of the interview is wide open, with the investigator striving to collect as much information as possible about the crime. During interrogation, there is a shift to a more adversarial attitude. Officers' attitudes and demeanor become more formal, antagonistic, challenging, and competitive. The direction of an interrogation is narrow and is specifically focused on the subject's direct or indirect involvement and knowledge about a crime or the concealment of an offense or an offender.

HISTORY

DURING THE EARLY MORNING HOURS OF MARCH 13, 1964, Catherine Genovese—whose friends called her Kitty—was returning home from her job as the manager of Ev's Eleventh Hour Club, a bar in Hollis, New York. As she approached her apartment in the upscale neighborhood of Kew Garden's Queens, New York, she was attacked and stabbed by an assailant. She screamed as she was stabbed, "Oh, my God, he stabbed me! Please help me! Please help me!" Lights came on in several neighbors' windows, and a man's voice cried out "Leave her alone." The assailant ran and hid, only to return in a few minutes to stab Kitty again. There were more screams, more lights, and Kitty's assailant fled a second time. Kitty managed to stagger to her doorway, bleeding profusely from her knife wounds. The assailant returned for a third time and completed his attack. When he was done, Kitty Genovese had been fatally stabbed. Throughout the attack, which by some accounts lasted nearly 15 minutes, only one individual of what police later reported were as many as 38 witnesses ever called the police. Witnesses would later explain their reluctance to call the authorities for a variety of reasons, including not wanting to speak with police because they simply didn't want to get involved, because they had warrants out against them, or because they assumed someone had already called the police (Rosenthal, 1999; Wainwright, 1964).

It is important to note that the characterization of interrogations as adversarial does not mean that all interviews are conducted with willing participants, nor that all people being interrogated must be forced or pressured to speak openly with investigators (Inbau, Reid, & Buckley, 2004). Witnesses and victims may have many reservations about speaking with the police or furnishing information. They may withhold information either knowingly or unknowingly. They may consider their information unimportant or insignificant, or they may be fearful of repercussions or retaliation against them or their family members. They may believe that they themselves are involved in some way or may simply feel distrustful of the police or afraid of media publicity. The best results are likely to be obtained if the officer is patient, courteous, open, understanding, and honest with the person being interviewed (Buckley, 2005; Milne & Bull, 1999).

Interviews

An investigator should begin an interview by establishing rapport with the person to be interviewed (Yeschke, 2002). **Rapport** is a relationship that develops between an officer and the person being interviewed in which the interviewee feels that the officer has empathy for him or her or identifies with his or her feelings (Richardson, 2000). Regardless of whether the person being interviewed is a witness, a victim, or a potential suspect, consider for a moment how he or she might be feeling. Showing a little compassion might go a long way in such a circumstance. If the interview occurs immediately after a crime, allow the person a few minutes to compose him- or herself. If necessary, separate the interviewee from large crowds, family members, the media, darkness, loud noises, or any anxiety-producing situation. Those things may interfere with creating rapport and a setting conducive to an interview.

Always treat the person to be interviewed with respect, and address him or her as Mr., Mrs., Miss, Ms., Sir, and so forth. Do not call a witness by his or her first name. It could negatively affect the interview.

rapport A relationship of mutual trust and emotional affinity that develops between an interviewer or interrogator and the person being interviewed or interrogated.

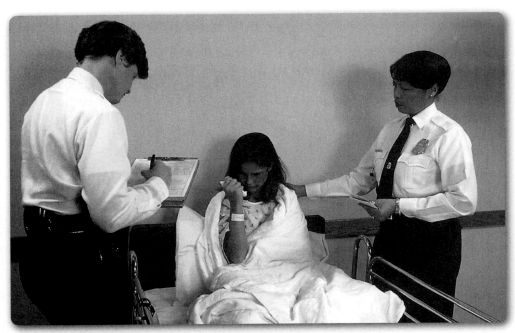

When interviewing victims immediately following a crime, allow them time to compose themselves.

aware hearing A technique of listening and literally hearing what is being said without interrupting the speaker.

Interviews are best conducted face-to-face in a courteous and sincere manner. Learn to listen with **aware hearing;** that is, focus your listening and hear more than the words being spoken (Berg, 2007; Yeschke, 2002). Avoid interrupting speakers to interject your own views or comments. In other words, do not interrupt the interviewee by saying such things as "Oh yeah, I've seen that sort of thing before," or "Gosh, that really was bad, but I know from experience it will be okay," or similar well-intentioned comments. Likewise, learn to distinguish between a pause for breath, a pause for the speaker to recompose him- or herself, and the completion of a statement. Good aware hearing in interviews and interrogations pays off. Experienced investigators know that as many as 95 percent of crimes are cleared through interviews and interrogations (Palmiotto, 1995).

If time permits, investigators should prepare for the interview. In some cases, such as hot crimes or emergencies, there may be no time for preparation. However, in most situations investigators should know, at minimum, who is being interviewed and who else might be involved in the case, what the crime involved, where events took place, how the interviewee was involved, and why things may have occurred as they did. The more information the investigator has regarding the case and the people involved, the better the investigator can control the process. Furthermore, demonstrating that one has some information can suggest to the interviewee that one actually has more information than he or she possesses. This can encourage the interviewee to open up and provide additional information.

Witnesses, victims, or others who are to be interviewed about a crime should be separated at the crime scene as soon as possible. Investigators need to know what each person saw, heard, and knows about the case. Allowing one person to hear what another person has to say, or to share their information, contaminates whatever information the investigator might eventually obtain.

Whenever possible, people involved in a criminal case should be interviewed in a logical order that provides the investigator with increasing amounts of information. The following order is recommended:

1. Victims or complainants
2. Eyewitnesses
3. Informants and others who have relevant information but are not eyewitnesses
4. Suspects

Not only will a well-conducted interview obtain the desired information, but it can also serve as an excellent public relations tool. Throughout the interview, the interviewee will be making assessments about the officer, and those assessments, in turn, reflect on the department. A well-handled interview leaves the interviewee feeling confident about the police and their ability to handle the case. A poorly executed interview may leave the interviewee feeling insecure about his or her safety or the ability of the police to solve the crime. It may even make it difficult to gain the continued cooperation of that witness or victim.

It is important to separate witnesses, victims, and others who may be interviewed about a crime.

The Cognitive Interview Research suggests that interview style is important in determining the amount and type of information subjects provide. The **cognitive interview** is a technique used in law enforcement interviewing and interrogation that involves jogging a witness's memory (Geiselman et al., 1987), or doing what social scientists might refer to as "triggering memories" (Berg, 2007). Geiselman and Fisher (1997) and Fisher and McCauley (1995) have outlined the scientific merits of the cognitive interview and summarized the major principles underlying the cognitive interviewing technique.

cognitive interview An interviewing technique that helps victims or witnesses mentally put themselves at the crime scene to gather information about the crime.

During more traditional interviews, interviewers usually ask witnesses and victims open-ended questions such as "What happened?" After a 10- or 15-minute narration by the subject, the interviewer then usually asks specific questions to gain additional information on certain key points. This passive approach to interviewing fails to aid a witness or victim in remembering details.

Many witnesses and victims are in a kind of shock and may have difficulty remembering such obvious details as the color of the criminal's shirt or whether the gun was blue or steel-colored. Cognitive interviewing includes four procedures for triggering these memories.

1. *Reconstruct the circumstance.* Ask the subject to try to reconstruct the incident and focus on it in the mind's eye. Say, "Close your eyes, and try to see yourself back at the scene." Also have the subject try to remember how he or she felt at the time of the event. Ask, "How were you feeling just before the robber entered?" or "What were you thinking just after the robber entered?"
2. *Report all information.* Have the subject focus on the event and tell all, trying not to edit or omit anything, no matter how trivial it may seem. Try not to interrupt this narration.

3. *Recall events in a different order.* Ask the subject to recall the events out of sequence. For example, ask the subject to begin with the most impressive or scariest part of the event. Or simply ask the subject to reverse the order of events.

4. *Change perspectives.* Ask the subject to try to recall the event from the point of view of someone else who was present. Tell the witness to place him- or herself in the person and perspective of some prominent actor in the event (for example, the victim) and imagine what he or she must have seen (Morgan, 1990).

The procedures involved in cognitive interviewing are designed to draw information along different memory paths (Fisher & McCauley, 1995). In turn, this allows the investigator to assist the subject in remembering details or triggering memories. For instance, regarding appearance, instead of simply asking, "What did the suspect look like?" the investigator might ask, "Did the suspect look like anyone you know?" or "Was there anything out of the ordinary about how the suspect looked?" For names, rather than asking, "Do you recall any names being mentioned?" the investigator might ask, "Do you recall the sound of the first letter of any suspect's name that may have been mentioned?" or "Do you recall if any of the suspects' names had more than one syllable?"

Cognitive interviewing techniques can be very effective for drawing out details of an event; however, there are also several drawbacks. First, it is much more time-consuming than traditional interviewing strategies. Second, it requires more control over the environment than other interviewing procedures. Finally, it requires that the interviewer be well practiced in the technique and have more skill than might be required for more traditional, straightforward question-answer interviewing techniques.

The Reid Technique of Interviewing Although not widely employed by law enforcement agencies, the Reid technique is used by some and is fairly commonly used in industrial settings. The Reid technique of interviewing involves a three-part investigative procedure. The first step is referred to as *factual analysis* and represents analysis of the information collected at the crime scene, including information about evidence, victims, witnesses, and possible suspects. This segment of the investigation helps the investigator prepare for the interview and determine the direction an investigation should take. It can also assist by potentially offering some insight into the possible offender. The second step of the process is the interview of possible suspects. This is a highly structured interview sometimes referred to as a **behavioral analysis interview (BAI).** The BAI is a nonaccusatory interview designed to identify whether a person is telling the truth or withholding relevant information concerning a specific crime or act of wrongdoing (Inbau, Reid, & Buckley, 2004). Individuals trained in the Reid technique spend considerable time learning how to interpret suspects' behavioral responses during the interview. When an interviewer believes that a suspect has not told the truth during the nonaccusatory interview, the third step in this technique is employed; namely, an accusatory interrogation. Although not necessarily called the Reid technique, many police agencies do engage in an assessment of deception by observing behavioral clues such as whether the suspect maintains eye contact, certain evasive head and body movements, monitoring breathing, and observing how hands and arms are held (Navarro & Schafer, 2001).

The underlying rationale for the behavioral analysis interview is the notion that all deception is motivated by the effort to avoid the consequences of telling the truth. These consequences may be real (being fired, going to jail, paying reparations or a fine) or personal (shame, embarrassment, humiliation, fear of disappointing family,

behavioral analysis interview A nonaccusatory interview designed to identify whether a person is telling the truth or withholding information.

and so on). One of the goals of the interrogation segment of the Reid technique is to reduce the perceived negative consequences of telling the truth. Legally, an investigator cannot reduce real criminal consequences for a suspect. Only the district attorney's office is authorized to formally offer a plea negotiation, which might include lesser penalties in exchange for cooperation or a confession. However, an investigator can use a number of legal and proper procedures to illicit information from a deceptive suspect and to encourage the suspect to perceive lesser consequences. These procedures are more fully discussed later in the chapter.

Complainants and Complaints

A **complainant** is an individual seeking satisfaction or action for an injury or for damages sustained as the consequence of another's activities or actions. The complainant may be the victim of a crime or someone who seeks action on behalf of a victim. For example, the parents of a juvenile who has been assaulted may file a complaint with the police. A **complaint** is a formal allegation by which a legal action is commenced against a party; it is a request for police action in some matter. In recent years officers have been provided with a means of filing a complaint in certain domestic violence situations in some jurisdictions. In such cases, the officer becomes the complainant.

Complainants are especially important during the initial stages of police investigations. Complainants provide basic information about the crime. They may be able to describe a suspect and the various details, events, and circumstances before and during commission of the crime. Data provided by complainants to an officer may seem trivial at times. But officers must remember that when a complainant tells the police something, he or she is likely to perceive this information as very important. Once again, the way an officer handles filing a complaint and interviewing the complainant may affect the public image of the officer's agency and, indirectly, of police in general.

All complainants should be taken seriously until their complaints are demonstrated to have no basis in fact or reality. Even mentally deficient and alcoholic or drug-impaired complainants may furnish valuable and useful information. For example, if an agitated alcoholic street person has just witnessed the mugging of another street person, she may be the only source of information about the crime. In this case the police will probably hold the complainant and reinterview her after she has sobered up. On the other hand, the complainant may be someone who claims that the silver foil helmet he is wearing protects him from the Martian invaders masquerading as store clerks in the supermarket. In this case the police may consider referring the man to a psychiatric facility for an intake examination and evaluation. Some police agencies keep a file near the complaint or information desk of repeat complainants who are troubled or psychotic. This provides a reference for officers to check when they suspect a complainant is mentally troubled.

The complaints that complainants bring to police fall into two general categories: specific or nonspecific. The classification of a given complaint depends on certain facts offered by the complainant. If a criminal offense is involved and there is supporting data, the matter may be considered a *specific complaint*. If there is no basis in fact or law to warrant police action, the matter may be considered a *nonspecific complaint*. After taking a nonspecific complaint, the police may refer the complainant to a more appropriate agency or department.

Specific Complaints Whenever a complainant provides information about a possible crime in an initial complaint, a more thorough investigation should be arranged. A detailed interview is the first important step in such an investigation. This

complainant An individual who seeks satisfaction or action for an injury or for damages sustained. It may be the victim of a crime or someone acting on behalf of the victim.

complaint A formal allegation by which a legal action is commenced against a party; a request for police action in some matter.

interview should be as exhaustive as possible and should obtain the following information: the name, address, telephone numbers, and occupation of the complainant; the time and location of the crime; the nature of the offense; the number of suspects and a description of each; the license number and description of any vehicle involved; the direction of the suspects' flight; the present location of the suspects, if known; a description of property involved; the weapons, if any, that the suspects may have used; and the identity of any witnesses. The success of most investigations depends on obtaining complete and detailed information during the initial interview with the complainant. If all the pertinent information is not obtained from a complainant during the initial interview, valuable time may be lost, and the case may go unsolved.

Nonspecific Complaints This type of complaint represents a large proportion of calls to police agencies. Complaints of this kind do not have any basis in fact and are often merely hearsay generalizations. An example of a nonspecific complaint is one in which a caller claims that a person who lives down the block is engaging in criminal activities. The complainant may tell the police that the person down the block has no visible means of support but drives a brand new expensive car and wears expensive looking clothing. The complainant may also tell the police that the person has no interactions with neighbors and keeps erratic late-night hours. Finally, the complainant may tell police that he or she has a "gut feeling" about this person. When questioned, the complainant may recall no specific criminal activities committed by the supposed offender but may still argue that this individual is "a suspicious character."

While maintaining a polite demeanor, the officer receiving this complaint should inform the caller that no police action is possible because no laws have been broken. The caller should be thanked for taking the time to contact the police and encouraged to call again should he or she learn about any specific violations of law by the suspicious neighbor. A brief record should be made of the complainant's information for future reference in the event additional information is received regarding the violation of a specific law.

Witnesses

Investigators solve many cases simply by talking with people and finding out what they may have seen or heard. When preparing to interview a witness, consider the kinds of questions a defense attorney might ask each witness at the trial. Questions by the defense are likely to challenge the credibility of the prosecution's witnesses. The challenge may be directed at such factors as witnesses' physical or mental condition, their emotional state, and their experience, education, and knowledge. Remember that witnesses do not have to be advised of their constitutional rights; however, do not threaten or promise anything to witnesses to obtain statements.

Witnesses are often hastily questioned on the spot, immediately after the reported violation, to get quick information that might lead immediately to the apprehension of the perpetrator. Following this preliminary interview at the crime scene, the investigating officer may want to conduct more extensive, formal interviews with witnesses and victims. Be sure to set appointments for interviews at the convenience of the witnesses. It may be necessary to interview them at work or at their homes rather than at the police station. Also, arrange for privacy so they will be comfortable speaking with you. In addition to the general guidelines already discussed, Figure 6.1 lists ten basic rules for interviewing witnesses. Let's next take a look at some of the kinds of witnesses likely to be encountered in the field and ways of establishing rapport with them.

FIGURE 6.1 Ten Basic Rules for Interviewing Witnesses

1. Plan ahead.
2. Arrange for privacy.
3. Identify yourself properly.
4. Assemble case facts in advance.
5. Have an intentional direction.
6. Be timely.
7. Avoid interruptions.
8. Be a good (aware) listener.
9. Adjust language level, pace, and demeanor as necessary.
10. Maintain rapport throughout the interview.

Willing Witnesses   Such people generally cooperate with the police and furnish all the information they have concerning a given event. They either seek out the police to furnish their information or cooperate fully when located and interviewed. Be mindful, though, that willing witnesses may not always be reliable and may have ulterior motives.

Eyewitnesses   Eyewitnesses are the most important type of witness. Allow them to state in their own words what they saw happen. Avoid asking a lot of questions until they have completed recounting their story. After hearing an eyewitness's account, ask specific questions to clarify inconsistencies or gaps in the story.

Reluctant Witnesses   Hostility toward police, stubbornness, fear, indifference, or a relationship with the suspect may make a person reluctant to furnish information. A reluctant witness is one of the most difficult problems an officer contends with in an investigation. Patience, tact, and persuasiveness should govern the investigator's conduct during this type of interview. Information from such a witness may be the link needed to convict or clear the suspect in the crime.

Silent or Disinterested Witnesses   These individuals want to offer no information or assistance to the investigator. Some simply do not want to become involved in a police matter. Others may fear any contact with the police or the courts. Still others may lack sufficient intellect to understand the need for their assistance or may be so oblivious to their surroundings that they can truly offer no information. There are also people who, for whatever reason, delight in seeing the police fail in their efforts, and they will remain silent. The interviewer must remain patient and persistent when working with such witnesses. Appealing to their sense of decency or fairness or attempting to have them emphasize with victims in the case may help in obtaining information.

Unreliable Witnesses   People in this category may be deficient individuals, publicity seekers, children with vivid imaginations, or pathological liars. If you allow witnesses to talk freely, you can call to their attention obvious discrepancies in their statements. To establish the reliability of statements, the interviewer should try to learn how the witnesses came by the information, how good their memories are, and what interest they might have in the case or the people involved. It is also wise to determine their credibility, personal feelings, and honesty. If a witness appears to be a pathological liar, this witness should be reminded that lying to the police has serious repercussions.

Frightened Witnesses   Such people fear that suspects or their associates will seek revenge should they cooperate with the authorities. They honestly believe that someone is lying in wait to harm them, and they will suffer loss of sleep and appetite worrying about this threat of harm. Investigators should try to gain their confidence and assure them that retaliation is extremely rare. These witnesses should be told to notify police immediately if they receive any threats.

Biased Witnesses　These individuals willingly furnish information, but their statements may be prejudiced toward the suspect or victim in some way. A close relationship between a witness and the suspect tends to bias the statement furnished by the witness. A desire to wreak personal vengeance on a suspect is often very strong. When dealing with such a witness, investigators should consider the manner of conversation, the inherent likelihood of the story, the number and character of contradictions in the story furnished, and the nature and extent of the witness's interest in the case.

Hostile Witnesses　These witnesses, who are not disposed to furnish any information to the police, are antagonistic and resist any form of questioning. Investigators should not let a hostile witness know that they resent this attitude. Instead, investigators should try to determine the reason for the hostility and then try to correct it. It is important to make such individuals feel that their information is greatly appreciated. Appeals to civic duty, personal pride, religion, decency, family, or justice may be helpful. Winning the cooperation of hostile witnesses may ultimately provide the margin of proof necessary to successfully prosecute a suspect.

Timid Witnesses　When witnesses are self-conscious or shy, lack confidence, or have poorly developed language skills, the investigator should make every effort to put them at ease. All conversations should be conducted in a relaxed manner and questions asked in a simple, straightforward, matter-of-fact way.

Deceitful Witnesses　When an investigator encounters deceitful witnesses, the investigator must listen attentively but should not immediately let on that he or she does not believe the story being offered. The witness should be allowed to recite many

Different types of witnesses require different approaches.

falsehoods before being confronted with them. Then the witness should have each false statement pointed out to him or her and be reminded that there are serious consequences for offering perjured testimony before a court of law. Tape-recording and playing back false statements can sometimes induce a deceitful witness to recognize the futility of deception. In some cases, asking the witness if he or she is willing to take a polygraph test (discussed later in this chapter) may result in a change of attitude and a willingness to speak more honestly.

Children   Information furnished by children is often unreliable, and corroborative testimony should always be sought. Children are very imaginative and often confuse facts with fantasy; judges and juries are hesitant to convict a suspect solely on the testimony of a child. On the other hand, it is very important not to disregard statements offered by children unless they are shown to be untrue. Investigators should be exceedingly careful about putting words in a child's mouth and should avoid asking leading questions.

Young Adults   People in this age bracket, whether married or single, are not as reliable or dependable as mature adults. They are usually preoccupied with their own personal lives and affairs, or problems.

Mature Adults   These individuals have a fuller appreciation of police responsibilities and are generally more dependable witnesses. Their personal adjustments have been made, and their social experiences have been widened. The powers of observation and retention of these adults are usually at their peak, and their opinions are more apt to be reserved.

Taking Notes

When, or if, one should take notes during witness questioning is a controversial issue. It is important for investigating officers to keep accurate field notes; however, whether the records should be handwritten notes or electronic recordings may depend on the witness and the technological sophistication of the investigating officer's department. Some witnesses are not comfortable having their conversation recorded—no matter how inconspicuous the recording device might be. Others prefer that the interview be taped to ensure that the officer gets all the information accurately and completely.

When using a recording device, the witness should be informed before the interview begins that a taped record is being made. The investigator should explain that the purpose of recording the interview is merely to ensure accuracy in what is included in the field record. If equipment is available, it may also be advisable to videotape the interview. In several jurisdictions persons suspected of driving under the influence of alcohol (or other substances) are routinely videotaped during their field sobriety tests and accompanying interview. Video records provide a means of assessing various physical behavioral cues that occurred during the interview or an interrogation (Gordon & Fleisher, 2006).

Even when an investigator chooses to use only a notebook during the interview, caution is advised. Some witnesses may be disturbed or distracted if they see the investigator taking too many or too frequent notes. Interviewers need to become sensitive to the verbal and nonverbal clues the witness gives during the interview. If the interviewer perceives that note taking is a problem, he or she should take few or no notes during the course of the interview. At the conclusion of the interview, the interviewer should quickly jot down relevant facts and names the witness has offered.

How and whether to take notes during the interview depends largely on the individual witness. Some people are fearful of any written record. The investigator's main objective is to obtain as much information as possible about the case; doing so may require a little extra effort on the interviewer's part.

INTERROGATIONS

Interrogating suspects is somewhat more difficult than interviewing witnesses or victims (Gordon & Fleisher, 2006; Zulawski, 2001). Once located by the police, a suspect involved in a crime may or may not be willing to make a statement, an admission of guilt, or a confession. Many investigators believe the central purpose of an interrogation is to obtain a confession, and the effort to obtain a confession as a means of solving a case is an integral part of police work today. Let us consider the larger purpose of interrogation in modern-day police work.

The central purpose of an interrogation is to elicit from a suspect—or from people related to or associated with a suspect—information about a criminal event. An interrogation, in modern police work, *is not* intended to be used as a weapon to get a guilty person to break down and confess. Rather, it is a procedure used to obtain *the truth* (Zulawski, 2001). In addition, the interrogation process may accomplish other goals. Possible goals of the interrogation process include the following (no hierarchy or order is intended):

- Learn the truth and possibly establish the innocence of a suspect.
- Obtain an admission of guilt (a confession).
- Ascertain the names of accomplices and accessories.
- Eliminate or incriminate other suspects.
- Gain additional facts and information about the circumstances surrounding the crime.
- Identify new leads either unwittingly offered or intentionally provided by the suspect.
- Locate or recover stolen property.
- Discover new or additional physical evidence such as weapons.
- Obtain additional facts to corroborate or disprove some fact.
- Develop information that might uncover other unlawful activities or resolve other cases.

When suspects under questioning demonstrate that they are innocent, the interrogation has served its professional purpose no less than when a confession is obtained from a guilty party. Many of the techniques used in interviewing are also used in interrogation, but there are some important differences. One of the most important is that the manner in which the investigator interrogates suspects must not violate their rights in order to ensure that their statements will be admissible in court.

Legal Aspects of Interrogation

Before being interrogated or questioned while in police custody, an individual must be advised of his or her legal rights. Recall that in Chapter 2 *custody* was defined as detainment of an individual by a police officer such that the individual believes he or she has lost the liberty to freely leave. These rights were established in the *Miranda* decision (*Miranda v. Arizona*, 1966).

Ernesto Miranda was a 25-year-old mentally impaired man. He was arrested in Phoenix, Arizona, and charged with kidnapping and rape. After his arrest, the complaining victim identified Miranda. Miranda was taken into a small room at the station

HISTORY

FOLLOWING THE SUPREME COURT'S DECISION, Miranda's rape charge was dropped. However, because Miranda had taken his victim's credit cards, a robbery charge was still valid. In a subsequent trial, Miranda was found guilty of robbery as the result of information provided by his wife about an admission of guilt on Miranda's part. He was returned to prison and was paroled in December 1972. During the next several years, Miranda was stopped numerous times for minor traffic offenses and eventually lost his driver's license. Subsequently he returned to prison due to a parole violation (possession of a gun) and served one year before being released. In 1976, following a card game at the La Amapola Bar, Miranda was stabbed and killed during a fight. Ironically, a suspect was arrested at the scene and read his *Miranda* warning.

and interrogated for more than 2 hours. During the course of this interrogation, Miranda asked to telephone his sister (with whom he resided), but his request was refused. He also asked to use the bathroom, and officers informed him he could as soon as he signed a confession. Eventually Miranda did sign a written confession. He was later convicted and sentenced to 20 years in prison. The conviction was affirmed on his appeal to the Arizona Supreme Court. Miranda continued his appeal, eventually being heard by the U.S. Supreme Court. The appeal's argument rested heavily on the facts that Miranda had never been warned that any statement he made could be used against him and that he had been unaware of his right to have legal counsel present during questioning (the interrogation).

The *Miranda* case was one of four similar cases heard simultaneously by the Supreme Court. Each case dealt with the legality of confessions obtained by police from suspects being held *incommunicado* (not being allowed to notify anyone of their whereabouts) and without benefit of knowing their constitutional rights and protections as suspects in a criminal case. The other cases heard by the Supreme Court in this regard were *Vignera v. New York* (1966), *Westover v. United States* (1966), and *California v. Stewart* (1966).

The Supreme Court's decision in *Miranda* concerned the Fifth Amendment and the admissibility of statements obtained from suspects questioned while in custody (or when otherwise denied their freedom). Under provisions of the Fifth Amendment, "no person . . . shall be compelled in any criminal case to be a witness against himself." Taken literally, this means that a defendant cannot be required to testify in court. It also means that a suspect cannot be coerced in any manner to confess nor made to confess under fear of duress. According to the Supreme Court's decision, Miranda had confessed as a result of the "third-degree methods" used by the police during their interrogation. Miranda's conviction was overturned, and the Court

FYI Immediately following the *Miranda* ruling, many police officers believed that cases would be lost as would their ability to obtain confessions. Research during that time, however, demonstrated that few cases were actually lost as a direct result of *Miranda* errors. In fact, the impact on convictions from *Miranda* was negligible (Wasby, 1970).

established a set of guidelines for police to follow prior to interrogating suspects in police custody. Decisions in subsequent cases have refined the rights of suspects set forth in the *Miranda* decision.

Because of television and movies, most people have at least heard of the *Miranda* warning. There are slight variations in wording in different jurisdictions across the country, but all share several basic elements. The *Miranda* warning informs a suspect who has been arrested or who is about to be interrogated that he or she is entitled to certain rights:

1. You have the right to remain silent. You are not required to make any statement or answer any questions. Anything you say will be taken down and can be used against you later in a court of law.
2. You have the right to speak to an attorney. You may consult with an attorney or have one present with you during any questioning.
3. If you cannot afford an attorney, one can be appointed for you. If you want to have an attorney present during questioning, one will be provided by the court at no charge.
4. You retain the right to counsel, even if you speak with the police. If you want to answer questions now, without an attorney present, you will still retain the right to stop answering questions at any time.

The *Miranda* warning is intended to protect the rights of accused persons held in police custody. However, a suspect can waive his or her rights and answer questions posed by the police. In many jurisdictions, an officer's or investigator's department or the prosecutor's office may require both an oral acknowledgment of one's rights ("Do you understand these rights as I've explained them to you?") and a signed statement of the waiver. Decisions in cases subsequent to the *Miranda* decision have refined the rights of suspects set forth in *Miranda*. (Figure 6.2).

FIGURE 6.2 Cases Affecting Interrogation Procedures

Escobedo v. Illinois	1963	A suspect in custody must be advised of the right to silence and the right to be advised by an attorney during interrogation.
Miranda v. Arizona	1966	Suspects cannot be questioned without first being advised of certain rights: The right to remain silent, the right to be told that anything said can be used in court, and the right to consult with an attorney before questioning and to have an attorney present during questioning.
Orozco v. Texas	1969	Interrogation does not have to take place in a police station to have a coercive effect, and being in police custody is defined as being deprived of freedom in a significant way.
Harris v. New York	1971	A defendant's statement made in violation of *Miranda* may be used to challenge the defendant's trial testimony.
Michigan v. Tucker	1974	Statements made in violation of *Miranda* may be used to locate prosecution witnesses.
Beckwith v. U.S.	1976	The application of *Miranda* depends on custodial police interrogation, involving questioning in a coercive, police-dominated atmosphere.

FIGURE 6.2 (*Continued*)

Oregon v. Mathiason	1977	Custodial interrogation is defined as questioning initiated by law enforcement officers after a person has been taken into custody or otherwise deprived of freedom.
Rhode Island v. Innis	1980	Disclosures offered outside the context of interrogation are not violations of *Miranda*.
Harry v. Estelle	1980	*Miranda* applies only in investigative interrogation.
California v. Prysock	1981	*Miranda* warnings are valid regardless of wording or order given.
Edwards v. Arizona	1981	Once a suspect in custody states that he or she wants an attorney, police must halt all questioning and may not engage in further questioning unless the suspect requests it.
U.S. v. Lane	1983	Voluntary statements made without questioning by police may be used against defendants at trial.
U.S. v. Dockery	1983	This case clarified the meaning of custodial interrogation and the appropriate use of deception.
California v. Beheler	1983	*Miranda* warnings are not required when suspects voluntarily go to a police station to make a statement.
New York v. Quarles	1984	The public safety exception to *Miranda* warnings exists when a public threat could be removed by the suspect making a statement.
Minnesota v. Murphy	1984	Probation officers are not required to give *Miranda* warnings to their clients.
Berkermer v. McMarthy	1984	*Miranda* warnings are not required for traffic violations.
Lanier v. South Carolina	1986	Illegal arrests invalidate voluntary confessions.
Illinois v. Perkins	1990	Jailed suspects need not be informed of their right to remain silent when they provide information to undercover agents.
New York v. Harris	1990	A suspect's statements made at the police station, after a questionable entrance by the police into the suspect's house, are not barred from being admitted at trial.
McNeil v. Wisconsin	1991	A suspect jailed for one crime can be questioned for the first time about a separate crime without the presence of his or her lawyer.
Davis v. U.S.	1994	When a suspect makes an ambiguous reference to an attorney during questioning, such as "maybe I should speak with an attorney," he or she is not protected by *Miranda,* and police may continue questioning.
Stansbury v. California	1994	Reaffirmation that the officer's subjective determination of custody is irrelevant and that when a suspect believes he or she has been deprived of freedom, that individual is in custody.
Dickerson v. U.S.	2000	The Supreme Court establishes *Miranda* as an indisputable cornerstone of the justice process.

An interrogation is an offensive-defensive situation in which investigators try to secure a confession.

Preparing for Interrogation

In preparing for an interrogation, investigators should review all available data concerning the *crime,* the *suspect,* and the *victim.* All materials related to the case file should be reviewed, especially the physical evidence and the *modus operandi* information. Investigators should check out all available information about the suspect. Such data may include personal background, relationship to the victim, motive and possible means to commit the crime, alibi, and opportunity to commit the crime. Additionally, the preparing interrogator should examine the suspect's identification record, previous employment history, occupation, known associates, family, hobbies, hangouts, and financial status, as well as the type of automobile he or she drives or has access to. As to the victim, scrutinize such information as marital status, reputation, financial situation, employment, and leisure activities. In addition, the investigator should look into personal habits, associates, places of amusement frequented, and other activities. This procedure is recommended particularly in those cases where there appear to be discrepancies in the victim's account of the reported incident. Alleged victims of robberies, burglaries, kidnappings, rapes, and arsons have been known to report fictitious crimes. This preparation for interrogation may appear time-consuming, but it takes only a matter of minutes. In some cases little information is available. Experienced investigators seldom conduct an interrogation without first going through as much of this process as time permits.

Interrogation Settings

Because of the slightly adversarial nature of an interrogation, whenever possible it should be conducted in a setting familiar to the investigator; this gives the investigator a psychological advantage similar to the home-court advantage in a basketball game.

As previously mentioned, interviews are often held at the convenience of witnesses or victims, in settings of their choosing (home, office, the station). Interrogations, however, are more firmly controlled by the police. The investigator determines when and where the interrogation will be conducted.

Most interrogations take place at the police station. However, if the suspect refuses to come to the station or if there is insufficient evidence for an arrest, the officer may conduct an on-the-spot interrogation. The suspect may be interrogated in the squad car, at home, or at work. Following apprehension at the scene of a crime, a suspect may consent to being interrogated and readily waive constitutional rights in an attempt to project an aura of innocence. This is similar to a poker game in which the suspect tries to bluff the arresting officers with an attitude of cooperation, hoping to convince "the law" that they have the wrong person. In these situations the officer should keep the suspect separate from any family or friends present at the scene. On-the-spot interrogations should be straightforward, and questioning should pertain to the crime and should seek answers about the *who, what, when, where, how,* and *why* of the crime.

In general, suspects should be interrogated as soon as possible after being identified or captured, once preparations have been made. Formal interrogations conducted at the station are sometimes more effective than on-the-spot confrontations. The mere fact that a suspect has been brought into the station for questioning can be fairly intimidating. For some people, it may assist in their opening up and admitting involvement in a crime, or knowledge about one.

As with interviews, interrogation settings should provide some degree of privacy, and distractions should be eliminated before the interrogation begins. Interruptions should be limited, whenever possible, to messages or intentional ploys that are intended to improve the results of the interrogation (Zulawski, 2001). Interrogation rooms in police stations should not have telephones, nor should they have windows, pictures on the walls, excessive furnishings, or anything else that might distract a suspect. The interrogation may occur in the presence of the suspect's attorney or, if the suspect waives his or her rights (Figure 6.3), without benefit of counsel.

Customarily, at least two officers are present during the interrogation of a suspect. When the suspect is female, at least one of the officers should also be female. Regardless of the number of officers present, only one officer should ask questions at a time. Other officers may question the suspect regarding a specific point or omission after the original interrogator has exhausted a line of questions; on some occasions, several officers may interject pertinent questions at appropriate times. As long as there is no conflict in the control of the interrogation, and it does not persist throughout, this tactic sometimes works very well. The advantage of having several officers present during the interrogation is that it safeguards against unfounded allegations of misconduct, unethical tactics, false charges of abuse, or other complaints that a suspect might make. Again, when and where possible, videotaping an interrogation provides a visual record that can easily safeguard against false allegations. It also provides a means of teaching inexperienced interrogators various interviewing and interrogation techniques.

Establishing a Tone

As with interviews, it is important to establish rapport with a suspect before beginning an interrogation (Gordon & Fleisher, 2006). Unlike the interview situation, however, this is often a more difficult task. If, in fact, the suspect is involved in the crime under investigation, he or she may not be open to friendly conversation. You might instead choose to instill a little fear in the suspect by indicating the very serious consequences

FIGURE 6.3 A *Miranda* Warning and Waiver Used by One Police Department

Your Rights

1. You have the right to remain silent.

2. Anything you say can and will be used against you in court.

3. You have a right to talk to a lawyer for advice before we ask you any questions and to have him or her with you during questioning.

4. If you cannot afford to hire a lawyer, one will be appointed to represent you before any questioning, if you wish.

5. If you decide to answer questions now without a lawyer present, you will still have the right to stop answering at any time. You also have the right to stop answering at any time until you talk to a lawyer.

Waiver of Rights

I have read the above statement of my rights, and I understand each of those rights. Having these rights in mind, I waive them and willingly make a statement.

SIGNED: _____ AGE: _____

Address _____

Date _____ Time _____ Location _____

Witness _____ Department _____

Witness _____ Department _____

that will arise if he or she is not cooperative. Alternatively, you might decide to appeal to the suspect's conscience or sense of guilt. For example, suggest how important it is to get bad things off your chest and to begin fresh. You might even use information you have about the suspect. For instance, if the suspect has strong family ties, the interrogator can ask how a member of the family, a mother or spouse, for instance, might feel about not seeing the suspect for many years should he or she be convicted and sent to prison (Paladin Manual, 1991). Use any approach or tone that results in cooperation rather than resistance to police questions.

Before an officer begins the interrogation, he or she will have to make certain decisions that will affect the tone of the procedure. First, the officer must decide whether or not to confront the suspect on his or her first apparent lie and on every successive falsehood. If the officer chooses to do so, the falsehoods can be used as a kind of leverage to make the suspect recognize that it is important to offer truthful answers. Second, the officer must decide how persuasive a stance to take with the suspect. The old saying that one can catch more flies with honey than with vinegar may apply here. An effective interrogator is good at **persuasion;** that is, at motivating and convincing a suspect to be honest and forthcoming. Using persuasive techniques often gets better results than coming on hard and strong (Zulawski, 2001).

Persuasive interrogating involves tapping into three sources of motivation: emotions, reason, and rationalization. *Emotions* include beliefs, desires, hopes, and feelings. *Reason* is more cognitive and includes the ability to understand situations, interpret and anticipate outcomes, appreciate the consequences of one's actions, and resolve problems. *Rationalization* denotes an ability to reason, but one that justifies one's actions and behaviors—whether they are objectively legitimate or not (Boetig, 2005). Interrogators can tap into these three areas to persuade a suspect to talk more openly and completely. An effective and persuasive interrogator should be able to convince a suspect that he or she is sincerely interested in establishing the truth and not merely in obtaining a confession.

Along similar lines, some sources refer to rationalization, projections of blame, and minimization as three categories of action or approaches persuasive investigators use to motivate suspects to speak openly (Boetig, 2005; Napier & Adams, 1998). In this case, rationalization is meant to offer suspects the opportunity to make their crimes appear socially acceptable or reasonable based on circumstances at the time of the incident. Projections of blame enable the suspect to distance him- or herself from sole responsibility or to shift some responsibility for the incident to someone or something else, such as the victim, others involved in the crime, drugs, or even society. Finally, a persuasive interrogator may seek to minimize the heinous nature of the crime so it produces less guilt or shame for the suspect (Boetig, 2005; Napier & Adams, 1998). This is sometimes accomplished by avoiding **affected words,** such as *kill, rape, torture,* and other unnecessarily graphic terms. In place of these affected terms, investigators should use milder words that permit the suspect to save face.

Additionally, interrogators should avoid displaying any sign of their own emotions during interrogations. For instance, one should not indicate signs of joy, surprise, disdain, or disappointment. The appearance of these emotions may seem judgmental to the suspect and may interfere with his or her willingness to speak freely. Interrogators should also remember to practice aware hearing.

When a suspect has concluded his or her statement, it should be compared with information and statements obtained from the victim and witnesses as well as with the physical evidence. It is important to remember that things left unsaid by a suspect may be just as important to the case as things said in the statement. Also, carefully monitor the suspect's nonverbal responses and body language throughout the interrogation (Walters, 2002). Emotional outbursts, facial expressions, voice inflection, pauses and delays in response, nervous mannerisms, and indications of surprise, sorrow, regret, remorse, or embarrassment may all be helpful in unraveling an explanation and getting a confession to the crime.

Liars and Telling Lies

In addition to behavioral clues that a suspect may be lying, there are a number of verbal clues. The old adage "I know you are lying because your mouth is moving" may not entirely hold true, but there are psychological and cultural give-aways or *tells* that can signal an interrogator that the suspect is being deceptive. According to Collett (2004),

persuasion Motivating and convincing a person to offer information or to comply with a request.

affected words Words that have negative connotations in certain contexts in a given culture.

FIGURE 6.4 Ways People Tell Lies

Beating Around the Bush Left to offer a description on his or her own, a liar will often beat around the bush. Liars tend to give lengthy, convoluted explanations with lots of digressions, but when asked a direct question, they tend to give a short answer.

Outlining Liars tend to omit details; instead, they offer explanations in broad strokes. Specifics such as the time or place of an event are generally lost in these absent details. For example, a liar might tell you he went for a hamburger, but he probably won't tell you where he went or whether he had fries and a coke with it. When liars do provide details, they are seldom in a position to elaborate on them. If you ask a liar to expand on his or her account, it's very likely that the liar will simply repeat him- or herself.

Smokescreens Liars often produce answers that are designed to confuse rather than answer the question; consequently, their answers may not always make sense. For example, during a press conference with President Richard Nixon, when he was confronted with the Watergate scandal, he once stated to the press, "Please stop trying to confuse me with facts; I know what I know."

Specific Word Choice Liars have a tendency to make fewer references to themselves. In other words, they do not frequently use words like "I," "me," and "mine." As well, liars tend to overgeneralize by making frequent use of words like "always," "never," "nobody," and "everyone," thereby mentally distancing themselves from the lie.

Disclaimers Liars are likely to use disclaimers such as "You are simply not going to believe this," or "I know this sounds unbelievable but. . . ." Disclaimers such as these are intended to acknowledge suspicions the other person may have and to dissuade them.

Speed of Speech Telling a lie takes a fair amount of mental gymnastics. After all, the liar must both construct the lie and keep it separate from the truth. As a result, the liar cannot speak as quickly as he or she might if speaking the truth. Consequently, liars often pause before they produce a lie, and weave this lie slowly—unless, of course, this is a well-rehearsed lie, in which case it will be delivered quickly, and each successive telling will be virtually identical to the preceding one, which a truth seldom is.

Verbal Pauses Liars have a greater tendency than truth tellers to add many verbal pauses to their speech ("um," "er," "ah," and so forth) between their words and sentences. These permit additional time for the liar to create his or her yarns.

Source: Adapted from Peter Collett, 2004.

several features of talk provide clues that an individual may be lying. Some involve the verbal content of what people say, others the way people articulate what they are saying. Figure 6.4 describes a number of telltale signs that people may be lying.

Interrogation Approaches

Interrogations are a process of questioning, probing, challenging, and gathering information. Interrogators must cast their nets and gather as much information from the suspect as possible while giving out as little of their own information as they can manage. To accomplish this, interrogators employ a variety of approaches.

Any remark or gesture made to suspects in an effort to elicit the truth could be considered an interrogation approach. For example, saying to a suspect, "Well, I guess you know why you're here," or "You sure did a foolish thing," could fall into this category. However, there are several ways we might more broadly delineate various approaches to the interrogation process. Before beginning an interrogation, an investigator must assess a suspect's personality and character traits and decide which approach is best to begin with. These approaches can also be used in interviews.

The Logical Approach   This approach is based on reason. It assumes that the person being interviewed or interrogated is reasonable and rational and that there is considerable evidence available. The logical approach is often used with suspects who have prior criminal records, with educated people, with mature adults, and with others who have good rapport with the investigator (Zulawski, 2001).

When using a logical approach, the investigator confronts the suspect with convincing evidence and overwhelming proof—pointing out all the specific elements that prove the suspect's involvement. Factual remarks that indicate the suspect's guilt or involvement make it difficult for him or her to deny involvement with any sincerity. However, if firm information or evidence about the suspect's involvement is not available, any reference to such material may expose the weakness of the officer's case. For example, if the investigator remarked that a witness took down the suspect's license plate number at the crime scene, when in fact the suspect used a borrowed automobile, the suspect will recognize the bluff. Bluffing, although useful in some situations, is fraught with danger and should be used cautiously.

Should the suspect offer an **alibi** during the interrogation, the suspect should be asked to repeat the story several times in minute detail. This tactic can sometimes uncover discrepancies in "manufactured" statements. A suspect in this situation has two stories to remember—the truth and the fabricated account (Collett, 2004). The interrogating officer should challenge the accused person on each and every inaccuracy to demonstrate the untenable nature of the suspect's story.

> **alibi**   A defense offered by a suspect or defendant that attempts to prove that he or she was elsewhere at the time of the crime in question.

The Emotional Approach   With this approach, the questioner appeals to a suspect's sense of honor, righteousness, decency, morality, family pride, spiritual beliefs, justice, fair play, restitution, or other such reasons for disclosing the truth. This approach is generally most successful with first-time violators who have committed a careless criminal act because of anger, passion, or other emotions. Calm confidence, understanding, and an interest in knowing the suspect's motivation can help the interrogator communicate with the accused. The following remarks may be successful when appealing to people's emotions:

- "You're not the first person who has gotten into trouble; however, I see no reason to lie about it."
- "Society can forgive people for their mistakes but will not condone lies, hypocrisy, or cowardice."
- "All of us have made mistakes, but the least a person can do is try to rectify them."
- "It takes courage to tell the truth. Don't compound your crime with lies."
- "Is it fair to your family to put them through all of this when telling the truth could set things right?"
- "Many decent people get into trouble, but they do not lie about it."

Indirect versus Direct Lines of Inquiry   An *indirect* approach attempts to draw out information without specifically addressing the actual topic or subject. For example, using an indirect approach, the officer might ask a suspect, "Have you ever been in the vicinity of Market and Gable streets?" This might be followed by, "Have you ever been in the convenience store on the corner of Market and Gable?" And, finally, "Do you have any information regarding a robbery that occurred in that store

FYI Many television programs and movies about police and crime investigation portray officers threatening suspects with physical harm or actually grabbing or striking suspects. Such behaviors appeal to some Americans' sense of justice and retribution and can be very dramatic, but they violate the U.S. Constitution. In the real world, upholding the Constitution is among the most important duties of every American law enforcement officer. Flagrant disregard for a suspect's rights jeopardizes the rights of all Americans, guaranteed by the Constitution, as well as the likelihood of obtaining a conviction, and is not tolerated.

last Thursday night?" A more direct line of questioning might have been phrased, "On Thursday night, September 7, did you rob the convenience store on the corner of Market and Gable streets?"

An indirect approach may be useful when subjects are being somewhat evasive or until stronger rapport is established. Coming on too strong or too directly may close down an otherwise cooperative suspect. On the other hand, following an indirect line of questioning, or maintaining this style too long, may fail to provide an investigator with necessary information.

Validation Questions Sometimes, after a suspect has answered a question, the investigator can attempt to validate the answer. For example, a suspect may have flatly denied any involvement in the burglary under investigation. The investigator might ask him or her, "So, what time was it when you got home after breaking into the house?" or "Was it still light outside when you finished up with the house?" Answering these questions forces the suspect to contradict his or her denial of involvement in the crime. The only way to consistently maintain one's innocence is to correct the investigator and say, "I told you I never did the burglary!"

Deflating or Inflating a Suspect's Ego Challenging a suspect's abilities, skills, or intellectual capacity sometimes results in angering him or her enough to admit criminal involvement. For example, an officer might say, "Look, we know you were involved, but you couldn't possibly have done this alone, you just aren't smart enough." Or a suspect might be told what a rank amateur job had been done in committing the crime in an attempt to challenge the suspect's sense of pride or professionalism. The purpose is to challenge the suspect in some manner and push the suspect into defending his or her criminal prowess in a statement. This strategy may also work by praising a suspect on pulling off a spectacular crime. A suspect may want to take credit for a crime that even the police seem impressed with.

Understating and Overstating Sometimes it is best to understate the nature and or penalties of a crime. If someone stands accused of a multiple murder with special circumstances, and is potentially looking at the death penalty, the officer might not choose to talk about *murder* or the *electric chair*. The interrogator might instead ask about the "accident," the "event," the "thing that happened," or some other understated description. Similarly, saying that cooperation might be viewed favorably by the prosecutor may go further than the vague statement, "Maybe you can beat the death sentence." Asking a suspect to admit the truth in a case may be better than asking the suspect to admit guilt.

Conversely, in some cases *overstating* the severity of a crime may arouse a response in a suspect. For example, telling the suspect that only a few hundred dollars of the

$5,000 stolen has been recovered and asking where the rest of the money is creates a dilemma for the suspect. The suspect, if guilty, likely knows the truth and may inadvertently correct the officer. Or the suspect may feel he or she is being cheated by an accomplice and may in anger offer up the truth. Furthermore, depending on the amount of the actual and claimed loot, the difference may change the charge from a misdemeanor to a felony. That change may also affect the way the suspect responds to questions. Hence, overstating crimes or penalties may motivate a suspect to provide information that implicates him or her in the actual crime.

The Third Degree The **third degree** is the use or threat of physical force, mental or emotional cruelty, or water or food deprivation to obtain information in a police interrogation. At one time in the history of policing, such tactics were used. Third-degree tactics are completely illegal. Officers cannot hit, punch, strangle, or in any other way cause physical harm to a suspect. They cannot refuse rests, toilet privileges, food, or water to a suspect. Furthermore, police cannot even hold a suspect for more than 48 hours without allowing the suspect an opportunity to contact the outside world (a loved one, an attorney, the media, and so on).

third degree The use or threat of physical, mental, or emotional cruelty, or water or food deprivation, to obtain a confession.

Although the use of the third degree is illegal, it is not illegal to make a suspect feel uneasy about the interrogator's level of actual information or knowledge about the suspect. Asking questions while looking directly into the eyes of the suspect is not unlawful, but it may make the suspect feel uncomfortable. Causing physical harm to the suspect is illegal; however, gently placing a comforting hand on the arm of the suspect is not, and may assist in rapport.

There are many television and movie depictions, and even some literary ones, of the good-cop, bad-cop method of interrogation. In these scenarios, one officer is angry, hostile, violent, and menacing. The other is calm, quiet spoken, and protective of the suspect. However, there is a fine line between the use of this sort of game theory in an interrogation and the violation of a person's rights. Role-playing that is too extreme may be considered unethical even if it is ruled legal. Interrogators should be cautious in their use of such tactics.

It is important to remember that suspects being interrogated are *suspects;* they have not yet been shown to be guilty. They are deserving of all of their constitutional rights and human and social amenities. No explanation, statement, admission, or confession can adequately excuse deliberate violation or debasement of these rights.

Interrogating Juveniles

As the result of the U.S. Supreme Court's decision in *In re Gault* (1967), police officers and probation officers are obligated to advise minors, upon taking them into custody, that they have a right to remain silent, a privilege against self-incrimination, and a right to be represented by private counsel or by counsel appointed by the court. Should the minor, because of youth, be unable to knowingly and intelligently waive these rights, the rights must be explained to the parents or legal guardian before the juvenile is interrogated. The parents or guardian can exercise the waiver on behalf of the child.

This change in juvenile proceedings came about as follows. In June 1964 in Gila County, Arizona, Gerald Gault, a 15-year-old boy, was taken into custody by a deputy sheriff following a verbal complaint by a female neighbor that he had made obscene telephone calls to her. The youth was placed in a children's detention home. The following day a petition was filed in juvenile court asking for a hearing regarding the care and custody of Gault. The petition gave a factual basis for the judicial action it initiated, but it recited that Gault was under 18 and needed the protection of the court. The petition also stated that Gault was a delinquent minor. Gault's parents neither were served with the petition nor saw it. No witnesses were sworn at the hearing or at the second hearing a week later.

The judge declared Gault a juvenile delinquent and committed him to a juvenile correction facility until the age of 21. This meant that Gault was given a sentence of 6 years for an offense that, if committed by an adult, could be punished by no more than 2 months in jail and a $50 fine. When Gault's case finally reached the U.S. Supreme Court, the Court held that a juvenile has due process rights in delinquency hearings when there is the possibility of confinement in a state institution. Specifically, the Court ruled that juveniles have a right against self-incrimination, a right to adequate notice of the charges against them, a right to confront and cross-examine their accusers, and a right to assistance of counsel.

In most jurisdictions a juvenile's parents or guardian must be notified when the child is arrested or taken into custody. Questioning of juveniles usually takes place in the presence of the parents or guardian, or in the presence of an attorney representing the juvenile.

When interrogating juveniles, an investigator should adjust his or her level of language to ensure that the young witness or suspect clearly understands every question. Adolescents may be physically and mentally more mature than younger children; however, their language skills and vocabulary may not necessarily coincide with their age. Adolescents are likely to respond differently in front of their friends or parents than away from them. Sometimes the same youth putting on a brash, tough-guy image in front of friends will actually speak quite openly when the interview or interrogation is conducted in private. Similarly, some juveniles are resistant when their parents are around, whereas others are more likely to offer admissions when Mom and Dad are in the room.

Juveniles may have very definite images and opinions about the police. Some juveniles have difficulties with adults in general; others are more selective and simply dislike officers. Like adults, however, many juveniles are cooperative and willing to assist police. Officers, therefore, should not draw conclusions prior to speaking with the specific juvenile in question.

When interrogating juvenile suspects, using profanity, vulgarity, or physical force (real or threatened) is reprehensible. In addition, officers must guard against becoming frustrated or angry with particularly trying or difficult juveniles. Empathizing with the juvenile and exhibiting a little patience may go a long way toward getting youthful suspects to answer questions.

CONFESSIONS AND ADMISSIONS

confession A voluntary statement—written, oral, or recorded—by an accused person, admitting participating in or commission of a criminal act.

A **confession** is a voluntary statement in which a person charged with the commission of a crime admits participating in or committing the crime in question. A confession may be written, oral, or recorded.

admission A voluntary statement by the accused person containing information and facts about a crime but falling short of a full confession.

An admission differs slightly from a confession. An **admission** is a statement by the accused that contains information and facts about the crime but falls short of a full confession. In connection with proof of other facts, an admission may be used to demonstrate a suspect's guilt. To be received into evidence in court, an admission must relate to relevant and material facts. Admissions, in themselves, may not necessarily incriminate the accused. In an admission, the person is not *confessing* the commission of the crime, only *admitting* certain facts.

For instance, if a suspect was shown a knife and in turn states, "Yes, that is my knife—I killed the dirty rat," this would be a confession. If, however, the suspect said, "Yes, that is my knife, but I was not present when the dirty rat was killed," this would be an admission only to the fact that the murder weapon was his. Admission of that fact, along with evidence demonstrating that the suspect was present at the time of the killing, would go toward proving that the suspect was actually guilty of the murder.

Guidelines for Taking Confessions and Admissions

There are no magic formulas for taking confessions or statements of admission. Officers are more or less on their own and are held strictly accountable by the courts for everything they do. Remember, the courts look at the transaction after it has occurred rather than during the time that it happens. This puts a large burden on the officer to use great care when obtaining any statements. The following are suggestions for taking statements; this is not, however, a complete list of everything one should do.

- The form of the confession is immaterial; it may be oral, narrative, question-and-answer, or a combination of question-and-answer and narrative type.
- The suspect should not be placed under oath; such precautions reflect a possible form of compulsion.
- Confessions may be handwritten (in pen not pencil) by the officer or suspect. They may be prepared first person and should be written in a language of the defendant. They may be typewritten, printed, recorded by a stenographer and transcribed into written form for the suspect's signature, tape-recorded, or video-recorded. Video-recording the confession in certain cases is of added value. However, the defense may question the failure of the police to use that method in all their cases, contending that such failure implies the possible use of improper methods that they did not want to show on video.
- A tape recorder, if used, should not be turned on until the officer is ready to obtain a concise statement from the suspect.
- When suspects confess orally to a crime, a written statement should be immediately prepared for their signature. Delays or postponements in obtaining a written confession may result in a change of attitude in an otherwise cooperative suspect.
- The basic guidelines, laid down in the *Miranda* decision, of advising the suspect of rights before any questioning or the taking of statements or confessions should be followed. This procedure should be adhered to even though the required warnings may have been given to the suspect at the time of his or her arrest. If the statement is recorded or video-recorded, the *Miranda* warnings should be offered on tape.
- Taking a statement should begin with the recitation of the suspect's legal rights and be followed by questions designed to identify the suspect; the type of crime involved; the name of the person being questioned; the date, time, and place the statement was taken; and the introduction of all parties present.
- The number of persons present at the taking of a confession should be kept to an absolute minimum. There may be an implication of coercion or duress if several officers are present, either as interviewers or as interested observers.

- Questions should be asked in the shortest and simplest manner so that the suspect easily understands them. This manner of questioning brings out all of the facts in the most effective way.

- Clarify all indefinite answers given by a suspect to questions asked during the taking of the statement. This is accomplished by asking specific questions of the suspect about the identity of a particular person, exact location of a place, meaning of terminology used, specific time, date, and so forth. For example, expressions such as "hot car" (stolen car), "junkie" (drug addict), and "kibbles and bits" (crack cocaine) should be explained.

- Statements should not include any crime other than that for which the suspect is charged unless it is tied in closely with that particular case. For example, where a suspect burglarized a residence and thereafter raped an occupant at the same location, both the burglary and the rape offense could be included in the same confession. If the suspect was involved in another burglary a block away prior to committing the aforementioned burglary-rape offense, then two separate statements would have to be taken.

- Confessions should be as brief as possible while including all the relevant details. There is no minimum length for a statement. The inclusion of details assists the officer in corroborating the statement of the suspect.

- When alterations, changes, corrections, or erasures are necessary in a statement, they should be made in the subject's own handwriting or made by the officer and initialed by the suspect to show that the suspect is aware of them. This procedure prevents the claim that other passages or pages were added to the statements.

- Each page of a statement should be initialed or signed by the subject unless, of course, the subject writes out his or her own confession.

- The concluding paragraph of a statement should say in the suspect's own handwriting that the suspect has read the statement and acknowledges it to be true. Each officer present should witness the statement with signature, date, and department.

Regardless of how effectively an investigator interrogates a suspect, or seeks to obtain a statement, experienced investigators understand the following about confessions:

- When dealing with experienced criminals, confessions are not readily given.

- Full confessions frequently originate with small admissions and can build to complete confessions.

- Guilty suspects seldom tell investigators everything they know about a crime.

- Many offenders are not proud of their violence and recognize that it was wrong; this can be used to obtain admissions or confessions.

- Guilty suspects omit details that cast them in a harsh or critical light.

- When an offender does offer a confession, it is typically in order to obtain a position believed to be advantageous to him or her. (Holmes, 1995; Napier & Adams, 2002).

TECHNOLOGY FOR SEEKING THE TRUTH

Throughout history many cultures have tried to develop a way to prove a person is telling the truth. In many early cultures, suspected liars were told that if they placed their hand into a cauldron of boiling oil, they could withdraw it uninjured if they were telling the truth. However, if they were lying, their hand would be severely burned. These early truth-seeking ordeals relied heavily on their psychological impact on a guilty person's mind. Lying also had many physiological effects, such as dryness of mouth, shaking or trembling, perspiration, and increased respiration and heart rate. These were well known among many cultures. The ancient Chinese, for example, made suspected liars chew a mouthful of uncooked rice. If the rice remained dry after chewing, the person was assumed to have been lying.

Criminal investigation has come a long way from dipping hands in boiling oil or filling people's mouths with rice. Today agencies more commonly use technology and science to try to assess the truthfulness of a suspect's statements.

The Polygraph

The **polygraph** is a mechanical device that permits an assessment of deception associated with stress as manifested in physiological data. The endocrine system and the nervous system gear up the body to protect it from impending stress or danger. This involves a change in blood volume and pulse rate, along with increased respiration. In addition, there is a change in skin resistance. Each of these changes is recorded by the polygraph (Elley, 2000; Hollien, 1990).

polygraph A mechanical device that permits an assessment of deception associated with stress as manifested in physiological data.

Typically, a polygraph simultaneously records respiration, blood pressure, heart rate, and even the skin's electrical resistance. Because the polygraph uses physiological data, a subject hooked to the machine does not really need to verbally respond to a question. The polygraph will measure and reflect the somatic and emotional effects of being asked the question. Two types of questions are traditionally asked during a polygraph examination. The first is *control questions,* which are used as standards of truthfulness against which the examiner can compare patterns created when the subject is asked questions about the crime, or *investigative questions.* By comparing the patterns produced by both sort of questions, the examiner judges whether deception is taking place (Bull, 1988). Experts believe that differences in the patterns are caused by stress and various somatic and emotional protective responses of the nervous system (Abrams, 1991).

More often than not, polygraphs fail to detect rather than verify truths. Nevertheless, they continue to prove beneficial for cross-checking and validating statements. One important reason to use the polygraph is to eliminate suspects or to verify a suspect's alibi. Many police departments and prosecutors use the polygraph to see if a suspect is telling the truth and can be removed from the primary list of suspects. Many criminals believe that polygraphs are *truth machines.* Consequently, polygraphs sometimes have a significant psychological effect on a suspect. When an investigator tells a suspect that he or she would like to verify the suspect's statement with a polygraph test, this sometimes leads to a confession.

Research suggests that polygraphs are inconclusive or incorrect about 15 to 20 percent of the time, often depending on the skill of the polygraph operator (Moore, Petrie, & Braga, 2003; Sullivan, 2007). It is likely one would not want a life-or-death situation to be determined with a 15 to 20 percent error rate. It is more than adequate, however, for verifying a suspect's alibi or a witness's statement.

Although the actual test is not admissible in court, the confession is. It is important to note that witnesses, suspects, and victims cannot be compelled to undergo a polygraph test because the Fifth Amendment against self-incrimination protects them. Subjects can, however, voluntarily submit to a polygraph examination.

COMPUTERIZED POLYGRAPH TESTING

Computer software that takes the burden of interpretation of results off the examiner is replacing mechanical and electronic polygraph systems. The software measures, records, and analyzes a person's physical reactions to questions. The software then reports the probability that the person has answered the questions truthfully.

Truth Serums and Hypnosis

Using injections of sodium pentothal, phenobarbital, or other fast-acting drugs that produce a deep-sleep-like condition has not achieved scientific acceptability as a reasonable and accurate means for establishing truth (Graham, 2004). The theory in the use of such drugs—often referred to as truth serums—is that the subject is relieved of inhibitions and will make true statements while under the influence of the drug. When a truth serum test is given, it should always be administered by a physician under controlled conditions. Individuals vary greatly in their reaction to truth serums, and the courts do not officially recognize truth serums or their reliability, nor do they admit the results of such tests as evidence.

As for the use of hypnosis, the courts have established guidelines for using testimony from such a procedure. The hypnosis must be performed by a trained

STATISTICS A study of law enforcement agencies in the United States (McCloud, 1991) found that 93 percent of the responding agencies use polygraphs in their investigations. Of these agencies, nearly 75 percent used sworn personnel as their polygraph examiners. Regardless of how frequently agencies use polygraphs in investigations, the question remains, "How accurate are they?" Even among avid polygraph supporters, opinions differ regarding reliability of the polygraph. Most agree that the machine can detect physiological changes in the subject at least 75 percent of the time, and perhaps as high as 85 to 90 percent of the time. However, most admit that variation does occur and that it is dependent on several distinct factors: the machine itself, the subject, and the operator or examiner. While continuing to be very useful in police investigations, polygraph results are not yet accepted in courts as absolute evidence. However, thirty states in the United States will allow polygraph results into evidence if both parties agree, and thirteen states do so even if opposing counsel objects (Rafky & Sussman, 1985).

professional, independent of either party in the case, after a thorough study of the subject and the case. Subjects must be advised of their rights and must give their consent to the procedure.

SUMMARY

Learning Objective 1

To solve a criminal case, investigators rely on physical evidence and the crime scene; information in investigative reports, *modus operandi* files, and other reports; and, especially, information gathered in interviews and interrogations.

Learning Objective 2

An interview is questioning to gather information from persons who are not suspects but know something about the crime or the persons involved in it. Like an interview, an interrogation seeks information about a crime, but it is more adversarial and is focused on persons suspected of direct or indirect involvement in the crime.

Learning Objective 3

There are several ways to improve communication and obtain useful information from witnesses: prepare in advance; arrange for privacy; establish rapport; practice aware hearing; use cognitive interview techniques; avoid interruptions; and remain adaptable, patient, objective, and sensitive.

Learning Objective 4

Before being questioned in police custody, a suspect must be advised of his or her rights under the *Miranda* decision. These include the right to remain silent, the right to be told that anything said can and will be used in court, the right to consult with an attorney before answering any questions and to have an attorney present during interrogation, and the right to court-appointed counsel if unable to afford an attorney.

Learning Objective 5

Many of the principles that apply to interviews also apply to interrogations. In addition, it is important to conduct the interrogation in a setting chosen by the investigator, use persuasive techniques, avoid affected words, and use a variety of approaches. Approaches include the logical approach, the emotional approach, indirect or direct inquiry, validation questions, deflating or inflating of the suspect's ego, and overstating or understating the crime or penalty. The third degree is an illegal interrogation technique.

Learning Objective 6

Special conditions must be observed when questioning juveniles. Obtain permission from parents or guardian before interrogating juveniles. Advise juveniles of their right to remain silent, to avoid self-incrimination, and to have counsel. Generally, question juveniles in the presence of their parents or guardian.

Learning Objective 7

A confession is a voluntary statement—written, oral, or recorded—by a person charged with a crime. The statement must admit participation in or commission of the criminal act in question. An admission differs slightly from a confession. An admission is a statement by the accused that contains information and facts about the crime but falls short of a full confession.

· ·

KEY TERMS

interview 104

interrogation 104

rapport 105

aware hearing 106

cognitive
  interview 107

behavioral analysis
  interview 108

complainant 109

complaint 109

persuasion 121

affected words 121

alibi 123

third degree 125

confession 126

admission 126

polygraph 129

· ·

QUESTIONS FOR REVIEW

Learning Objective 1

1. When physical evidence from a crime scene is insufficient to establish a lead in a case, how can an investigator gain more information?

Learning Objective 2

2. How would you distinguish between an interview and an interrogation?

Learning Objective 3

3. How does rapport affect an interview?
4. What is meant by *aware hearing,* and why is it important for a criminal investigator?
5. What are four procedures used in a cognitive interview?
6. Why should all complainants be taken seriously?
7. What are some characteristics of an unwilling witness?

Learning Objective 4

8. Does the *Miranda* decision prevent a suspect from answering questions posed by police investigators?

Learning Objective 5

9. What is the central goal of any interrogation?
10. How does the tone of an interrogation affect a suspect's responses?
11. Why should an investigator know as much as possible about the crime, the victim, and the suspect prior to the interrogation?
12. In which interrogation approach do you try to draw out information without specifically addressing the actual topic?
13. How might deflating a suspect's ego bring him or her to admit involvement in a crime?

Learning Objective 6

14. How did the *Gault* decision affect juveniles?

Learning Objective 7

15. How would you distinguish between a *confession* and an *admission?*
16. How accurate are polygraph tests?

CRITICAL THINKING EXERCISE

Pair up with another member of the class. Each of you will take a turn practicing interviewing, using the following questions. Work hard to use aware hearing. Do not interrupt the subject in the middle of a sentence or interject comments or value judgments about the answers. Be sure to thank the subject for taking the time to be interviewed.

1. What is your name?
2. Where do you live?
3. Who else lives with you?
4. Do you have any identification with you that I can look at? (If the subject has no identification with him or her, ask the following.) Is there some reason you are not carrying any identification?
5. What were you doing just before we began this interview?
6. Where did you park your car this morning? (If the subject has no car, ask the following.) How did you get to school this morning?
7. Where do you usually buy your groceries?
8. Have you ever purchased groceries at (name a different local store)?
9. What did you have for breakfast this morning?
10. What were you doing last night at about 8:00 p.m.?

INVESTIGATIVE SKILL BUILDERS

Acquiring and Evaluating Information

An officer is dispatched to an apartment complex to respond to a call that a young woman has been raped. Upon arriving at the complex, the officer goes directly to the apartment number the dispatcher provided. A woman in a tight-fitting jumpsuit answers the door and tells the officer to come in. She leads the officer into the living room where a second young woman, about 16 years old, is lying on the couch. The first woman says that her niece (referring to the other woman) has been raped.

The young woman on the couch is dressed in a torn, see-through white blouse and a pair of light blue short-shorts. She does not appear to be injured physically, but her hair is messed up, and her makeup has run from crying. The living room does not look as if any violence has taken place. A glance into the adjacent bedroom suggests that there may have been some sort of struggle in there. The bed is unmade, blankets and pillows are on the floor, and a lamp is overturned.

The officer begins to interview the girl. "What's your name?" "Olive," the girl replies as she sits up on the couch. The officer asks Olive if she knows who attacked her. She looks toward the other woman and then looks back at the officer and stammers, "No, no, no, I never saw him before." When asked if she can describe him, again she looks at her aunt before speaking. "Yes," she says, "I think I can." She gives a description, including a first name of Jimmy. "So you do know him?" the officer asks. Fear crosses the girl's face. "No, . . . yes, well, I've . . . I think I've seen him around." She nervously looks at her aunt, who has now moved closer to the couch. "Jimmy? Did you say Jimmy?" the aunt questions the girl. "Did Jimmy Jacks do this? My Jimmy Jacks?" The girl begins to cry. The aunt slaps her. "You little slut!" the aunt continues. The officer moves between the aunt and Olive saying, "Hey, there will be none of that." "Who is Jimmy Jacks?" the officer asks. The aunt composes herself. "He's a gentleman friend of mine," she says and moves away from the couch. The officer begins to suspect that the aunt is a prostitute and that perhaps Olive is too. "Exactly what do you do for a living?" the officer asks the aunt. "Me?" she replies. "I'm an escort hostess." When asked if she is in school, Olive shakes her head no and says she works for the same escort service as her aunt. Convinced that both women are prostitutes and that Olive slept with a regular client of her aunt's and didn't get paid, the officer asks Olive, "Are you prepared to press charges against this Jimmy Jacks if I arrest him?" Olive thinks for a minute, glancing first at her aunt, then back at the officer. "I . . . I don't really think so," Olive replies as she looks back at her aunt. "Well, there isn't very much I can do for you then," the officer tells her. Then the officer leaves.

1. Did the officer handle the situation properly?
2. How else might the officer have handled the situation?

Integrity/Honesty

In the preceding scenario, should the officer have arrested the aunt on a domestic violence charge after she struck the niece? Explain your answer.

Responsibility

In the preceding scenario, should the officer have pursued a charge of rape against Jimmy Jacks? A charge of prostitution against Olive?

Fingerprints

After completing this chapter, you will be able to:

1 Explain the importance of fingerprint identification in criminal investigation.
2 Distinguish among the basic fingerprint patterns.
3 Identify the types of fingerprints that may be found at a crime scene.
4 Describe various methods for developing invisible fingerprints.
5 Tell how computer technology aids in fingerprint identification.
6 Trace the development of the admissibility of fingerprint identification as evidence in court cases.

FINGERPRINT IDENTIFICATION

Fingerprints and palm prints are among the most valuable types of physical evidence found at a crime scene. Prints of bare feet occasionally play an important role as well. These prints are direct evidence of an individual's presence at a crime scene and of his or her identity. Frequently, the principal evidence found at a crime is a fingerprint, or partial fingerprint, that becomes the key to locating and identifying the perpetrator. Of all methods of identification, fingerprint identification has proven the least fallible.

In this chapter, the term **fingerprint** refers to any impression of the friction ridges on a person's hands and feet. **Friction ridges** are minute raised lines on the surface of fingertips, palms, toes, and heels. Grease, oil, salts, and perspiration transferred to an object touched by fingertips, palms, toes, and heels cause the prints. Sometimes prints are created by a substance covering the hand or foot, as when a barefoot killer walks through the spilled blood of his victim. Prints may even be formed by the negative impression created when a liquid substance is touched and then allowed to dry. For instance, touching wet paint or freshly plastered walls creates a negative impression of the friction ridges that press against the surface. Upon first examination, it is often difficult to discern whether a print was left by a finger, the palm of a hand, or even the sole of a foot.

There are several different systems for filing fingerprints, each based on a classification of common characteristics. It should be noted that *classification* of fingerprints is not identical to *identification* of fingerprints. **Classification** is a method of organizing fingerprints into certain formula sets based on particular characteristics common to all fingerprints. Identification involves comparing the fingerprints of a suspect with any prints found at a crime scene to determine a possible match. In other words, the fingerprint classification of a suspect is a major point of identification. Because a print of one person's finger has never been known to exactly duplicate that of another—not even an identical twin's—fingerprints are important in identifying suspects in criminal investigations (Collins, 2001; Maltoni et al., 2005).

fingerprint An impression created by the friction ridges on a person's fingers, palms, or feet.

friction ridges Minute raised lines on the surface of fingertips, palms, and heels of feet.

classification A method of organizing fingerprints based on particular characteristics.

FYI The science of fingerprint identification is known as dactylography. The word *dactyolography* is a compound word consisting of the prefix *dactylo*, meaning "finger, toe, or digit" (deriving from the Latin *dactylus* and the Greek *daktylos*) and the suffix *graphy*, meaning "a representation of a specified object" (derived from the Latin *graphia* and the Greek *graphein*).

dactylography The scientific study of fingerprints as a means of identification.

The study of fingerprints as a means of identification is known as **dactylography.** It has long been regarded as the greatest scientific contribution to law enforcement and criminal identification. Many of the people who contributed to the development of this science are listed in Figure 7.1. The science of fingerprint identification provides an important service in the administration of justice and in many other areas in which positive identification is crucial. Some of the uses of fingerprints include the following:

- Identification of criminals whose fingerprints are found at the scene of a crime.
- Identification of fugitives through comparison with fingerprints in a database.

- Exchange of criminal identification information with identification bureaus of other states or foreign countries in cases of common interest.
- Identification of children kidnapped by family members.
- Identification of bodies, as in the case of homeless persons or persons killed in traffic, train, or airplane accidents.
- Prevention of hospital mistakes in identification of infants.
- Prevention of fraud by people taking specialized examinations or selling valuables to pawnbrokers.
- Identification of unconscious people or those suffering from amnesia or other cognitive problems.
- Identification of missing persons.
- Identification of applicants for licenses for drivers, firearms, aircraft, and other equipment.
- Identification of applicants and assessment of their background when determining suitability for certain jobs (for example, child care workers or law enforcement officers).

FIGURE 7.1 Precursors of Fingerprint Identification

Nehemiah Grew	1684	English physician who first called attention to the system of pores and ridges in hands and feet
Marcello Malpighi	1686	Italian anatomist who first wrote about elevated ridges of tips of fingers and figures on palms.
Johannes Purkinje	1823	Bohemian anatomist who wrote on the diversity of ridges on finger tips; first outlined broad system of classification.
William Herschel	1858	British administrator in India who first used fingerprints for governmental identification purposes.
Henry Faulds	1880	British missionary in Japan who first developed a method for lifting prints using a thin film of printer's ink as the transfer medium and who concluded that fingerprint patterns remained unchanged throughout a person's life.
Alphonse Bertillon	1883	French police officer who developed the concept of criminal identification using physical measurements and photographs of criminal suspects.
Francis Galton	1892	British anthropologist who presented statistical proof of the uniqueness of fingerprints and outlined principles of fingerprint identification.
Juan Vucetich	1894	Argentinean police officer who published a book outlining a method of fingerprint classification.
Edward Henry	1897	British police officer in India who developed a method of fingerprint classification that is still widely used.
Edmond Locard	1918	Established that if twelve points are the same between two fingerprints it is sufficient as a positive identification.

THE NATURE OF FINGERPRINTS

bulb The rounded area at the end joint of every finger and thumb.

The various lines and ridges on the rounded area, or **bulb,** of the end joint of every finger and thumb create fingerprints. These ridges form distinct contours and patterns that distinguish one person from another, and these patterns remain unchanged throughout an individual's life (Jones, 2000).

When crude attempts are made to alter these patterns with abrasives, such as sandpaper, or various chemicals, the ridges eventually return to their original pattern. Skin conditions such as warts, wounds, blisters, or temporary damage caused by certain occupations have no permanent effect on the pattern (Fisher, 2003). Once the condition changes or the skin heals, the original contours and ridge pattern return.

Fingerprint Patterns

Generally, fingerprints are classified into three main patterns: arched, looped, and whorled. Further divisions into subgroups results in the basic fingerprint patterns shown in Figure 7.2.

The ridge detail of fingerprints—including the ends of the ridges, the ridge formation, and the relationships between ridges—forms the basis of identification. For instance, look at the two examples of arched prints in Figure 7.2. In the *plain arch,* the ridges enter on one side of the impression and flow (or tend to flow) out the other side with a wave in the center. In a *tented arch,* the ridges enter on one side and flow out the other, as in the plain arch, but the ridge or ridges at the center have a decided upward thrust.

Now look at the two looped patterns. In such patterns, one or more ridges enter from one side, make a hairpin turn, and exit on the side from which they entered. At least one ridge must follow this course and pass between the delta (a triangular area) and the core, or approximate center of the finger. Note that the loop pattern has only one delta. In a *radial loop,* the ridges slant toward the thumb, or radial bone of the forearm. In an *ulnar loop* pattern, the ridges slant toward the little finger, or the ulnar bone of the forearm.

Fingerprints can sometimes help police identify children or other missing persons.

In whorl patterns, at least one ridge must pass completely around the core of the finger. Its path may form a spiral, a circle, an oval, or any variant of a circle. It must make at least one recurvature in front of each delta. A whorl has at least two deltas, one at the right side and one at the left side. The *plain whorl* is the simplest and most common of the whorl subdivisions. It has two deltas and at least one ridge that makes a complete circuit about the core of the finger. The *double-loop whorl* finger impression consists of two loop formations with two separate and distinct sets of shoulders and deltas. In a *central-pocket loop whorl,* most of the ridges form a loop, with one or more ridges curving completely around the core to form a pocket. An *accidental whorl* is a combination of two or more types of patterns (except the plain arch). Look again at Figure 7.2 to see examples of the four types of whorl patterns.

To determine whether two fingerprints are the same, fingerprint analysts compare various characteristics, depending on the types of patterns being examined. These characteristics have to be pointed out as the identifying features to demonstrate that two fingerprint impressions are or are not the same. If the fingerprint exhibits a loop pattern, ridge counting may be used. The analyst counts the ridges that touch or cross an imaginary line drawn between the core and the delta of a loop. Ridge endings—, bifurcations (forks) —C, and islands —⊂⊃— are the most common ridge characteristics in such an analysis. See Figure 7.3 for several examples of ridge counting (Maltoni et al., 2005).

FIGURE 7.2 The Basic Fingerprint Patterns

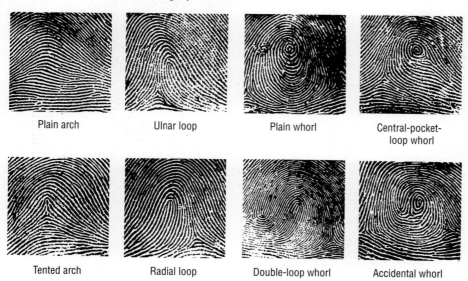

| Plain arch | Ulnar loop | Plain whorl | Central-pocket-loop whorl |
| Tented arch | Radial loop | Double-loop whorl | Accidental whorl |

FIGURE 7.3 Methods of Comparing Fingerprint Impressions

Ridge counting

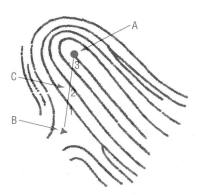

Ridge count three

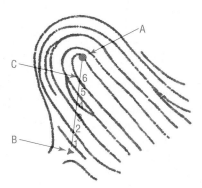

Ridge count six

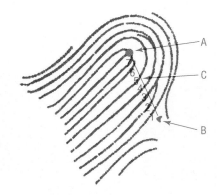

Ridge count seven

A. Core (center)
B. Delta
C. Imaginary line between A and B used to count the total number of ridges touching or crossing it

Ridge tracing

Ridge A is traced from the left delta to the right delta. At a point nearest the right delta, should tracing ridge A pass inside the right delta with three or more ridges intervening between tracing ridge A and the right delta, the tracing is designated as *inner*.

Ridge A is traced from the left delta toward the right delta. At a point nearest the right delta, should tracing ridge A pass outside the right delta with three or more ridges intervening between tracing ridge A and the right delta, it is designated as an *outer*.

Ridge A is traced from the left delta toward the right delta. At a point nearest the right delta, should ridge A pass inside or outside the right delta with less than three intervening ridges between ridge A and the right delta, the tracing is designated as *meet* or *meeting*.

If the fingerprint has a whorl pattern, then ridge tracing may be used. Once the deltas are located, the analyst traces the ridge that emanates from the lower side of the left delta toward the right delta until it reaches the point nearest or opposite the extreme right. The ridges between the tracing ridge and the right delta are then counted (Ashbaugh, 1999; FBI, 1984). Figure 7.3 illustrates this process.

Fingerprint Procedures

The use of digitized fingerprinting, or the electronic reproduction of fingerprints for computer systems, is a growing phenomenon in the United States. However, many agencies continue to use inked fingerprints.

To create an inked fingerprint, under ordinary circumstances, the surface of the fingers is inked and the ridges and patterns are transferred to a standard 8 × 8-inch form called a **ten-print card.** This serves as the basic document used in fingerprint files. As will be discussed later, even when fingerprints are digitized for computer record keeping, the format of the ten-print card continues to be used. There are variations in the materials used to create fingerprints, but there are several common basic elements.

ten-print card A card or form onto which fingerprints and other personal data are transferred and filed for future retrieval.

First, one needs a transferring material or medium, such as ink. This may be an inked pad, a tray with ink from a tube of printer's ink, or an inkless, colorless chemical that will create an impression when contacted by special chemically treated paper. Second, one needs a medium on which the impressions can be made. This may be paper, cardboard, celluloid, or glass. Third, one should have a solid surface on which to work. A table or desk serves this purpose. Finally, one should have materials to clean up with, such as denatured alcohol, soap and water, and towels.

The basic method for taking fingerprints is quite simple and usually proceeds as follows:

1. The subject stands about an arm's length from the work area.
2. The subject should be told to relax the hand and let the technician or officer do all the work.
3. The subject's right hand should be taken so that the thumb will be the first to be printed. Press the thumb gently but firmly into the ink medium. Ink the entire bulb of the thumb.
4. Next, the subject's right thumb should be pressed onto the card or paper intended to receive the fingerprint impression. The thumb should be rolled gently from one side to the other to get a complete fingerprint.
5. This process should be repeated for each of the remaining fingers on the right hand.
6. Next, this procedure should be repeated for the thumb and each finger of the left hand.
7. When using a ten-print card, a second impression of the four fingers of each hand and a second impression of each thumb are made in the spaces provided.
8. After all impressions have been taken and the subject's hands are clean, the subject should sign the fingerprint card, which is usually cosigned by the technician or officer who took the fingerprint impressions.

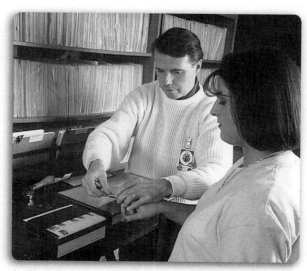

A subject's fingers are gently rolled in ink before being printed.

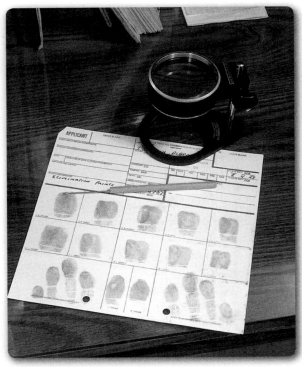

A ten-print card.

On occasion, there may be exceptions to these basic procedures. For example, if a subject has an amputated or missing finger, the technician or officer will naturally have to leave the appropriate space blank. Similarly, temporary injuries may create problems. For instance, the subject may have a fresh cut or an infection or a bandaged wound on a finger. Such problems should be annotated in the blank space on the card. Expressions such as *amputated, fresh cut,* or *bandaged* written in the blanks will inform others of why the impression is missing from the record.

Types of Fingerprint Impressions

Several types of fingerprints can be found at crime scenes. These include latent prints, visible prints, plastic prints, and invisible prints. Many television shows—and even some police agencies—have taken to generically calling all fingerprints found at the crime scene "latent prints," but this is not entirely accurate. Let's consider the various types of fingerprints.

Latent Prints Impressions transferred to a surface by perspiration or oil from the ridges of fingers, toes, palms, and heels are usually classified as **latent prints.** These sorts of impressions may also be made by a residue of mud, blood, paint, or some other sticky substance, such as syrup, adhesive, or lacquer, carried on the hands or feet. Latent prints may be visible or invisible but are more commonly not visible without some sort of development (discussed later in this chapter).

Visible Prints These are prints made by soil or stained fingertips or palms. They may include impressions left in dust on solid, nonporous surfaces. **Visible prints** are readily observable on the surfaces of objects that have been touched or carried. Fingerprints of this sort may or may not have identification value, depending on how distinctly friction ridge impressions have been transferred to the object's surface.

Invisible Prints These prints are not readily observable, but various powders, chemicals, gases, and light sources can make them visible. **Invisible prints** typically are found on nonporous surfaces such as glass, metal, finished wood, doorknobs, window moldings, telephones, and other hard smooth surfaces. However, invisible prints may also be found on paper documents, cloth material, and other porous materials.

Plastic Prints These are a form of visible print created in soft substances in which a negative impression of the friction ridges is made upon contact. For example, a damp bar of soap, butter, putty, grease, paint, or even peanut butter can form a kind of mold of the fingerprint when touched, thereby creating a **plastic print.**

When police officers are looking for fingerprints at a crime scene, they frequently find a number of prints—sometimes many fingerprints—that belong to the various people residing in the premises or who work or frequent the business establishment. These prints belong to individuals who have a legitimate reason to have been at the scene. Before checking all of the fingerprints found at a crime scene, investigating officers should seek to eliminate those individuals with legitimate reasons for having left prints at the scene. **Elimination prints** are fingerprint impressions made of these

latent print An impression transferred to a surface by sweat, oil, dirt, blood, or some other substance on the ridges of the fingers; it may be visible or invisible.

visible print A fingerprint found at a crime scene that is immediately visible to the naked eye.

invisible print A latent print not visible without some form of developing.

plastic print A type of visible print formed when substances such as butter, grease, wax, peanut butter, and so forth that have a plasticlike texture are touched.

elimination print Fingerprints taken of all persons whose prints are likely to be found at a crime scene but who have a lawful reason to have been there and are not suspects.

persons in order to compare them against prints found at the crime scene by other than those with legitimate reasons for being there—the suspect(s).

Methods of Developing Invisible Prints

Latent or invisible prints left on surfaces are delicate liquid or semi-liquid deposits. They are composed largely of water or other adhering materials, which can bond to various powders to make them visible, or they can be made visible through other print development techniques (Champod et al., 2004; Lee, 2001).

Powders Traditionally, fingerprint powders were white or black; today, they may also be silver, red, or gray. The color of the background on which the print is made determines the color of powder to use to provide a good contrast: Light-colored powders help prints stand out on a dark background, and dark powders are more useful on a light background. To develop the print, one applies a small amount of fingerprint powder to the area believed to have been touched. Typically, the powder is applied with a small feather brush, spreading the powder very gently to discover the print without destroying the impression. The powder should never be sprinkled directly on the print.

Powders also come in an assortment of fluorescent colors such as orange, red, blue, and yellow, and they may be magnetic or nonmagnetic, depending on whether the object or surface to be dusted is a ferrous, or iron-containing,

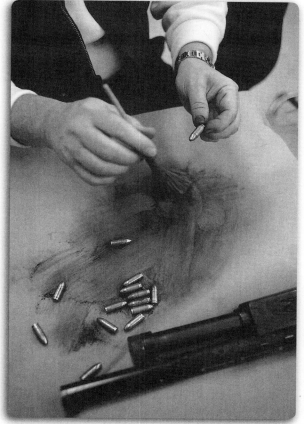

When dusting for latent prints, it is important to use the correct amount of powder.

material. Fluorescent powders are very strongly fluorescent and can be detected with a low-power ultraviolet lamp or an alternate light source such as the blue light special or blue light ultra. These fluorescent powders make the prints glow and become visible (Trozzi, Schwartz, & Hollars, 2000). Magnetic brushes and powders are particularly useful for dusting overhead, slanted, or vertical surfaces.

Lifting Prints Generally, fingerprints are lifted with a length of clear tape. One end of the tape is placed just beyond the end of the print, and the tape is then gently pressed over the print with an even pressure. Care must be taken to avoid or eliminate any tiny air bubbles. Once the tape is in place, the tape may be left in place on the object to protect the print, and the entire object may be sent to the crime lab. If the object is too large or it is not feasible to send it to the lab, the tape may be lifted from the surface of the object and carefully transferred to a card. The powder that originally adhered to the latent fingerprint will now adhere to the tape in the same pattern. The card with the transferred print should be annotated with all pertinent data—including who found and lifted the print, where it was recovered, and what type and color powder was used—and should have the officer's or technician's signature.

Rubber lifters may also be used to recover fingerprints. These are particularly useful for removing prints from surfaces that are curved or that are difficult to photograph. The rubber lifter consists of a thin black or white flexible material coated on one side with an adhesive. To take a latent print, the officer must first apply print powder to the area. Then, after removing the protective celluloid covering from the adhesive, the

RUVIS SceneScope provides more sensitivity than traditional methods of enhancement and without any treatment.

officer places the adhesive side of the lifter against the print and slowly pulls it away. The covering is replaced over the adhesive side, protecting the lifted print.

As a rule of thumb, all invisible prints, once developed, should be photographed with a fixed-focus fingerprint camera before being lifted. It is also important to photograph visible and plastic prints because they too may be damaged beyond recognition once lifted. Photographs provide an accurate record of the prints should lifting fail and the print be damaged or destroyed.

One of the difficult tasks associated with detecting fingerprints at crime scenes is locating invisible ones. At one time, crime scene investigators simply dusted areas where there was some likelihood that fingerprints might have been left by a suspect. Today, however, an ultraviolet image converter assists many crime scene investigations. This device, called the reflected ultraviolet image system (RUVIS), is able to locate invisible latent prints on most nonabsorbent surfaces without the additional use of chemicals or powders. RUVIS detects the prints in their natural state by aiming ultraviolet light at the surface suspected of containing prints. When the ultraviolet light strikes the fingerprint, the light is reflected back to the viewer, differentiating the print from its background. The transmitted ultraviolet light is then converted to visible light by an image intensifier, thereby making the print visible. Once detected, the print can be made visible using conventional development techniques (Safferstein, 2003).

Fuming   In some situations invisible prints can be made visible by using cyanoacrylate vapors that polymerize, or bond, with an invisible print, producing a visible chemical reaction in the form of a white deposit on the print. At one time this technique involved placing small objects, such as credit cards, soft drink cans, or photographs, in a closed container with superglue and a heat source. The effect was to create a chemical vapor from the cyanoacrylate in the glue, which developed the fingerprint on the small object (Almong & Gabay, 1986). Today many police agencies and crime labs use commercially developed fuming chambers and fuming wands to develop invisible prints in the laboratory or at the crime scene (Lewis et al., 2001).

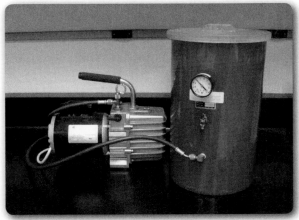

Many of the methods used to develop invisible prints, such as this cyanoacrylate vacuum fuming chamber, require technicians to take safety precautions.

Superglue is no longer used, but the process is still sometimes referred to as "superglue fuming." Safety precautions must be followed with any fuming device because hydrogen cyanide, a poisonous, highly flammable liquid, can form at high temperatures.

Developing Fingerprints on Bodies

Television would have one believe that lifting fingerprints from the skin of a dead body is a simple and commonplace event—yet it is not quite so simple or commonplace. There have been occasional successes using one or another of several techniques, including lasers and powders, fuming the body with cyanoacrylate vapors, and applying magnetic powders (Futrell, 1996). In Canada the Royal Canadian Mounted Police (RCMP) have even had some limited success using a technique referred to as alpha-napthoflavone, which involves exposing the body to iodine fumes and then spraying it with another chemical, which turns fingerprints on the body a highly visible blue (Willett, 1997). The basic problem in developing fingerprints on human bodies is that the victim's skin contains the same sweat and oils as fingerprints are made from. Researchers have been grappling with this problem for years. A few prints have been successfully retrieved, but it tends to be a time-consuming process usually resulting in a uselessly blurry print, or none at all. One strategy that avoids this problem is the use of static electricity. Static electricity attracts dust. By using a *polyethylene terephthalate* (PET) semirigid sheet coated with printing ink, it is possible to visualize impressions of fingerprints on the skin of living and dead bodies. Compared with visualization methods for fingerprints produced from perspiration, this method recovers better images for a longer time after the fingerprint has been deposited on skin, but it does not always yield results (Guo & Xing, 1992).

Using Chemicals to Develop Prints

Many methods can be used to develop invisible prints, such as a fuming chamber.

Many chemical methods have been successfully used to develop fingerprints on various surfaces. The following four methods are widely used.

Iodine Method   Fuming with iodine crystals causes the latent prints containing fat or oil to develop visible prints. The iodine fumes are absorbed and react with perspiration or fatty matter, creating a yellowish or brownish impression. Iodine fuming is effective in developing latent prints on greasy surfaces, paper, cardboard, wood, metal, and other materials.

Silver Nitrate Method   The suspect material is immersed in a silver nitrate solution in a tray. This is called *silvering*. When taken from the solution, the material is placed between two clean, white photo-blotting papers to remove the excess solution and is allowed to dry. The dry specimen is then exposed to a strong light source, such as a photoflood light, an ultraviolet lamp, a carbon arc, a halogen lamp, or even sunlight. When satisfactorily developed, the print becomes visible as a dark brown outline that can be photographed. This method is sometimes called the *silver chloride method* because the sodium chloride from perspiration that has formed a latent print reacts with the silver nitrate solution to form silver chloride. This method is useful for developing latent fingerprints on paper, unpainted wood, and other porous materials.

FYI Inkless or colorless chemical processes are cleaner to work with, but they do not produce as sharp a fingerprint image as ink. As a result, many police agencies either use the messier real-ink method, or a *live-digitized* version.

Ninhydrin Method   Powdered ninhydrin is suspended in ethyl alcohol or acetone and applied to the suspect document or surface by spraying, brushing, swabbing, or immersing. Commercially prepared sprays are available that require no mixture or preparation. If the surface is allowed to dry at room temperature, a purple-reddish-brown stain of the ridge pattern in latent prints will develop in about 2 hours. Applying heat can speed the development process, but it may affect the final product. This method is particularly effective on porous materials such as paper and certain types of fabrics. It is especially effective on older prints because it reacts with the amino acids in human perspiration, which remain longer than the salt deposits that the silver nitrate method reveals.

Chem Print Method Chem Print is a trade name for a ninhydrin solution sold in an aerosol container. The benefit of this commercial spray is that it contains no acetone and will not destroy inks or printing on most documents. The suspect specimen is sprayed until moist on all sides, and then allowed to dry. When dry, it is subjected to low heat (about 200 degrees Fahrenheit), and latent prints, if present, will develop. When speed of development is not critical, the material should be warmed to about 75 to 110 degrees Fahrenheit for about 24 hours. Chem Print is particularly effective for developing latent prints on objects made of cardboard, paper, and wood, and for objects with printed words on them. It also is effective on certain types of fabrics. Latent prints developed using Chem Print remain stable for approximately 6 months before fading. It is important, therefore, to photograph the prints as soon as possible after developing to ensure their preservation.

Fingerprint Kits

Because of police shows on television and depictions of police in the movies, the average citizen knows something about "dusting for prints." Unfortunately, many citizens now expect the police to dust for prints whenever a crime occurs—no matter how small the loss or how futile the dusting might be.

Dusting for prints in a supermarket following a robbery, for example, would yield literally hundreds of fingerprints throughout the store—with no way to know when they were created. On the other hand, if particular objects are witnessed as having been touched by a suspect, these objects (rather than random areas of the store) should be dusted for latent prints. In the DC Sniper case of 2002, for example, police found a magazine at the scene of a store robbery in Montgomery, Alabama, with John Lee Malvo's fingerprint on it. Malvo was identified by witnesses as one of the men involved in the robbery. Police then traced Malvo to Tacoma, to a house where he had been living with former soldier John Allen Williams, also known as John Allen Muhammad, and ultimately linked both men to the murder rifle through fingerprint analysis (CBS News Online, 2002; CNN.com, 2002).

Although dusting for fingerprints may not always turn up prints or a suspect, it should nonetheless be taken very seriously. Given the advances made in fingerprint identification technology, there is an increasing possibility that dusting, even in some lesser crimes, will produce useful evidence. For example, a number of police departments across the nation have begun having patrol officers or crime scene investigation teams dust stolen cars for fingerprints to identify possible theft suspects (Silver, 2003). A simple field fingerprint kit might include the following basic items:

- Flashlight
- Tongs or tweezers
- Latex gloves
- Large and small collection envelopes
- Evidence tags or stickers
- Notebook and pencil
- Pen and a marker
- Transparent lifting tape
- A pair of scissors

- Magnifying glass
- Ruler or tape measure
- Fingerprint powders (assorted colors and magnetic and nonmagnetic forms)
- Fingerprint brushes (including a magnetic brush)
- Latent print transfer cards
- Rubber lifters (several sizes)
- Fixed-focus fingerprint camera and film, or a digital camera

Even simple fingerprint kits can aid in the identification of possible suspects.

FINGERPRINT FILES AND SEARCHES

At one time all fingerprint identifications were done by hand. A fingerprint analyst literally went through every relevant file copy of a fingerprint to visually compare it with a suspect specimen. For the most part, the Henry system of fingerprint identification was used. When a suspect's fingerprints were received, the analyst would search for the suspect's name in the name index file. These manual searches began with a fingerprint classifier determining the primary fingerprint classification in order to assist in distinguishing between people with the same name. If a match was found in the name index file, the case jacket folder number or the master fingerprint classification for that name was noted so the fingerprints could be manually checked with the prints on file. Starting with the name of the suspect and consulting the name index file was much faster than completely classifying a set of fingerprints and then searching the main fingerprint files for matches of these classifications. But this could only be accomplished if there was a known suspect; it was not useful for anonymous latent prints.

When efforts to identify a suspect by name failed, or when there was no known suspect, fingerprints would be fully analyzed and classified and manual searches would be undertaken to locate matches with specimens in the main files. This was a long and laborious task, often requiring many hours of tedious work. The searching officer would have to visually compare the set of suspect prints and the hundreds of sets of prints on file with similar classifications. Figure 7.4 shows the characteristics a fingerprint technician might try to match when comparing file prints with latent prints recovered from a crime scene.

Automated Fingerprint Identification Systems

Computer technology has significantly altered and improved many aspects of police work. Among the most important advances is the **integrated automated fingerprint identification system** (IAFIS). This computer technology uses a mathematically created image of a fingerprint and identifies up to 250 characteristics for each print (Buracker & Stover, 1984; FBI, 2000). IAFIS is maintained by the FBI and contains the largest centralized biometric database in the world. In full, IAFIS contains the fingerprints and corresponding criminal history information for more than 47 million subjects in its Criminal Master File. State, local, and federal law enforcement agencies

integrated automated fingerprint identification system (IAFIS) A computer system maintained by the FBI that uses a mathematically created image identifying up to 250 characteristics of each print; this is the largest centralized biometric database in the world.

FIGURE 7.4 Enlarged, Inked Fingerprint Showing the Location of Twelve Ridge Characteristics

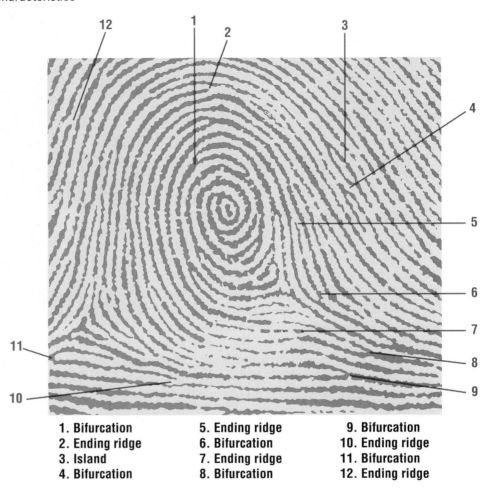

1. Bifurcation	5. Ending ridge	9. Bifurcation
2. Ending ridge	6. Bifurcation	10. Ending ridge
3. Island	7. Ending ridge	11. Bifurcation
4. Bifurcation	8. Bifurcation	12. Ending ridge

submit these fingerprints, and their corresponding criminal history information, to this database voluntarily. At the state and local levels a similar database is maintained, more commonly referred to as AFIS (automated fingerprint identification system), which contains the materials submitted to the FBI's IAFIS database for a specific locality.

In addition to scanning, storing, searching, and retrieving digitized fingerprint images, AFIS technology can reproduce these prints on a plotter or a terminal screen for visual comparisons. Standard ten-print cards can be scanned electronically, digitized, and made readable by the computer system to create the database of fingerprint records. In addition, AFIS technology can create live-digitized fingerprints. This process involves placing a hand on a scanning instrument not unlike the flatbed scanner many readers may have sitting on their desks. The digital scanner uses laser technology to scan the fingerprints, converting the resulting image into a digitized form. From this, images can be sent to the printer or the computer monitor.

The processes of digital fingerprinting and inked fingerprinting are similar, but many law enforcement administrators believe the digitally produced prints are of better quality than those produced by ink (Burker, 1992). Also, AFIS technology permits an agency to compare an applicant's or a suspect's fingerprints with thousands or even millions of prints in a matter of minutes. The same search would take weeks or months if done manually.

HISTORY

AFIS TECHNOLOGY ROSE TO NATIONAL PROMINENCE IN 1985 when the Los Angeles police department identified and arrested Richard Ramirez as the notorious Night Stalker. The Los Angeles police had used an AFIS built by Nippon Electronic Company of Japan to sort through 380,000 electronically stored ten-print cards. The computer had identified Richard Ramirez as the most likely match with the latent prints found at the crime scenes. Ramirez was arrested just 2 hours after the computer identified his fingerprints. He was charged with killing fifteen people. Experts have estimated that a comparable search of ten-print cards done manually would have taken a single technician 67 years to complete (Elmer-DeWitt, 1985).

AFIS technology has improved, become less expensive, and even more portable during the past decade. Some private companies have even begun to use live-digitized fingerprinting on prospective employees and electronically submitting these finger-prints to the FBI for background investigations ("DigitalPrints," 2002). This type of submission can reduce the time required to undertake an IAFIS search by weeks. In 2004 the Department of Homeland Security began a national program of digitally photographing and fingerprinting suspect foreign visitors at the Los Angeles International Airport in an effort to ferret out persons on the terrorist watch list (Xinua News Agency, 2004). Because the scanning instruments can be made small enough to be portable, the U.S. Army has even begun using digital fingerprinting in its efforts to uncover insurgents in Iraq, and army patrols carry portable digital scanners with them (McDougall, 2006). These patrols use what is called a biometric automated toolset to do on-the-spot scanning of fingerprints. The data are later transmitted by satellite to the Department of Defense for inclusion in its automated biometric identification system database and to the FBI for entry into its IAFIS database.

AFIS technology operates with incredible speed and is capable of making extremely fine distinctions between classification points, providing considerable accuracy in a matter of minutes. The system can compare more than 90 minute points along ridges, whorls, bifurcations, islands, and contours on each finger. A given print might not provide 90 points of match, but accurate identifications can be made with as few as 12 or 15 matches.

AFIS technology is credited with 98 to 100 percent accuracy; this does not mean, however, that the computer makes matches 98 to 100 percent of the time. First, the computer cannot identify a print that is not present in the system's database. If a suspect's prints have never been taken, they will not be available to compare with the latent prints. Second, the system does not necessarily identify a single suspect. Rather, the computer generates a list of *candidates* whose prints match at various classification points. A qualified fingerprint examiner must determine the best match among the candidates.

ADMISSIBILITY OF FINGERPRINT EVIDENCE

The admissibility of fingerprint evidence can be traced to the case of *People v. Jennings* (1911). This case held that fingerprint evidence was admissible as a means of identi-fication. The court also ruled that people experienced in fingerprint identification may give their opinion about whether the fingerprints found at the scene of the crime belonged to those of an accused individual. The court's conclusions were based on a

FOCUS ON TECHNOLOGY

AUTOMATED FINGERPRINT IDENTIFICATION SYSTEM (AFIS)

With AFIS, latent prints or prints recovered from a crime scene can be quickly searched and compared against existing fingerprint databases for possible matches. Because AFIS technology has improved and become less expensive, more municipal agencies are able to use this system.

comparison of the photographs of such prints with the impressions made by the defendant. The court stated that the weight of the testimony of experts in fingerprint identification is a question for the jury to determine.

Cases that followed the *Jennings* decision strengthened the legitimacy of fingerprints as a means of identification. For instance, in 1914 in the case of *New Jersey v. Cerciello,* the trial judge had permitted fingerprint evidence to be introduced. On appeal, the defendant argued that it was an error to allow testimony by fingerprint experts, who had compared fingerprints obtained from the defendant voluntarily with fingerprints found on a hatchet near the body of the murdered victim. The New Jersey Court of Appeals disagreed:

> In principle its admission as legal evidence [fingerprint comparisons] is based upon the theory that the evolution in practical affairs of life, whereby the progressive and scientific tendencies of the age are manifest in every other department of human endeavor, cannot be ignored in legal procedure, but that the law in its efforts to enforce justice by demonstrating a fact in issue, will allow evidence of those scientific processes, which are the work of educated and skillful men in their various departments, and apply them to the demonstration of a fact, leaving the weight and effect to be given to the effort and its results to the consideration of the jury.

The U.S. Supreme Court agreed with the New Jersey appellate court, and in two other New Jersey cases several years later, the Court held admissible as evidence a photograph of fingerprints on a balcony post of a house, in lieu of producing the actual post, and a photograph of the fingerprints on a car door, along with an expert's identification of these prints as belonging to the defendant (*Lamble v. State,* 1921; *State v. Connors,* 1915).

In *Commonwealth v. Albright* (1931) a fingerprint expert had testified in the court trial about a fingerprint on a piece of glass, established to be from a pane in a door of a burglarized house. The expert affirmed that the impression on the glass was the same as that of the defendant's left index finger. The Pennsylvania State Supreme Court confirmed the conviction on the basis of the fingerprint evidence, stating:

> It is well settled that the papillary lines and marks of the fingers of every man, woman, and child possess an individual character different from those of any other person and that the chances that the fingerprints of two different persons may be identical are infinitesimally remote.

A case decided during the civil rights movement of the 1960s established another important principle of admissibility of fingerprint evidence. In *Schmerber v. California* (1966) the U.S. Supreme Court held that the introduction into evidence of fingerprint impressions taken without the consent of the defendant was not an infringement of the constitutional privilege against self-incrimination. The Court ruled that it is constitutional to obtain real or physical evidence even if the suspect is compelled to give blood in a hospital; submit to fingerprinting, photography, or measurements; write or speak for identification; appear in court; or stand or walk. It also held that it is constitutional to compel a suspect to assume a stance or make a particular gesture, put on a blouse to see if it fits, or exhibit his or her body as evidence when it is material. The *Schmerber* case points out that the privilege against self-incrimination is related primarily to "testimonial compulsion."

Numerous U.S. Supreme Court decisions have reinforced the admissibility of fingerprint identification evidence.

SUMMARY

Learning Objective 1

Fingerprints, palm prints, and sometimes footprints are among the most valuable types of evidence found at a crime scene. Fingerprints are created by the various lines and ridges on the end joint, or bulb, of every finger and thumb. These ridges form distinct patterns that are uniquely distinguishable from one person to another. These patterns remain unchanged throughout an individual's life.

Learning Objective 2

Fingerprints are classified into three main groups of patterns: arches, loops, and whorls. There are eight subclassifications of the main groups. Matches of fingerprints are made by comparing numerous characteristics within these classifications.

Learning Objective 3

Several types of fingerprints can be found at crime scenes. They include latent prints, visible prints, plastic prints, and invisible prints.

Learning Objective 4

Invisible prints at a crime scene may be developed using a number of techniques. These include the use of powders, fuming, and chemical developers. Many agencies now examine for fingerprints in mundane criminal cases such as auto thefts and even some residential home burglaries.

Learning Objective 5

At one time fingerprint searches were conducted manually. Today, most fingerprint searches are conducted by computer, often by means of an automated fingerprint identification system (AFIS).

Learning Objective 6

The admissibility of fingerprint identification as evidence in a criminal court case can be traced to the Illinois case of *People v. Jennings,* upheld by the U.S. Supreme Court in 1911. Subsequent decisions in other cases refined and strengthened the legitimacy of fingerprints as a means of identification.

KEY TERMS

fingerprint **136**

friction ridges **136**

classification **136**

dactylography **136**

bulb **138**

ten-print card **141**

latent print **142**

visible print **142**

invisible print **142**

plastic print **142**

elimination print **142**

integrated automated fingerprint identification system (IAFIS) **147**

QUESTIONS FOR REVIEW

Learning Objective 1

1. Define *friction ridges* and *dactylography*.
2. What direct evidence do fingerprints provide about people and a crime scene?

Learning Objective 2

3. Describe the three main fingerprint patterns.
4. On what portion of the finger are friction ridges found?

Learning Objective 3

5. Define *latent prints, visible prints, plastic prints, invisible prints,* and *elimination prints.*

Learning Objective 4

6. Why might an investigator use a particular color of fingerprint powder?
7. How is cyanoacrylate, a chemical used in special glues, useful in developing some invisible fingerprints?
8. What is meant by the term *silvering*?

Learning Objective 5

9. Why do many police agencies rely on computers to electronically search for fingerprints that match specimens recovered at crime scenes?

Learning Objective 6

10. To what U.S. Supreme Court decision can the admissibility of fingerprints as evidence be traced?

CRITICAL THINKING EXERCISES

You will need a magnifying glass, an ink pad, some blank white paper cards, and cleanup supplies such as a towel, soap and water, or denatured alcohol.

1. Divide the class into small groups (about four to six students in each; try to keep it an even number). Have each person take the fingerprints of another person in the group, using the steps described in the chapter. Create a ten-print card for each person in every group: be sure to affix the name of the student belonging to the fingerprint on the back of the cards. Exchange cards. Using Figure 7.2 as a guide, determine the fingerprint pattern of each print card. Return the card to the owner for review and to verify the classification of the fingerprint patterns.

2. Using the technique described in the chapter, the instructor fingerprints six members of the class selected at random—*do not* place the names of these students on the cards. These individuals will be the class "suspects." Next, the instructor mixes up the six ten-print cards and selects one; the other cards may be placed aside for possible future use. Using copies of the class set of fingerprint ten-print cards as your database, see how long it takes each group to correctly identify the "suspect."

. . . .

INVESTIGATIVE SKILL BUILDERS

Applying Technology to Tasks

You are the first to arrive at a home where a bad drug deal resulted in the shooting deaths of three people. There is a coffee table in the living room with a thin layer of white powder—possibly heroin or cocaine—spread across its surface. A revolver rests on the table as well. With latex gloves on your hands, you carefully lift the gun by placing your thumb and forefingers on the outer edges of the trigger ring. You carefully examine the pistol and can see that five bullets have been fired. You also notice that the powder from the table has adhered to the butt of the gun (its handle). There appear to be fingerprints on the butt made visible by the powder.

1. How will you lift the prints from the gun?
2. How will you determine whether these fingerprints are from the assailant or one of the victims?

Integrity/Honesty

You are still investigating the crime scene described in the preceding scenario. You notice that sticking out from under the couch is a bundle of hundred dollar bills. You are alone. You count the money and determine that there is a total of $10,000. Do you include this money in your evidence list and inventory or say nothing and keep it since no one is likely to know you took it?

From Surveillance to Records and Files

CHAPTER OBJECTIVES

After completing this chapter, you will be able to:

1 Explain what is meant by *surveillance.*
2 Discuss the purpose of surveillance and how to prepare for surveillance operations.
3 Describe the various types of surveillance used by police agencies.
4 Detail several tips for surveillance officers and investigators.
5 Discuss the importance of police agency files and records in conducting surveillance.
6 Explain how people may be connected and traced through public and private records.

SURVEILLANCE: OBSERVING THE SCENE

Most people have seen an old movie in which the hero jumps into a cab and while pointing to another vehicle pulling away from the curb shouts to the driver: "Follow that car!" This is the underlying principle of surveillance: watching and following others. As this chapter will reveal, however, there is much more to surveillance than simply following someone in another vehicle (although that is one task associated with surveillance). Today extremely sensitive parabolic microphones, sonic wave detectors, and digital audio listening devices permit officers to listen in on conversations almost anywhere and from a considerable distance (Brookes, 2001). Even wiretapping has become enormously more sophisticated during the past several decades. Police are not limited to placing a "tap" on a land-line telephone; rather, conversations can be intercepted and traced when they occur over cell phones, satellite phones, and even between computers (Siljander & Fredrickson, 2003).

Officers can also now *see* what's going on from a significant distance using a telephoto lens or satellite cameras powerful enough to read the back of a pack of matches held in the hand of a suspect standing in his or her backyard. Even darkness is no longer an obstacle due to advances in night vision technology such as thermal infrared imaging and helicopter surveillance with forward-looking infrared (FLIR) devices. In addition, tiny cameras are now available that can be concealed in a lipstick, one's eyeglasses, a smoke detector, or even a tie pin (Brookes, 2001; Monmonie, 2003). But perhaps we are getting a little ahead of ourselves. Let's begin with a simple definition of surveillance.

surveillance The secret observation of people, groups, places, vehicles, and things over a prolonged period in an effort to gather information about a crime or criminal behavior.

Surveillance is the secret observation of people, groups, places, vehicles, and things over a prolonged period to obtain information. The word *surveillance* derives from the French word *surveiller,* which means "to watch over." Surveillance is a valuable investigative tool that can provide information about the activities and identities of individuals. To conduct a successful surveillance, officers must be alert, discreet, and cautious. Surveillance requires great patience, versatility, careful observation skills, and a good memory. The ability to role-play also helps. To better understand surveillance, it is important to understand some of the law enforcement jargon related to it. A number of the more common terms are described in Figure 8.1.

Unlike other aspects of police work, for which the officer can prepare and plan, surveillance depends largely on the actions of the subject. When conducting surveillance without advance knowledge of the subject's plans and activities, officers must simply wait, watch, and respond. In some situations, an investigator may obtain information about a subject's plans from an informant or from a wiretap or other listening device. In these instances, the subject's movements may be anticipated to some degree.

There are no hard-and-fast rules governing how surveillance operates. In fact, actions and activities that work in one situation may prove useless in another. Surveillance takes time, personnel, and expensive equipment, so each case must be carefully considered and resources allocated accordingly (Adams, 2007).

The Purpose of Surveillance

In general, surveillance is used to obtain information—about people, their friends and associates, and activities—that may assist in solving a criminal case, protecting a witness, or locating a fugitive. It is important to keep the purpose of a particular surveillance in mind so the objectives of the case can be met. Here are some reasons surveillance is undertaken:

- Gather information to develop a criminal case
- Detect or prevent crime

FIGURE 8.1 Surveillance Terms

Basic Terms

Subject	The person or object being observed
Surveillant	The officer or investigator conducting the surveillance
Surveillance	Careful observation of a person, group, place, vehicle, or thing, undertaken in a secretive manner

Other Terms

Fixed surveillance	A stationary location from which surveillance is undertaken
Mobile surveillance	A surveillance undertaken using any of a variety of mobile conveyances, including walking (tailing)
Aerial surveillance	Use of an aircraft to observe and follow a subject or a subject's vehicle
Being made	Recognition of a surveillant by the subject
Being burned	Another term for a surveillant being recognized by the subject
Blown cover	Synonymous with being made
Bugging	Use of various small electronic listening devices, or "bugs," located near or on the subject
Loose surveillance	Following a subject, but not very closely, in an effort to avoid detection
Close surveillance	Opposite of loose surveillance; investigators keep the subject under constant surveillance, even at the risk of being identified as surveillants
Cover or cover story	A surveillant's use of false identification or a false identity to gain access to or remain undetected in a location or among persons under surveillance
Covert	Secret, undercover, or unannounced
Discreet surveillance	Observations at a discreet, or cautious, distance from the subject; in such situations, losing sight of the subject may be better than being identified
Electronic surveillance	Use of various cameras and listening and recording devices to monitor a surveillance location
Homing or tracking device	Small electronic device that emits a radio signal that permits tracking by means of an associated tracking device; also called a *beeper,* a *signal,* a *transponder,* and a *beacon*
Picking up a tail or growing a tail	Recognition by a subject that he or she is being followed (see tailing)
Planted	Intentionally placed in a location, without the knowledge of others at that location, in order to make observations
Shadowing	Closely but secretly following a subject
Stakeout	Same as a *fixed surveillance*
Tailing	Following a subject without detection
Tap or wiretap	Placing a listening and recording device on the telephone line of a subject or intercepting the signal of a cell or satellite phone; wiretaps cannot be undertaken without a court order
Tight surveillance	Very close observation of the subject; a minimum distance is permitted between the surveillant and the subject, but secrecy is maintained
Undercover	Using a *cover* or *cover story* to gain entry to a location or when *planted* in a location
Visual contact	Ability to see the subject; to maintain a line of sight on the subject

- Detect and prevent terrorist attacks
- Locate a wanted fugitive
- Learn about various contacts and associates of a particular suspect or group
- Gain information sufficient to establish probable cause for issuance of a search or arrest warrant
- Discover the activities and movements of suspected individuals
- Verify statements made by witnesses or informants
- Observe and monitor communications of known members of terrorist organizations
- Recover stolen property
- Intercept criminals in the act of committing a crime
- Prevent a crime from being committed
- Develop intelligence on criminals and criminal organizations
- Develop intelligence on terrorists and terrorist organizations
- Obtain information to use during an interrogation

Preparing for Surveillance

Investigators may not be able to anticipate every move of a subject under surveillance, but preparations are very important nonetheless. The personnel and equipment needed and the type of surveillance (loose, tight, stationary, or moving) must be determined in advance. The use of code words, methods of summoning aid, methods of entrance and exit from the surveillance location, dress, and safety precautions should all be considered.

Before beginning surveillance, an investigator should become familiar with all the available facts of the case and the purpose of the surveillance. It is important to know the subject's full name, nicknames, and aliases; residence and business address and telephone numbers; known hangouts; and complete physical description. Information on a suspect's habits, mannerisms, friends, and peculiarities may also prove useful (Jenkins, 2003).

The type of vehicle the suspect drives, has access to, or prefers driving all may be important. Surveillance team members should know the subject's driver's license number, car tag number, and general driving habits, if available. Whenever possible, team members should become familiar with the streets and the neighborhood where the surveillance will take place as well as the kind of people residing in the area. To blend in better, officers should dress as people do in the neighborhood. Finally, each team member should have fictitious credentials and a plausible cover story in case he or she is detected or questioned by the subject or the subject's associates.

TYPES OF SURVEILLANCE

There are a number of different types of surveillance strategies. Two of the broadest categories are (1) fixed, or stationary, surveillance and (2) moving, or mobile, surveillance.

Fixed Surveillance

fixed, or stationary, surveillance Close watch on a subject or object from a single location and vantage point, such as a building or vehicle.

Fixed, or **stationary, surveillance** uses a single location from which the surveillants operate and observe the target (the subject of the surveillance). Fixed surveillance is sometimes referred to as a *stakeout* or a *plant*. The location may be a room, office, storefront, or surveillance van or truck (Figure 8.2). During a fixed surveillance, a surveillant may assume the guise of a gardener, street repairer, painter, or other laborer, or even a street person. Such covers enable the officer or investigator to move more freely around the area and the subject (Staples, 2000).

Fixed surveillances, or stakeouts, are usually limited in their duration. For example, imagine that there had been a series of burglaries in a certain type of business establishment in a particular neighborhood. One strategy the police might use is to stake out a similar type of establishment in the area.

A stakeout may also be initiated to identify a suspicious individual or vehicle in the area of high crime. Or a fixed surveillance may be ordered because a contemplated robbery, burglary, narcotics operation, or other criminal activity has been reported to the police. Sometimes a stakeout provides the means of identifying a suspect informants or witnesses have said was involved in a crime. As in any surveillance, the success of a stakeout depends on how well the officers involved have prepared for and understand their assignment.

When establishing a fixed surveillance, the primary requirement is good visibility of the suspect or location being watched. The goal of fixed surveillance is more often to gather information than to seize a suspect. The quality of the information obtained will only be as good as the surveillant's ability to see and hear (Acm IV Security Services, 1993; Staples, 2000). Before starting a fixed surveillance, the officer must carefully survey the area in question. This survey should take into account such things as the investigator's ability to hear and see the identities of the residents of the immediate area and their businesses and occupations. It also may include social activities occurring in the area and the trustworthiness of residents in the area.

FIGURE 8.2 Fixed Surveillance

Key
A Primary fixed surveillance location
B Suspect's location
C Secondary fixed surveillance (rooftop)
D Mobile surveillance team
E Suspect's car

Moving Surveillance

Surveillance becomes increasingly more complicated and difficult when an investigator must follow, or tail or shadow, a suspect in a **moving surveillance.** The risk of detection increases with movement regardless of whether the investigator follows on foot (foot surveillance) or in a car or truck (vehicle or automobile surveillance) or even observes from the air (aerial surveillance). Moving surveillance requires more officers and vehicles as well as more extensive planning and communications systems. Complications may include the amount or flow of pedestrian traffic and road congestion caused by an accident or heavy vehicular traffic. Let us consider several variations on traditional mobile surveillance.

moving surveillance The observation of a subject while moving on foot, in a vehicle, or in an aircraft.

Foot Surveillance   In foot surveillance, the number of officers may depend on the amount of pedestrian traffic and the locale of the surveillance. There are three major types of foot surveillance: one-investigator, two-investigator, and three-investigator surveillance (Siljander & Fredrickson, 2003).

- **One-investigator surveillance.** In a one-person surveillance, a single investigator watches and follows the subject. There is little margin for error, and there is a fairly high risk of detection if surveillance continues for a long time, because the surveillant must maintain visual contact with the subject at all times.

- **Two-investigator surveillance.** In an effort to avoid detection, a mobile surveillance may use a two or more person surveillance team. Using two surveillants provides greater flexibility. For example, with two investigators, the position of the investigator directly behind the subject can be changed periodically. Furthermore, the use of two investigators reduces the likelihood of losing the subject in heavy pedestrian traffic. When pedestrian traffic is not too heavy, one investigator may walk behind the subject while the other walks parallel to the subject on the opposite side of the street.

- **Three-investigator surveillance.** Three-investigator surveillance is sometimes referred to as **ABC surveillance.** This procedure further reduces the chances of a subject detecting the surveillance. In ABC surveillance, Officer A follows the subject, maintaining visual contact from a reasonable distance. A second investigator, Officer B, follows A. The distance between A and B may be somewhat greater than between A and the subject. A third investigator, C, participates in the surveillance from across the street (Figure 8.3). Typically, Officer C is approximately where Officer A is on the opposite side of the street, or slightly behind A. Investigator C has to keep both A and B in sight. A variation of this technique places one of the officers ahead of the subject. This procedure, called a **leading surveillance,** is useful when the suspect's route is well established and known to the investigators. Sometimes officers coordinate their movements in advance and exchange places at designated times or locations to make it more difficult for the subject to notice that he or she is being followed.

The three-investigator procedure can be very effective, and having a fourth officer standing by in a car can be even more effective. In addition to providing a measure of safety in an emergency situation, the fourth officer can be exchanged for one of the others if the subject begins to act suspiciously about being followed.

ABC surveillance A three-officer foot surveillance in which Officer A follows the subject and in turn is followed by Officer B. The third surveillant, Officer C, normally walks on the other side of the street parallel to subject.

leading surveillance Type of mobile surveillance where the surveillant walks ahead of the subject.

FIGURE 8.3 ABC Foot Surveillance Method

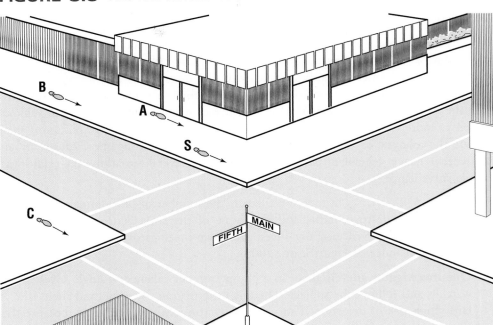

Vehicle Surveillance As in foot surveillance, the officer should stay as close to the suspect as possible without becoming conspicuous. Vehicles used for surveillance should be plain and nondescript and fit into the flow of traffic without being noticed.

Before a vehicle surveillance begins, the communications equipment should be checked to make sure it is in good working order. Police radios, however, should be mounted where they cannot be seen should someone look inside the driver's compartment. Similarly, no police objects, such as handcuffs, hats, manuals, official papers, or clipboards, should be visible from the outside.

Mobile surveillance may be undertaken with one, two, or several cars. There may even be a combination of foot and vehicle surveillance. For example, a subject may be walking, followed by an officer on foot and an officer in a car. Suddenly the subject sees a bus and gets on. The foot officer can continue **close surveillance** by getting on the bus with the subject. The officer in the car can continue following the bus. Similarly, a subject driving a car may park and enter a shopping mall. In this situation, an officer may have to park and leave the car to maintain surveillance of the subject on foot through the mall.

Many police agencies use a strategy called **perimeter box surveillance.** Typically, this procedure involves four cars, with at least two carrying extra foot officers. One car stays ahead of the subject's car, one car follows the subject's car, and the other two cars maintain positions on streets parallel to that of the subject (Figure 8.4). This method permits coverage of all turning contingencies that the subject might choose, even if the subject suddenly turns at an intersection or when the light is yellow or has just turned red.

Whether following a subject with one, two, or more cars, it is prudent to alter the distance and location of the cars regularly. An officer driving ahead of the subject

close surveillance Surveillance conducted while remaining very close in proximity to the subject.

perimeter box surveillance a vehicle surveillance technique that allows surveillants to maintain coverage even if the subject suddenly turns at an intersection.

FIGURE 8.4 Perimeter Box Surveillance Method

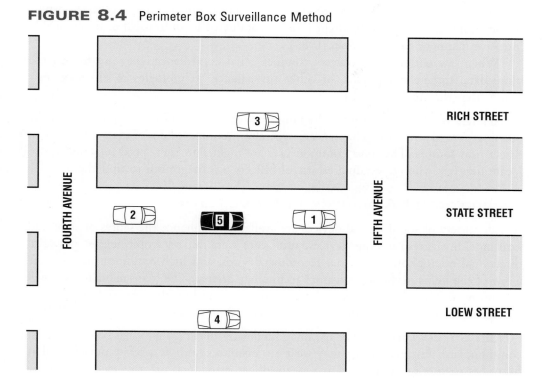

should keep in contact with fellow officers by radio and should watch the subject in rearview mirrors. In such situations, it is helpful to have a second officer in the lead car as an observer.

Electronic Vehicle Tracking In some situations police may attach a bumper beeper or similar global positioning system (GPS) device. These devices can be secretly attached to or placed in the vehicle of a subject to be followed. A warrant is not necessary to secretly attach a device to a car provided the car is parked in a public place at the time. A warrant is also not required to follow a tracking device placed on a vehicle so long as it is traveling on public streets or through public places. In *United States v. Knotts* (1983), the Supreme Court ruled that "a person traveling in an automobile on public thoroughfares has no reasonable expectation of privacy in his movements from one place to another." Sophisticated receivers in the police units, or in helicopters, monitor these device signals and can locate and follow the vehicle under surveillance. These kinds of devices are particularly helpful during investigations of ongoing, conspiratorial criminal activities involving a high degree of organization (gambling, frauds, drug sales) and in situations where the subject under surveillance is likely to identify one or more of the people or vehicles in the mobile surveillance if they get too close. Similarly, such devices are sometimes concealed in satchels containing ransom money to permit police to monitor the whereabouts of the ransom from a safe distance.

Aerial Surveillance The use of planes and helicopters for aerial surveillance has become fairly common. Warrants are not required to undertake aerial surveillance over public or private property for several reasons. Originally, landowners owned all airspace directly above their property, but in *United States v. Causby* (1946) the Supreme Court ruled that the sky is a "public highway." This ruling did not clearly specify whether landowners retained any rights to restrict overhead nontransportation activities, but it certainly made it possible to fly over private property to conduct surveillance. Today air traffic has become so common place that people cannot reasonably expect privacy from the air unless the flight is being conducted in an unusual or unreasonably intrusive manner (*Florida v. Riley,* 1989).

When law enforcement officers conduct aerial surveillance, they are free to use binoculars, camera equipment, or other surveillance technologies to enhance their vision from the air.

Thermal Imaging Forward-looking infrared devices (FLIRs), mentioned in the opening paragraph of this chapter, are typically mounted under aircraft and used to detect heat sources. The most common uses are nighttime high-speed pursuits and to locate fugitives who are evading efforts of officers on the ground to find them.

Technological Advances in Surveillance

A wide variety of sophisticated devices are available to enhance the senses of sight and hearing. Tiny eavesdropping devices, miniature cameras, telescopic lenses, powerful directional microphones, compact recording devices, and high-resolution imaging are a few of the items in the investigator's technology arsenal. The items actually used will depend on the type of surveillance being undertaken and on the financial resources of the agency conducting the surveillance (Brookes, 2001; McKeown & Stern, 2000).

Audio Surveillance The use of audio devices in surveillance has become almost commonplace. An investigator may wear a transmitter both as a safety device to alert his or her partner to trouble and as a means of gathering incriminating evidence during a conversation with a subject. A subject's room or vehicle may be bugged, or the subject's telephone may be wiretapped. In some situations, a listening or tracking device may be attached to the subject's purse or clothing. It is important to make sure audio surveillance is done legally. Whenever police agencies use electronic listening devices, they must consider the provisions of the Fourth Amendment and various federal and state privacy acts. Many forms of electronic surveillance and wiretapping are considered by the courts to be searches and must follow the same regulations as would a physical search. Thus they require showing sufficient probable cause and obtaining an order from the court.

Provisions for using electronic listening devices can be traced to the landmark case of *Katz v. United States* (1967). In the *Katz* case, the Supreme Court ruled that the Constitution protects private telephone conversations from unauthorized government intrusions—such as wiretapping or electronic surveillance—even when calls are made from a public telephone booth. According to the *Katz* decision, electronic surveillance and wiretapping are permitted only with probable cause and by court order.

In June 1968 the United States Congress enacted legislation outlawing wiretapping and electronic eavesdropping. However, the act provided for closely supervised, court-approved electronic eavesdropping by federal investigative officers to combat certain serious criminal activities (primarily organized crime). The introduction to Title III of the Omnibus Crime Control and Safe Street Act of 1968 states this provision:

> Organized criminals make extensive use of wire and oral communications in their criminal activities. The interception of such communications to obtain evidence of the commission of crimes or to prevent their commission is an indispensable aid to law enforcement and the administration of justice.

The Crime Control Act of 1968 permits federal officers to use wiretaps or electronic eavesdropping, provided they first obtain a court order from a federal judge after demonstrating probable cause. Similarly, the act permits state and local officers to tap wires under similar circumstances, provided the state has a statute authorizing such procedures. In the absence of an authorizing statute or a court order, it is a criminal offense to participate in wiretapping or electronic eavesdropping.

Complicating wiretapping and electronic eavesdropping legality issues are the more recent changes set forth by the Patriot Act and the Patriot Act II. Under provisions of these acts, wiretaps without any court order for up to fifteen days after a terrorist attack are permissible if a subject is considered a reasonable suspect of terrorist involvement (ACLU Fact Sheet, 2003; Etzioni, 2004). Many of the electronic surveillance provisions in the Patriot Act and Patriot Act II would have faced serious opposition prior to September 11, 2001, but these events convinced many Americans and an overwhelming majority in Congress that law enforcement and national security officials need new tools to fight terrorism. These legal enhancements should not, however, provide opportunities for law enforcement and the intelligence community to harass individuals who are merely exercising their First Amendment rights to free speech (Podesta, 2002).

Video Surveillance   At the current rate of technological advancement, today's science fiction is tomorrow's science. With advances in microminiaturization, high-resolution and digitized imaging, and satellite video capabilities, many law enforcement agencies are now able to take advantage of video surveillance to extend what they see and record it for later use. Fiber optics and high-quality reproduction from miniaturized and remote cameras and recorders allow investigators to view and record criminal activities with little danger of discovery by subjects under surveillance. When played in a courtroom, a video or digital recording of a criminal's activities can be very convincing to a jury. Among the more interesting visual technological advances currently being developed is facial recognition imaging.

facial recognition systems
Computer-based security systems that are able to automatically detect and identify human faces.

Facial recognition systems are computer-based security systems that can automatically detect and identify human faces. These systems depend on a recognition algorithm. The first step for a facial recognition system is to recognize a human face and extract it from the rest of the scene. Next, the system measures nodal points on the face, such as the distance between the eyes, the shape of the cheekbones, and other distinguishable features. These nodal points are then compared to the nodal points computed from a database of pictures to find a match. Facial recognition systems have rather obvious limitations, including the angle of the face when captured, lighting conditions, and the comparisons available in the photo face database. Some systems claim to be highly accurate, even when the subject is wearing a disguise, but critics suggest that these systems can be fooled by simple disguises such as a beard (ACLU Fact Sheet, 2002; Feder, 2004).

Current systems are limited based on the angle of the face captured and the lighting conditions present. New technologies are in development to create three-dimensional models of a person's face based on a digital photograph to create more nodal points for comparison. However, such technology is inherently susceptible to error given that the computer is extrapolating a three-dimensional model from a two-dimensional photograph.

The focus on facial recognition has shifted in recent years to its use as a way to secure borders and airports. The most elaborate system of identification in the United States began development in 2004 and is currently deployed by the Department of Homeland Security (DHS). The United States Visitor and Immigrant Status Indicator Technology (US-VISIT) is an integrated federal government program intended to improve the nation's capability to collect information about foreign nationals who travel to the United States, as well as to control the preentry, entry, status, and exit of these travelers. The program requires visitors to the United States to provide fingerprints and a digital photograph at their port of entry. US-VISIT then interfaces with the Automated Biometric Identification System (IDENT) database to see if the visitor is a "person of interest."

TIPS FOR SURVEILLANCE OPERATIONS

Officers and investigators on any surveillance operation must maintain constant vigilance. Inattention or unnecessary distraction, even for brief periods, may result in losing the subject or following the wrong vehicle. During foot surveillance, it is important to be sure that the surveilling officer is not also being followed. Sometimes a wary criminal will enlist a confederate to intentionally follow him or her to make sure there are no police doing likewise. This is sometimes referred to as a **convoy.**

convoy Following a subject using multiple surveillants in tandem.

Subjects of surveillance may try an assortment of techniques to detect surveillance. Becoming familiar with a subject's possible countermeasures may help an investigator avoid exposure (Jenkins, 2003). Figure 8.5 lists a number of common techniques used to detect surveillance.

Officers on surveillance should try to blend in with other people and activities in the area. Clothing should be appropriate to the locale. Officers should engage in conventional activities, like buying and reading a newspaper, purchasing and drinking a cup of coffee, or shopping in a grocery store. In short, the surveillant should do whatever others in the immediate vicinity are doing.

FIGURE 8.5   Countermeasures Used to Detect Surveillance

During Foot Surveillance

- Riding backwards up an escalator
- Riding an elevator to the top floor and then back down again
- Taking an elevator to a floor several floors above the desired floor and then using the stairs to go back to the desired floor
- Getting on or off buses or other forms of transportation
- Entering a subway station and then immediately exiting it
- Stopping and talking with a stranger and then watching to see if this person is questioned by anyone
- Moving quickly around a corner and then waiting to see if anyone hurries around in pursuit
- Walking through a crowded store, hotel lobby, courtyard, sporting event, or other public place
- Entering a darkened movie theater and leaving through an emergency door
- Feigning a call at a pay phone to size up people in the vicinity

During Mobile Surveillance

- Driving down a dead-end street
- Speeding up or slowing down
- Rounding a corner and doubling back
- Making a sudden U-turn in the middle of the street
- Running a red light
- Turning a corner on a red or yellow light
- Discarding something from a window to see if anyone stops to pick it up
- Changing lanes frequently
- Pulling into a parking lot and parking to see if a pursuing vehicle does likewise
- Pulling into a parking lot, and then immediately leaving, to see if anyone else does the same thing
- Stopping at the side of the road to check a tire and seeing if anyone else stops

---

Many officers who work undercover carry an assortment of disguises and clothes in their vehicles. This allows them to change disguises very quickly. In some cases, the undercover officer may choose to use a pet: for example, walking a dog. In other situations, the officer may ride a bicycle or a motorcycle, walk along with another officer, stop to make a purchase, and so forth. Inventiveness and originality are important attributes in surveillance.

During any surveillance, the officer must be both stealthful and observant. If the subject stops to make a telephone call, make a purchase, or secure a train or airplane ticket, the surveillant should try to remain as close as possible to the subject. It is important that the officer knows what goes on during the transaction. Should it prove impossible to remain close, asking for a ticket to the same place or saying, "I'd like something like that last person bought," might obtain the necessary information. Should the subject enter a hotel, the desk clerk, manager, and security officer (if trustworthy) can help considerably. With their aid, the surveillant can learn about the subject's phone calls and messages, possible contacts, trash, comings and goings, and any other pertinent information.

Sometimes the subject may approach a surveillant. The surveillant should never immediately conclude that he or she has been *made* (identified as an officer). The subject may be suspicious and may even be trying to detect whether he or she is being followed, but it does not automatically mean that the surveillant has been identified. The sputterings of an inexperienced surveillant, however, are likely to ensure that the subject has now become aware of his or her tail. An experienced officer knows that the subject may look into the eyes of many people around him or her, and may even stop to converse with several in an effort to test their responses and detect a possible tail. A subject worried about being followed may walk up to someone and ask directions, request a match, ask the time, or engage in any number of other simple pleasantries. When conducting surveillance, it is always advisable to have a well-rehearsed story ready in case of a confrontation. If a subject accosts a surveillant and accuses the officer of following him or her, the officer should act surprised and deny it. The officer might say, "Why on earth would I follow you? Do I know you?" Or the officer might act insulted or annoyed at being bothered by this "stranger." In any event, the officer should maintain a consistent role and strongly deny following the subject. Of course, the officer will now need to drop out of the surveillance and be replaced by someone who has not been *burned* (identified).

RECORDS AND FILES

The department's records and reports are an important aid in conducting investigations or surveillance. These include preliminary reports of criminal incidents, follow-up reports, offense and arrest records, *modus operandi* files, missing persons reports, gun registrations, Wanted bulletins and updates, surveillance reports, and even various officers' personal information files. An example of a typical surveillance form is shown in Figure 8.6.

FIGURE 8.6 Sample Surveillance Form

SURVEILLANCE REPORT

Date: 04-20-07   Start Time: 1030   Finish Time: 1130   Case No.: 2251

Address (Location or Subject Name): JOHN BURTON (2240 Maple Street)

Purpose of Surveillance: Follow subject, establish his routine route; possible book making enterprise.

Weather Conditions: Cloudy   Equipment Used: None

Conversation with Subject: None

Telephone Calls Made: One (555-3458); made from telephone booth on Maple and Oak St.

Personal Contacts by Subject: None

Record of Observations During Surveillance:
Time: 1040: Subject entered Joe's Pizza shop (1406 Maple).
Time: 1050: Subject left Joe's but entered Mike's Bike Shop (1408 Maple).
Time: 1100: Subject exits Mike's, enters Wang's Hardware Store (1410 Maple).
Time: 1130: Subject leaves Wang's, goes to corner phone booth and makes call.

Signature of Officer:

In addition to files housed in the department, there are literally hundreds of persons, places, indexes, directories, file systems, places of business, organizations, newspapers, libraries, and municipal, county, state, and federal sources of records available to investigators. The more sources an investigator accesses, the easier investigations become. The ability to find information may well be as important as or more important than the information itself. By gaining information from various sources, an investigator can shorten an investigation by days or even weeks. Early solutions in an investigation may make the difference between apprehension and escape or between recovery and loss of property. They may also prevent unnecessary use of expensive personnel and equipment.

Linking People to Records

In many investigations, all the officers have on a suspect is a past address, yet they are expected to locate that suspect. A number of obvious records contain information about people, and they may aid in the search for a fleeing felon or suspect. These include fingerprint and photograph files and *modus operandi* files. These files, along with others, can assist an investigator in identifying or locating a suspect. Computer technology also allows police investigators to gain a wide assortment of identifying elements about a suspect.

Tracing and Locating People

When it is apparent that a suspect has *skipped* (fled the area), police will need to use a variety of techniques and types of records to trace him or her. Fortunately, humans are creatures of comfort and habit. Remembering this can sometimes help an officer locate or trace a person who dropped from sight or left the area. Ironically, many criminals head for home when they are in trouble—not necessarily their own home but that of their parents, a sibling, or a close relative living in the area. An investigator would be wise to locate and check such locations and to speak with relatives. Placing known relatives under surveillance would be a good idea.

Sometimes a simple trip to the post office to see if a forwarding address has been supplied is all it takes to locate a suspect. In some cases the suspect's bank may provide an address to which statements are now being forwarded or the name of the bank to which money has been transferred. Utilities often require deposits from customers who have never had a utility account or who may have a bad credit history. To avoid paying a deposit to initiate telephone or electric service, a suspect may admit that he or she had previously had an account. When the utility office in the original area has been contacted to verify information, officials can inform the police of the new location of the suspect. With a little bit of thought, investigators can find numerous sources of records to assist them in tracing a missing suspect.

Types and Sources of Recorded Information

The quantity and variety of stored information available to investigators is extremely large, so an organization scheme or classification system is useful. Let us consider some major categories or sources of information linking people to records.

Law Enforcement Agencies
The first files used to identify or learn more about a suspect are those immediately available to the police; that is, those housed in the police department such as **criminal jackets,** the files on criminals that list their arrests and convictions. Also included are all arrest and incident files housed at the

criminal jackets Official police records of criminals.

FOCUS ON TECHNOLOGY

SURVEILLANCE TECHNOLOGIES

Technical surveillance equipment and techniques extend an investigator's senses of seeing and hearing. (Top left) wire and recorder used in audio surveillance; (Top right) night vision equipment used for video surveillance when there is no light or very poor lighting; (Bottom) undercover officer being fitted with a hidden recording device.

agency; files on fences (people dealing in stolen property), pawnbrokers, and known or habitual criminals residing in the area; Stop and Wanted bulletins; *modus operandi* files; and other files. The kinds of information one might obtain from these records include last known address or residence, telephone numbers, friends, relatives, and associates, usual occupation, last known place of business, and so forth.

It also may be useful to consult local jail or prison records if a suspect has been incarcerated previously. Such records may provide investigators with leads regarding the suspect's visitors, cellmates, previous addresses, and perhaps other places of incarceration.

Investigators should also consider speaking with probation officers and consulting their files. Many probation offices across the country are not computerized. Consequently, it is sometimes easier and faster to talk with the suspect's probation officer than to wade through volumes of written records. The probation officer may have information about the suspect, his or her friends, relatives, and even places the suspect may like to hang out.

Federal Agencies   Federal agencies with files of information on people include these major agencies: the Federal Bureau of Investigation (FBI), which has various standard reference files and computerized identification databases; the Drug Enforcement Administration (DEA), which holds records on both individuals and companies that have violated various drug laws; the U.S. Marshals Service and the Treasury Department, which includes the Bureau of Alcohol, Tobacco, and Firearms (ATF) and the Internal Revenue Service (IRS). Each of these agencies has files on suspects and criminals that have been involved with that organization. In addition, investigators might contact the Department of Homeland Security and subdepartments such as Customs and Border Protection, Immigration and Customs Enforcement (ICE), or the U.S. Secret Service.

The U.S. Postal Service can be useful in certain investigations, and the U.S. Department of State may provide information about suspects planning to leave the country and in need of a passport. Finally, the military may be an excellent source of information, especially if a base is in the area. If the suspect is in the military—either active or reserve—it may be simple to locate him or her.

State and Local Agencies   Most regulatory and licensing powers are in the hands of state agencies. Applying for something as mundane as a fishing license provides information about the applicant to a state agency (fish and wildlife or a similar department). Agencies where information about suspects may be available to investigators include the state department of motor vehicles or the motor vehicle registry, the office of employment or unemployment, and various social service agencies. In addition, local agencies such as the county or township clerk's office or various offices typically housed in the local courthouse may have information on a suspect and his or her whereabouts.

Public Records Offices and Business Organizations   Today it is virtually impossible to live and work in society without taking part in many business transactions. People enter into contracts for housing, credit, various business dealings, and even social or recreational activities. All of these activities are likely to leave a paper trail because they require a person's name on some form of record.

Having the water or electricity or gas turned on in one's apartment involves contacting the utility and providing an address and telephone number. If a person has even a single gasoline credit card or department store credit card, a credit record exists. In addition to information filed with the company actually distributing the credit card, credit reporting agencies maintain and report information on a customer's credit history, including a current address.

Many people, including criminals, are concerned about their welfare and that of their family members. Therefore, they may at some point try to obtain some form of insurance. Whether is it automobile, health, or life insurance, application records will be on file somewhere.

Miscellaneous Sources and Files   The space needed to list all possible miscellaneous sources of files would exceed the limits of this book. However, some widely available sources bear mentioning. These include public libraries, libraries on college and university campuses, auto rental and leasing agencies, city directories, the chamber of commerce, hospitals, hotels, taxi and livery companies, travel agencies, moving companies, and Internet sources such as USA People Search (www.usa-people-search.com), where for a small fee (about $40) anyone can have the following pieces of public information provided for a name where records exist:

- Current address
- Current phone
- Up to 20 years' address history
- Birth date
- Aliases/maiden names
- Property ownership
- Bankruptcies
- Tax liens and judgments
- Relatives
- Roommates
- Neighbors
- Personal assets
- Marriages and divorces
- Website ownership

SUMMARY

Learning Objective 1

Surveillance is the secret observation of people, groups, places, vehicles, and things over a prolonged period to gather information about a crime or criminal.

Learning Objective 2

The purpose of surveillance is to obtain information about people, their friends and associates, and activities that may assist in solving a criminal case, protecting a witness, or locating a fugitive. Considerations of personnel, equipment, and the type of surveillance influence the success of any surveillance operation.

Learning Objective 3

The major categories of surveillance are fixed, or stationary, surveillance; moving surveillance; and technical surveillance. Moving surveillance can include one-, two-, or several investigator foot surveillance; vehicle surveillance; and aerial surveillance. Technical surveillance can include audio surveillance, video surveillance, and tracking subjects.

Learning Objective 4

In surveillance operations, officers must maintain constant vigilance, be stealthful and observant, maintain their cover or disguise, be aware of the suspect's countermeasures, and try to blend in with other people and activities in the area with regard to clothing, vehicles, and actions.

Learning Objective 5

An important aid in conducting surveillance can be the police agency's records, files, and reports. These include preliminary reports of crimes, follow-up reports, offense and arrest records, *modus operandi* files, fingerprint files, and other such records and reports.

Learning Objective 6

Various public and private agencies can provide information about people and assist a surveillance operation. These include federal agencies, state and local agencies, public records offices, and private business organizations.

KEY TERMS

surveillance **156**

fixed or stationary
  surveillance **158**

moving surveillance **159**

ABC surveillance **160**

leading
  surveillance **160**

close surveillance **161**

perimeter box
  surveillance **161**

facial recognition
  systems **164**

convoy **164**

criminal jackets **167**

QUESTIONS FOR REVIEW

Learning Objective 1

1. What does the term *surveillance* mean?

Learning Objective 2

2. In general, what is the purpose of surveillance?

3. List six reasons surveillance might be undertaken.

4. Why is preparation for surveillance important?

Learning Objective 3

5. What are the major categories of surveillance?

6. At what point should a fixed surveillance become a mobile one?

7. What type of surveillance should be used to gather information on a suspected terrorist?

8. What might the police do if there were a series of burglaries in a given neighborhood?

9. What are some problems associated with a one-officer moving surveillance?

10. What is an *ABC surveillance* method?

11. How does the strategy of *perimeter box surveillance* work?

12. What is the landmark case that defines the legality of police use of listening devices?

Learning Objective 4

13. What might you suggest that a surveillant do before beginning a surveillance operation?

14. How should surveillants dress when doing a surveillance operation?

Learning Objective 5

15. Why is it important to maintain accurate police records and files?

Learning Objective 6

16. How might someone's old mailing address help an investigator locate the individual's current address?

17. How might a credit card bill found in the trash assist the police in locating a missing felon?

18. Why do fleeing felons frequently go to their parents' or a relative's home?

CRITICAL THINKING EXERCISES

1. Along with other members of the class, write your name on a slip of paper. Have your instructor place all these slips in a paper bag and shake the bag to mix up the slips of paper. When the bag is passed to you, draw out one slip. If you draw your own name, take another and replace you own name slip. Do not read aloud the name on the slip you chose or in any other way disclose whose name you have drawn. Using information in this chapter, decide how you will complete the following tasks without directly asking the person named on your slip of paper:

   a. Find out his or her current local address and telephone number.

   b. Find out the home address and telephone number of the person's parents (or nearest relative if the parents are deceased or the individual currently resides with parents).

   c. Determine where and when the person *usually* goes grocery shopping.

   d. Identify the types of foods the individual typically purchases while grocery shopping.

2. In a follow-up class session, compare your surveillance results with others in the class. Determine how many surveillants were *made* by their subjects.

3. Break into groups and discuss how you, as investigators, might go about developing information about the manager of the restaurant described in the following scenario:

   The Hot Hot Spot is a restaurant and bar located just outside of town in a one-story wood-framed building. It is adjacent to a small shopping area, a pocket mall, consisting of a grocery store and four other businesses. Directly across from the pocket mall, slightly diagonal to the restaurant, is a paint and wallpaper store. The Hot Hot Spot employs 15 people (7 men and 8 women).

   The restaurant's bar has been reported as having sold alcohol to minors, but there has been no investigation of these allegations. Both the bar and the restaurant are frequented by a variety of suspicious characters. The manager is new to the community and claims to have previously owned and managed a restaurant in Boise, Idaho.

   Be sure to include in your answer the types of surveillance and tracing techniques you might use in your investigation of the manager.

INVESTIGATIVE SKILL BUILDERS

Organizing and Maintaining Information

You receive a bulletin that, on route to the state prison, the prisoner bus has broken down and one of the inmates has escaped. The bulletin includes a description of the fugitive, as well as his last known home address and that of his parents. What are some of the techniques and sources of information you might use in an effort to locate and apprehend this fugitive?

Integrity/Honesty

An officer arrives at the home of a man believed to be the friend of a fugitive you (a police officer) are seeking. You have been tracking this fugitive for nearly two months. The fugitive is wanted for two forcible rapes and a rape-murder. When you ring the doorbell, nobody answers. You knock on the door, and it swings open. From the doorway, you call to see if anyone is home inside, but there is still no answer. As you glance into the living room, you notice a phone bill on the coffee table. You think to yourself, "This individual may have made a call to the fugitive, and there may be a record on the phone bill." You decide to enter the house and copy the phone numbers on the bill. When you finish writing down the numbers, you carefully replace the bill on the coffee table and leave. Using the telephone numbers, you are able to locate and apprehend the fugitive.

1. Given the seriousness of the crimes that the fugitive is believed to have committed, was the officer justified in entering the "friend's" house and writing down the phone numbers?
2. The phone numbers enabled the police to locate and apprehend the fugitive, but were police justified in obtaining the phone information in this manner?

Creative Thinking

You must locate a father who has taken his two children from their mother. The mother had been granted legal custody of the children after a divorce. You speak with the mother and obtain a list of her ex-husband's friends and relatives. You also learn that he is a master electrician by trade.

1. What strategies might you try in your effort to locate this man? Be creative in your approach.
2. How might knowing that the man is a master electrician help in your search?

Writing Reports

After completing this chapter, you will be able to:

1 Understand the importance of good investigative reports.
2 State the basic questions a good report should answer.
3 Explain some of the uses of police reports.
4 List and describe the characteristics of a good report.
5 Identify the major types of police operations reports.

COMMUNICATING THROUGH REPORTS

Effective communication is essential in all police work, and criminal investigation is no exception. If investigators are to communicate effectively on a witness stand, during interviews and interrogations, and among themselves, they need solid oral and written skills. Their oral skills should include clear enunciation, well-ordered and simple presentation, and suppression of **cop speak,** or police jargon. Written skills such as note taking and report writing are critical tools in the investigation of crimes. Among the more accurate elements of many television and movie versions of police work is the need to write reports. Underplayed in these fictionalized accounts is the damage that a poorly written report can do to the investigation or prosecution of a criminal case.

Police reports must set forth information in an accurate, concise, clear, and complete manner (Meier & Adams, 1999; Routledge, 2000). These reports serve as records of the investigation efforts and the criminal incident. Police reports are official records of the activities of a government agency and are used in a variety of ways. Every investigation should be complemented by an accurate report (Frazee & Davis, 2004). Report writing is so important that a number of police agencies in the United States have hired technical writers to coach their officers on proper writing skills.

Reports provide information to fellow investigators working on a case, to supervisors and administrators who may need to allocate resources for a case, and to the prosecuting attorney who may try the case. Reports may also be used in court to outline a case to the jury. Investigative reports play a key role throughout the criminal justice process. They begin as notes taken during the preliminary investigation, continue as records of the follow-up investigation, and emerge again during the trial and perhaps even during an appeal. Because reports sometimes create the foundation for a criminal prosecution, it is important that investigators are mindful about how reports are produced (Frazee & Davis, 2004; Hess & Thaiss, 1998).

In the double-murder trial of O. J. Simpson, the defense initially sought to impugn the police investigation by showing that investigators had botched their reports. The defense team claimed that the investigators had failed to maintain an accurate chronology of events, that specific forms were not always filled out completely, and that contrary to department policy plain sheets of paper had been substituted for certain forms.

These concerns regarding report writing may seem to be nit-picking to the uninitiated, but even minor flaws such as these could damage a prosecution. Reports communicate factual information, describe events and actions, and frequently even state motives. If there are errors in police reports, a judge or jury may infer that there are errors in the facts or mistakes in procedures.

cop speak Specialized vocabulary, or jargon, used by police.

Report-Writing Guidelines

One cannot take a magic potion to become a proficient writer; however, a number of structural elements are typically included in a well-written report. These elements answer six basic questions: who, what, when, where, how, and why (Hess & Wrobleski, 2002). Answering these questions ensures that the necessary elements of the investigation are included in the report and that the report will at least be acceptable. You may recall from Chapter 2 that these are the same six questions that must be answered as investigators take notes in the field.

Who were the People Involved? Who are the complainant, the victim, the witnesses, and, if known, the suspects? who are the investigators in the case, and what are the names of the officers who first arrived on and secured the scene?

What Happened?   What was the crime? What events surrounded the criminal event? If there are victims, in what ways were they injured or victimized? If property was stolen, a detailed account and description of missing items or objects should be included. The report should also include such information as the actions of suspects; the evidence located; any special knowledge, skills, or expertise needed to accomplish the crime; anything reported that was not substantiated by facts or physical evidence; and further actions that may be warranted.

When did the Crime Occur?   At what time of day did the crime take place? What was the day of the week? The month? When was the matter discovered and reported?

Where did the Crime Occur?   It is important to provide correct information concerning the address of the crime location in the report—including street name, street number, and type of building (house, apartment building, store, warehouse, etc.). Telling exactly where in a given location a crime or a portion of a criminal event took place is also important. If a criminal matter occurred outdoors, the exact location should be recorded, with stationary objects used as reference points for measurement. For example, a report might say an event occurred 12 feet west of the Oak Park street sign on the west curb of Maple Street.

How was the Crime Committed?   An investigator should include all information that shows or suggests how the event took place. This may include the *modus operandi* as well as information about how the suspect or suspects arrived or fled the scene. The report should also contain information, if available, regarding how the suspect may have obtained information necessary to commit the crime (for example, lock combinations, alarm system details, or floor plans).

Why was the Crime Committed?   Information on motives is usually nothing more than deductions based on experience, evidence, and available facts; in other words, motives are frequently based on conjecture. Nonetheless, this question should not be omitted or overlooked. Consider such things as how much time elapsed before the crime was reported, why a witness is so eager to point out a guilty party, why the victim was so afraid to speak with the police, and why a particular suspect committed this crime against this particular party. It is also worthwhile to consider why a suspect chose a particular victim over another or chose one location or building over another.

In some cases, such as robbery or burglary, it may be assumed that the crime was committed to obtain possessions, most likely to sell for cash. Certain crimes, such as traffic accidents, seldom have motives. For other crimes, such as homicides, a lengthy investigation may be required to uncover the motive. Information on motives may not be available for preliminary reports for a variety of reasons.

Answering these six basic questions provides a kind of skeleton on which the reporting officer can hang the facts of the case. Naturally, the order in which these questions are presented and answered will vary with the facts of the case and the reporting officer's own writing style (Guffrey, 2004; Hess & Worbleski, 2002). In some cases, it may not be possible to answer all six questions. Furthermore, these questions should not be literally transcribed in a report. Nowhere in the report does one actually write "Where did the crime occur?" and the answer to that question. The questions are a guide, especially for inexperienced report writers, to ensure that all necessary information is provided in an investigative report.

When writing reports, as with all other phases of police work, good judgment, a good working knowledge of procedures and department policy, and some practice are

FOCUS ON TECHNOLOGY

REPORT-WRITING AIDS

Police agencies use a variety of technologies to make report writing more efficient. A laptop or notebook computer enables officers to input crime scene data, access department records, or search computerized databases from their patrol car. In some departments officers can use a cellular telephone to dictate their reports from a cruiser to a central processor, thereby allowing them to remain in the field.

necessary elements for success. As in all writing, consider your *audience*. As an officer or investigator, your audience is likely to include other officers, supervisors, administrators, and prosecuting attorneys. Whenever possible, get advice from more experienced writers about improving your writing skills.

Tests of a Report

For reports to be useful in an investigation, they must have certain basic characteristics. A checklist of traits of a solid report would include clarity, pertinence, brevity, comprehensiveness, accuracy, and a long list of other elements. All the recommendations would be relevant to good report writing. However, all these principles can be inferred from three simple tests of a report:

1. Is the report complete, concise, clear, and accurate?
2. Will an oral explanation be required to explain what is already included in the written report?
3. Can the statements made in the report be proved, corroborated, or demonstrated by evidence?

If you answer "No" to the first and third questions and "Yes" to the second, your report is not yet ready for others to see. You want a "Yes" to question 1, a "No" to question 2, and a "Yes" to question 3.

The Value of Reports

Reports provide the data needed to investigate and apprehend criminals and to solve crimes. In some departments, officers come back to the station and type their reports on typewriters or computers. Others use computers to input their reports directly into the department's information storage system and database. Some departments have a digital dictation system, in which officers use a telephone to reach a special digital computer processor that handles the officer's voice data like data keyed from a computer (CNN.com, 2003; Manning, 2000). However the data are stored, the reports are a valuable asset to the department and perform the following functions:

- Provide a written record and a readily accessible memory bank of police business and information
- Refresh an officer's memory regarding further investigation and administration
- Provide a means of controlling communication throughout the police department and its associated agencies
- Provide a database of information for solving similar crimes, perhaps committed by the same criminal
- Furnish a base of accurate statistical information on which decisions about resource allocation and policy may be based
- Aid in identifying criminal patterns, which in turn allows the development of intervention plans
- Aid in assessing the effectiveness of personnel distribution and analyzing overall agency operations
- Assist in identifying unusual or periodic intra-agency problems
- Assist in documenting needs for budget requests and justifications
- Produce statistical information to be contributed to local, state, or FBI crime databases
- Provide a vital tool for a department in carrying out its varied objectives
- Provide a source of accurate, detailed, and succinct information to prosecute a criminal when a law has been violated

In addition to these benefits, reports permit accountability, oversight, and supervision, both inside and outside the agency (Pailca, 2003). Outside the agency, police provide information to their respective communities concerning the local crime rates and efforts planned or undertaken to reduce these rates. Internally, reports provide supervisors and administrators with information necessary for considering an agency's policies, resources, procedures, and all other matters concerning the work in the organization. Reports also provide means for evaluating the effectiveness of special units or personnel. In all these situations, reports may serve the additional purpose of interpreting facts, transmitting information, analyzing problems or situations, and educating employees and others about policies and how these policies affect the organization and the community.

CHARACTERISTICS OF A GOOD REPORT

A report may contain all the necessary information, but if it is poorly written, points may be lost in the prose. Some officers dread report writing and find it difficult to master. Others seem to be gifted in this area and create effective, well-written documents. Police reporting, however, is not an innate trait that some officers are born with and others are not. Similarly, while some officers speak more effectively than others, their ability may not translate into good writing skills. One can learn to write effective reports by practice and by following some basic rules. Reports should be complete, concise, clear, and accurate (Brown & Cox, 1998). By directing attention to these characteristics, an officer can make writing a more positive experience.

Completeness

Completeness means that the report contains all pertinent information. Partial facts create a false picture of the events. Negative results of investigative leads should be included, along with more successful ones. For example, if an investigator searched a suspect's room and found nothing, this information should be included in the report. Having the information in the report will indicate which actions have been taken and which have not, which can help avoid duplication of efforts and wasting time.

To evaluate your report, have a fellow officer read it. If the other officer has questions about what you have described in the report, needs to have certain points clarified, or does not understand the sequence of events, revise your report. Unanswered questions or confused descriptions create problems for a person who may not have been at the scene or present during an interview with a witness. Consider the follow-up investigator or the prosecuting attorney. Will he or she need to call in the morning because information in the report is not complete? Will follow-up investigators or the prosecuting attorney be able to locate listed witnesses from the information presented in the report? Will follow-up investigators have to duplicate any work that has already been accomplished because it is not mentioned in the report? The report writer (in this case likely the initial officer on the crime scene) should ask him- or herself these kinds of questions before turning in a finished report.

One commonly overlooked piece of information that should be included in contemporary reports when possible is the subject's e-mail address. In most police departments each officer has an e-mail account, and follow-up investigators can use e-mail to correspond with witnesses and victims. When the investigator only needs to ask a simple question or confirm a statement, e-mail can be efficient. An added benefit is that e-mail interviews can be printed out and attached to the supplementary report. E-mail correspondence is a little like having a written statement instantly delivered. Naturally, the use of e-mail in this regard is not always feasible, but if an e-mail address is available, it should be recorded in the initial report (Pasquale, 2006).

Conciseness

Reports should be as *concise* as possible while retaining all essential features and details in an understandable manner. Reports should be written as a narrative but should eliminate nonessential modifiers or descriptors. Similarly, technical jargon and unnecessary words should be avoided. Sentences should be kept simple and direct and in active rather than passive voice. Long, convoluted sentences are confusing and sometimes difficult to follow (Frazee & Davis, 2004). Do not use meaningless or unnecessary words and phrases. For example, one could write, "I observed a very nice reddish or dark pinkish kind of colored big car pass at a very, very high rate of speed, maybe as fast as 75 mph." Or one could write a more concise version: "I observed a red Ford Mustang traveling at an estimated speed of 75 mph."

An inexperienced police report writer might practice by writing a composition of at least seventy-five words on any police topic. The description should then be corrected and condensed to a narrative. After completing this task, the writer should seek advice and suggestions from a more experienced report writer about how to improve the practice report.

Clarity

A report must exhibit *clarity;* that is, it must clearly explain exactly what the officer saw, heard, and did. Short active-voice sentences lead to clear meaning and understanding.

For example, one might write, "When the officer arrived, the victim was found lying there with the gun next to him having been fired once." A more active and clearer version might be written as follows: "Officer Thomas Jones arrived to find the victim, Morris Kupnick, lying on the floor. To the left of Kupnick's head, Officer Jones found a blue-barreled revolver with one round discharged." While brevity is important, it should not be accomplished at the expense of clarity. Clarity can best be accomplished by the use of Standard English, including good sentence structure, correct punctuation, accurate spelling, proper capitalization, and standard paragraphing. The words and phrases selected should enable a reader to easily understand the report. Errors in punctuation, misplaced pronouns, or words used incorrectly detract from the value of the report and could cast doubt on an officer's testimony in a court trial (Frazee & Davis, 2004; Godwin, 1993; Goodman, 2007).

Accuracy

Reports must demonstrate *accuracy* to be valuable. Concentrate on specifics and avoid generalities. For example, one might write, "The suspect is big and carried several weapons on his person." A more accurate statement might be, "The suspect, Martin Sayre, is approximately 5 feet 9 inches tall and weighs approximately 250 pounds. After being advised of his rights, Sayre was searched by Officer McCarry. Officer McCarry found that Sayre was concealing on his person, a .32-caliber derringer, a .38-caliber Smith & Wesson revolver, a folding pocket knife with a single 4-inch blade, and a 6-inch length of steel pipe."

It is equally important not to confuse fact with hearsay. Information reported must be only what actually transpired and has been verified by the investigation. Reports should not contain conclusions that the officer has made by supposition or guesswork. Nor should the report contain an officer's personal opinion about the matter. Personal opinions tend to lessen the value of a report. If one is included, a clear visual signal should indicate that it is the opinion of the investigator: "It is the opinion of the reporting officer that . . ." It is important to remember that every suspect deserves a fair and unbiased day in court and that in the United States a person is considered innocent until proven guilty in a court of law. Describing a suspect in an inappropriate manner or giving unsolicited opinions can taint this aspect of due process.

sexist language Insensitive, politically incorrect language used in reference to gender or gender issues, occupations, and the like.

Conscientious efforts also must be made to avoid **sexist language.** Neutral or inclusive wording can usually describe the event or situation without creating a sexist atmosphere. When describing occupations with the traditional ending *—man,* select gender-neutral titles. For example, instead of using the label *mailman* or *policeman,* substitute *letter carrier* or *postal worker* for the former and *police officer* for the latter (Gastil, 1998; Swift & Miller, 2001). Use proper names rather than the pronoun "he" or the expressions "he or she," "him or her," and so forth. Gender-specific references can also be avoided by writing in the third-person plural and using proper nouns when possible (Lester & Beason, 2004).

affected terms Words or phrases that convey negative judgments or carry negative or pejorative attitudes about something.

In addition to avoiding sexist language, one should avoid **affected terms.** Affected terms are words or phrases that convey negative judgments or carry negative or pejorative attitudes about something. For example, one should not write about the "criminal," the "rapist," or the "murderer;" each of these terms conveys a harsh and negative connotation about the category of behavior it represents and could be viewed as biased. Instead, refer to the "suspect," a more neutral term. After a warrant has been issued, reports may refer to suspects as "defendants." A juvenile or a person not involved with the criminal charges may be referred to as "an interested party" or as a "subject."

It should also be noted that as a matter of practice one should not use profanity in reports. Some departments permit the use of profanity in a report if it is an exact quote from the suspect or witness; otherwise such quotes may be kept in the officer's personal notes. In formal police reports in agencies where even the direct quoting of profanity is banned, blanks can be used. For instance, one might write: Suspect Peters stated, "Yes I killed the _____ [profane expletive]." Use abbreviations for profanity, such as SOB or other epithets—unless it is an exact quote. It is nearly always sufficient (with the possible exception of a capital crime) to say, "Peters called Hogan a profane name, and Hogan struck Peters in the mouth." or "Calhoun was yelling loudly and profanely at Officer Jones and Carter." However, the exact words of Peters and Calhoun should be recorded in the officer's notes in the event that a judge in court wants to hear exactly what was said in the defendant's or victim's own words.

The decision to prosecute a case or to continue an investigation is frequently made solely on the basis of a criminal investigation report. Absolute, unbiased accuracy is essential. Care should be taken when writing up field notes to ensure that later reports indicate correct times, dates, names of all parties involved, complete addresses, phone numbers, and, when possible, e-mail addresses; contain carefully crafted descriptions of suspects and the crime scene; and list all items of evidence and their chain of custody. As well, all investigators and their activities should be properly annotated.

Errors or omissions in reports raise doubts about the thoroughness, accuracy, reliability, and, indeed, the truthfulness of the report writer. A suspect's fate often hinges on the accuracy of the information in a police report.

Mechanical Elements Common to Police Reports

Police reports are typically based on the various field notes taken by an officer or officers during the preliminary investigation. There are several methods for taking field notes; some are fairly commonly known and others are unique to particular jurisdictions (Meier & Adams, 1999). Field note methods all share at least one common trait: They provide a guide to ensure that the necessary information for the report has been gathered. One can think of field notes as pieces of a puzzle and the final written report as the finished picture. One big difference between the field notes an officer or investigator writes and the final investigative report is that the field notes are largely written for an audience of one—namely, the officer writing them. The investigative report is directed to a much broader audience, which may include other officers and investigators, supervisors, the prosecuting attorney, the defense counsel, the judge, and in some cases even members of the jury.

The structure and the content of a police report may vary. For example, departments may have different policies on report contents, diverse needs or uses for portions of the information, varying levels of computer-entry sophistication, and different statistical or informational requirements. Overarching these disparate departmental needs, however, are certain broad categories of information that are required for the type of report being written (Rupp, 2004). We look at these categories next.

Names The names (real names and aliases) of complainants, witnesses, possible suspects, and any parties of interest related to the criminal event should be included in field notes and in the final report. The names of individuals involved should be listed first. The sequence should be last name, first name, and middle initial, if any. In many departments, the family name is written in capital letters: for example, "WILSON, John Edward." In some departments, names are written entirely in capital letters: "WILSON JOHN EDWARD." This convention can help a reader find a name in a length report, but capitalization should conform to the department's policy.

Be aware that in some cultures the order of names may be reversed. The family name is first and the given name is second in many Asian cultures; this is also the case in some Middle Eastern and African cultures. For example, if a person from mainland China has the name Kang Xie, the family name is actually Kang, but if the person is from Hong Kong, the family name may be Xie. It is important to determine the cultural context of the subject's name when writing up the full report.

The designations Mr., Miss, Ms., and Mrs. are not used with names in a report. For instance, it would not be correct to use "*Mr.* John Paul JONES," or "*Mrs.* John Paul JONES." Instead, one would expect to find the names written as. "Jones, John Paul," or "JOHN PAUL JONES," and "JONES, Mary Jane (Mrs.)" or "MARY JANE JONES (Mrs.)." It is preferable to use the full middle name of a person rather than only the middle initial. When a middle name is actually only a single initial, it should be enclosed in quotation marks, as in MOORE, Alice, "P," or Alice "P." Moore. If the subject has no middle name, indicate this as "MOORE, Alice (NMN)" or "ALICE (NMN) MOORE."

Race and Sex Race and ethnicity should always be presented in a proper, nonderogatory manner. Race is ordinarily indicated by abbreviations, such as *W* for Caucasian (white), *B* for African American (black), *H* for Hispanic, *A* for Asian, *I* for American Indian, and *U* for unknown. Sex is always designated by *M* for male, and *F* for female. The usual sequence is race first, then sex. A listing of *W/F* refers to a Caucasian female.

Age For the report, the age of a person should be based on his or her last birthday. Typically, the first reference to a person's age consists of his or her *date of birth* (DOB), if known. When such information is not known, as in the case of an unidentified deceased victim or an uncooperative suspect, age may be recorded as an approximation or a limited age span: for example, "The victim appeared to be approximately 40 years old" or "The victim appeared to be 35–40 years of age." Again, age should be handled in a proper and neutral manner, without derogatory or unwarranted reference to senility. Dates of birth should be written in the following sequence: *month/day/year.*

Addresses It is important to obtain, and when possible confirm, the addresses of all crime scene victims, suspects, and witnesses. Each address, whether residence or business, should include the street number and an apartment, suite, condominium, or room number if there is one. When such detail is not available, a general description of the area where the business or residence is located should be obtained (stating cross streets and so forth) so that the location can be identified and found later if necessary. Ask for identification with the proper address affixed to it to confirm the addresses given.

Telephone Numbers One should always get as many telephone number contacts as possible, so it will be easier to reach the victims and witnesses. Be sure to include the area code, home and office numbers (including any possible extensions), and the cellular phone and pager numbers, if available.

E-mail Addresses Most people today have at least one e-mail address; many people have several. As mentioned previously in this chapter, this can be a fast and efficient way of contacting a witness or victim to arrange a meeting or to ask a simple question. Many people have wireless Internet capacities on their telephones, and they may even check their e-mail while on the run.

Descriptions of People Whenever there is a witness or a victim of a crime, it may be possible to obtain a description of a suspect. Some report forms contain checklists for recording a person's physical description. The following informational items are typically included when writing up a personal description: height, weight, hair color and general characteristics (e.g., wavy, long, short, fringe, bald), eye characteristics and color, build, complexion, facial hair, identifiable marks (e.g., scars, birthmarks, tattoos, a limp, amputations), teeth (color, gaps, shape, etc.), unusual mannerisms or voice, and style and color of dress.

Additionally, in a felony report, under the heading "Details of the Crime," investigators should provide the following information about the suspect if they are aware of it: education; occupation (present and past); hobbies; information about parents, siblings, relatives, known associates, and friends; military service; Social Security number; marital status and wife's maiden name, if applicable; and any other pertinent information.

Descriptions of Property When property is taken, a complete and accurate inventory and description of items may assist in their recovery. If property has been damaged or destroyed, a thorough description may be required by an insurance agency. Whenever property is involved in the crime, the minimum description should include the following: quantity; kind; physical description, including model, style, design, shape, size, and serial number, if known; color; condition, including age and apparent wear; approximate value at the time of the loss (indicate how this was determined, such as "owner's estimate," "receipts," "written appraisal"); trade name; and any unique markings. The owner should also be asked if he or she has a picture of the item; many homeowners photograph their possessions for insurance purposes.

Stolen property should be listed in orderly groups. Property that can be distinguished by identification or serial numbers should be grouped together. Items that are listed by brand or trade names should be in a separate group. Articles that have neither identification numbers nor trade names can be placed in yet another group. When recording the information on the crime report, give every item on each list a unique number. In a separate column describe each item, and in a third column show the value of each item.

All items should be described as completely as possible, with emphasis on special features of identification—even when the manufacturer's name is not known and the item bears no identification marks or numbers. For instance, an important identifying piece of information about a stolen gold necklace may be that the barrel catch has been resoldered. Knowing that a man's gold wedding ring has the words "Love is Forever, *Grace*" engraved on the inside could help identify the article when it is recovered.

Descriptions of Vehicles When a vehicle is involved in a crime, a description of it should be carefully worked out. In addition to a general description of the vehicle's condition, the report should contain the following basic information: the vehicle's year, make, and model; body type (e.g., coupe, sedan, convertible, two-door, three-door hatch); color; license number; motor number or vehicle identification number (VIN); accessories; distinguishing marks or characteristics, including upholstery, interior of vehicle, dashboard, seat covers, ornamentation; registration information; and owner's name, address, telephone number, and, if available, e-mail address.

Description of Physical Areas All pertinent information regarding an area where a crime has occurred should be included in a description entered on the crime report. The data should include various dimensions, typography, vegetation, access and egress, types of buildings or structures, and even the size and height of various buildings or structures.

FIGURE 9.1 Military System of 100 Hours

Clock Time	100-Hour Time	Clock Time	100-Hour Time
12:01–12:59 a.m.	0001–0059	12:01–12:59 p.m.	1201–1259
1:00–1:59 a.m.	0100–0159	1:00–1:59 p.m.	1300–1359
2:00–2:59 a.m.	0200–0259	2:00–2:59 p.m.	1400–1459
3:00–3:59 a.m.	0300–0359	3:00–3:59 p.m.	1500–1559
4:00–4:59 a.m.	0400–0459	4:00–4:59 p.m.	1600–1659
5:00–5:59 a.m.	0500–0559	5:00–5:59 p.m.	1700–1759
6:00–6:59 a.m.	0600–0659	6:00–6:59 p.m.	1800–1859
7:00–7:59 a.m.	0700–0759	7:00–7:59 p.m.	1900–1959
8:00–8:59 a.m.	0800–0859	8:00–8:59 p.m.	2000–2059
9:00–9:59 a.m.	0900–0959	9:00–9:59 p.m.	2100–2159
10:00–10:59 a.m.	1000–1059	10:00–10:59 p.m.	2200–2259
11:00–11:59 a.m.	1100–1159	11:00–11:59 p.m.	2300–2359
12:00 noon	1200	12:00 midnight	2400

Dates   The written sequence for dates should be *month/day/year,* using two digits for each. For instance, one should write September 7, 2007, as 09/07/07. Officers need to be careful when recording dates. Errors in dates can create havoc when discovered during a trial and can draw into question the reliability of other aspects of the report.

Time   Most police agencies use the military system of 100 hours in their reports (Figure 9.1). The only exception is when reporting the exact words of a witness or subject regarding time.

Format of a Report

Reports and reporting forms used by police agencies vary considerably. Differences in reporting forms are the result of department needs, requirements, policies, data collecting strategies, and preferences. In spite of the variations in reporting forms, the information sought by officers regarding crime detection, apprehension of criminals, solving crimes, and rendering police services is essentially the same. Many report forms used by police agencies contain two major parts (Figure 9.2), a form section and a narrative section.

form section   A boxed section of a police report form designed for fill-in and check-off informational items.

The first section of most police report forms is a printed **form section** that can vary in length and content. In some departments report forms appear as templates in a computer program, allowing officers to fill them in directly on a computer. Typically, these forms consist of labeled fill-in blocks and blank spaces that call for specific short or check-off responses from the officer completing the form. Whether printed or electronic, the spaces and blocks guide the officer through important information that should be included on the report.

FIGURE 9.2 Major Parts of Police Reports

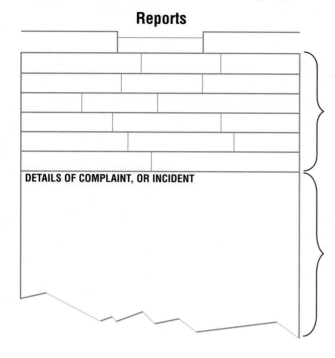

Reports

DETAILS OF COMPLAINT, OR INCIDENT

Part I
Information required:
In crime reports, this
section provides statistical
data for local, state, and
federal computer analysis.

Part II
Narrative portion:
This section states
all the facts, establishes
the crime, identifies
the suspect, and aids
in prosecution.

The types of information required in the form section of the report generally include the case or file number; the date and time of the report; the type of offense and the classification if applicable; the date and time the incident was reported; the name of the victim, complainant, or source of the complaint; addresses; telephone numbers; the officer(s) involved; and descriptions of suspects and vehicles. It is very important that all the labeled spaces provided on the form section of the report be filled in. When information requested on a form blank is not known, the word "unknown" should be written in the space. This assures a reader that the information was not overlooked but was not known by the reporting officer. In most agencies, separate forms are used for felonies or misdemeanors. A felony crime report is typically longer and has a more detailed form section than does the misdemeanor form or other nonfelony report forms.

The second portion of a police report form is the **narrative section,** or body of the report. This section sets forth the details of the matter being reported. There are no hard-and-fast rules about how to begin the narrative. Many officers prefer to begin with the suspect's first known act and to record successively each subsequent act separately in sequence. It is important throughout the narrative to describe exactly what each witness saw, heard, or did. In the narrative portion of the report, officers must be mindful to refer to individuals as suspects, witnesses, and victims. Reference, for example, may be made to witness KAZINSKI, suspect BOURNE, defendant NOOJIN, or victim MYERS.

The narrative should be direct and clear, without tangents. Details of the incident, descriptions of evidence, explanations of who found what and where it was found, descriptions of suspects, and dispositions of the case should be carefully spelled out in the narrative section of the form. All details connected with the incident should be set forth. Stolen property should be itemized and described completely and accurately, and its value should be listed (according to the owner's estimate) or approximated.

narrative section A lined or blank section of a police report form designed for detailed descriptions and accounts of events.

synopsis A summary or abstract of a larger body of writing, such as a police report.

Some agencies require a summary, or **synopsis,** of the full report as the first item in the narrative section. Statements made in the synopsis must be substantiated by information set forth in the full report.

TYPES OF REPORTS

Reports and reporting forms vary considerably in local, state, and federal agencies. Variations occur because of such factors as the responsibility and jurisdiction of an individual department or agency, the nature of the subject matter, and agency preferences and particular needs. Regardless of the variations and differences, police agencies tend to concern themselves with four basic categories of forms and reports: internal business-related reports, technical and specialized equipment reports, intelligence reports, and day-to-day operations reports. Operations reports are most commonly prepared by officers and include misdemeanor and/or miscellaneous reports, felony reports, follow-up reports, arrest reports, and vehicle accident reports. Each of these types of operations reports is described more fully in the following sections. The reports depicted are only samples of reports that a law enforcement agency might use.

Misdemeanor and/or Miscellaneous Reports

complaint or incident report A police report written to document events surrounding misdemeanor and miscellaneous incidents.

Misdemeanor reports record all lesser crimes and miscellaneous incidents. Sometimes such a report is called a **complaint report** or an **incident report.** The complaint report contains such identifying data as the nature of the complaint; the code violation, if any; the file number; the date and time the complaint was received; the location of the incident; names of the victims, witnesses, and subjects involved; addresses, telephone numbers, and e-mails of all persons involved; and descriptions of suspects.

Occasionally officers may encounter obstacles in completing a report. Frequently, victims of minor crimes do not want a report made and indicate that even if one were drawn up, they would not sign it. Victims are often unwilling to sign a complaint on a misdemeanor because they "do not want to cause any trouble." It is important, though, to record the information concerning the misdemeanor for the following reasons:

- It provides intelligence for detectives and uniformed officers about the types of crimes being committed in the area and can serve as a database from which to establish a crime pattern.
- Victims may change their minds later or may discover additional loss or damage.
- Most insurance claims cannot be processed unless a police report has been filed.
- Known suspects for unreported crimes may be sought for similar crimes in reported cases.

A sample completed misdemeanor and/or miscellaneous report involving a prowler complaint appears in Figure 9.3.

After completing a misdemeanor or miscellaneous report, an investigator may sometimes determine that the incident is actually a felony, an attempted felony, or a crime that requires filing a felony report. Under such circumstances, in the narrative section of the misdemeanor report, often titled "Details of the Incident," the reporting office should write, "See crime report." The crime report or felony report should then

FIGURE 9.4a Felony Crime Report

Robbery		**1. CASE NO.** 07-1024
	Felony Crime Report **Jackson Police Department**	

2.CODE SECTION 211a PC	**3. CRIME** Armed Robbery		**4.CLASSIFICATION** Market w/revolver		**5. REPORT AREA** 5
6.DATE AND TIME OCCURRED - DAY 06/29/07 0700 Friday		**7.DATE AND TIME REPORTED** 06/29/07	**8. LOCATION OF OCCURRENCE** 100 North "C" St., Jackson 92410		
9. VICTIM'S NAME LAST, FIRST, MIDDLE (FIRM IF BUSINESS) McDaniel's Market			**10. RESIDENCE ADDRESS**		**11. RES. PHONE**
12. OCCUPATION Grocery Store	**13.RACE-SEX**	**14. AGE**	**15.DOB**	**16. BUSINESS ADDRESS (SCHOOL IF JUVENILE)** Same as 8	**17. BUS. PHONE** 555-1505

CODES FOR V = VICTIM W = WITNESS P = PARENT RP = REPORTING PARTY DC = DISCOVERED CRIME **BOXES 20 AND 30**					**18.CHECK IF MORE NAMES IN CONTINUATION** X
19. NAME - LAST, FIRST, MIDDLE McDaniel, John Joseph			**20. CODE** RP	**21. RESIDENCE ADDRESS** 1234 Elm Avenue	**22. RESIDENCE PHONE** 555-3210
23. OCCUPATION Owner	**24. RACE -SEX** MWA	**25. AGE** 54	**26. DOB** 9/9/52	**27. BUSINESS ADDRESS (SCHOOL IF JUVENILE)** Same as 8	**28. BUSINESS PHONE** 555-1505
29. NAME - LAST, FIRST, MIDDLE Johnson, Mary Lois			**30. CODE** W	**31. RESIDENCE ADDRESS** 955 North "C" Jackson	**32. RESIDENCE PHONE** 555-1433
33. OCCUPATION Housewife	**34.RACE-SEX** WFA	**35. AGE** 48	**36.DOB** 12/12/58	**37. BUSINESS ADDRESS (SCHOOL IF JUVENILE)** None	**38. BUSINESS PHONE**

MODUS OPERANDI   (SEE INSTRUCTIONS)

39. DESCRIBE CHARACTERISTICS OF PREMISE AND AREA WHERE OFFENSE OCCURRED
Large groc. mkt. in downtown area next to hotels. Alley in rear, Pkg. lot on E. side

40. DESCRIBE BRIEFLY HOW OFFENSE WAS COMMITTED
Climbs fire escape on adjoining hotel, jumps to roof of mkt., drills out 20" hole in roof, lowers self

via rope to floor of store, waits till opening, forces mgr. to open safe, locks victims in walk-in
cooler, leaves through rear alley exit.

41. DESCRIBE WEAPON, INSTRUMENT, EQUIPMENT, TRICK , DEVICE OR FORCE USED
2" B/S Rev. 1-1/4" drill, chisel, hammer, rope

42. MOTIVE - TYPE OF PROPERTY TAKEN OR OTHER REASON FOR OFFENSE
Money & Checks

43. ESTIMATED LOSS VALUE AND/OR EXTENT OF INJURIES - MINOR, MAJOR
$8,110.

44. WHAT DID SUSPECT/ S SAY - NOTE PECULIARITIES
"This is a robbery, behave and you won't get hurt. Get over here 'fass'."

45. VICTIM'S ACTIVITY JUST PRIOR TO AND/OR DURING OFFENSE
Opening Store

46. TRADEMARK - OTHER DISTINCTIVE ACTIVITY OF SUSPECT/S
Ate on premises, drank Vodka

47. VEHICLE USED - LICENSE NO. - YEAR - MAKE - MODEL - COLORS (OTHER IDENTIFYING CHARACTERISTICS)
None seen

48. SUSPECT NO. 1 (LAST, FIRST, MIDDLE) S-1 Name Unknown	**49. RACE- SEX** WMA	**50. AGE** 30-35	**51. HT.** 6'	**52. WT.** 200	**53.HAIR** Dk	**54.EYES** brn	**55. ID. NO. OR DOB**	**56. ARRESTED** YES ☐ NO ☒

57. ADDRESS, CLOTHING AND OTHER IDENTIFYING MARKS OR CHARACTERISTICS
Work clothes, wore flashy ring with large brilliant stone

58. SUSPECT NO. 2 (LAST, FIRST, MIDDLE) S-2 Name Unknown	**59. RACE- SEX** WMA	**60. AGE** 30-35	**61. HT.** 5'8	**62. WT.** 180	**63.HAIR** blk	**64.EYES** brn	**65. ID. NO. OR DOB**	**66. ARRESTED** YES ☐ NO ☒

67. ADDRESS, CLOTHING AND OTHER IDENTIFYING MARKS OR CHARACTERISTICS Work clothes, Army type boots, small blue dot left cheek under eye	**68. CHECK IF MORE NAMES IN CONTINUATION**

REPORTING OFFICERS Samons #18 / Jacobs #35	**RECORDING OFFICER** Jacobs	**TYPED BY** mmk	**DATE AND TIME** 06/29/07 1300	**ROUTED BY** Owens

FURTHER ACTION ☒ YES / ☐ NO	☒ DETECTIVE / ☐ JUVENILE / ☒ DIST. ATTNY / ☒ SQ./P.D.	☒ C11 / ☐ PATROL / ☐ OTHER_____ / ☐ OTHER_____	**REVIEWED BY** Moore, R.L. Lt	**DATE** 6/29/07

FIGURE 9.4a (*Continued*)

Robbery			69.CASE NO. 07-1024
	(2) **Jackson Police Department**		

70.CODE SECTION 211a PC	71. CRIME Armed Robbery	72. CLASSIFICATION Market w/revolver		
73.VICTIM'S LAST NAME, FIRST, MIDDLE (FIRM IF BUS.) McDaniel's Market		74. ADDRESS 100 North "C" St.	RESIDENCE □ BUSINESS ☒	75. PHONE 555-1505

W 2 RENTS FROM, Josephine MARY, Rm 410 Shasta Hotel, 555-1349
    Beauty Operator, WFA, 52, 2/18/55, Classic Beauty Salon, 19th and K Sts.; Phone 555-1000

06/29/07 0700 RP after unlocking front door of store, proceeded to the rear storeroom where
    he was confronted by two unknown suspects. S-1, the taller of the two, pointed a 2" B/S
    revolver at RP stating—"This is a robbery, behave and you won't get hurt, get over here
    fast (the word fast slurred to sound like 'fass')."
S-2, an African-American, short and stocky, did not speak. At that time W-1 entered the
market at which time S-2 escorted her to the rear of the store where RP and S-1 were
standing.

S-1 then ordered RP into rear office where he commanded RP to open the floor safe
(combination Mosler) and get the money. $8,110 in used currency and checks given
to S-1. (Three $100 bills, two $50 bills and about 20 checks were included).

Subsequently, S-1 ordered RP and W-1 into the walk-in refrigerator at which time the
door was closed, the outside strap latch locked, and a stick of wood put in the hasp to
secure the lock. After about 24 minutes, RP succeeded in opening the door.

Entrance to the market was gained by cutting a 20" square hole through the roof. A
series of holes were cut through the tar paper and wood with a $1\frac{1}{2}$" bit. Some holes
overlapped; where they did not, the wood between the holes appeared to have been cut
with a chisel. Two sets of shoeprints were observed leading from the edge of the roof to
the hole, but did not return. It was noted that the Shasta Hotel is located adjacent to the
market. The hotel has a fire escape opposite the edge of the roof where the shoeprints start.
In the market attic, trails in the dust led from a point just below the hole in the roof to a
trap door in the store's ceiling. The trap door had been closed at the end of the previous
business day, but was now open. From this point there was a 12' drop below to the open
storeroom floor. Dust, scuff marks, and partial shoeprints of the same pattern observed on
the roof were found on the linoleum floor just below the trap door.

Two $\frac{1}{2}$" holes, 4'8$\frac{1}{2}$", and the other 5'2" above floor level had been drilled through the
storeroom wall which faces the front of the store.

REPORTING OFFICERS Samons #18/ Jacobs #35	RECORDING OFFICER Jacobs	TYPED BY mmk	DATE AND TIME 06/29/07	ROUTED BY Owens

FURTHER ACTION	☒ YES □ NO	COPIES TO	☒ DETECTIVE □ JUVENILE ☒ DIST. ATTNY □ SQ./P.D.	☒ C11 □ PATROL □ OTHER___ □ OTHER___	
			REVIEWED BY Moore, R. L. Lt.		DATE 06/29/07

FIGURE 9.4a *(Continued)*

Robbery		69.CASE NO.
		07-1024

(3)
Jackson Police Department

70.CODE SECTION	71. CRIME	72. CLASSIFICATION
211a PC	Armed Robbery	Market w/revolver

73.VICTIM'S NAME LAST, FIRST, MIDDLE (FIRM IF BUS.)	74. ADDRESS	RESIDENCE	BUSINESS X	75. PHONE
McDaniel's Market	100 North "C" St.			555-1505

Fresh sawdust and plaster were found on the floor on both sides of the wall, just below the holes. Remnants of three packages of Gallo salami, three empty milk cartons, a half-pint of Samarov Vodka and a brown plastic satchel were found in the storeroom. A 16" length of 1/2" hemp rope tied to its handle was found in the satchel along with the following tools: a wood brace, four wood bits, a carpenter's hammer, wood chisel, linoleum knife, 12" crow bar, pair of side cutters, and a keyhole saw. The tools, satchel, and rope were foreign to the crime scene and were not recognized by anyone who had legal access to the property.

W-2   A guest of the Shasta Hotel reported that at about 0200 hours she got up to take an Alka-Seltzer and saw a black man and a white man ascending the fire escape of the hotel. She returned to bed and did not notify anyone. W-2 advised that she did not believe she could identify either of these suspects.

PROPERTY REPORT ATTACHED.

Investigation continuing.

REPORTING OFFICERS	RECORDING OFFICER	TYPED BY	DATE AND TIME	ROUTED BY
Samons #18/ Jacobs #35	Jacobs	mmk	06/29/07 1300	Owens

FURTHER ACTION	X YES	COPIES TO	X DETECTIVE	X C11		
	NO		JUVENILE	PATROL		
		X DIST. ATTNY	OTHER_____			
		SQ./P.D.	OTHER_____	REVIEWED BY		DATE
				Moore, R.L., Lt.		06/29/07

FIGURE 9.4b (*Continued*)

Robbery	69. CASE NO.
Jackson Police Department	07-1024

70. CODE SECTION	71. CRIME	72. CLASSIFICATION		
211a PC	Armed Robbery	Market w/revolver		

73. VICTIM'S LAST NAME, FIRST, MIDDLE (FIRM IF BUS.)	74. ADDRESS	RESIDENCE	BUSINESS X	75. PHONE
McDaniel's Market	100 North "C" St.			555-1505

PROPERTY REPORT

ITEM	DESCRIPTION	VALUE
1.	Currency in denominations of $1, $5, $10, $20s; 3 — $100s; 2 — $50s and approximately 20 checks (owner's estimate). Checks taken were personal type checks under $50 and drawn on the Bank of America or Wells Fargo Bank.	$8,110.00

REPORTING OFFICERS	RECORDING OFFICER	TYPED BY	DATE AND TIME	ROUTED BY
Samons #18/ Jacobs #35	Jacobs	mmk	06/29/07 1300	Owens

FURTHER ACTION	[X] YES [ ] NO	COPIES TO	[X] DETECTIVE [ ] JUVENILE [X] DIST. ATTNY [ ] SQ./P.D.	[X] C11 [ ] PATROL [ ] OTHER_____ [ ] OTHER_____	

REVIEWED BY	DATE
Moore, R. L., Lt.	06/29/07

FIGURE 9.4c *(Continued)*

Robbery			69.CASE NO.
			07-1024

Jackson Police Department

70.CODE SECTION 211a PC	71. CRIME Armed Robbery	72. CLASSIFICATION Market w/revolver	
73.VICTIM'S LAST NAME, FIRST, MIDDLE (FIRM IF BUS.) McDaniel's Market		74. ADDRESS RESIDENCE ☐ BUSINESS ☒ 100 North "C" St.	75. PHONE 555-1505

EVIDENCE REPORT

ITEM   DESCRIPTION

1.   One brown satchel (plastic material), 18" x 14" x 8",
       with a 16' length of hemp rope tied to its handles.
       Contents of bag included: 1—wood brace (red in color),
       4—$1\frac{1}{4}$" bits, carpenter's hammer, wood chisel,
       linoleum knife, 12" crowbar, side cutters, keyhole saw.

2.   3 empty pint milk cartons (Arden Farms Dairy).

3.   Remnants of 3 packages of salami (Gallo brand).

4.   One half-pint empty bottle of vodka (Samarov label).

    The above items were collected and marked for identification
by Officer JACOBS #35, with the initials "L.J." and maintained
by him until delivered to Lt. John WILSON, Police Crime Laboratory
on 06/29/07. Specimens of tar paper, insulated material,
wood chips, and ceiling plaster were obtained by Officer
JACOBS from area of roof breakthrough for possible future
comparison purposes. Ten photographs of shoeprints taken from
the surface of the market roof, the attic, and from the area
below the trap door of the market ceiling were also taken by
Officer JACOBS for comparison with the footwear of suspects
developed in this investigation.

REPORTING OFFICERS Samons #18 / Jacobs #35	RECORDING OFFICER Jacobs	TYPED BY mmk	DATE AND TIME 06/29/07 1300	ROUTED BY Owens

FURTHER ACTION ☒ YES ☐ NO	COPIES TO ☒ DETECTIVE ☐ JUVENILE ☒ DIST. ATTNY ☐ SQ./P.D.	☒ C11 ☐ PATROL ☐ OTHER___ ☐ OTHER___		
		REVIEWED BY Moore, R.L., Lt.		DATE 06/29/07

each dwelling entered during the commission of the crime. Crime reports are recorded in all felony cases, regardless of whether the victims are willing to file a report or sign a complaint.

Follow-Up, Continuation, and Supplemental Reports

follow-up or supplemental report A report written during the secondary level of criminal investigation, indicating any actions or information obtained after the initial report was written.

A **follow-up report,** or a **supplemental report** as it is sometimes called, is made after the initial report. Any officer who obtains additional information on a case under investigation will complete a supplemental report. The label *continuation report* or *supplemental report* is sometimes used on reports describing crimes incidental or secondary to the primary felony. For example, a suspect might carjack a vehicle to make his or her escape after killing a person. The suspect may even injure the driver of the carjacked vehicle. The homicide will be written up on an initial felony crime report, but the carjacking and the possible aggravated assault on the driver will be recorded in a continuation or supplementary report that also becomes part of the full case file of the offense.

In many felony cases, the investigation spans several days or weeks. Whenever an officer rechecks any offense previously reported, he or she must fill out a supplementary report describing what actions were taken, what was discovered, or what additional property was recovered. The value of such a report depends on the thoroughness of the investigating officer drafting the report.

In most instances, officers assigned to the case will draft the follow-up reports as work progresses. However, if other officers receive information regarding the case, they too should complete follow-up reports. For example, during a routine drug bust, a uniformed officer notices that the drug dealer is wearing an unusual ring. Because it is so unusual, the officer recalls that such a ring was described as having been taken during a recent burglary. After discussing this with the dealer, the officer learns the name of the person who sold the dealer the ring. All of this information should be submitted in a follow-up report and filed with the initial burglary report. The information can help to establish or verify a *modus operandi,* as well as lead the investigators of the burglary to someone who may possess information about the burglary.

Follow-up reports always carry the same numbers as the original case, regardless of the number of supplemental reports created. Figure 9.5 is an example of a supplemental report in a burglary investigation. The report covers an interview with a witness two days after the burglary and subsequent arrest of a suspect.

Arrest Reports

arrest report A report that documents the circumstances of the arrest or detention of individuals by the police.

An **arrest report** documents the circumstances of the arrest or detention of individuals by the police. Its purpose is to serve as a basis for prosecution. To accomplish its purpose, the report must meet two qualifications: (1) it must demonstrate a legal, proper arrest for which there was probable cause; and (2) it must be complete and correct to serve as an adequate guide for follow-up investigation.

The effectiveness of the prosecution is generally equal to the effectiveness of the arrest report. Evidence located by the follow-up investigation does not carry the same weight as facts and evidence discovered at the time of arrest. The defense attorney may try to rebut follow-up evidence by asking the court or jury, "Why didn't the officer who made the arrest find this damaging bit of evidence?" Many cases are lost in court because of poor investigations, but more are lost because evidence was not properly reported. An officer who demonstrates the most commendable initiative and intelligence in making an arrest will fail to bring about a conviction in court if the arrest report is not correct and as complete as possible.

FIGURE 9.5 Follow-Up Report

Robbery	**69. CASE NO.**
	07-313

Jackson Police Department

70. CODE SECTION	**71. CRIME**	**72. CLASSIFICATION**		
459 PC	Burglary	Commercial Jewelry Store		

73. VICTIM'S LAST NAME, FIRST, MIDDLE (FIRM IF BUS.)	**74. ADDRESS**	RESIDENCE	BUSINESS X	**75. PHONE**
Sparkle's Jewelry Store	246 Barnard St			555-1505

<u>FOLLOW-UP REPORT</u>

On 07/15/07, 1030 hours, WALTER J. SAUGER, Mgr., Fidelity Loan Co., 208 S. Spring Street, contacted the station and advised Officer TUSCILLO that an unknown individual had tried to pawn a lady's W/G diamond ring, set with a 1/2 karat diamond in a basket setting, engraved "J.A.". SAUGER stated that he did not like the looks of the suspect and refused to take the item. The unknown person left the store and walked south on Spring St., according to SAUGER. Suspect is described as M/W/A, 35–38 yrs, 5'7–9", 160–170, wearing dark trousers, a faded blue shirt with white square buttons; dk. brn. hair, neck length; and dk. sunglasses.

Since the above jewelry fit the description of some of the property taken in the burglary of the SPARKLE'S JEWELRY STORE on 07/13/07, reporting officer proceeded to S. Spring Street, where an individual similar to the person described by SAUGER was observed walking south on the east side of Spring St. Suspect was placed under arrest by Officer TUSCILLO at 1040 hours. At that time Officer TUSCILLO informed the suspect that he had the right to remain silent and that any statement he might make could be taken down and used against him in a court of law. He was also advised that he had the right to an attorney of his own choice and to have an attorney present during questioning; that if he so desired and could not afford an attorney, one would be appointed for him without charge. At that time suspect stated that he understood his rights, but was willing to make a statement.

A search of the suspect discovered several articles of jewelry similar to the items taken in the SPARKLE store burglary as well as an eight-inch screwdriver. The screwdriver tip appeared similar to the tool impression left on the window ledge of the victim jewelry store.

Suspect was identified as HARRY AMES, 406 Maple St., San Francisco, California 94118, and claimed he had just been released from Soledad Prison on 07/10/07, where he had served four years for burglary. He was booked at Central Jail on suspicion of Burglary, Booking #6345K.

BENJAMIN SCHWARTZ, owner of Sparkle's Jewelry Store, identified the three rings and a lady's Bulova watch recovered during the search of AMES, all part of the stolen jewelry taken in instant case on 07/13/07.

(Include in report)
<u>SUSPECT</u>:   (description)
<u>PROPERTY</u>:   (list of items, description, value)
<u>ARREST REPORT</u>: (attach copy of arrest report)

REPORTING OFFICERS	**RECORDING OFFICER**	**TYPED BY**	**DATE AND TIME**	**ROUTED BY**
Tuscillo, Michele #436	Tuscillo	mmk	07/15/07 1030	Miller

FURTHER ACTION	X YES	**COPIES TO**	X DETECTIVE	X C11			
	NO		JUVENILE	PATROL			
			X DIST. ATTNY	OTHER____	**REVIEWED BY**		**DATE**
			SQ./P.D.	OTHER____	George Aplin, Capt.		07/15/07

Arrest reports are generally completed by officers immediately after making an arrest, with or without a warrant. A report must be submitted for an arrest in any of the following situations:

- Misdemeanor or felony
- Commitment to a mental institution
- Service of an arrest warrant
- Desertion or other crime by military personnel
- Transfer of custody of a suspect arrested by another agency

The arrest report form, like most other reports, has a form section and a narrative section. Generally, the arrest report is typed, but when the arresting officer does not have the opportunity to type or print the report it may be hand-printed or hand-written. In most agencies today, officers type their reports directly into a computer and print them out as a prestructured form. Figure 9.6 shows an example of an arrest report form.

The circumstances of the arrest and the *corpus delicti* of the crime should be set forth. The report should describe what happened in chronological order, beginning with the first act of the suspect. The arrest report should include what was said and to whom and all statements made by witnesses and victims as well as with suspects. Statements made by the suspect should be recorded as accurately as possible. If there is any physical evidence associated with the arrest, such evidence should be itemized and include the following information: where it was found, the person who found it, the date, and the final disposition of the item.

For arrests in which large amounts of property are recovered, there may not be enough room on the arrest report to fully itemize each article. In such instances it is customary to create a full description on a separate continuation sheet entitled, *Evidence Report*. This report should carry the names of the people arrested, the crime for which each suspect was arrested, and his or her booking and case numbers. This evidence report should be attached to the original arrest report. The arrest report should include the statement "See attached evidence report."

Injuries Associated with an Arrest People arrested are sometimes injured during the arrest or have been in fights or accidents before the arrest. As a result, special attention is required to protect both the prisoner and the police agency. The injury or any illness noted should be described in the arrest report, and any medical or first-aid treatment administered at the scene should be documented. If the injury was the result of force used to overcome resistance to the arrest, the officer should outline the details of the force and the resulting injury in the narrative part of the arrest report. As soon as possible after the injury is discovered, if it is not minor, the prisoner should be examined by a licensed physician because officers are not qualified to determine the seriousness of illness or injury. The arresting officers should photograph any visible marks or bruises. Some departments have special forms for reporting injuries during an arrest. Recording injuries during the arrest serves two purposes: it protects prisoners and ensures that they receive adequate medical examination and treatment; and it protects the police agency by recording appraisals by a competent medical authority of the extent of prisoners' injuries.

Property or Evidence Held in an Arrest When evidence is held or property is impounded as part of an arrest, all items should be accurately identified and described so that they can be released to a suspect or victim when they are no

FIGURE 9.6 Arrest Report

Arrest Report
Irvine Police Department

CA0303600   Arrestee #_____   DR #_____

INVOLV. CODES: ARR – ARRESTEE	DATE	TIME	LOCATION
(BOXES 1 & 39) DET – DETAINED			
MHD – MENTAL HEALTH			

1. INV CODE	2. NAME (LAST) (FIRST) (MIDDLE)	3. SEX M ☐ F ☐	4. RACE W B H C J F I P O A U	5. DOB	6. AGE

7. ALIAS, SCARS, MARKS, TATTOOS, NICKNAMES	7A. G.E.T. ☐ Y ☐ N

8. HT.	9. WT.	10. HAIR	11. EYES	12. OLN	13. OLS ☐ CA	14. POB	15. SOCIAL SEC. #	16. CII #

17. BOOKING #	DATE	TIME	18. ADDRESS	19. CITY	20. STATE	21. ZIP

22. RESIDENCE PHONE ( )	23. OCCUPATION	24. EMPLOYER/ADDRESS (SCHOOL IF JUVENILE)	25. BUSINESS PHONE ( )

26. CODE SECTION / DESCRIPTION

OF WARRANTS ATTACHED ☐

27. PARENT/GUARDIAN NOTIFIED (LAST) (FIRST) (MIDDLE) (IF JUVENILE) ☐	28. DOB	29. PHONE # ( )	30. NOTIFIED BY	31. DATE/TIME

32. ARRESTEE'S VEHICLE DESCRIPTION	VYR	VMA	VMO	VST	COLOR(S)	33. IDENTIFYING FEATURES OF VEHICLE

34. DISPOSITION OF VEHICLE
☐ IMPOUNDED ☐ LEFT AT SCENE ☐ OTHER

35. ARRESTEE STATUS (ADULT) ☐ OCJ ☐ BAIL ☐ 849 ☐ PROMISE TO APPEAR ☐ RELEASED TO_____	36. ARRESTEE'S STATUS (JUVENILE) ☐ OCJH ☐ RELEASED TO PARENTS ☐ RECOMMEND CSP ☐ REFER TO PROB ☐ OTHER_____	37. MIRANDA YES ☐ NO ☐ DATE: BY: TIME:	38. INVOKED? ☐

Arrestee #_____

39. INV CODE	40. NAME (LAST) (FIRST) (MIDDLE)	41. SEX M ☐ F ☐	42. RACE W B H C J F I P O A U	43. DOB	44. AGE

45. ALIAS, SCARS, MARKS, TATTOOS, NICKNAMES	45A. G.E.T. ☐ Y ☐ N

46. HT.	47. WT.	48. HAIR	49. EYES	50. OLN	51. OLS ☐ CA	52. POB	53. SOCIAL SEC. #	54. CII #

55. BOOKING #	DATE	TIME	56. ADDRESS	57. CITY	58. STATE	59. ZIP

60. RESIDENCE PHONE ( )	61. OCCUPATION	62. EMPLOYER/ADDRESS (SCHOOL IF JUVENILE)	63. BUSINESS PHONE ( )

64. CODE SECTION / DESCRIPTION

OF WARRANTS ATTACHED ☐

65. PARENT/GUARDIAN NOTIFIED (LAST) (FIRST) (MIDDLE) (IF JUVENILE) ☐	66. DOB	67. PHONE # ( )	68. NOTIFIED BY	69. DATE/TIME

70. ARRESTEE'S VEHICLE DESCRIPTION	VYR	VMA	VMO	VST	COLOR(S)	71. IDENTIFYING FEATURES OF VEHICLE

72. DISPOSITION OF VEHICLE
☐ IMPOUNDED ☐ LEFT AT SCENE ☐ OTHER

73. ARRESTEE STATUS (ADULT) ☐ OCJ ☐ BAIL ☐ 849 ☐ PROMISE TO APPEAR ☐ RELEASED TO_____	74. ARRESTEE'S STATUS (JUVENILE) ☐ OCJH ☐ RELEASED TO PARENTS ☐ RECOMMEND CSP ☐ REFER TO PROB ☐ OTHER_____	75. MIRANDA YES ☐ NO ☐ DATE: BY: TIME:	76. INVOKED? ☐

longer needed. Property receipts should be issued whenever possible. If property taken from an arrestee is identified by number or inscription, it should be checked against the stolen property file of the arresting agency or of other state and federal agencies when warranted. A list of property taken from a prisoner may serve to connect the prisoner with unsolved crimes. When the suspect arrested has a vehicle, the disposition of the vehicle should be shown in the report: for example, "released to witness LOPEZ," "left at scene," "released to Boatman Towing Company," or "held for processing." Some agencies include this vehicle disposition in their boxed area of the arrest form (see Figure 9.6, boxes 34 and 72). Impound reports are also prepared by many agencies to document the condition of vehicles when impounded.

Vehicle Accident Reports

Vehicle accidents, or collision reports, as they are referred to by some agencies, are an important source of information in a number of areas. First, in a traffic fatality, the collision report is part of a homicide investigation. As a result of such an investigation, a surviving driver may face aggravated vehicular homicide or vehicular homicide charges. Furthermore, the families of the victims deserve a thorough investigation of the victims' deaths. Second, information from collision reports can help courts assess liability in personal injury or property damage cases. Third, enactment of traffic and vehicle safety laws often results from information gathered from collision reports (National Highway Traffic Safety Administration [NHTSA], 2006). Finally, many safety advances in vehicles, such as hydraulic brakes, safety glass, shock-absorbing bumpers, and front and side air bags, as well as accident reduction techniques, have resulted from accident investigation reporting and crash research.

Policies, laws, and ordinances dictate whether a written report must be made for every traffic accident that comes to a police department's attention. Most police agencies require a written report in accidents involving appreciable property damage but do not require a report covering minor damage, such as a slightly dented fender. However, damage does not have to exceed a specified amount for an accident to constitute a traffic accident. Investigation and reporting all known vehicle accidents in public places is recommended because the only difference between a fatal accident and one involving only property damage is a matter of chance, a small difference in position or time, or a slight variation in speed. Information in a vehicle accident report must be written in such a way that anyone who refers to the report will have as much knowledge of the circumstances as the investigator does. The report must contain all facts about the accident.

traffic collision report
A report that contains all the facts about the accident.

A **traffic collision report** is generally a form that supplies a detailed framework. The officer completes the form by filling in the blanks with the requested information and placing an *X* in the appropriate boxes. Additional information about details or a summary of the accident is recorded on supplementary sheets, which are attached to the face sheet (the collision form). Figure 9.7 shows the first page of a sample collision report.

FYI In 2004 there were an estimated 6,181,000 police-reported traffic crashes, in which 42,636 people were killed and 2,788,000 were injured; 4,281,000 crashes involved property damage only (NHTSA, 2004).

FIGURE 9.7 Traffic Collision Report

TRAFFIC COLLISION REPORT

PAGE _1_ OF _5_

SPECIAL CONDITIONS	NO. INJ. 1	H & R FELONY ☐	CITY Jackson		JUDICIAL DISTRICT	NO. 07-233T
	NO. KILLED 0	H & R MISD.	Jackson	REPORTING DISTRICT 024x0	BEAT 5	

LOCATION

COLLISION OCCURED ON

	MO. 1	DATE 24	YR. 07	TIME(2400) 0800	OFFICER I.D. 1408

☐ AT INTERSECTION WITH
☒ OR 40 FEET /MILES _S_ OF "A" Street

INJURY, FATAL OR TOW AWAY ☒ YES ☐ NO   STATE HWY ☐ YES ☒ NO

PARTY 1

DRIVER ☒ | PEDES-TRIAN ☐ | PARKED VEH. ☐ | BI-CYCLIST ☐ | OTHER ☐

NAME (FIRST, MIDDLE, LAST) Robert Edward Young	STREET ADDRESS 845 Taylor St.

DRIVERS LICENSE D543104 Ca.	BIRTHDATE MO. 4 DAY 8 YR. 50	SEX M	RACE C	CITY Ontario,	STATE Ca.	91761	PHONE 555-4543

VEHICLE YR. 2000	MAKE Chev.	LICENSE NO. 129 SUZ	OWNER'S NAME ☒ SAME AS DRIVER

DIRECTION OF TRAVEL N	ON/ACROSS (STREET OR HIGHWAY) 2nd Street	OWNER'S ADDRESS ☒ SAME AS DRIVER

SPEED LIMIT 35	DISPOSITION OF VEHICLE Towed to Wise's Garage	☐ BY DRIVER	ON ORDERS OF Driver	VEHICLE DAMAGE ☐ MINOR ☒ MOD. ☐ MAJOR ☐ TOTAL R. F. Fender	VIOLATION CHARGES 1 _____ 2 _____

PARTY 2

DRIVER ☒ | PEDES-TRIAN ☐ | PARKED VEH. ☐ | BI-CYCLIST ☐ | OTHER ☐

NAME (FIRST, MIDDLE, LAST) Walter Joseph Murray	STREET ADDRESS 643 Broadway

DRIVERS LICENSE W533421 Ca.	MO. 9 DAY 15 YR. 78	SEX M	RACE C	CITY Ontario,	STATE Ca.	PHONE 555-4321

VEHICLE YR. 2000	MAKE Ford	LICENSE NO. 155 OLC Ca.	OWNER'S NAME ☒ SAME AS DRIVER

DIRECTION OF TRAVEL W	ON/ACROSS (STREET OR HIGHWAY) Private Drive to 2nd St.	OWNER'S ADDRESS ☒ SAME AS DRIVER

SPEED LIMIT	DISPOSITION OF VEHICLE Cared for	☒ BY DRIVER	ON ORDERS OF	EXTENT VEHICLE DAMAGE ☐ MINOR ☒ MOD. ☐ MAJOR ☐ TOTAL	LOCATION L.F. Fender	VIOLATION CHARGES 1 21804a VC 2 268483 VC

PROPERTY

DESCRIPTION OF DAMAGE

OWNER'S NAME	ADDRESS		NOTIFIED ☐ YES ☐ NO

INJURED/WITNESS

WITNESS ONLY	AGE	SEX	FATAL INJURY	SEVERE WOUND DISTORTED MEMBER	OTHER VISIBLE INJURIES	COMPLAINT OF PAIN	DRIVER	PASS.	PED.	BI-CYCLIST	OTHER	IN VEH. NUMBER
☐			☐	☐	☐	☒	☒	☐	☐	☐	☐	2

NAME Walter Joseph Murray   PHONE 555-4321
ADDRESS 643 Broadway, Ontario, Ca.   TAKEN TO (INJURED ONLY) Refused medical care

☐			☐	☐	☐	☐	☐	☐	☐	☐	☐	

NAME   PHONE
ADDRESS   TAKEN TO (INJURED ONLY)

☐			☐	☐	☐	☐	☐	☐	☐	☐	☐	

NAME   PHONE
ADDRESS   TAKEN TO (INJURED ONLY)

SKETCH

◯ INDICATE NORTH

(see page 3)

MISCELLANEOUS

Suggested:

Vehicle Description

and

Driver Description

(put in this section)

VEHICLE TYPE			
PARTY 1	01	PARTY 2	01
ROAD TYPE			
A CONVENTIONAL, ONE WAY			
X B CONVENTIONAL, TWO WAY			
C EXPRESSSWAY			
D FREEWAY			
E OTHER (EXPLAIN IN NARRATIVE)			

555 (REV 11-93)

57698- 456 555 REV 11-93 500M OSP

In addition to these general report forms, many departments have forms to report the occurrence of graffiti in the area, private person arrest forms (where a community member makes an arrest), custody/visitation court order violation reports (when separated or divorced parents have restricted parental visitation rights), domestic violence crime reports, intoxication reports, and even drug influence evaluation reports (to record field sobriety test results and observations).

THE COMPLETED REPORT

When a written report is completed, it is reviewed by the officer's immediate supervisor. It may also be read by a number of others inside and outside the department. These people include the following:

- Department administrators
- Chief or sheriff
- Record clerks
- Court administrator
- Other law enforcement agencies
- Various assistant district attorneys
- District attorney
- Grand jury (in jurisdictions where they apply)
- Defendant
- Defense counsel
- Trial judge
- Various court officials
- Media

Police reports carry information needed for making a wide variety of important decisions about the liberty of a suspect in a crime or the role of parties involved in an accident. It is critical, therefore, that reports be forthright, clearly written, and accurate so that they can withstand attacks from any quarter. Reports are the professional tool of law enforcement used in the administration of justice.

SUMMARY

Learning Objective 1

Effective communication is essential in all police work. Writing skills, as evidenced in good report writing, are among the most important tools in the investigation of crimes, apprehension of suspects, and prosecution of criminals.

Learning Objective 2

A well-structured police report contains all the essential information to answer the questions who, what, when, where, how, and why about a crime that has been committed.

Learning Objective 3

In addition to serving as a record of an investigation, a basis for prosecution, and an aid in developing a database of crime statistics, written reports can also help in making departmental decisions regarding resources and personnel allocations, and in assessing accountability within and outside the agency.

Learning Objective 4

A good police report has four characteristics: it is complete, containing all pertinent information; it is concise, presenting all essential features while eliminating nonessential details; it is clear, relating exactly what an officer saw, heard, and did; and it is accurate, concentrating on specifics and avoiding generalities.

Learning Objective 5

Police agencies tend to concern themselves with four basic categories of reports: internal, technical and specialized equipment reports, intelligence reports, and operations reports. Operations reports are the type most often prepared by line officers and investigators. They fall into these four categories: misdemeanor and/or miscellaneous reports, felony reports, arrest reports, and traffic collision reports.

. . . .

KEY TERMS

cop speak 175	synopsis 186	evidence report 188
sexist language 180	complaint or incident report 186	follow-up or supplemental report 194
affected terms 180		
form section 184	felony report 188	arrest report 194
narrative section 185	property report 188	traffic collision report 198

. . . .

QUESTIONS FOR REVIEW

Learning Objective 1

1. How may poor oral or writing skills adversely affect a criminal investigation?
2. Why might a prosecutor be concerned about how well police officers communicate in writing?

Learning Objective 2

3. What are the six basic elements of a well-written report?

Learning Objective 3

4. How could an investigative report help an officer testifying in court?

Learning Objective 4

5. What are the characteristics of a good report?
6. Why must police reports be concise?
7. Why must police reports be accurate?

8. What should officers be aware of concerning different cultures when writing names in their reports?

9. How should affected words be handled in police reports?

10. What time is it on 100-hour time at four o'clock in the evening?

Learning Objective 5

11. What is the difference between a felony report and a misdemeanor report?

12. When are traffic collision reports typically written?

13. What are some of the purposes of traffic accident reports?

CRITICAL THINKING EXERCISES

1. Drop a small item of person property (e.g., a ring, watch, pen, necklace, broach, or pin) into a large box that your instructor will provide. Then write a lost property description of the "missing property." Be sure to include a value for each item. Read your property description aloud and see if you instructor or a fellow classmate can retrieve your "missing item" from the box based on your description.

2. The following narrative of a homicide is written in an unacceptable manner. The report contains many unnecessary words and sentences. It contains accurate facts, but they are presented in an awkward fashion. Rewrite this report, correcting the various errors. Be certain to use good sentence structure, punctuation, and proper paragraphing and organization.

> On December 21, 2007 at four thirty or so in the afternoon, just before the sun began to set, Officer Jack Jones was notified by Mrs. Janet Parson, the department dispatcher, that someone had been shot at the Ralph's supermarket, down the road from the Pressly Dry Cleaning store, in Irvine, CA. The Ralph's is located on the West side of Walnut Boulevard, and faces, Culver Ave.; sitting right next door to a Starbucks coffee shop. Its address is 1609 Culver Ave. A white man was shot by another white man, according to several people who must have seen the crime, including Mark LaPage, who lives at 242 Golden Glow street, in the city of Irvine, not too far form the University of Irvine campus.
>
> After having a cup of coffee, Officer Jack Jones, the reporting officer, got to the scene of the crime. He spoke with another witness, JUDY WILLSON who said she could recognize the man who had shot Mr. Peitry, the Ralph's manager. The shooter was described as having a baseball cap on, so Judy Couldn't see his hair color. He had on blue jeans, with the left pocket torn off. A light brown colored jacket over a beige colored shirt that also had dark brown stripes on it. JUDY told me that things happened to fast to get any more information or details about the murderer, but that she could recognize him if she saw him again, even though she doesn't think she has ever seen him before, and could not see his hair color.
>
> Mr. Gary Peitry was laying on the ground when Officer Jack JONES arrived. There was a lot of blood pooling around his head and several of he onlookers were turning kind of green. There was a star shaped entry wound by the left side of Mr. Peitry's neck and the base of his head, just below his ear. There was an erring in Mr. Peitry's left ear, kind of a bluish or greenish stone set in silver. Mr. Peitry wasn't breathing, and OFFICER Jones could find no pulse, even though he looked for a few minutes, and even checked his ankles. Mr. Peitry's body was laying on the East side of the parking lot, with his head facing Culver Avenue.

INVESTIGATIVE SKILL BUILDERS

Acquiring and Evaluating Information

You have been working as a small-town police officer for five years. You work in a college town, where the campus police force numbers sixteen officers. You have been working as one of the town police department's three investigators, a rotating position that each officer holds for ninety days at a time. During the current period, you have investigated several rapes, robberies, burglaries, and assaults. You have recently been asked to assist in the investigation of a string of rapes; three have actually occurred in dormitories on the college campus, and two in your jurisdiction in apartments.

The college is a medium-sized, four-year residential campus, with approximately 12,000 students. The campus police serve largely as security guards and lack the capacity and training to conduct a criminal investigation of this nature.

You receive copies of the incident reports completed by the campus police and copy these with those completed in your department. All of the rapes have occurred at night. The assailant seems to choose women who are walking home alone from a night class, follows them to their doors, and as soon as these women unlock their doors, pushes them in and down to the ground. Once the woman is on the floor, the assailant brandishes a large knife, threatens to cut her throat if she screams or resists, and then proceeds to rape her.

The description of the attacker is sketchy, but all of the victims agree that the man is white, 20–25 years old, and 5 feet 8 to 5 feet 10 inches tall, and that he wore an unusual and overpowering aftershave or cologne that smelled of citrus. All of the women agree that the knife was some sort of folding pocketknife.

One morning as you sip your coffee and review the criminal reports, you receive a call from the campus police. They tell you that they think they have captured the rapist. You rush to the campus and are met by Officer Dave Martin. Officer Martin tells you, "It's the wildest thing I have ever seen. This guy came in this morning and told us he did it. That he was the rapist. We read him his rights, and he has already given us a statement." Martin hands you a written statement.

When you meet the man, you introduce yourself as a police officer and, as a safety measure, your reiterate his *Miranda* warnings. You ask his name, and he tells you it is Jason Gibbon. You look over his statement and ask him if he wrote it. He nods affirmatively. The statement contains superficial information, the type anyone might have obtained from reading accounts of the attacks in the campus or local newspapers. You ask him to tell you some details that were not in the papers, and he becomes angry and agitated.

You take out the case reports and look through the evidence reports. You see that there is little physical evidence to connect anyone to the crime. There were no semen stains or samples, because the rapist wore a condom and took it with him. Although the rapist had knocked down each of the women, there had been no real struggles, scratches, or blood samples. You ask Officer Martin whether Gibbon had any weapons on him when he came in. Officer Martin says he was carrying a knife. You ask to see it. The reports indicate that the women had described a folding pocketknife, and Gibbon was carrying such a knife; however, folding pocketknives are fairly common. You sniff the air and notice that Gibbon has no particular scent about him. Yet all of the victims agreed that the attacker had been wearing an overpowering amount of cologne or aftershave with a distinctive citrus odor. You are not comfortable that this is your man.

1. Should you keep this man in custody?

2. What actions might you take to confirm whether Gibbon is the right suspect?

3. What sort of defense might Gibbon mount in court?

4. Should you include your doubts in your own felony report?

Decision Making

Using the information in the preceding story, answer these questions:

1. Should you continue the investigation, even though Gibbon has already confessed?
2. What should you tell the victims, if anything?
3. Should you share your concerns with your supervisor?

Integrity/Honesty

Using the information in the preceding case, consider these questions:

1. Should you mention to anyone else that Gibbon does not have the cologne smell, or should you wait to see if others notice that missing element on their own?
2. Since your evidence is largely circumstantial, and you are not really comfortable with Gibbon as a suspect, will you try to find another suspect?

Robbery

After completing this chapter, you will be able to:

1 Provide an overview of the crime of robbery in the United States.
2 Explain the legal elements of robbery.
3 List and describe the main categories of robberies.
4 Name and describe the principle classes of robbers.
5 Enumerate basic procedures used in robbery investigations.

FIGURE 10.1 FBI Crime Index

Violent Crime

- Murder and nonnegligent manslaughter
- Forcible rape
- Robbery
- Aggravated assault

Property Crime

- Burglary
- Larceny-theft
- Motor vehicle theft
- Arson

---

crime index A collection of statistics in the FBI's Uniform Crime Reports on the number of murder, rape, robbery, assault, burglary, larceny-theft, motor vehicle theft, and arson crimes reported in a calendar year.

index crime One of the eight crimes (murder, rape, robbery, assault, burglary, larceny-theft, motor vehicle theft, and arson) that the FBI considers the most serious and that are combined to create the crime index.

clear cases To solve criminal cases by arresting, charging a suspect with a crime, and turning the case over to the courts for prosecution.

FIGURE 10.2 Percentage Distribution of Index Crime Offenses

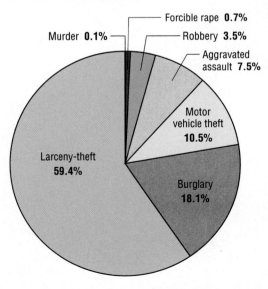

Source: Federal Bureau of Investigation, *Crimes in the United States.* USGPO, 2002, Figure 2.2.

OVERVIEW OF ROBBERY

Television and movies have created an image of robbers as romantic and colorful characters. Bonnie Parker and Clyde Barrow, John Dillinger, Lester Gillis—A.K.A. "Baby Face Nelson"—Benjamin "Bugsy" Segal, and Salvatore "Lucky" Luciano, to name but a few, all conjure up images of exciting and adventurous desperados of old, and each has been depicted almost lovingly in books and films. Even less vintage robbers such as Jack Roland Murphy—A.K.A. Murph the Surf—the man who stole the Star of India sapphire, a crime so spectacular that it inspired a book and the film *Topaz* in 1969 (see also Uris, 1983), have been romanticized. But these poorly cast folk heroes killed dozens of people, exhibiting a lack of concern over human life and a dedication to lethal violence along with their "colorful" robberies.

Robbery is a very serious crime that costs citizens and the government millions of dollars each year. The FBI identifies robbery as one of the eight most serious crimes in our society and reports yearly statistics on robbery in its Uniform Crime Reports (UCR). In 2004, 401,326 robberies occurred in the United States (FBI, 2005a). The UCR tracks the fluctuations in the overall volume and rate for murder, rape, robbery, assault, burglary, larceny-theft, motor vehicle theft, and arson. The reported incidence of these crimes is combined to create the **crime index** (Figure 10.1). These crimes are part of the crime index because they are believed to be important crimes. Each of these offenses is also referred to as an **index crime** (except arson because of problems with accurate reporting). As Figure 10.2 shows, most index crimes are property crimes, not violent crimes.

Robbery is among the leading criminal problems facing U.S. law enforcement today. Perpetrators include people of every age group, occupation, social stratum, gender, and race. The single defining characteristic linking people who engage in robbery is their desire to obtain money or property without working or paying for it.

Robbery is not always confined to loss of money or property. Violence or the threat of violence often accompanies the commission of a robbery. In 2004 offenders used firearms in 40.6 percent of robberies. Offenders used knives or other cutting instruments in 8.9 percent of these crimes. In the remaining 9.4 percent of robberies, the offenders used other types of weapons (FBI, 2005b). Robberies are a major concern to law enforcement officials because of their economic effects, the fear and death they cause, and the difficulty of investigating and clearing cases of robbery. For UCR purposes, law enforcement agencies **clear cases,** or solve criminal offenses, when at least one person is arrested, charged with the crime, and turned over to the courts for prosecution.

FIGURE 10.3 Percentage of Crimes Cleared by Arrest, 2004

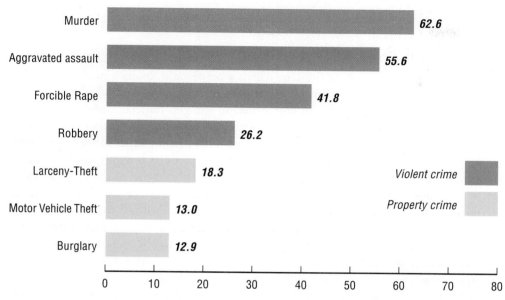

Source: Federal Bureau of Investigation, *Crimes in the United States*, USGPO, 2004, Figure 3.1.

Figure 10.3 shows the proportions of index crimes cleared by arrest for the year 2004. Although the number of reported robberies has decreased during recent years, because of its personal and often violent nature, robbery remains one of the crimes most feared by the American public.

LEGAL ELEMENTS OF ROBBERY

Robbery is the unlawful taking or attempted taking of another's personal property in his or her immediate possession and against his or her will by force or threat of force. To legally qualify as robbery, the *force* must be more than merely enough to lift and remove the property; it must be sufficient to overcome even slight resistance. Furthermore, *fear* must be present for a crime to be considered a robbery. This fear must be (1) fear of threatened injury to the victim, the victim's property, or a relative of the victim; or (2) fear of immediate injury to the victim or the victim's property or to anyone in the immediate company of the victim at the time of the offense.

State statutes precisely define the crime of robbery. Some states have only one degree of robbery; others have simple and aggravated categories. Some states even have first-, second-, and third-degree robbery. Investigators should be familiar with the criminal definitions of robbery in their own state and be able to recognize the *corpus delicti* of the crime. Generally, robbery is distinguished from theft or burglary in that robbery (1) involves the wrongful taking of personal property (2) in the presence of or from the owner in control of the property and (3) against the person's will, by force or threat of force, in the presence of fear.

CATEGORIES OF ROBBERY

In addition to knowing the elements of the crime of robbery, an investigator also should be familiar with the kinds of robberies possible. Robberies can be divided into four broad categories, depending on the *modous operandi* of the perpetrator. These

robbery The unlawful taking or attempted taking of another's personal property in his or her immediate possession and against his or her will by force or the threat of force.

categories include residential robberies, commercial robberies, street robberies, and vehicle-driver robberies or carjackings.

Residential Robberies

residential robbery

A robbery in which the target is a person in a private residence, hotel or motel room, trailer or mobile home, or other attached areas of a residence.

Residential robberies include those in which a perpetrator enters a home or hotel or motel room and uses force against the occupant to steal money or valuables. In addition, such crimes include robberies committed in garages, trailers, mobile homes, and even elevators. Residential robberies occur with less frequency than other types of robberies. In 2004 residential robberies represented 11.8 percent of all robberies reported in the UCR. It is not unusual for robber and victim to be at least acquainted and for the robber to have selected the victim because the robber believes there is money or other valuables in the home. Even when victim and robber are not acquainted, the victim is likely to have been selected because of the robber's belief that valuables were kept in the home. In hotel or motel robberies, robbers may gain their information from an employee who believes valuables may be found in the victim's room.

Perpetrators of residential robberies are typically armed with firearms, knives, or other weapons (Kellerman et al., 1995). In hotel, motel, garage, or elevator robberies, the crimes are swift and frequently involve violence. Neither gang violence nor residential robberies are new in the United States. However, one of the more recent incarnations of residential robbery—home invasion—presents law enforcement with a new twist. Beginning around 1990, there were reports that groups of young men were traveling around the country terrorizing selected community members. In Fairfax County, Virginia, police reported seven such home invasions during the first six months of 1990 alone. The interesting twist in these cases is that the "invaders" are often young Asian men (mostly in their twenties) who rob Asian families (Dunlap, 1997). Their rationale for targeting Asian families was that these individuals often distrust banks and therefore were likely to have large sums of money and jewelry in their homes.

These Asian home invaders operated in a very organized manner and usually worked in groups of two to nine people. Entrance into the victim's home varied. In some cases, entry was through an open door or window. In other cases, brute force was used to gain entry through the front door.

Home invaders are terroristic, using violence or threats of violence to intimidate the victims into submission. Their actions might include aiming their guns at children and threatening to shoot or even firing warning shots. Furthermore, invaders threaten to return and retaliate should the crime be reported.

Not all jurisdictions have had identical types of invaders. For example, in Florida, where home invasions have been occurring since the 1970s, the original perpetrators were cocaine smugglers (Hurley, 1995). But during the late 1990s and early 2000s, home invasions were perpetrated more frequently by young African Americans between the ages of 18 and 30. Police in Florida continue to report that their home invasions tend to be drug-related. In California, during the mid-1990s, a wave of home invasions were perpetrated by Mexican gang members who targeted successful Mexican businessmen. However, these robberies were largely fruitless; unlike Asian businessmen, their Mexican counterparts have no problem keeping their money and jewels in banks and bank vaults.

Today there is no reason to expect home invasions to be restricted to certain ethnic or cultural groups. Police agencies in many areas across the United States work with community members to increase awareness of the continuing problem of home invasions.

> **FYI** Bank robbery is both a federal and a state offense. United States Code Title 18, Section 2113, defines the elements of the federal crime of bank robbery. Thus bank robberies are within the jurisdiction of the FBI and the state and the local community where the crime occurred and are jointly investigated.

Commercial Robberies

Perhaps the most obvious **commercial robbery** is that of a bank. However, small businesses, service stations, convenience stores, bars, video rental stores, fast food establishments, automatic-teller machines, or any commercial businesses open late at night or all night may become targets of commercial robbery. Commercial robbers may also invade restaurants, markets, or jewelry stores and rob patrons of their cash, jewelry, and other valuables.

commercial robbery - Robbery of a commercial location such as a bank, service station, restaurant, or other commercial enterprise.

With the exceptions of banks, commercial robberies usually occur toward the end of the week and in the twilight to early-morning hours, from around 6:00 p.m. to around 4:00 a.m. Stores where visibility from the street or lighting conditions are poor make good targets for robbery. Similarly, businesses near on and off ramps of highways are likely targets.

In an attempt to deter robbers, many small businesses use video cameras, armed guards, and alarm systems. Some have conspicuous signs indicating that all money is kept in a safe and that the employees do not possess the combination or the key.

With the exception of bank robbers, who may either be professional or amateur, a great many commercial robbers are experienced criminals. This means they are more likely to have previous records and to be following an identifiable *modus operandi* (Martin, 2000).

Street Robberies

Street robberies are likely to occur on public streets and sidewalks or in alleys and parking lots. Street robberies, or muggings, are among the most common type of robbery. Often they occur so fast that the victim is unable to offer police anything but a vague general description of the offender. Many jurisdictions classify purse snatching as robbery. A purse snatcher can run past the victim and grab her purse so quickly that the victim may never have an opportunity to clearly see her attacker.

street robbery Any of an assortment of robberies that occur in street settings.

In a typical street robbery, victims may be injured when pushed to the ground or struck as the robber flees. Street robbers commonly use weapons, rely on speed, a punch, or a shove, and the element of surprise to accomplish their robberies. Elderly people are often the target of street robberies because they are perceived as likely to offer little resistance. However, as street robberies are frequently opportunistic, younger victims are also fairly common.

In larger cities with diverse immigrant groups, special problems arise, particularly among those illegally in the country. People who are in the country illegally are less likely to report being the victims of a robbery. They fear drawing attention to themselves and being discovered as illegal. A further complication may be the residual fear or mistrust of the police from negative experiences in their native countries.

Automatic-Teller Machine (ATM) Robberies
ATMs were first introduced in the mid-1960s in the United Kingdom and in the late 1960s in the United States

(Scott, 2003). The number of ATMs in the United States has increased exponentially since their initial appearance. ATM users now annually conduct billions of dollars of financial transactions, mostly cash withdrawals. ATMs were initially found only on bank premises, but today ATMs are located in convenience stores, airports, shopping malls, restaurants, casinos, and even game arcades. ATMs were originally owned and operated by banks, but they have become so prolific and profitable that private individuals now purchase and operate their own machines (Guerette & Clarke, 2003). Americans traveling in foreign countries have come to expect to find ATMs that will accept their U.S. bank cards—and they are usually not disappointed. But to some extent, ATM users have traded convenience for safety.

ATM robberies frequently follow a basic pattern, including invasion of a user's personal space (Holt & Spencer, 2005):

- Most ATM robberies are committed by a single offender who wields some type of weapon against a lone victim.
- Most occur at night, with the highest risk to users being between midnight and 4 a.m.
- Most robberies occur moments after the ATM user has made a withdrawal.
- Robberies are somewhat more likely to occur at walk-up ATMs than at drive-through ATMs.
- About 15 percent of ATM robbery victims are injured during the robbery.
- The average loss to an individual robbed at an ATM is between $100 and $200 (owing in part to the limits of cash removal at ATMs).

Vehicle-Driver Robberies

vehicle-driver robbery Robbery of an object of value in or attached to a vehicle or from the driver of the vehicle.

Vehicle-driver robberies may be committed against drivers of commercial vehicles, such as taxicabs, buses, long-haul trucks, delivery vans, armored vehicles, and even package or messenger service trucks. With the exception of armored vehicles, and perhaps delivery vans, vehicle-driver robberies typically occur at night.

Taxicab drivers and pizza delivery people are likely robbery targets because they can easily be lured to secluded locations with a simple telephone call. Once they arrive at the destination, the criminal can execute the robbery. Many cab services have placed bulletproof barriers between the passenger and the driver. However, such a separation fails to accomplish anything if a single rider is permitted to sit in the front seat next to the driver.

Drivers of personal cars are also potential victims of vehicle robberies. When stopped at a light or a stop sign, a driver may be approached and robbed at gunpoint. In some cases the robber may come from the passenger side of the car, smash the window, and grab a purse carelessly left on the seat. Whenever a driver picks up a hitchhiker, the driver is inviting a robbery—if not a more serious assault or homicide. Sometimes robbers feign car trouble or an accident to lure a Good Samaritan to stop and assist. Once stopped, the motorist is robbed.

Armored-Vehicle Robberies Armored-vehicle robberies are a particular problem because they are generally well planned and organized and carried out by professional robbers. Given the large amounts of money or valuables typically at stake in an armored-vehicle robbery, robbers are likely to use lethal force, and guards are likely to be injured or killed.

carjacking Robbery of a car with the driver and or occupants still in it.

Carjacking In the early 1990s, the news media began reporting stories about a category of violent crime called **carjacking.** This type of robbery involves the completed or attempted robbery of a motor vehicle by a stranger to the victim. It differs from other motor vehicle thefts because the victim is present and the offender uses or threatens to use force (Klaus, 2004). This crime is similar to hijacking long-haul trucks or airplanes. The Pamela Basu case made *carjacking* a household word:

> On Tuesday, September 8, 1992, two men hijacked Pamela Basu's car by pushing Mrs. Basu out of the vehicle at a stop sign. Entangled in her seat belt, Mrs. Basu was dragged for almost two miles after her vehicle was commandeered. Her 22-month-old daughter, who was strapped in a car seat, was tossed onto the roadway a few blocks after the vehicle was seized. Mrs. Basu was killed, but her daughter survived the attack.

Carjackers use surprise and weapons to carry out their robberies. Sometimes they choose victims who are waiting for a light to change or who have stopped at a stop sign. Frequently, they strike in supermarket or shopping mall parking lots. What is even more frightening to potential victims is that carjackings occurs randomly, at night or during the daytime. The violence now commonly associated with this crime is so widespread that extra guards, roaming patrols, and escort services have been added at many shopping malls.

The basic *modus operandi* is to operate in small groups of two to five individuals, to use fear and force to quickly separate the individual from the vehicle, or to push the vehicle inhabitant over and take control of the car. Young mothers with babies or small children are particularly targeted because their child can be threatened with harm to gain the cooperation of the mother/driver. One variation on carjacking began in April of 1993 when a series of unrelated "bump-and-stop" carjackings began to arise in Florida. The initial targets were tourists driving rental vehicles. In the first of these crimes, Barbara Meller-Jensen, a German visitor, was driving from the airport in a rental car with her 6-year-old son and 2-year-old daughter. Suddenly she felt her car being struck from behind. She pulled over to check things out and was grabbed by the drivers of the vehicle that had just struck her. The men took her purse and ran back to their car. Mrs. Jensen ran after them seeking to retrieve her purse. After banging on their window and grabbing the door handle, she tripped and fell under the Cadillac as it sped off. Her skull was crushed as her horrified son and daughter looked on (Navarro, 1995).

Among the various motives for carjacking are to acquire transportation away from or to a crime scene, to acquire money and valuables from the driver, to acquire a vehicle for use in a drive-by shooting, or to sell the vehicle for cash or trade it for drugs (Jacobs, Topalli, & Wright, 2003).

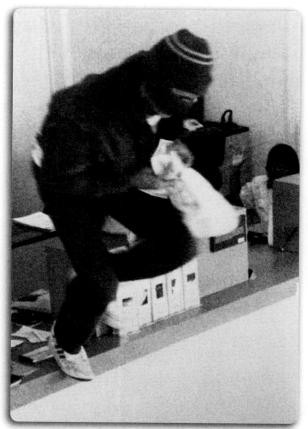

Bank robbers often use disguises to make it difficult for witnesses to identify and describe them.

CLASSIFICATION OF ROBBERS

Recognizing the type of person who commits a robbery can help an investigator build a case. Robbers can be classified by their techniques, their motives, and even their world-view or outlook on life. Borrowing from a typology suggested by John Conklin (1972), robbers can be separated into four groups: professional, opportunistic, drug-addicted, and alcoholic.

Professional Robbers

professional robber
A person who has incorporated robbery into a lifestyle and who robs as a means of economic support.

Professional robbers have incorporated robbery into their lifestyle and have committed themselves to this crime as a means of economic support. Professional robbers tend to plan and organize their crimes before committing them. Because professionals are well organized, they may divide the tasks related to a robbery and may subcontract some of these tasks to other professionals. For example, a driver of a getaway car may be engaged, or an alarm specialist may be included on the team.

Professionals see robbery as their job, and they treat their criminal activities as others treat going to work. Many professionals are exclusively robbers, but others engage in various criminal endeavors. However, they take all their criminal involvements seriously. Typically, professional robbers are highly skilled at their chosen work. Professionals are likely to target large commercial establishments rather than mom-and-pop businesses, seeking the largest financial return for their efforts.

Opportunistic Robbers

opportunistic robber
A person who steals small amounts of property or cash whenever the opportunity presents itself.

Opportunistic robbers are the most common type. Opportunists typically steal small amounts of money whenever a likely target presents itself. Opportunists are likely to engage in a variety of other crimes of opportunity, such as shoplifting, petty theft, and various larcenies. Hence, opportunistic robbers are seldom committed to robbery as a career in the way that professionals are. Opportunists tend to be young minority group members, frequently gang-involved, and are seldom well organized or highly skilled. They spend little time organizing or planning a robbery and generally do not use weapons.

Drug-Addicted Robbers

drug-addicted robber
A person who robs others to sustain an addiction to some type of illegal drug.

Another large category of robbers is made up of drug addicts. **Drug-addicted robbers** typically rob to support their drug habit. Addicted robbers have a relatively low commitment to robbery per se, and a high commitment to drugs. They commit robberies simply as a means of getting money to buy drugs. Because robbery is more dangerous than other forms of crime, addicts resort to it less often than other forms of criminal activity, such as theft or burglary. Addicted robbers tend to be desperate and careless in their handling of a robbery and may choose their targets poorly. They are seldom interested in a planned or organized "big score" and usually seek only enough money to purchase their next drug fix.

Alcoholic Robbers

alcoholic robber   A person who robs to sustain an addiction to alcohol or who attributes criminal actions to the influence of alcohol.

Like addicted robbers, **alcoholic robbers** tend to be disorganized and opportunistic. Some alcoholic robbers attribute their crime to a state of alcohol-induced disorientation. Others may simply engage in robbery as a method of obtaining money for alcohol, much as addicts seek funds to satisfy their drug habit. In some cases, alcoholics whose condition has caused them to lose their jobs may engage in robbery as a method

STATISTICS   In 2002 about 25 percent of convicted property and drug offenders had committed their crimes to get money for drugs, compared to 5 percent of violent and public order offenders. More than 68 percent of local jail inmates were found to be dependent on drugs or alcohol or abusing them according to this same survey of men and women held in local jails (Karlberg & James, 2005).

of economic support. More commonly, however, alcoholic robbers are not committed to robbery, are not very skilled at it, seldom plan their crimes in advance, and haphazardly choose their victims. Alcoholic robbers are among the most likely type of robbers to be apprehended, owing to their generally disorganized and haphazard attitude toward the robberies they commit. Some alcoholic robbers may be impelled to rob by forces similar to those that impel them to drink alcohol abusively.

INVESTIGATION OF ROBBERIES

Robbery has a comparatively low rate of clearance by arrest. The UCR indicates that the 2004 clearance rate for robbery was just slightly above 26 percent nationally (FBI, 2005a). A number of things hamper the investigation of robberies and contribute to this low rate of clearance. For instance, physical evidence may not be found, the crimes are often committed swiftly, and victims and witnesses are frequently so terrified that they cannot provide much of a description or other information.

When the police are informed of a robbery, the robber has usually already fled the scene. In some situations, however, as in the case of silent alarms, the police are informed while the robbery is in progress. In either case, once the police are aware that a robbery has occurred, *time* becomes a critical factor. The lag between a robbery's commission and its being reported to the police, the response time of the police, and the number of personnel devoted to a particular robbery all affect the potential for successfully solving the crime.

Response and Approach to the Robbery Scene

Because circumstances vary, procedures or strategies for investigating robberies must be flexible. An in-progress robbery reported through a silent alarm justifies an "all-units" emergency response. All-units broadcasts are justified by police incidents that involve violence, physical danger, or the presence of felony suspects at the scene. The obvious reason for an all-units call is to ensure that police units arrive at the scene as quickly as possible. It is the radio dispatcher's job to direct enough units to the scene and to identify the units closest to the location. **Response time,** the amount of time it takes police to arrive on the scene after being informed of the crime, can be a critical factor in both saving lives and apprehending felony suspects. The National Crime Victimization Survey conducted by the Bureau of Justice Statistics in 2003 found that nearly 31 percent of all violent crimes have response times of less than five minutes, and nearly 60 percent of violent crimes have response times of ten minutes or less. Property crimes, on the other hand, typically have a response rate of about 11 percent where response time is within five minutes, and about 28 percent in less than ten minutes (Bureau of Justice Statistics [BJS], 2005).

response time The lag time between a crime being reported and the arrival of police at the crime scene.

En route to the crime scene, officers should make sure that all available information has been received accurately from the dispatcher. Such information should include the address of the location and, if known, whether the robbery is still in progress, how many suspects there are, what sort of weapon was shown or used, and whether there is any description of the suspect or suspects.

As an officer approaches the scene, he or she must be alert for a number of possibilities:

- A fleeing suspect may be lurking in a doorway, walking on the sidewalk, or feigning interest in the activities of the police.
- A fleeing suspect may open fire on approaching officers.

- The dispatcher may provide information on the direction in which a suspect fled or the type of vehicle the suspect used to escape.
- The officer may notice evasive actions by another driver or by pedestrians, suggesting implication in the robbery by these individuals.

In addition, it is a good practice to shut off the siren and red lights when in the vicinity of the robbery to avoid warning the suspects. An exception is when the dispatcher has indicated *an officer in need of assistance* or *an officer down*.

An officer arriving on the scene of a robbery has three primary objectives: public safety, officer protection, and control over the crime scene. Investigating officers should remain alert, curious, and identification-conscious. Officers should proceed cautiously until the true situation is known and should avoid action stereotyping, physical stereotyping, and situational stereotyping (Baker & Florez, 1980; Goffman, 1982).

action stereotyping Misreading common or stereotypic behaviors and interactions of people at or near a crime scene who may actually be the offenders.

Action stereotyping occurs when an officer misreads common or stereotypic behaviors of people at or near a crime scene. For example, a person may call out to the officer, saying, "Everything is OK," but may not be telling the truth. The apparently helpful person may actually be the robber, counting on the officer misreading this interaction ritual (Collins, 2005; Goffman, 1982). Or a bandit may force an employee to make the statement in an attempt to fool the police, again hoping for a misreading of what action is actually happening. It may be wise and cautious to call people over from where they may be standing and speak with them privately. This can help ensure that the person talking is not literally under the gun of the bandit. Any strange actions on the part of employees at a robbery scene should be cause for suspicion and should be carefully investigated.

physical stereotyping A misconception that a criminal is a certain type of person.

In the absence of a physical description of a suspect, officers must avoid possible **physical stereotyping**—that is, expecting that a robber is a certain type of person. The expectation that a convenience store robber is a young male member of a minority group may allow the middle-aged white female robber to escape unnoticed. One must be cautious and suspicious of everyone until identities of those present can be determined.

situational stereotyping False or mistaken conclusions from the manifest appearance of certain situations.

In a similar manner, **situational stereotyping,** or mistaken conclusions from the appearance of a situation, can create serious problems in a robbery investigation. Even if a jewelry store's owner is a nervous person who has previously triggered several false silent alarms, this time it may be the Real McCoy. The misuse of silent alarms in many jurisdictions is handled by fines and sometimes by suspension of privileges. However, whenever a silent alarm is received, it must be handled diligently and with all necessary precautions. In some jurisdictions, a silent alarm results in a telephone call to the store for a prearranged false alarm code. If the code cannot be given or is given incorrectly, police are dispatched to investigate.

Duties at the Scene

The order of investigative activities in robbery cases is dictated by the facts of each situation. In all crimes, however, patrol officers typically are the first to arrive at the scene, and they have certain responsibilities. These responsibilities include apprehending the suspects, if possible; securing the names, addresses, telephone numbers, and e-mail addresses of all witnesses and victims as soon as possible; and safeguarding any evidence.

The first officers to arrive at the scene should conduct brief interviews with all parties concerned. These individuals should be separated from each other to avoid contaminating one another's stories. Using this information, investigating officers should transmit the initial broadcast data as quickly as possible. As previously mentioned, time is the enemy of the investigator in a robbery case. The sooner robbery information is broadcast, the greater the likelihood of other officers' spotting a fleeing suspect. The information needed for the initial broadcast includes the following:

- Type of robbery
- Type of premises
- Location of occurrence
- Time of occurrence
- Number of suspects
- Direction suspects are believed to be heading
- How suspects left the scene (on foot, by car, by bicycle)
- Description of the escape vehicle
- Type of weapon used, if any

As soon as possible, a supplemental broadcast should be made. The supplemental broadcast should contain a detailed description of the suspect(s), including clothing worn, any visible characteristics, and any special equipment that might have been carried. The vehicle used in the escape should be described as completely as possible, including color, make and model, and noticeable damage (e.g., crushed fenders, broken lights, or rusted areas). A supplemental broadcast should also be issued to advise other officers if a previous robbery call has turned out to be a false alarm.

Witness Descriptions and Identification of the Suspect

The various strategies discussed in Chapter 2 regarding identification of a suspect are relevant here. If a suspect can be located and apprehended in a short time (15–20 minutes), he or she may be immediately taken back to the crime scene for identification by witnesses. Alternatively, victims and witnesses may be transported to where the suspect is being held. If a suspect is not found for several hours, a photo line-up, sometimes referred to as a *photo pack* or *photo array*, may be used to secure a positive identification.

To expedite obtaining information from witnesses at the scene of a crime, some police agencies use a standardized form to record witness data. A form, however, is not intended to replace a face-to-face interview. Rather, it is meant for quickly obtaining some basic information. Forms can be especially useful when police personnel are in short supply and there are many witnesses or victims to speak with.

Preserving the Crime Scene

Preserving the crime scene, as described in Chapter 3, is the responsibility of the first responding officer who arrives at the scene. All available evidence must be safeguarded if it is to be useful in the investigation. Only those officers whose presence is necessary should enter the immediate crime scene area. Officers involved in collecting evidence should not move any item until notes are made, photographs are taken, sketches are drawn, and measurements are recorded.

Robbers generally leave little physical evidence for the police to collect and use. However, in some cases investigators may find useful footprints, fingerprints, or discarded articles belonging to the robber, including cigarette butts, gum or gum wrappers, soft drink cups, clothing fibers, or even bullet casings. Eye-witnesses may change their testimony, so a search for physical evidence should be undertaken at any robbery scene. The actual nature and extent of a search for evidence depends on the type of property

FOCUS ON TECHNOLOGY

COMPUTER FACIAL COMPOSITES

SOPHISTICATED SOFTWARE makes it possible to generate a likeness of a suspect from a victim's or a witness's description. A sketch is automatically assembled from a stored library of thousands of features on the basis of the description given. The initial sketch can then be modified to portray unique characteristics, different hair colors, and disguises.

taken, the location of the robbery, and the kinds of articles or materials involved. In a bar or restaurant, for example, investigators might ask witnesses whether the robber sat down and, if so, where? The counter or tabletop could be processed for fingerprints, as could the menu or the salt and pepper shakers or the glass of water he or she may have drunk from. In a convenience store robbery, the front doors could be examined to see if the subject has left prints on the glass or handle. All physical evidence must be collected in accordance with department policy and recorded and transferred according to strict guidelines for chain of custody to remain intact.

Surveillance Cameras and Robbery Investigations

Although physical evidence in robberies is often scant, an establishment that has been robbed may have had a surveillance camera operating during the robbery. The tape from such a camera can be an important tool for identifying the suspects and can serve as evidence in court after their capture. Hidden surveillance cameras have been used successfully in solving robberies in banks, large department stores, and even small convenience stores. When installed and positioned properly and when the lighting is adequate, surveillance cameras can provide investigators with particularly useful information.

Photographs of three fugitive bank robbers taken by hidden surveillance cameras.

During recent years, banks have begun using digital surveillance cameras, which can provide high-quality images of suspects to police and the media almost immediately following a robbery. Digital surveillance cameras have also benefited banks in their effort to foil robberies in recent years as the FBI has reallocated its resources away from chasing bank robbers and toward averting acts of terrorism. With the FBI reducing attention toward bank robberies, a greater burden has fallen on state and local police departments, which lack the training and assets of an FBI field office. The improved images from surveillance pictures have enabled police detectives to make matches with their criminal files faster than in the past ("Digital Technology," 2004).

SUMMARY

Learning Objective 1

Robbery is a very serious crime that costs citizens and the government millions of dollars each year. Robbery is one of eight crimes that the FBI considers the most serious crimes in American society. The FBI reports yearly statistics on robbery in its Uniform Crime Reports (UCR). In 2002 robbery made up 3.5 percent of the crime reported in the UCR. Although the percentage of robbery crimes is low, robbery is a crime feared by many people because of its potential for violence.

Learning Objective 2

State statutes define what constitutes the crime of robbery in each state. Generally, these statutes have the following elements in common: Robbery is (1) the wrongful taking of personal property (2) in the presence of or from the owner or person in control of the property, (3) against the person's will by force or the threat of force, and (4) fear is present.

Learning Objective 3

Robberies can be divided into four categories: residential, commercial, street, and vehicle-driver.

Learning Objective 4

Robbers can be divided into four types: professional, opportunistic, drug-addicted, and alcoholic.

Learning Objective 5

Because the circumstances of the crime vary, any procedures or strategies used in investigating a robbery must be flexible. En route to the crime scene, officers should make sure all information available has been received accurately from the dispatcher. The responding officer should check the address of the location and, if known, whether the robbery is still in progress, how many suspects there are, what sort of weapon(s) is being used or shown, and whether there is any description of the suspects. The three primary objectives of an officer arriving on the scene of a robbery are (1) public safety, (2) officer protection, and (3) control over the crime scene.

KEY TERMS

crime index 206	street robbery 209	alcoholic robber 212
index crime 206	vehicle-driver robbery 210	response time 213
clear cases 206	carjacking 210	action stereotyping 214
robbery 207	professional robber 212	physical stereotyping 214
residential robbery 208	opportunistic robber 212	situational stereotyping 214
commercial robbery 209	drug-addicted robber 212	

QUESTIONS FOR REVIEW

Learning Objective 1

1. Why do many Americans seem to especially fear being robbed?
2. Robbery is considered an *index crime;* what does that mean?

Learning Objective 2

3. What are two key elements that distinguish *robbery* from *theft*?
4. How much force must be used to qualify as an element of robbery?
5. What kind of fear is necessary for the crime of robbery?
6. What are the legal elements necessary for a crime to be classified as a robbery?

Learning Objective 3

7. How would you classify the robbery of someone living in a trailer?
8. If the patrons of a coffee shop are robbed in broad daylight, how would you classify this robbery?
9. Why do some jurisdictions classify purse snatching as a street robbery?
10. Why do street robbery victims sometimes offer little information about their attackers' descriptions?
11. Why are taxicabs frequently targets of vehicle robberies?
12. How is a carjacking different from a car theft?

Learning Objective 4

13. What may motivate an alcoholic robber to commit robbery?
14. Describe some characteristics of a professional robber.

Learning Objective 5

15. What is meant by *action stereotyping*?
16. When is a supplemental broadcast sent?
17. How might a surveillance camera aid in the investigation of a bank robbery?
18. How have digital cameras aided in resolving bank robberies?

CRITICAL THINKING EXERCISE

Divide the class into several small groups of five or six people. Read the scenario that follows, and devise a group response to the question. Compare you group's response to the response of other groups.

> You and your fellow officer have just responded to a robbery call at a supermarket. Upon arriving at the scene, the two of you split up. While conducting an immediate investigation, you are confronted by a robbery suspect who has surprised and disarmed your partner. The suspect shouts angrily for you to drop your gun and threatens to kill your partner if you do not comply. What will you do?

INVESTIGATIVE SKILL BUILDERS

You answer a robbery-in-progress call at a drugstore. When you arrive, a middle-aged man wearing a white lab coat is behind the counter. He assures you that the call must have been a prank or a false alarm and that everything is fine. What should you do before leaving?

Integrity/Honesty

You have been working a foot-patrol beat for several months. During that time, you have regularly eaten your lunch at Big John's Diner. Normally, when you eat at the diner, you receive your bill and pay it like any other customer. However, last week you foiled an armed robbery at the diner. To show his appreciation, Big John has told you that he really does not want you to pay for your meals there. Today, when you leave the money for lunch, Big John comes running after you with the money. He pushes it back at you and says, "If you keep paying for your meals, I am going to be insulted." How should you handle this situation?

11 Assault

FIGURE 11.1 Aggravated Assault Crime Index Totals

Year	Number of Offenses	Crime Index Total	Rate Per 100,000 People
2000	911,706	11,608,070	324.0
2001	907,219	11,849,006	318.5
2002	891,407	11,877,218	310.1
2003	859,030	1,383,676	295.4
2004	854,911	1,367,009	291.1

Source: Federal Bureau of Investigation, *Crime in the United States, 2000, 2001, 2002, 2003, 2004*. Washington DC: U.S. Government Printing Office.

OVERVIEW OF ASSAULT

An assault is an unlawful attempt or threat to commit a physical injury to another through the use of force. In 2004 the FBI reported 854,911 assaults, indicating a decrease of approximately one-half percent from the preceding year. As Figure 11.1 shows, the number of aggravated assaults has decreased for a fourth consecutive year; nonetheless, aggravated assaults represented 62.5 percent of the violent crimes committed in the United States during 2004, making it the most frequent of the crimes against people (FBI, 2005).

LEGAL ELEMENTS OF THE CRIME OF ASSAULT

At one time, in many states the term **assault** referred to threats of or attempts to cause bodily harm. The term **battery** referred to actually carrying out these threats of physical harm. Actual physical contact was not required for an assault to have taken place. The mere threat or fear of an attack coupled with the ability of the attacker to carry out the threat was sufficient.

Today most states have revised their statutes, and the term *assault* is used virtually synonymously with *battery;* thus the once separate crimes have been combined in a single crime called *assault.* Some states do, however, retain separate statutes for assault and battery: *assault* typically remains threats of or attempts to cause bodily harm, and *battery* is typically understood as any unwanted touching or carrying out threats to do bodily harm. It is important to become acquainted with your state's particular statutes. In this chapter, the term *assault* includes the more serious charge of battery as well.

assault An unlawful attempt or threat to commit a physical injury to another through the use of force.

battery Once used commonly to refer to actually carrying out the threat of physical harm in an assault; today most jurisdictions use the terms synonymously and call the crime *assault.*

FYI The California Penal Code defines *assault* as "an unlawful attempt, coupled with a present ability, to commit a violent injury on the person of another." It defines *battery* as "any willful and unlawful use of violence upon the person of another." These statutes were originally enacted in 1872.

SOURCE: *California Penal Code.* 2006. Belmont, CA: Thompson/West, pp.100, 102.

Classification of Assault

Assaults are frequently divided into two general categories: simple assault and aggravated assault (or felonious assault).

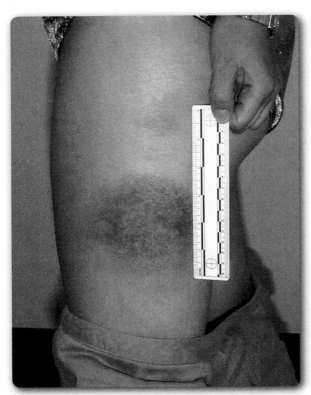

A punch to a person's body may be considered a simple assault.

Simple Assault **Simple assault** can be defined as intentionally causing fear in another person or immediate bodily harm or death. It also may include intentionally inflicting or attempting to inflict bodily harm on another person. Simple assault is usually a misdemeanor. Different jurisdictions may have slightly varying statutes, but most share several common elements, which include:

1. Intent to do bodily harm to another individual
2. Actual and present ability to do bodily harm
3. Commission of some overt act demonstrating intent to carry out the assault

The purpose of the first element is to ensure than an *accident* did not cause the injury and that the person acted intentionally. For instance, while a person is trying on a pair of tight-fitting driving gloves in a department store, his or her hand slips and strikes another person who is also trying on gloves. The striking is an accident and therefore not legally an assault.

The second element ensures that the accused person was physically capable of committing the act at the time of the alleged assault. For example, someone throwing a baseball at the head of a person 800 yards away is unlikely to have the ability to hit his or her victim.

The third element ensures that more than an empty threat or meaningless gesture occurred or was perceived. If a subject was in range of striking another and took a menacing step in the direction of the would-be victim with his or her fists clenched, an assault can be proved—even if a third party interrupted the act by stepping between the two individuals.

simple assault Intentionally causing fear in a person of immediate bodily harm or death.

aggravated (felonious) assault An unlawful attack on another person with the intention of causing severe bodily harm.

Aggravated Assault In an **aggravated assault** an individual unlawfully attacks another person with the intention of causing severe bodily harm. Aggravated assaults are considered felonies. An aggravated assault must include all three elements of a simple assault and an additional element:

4. Intentional inflicting of bodily harm that has resulted in one or more of the following:
   a. Sufficient injury to cause a high probability of death
   b. Severe physical disfigurement
   c. Permanent loss of prolonged impairment of the use or function of any body part or organ, or any injury to the body

Aggravated assaults are usually committed with a weapon that is likely to produce serious injury or a potentially fatal wound. Thus, if a blow to the head with a golf club is sufficient to cause unconsciousness, the blow is classified as an aggravated assault. A knife or gunshot that causes massive bleeding is likewise considered an aggravated assault. The loss of an eye after a severe trauma, such as being struck by a fist or club, makes the striking an aggravated assault. Finally, maiming, such as inflicting a wound that resulted in the loss of an arm or a leg, is also considered aggravated assault.

HISTORY

STALKING CAME TO NATIONAL FOCUS IN 1989 when a young rising starlet by the name of Rebecca Schaffer was killed by Robert John Bardo as she answered the door to her apartment. Schaeffer was a vibrant 21-year-old actress who played a character in the popular 1980s sitcom *My Sister Sam*. Shortly before her murder, she had starred in her first movie. Bardo, a 19-year-old man from Tucson, Arizona, had been writing to Schaffer for some time, and she had written back and even sent him an autographed photograph. Bardo became fixated on the young actress, going so far as to build a shrine to her in his room using media photographs. He employed a detective agency to track down her home address and also used a computer database to determine what kind of car she drove and where she generally shopped. Having located her West Hollywood home, one day he simply waited in front for hours. After a studio person dropped off materials for her to review, he went to the door. At first he was rebuffed by Schaffer, who politely told him she was too busy to speak with him. He then returned, and when Schaffer opened the door this time, he shot her point blank. Bardo was located the next day in Tucson, Arizona, and arrested. He was extradited to California where he was convicted of first-degree murder and sentenced to life in prison without parole (Layton, 2002).

Any of these additional elements changes the assault from simple to aggravated. In some jurisdictions the statutes do not require actual damage to the body to shift from simple to aggravated assault. In these states, it is sufficient that the attacker employed a weapon that caused another to fear or expect immediate harm or death.

Stalking: A New Assault Technique

Stalking is behavior in which a person "intentionally and repeatedly follows, attempts to contact, harasses, and/or intimidates another person" (Geberth, 1992, p. 139). Meloy (1999) claimed, that while stalking is actually an old behavior, it is a relatively new *crime*. In 1991 the California legislature passed the country's first antistalking law (Penal Code Section 646.9). California's stalking law went through several revisions until it developed in 1994 into this current version:

> Any person who willfully, maliciously, and repeatedly follows or willfully and maliciously harasses another person and who makes a credible threat with the intent to place that person in reasonable fear for his or her safety, or the safety of his or her immediate family is guilty of the crime of stalking, punishable by imprisonment in a county jail for not more than one year, or by a fine of not more than one thousand dollars ($1,000), or by both that fine and imprisonment, or by imprisonment in the state prison. (*California Penal Code*, 2006, p. 392)

In some cases the stalker is an individual enamored with a famous person, but the majority of stalkers are estranged husbands or boyfriends, or in some way are known to the victim (Hoffman, 2005; Tjaden & Thoennes, 1998; Tucker, 1993).

Traditionally, most police agencies have responded to stalking by recommending that the victim seek a **restraining order** against the stalker. Until recently, however, restraining orders were really not worth the ink they were printed with. In 1994 Colorado led the way by passing a domestic violence act that included arrest for violating a restraining order. Also, a number of states began establishing specific stalking laws. Currently, all fifty states have stalking laws of some form (Hoffman, 2005).

stalking Intentionally and repeatedly following, attempting to contact, harassing, or intimidating another person.

restraining order Court order requiring a person to do or refrain from doing a particular thing.

Research suggests that nearly 90 percent of all stalkers are men, and 81 percent of the women being stalked are stalked by current or former intimate partners (Stalking Fact Sheet, 2005).

Not all stalkers are alike, however. Zona, Sharma, and Lane (1993) developed a typology that identifies three stalker categories: erotomania, love obsessional, and simple obsessional.

Erotomania   In erotomania the stalker develops the delusional belief that he or she is passionately loved by another person (the stalking victim). This is a rather rare form of stalking.

Love Obsessional   The love obsessional group of stalkers shares many of the attributes of those in the erotomania group, including the false belief that the victim is in love with the stalker. However, for stalkers in the love obessional group, this belief is only one of many delusions they may experience. Some members of this categorical grouping may only be obsessed with *their love* for a victim, without believing the victim loves them in return. Typically, celebrity stalkers are classified as *love obssessional.*

Simple Obsessional   Stalkers classified as *simple obsessional* are among the most common type. The stalker usually has had a prior relationship with the victim, often an intimate one in the context of some form of domestic violence (Hoffman, 2005).

INVESTIGATING ASSAULTS

In many assault cases the assailant and the victim know each other well or are at least acquainted with one another. The Bureau of Justice Statistics regularly conducts a national survey of the victim–offender relationship in crimes of violence. Information from the 2004 survey indicates that 3 percent of the aggravated assaults were between intimately known persons, 7 percent involved victims and assailants who were other types of relatives, and 35 percent of the aggravated assaults reported were between persons who knew each other (friends and acquaintances). Taken together these three categories of nonstranger assailants represent 44 percent of the aggravated assaults reported in 2004 (Criminal Victimization, 2004).

The relationship between parties in an assault can create certain investigative problems. Friends or relatives may be unwilling to file a complaint against an assailant. In addition, it is difficult to determine who is the actual victim in some assaults. This is particularly true when a fight has occurred. Furthermore, responding to an assault call—especially between family members—can be particularly dangerous for officers.

Usually, patrol officers make the initial response to an assault call. According to the UCR, each year more officers are injured and killed answering assault and **domestic assault** (assault between family members) calls than calls for almost any other category of crime (Sourcebook, 2004). Officers must use extreme caution when answering assault calls.

Investigating assault cases has a number of dangers. For example, officers frequently arrive on the scene when the parties are in a heated emotional state or in the middle of a fight. The officer's immediate task is to take control of the situation, separate the parties, and check for injuries. If injuries are found, they should be treated with first aid, and, if necessary, medical personnel should be summoned.

Next, the officer should find out what happened and try to determine who is an assailant and who is a victim. It is important that the officer remain emotionally detached and not take sides in a dispute. Arguments and problems arising from simple assaults are not always that simple to resolve. The assault may be the culmination of a long history of complicated disagreements. Moreover, what an officer sees immediately

domestic assault   Any type of battery that occurs between individuals who are related or between individuals and their significant others.

upon arriving may not be what it seems. A wounded or unconscious person lying on the couch may not be the victim. It may be the assailant, overcome by the victim.

A second danger to officers investigating assaults is **complacency,** or taking things for granted. Officers on patrol sometimes grow accustomed to being dispatched to a particular address for a domestic violence call. Because they have been there before and feel they know the parties involved, they can become careless. Officers must stay guarded and alert whenever answering assault calls. The victim of domestic violence can quickly shift gears and become an ally to the attacker when the police arrive. Suddenly, both parties may be attacking the officer (Jackson, 1996).

After carefully separating, interviewing, and checking the suspect and the victim, the officer should determine whether a crime has occurred and whether the assault is simple or aggravated. Next, the officer must determine whether an arrest is warranted. A simple assault committed outside the officer's presence is a misdemeanor, and the victim must file a complaint for action to be taken. The officer should advise the victim that he or she can file a complaint against the assailant, and the officer should explain how to file one. In some jurisdictions, the victim can even make a private person's arrest—often called a **citizen's arrest.** Officers can assist the victim in making an arrest if that is the victim's desire. If necessary, the victim should be referred to an appropriate social service agency for follow-up counseling or assistance.

John Wayne Bobbit came to fame in 1993 when his wife, Lorena Bobbit, cut off his penis as he slept and used *Battered Wife Syndrome* as her successful defense at trial. In 2002, John Wayne Bobbit was arrested and charged with domestic violence in a separate case and with a different woman.

When investigating an aggravated assault, investigators must be sure to obtain all the facts relative to a complaint. As in other criminal investigations, a series of ordered steps is suggested for investigating aggravated assault:

- Assess the scene and render first aid if needed; determine if additional medical support is needed.

- Determine whether a crime has been committed. If so, what specific crime or crimes?

- Protect the crime scene. Officers should follow the usual procedures for finding and securing evidence. Two important pieces of evidence are photographs of injuries and the weapon used in the assault.

- Identify and locate witnesses, victims, and suspects. Keep all parties separated so that in interviews they will state their own observations and accounts.

- Identify and arrest the assailant, if possible, or determine whether a fresh pursuit would be of value and whether the suspect is even in the vicinity.

- Initiate a radio broadcast of the suspect's description, including any other pertinent information.

DOMESTIC ASSAULT

Many of the nation's assaults occur between family members. **Intrafamily violence,** as many sociologists now call this phenomenon, has become a serious and perplexing problem in the United States in recent years. Assaults by strangers often occur in public, such as on the street, at a store, a park, or a parking lot. These crimes are

complacency   Lack of care resulting from having grown accustomed to a given pattern of events or behavior; taking for granted certain events and circumstances.

citizen's arrest   An arrest by a private individual, as contrasted with a police officer, permitted under certain circumstances for a felony or for a misdemeanor amounting to a breach of the peace.

intrafamily violence   Any type of violent behavior directed toward a family member.

preventable through police patrols or other police intervention strategies. Domestic assaults usually occur in private residences and were believed to be largely inaccessible to police. As a result, the police were thought to be unable to do anything to prevent them unless summoned by one of the parties.

The Police Foundation examined domestic assaults and domestic homicides that occurred in Kansas City, Missouri, during a two-year period. This study revealed that in the two years preceding a reported domestic assault or homicide, the police had been called to the address of the incident five or more times in half of the cases (Police Foundation, 1977). In short, in a number of instances police intervention may reduce or prevent intrafamily violence. Failure to take more serious action when arriving at the scene has caused many states to adopt laws that mandate an arrest in an apparent domestic violence assault case.

In another study, Sherman and Berk (1984) found that when police made an arrest the suspect was less likely to assault his spouse or girlfriend again than if the police merely gave advice or ordered him to leave the premises. This study concluded that in cases of domestic assault, whenever possible, officers should make an arrest unless there is a clear reason to believe an arrest would be counterproductive.

A third study, conducted by Langan and Innes (1986), examined whether calling the police had any impact on subsequent violence in domestic assault cases, and they found that it did. Calling the police was associated with lower rates of subsequent violence. Moreover, even when violence *did* occur after a call to the police, it was no more serious than violence against women who had not called the police.

Taken together, these studies strongly suggest that police can reduce intrafamily violence. It is important that officers consider carefully whether to make an arrest on a domestic assault call. As will be discussed, in some jurisdictions this decision is enforced by statutes.

Assaults against Spouses

The shadowy figures of death and mayhem related to domestic assaults and homicides have always been with society. They came to the forefront of social concern in 1994 with the enormous media coverage of the O. J. Simpson murder trial and allegations of Simpson's spousal abuse throughout his marriage to Nicole Brown Simpson. The Simpson case showed many American women that clinging to destructive relationships can place them in dire jeopardy.

In New York, only weeks after the murder of Nicole Simpson, the state legislature unanimously passed a sweeping bill that mandates arrest for any person who commits a domestic assault. In 1994 Colorado established one of the toughest anti-domestic-violence laws in the country. Not only are police officers required to take assailants in domestic assaults into custody at the scene of violence, but they are also required to arrest a subject for a first-time violation of a restraining order! Subsequent violations of the restraining order carry mandatory jail time. Domestic violence coalitions across the country used the media coverage of the O. J. Simpson trial in many ways to educate the public on domestic assaults and homicides (Blackman et al., 1994).

Slightly more than a third of all visits to emergency rooms by women are for injuries that occur during domestic assaults. Some studies have reported that women are just as likely to start a fight as men; however, many other studies indicate that women are six times as likely to be seriously injured in a fight. In 1992 the American Medical Association, along with the surgeon general, declared that violent men constitute a major threat to women's health in the United States. In 1993 the National

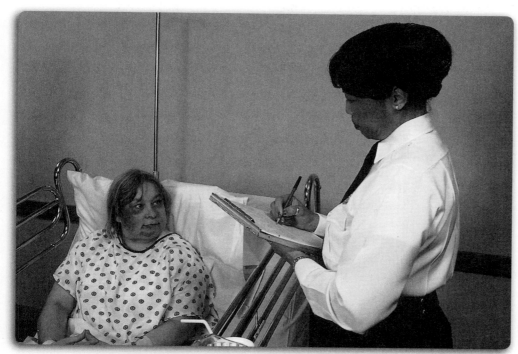

Slightly more than a third of all visits to emergency rooms by women are for injuries from domestic assault.

League of Cities estimated that as many as half of all American women will experience violence from their spouses or boyfriends at some time during their relationship (Booth, McDowell, & Simpson, 1993).

Perhaps the most gruesome report is one by the March of Dimes, which concluded that the battering of women *during pregnancy* causes more birth defects than all the diseases for which children are usually immunized combined (Booth, McDowell, & Simpson, 1993).

It has been estimated that nearly 5.3 million incidents of Intimate Partner Violence (IPV) occur each year among U.S. women age 18 and older (Tjaden & Thoennes, 2000). In 2001, 20 percent of all nonfatal violence against females was committed by a husband or boyfriend (Rennison, 2003). Because of the enormity of violence against women and especially domestic partners, most jurisdictions across the United States have established domestic violence statutes.

Domestic violence statutes require officers to make arrests even without a signed complaint (Connor, 1990; Roberts & Kurst-Swanger, 2002). In effect, the officer becomes the complainant. Under these statutes, a responding officer must make an arrest even if the victim does not desire to file a complaint and the officer was not present during the attack. Typically, these statutes require that the officer have probable cause to believe that there has been some form of physical violence. This might be fresh scratches or bruises on the arms or the face of the victim, or trickles of blood from a small cut on the victim's lip or nose.

domestic violence statutes Laws that outlaw physical violence against any family member; responding officers serve as the complainant in domestic assault situations under certain circumstances.

Assaults against Children

No one knows for sure how many children are assaulted in families each year. The statistics represent only reported cases, and it is likely that many instances of child

child abuse Physical harm, including sexual abuse, or emotional harm inflicted on children.

battered child syndrome The group of injuries suffered by physically abused children.

assaults and abuse go unreported. **Child abuse** can be physical harm, including hitting and sexual abuse, as well as emotional harm from psychological degradation (calling the child by derogatory or insulting names and creating a sense of humiliation, shame, and worthlessness). Generally, the abusers are parents or close relatives, and the incidents happen repeatedly (Crosson-Tower, 2005). In many cases, parents and other relatives who assault children were themselves abused as children (Palacios, 2006).

The clinical term for the injuries suffered by physically abused children is **battered child syndrome.** The physical abuse of children takes many forms, from minor assaults to outright physical torture. Children may be beaten with a belt or cord; burned with cigarettes, flames, or hot liquids; or slapped, punched, thrown, knocked down, or kicked. Abusive parents are generally isolated. They may have no one to turn to for relief from everyday frustrations. In many cases, such parents lack information and resources about child development. They do not know what a child can reasonably be expected to do or how a child may act at certain ages. The tendency to abuse children is increased by such problems as unemployment, low self-esteem, poor stress management skills, marital conflicts, and drug and alcohol use (Palacios, 2006).

Parents or caregivers may give various reasons for injuries to their children. They may blame an injury on an accident or on actions of a sibling. Explanations such as falling down stairs, running into walls and doors, and tripping on sidewalk cracks are common explanations offered by parents for their children's injuries. Investigators should always be suspicious of explanations that seem inconsistent with the injuries a child has sustained. Intentional injuries to children generally occur on the face, back, ribs, buttocks, genitals, palms, or soles of the feet.

One form of child abuse that has begun to intrigue many law enforcement agencies is Munchausen syndrome by proxy (MSBP or MSP). Munchausen's syndrome, in general, refers to a psychiatric disorder in which patients pretend to have illnesses to garner attention by having many medical tests, hospital stays, and surgical procedures. **Munchausen's syndrome by proxy** (MSBP) is a parenting disorder in which parents or caregivers, usually the mother, fabricate symptoms in the child to gain attention through pity and sympathy as the child is subjected to unnecessary medical tests or surgical procedures. In some cases the parents or caregivers also inflict injury, expose the child to contaminants or even poison, and sometimes inadvertently kill the child in the process. For example, subjects may report finding blood in the child's urine and actually prick their own finger to introduce blood into a urine sample. Repeated retesting of new samples of urine, taken when the suspected MSBP offender is not present,

Munchausen syndrome by proxy A parenting disorder in which parents or caregivers, usually the mother, fabricate symptoms in their children to gain attention.

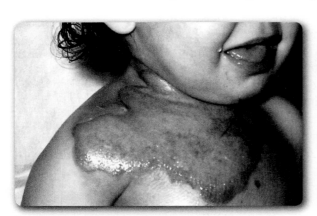

will fail to uncover blood. In some instances the offender will tamper with a medical chart once the child has been hospitalized, indicating fevers or other symptoms that were never actually detected. Some offenders have suffocated children to cause respiratory distress or injected feces diluted with water or household chemicals into a child to create a toxic reaction. Many time these events become genuinely life-threatening to the child (Geberth, 1994; Hayward-Brown, 2004).

When police are contacted about a possible case of MSBP, it is usually because of the suspicions of a health professional. Investigators should make use of this medical contact and any other relevant contacts with social services or social welfare agencies, as well as the prosecutor's office (Hanon, 1991; Lasher & Sheridan, 2004).

Assaults against children have increased dramatically. The abuse of children takes many forms.

As in any assault case, evidence is an important investigative goal. Among the most common procedures for securing evidence in an MSBP case is separation of the suspect and the victim. If the symptoms of illness cease or dissipate when the two are kept apart, and if the symptoms reappear shortly after the two are reunited, the inference of MSBP is quite strong.

Hidden cameras are also effective in investigating MSBP cases. Video surveillance can be particularly effective for confronting the offenders, who frequently lie pathologically about their involvement in making their child ill. Extreme care must be taken when surveillance is used because the suspect has access to the victim and may cause further harm.

Assaults against Elders

Elderly family members may also be the object of physical violence. A family member may take out his or her frustration on elderly parents or aunts or uncles who cannot defend themselves. Such abuse may also take place in retirement and elder care home and nursing facilities (Payne, 2005). As in child abuse cases, investigators should look for an injury that does not fit the explanation for the injury. Common injuries inflicted on elders include burns, cuts, pinches, bruises and welts, dehydration or malnutrition, soiled clothing or bedding, and injuries to parts of the body normally hidden by clothing.

SUMMARY

Learning Objective 1

Assault is an unlawful attempt or threat to commit a physical injury to another through the use of force. Aggravated assault is one of the eight crimes that the FBI considers the most serious. The FBI reports yearly statistics on aggravated assault in its Uniform Crime Reports (UCR). In 2004 aggravated assaults represented 62.5 percent of the violent crimes committed in the United States, making it the most frequent of the crimes against people.

Learning Objective 2

Assaults are classified as *simple assaults* and *aggravated* (felonious) *assaults,* which are defined by state statutes. Generally, simple assaults have these elements: intent to do bodily harm to another individual, actual present ability to do bodily harm, and commission of an overt act demonstrating intent to carry out the assault. An aggravated assault has these elements in addition to an intentional infliction of bodily harm that results in (a) injury sufficient to cause a high probability of death, (b) severe physical disfigurement, or (c) permanent loss or prolonged impairment of the use or function of any body part or organ or any severe injury to the body.

Learning Objective 3

When responding to an assault complaint, the responding officer's immediate task is to take control of the situation, separate the parties involved, and check for injuries. Next, the officer should find out what happened and try to determine who is an assailant and who is a victim. After separating, interviewing, and checking the parties involved, the officer should determine whether a crime has occurred and whether the situation is a simple or aggravated assault. The crime scene should then be secured and preserved, and evidence should be collected. Investigating an assault requires extreme care because the responding officer frequently enters an emotionally charged situation that can quickly shift from one of appreciation to one of attack on the officer.

Learning Objective 4

Assaults among family members are a serious and growing problem. Intrafamily violence can take the form of spousal abuse, child abuse, or elder abuse. Many police agencies are taking a proactive approach to domestic violence and are using intervention strategies to reduce or prevent intrafamily violence. Some states have passed domestic violence statutes that allow the responding officer to serve as the complainant in a domestic assault under certain circumstances.

KEY TERMS

assault 221
battery 221
simple assault 222
aggravated (felonious) assault 222
stalking 223

restraining order 223
domestic assault 224
complacency 225
citizen's arrest 225
intrafamily violence 225

domestic violence statutes 227
child abuse 228
battered child syndrome 228
Munchausen syndrome by proxy 228

QUESTIONS FOR REVIEW

Learning Objective 1

1. What are the essential elements (*corpus delicti*) of a simple assault?

Learning Objective 2

2. What elements distinguish an *aggravated assault* from a *simple assault?*
3. If a victim lost an eye after being intentionally punched, how would you classify the assault?
4. If a victim lost an eye due to a wild pitch at a high school baseball game that struck him in his eye, how would you classify that assault?
5. What is *stalking*, and how is it related to assault?

Learning Objective 3

6. Why is an immediate police response to assault calls recommended?
7. Why is it important to consider the relationship between parties in an assault case during an investigation?

Learning Objective 4

8. Why might it be better to arrest an assailant in a domestic assault rather than just advise him at the scene to behave?
9. What is meant by *intrafamily violence?*
10. Why should officers never take any domestic assault call—even a repeated one—for granted?
11. How can *complacency* become a serious risk to an officer's safety on a domestic assault call?
12. What is meant by *Munchausen syndrome by proxy?*

CRITICAL THINKING EXERCISES

1. Consult your state's criminal statutes and locate the definitions of all the classes of the crime of assault in your state. Using these definitions, create a list of possible misdemeanor and felony assaults that would fit into the various classes. Share your list with others in the class and resolve any disagreements about classification.

2. In your local newspaper, find a recent article that describes a domestic assault or homicide. Discuss the facts of the case in class, and consider what the police might have been able to do to prevent the assault or homicide.

INVESTIGATIVE SKILL BUILDERS

Acquiring and Evaluating Information

You arrive at the scene of a domestic assault call. After you and your partner have separated the man and women at the scene, you interview the man. He tells you that he is tired of seeing his kid sick all the time. Every time the man goes on a business trip, he comes home to find that his son, Gerald, has gone to the emergency room. You learn that this seems to have started about three years ago, about the time the man began a job that took him out of town twice a month. You ask what types of problems Gerald has been having, and the man tells you, "That's the funny thing, officer. He seems to keep getting these strange infections. Sometimes he has violent vomiting that the doctors just can't figure out the cause for." You ask if Gerald has seen a regular doctor to monitor any of these mysterious illnesses. He tells you that his wife has trouble keeping doctors because they can never determine the cause of Gerald's illnesses.

1. Should you investigate anything more than what actually caused the domestic disturbance?
2. Do you have any suspicions about what may be going on with Gerald?
3. Should any follow-up investigation be undertaken? If so, what should the investigators consider doing?

Integrity/Honesty

You and your partner receive a call that a fight has broken out at a local neighborhood bar. When you arrive, you realize that one of the two men fighting is a good friend of yours. When you separate the two of them, you take your friend aside and have your partner take the other man to discuss what happened. From your friend you learn that both men had been drinking and that they had gotten into an argument over a football game bet. Your friend also admits to you that he threw the first punch—and maybe even the second punch. The other man is bleeding from his mouth and lip and is insisting on filing charges of assault against your friend.

1. What type of assault has taken place?
2. Should you arrest your friend or try to talk the other man out of filing charges?

12 Sexual Assault and Rape

After completing this chapter, you will be able to:

1 Provide an overview of sex crimes in the United States.
2 Identify six categories of sex offenses.
3 Explain the legal elements of the crime of rape (sexual assault).
4 Distinguish between *forcible rape* and *statutory rape.*
5 Discuss the special circumstances of rape and sexual assault investigations.
6 List the categories of sex crimes against children.
7 Describe the special demands required when investigating sex crimes against children.
8 Specify the five basic stages of child development and tell how knowledge of these stages can assist an investigator.

OVERVIEW OF SEX CRIMES

Sex crimes represent a broad classification of illegal behavior. They range from nuisance crimes, such as voyeurism and exhibitionism, to offenses such as forcible rape and lust crimes, which are a significant threat to society. Investigating sex crimes is a challenge for criminal investigators. Discussing sexual topics is a fairly sensitive and guarded area of conversation in most social settings, making what is already a difficult task more difficult. Those committing sexual crimes are generally regarded as vile and contemptible, and officers who investigate these criminals sometimes become tainted just by contact with these offenders. As with other crimes, the quality of the investigation will significantly affect the outcome in a court case. However, in serious sex crimes, the manner in which the investigation is conducted will also have an effect on the victim's psychological well-being. Consequently, sex crime investigators need to be especially sensitive to the victims they interview and often seek avenues to increase their skills for work with such victims, such as attending seminars, taking specialized in-service courses, and undertaking specialized readings (Carney, 2003).

Forcible rape is the only sex offense that is classified as an index crime. According to the Uniform Crime Reports (UCR) definition, the victims of forcible rape are always female. During 2004, approximately 94,635 females nationwide were victims of forcible rape (Figure 12.1). This estimate represents a small increase of 0.8 percent from the 2003 number and a 4.9 percent rise from the 2000 figure. However, the 2004 data showed a 2.9 percent decrease when compared to the 1995 estimated volume of female forcible rapes.

Rape is the least reported of all index crimes. If you look again at Figure 10.2 in Chapter 10, you will see that forcible rape comprised less than 1 percent (.7) of all offenses reported in 2002. The low rate of forcible rape in comparison with other index crimes does not diminish the violence of this act or the seriousness of this crime. Except for murder, no other crime generates more public concern and causes more personal devastation than forcible rape.

This chapter is not designed to explore what prompts a person to commit sex crimes, what course of therapeutic treatments may be appropriate, or even whether criminals who commit sex crimes can be rehabilitated. The evaluation, diagnosis, treatment, and possible rehabilitation of such criminals are within the realm of the courts and in the hands of psychological and correctional professionals. The purpose of this

FIGURE 12.1 Forcible Rape Crime Index Totals

Year	Number of Forcible Rapes	Rate per 100,000 Inhabitants
1995	97,470	37.1
1996	96,252	36.3
1997	96,153	35.9
1998	93,144	34.5
1999	89,411	32.8
2000	90,178	32.0
2001	90,863	31.8
2002	95,235	33.1
2003	93,883	32.3
2004	94,635	32.2

Source: Federal Bureau of Investigation. 1995–2004. *Crimes in the United States.* Washington, DC: U.S. Government Printing Office.

chapter is to help you gain a better understanding, in a general sense, of sex offenses and to provide you with a working vocabulary of relevant terms and knowledge of the ramifications of specific violations. The sex crimes discussed in this chapter are limited to some of the more common offenses that an investigator might encounter in the field. That does not mean that more exotic, perverse, and bizarre crimes do not occur—they do, and they do so with some regularity.

CLASSIFICATION OF SEX CRIMES

sex crime Any of an assortment of criminal violations related to sexual conduct.

mutual consent Willing participation by both parties in sexual acts.

The term **sex crime** covers a multitude of offenses ranging from indecent exposure and obscene phone calls to forcible rape. Some people try to classify sex crimes on the basis of consent, or more precisely, mutual consent. However, the exact definition of **mutual consent** can be quite elusive. It is not clearly defined in law and is often misinterpreted by defendants who look to it as a defense. For example, in the now infamous Duke University Lacrosse scandal, members of the Duke Lacrosse team were accused of having repeatedly raped an exotic dancer they had employed for a party. One might initially question when an exotic dancer, who upon investigation is found to have performed sexual acts for previous employers, her driver, and her boyfriend, does and does not express consent (Meadows, 2006). Under the law, any implied or expressed consent is immediately withdrawn once a woman indicates she no longer desires to continue whatever sexual activity she may previously have consented to. However, one can readily see where there might be confusion in a court case. Similarly, a person under the temporary influence of alcohol or drugs may not be able to actually or legally consent to a sexual act. A wife who is unwilling to have intercourse with her husband does not consent to sex merely by virtue of marriage vows. Moreover, children cannot legally consent to sex even if they do so verbally and without duress or coercion.

Even when there is mutual consent, a number of acts remain illegal. For instance, in most jurisdictions, prostitution is illegal regardless of whether both parties consent or not. Homosexual sexual encounters and even certain nontraditional sexual acts between heterosexuals, such as anal intercourse, are illegal in some jurisdictions.

It is not necessary to classify each of these crimes separately, or on the basis of mutual consent. Instead, let us consider a classification scheme that encompasses six categories (Figure 12.2). From the perspective of the general public, the most serious offense remains forcible rape, or forcible rape and murder. Rape can be difficult to prove in a court of law. It is up to the investigator to obtain sufficient evidence to make a solid case against a rapist or rapist-murderer.

LEGAL ELEMENTS OF THE CRIME OF RAPE

forcible rape Sexual intercourse against a person's will by use or threat of force.

Rape is usually classified as either forcible or statutory. **Forcible rape** is frequently defined in penal codes as a crime where any of the following conditions have occurred: (1) sexual intercourse against a person's will by use or threat of force, violence, duress, or fear of immediate bodily injury; (2) where a person is prevented from resisting by any intoxicating or anesthetic substance or any controlled substance; (3) where a person is at the time of the act unconscious or asleep; (4) where a person is incapable of giving legal consent because of a mental or developmental disorder or physical disability.

statutory rape Sexual intercourse with a minor, with or without the minor's consent.

Statutory rape is sexual intercourse with a minor, with or without the minor's consent. The definition of a *minor* varies from state to state. Some states define a minor simply as someone under the age of 18. Others have more complex definitions, which may distinguish victims under 14 from those between 14 and 18 or may make a

FIGURE 12.2 Typology of Sexual Offenses

Voluntary (but with inappropriate partners)

- Fornication
- Adultery
- Incest
- Bigamy
- Lewd and illegal cohabitation

Involuntary

- Forcible rape
- Seduction
- Abduction for sexual purposes

Commercial

- Prostitution
- Pimping and pandering
- Indecent publications
- Obscene pornography
- Sale via the Internet of obscene pornography

Abnormal

- Sodomy
- Bestiality
- Sexual perversion
- Lewd and lascivious behavior with a child

Nuisance

- Voyeurism
- Indecent exposure (exhibitionism)
- Frottage
- Transvestism
- Fetishism
- Coprophilia
- Obscenity by telephone, letter, literature, or transmission over the Internet
- Public obscenity by gesture or statement

Dangerous

- Sexual asphyxiation (gasping)
- Flagellation
- Anthropophagy (cannibalism)
- Sexual pyromania
- Piquerism
- Pedophilia
- Lust murders
- Rough sex

rape An act of sexual intercourse, or penetration of the victim's vagina, without consent from the victim and against the victim's will by force, coercion, or duress.

similar distinction between different consenting parties of different ages (for example, a 14-year-old female with a 20-year-old male).

Although each state has its own statutes defining **rape,** all definitions share these *corpus delicti* elements:

- An act of sexual intercourse or penetration of the victim's vagina
- Without consent from the victim
- Against the victim's will and by force, coercion, or duress

date rape Forced sexual intercourse that occurs between friends or acquaintances or while a couple is on a date; also called *acquaintance rape.*

To create more flexible sexual offense laws, a number of states have substituted the words *sexual assault* for the word *rape* in their statutes. In some states, if the suspect is prevented from completing the act, it is classified as *assault with intent to commit rape* or *attempted rape.* Attention has became more focused on sexual offenses that occur between friends or while a couple is on a date. Such crimes are usually labeled **date rape** or *acquaintance rape.* In addition, in keeping with the changing values of society, several states now provide that the victim and the assailant may be of either sex. Even though victims may be either male or female, the offenders tend to be overwhelmingly male (Bureau of Justice Statistics, 2005).

FYI Society is becoming increasingly aware of male rape. Many experts believe that the current male rape statistics vastly underrepresent the actual number of males age 12 and over who are raped each year. Rape crisis counselors estimate that only 1 in every 50 women report their rape to the police, and counselors believe the rates for underreporting by men are even higher (Brochman, 1991). Until the mid-1980s, most research ignored male rape, and much of the literature discussed this violent crime in the context of women victims only.

When one investigates sexual assault crimes, it is important to remain aware of several common reactions of victims of such crimes. Many victims develop an overwhelming feeling of guilt, shame, and worthlessness after a sexual assault. Some fear that their friends and relatives will blame them for the attack and will treat them differently. Others may have had a close relationship with their attacker, or may even be related, and fear that a charge of rape will create family problems. Some victims fear having to go to court and relive their sexual assault. Figure 12.3 shows a national survey of the relationship between rape victims and their attackers.

FIGURE 12.3 Victim and Offender Relationship

Offender	Number of Victims	Percent of All Victims
Nonstranger	136,550	67%
Intimate	35,340	17
Other Relative	5,600	3
Friend/Acquaintance	95,610	47
Stranger	64,040	31
Relationship Unknown	3,090	2
Total	203,680	

Source: Catalano, Shannan M. 2005. *Criminal Victimization, 2004.* Bureau of Justice Statistics, U.S. Department of Justice, Office of Justice Programs, NCJ 210674. Washington, DC: U.S. Government Printing Office.

Rape-Murder

Keppel and Walter (1999) suggested a model for understanding rape-murder, and Salfati and Bateman (2005) recently used this model to assess homicidal behavioral consistencies among offenders to distinguish between instrumental and expressive crimes. The Keppel and Walter (1999) typology includes four categories: power assertive, power reassurance, anger retaliatory, and anger excitation.

Power Assertive Rape-Murder The power assertive rape-murderer plans a series of activities leading up to the rape, but the murder is not part of this careful planning. Rather, the murder is the result of increased aggression on the part of the rapist in his attempt to control the victim.

Power Reassurance Rape-Murder In the power reassurance rape-murder, a planned single rape attack is followed by the murder of the victim. The power reassurance rape-murderer has an idealized seduction and conquest fantasy, which he acts out and fuels by insisting that his victim offer verbal reassurance of his sexual prowess: "It feels good, doesn't it baby?" "I'm the best lover you've ever had, aren't I?" When the victim does not fall in line with the attacker's fantasy, a sense of failure overwhelms the attacker, catapulting him into a murder assault. The power reassurance type of rape-murderer seeks to express his sexual competence through seduction. That failing, the murder of the victim permits him to continue his fantasy.

Anger Retaliatory Rape-Murder The anger retaliatory rape-murderer typically plans a rape, and the murder involves overkill. The murder itself is an anger venting, near cleansing act expressing some sort of symbolic revenge on a female victim. It suggests that the attacker has had poor or failed relationships with women, and he focuses his anguish and contempt for these women into the act of rape and murder. The attacks are not predicated on a fantasy system, but they are often triggered by a woman with power over the assailant criticizing, chiding, or reprimanding him. In an effort to express his revenge for being disciplined, the anger retaliatory rape-murderer lashes out either at the target of his frustration (the woman who disciplined him) or at a substitute woman who symbolically represents this woman.

Anger Excitation Rape-Murder Anger excitation rape-murderers enjoy inflicting pain and fear in their victims. These attackers may torture their victims for prolonged periods of time; the various acts of torture energize the killer's fantasies and temporarily satisfy his desire for domination and control over the victim. Torture and mutilations tend to be ritualized and serve to increase the killer's enjoyment of the process of killing.

INVESTIGATING SEX OFFENSES

An investigator should attend to two tasks right away in a sex crime investigation. First, he or she should make sure that the victim receives any medical attention needed and that a physical examination is done to establish that a rape or sexual assault has occurred. Second, the investigator must protect and preserve the crime scene and any evidence therein. If a suspect is identified incident to or soon after an assault, the suspect's clothing and any other physical evidence should also be secured.

Understanding and sensitivity are essential when working sexual assault cases. As previously mentioned, victims of sexual assault are often on tenuous psychological ground; they are likely to feel frightened, insecure, and sometimes desperate. Some large departments have special sex crime units whose sole task is to investigate sexual offenses. In these

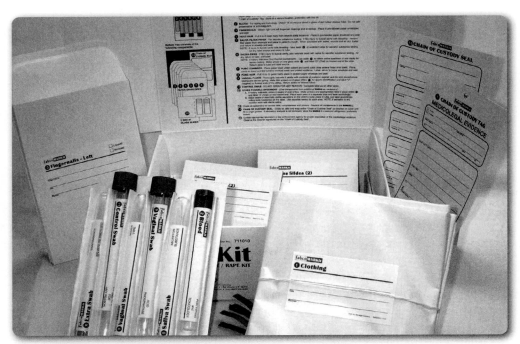

Rape kits are commonly housed in emergency rooms at hospitals.

rape kit An evidence kit typically housed in hospital emergency rooms and used to secure physical evidence specimens in rape cases.

situations, the investigators are likely to have developed relationships with medical professionals in the local hospitals. Investigators may even have fostered alliances with hospital social workers, who can assist in calming and communicating with victims. During the past several decades, many police departments have developed **rape kits,** which are usually housed in the emergency room of the local hospital. A typical rape kit contains tags and containers for specimens taken from a victim of a sexual assault. There may be no evidence at the scene and no witnesses in a sexual assault case; therefore, it is crucial to collect and properly label any evidence found on the clothing or person of the victim. Some kits include a saliva kit, which that can further aid in detecting the presence of saliva as well as extracting DNA for testing ("New Saliva Kit," 2006).

As a matter of practice, the preliminary interview is usually undertaken by the responding officer. While the responding officer may not be female, the officer should be trained to handle preliminary interviews with victims of sexual assault. Many police academies are now including such sensitivity training in their curriculum. After a victim has received medical attention and any evidence has been collected, a follow-up interview should be conducted. In a further effort to consider the feelings of the victim, many departments assign a female officer to interview the victim and to investigate sexual assaults on women and children.

Preliminary interviews with victims should seek information about the attacker, where the assault occurred, and any relevant circumstances surrounding the offense. The preliminary interview should be conducted in a manner that protects the modesty of the victim. If a female officer is not available, the assistance of a female nurse, social worker, or doctor should be requested. Having another woman present during the interview often helps to reassure the victim.

Frequently, preliminary interviews with sexual assault victims take place shortly after the actual assault. This means the trauma and feelings surrounding the attack are still very intense. Investigators should not focus too much on the specific details of the assault. If the victim claims she has been raped, the officer should assume that this is an accurate statement and proceed. If the victim is talking and describing the assault, it is advisable not to interrupt with questions but to allow the story to flow at the victim's own pace. Good investigative techniques in sexual assault cases include careful word choices and questions. Avoid accusatory questions such as "Why did you go back to his apartment?" or "Why were you drinking so heavily?" Such questions have little investigative value and are likely to close down communication channels with the victim (Zulawski, 2001).

> **FYI** The presence of semen is not evidence of rape, nor does its absence mean that a rape has not occurred. Some rapists experience sexual dysfunction. The rapist may be unable to achieve an orgasm, may have difficulty in achieving and sustaining an erection, or may experience premature ejaculation.

Certain essential pieces of information should be gathered during sex crime investigations, including the following:

- Name and contact information of the victim.
- Date and time of the offense.
- Type of assault.
- Age of the victim.
- Physical description of the attacker.
- Location of the assault, including description of the room, alley, park, car, and so on.
- Description of weather conditions, lighting, visibility, or other environmental factors.
- General condition of the victim: emotional state, presence of drugs or alcohol, physical condition (bruises, scratches, cuts, bleeding), medical examination findings, and any indication of pregnancy.
- General condition of the attacker: torn clothes, scratches, or wounds inflicted by the victim.
- Identity and contact information of any possible witnesses, either witnesses to the crime or people who may have seen the victim shortly before or after the crime.
- Any special features, mannerisms, or statements of the suspect or any unusual occurrences recalled by the victim.
- Description of the circumstances leading to the attack, according to the victim, and any possible *modus operandi.*
- Description of any weapon shown or used in the assault.
- Any information about how the attacker fled: description of car or other vehicles, direction of flight, and so forth.
- All physical evidence collected from the victim's body and clothing that might show that a sexual act took place or that might link an act with a suspect.
- All physical evidence found at the scene of the crime that might connect a suspect with the crime.

SEX CRIMES AGAINST CHILDREN

Perhaps more heinous than the crime of rape is the crime of sexual assault against a child. Even violent inmates in prison place child molesters ("short-eyes" in prison slang) at the bottom of the pecking order. Child molesters in prison are sometimes found beaten or killed simply because others have learned that their crimes include the rape of a small child or infant.

Categories of Sexual Assault against Children

child molesting Broad term encompassing any behavior motivated by an unnatural sexual interest in minor children.

Child Molesting
A definition for the sexual abuse of children, **child molesting,** typically includes acts such as fondling, kissing, or sexual penetration of a child under the age of legal juvenile jurisdiction (Hickey, 2006; Murray, 2000). Child molesting, however, is a broad term that may include any behavior motivated by an unnatural or abnormal sexual interest in children. Many states have specific statutes defining this type of sexual offense. Several states have broadened penalties to allow them to fit the severity of the crime, especially when the victim is very young or an infant.

Research suggests that certain characteristics can be associated with typical child molesters. (Litton, 2006, p. 327):

- They are mostly male, although research suggests there have been female perpetrators in some day-care facilities.
- They are likely to have irregular employment histories, previous arrests, and are likely to be married.
- They are more likely than pedophiles to engage in intercourse with their victims.
- When it is not a family member, the perpetrator is not likely to know the victim.
- In family or incest cases, the victim may experience more severe forms of violence and aggression than in nonfamily cases.
- Older victims suffer more brutal forms of abuse.
- Overall more force is used during their offenses, and offenders may use substances such as alcohol to coerce their victims.

pedophile An adult who is sexually attracted to children or performs sexual acts with children; usually a man with a female victim.

Pedophilia
The term **pedophile** is sometimes inaccurately used as a synonym for *child molester;* they are, however, separate conditions. Pedophiles are people who meet the following criteria (American Psychiatric Association, 2000, p. 572):

A. Over a period of at least 6 months, recurrent, intense sexually arousing fantasies, sexual urges, or behaviors involving sexual activity with a prepubescent child or children (generally age 13 years or younger).

B. The person has acted on these sexual urges, or the sexual urges or fantasies caused marked distress or interpersonal difficulty.

C. The person is at least 16 years and at least 5 years older than the child or children in Criterion A.

According to Fontana-Rosa (2001), pedophiles typically have immediate access to children and, unlike child molesters, are more often unmarried. Pedophiles are generally male and at least 25 years old. Pedophiles may live with their parents or alone. They are habitual offenders, and their likelihood of repeating assaults on children is high.

Characteristics associated with pedophiles include the following (Litton, 2006, p. 327):

- Most are male and choose mostly female victims.
- They usually live alone or with their parents (not with roommates).
- They are likely to maintain steady employment histories, and tend to work where they can be close to children such as in schools, parks, or youth clubs.
- They seek affection and affirmation; they want the children they victimize to be their friends.
- They are unlikely to force sexual intercourse on their victims; rather, they are more likely to fondle or touch their victims.
- They perceive themselves as shy, introverted, sensitive, or depressed.

Sexual Seduction   Similar to statutory rape, **sexual seduction** involves encouraging a younger (minor) or less mature person into an illegal sexual situation, such as intercourse. It may additionally represent various forms of sodomy, anal intercourse, cunnilingus, or fellatio committed by an adult with a willing child.

sexual seduction   Sexual intercourse, or other illegal sexual acts, between an adult and a willing minor child.

Lewd and Lascivious Behavior with a Child   The elements of **lewd and lascivious behavior with a child** include touching any part of a child to arouse, appeal to, or gratify the sexual desires of either the child or the perpetrator. Laws against such behavior generally apply to any gender combination of perpetrator and victim. If elements of the crime are present and the suspect is positively identified, a private person can arrest the victim as a public nuisance at the scene. If the act is observed by an officer, he or she can make the arrest.

lewd and lascivious behavior with a child   Touching any part of a child to arousal with a child appealing to or gratifying the sexual desires of either the child or the perpetrating adult.

Indecent Exposure   The crime of **indecent exposure** is among the most common of the standard sex offenses. It involves publicly exhibiting one's genitals. Victims can be either children or adults. The exhibition may occur in any public location, such as in a street or park or from an automobile. The reaction to the offense is a source of sexual pleasure for the offender.

indecent exposure   Exhibiting the private parts of one's body in a lewd or indecent manner to the sight of others in a public place.

Contributing to the Delinquency of a Minor   Statutes pertaining to **contributing to the delinquency of a minor** impose a duty on parents, caregivers, or other adults to refrain from committing any act or omitting the performance of any duty if the act or omission causes or tends to cause or encourage a minor to violate any law or might encourage the minor to lead a dissolute, lewd, immoral, or criminal life. It is often a lesser crime included in other offenses, such as statutory rape, procuring alcohol for a minor, or other felonies in which a minor is a principal in a crime committed by an accompanying adult.

contributing to the delinquency of a minor   An act or omission that contributes to making or tends to make a child delinquent.

Incest   The laws surrounding the offense of **incest** vary from state to state. Most focus on the general prohibition of sexual intercourse between biological relatives. These usually include mother and son, father and daughter, and siblings. However, some state statutes merely prohibit marriage between biological relatives through first cousins, with no specific mention of sexual behavior or regard for the ages of parties involved.

incest   Sexual acts, usually intercourse, between persons who are so closely related that their marriage is illegal or forbidden by custom.

It is commonly thought that incest taboos, which are nearly universal, originated as a means of avoiding the disastrous results of genetic inbreeding. This logic, however, is faulty because many societies in the world do not understand biology or paternity, let alone genetics. More likely, this "natural law" evolved to promote harmony within the family and the society. If a father and a son competed for the sexual and romantic attentions of the father's daughter, the unity of the family would be seriously disrupted. Furthermore, there would be serious role confusion for all members of the family.

In spite of existing laws and the social taboo against incest, it continues to occur at alarming rates (Courtois, 1996). Perpetrators of incestuous assaults on children come from all walks of life and all educational levels. Because an older relative usually perpetrates the sexual assault, it is difficult for a child to come forward or to admit that such behavior has occurred. The most frequently reported form of incest is between fathers and daughters (Wilson & Bolton, 2000).

Various other crimes that sexually exploit children may be defined by statute, including visual or commercial exploitation of children through pornography or pandering (catering to the lower tastes and desires of others). Congress passed the Child Protection Act in 1984, which was designed to protect children from exploitation. The act specifically prohibits child pornography and significantly increases the penalties for it.

Investigating Sex Crimes against Children

Newspapers, magazines, and even the television news bombard the public with stories of children who have been molested or sexually abused. For example, in 2005 pop singer Michael Jackson was accused and tried for the alleged molestation of a 13-year-old boy at his Neverland ranch. Jackson was eventually acquitted, but the case held viewers riveted to their television screens each day for nearly a year. Despite being acquitted, many still believe that Jackson was guilty (Rosenberg, 2005; Showalter, 2005). There have been cases of mothers having their 11-year-old daughters perform sexual favors for men in exchange for crack cocaine, children being held in basements by foster parents and made to perform sexual acts for friends and the foster parents, even social and religious organizations whose members have engaged in sexual misconduct with children. Many people do not believe that such incidents have radically increased in number in recent years. Rather, they suggest that parents and children are more aware and better educated and that reporting techniques have become more effective.

Some perpetrators of child sexual abuse will never be prosecuted. Some remain secretly in the same community, and others move from one community to another to avoid detection. However, relocating may no longer be a solution for convicted offenders. Megan's Law, named after a child who was raped and killed in 1994, was signed by President Clinton in 1996. That law requires convicted rapists to register with the police when they move into a new community. The police in turn notify schools, day cares facilities, and so on.

FYI Most states have a Megan's Law website that provides information on where registered child molesters live. Go to www.megans-law.net and click on your state to see what information is available about child molesters residing in your neighborhood.

A number of federal and state regulations require teachers, doctors, and child-care workers to report to the police any suspicion of child abuse. Frequently, concerned neighbors contact the police with allegations or fears of a child's abuse, neglect, or sexual assault. When such a report reaches the police, they sometimes investigate the allegations on their own. In other cases, police agencies cooperate with the local social service agencies to investigate potential crimes against children.

FOCUS ON TECHNOLOGY

COMBINED DNA INDEX SYSTEM

CODIS (Combined DNA Index System) is a national DNA database that enables state and local law enforcement agencies to link serial violent crimes, especially rapes, to each other and to identify suspects by matching DNA from crime scenes with state databases of convicted sex offenders. As of 1998, all fifty states had passed legislation requiring convicted sex offenders to provide biological samples for the DNA database. Federal, state, and local crime labs can exchange and compare DNA profiles electronically using CODIS, thereby linking crimes to each other and to convicted offenders.

Under welfare regulations and codes, an investigating officer or welfare agent is empowered to place a child in temporary custody—even without a court order—if there is an apparent emergency or if the officer believes the child would be in imminent danger if left in the situation. This power is provided for in the law for the protection and welfare of children at risk.

Multidisciplinary Approach Child sexual abuse is difficult to investigate and even more difficult to prosecute for a number of reasons. First, in small communities, no one wants to believe such crimes could occur. This sort of denial is more acute when it appears the offender is a friend or relative. Evidence in these cases is often difficult to obtain, and blame is shifted from one child protection agency to another when cases are mishandled (Overton, Burns, & Atkins, 1994). Similarly, local community members and child protection agency workers tend to blame the prosecutor's office when child molesters escape justice.

The explanation for these problems rests in part on the way we have historically approached child sexual abuse—namely, as a *family problem* rather than as a *criminal offense*. As a family problem, it has traditionally been handled by child protection agencies. For a very long time, it was handled discretely by counselors and social service agency personnel (Tobin & Kessner, 2002). During the past two decades, however, police have become more inclined to respond to child sexual abuse as a serious and insidious crime. Today, most child sexual abuse cases are referred to the criminal justice system and not simply to a child welfare agency (Overton et al. 1994).

Police agencies have also recognized that child sexual abuse cases require investigators with special training and skill, yet most police academies offer only minimal training in child molestation and sexual abuse cases. Consequently, many—perhaps most—police agencies do not have personnel with the skills needed to effectively investigate such cases.

Police and social service agencies need to work in concert and form multidisciplinary teams. These investigations require the combined talents of police departments, social welfare agencies, and the prosecutor's office. Police personnel process the evidentiary elements of the case, social welfare agency personnel provide therapeutic input, and assistant prosecutors ensure that the rights of both victims and defendants are protected. All these elements are needed to effectively handle the victim and the perpetrator in a child sexual abuse prosecution.

Multidisciplinary teams provide several distinct advantages over more traditional practices, which were more adversarial. First, procedural policies and planned activities can be established, minimizing the number of times the same ground must be covered with victims in interviews. Second, team members can be trained to work together to conduct more effective and therapeutic interviews that yield prosecutable findings. Finally, a team that has worked together on similar cases for a long time increases its shared sensitivity to various issues. For example, team members become more adept at recognizing whether child victims are hiding facts, lying, or telling the truth. Often these cases consist mainly of the child's claim of abuse against the denial of an adult. If there is any question about the truthfulness of the child's testimony, it may be very difficult to obtain a conviction.

The multidisciplinary approach to investigating child sexual abuse cases offers a way to streamline and coordinate prosecution. Furthermore, it tends to reduce the secondary harm and anguish caused by the prosecution of such cases.

Interviewing Child Victims Although interviewing any victim of a sexual assault requires care and concern, interviewing a child victim requires even greater sensitivity. Unless there is a reason for urgency, investigators should interview child victims of sexual assault with the assistance of a qualified professional. Investigators should assess the situation and consider the extent of the child's physical injuries as well as his or her emotional condition.

Children who have been severely brutalized may not be able to provide much information. In addition, it is difficult to predict the quantity or quality of information that may be offered by very young children. It is important, therefore, that the investigator carefully consider when and how to interview the child.

It is also important for investigators to have some understanding of child development. That will allow them to choose appropriate methods and language to gain information and assess a child victim's responses. There are five basic stages in a child's development: infancy, early childhood, preschool age, school age, and adolescence (Gullo, 1994). Investigators familiar with these developmental stages can better determine how likely it is that a victim of a certain age understands the events that occurred and what kinds of questions would be most appropriate to ask. Successful communication with the victim is the key to a favorable outcome in a prosecution.

For example, if an investigator knows that children ages 4 to 6 do not generally understand concepts of relative time, physical space, and distance, the investigator can avoid questions such as "What time was it when Uncle Dan touched your private place?" or "How long was Uncle Dan in the bed with you?" Instead, a time frame relevant to the child might be used: for example, "Was it before supper or after supper that Uncle Dan touched you?" or "Would you say Uncle Dan was in your room for about the same time as one whole cartoon show?"

Although interviewing any victim of sexual abuse requires care and concern, interviewing child victims requires even greater sensitivity.

FIGURE 12.4 Stages of Child Development

Infancy (birth to 2 years old)

Infants rely on *sameness* and continuity of caregivers. They are dependent on their caregivers and begin to develop *basic trust* or *mistrust.* Infants have limited cognitive abilities, are unable to form complex concepts, and have little language ability.

Early childhood (2 to 4 years old)

For the first 2 years, children try to make their bodies do what they want. By age 3, they have gained sufficient muscle control to walk, grasp, control their bowels, and use language. They experiment with *autonomy* and develop a sense of control over their environment. They also begin to develop *preconcepts.* This means that the child is able to respond to symbols and signs but still lacks the capacity to understand most common concepts.

Preschool age (4 to 6 years old)

The child develops *initiative,* which adds to the already developing autonomy. The child uses free choice and begins to manipulate and control his or her environment. This period is sometimes referred to as the *play stage.* Children begin to act out adult roles and, importantly, begin to initiate purposeful activities on their own. They have only limited abilities to understand abstract concepts, and their verbal skills may imply greater understanding than they actually possess. Children in this stage frequently begin to read words, but they have only limited comprehension of meanings. Memory may be spotty, and some may have difficulty distinguishing fantasy from reality. Children at this development stage are fully capable of lying and do so frequently to avoid punishment or difficult situations.

School age (6 to 11 years old)

The social arena shifts from the home and family to school and peers. Language skills increase, and children begin to understand technology around them. As children begin to master skills, they also begin to take pride in being industrious. This period of *industry* is also characterized by chumming with members of the same gender and a general tendency toward truthfulness on most important issues.

Adolescence (12 to 18 years old)

Adolescence is a difficult time for young people. The child stands on the threshold of adult emotional feelings and physiology yet is still drawn to childish ways of play. Rapport with adults may be strained or difficult. It is a period of searching, testing, and experimentation and a time of *identity* development. Interest in intimate relationships begins to emerge. Some adolescents may be shy and reserved in discussions of intimate matters. Others may be outgoing and boisterous about intimate issues. Adolescents are fully capable of fabricating elaborate lies to protect themselves or friends they think need protection. They have a full understanding of abstract concepts and considerable mastery of language, reading, and writing.

It is important for investigators to know that children develop at varying rates. The different levels of maturation are summarized in Figure 12.4 and are based chiefly on the classic work of Erickson (1963) on childhood development.

A number of police agencies and courts have made active use of anatomical dolls in interviews with child sexual abuse victims. **Anatomical dolls** are male and female dolls with gender-appropriate genitalia. Research has shown that children who have been subjected to sexual abuse react differently to anatomical dolls than do children who have not had these experiences (Bower, 1991; Jampole & Weber, 1987).

anatomical dolls Dolls or puppets with sex-appropriate genitalia, used in interviews with suspected child victims of sexual abuse or assault.

A variety of techniques are used to help children explain what happened to them during a sexual assault.

Typically, sexually abused children bring sexual behavior into their play with anatomical dolls whereas children who have not been sexually abused do not.

As abhorrent to society as child sexual abuse is, investigators must be cautious to protect the innocent. Anyone who has worked extensively with children knows they can have vivid imaginations and will often lie to avoid getting into trouble. Although most child abuse reports are accurate, investigators should be mindful that some reporters of child sexual abuse may be liars or may have other axes to grind with the adult alleged to have committed the crime. Some children may also lie as a form of revenge or to avoid unpleasant situations, such as the disapproval of a parent or the admission of some misdeed. For example, a mother who discovers that her 13-year-old daughter is pregnant may jump to the conclusion that her daughter has been molested. The daughter, who was actually a consenting participant in a sexual relationship, may lie and claim that someone—perhaps the bus driver or a teacher—molested her.

The Office for Victims of Crime (OVC, 2000), a component of the Office of Justice Programs, has produced a handbook to assist police officers working with vulnerable populations such as children who are victims of crime. This document outlines how child victims should be interviewed and begins with the recommendation that the investigator choose a secure, comfortable setting for interviewing the child victim, such as a child advocacy center. If such an interview setting is not available, choose a location that is as comfortable as possible, and take the time to establish trust and rapport. Much of what the handbook suggests follows a similar developmental outline to that shown in Figure 12.4. For example, the handbook includes the following suggestions:

- Preschool children (ages 2–6) are most comfortable at home—assuming no child abuse took place there—or in a very familiar environment. A parent or some other adult the child trusts should be nearby.

- For elementary school children (ages 6–10), the presence of a parent is not usually recommended because children at this age are sometimes reluctant to reveal information if they believe they or their parents could "get into trouble." However, a parent or some other adult the child trusts should be close by, such as in the next room.

- Preadolescents (ages 10–12 for girls and 12–14 for boys) are peer oriented and often avoid parental scrutiny. For this reason, they may be more comfortable if a friend or perhaps the friend's parent is nearby.

- Adolescents (generally ages 13–17) may be fearful of betraying their peers, so it may be necessary to interview them in a secure setting with no peers nearby.

Another problem investigators face when interviewing child victims is that young children tend to have very short attention spans (Lynch & Bussiculo, 1991). It is best to keep interviews with young children brief, perhaps only 15 to 20 minutes long. It is also important when investigating sexual abuse of children that investigators understand what the child means when he or she describes behaviors. To a 5-year-old, "sex" may mean kissing someone on the lips or taking a nap on someone's lap. It is important to be sure both the child and the investigator understand *what the child means.* Investigators should refrain from defining words for the child and, instead, should ask the child to explain what he or she means.

In addition to obtaining the essential information already discussed, investigators must be mindful of the special circumstances of child victims. A number of things may affect the information provided by children:

- The closeness of the child's relationship with the offender.
- The duration of the sexual abuse (whether it went on for a long period or was a sudden attack).
- The amount of violence or threat of violence associated with the assault or assaults.
- The age and understanding (general developmental level) of the child.
- The child's ability to read, write, count, and tell a story.
- Knowledge and understanding of names for body parts.
- Knowledge and understanding of sexual behaviors.
- The child's recent sleep and behavior patterns (moodiness, fighting, night frights, and so on).

It is advisable for investigators to consult the child's parents regarding many of these issues before interviewing the child victim. Having this background information about the child will help investigators know what to expect and how best to phrase questions to the child.

SUMMARY

Learning Objective 1

Sex crimes represent a broad classification of illegal behavior. They range from nuisance crimes, such as voyeurism, to offenses that are a significant threat to society, such as rape. Forcible rape is one of eight crimes that the FBI considers the most serious in American society. The FBI reports yearly statistics on forcible rape in its Uniform Crime Reports (UCR). Forcible rape made up 0.7 percent of all index offenses in 2004.

Learning Objective 2

Sex offenses can be put into these six categories: voluntary, involuntary, commercial, abnormal, nuisance, and dangerous.

Learning Objective 3

Rape is a crime of violence and control, not sexual satisfaction. Each state has its own statutes defining the crime of rape, and all the definitions share certain elements: (1) an act of sexual intercourse, or penetration of the victim's vagina, (2) without consent from the victim, (3) against the victim's will, by force, coercion, or duress. In addition, some states may define other classes of crimes, such as *attempted rape* or *date rape*.

Learning Objective 4

Rape is usually classified as either *forcible rape* or *statutory rape.* Forcible rape is sexual intercourse against a person's will by the use or threat of force. Statutory rape is sexual intercourse with a minor with or without the minor's consent. The definition of a *minor* varies from state to state, and for statutory rape it may include a specific difference in the ages of the victim and the offender.

Learning Objective 5

Special circumstances of rape and sexual assault investigations include the sensitive nature of the offense, society's attitudes toward it, and the victim's embarrassment and possible reluctance to discuss the crime. Investigating a rape requires tact and understanding on the part of the investigator. Important information to obtain about a sex offense includes date and time of offense, type of assault, age of victim, physical description of attacker, location of assault, weather conditions, general condition of victim and attacker, words spoken, weapon used, method of attack, witnesses, and any physical evidence that can connect the attacker to the victim and establish that a crime was committed. Investigating rape and sexual assault often requires cooperation among many different agencies and organizations.

Learning Objective 6

Sex crimes against children include child molestation, pedophilia, sexual seduction, lewd and lascivious behavior, indecent exposure, contributing to the delinquency of a minor, incest, and several other statutory offenses. Child molesters generally are under age 35 at the time of their first arrest, know their victims at least casually, and may maintain their sexual interest in children while also performing sex normally with an adult partner. Pedophiles are usually single, maintain stable work histories, and tend to select female victims.

Learning Objective 7

Sexual abuse of children is difficult to investigate and even more difficult to prosecute. Interviewing child victims requires extreme sensitivity to the child's emotional and physical welfare. In recent years, police have come to recognize child sexual abuse as a criminal offense, not a family problem. Police, social service agencies, and prosecutors often cooperate in multidisciplinary teams to effectively deal with the victim and the perpetrator in child sexual abuse cases.

Learning Objective 8

The five basic stages of child development are infancy, early childhood, preschool age, school age, and adolescence. Knowing the characteristics of children at these various stages can help investigators know better how to interview children who are victims or witnesses of a crime.

. . . .

KEY TERMS

sex crime **234**

mutual consent **234**

forcible rape **234**

statutory rape **234**

rape **236**

date rape **236**

rape kit **238**

child molesting **240**

pedophile **240**

sexual seduction **241**

lewd and lascivious behavior with a child **241**

indecent exposure **241**

contributing to the delinquency of a minor **241**

incest **241**

anatomical dolls **245**

Kidnapping and Extortion

KIDNAPPING

kidnapping Taking another person from one location to another against that person's will using force or coercion.

ransom Money, property, or other consideration paid or demanded in exchange for the release of a kidnapping victim.

As we have seen, crimes against people encompass a range of conduct that injures, inflicts property losses, invades personal sexual integrity, and exploits children. Also among these crimes against people are the crimes of kidnapping and extortion. Kidnapping, extortion, and the threat of violence associated with them have increased in recent years. **Kidnapping** is taking someone away by force, often for **ransom,** or some form of payment.

In many kidnappings, the victims are relatives of the kidnapper. A divorced mother, fearing for the safety of her children when they are in the custody of their father, may take the children and leave the state, committing a kidnapping. In other kidnappings, the perpetrators demand hundreds of thousands of dollars in ransom from wealthy people or civic leaders. Or the ransom demand may be made against a corporate or industrial enterprise with which the victim is associated. Terrorists (see Chapter 22) have for years used kidnapping to coerce governments into changing policies or releasing prisoners, and sadly it has become a fairly common way for Al-Qaida and Al-Qaida-linked groups to garner attention (Associated Press, 2006). In one highly publicized case in 2002, 14-year-old Elizabeth Smart was taken at gunpoint from her bedroom, in Salt Lake City, Utah. The gunman warned her younger sister he would hurt Elizabeth if the girl told anyone what she had seen (CourtTV, 2002). No ransom was demanded, and despite national publicity and a nationwide search, Elizabeth remained missing for nine months. She was found and reunited with her parents on March 12, 2003 (Haberman & MacIntosh, 2003).

Kidnapping and similar crimes are among the most reprehensible encountered by law enforcement agencies, and they are often among the most difficult crimes to investigate. Although apprehending the perpetrator is important in every kidnapping case, the safety and welfare of the victims often become the primary concern of investigators.

People take a keen interest in kidnapping cases. In no other crime does public sympathy extend so thoroughly to the victim and the victim's family. In cases of kidnapping, people are usually quite cooperative with law enforcement efforts to locate and free the victims. Unfortunately, some cases of kidnapping turn out to be hoaxes. When the hoax is discovered, the public feels betrayed. This occurred in a small town in South Carolina in October 1994. For nearly two weeks, Susan Smith made tearful pleas on national television to the alleged kidnapper of her two small sons. Then she broke down and confessed to having drowned the two boys herself.

In kidnapping cases, particularly when the fate of the victims remains uncertain, the media tend to show considerable interest. Who, for example, can forget the media circus that surrounded the tragic Danielle Van Dam kidnapping and murder by her neighbor David Westerfield in 2002 (Kirn, 2002). Yet the media must exercise restraint to ensure the safety of the victims. Kidnapping for ransom, and other variations on this crime, are typically investigated in two phases. The first occurs while the victim's fate remains in question, and the second occurs after the victim has been released or is found.

The Lindbergh Case

Federal kidnapping legislation was a response to a series of kidnappings for ransom in the 1920s and 1930s. Rival gangs seized each other's members and held them for ransom. In many of these seizures, victims were snatched in one state and held in another. These seizures were followed by similar kidnappings of members of wealthy families. Each time, ransom demands went up.

HISTORY

ON MARCH 10, 1932, AL CAPONE, who had recently been sentenced to prison on a tax evasion charge, sent word to Charles Lindbergh through Arthur Brisbane, a writer and spokesperson for the William Randolph Hearst newspaper empire. If Lindbergh could arrange Capone's release from prison, Capone would personally try to find the kidnapped Lindbergh baby through his connections to the underworld. Initially, the kidnapping was thought to be connected to the underworld, because many such kidnappings had taken place as rival gangs competed for power. Capone's offer was declined (Messick & Goldblatt, 1974).

The most notorious of these seizures was the kidnapping and murder of the son of Charles Lindbergh, a hero because of his trans-Atlantic flight, and Anne Morrow Lindbergh. On March 1, 1932, the couple's 20-month-old son was kidnapped from their home in New Jersey. Although the child was seized in New Jersey, most of the ransom negotiations were conducted in other states. About ten weeks after the kidnapping, the child's badly decomposed body was found partially buried near the Lindbergh estate. Although the Lindbergh's had paid the ransom, their child had been murdered by a blow to the head, and the body had been partially dismembered. Two years later, police arrested Bruno Hauptmann, a carpenter, after he bought gas with a $10 bill from the ransom money and a search of his garage yielded more than $13,000 of the ransom money. In spite of inconsistencies in police reports and testimony in court and Hauptmann's claim of innocence, he was convicted and was executed on April 3, 1936.

The Lindbergh case led to passage of a federal kidnapping statute, sometimes referred to as the **Lindbergh law,** which was passed on June 22, 1932. This law made it a federal offense to transport in interstate or foreign commerce a kidnapped person for purposes of ransom, reward, "or otherwise" (Figure 13.1). Included in the "or otherwise" clause of the kidnapping statute are such offenses as sexual assault, bank robbery, and the taking of a child by a parent without legal custody. State legislatures followed the federal model in their kidnapping statutes, which were often nicknamed "little Lindbergh laws."

Lindbergh law Federal antikidnapping legislation passed in 1932.

Legal Aspects of the Crime of Kidnapping

By modern statutes, kidnapping is the unlawful taking of an individual against his or her will. Many states have separate statutes to prohibit the unlawful taking of a person

FIGURE 13.1 Title 18, U.S. Code, Section 1201

(a) Whoever knowingly transports in interstate or foreign commerce, any person who has been unlawfully seized, confined, inveigled, decoyed, kidnapped, abducted, or carried away and held for ransom or reward or otherwise, except, in the case of a minor, by a parent thereof, shall be punished (1) by death if the kidnapped person has not been liberated unharmed, and if the verdict of the jury shall so recommend, or (2) by imprisonment for any term of years or for life, if the death penalty is not imposed.

(b) The failure to release the victim within twenty-four hours, after he shall have been unlawfully seized, confined, inveigled, decoyed, kidnapped, abducted, or carried away shall create a rebuttable presumption that such person has been transported in interstate or foreign commerce.

(c) If two or more persons conspire to violate this section and one or more of such persons do any overt act to effect the object of the conspiracy, each shall be punishable as provided in subsection (a).

against his or her will for ransom and have harsher penalties for such a crime. State statutes vary with regard to whether kidnapping is a felony (Chamelin, 2005). In some states, simple kidnapping is a felony; in other states only more serious forms of kidnapping, such as those for ransom, rape, or revenge, are felonies. Some states define more than one degree of kidnapping, requiring aggravating circumstances for the more serious offense of first-degree kidnapping. For the more serious forms of kidnapping, a number of states impose the death penalty or life imprisonment. Since statutes vary, investigators must know what constitutes the crime of kidnapping in their respective jurisdictions. Although state statutes define kidnapping differently, the definitions have certain key elements in common:

1. Unlawful taking or seizing of a person without his or her consent.
2. Carrying away or transportation of the victim.
3. Unlawful confinement of the victim.

Kidnapping Investigations

The investigator must try to learn the *who, what, when, where, why,* and *how* of the situation. People tend to label every disappearance a kidnapping, but police must distinguish between legitimate cases and hoaxes. Alleged kidnappings may actually be attempts to cover up murders. Disappearances may involve youngsters who have run away from home, spouses who have fled their partners, or parents who have taken children not legally in their custody. As the investigator determines the likelihood that the disappearance is a genuine kidnapping, he or she also needs to determine the specific type of kidnapping it is. Is it a kidnapping in connection with another crime, such as a robbery? Is it a kidnapping for sexual assault? Is it a kidnapping motivated by politics or business? Gathering information to establish that a kidnapping has taken place should be an investigator's first consideration.

On occasion, investigation may determine that a kidnapping is, in fact, a hoax. This was the case in 2005 when Jennifer Wilbanks, the so-called run-away bride, jilted her husband to be. Wilbanks fled her Georgia home just days before her wedding, only to return later claiming that she had been kidnapped to Mexico, but escaped. Upon questioning, she admitted that she had voluntarily left the state.

If the information gathered establishes that a kidnapping has occurred, a broadcast should be made, the watch commander notified, and an immediate investigation begun. The investigation should include a thorough interview with the kidnap victim, if available, or with the complainant or family members as soon as possible. Investigators

FYI A change in U.S. monetary policy had a significant effect on the investigation of the Lindbergh kidnapping case. In April 1933 President Roosevelt ordered the recall of all gold and gold certificates to the U.S. Treasury. Because $40,000 of the ransom for the Lindbergh child had been paid in gold certificates in 1932, when sixteen gold certificates turned up in the metropolitan New York area between August and September 1934, investigators were extremely interested in the source of these bills. Several more gold certificates appeared, including one at a gas station. The description the suspicious attendant gave of the driver matched descriptions others had given of a man who also paid them in gold certificates. The license plate number copied down by the attendant led to Bruno Hauptmann, who lived in the Bronx.

should search the crime scene, interview any witnesses, and broadcast follow-up information. Additionally, information should be updated in the national missing persons computer network that the department uses. Investigators should also have witnesses try to identify suspects through mug books—whether traditional or electronic—and should examine cases with similar M.O.s.

Kidnapping with Ransom Demand   The first concern of law enforcement personnel during the primary stages of a kidnapping involving ransom is the life of the victim, and it involves two major objectives: (1) the safe return of the victim and (2) identification and apprehension of the responsible party or parties (Chrabot & Miller, 2004).

When a call is received indicating a kidnapping in which a ransom demand has been made, the officer or 911 operator should obtain the basic information already outlined and forward the call to the proper authority. In larger agencies, a particular unit or division may handle such cases; in smaller agencies, the operator or officer may gather the preliminary information and advise the complainant or caller about specific actions to take.

It is important to obtain the exact wording of the ransom note, letter, or telephone call. The complainant should be asked to avoid handling the note or letter and to see that no one else handles it. Officers should determine whether anyone else knows the contents of the ransom note, letter, or telephone call; if so, find out who. Furthermore, the officer should advise the caller not to discuss or divulge the contents of the note, letter, or telephone call to anyone except police officials and to treat everything concerning the note, letter, or telephone call with the utmost secrecy. Emphasis should be placed on the importance of silence to protect the safety of the kidnapped victim. Also, the complainant should be advised not to disturb anything at the kidnapping scene and to try to keep others away from the area as well.

The officer assigned to the investigation should immediately start a log and begin chronologically recording the facts of the case, procedures undertaken, and assignment of personnel. Most important to the preliminary investigation is arranging an interview with the complainant and any other witnesses to obtain firsthand information about the crime. After compiling the information necessary to determine that a kidnapping with ransom demand has occurred, the investigator should broadcast a general alert concerning the kidnapping and ransom demand. To aid the investigation, the officer should contact the local office of the FBI and notify it of the status of the kidnapping.

All activity around the victim's residence should be kept at a low profile to avoid arousing the suspicion of the kidnapper, the neighbors, or the public. The investigator's interview with the victim's family should include an explanation of police procedures in kidnapping cases and the assurance that everything humanly possible is being done to effect the safe return of their loved one. The cooperation and confidence of the family should be sought and as much information as possible obtained from them.

If the media do learn of the kidnapping, the officer in charge should solicit their cooperation to help bring about the safe return of the victim. All press inquiries should be handled by the ranking officer or by a public relations officer if the department has one. Members of the media can unwittingly destroy evidence, frighten or alarm the kidnapper, and block efforts to return the victim or complete ransom negotiations. Withholding information from the media is temporary and does not infringe on the "people's right to know" because the information will be

Elizabeth Smart was kidnapped at gunpoint in 2002 and was reunited with her family nine months later.

published when the immediate danger to the victim has passed. If kidnappers are kept in the dark, they can only guess whether the family has contacted the authorities, what investigative measures have been taken, what evidence has been located, and so on.

The following procedures are often helpful in investigating a kidnapping with ransom demand:

- Determine the method of entry used so that the area can be processed for possible evidence.
- Obtain and preserve the ransom note for laboratory processing.
- Furnish the family with an exact copy of the note in case they need it for negotiations.
- Review the ransom note, letter, or telephone instructions with the family to make sure they understand the contents.
- Make sure that the person answering the suspect's telephone call follows the instructions of the officer in charge.
- Determine the financial status of the family.
- Determine if the family intends to pay the ransom; avoid giving any opinion about the ransom.
- Find out how the members of the family can raise the ransom money and have it available if they decide to meet the demand.
- Help family members decide who should make the payoff.
- Obtain descriptions and license plate numbers for all cars that might be used in payoff negotiations.
- Discuss with family members ways in which they can verify that the victim is still alive.

- Obtain permission for officers to stay in the home of the family during the crisis.
- Arrange for a private telephone line and tapping and tracing of all incoming calls.
- Obtain permission from the family to intercept any mail and telegrams.
- Obtain a complete description of the victim (including clothing worn) and the best available photograph of the victim.
- Obtain a family history, particularly pertaining to the victim.
- Request permission from the family to examine personal possessions of the victim for possible leads.
- Ask whether the victim's fingerprints are available.
- Arrange to record all calls.
- Obtain specimens of the victim's handwriting.
- Ascertain the identity of local tradespeople and delivery people with whom family members may have had disagreements or arguments.
- Obtain information about the victim's place of employment.
- Determine what each family member was doing for an appropriate period before and on the day of the kidnapping.
- Assign unmarked police cars to strategic areas for surveillance and for backup if needed.
- Depending on the facts and circumstances, conduct any other appropriate investigation that can be accomplished without endangering the life of the victim.

Return or Discovery of the Victim   The second stage of a kidnapping investigation begins once the victim has been returned or the victim's body has been found. When a victim is returned, the first thing to do is notify family members that their loved one has been found alive and well. This is especially important when the victim is a child. Once this task is accomplished, the investigation changes. An all-out, no-holds-barred investigation is conducted to meet the second objective—namely, to identify and apprehend the person or persons responsible for the kidnapping.

Because the life of the victim is no longer at risk, the media can be kept apprised of the situation. In fact, the media may be of great help in this phase. Broadcasting or publishing descriptions or pictures of the suspected kidnapper, information concerning the kidnapper's vehicle or the ransom, or other pertinent facts may bring in new leads.

Some facts of a kidnapping case *should not be given to the media.* These include confidential investigative techniques, current plans for the investigation, investigative steps being taken, identities of witnesses, details of the ransom note, information about the payoff spot, or any other confidential information. Some information may need to be withheld to ensure that the defendant will ultimately receive a fair trial. Other information about the crime, such as the type of bindings used on the victim's hands or the type of weapon used to force the victim into the car, may be intentionally withheld. Kidnappings, like many other crimes that attract media attention, sometimes draw out celebrity wannabes who crave attention so much that they claim responsibility for crimes they did not commit. Details of the crime that are withheld can be used to verify that a suspect has direct knowledge of the crime, not merely information published in the newspaper or reported on the evening news.

During this phase of the kidnapping investigation, the officer in charge should conduct regular briefings to keep all the investigative personnel who are working on the case informed of developments. An investigation should be conducted into every aspect of the case suggested by the information received. Activities and procedures during this phase of the investigation should include the following:

- Thoroughly interview the victim, obtaining every minute detail.
- Obtain victim's clothing for laboratory examination for possible transfer evidence, such as hair or fiber.
- Thoroughly search the crime scene for physical evidence, including sites where the victim was kidnapped, where he or she was held (if known), and where the ransom was dropped off or paid.
- Take soil samples from the crime scene and from locations in the immediate vicinity (distances of approximately 10, 50, and 100 feet from the immediate crime scene).
- Carefully process all fingerprints found at the crime scene and compare them with those of possible suspects.
- Reinterview witnesses when necessary.
- Place stop and question notices against suspects and their vehicles.
- Have drawings or computer-generated pictures created, with the assistance of the victim, to aid in identifying the suspect.
- Consult usual informants on the street for possible leads.
- Undertake surveillance of possible suspects or their associates as needed.
- Try to determine why this particular victim was kidnapped.
- Determine whether the kidnapper is familiar with the victim's neighborhood, habits, financial status, and so forth.
- Obtain handwriting, fingerprints, and palm prints from all members of the victim's family and household and from all the victim's associates.

- Canvass pertinent neighborhoods for possible leads or suspects and interview neighbors, local storekeepers, and delivery persons.
- Maintain liaison with other law enforcement agencies for possible suspects and coverage of leads.
- Maintain a chronological log of all investigative attempts and findings.

It is important not to immediately rule out family members or trusted friends of the family in kidnappings. As the case of Susan Smith discussed earlier in the chapter illustrates, kidnappers are not always strangers. Be tactful but thorough in considering the involvement of a family member or close friend in the kidnapping. A kidnapping victim's life may depend on determining who is involved, so it is better to err on the side of rudeness than to overlook a relative or friend of the family who is actually the culprit.

HOSTAGE TAKING

The taking of hostages by a career criminal, a psychopath, or a would-be robber presents a highly sensitive situation for police personnel. Hostage takers are usually criminals whose escape from a crime scene has been interrupted, either by the police or by another individual. Realizing their dilemma, they take hostages to bargain for freedom, money, or means of escape. Resolving a hostage situation requires careful application of proper police response tactics.

Many large municipal police departments, the FBI, and a number of other federal agencies now have hostage negotiators ready to deal with cases involving **hostages,** or people being held against their will for various reasons. The Crisis Negotiation Unit (CNU) is an integral part of the FBI's Critical Incident Response Group and is responsible for the FBI's Crisis (Hostage) Negotiation Program. **Hostage negotiators** are usually people specially trained to communicate with felons holding hostages with the intention of obtaining the release of these hostages. Smaller departments frequently have arrangements with local clinicians skilled in negotiating with troubled people. The idea behind negotiating is to resolve hostage incidents without bloodshed—to defuse potentially lethal situations by talking with the suspect before deaths occur. Hostage negotiation was pioneered by a volunteer team of three New York City detectives. The FBI now has trained hostage negotiators in each of its field offices. A number of larger departments also have highly trained SWAT (special weapons and tactics) units capable of containing a suspect or handling barricaded suspects and other hostage situations.

When people are taken as hostages, the last thing their captors want is to have to kill them. Once the hostage is killed, the captor no longer has bargaining power. Hostages may not be part of a criminal's original plan. For example, when a bank robbery is interrupted by a passing police car, the robber may take bank clients and workers hostage. In such a situation, a hostage negotiator might have to work with the personality of the robber and the specific circumstances of the situation. No hard-and-fast rules can be laid down to cover all hostage situations (Whitcomb, 2002). Nonetheless, some general principles concerning hostage or kidnapping situations can be suggested. The first general rule is: *Give the culprit a chance to save face.* Orders for unconditional surrender place the hostage in needless peril. It has been said that strategy takes place in the area of ego. To be sure, the kidnapper has an ego, the investigator in charge of the scene has an ego, and all the back-up officers have egos. Law enforcement personnel working in these situations must remain flexible. Efforts must

hostage An innocent person held captive by one who threatens to kill or harm the person if his or her demands are not met and who uses the person's safety to negotiate for money, property, or escape.

hostage negotiator An individual specially trained to deal with persons holding hostages.

Hostage negotiators are usually persons specially trained to communicate with individuals who are holding hostages.

be made to let suspects feel that they can walk out and still be human beings. Law enforcement officers should use toughness only as a last resort. In rare cases a culprit may be bent on wanton killing or self-destruction, and negotiation techniques may be ineffective. In such cases, an armed assault may be in order. There are times when words have to be replaced with stronger tools, such as weapons. Negotiating is not the solution to every situation, but hostage negotiations give the police an important tool with which to do their job.

The second general principle or rule is: *Always tell the truth.* Lying weakens the position of the negotiator. Negotiators must establish credibility; getting caught in a lie destroys any possibility of being viewed as credible. It is much better to honestly tell the captor that his or her demand is impossible to meet than to make a promise that cannot be kept.

The third rule is: *Be patient.* No effort should be made to force the situation. Time is the ally of the police in a hostage situation. One basic concept to follow in critical situations is that good decisions are based on complete and accurate facts. The fundamental goal should be that no one gets hurt. Kidnappers can be caught and property replaced, but human life can never be restored.

Hostage takers may be categorized as follows: (1) the ordinary or professional criminal, (2) the mentally unbalanced or psychotic captor, (3) the political terrorist, and (4) the hijacker or carjacker. Hostage takers in the first category are the most predictable. They usually do not intend to take hostages, but when they are trapped, they use their victims to bargain for escape. Even when hostages are intentionally taken by professional criminals, it is unusual for the plan to include intentionally killing them. Sometimes a criminal will take hostage the family of a bank manager or supermarket manager. In these cases, the criminal uses the hostages as leverage to get money from the bank or market manager.

Mentally unbalanced or psychotic hostage takers are usually looking for a forum to make a statement or to get some message out. They regard themselves as trapped by society or some other imagined constraints or unknown force. They often have a wish for someone to take control and talk them out of dying—and killing. This is one of the areas where negotiators can best function. It is not uncommon for those who harbor strong feelings of frustration to commit suicide.

Hostage takers in category three are extremely dangerous and somewhat unpredictable. Terrorists (see Chapter 22) seldom agree to negotiate and are usually acting in accordance with their ideals or a cause. Because they may be religious or political zealots, reason is not always an avenue that works. Nonetheless, negotiators must attempt to channel the hostage taker's thinking toward more realistic terms.

The final category, hijackers and carjackers, is sometimes related to terrorist behavior. Terrorists may undertake a mass kidnapping, such as commandeering an airplane, a situation in which immobilizing them may cause a catastrophe. Airplane hijacking requires a friendly power that will allow the kidnappers to land and receive sanctuary, and these hijackings are usually politically motivated. Carjackings, on the other hand, are generally crimes for profit (see Chapter 10). Carjackings are perilous situations because the victim is frequently beaten, shot, or stabbed. If cornered, however, the carjacker will use the victim as a hostage to try to engineer an escape.

In any hostage situation, one of the initial steps is to establish a line of communication with the captor. A **line of communication** may involve direct, face-to-face conversation with the captor or the use of a telephone. Using the telephone allows the negotiator to develop a one-to-one relationship with the hostage taker. Negotiators can also be valuable in a hijacking in which hostages are being held aboard a grounded airplane or in instances in which a criminal is trapped with hostages in a bank or store. Negotiators try to formulate a psychological profile of the suspect after the first contact. Friends, neighbors, associates, and relatives are quickly contacted and interviewed regarding various aspects of the captor's life and personality. Having an idea about how the hostage taker acts in various circumstances helps the negotiator to tailor police tactics and strategies to the specific situation and the suspect.

Throughout all negotiations, the hostage taker and the victims should be contained within a confined area. In addition, an outer perimeter should be established to keep out traffic and curious people who might interfere with police operations.

line of communication A channel for communicating with another person.

CHILD STEALING

Stranger kidnapping (the abduction by someone not known to the victim) is a serious problem, but another form of kidnapping that has become prominent is parental child abduction. This offense is committed against the parent or other legal guardian and not against the child. Increasing numbers of noncustodial parents are no longer willing to endure long periods without seeing their children (Hoff, 2000). In many cases, the parent simply refuses to accept the noncustodial role. Instead, he or she takes desperate action and steals the children from the custodial parent or guardian. The taking of a child must only be against the will or without the consent of the parent, guardian, or person with legal custody for it to be classified as child stealing. If no judicial decree grants the custody of the child to one spouse, however, the other spouse is not guilty of child stealing if he or she takes the child away against the other's will. In the statutes on child stealing, the consent of the child under the age specified is no defense to a charge of the crime because the child is considered incapable of giving legal consent.

In one case, a woman stole her 4-year-old son during a visit with him, arranged through the county welfare department adoption agency at an agency office. The boy was a ward of the court at the time. He was in the custody and care of foster parents, who were in the process of adopting him. When he disappeared, the foster parents were waiting for him in a car parked outside the adoption agency. In this case, the mother was prosecuted for child stealing. In another case, a divorced mother in Nevada hired a security professional and convinced him, on the pretext of fighting conflicting custody decrees, to help her take her children from their father, who had moved with the children to Arizona. The plan failed, but the security professional was convicted of kidnapping and his conviction was upheld on appeal.

FYI The Christmas season brings a yearly leap in the theft of children by noncustodial parents. The National Center for Exploited and Missing Children issues yearly warnings to custodial parents to keep tight control of their children at the mall, to make sure they know who is chaperoning holiday parties, and not to let the good cheer of the season lull them into a false sense of security. The U.S. Department of Justice has estimated that upward of 350,000 children a year are stolen by family members.

FOCUS ON TECHNOLOGY

AGE PROGRESSION TECHNOLOGY

COMPUTER TECHNOLOGY to age-enhance photographs has become an important tool in searching for children who have been missing for a long time. From photographs and videotapes of the child and the child's family, as well as descriptive information about the child, the imaging technology produces an image of the child as he or she might currently appear.

EXTORTION

extortion Obtaining money or property from another by wrongful use of actual or threatened force, violence, or under color of official right; refers to such acts by public officials.

Like a kidnapping with ransom demand, extortion is a hybrid crime against the person and against property. **Extortion** is obtaining money, property, or other consideration by one party from another with the appearance of consent. However, the consent has actually been induced by force, fear, or coercion. Extortion is also the use of threats to force or manipulate a public officer to take some official action. A public officer is one who works for a government or holds elective office. This includes municipal, county, state, and federal officials.

Legal Aspects of the Crime of Extortion

To constitute extortion, the wrongful use of force or fear must produce consent. Although most states have separate criminal extortion statutes, extortion can also be found in the bribery or theft statutes of some states. The definition of extortion found in the Model Penal Code (Figure 13.2) provides an expanded definition of this crime.

blackmail The unlawful demand of money or property under threat to do bodily harm, to injure property, to accuse of a crime, or to expose disgraceful defects; commonly included under extortion statutes.

More typical today are ordinary cases of blackmail. In fact, in some jurisdictions, extortion is simply referred to as "blackmail." However, extortion and blackmail can be differentiated as follows: Demands made by public officials in their official roles for illegal payments or presents are extortion. Illegal payments or demands for property made by private citizens are better known as blackmail. **Blackmail** is typically classified as a person's use of written or oral threats of force or terror to demand money or property to which he or she is not actually entitled (Chamelin, 2005). Extortion can

FIGURE 13.2 Model Penal Code, Section 223.4

A person is guilty of theft by extortion if he purposely obtains property of another by threatening to:

(1) inflict bodily injury on anyone or commit any other criminal offense; or
(2) accuse anyone of a criminal offense; or
(3) expose any secret tending to subject any person to hatred, contempt or ridicule, or to impair his credit or business repute; or
(4) take or withhold action as an official or cause an official to take or withhold action; or
(5) bring about or continue a strike, boycott or other collective unofficial action, if the property is not demanded or received for the benefit of the group in whose interest the actor purports to act; or
(6) testify or provide information or withhold testimony or information with respect to another's legal claim or defense; or
(7) inflict any other harm which would not benefit the actor.

---

also be distinguished from robbery in that a kind of choice is given to the victim of extortion. In robbery, the intimidation is so extreme as to overpower the will of the victim and coerce him or her to give up money or property without consent.

Victims of extortion may include railroads, airlines, banks, amusement parks, utility companies, sports stadiums, celebrities, politicians, corporate executives, and even ordinary people. Extortionists have been known to select names at random from newspaper articles, telephone directories, or organization membership lists.

Threats to kill, kidnap, or injure a person; ransom demands for the release of a kidnapped person; and threats to destroy private or public property are investigated by the FBI under the Federal Extortion Statute (U.S. Code, 1970). The FBI can investigate these threats if they are transmitted in interstate commerce or sent through the U.S. Postal Service. If letters accusing a person of a crime or injuring his or her reputation are sent through the mail, they are investigated by postal inspectors. Federal prosecution under the Hobbs Act is often used against extortionists who attempt to obtain money from federally insured banks or loan companies by threats against employees and their families. The Hobbs Act regulates extortion and robbery, which Congress has determined have a substantial effect on interstate and foreign commerce by reason of their repetition and aggregate effect on the economy. This act prohibits interfering with commerce by robbery or extortion or attempting or conspiring to do so.

Extortionists deliver their threats by various means, including telephone, electronic computer communications networks or bulletin boards, and letter. Threats may be of personal injury, mutilation, kidnapping, or killing. Or they may involve burning, blowing up, or in other ways damaging or destroying property. In some cases, threats are used merely to antagonize or frighten a victim or to cause mental anguish. An extortionist often sends letters to families of kidnap victims, demanding money for the return of the victim, thereby taking advantage of the family's predicament. Invariably the threats indicate that harm or injury will befall the loved one should the police be notified. The extortionist usually works alone, although the messages may carry the pronoun "we." Threats are seldom actually carried out. However, threats against life or property cannot be ignored. Appropriate and timely police action must be taken.

The payoff location chosen by an extortionist may be any place that suits the culprit's purpose. It may be a church, a trash barrel in a park, an alley, a telephone booth in front of a police station (for an ironic twist), a cemetery, and so forth. Would-be extortionists have been known to send victims on wild goose chases during payoff runs to make sure police are not following or watching a payoff area.

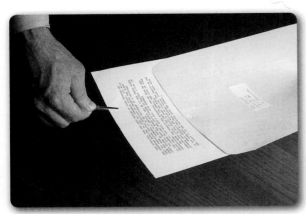

Extortion letters can sometimes reveal important information about their authors.

Sometimes a suspect will ride a bus or drive a car past the location, hoping to spot police surveillance activities. The extortionist may even call the victim and accuse him or her of contacting the police, hoping to further intimidate the victim into full cooperation.

Extortion Investigations

Solving an extortion case requires the complete cooperation of the victim. In extortion cases, the first concern of the police is the safety of victims. The recovery of extorted money or property and the apprehension of the suspect are a secondary concern. If a letter is involved, both the letter and the envelope may furnish valuable evidence about the educational background of the writer. Spelling, word choice, punctuation, and other writing elements can be studied and may offer insight. A thorough interview with the victim often results in the description of a logical suspect. The suspect may be a discharged or disgruntled employee, a business competitor, or a jealous suitor. She or he may be someone seeking revenge for some past incident, someone with a long-standing hatred or jealousy of the victim, or a vindictive neighbor. Seemingly irrelevant information that does not mean much to the complainant during an interview may become valuable to the investigator in identifying a suspect.

When covering an extortion payoff, the investigator must take many things into account. These include coordination, the number of surveillants needed, communications equipment, photographic and video equipment, and the type and number of surveillance vehicles. Specific considerations vary, of course, depending on the facts of the case, the location and terrain of the payoff area, and various unique circumstances in each case.

In many respects, extortion investigations are similar to kidnapping investigations. Investigators must focus on the identity and lifestyle of the victim, the location of the occurrence, and other routines and activities of the victim—employment, recreation, health needs, social practices, and so forth.

Extortion Threat by Telephone

The following procedures are in order when investigating telephone extortion threats:

- Ascertain the date and exact time the call was received.
- Determine what was said and by whom.
- Find out what threats were made and what instructions were given.
- Ask whether any background noises were heard, such as music, traffic, bells, or train or boat whistles.
- Ask whether the suspect said that he or she would call again and, if so, when.
- Determine whether any regional or foreign accent was detected in the suspect's voice; similarly, ask about speech impediments.

The victim should be advised that if any additional calls are received, he or she should cooperate with the caller, take detailed notes of the message, note the exact date and time of the call, and write down any directions for a payoff. As soon as possible, arrange to monitor and record calls at the victim's home or place of work or both. Instruct the victim to have the caller repeat instructions, even if he or she understands them, to ensure that they are clear. Endeavor to have calls traced by keeping the caller on the line as long as possible. The victim should ask such questions as, "With whom am I speaking?" "How do I know you're not joking?" "Why did you pick me?" "What denominations of money do you want?" "Where is the money to be delivered?" "When will I get additional instructions?" "How will I know when I have reached the location?" "What guarantees do I have that you will keep your word?" It is useful to have the victim ask as many of these types of questions as possible to get all the necessary information and to try to determine who the extortionist is or where he or she may be.

In one attempted extortion case, the manager of a supermarket received a telephone call from an unknown person who stated that he was holding the manager's wife and children hostage in his car. He advised the manager to meet him at a designated spot and to bring all the money in the store to secure their safe return. The manager immediately telephoned his home, knowing that his wife had not planned to leave the house that afternoon. The manager received no answer at his home. Next, he called the police, who sent a unit to the manager's residence. The officers determined that the wife and child were at home unharmed. The arranged payoff spot was covered by police, but the extortionist failed to appear.

When asked why she had not answered the telephone when her husband called, the wife replied that she had received a call shortly before her husband telephoned. The caller had identified himself as a telephone company employee. He told her that the phone line was being worked on, and that though the phone might ring, she should not answer it for at least one hour.

Later that same day, the manager of a supermarket in a city 70 miles away from the original store received a similar extortion call. This manager, like the other, called his home, and when he received no answer, he notified the police. The same M.O. had been used, but in this case, the extortionist showed up at the payoff location, where he was arrested by waiting police and charged with extortion. When arrested, the extortionist was carrying a loaded automatic pistol and a loaded revolver.

Extortion Threat by Letter

The following procedures are useful when investigating extortion threats involving letters:

- Ask when the letter was received.
- Find out how it was delivered.
- Get the postmark and date of the letter.
- Determine whether the letter was handwritten, hand-printed, typed, or computer-printed.
- Note the signature on the letter.
- Ask the recipient to maintain absolute secrecy and not to handle the letter or envelope or permit anyone else to touch them; instruct the complainant not to reveal the contents to anyone except law enforcement authorities.
- Instruct the complainant to maintain a normal routine around the house and place of employment.
- Ask the complainant if he or she suspects anyone of sending the letter.
- Find out if any prior communication had been received.
- Obtain and preserve the extortion letter for laboratory examination.
- Obtain permission to tape-record all telephone calls to the complainant's home and place of employment.

CAREERS FOCUS

FBI SPECIAL AGENT

FBI SPECIAL AGENTS INVESTIGATE VIOLATIONS of federal law. Violations may include such crimes as kidnapping, extortion, bank robbery, fraud and theft against the federal government, espionage, interstate transportation of stolen property, mail fraud, and sabotage. Agents may be required to do sophisticated surveillance, monitor court-authorized wiretaps, examine business records, collect evidence, interview and interrogate witnesses, or participate in sensitive undercover operations.

U.S. citizenship, availability for assignments anywhere in the Federal Bureau of Investigation's jurisdiction, and being between the ages of 23 and 37 are the initial requirements. All applicants must also pass vision and hearing tests. Finally, applicants must have a valid driver's license and be in excellent physical condition with no physical defects that would interfere in firearm use, raids, or defensive tactics.

If candidates meet all of the general requirements, there are five special agent entry programs for which applicants must meet specific requirements: law, accounting, language, engineering/science, and diversified. Those qualifying for appointment as special agents must pass a written examination and undergo a thorough background check. New agents receive intensive training in federal criminal law and procedures, investigative techniques, physical fitness, and firearm use.

Jobs with the federal government are based on a graded scale, from GS-1 (lowest) to GS-18 (highest). An entry-level special agent can expect to earn a base salary of about $39,700 and, with overtime, earn about $48,000 annually (Johnson & Locy, 2004).

- Arrange for tapping and tracing all telephone calls to the victim's home and place of employment.
- Brief all personnel involved with the case.
- Make certain that the victim's movements are coordinated with police instructions at all times during the crisis.
- Arrange personnel, vehicles, and equipment for any required surveillance.
- Obtain fingerprints and palm prints of the victim and others known to have handled the letter or envelope.
- Investigate the area of the victim's residence if it is relevant to the facts, circumstances, location, or other elements of the case. Extortionists have been known to observe their intended victims before and during the period of the extortion demands.
- Oversee the preparation of the payoff package.
- Alert all personnel and the victim to the danger of the suspect's stopping or intercepting the victim at any point along the payoff route.
- Check the anonymous-letter file of the local and state police and the FBI for similar letters.
- Record the license plate numbers of all cars that pass a payoff location; a video camera or a still camera with a telephoto lens can assist in this surveillance.

If a suspect is taken into custody, fingerprints and palm prints should be taken for comparison with the unidentified prints obtained during the course of the investigation. Handwriting or hand-printing specimens should also be obtained from the suspect, depending on whether the letter was written or printed. Voiceprint samples may also be taken for comparison with tape recordings made during extortion calls. It should also be determined whether the suspect has access to the particular make of typewriter or computer printer used to prepare any extortion notes (if the extortion note was printed or typed).

SUMMARY

Learning Objective 1

Kidnapping is taking someone away by force, often for ransom or some form of payment. In many cases of kidnapping, the perpetrators demand large sums of money from wealthy people or civic leaders, or from a corporation or industrial enterprise. Terrorists have used kidnapping as a means of coercing governments into changing policies or releasing prisoners.

Learning Objective 2

The Lindbergh kidnapping case in the early 1930s received worldwide attention and led to the passage of federal antikidnapping legislation. The Lindbergh law, as it came to be known, made it a federal offense to transport a kidnapped person in interstate or foreign commerce for purposes of ransom, reward, or otherwise.

Learning Objective 3

State statutes define what constitutes the crime of kidnapping in each state. Despite variation among the states, state kidnapping statutes have certain key elements in common. Kidnapping is (1) the unlawful taking or seizing of a person without his or her consent, (2) the carrying away or transportation of the victim, and (3) the unlawful confinement of the victim.

Learning Objective 4

As in any criminal investigation, it is important to ascertain the *who, what, where, when, why,* and *how* to establish that a kidnapping has indeed taken place. In addition, extreme tact, care, and control of dissemination of information regarding the kidnapping must accompany the investigation to ensure the safe return of the victim and to avoid tipping off the kidnapper as to what measures have been taken or what evidence has been located.

Learning Objective 5

A hostage taking is a highly tense and extremely sensitive situation for police personnel to resolve. Three general rules are helpful in dealing with such a situation: Give the culprit a chance to save face. Always tell the truth. Be patient.

Learning Objective 6

Recently a new form of kidnapping—child stealing—has become prominent. This is an offense against the parent or other legal guardian of a child and not against the child. In many cases, the noncustodial parent refuses to accept the noncustodial role and takes desperate action to steal his or her own child from the custodial parent or guardian.

Learning Objective 7

Extortion is obtaining money, property, or consideration by one party from another with the appearance of consent. However, the consent has actually been induced by force, fear, or coercion. Generally, extortion refers to such criminal acts by municipal, county, state, or federal officials. Illegal payments or demands for money, property, or special consideration made by private citizens are better known as blackmail. State statutes define what constitutes extortion or blackmail and may include such definitions in bribery or theft statutes.

. . . .

KEY TERMS

kidnapping **252**

ransom **252**

Lindbergh law **253**

hostage **259**

hostage negotiator **259**

line of communication **261**

extortion **262**

blackmail **262**

. . . .

QUESTIONS FOR REVIEW

Learning Objective 1

1. Define *kidnapping* and *ransom.*
2. Name some possible reasons for a kidnapping.

Learning Objective 2

3. What was the popular name for the federal kidnapping statute?
4. What was the big break in the Lindbergh kidnapping investigation?

Learning Objective 3

5. What elements do most state statutes have in common in defining the crime of kidnapping?

Learning Objective 4

6. What is the primary objective of a kidnapping investigation?
7. What kind of information is important to obtain during a kidnapping investigation?
8. Why should investigating officers not offer advice about whether family members should pay a ransom?
9. When investigators learn that a ransom note has been received, what should they tell the person to do?
10. Who should conduct the interview with a kidnapping complainant?
11. When a kidnapping victim has been released and the kidnapper is still at large, should the media be given the full story? Explain.

Learning Objective 5

12. Should a hostage negotiator ever lie to the hostage taker?
13. One of the three basic rules of hostage negotiation is *Be patient.* What are the other two?

Learning Objective 6

14. Under what circumstances would child stealing not be considered illegal?
15. Against whom is the crime of child stealing directed?

Learning Objective 7

16. What are some of the questions an investigator should ask the victim of an extortion call?
17. How would you differentiate between extortion and robbery?

CRITICAL THINKING EXERCISE

You are the desk sergeant in a small-town police department. A young woman runs into the station with tears streaming down her cheeks. "He's taken my children, he's taken my children," she screams. After she calms down, she offers the following account:

> I was getting into my car after shopping down at the Ralph's Market. I had just put the baby into his car seat and checked on my big boy's seat belt when a man wearing a ski mask rushed over to the car. He had a gun and ordered me out of the car. He jumped in and would not even let me get my kids out of the back seat. He promised that he would not hurt my boys but said that it would cost me money to get them back. He took my wallet and said he'd be in touch about the ransom.

1. What questions would you ask the victim?
2. What actions and activities would you suggest the police take to secure the release of the children and the apprehension of the carjacker-kidnapper?
3. What information should be released to the media?

INVESTIGATIVE SKILL BUILDERS

Participating as a Member of a Team

You are a member of a hostage negotiation team. You have been called to the scene of a carjacking standoff between local police and two would-be carjackers. They have a woman and two children hostage in the woman's car. One of the men has a handgun and the other a hunting knife. After nearly an hour of coaxing, your team leader has opened a line of communication with the carjackers. During his conversation with these men, he has learned the following:

- Both men are two-time losers for armed robbery.
- Their names are Darryl and Wayne.
- They might be willing to give up one of the hostages for some food and water.
- The woman has a superficial knife wound on her left arm from the carjackers' first effort to take control.

The two men are demanding to be allowed to drive away with one hostage. They claim that they will release the others as a sign of good faith. They say that they will release the last hostage after getting some distance away—if they are not followed.

If the police try to move in on them, they say they will kill the children first and then the woman. They say they want an answer in fifteen minutes.

Your team has now assembled to discuss possible actions.

1. What actions would you suggest?
2. Should the negotiating team capitulate on *any* of the demands?
3. What other information might the team leader try to solicit from these men?

Integrity/Honesty

You are working on a kidnapping case involving a divorced couple. The father had been granted legal custody of the 7-year-old girl. Yesterday the girl was picked up from school by a woman and has not been seen or heard from since. At the time of the incident, the girl's mother claims to have been working, but she cannot account for her whereabouts or provide any witnesses. The father maintains that they had gone through a terrible divorce and custody battle and says that he believes his wife is responsible for the kidnapping.

The mother of the girl maintains her innocence and suggests that her ex-husband has contrived this situation to make her look bad. She suggests that one of her ex-husband's girl-friends might have taken the girl at his request. During the interview with the mother at her home, your partner finds himself extremely attracted to her. They get to talking, and you overhear that he has made a date to see her socially later that evening. As you leave with your partner, he begins to suggest following up on the woman's suggestion that the ex-husband may have had something to do with the crime. He also suggests that you and he should drop the woman as a suspect.

1. How will you respond to your partner's suggestion?
2. Should you report his activities to your superior?

Homicide

HOMICIDE AND THE LAW

On August 6, 2006, at 800 hours, you and your partner are dispatched to a home because a woman has telephoned the station and reported finding her husband dead in their bed. Upon arrival, your partner begins to take the woman's statement while you are directed by her to the bedroom. You find a 51-year-old man in an undershirt and boxer shorts lying on his back, on top of crumpled sheets. His eyes are closed, his body still, and you can see from the soiled shorts and linens that his sphincter muscles have released, which is not uncommon in a *natural death*. But you also notice a half-filled open bottle of vodka and a pill bottle on the nightstand to his immediate right. You bend over to better read the pill bottle (being careful not to touch anything) and see that it is sleeping pills. The lid is off, and you count only six tablets inside. The prescription is dated August 5, 2006, and called for eighteen tablets; you now begin to consider this as a possible *suicide*. You check his eyes and see that they are fixed and dilated, an indication of death, but there are also broken blood vessels in the white of his eyes (petechiae), which are typically indicative of asphyxia. You also notice what may be faint ligature marks on the man's neck and consider that this may actually be a *homicide* someone is trying to conceal.

Only the third inductive explanation actually involves a criminal action and warrants a criminal investigation. However, because the police have been notified, they will need to consider and rule out the other two possible explanations. The first thing that must be undertaken in a homicide investigation is to establish that a crime has actually occurred.

Of all the serious crimes committed, homicide investigations demand the greatest effort by the police. Human life, in our society, simply has no price; it is an incalculable and irreplaceable commodity. The seriousness of homicide is reflected in the penalties for its commission, which include lengthy prison sentences and sometimes even death. The types of deaths that confront the police can be divided into four major categories: homicide, natural causes, suicide, and accidental causes. The goal of classifying a death in one of these categories is to assign *responsibility* in both a moral sense and a legal sense. Let us now consider some of the legal implications.

Homicide is the killing of one person by another. It is important to note, however, that not all homicides are criminal. Some homicides may occur because of an accident, owing to negligence, in self-defense or in the defense of another, or as the only way of apprehending a dangerous fleeing felon. Even self-inflicted deaths are generally treated as homicides until the police can establish them as suicides. **Justifiable homicide** is the intentional killing of another person in the performance of a legal duty or the exercise of a legal right. The shooting death of an armed robber by a police officer who has arrived on the scene only to be met by the robber's gunfire or a victim killing her rapist in her efforts to stop the rape or escape fall into this category. **Excusable homicides** are accidental killings where there is no gross negligence. Every year there are hundreds of accidental, but fatal, shooting accidents when one hunter mistakes another hunter for quarry. Although the question of gross negligence may be raised in a hunting incident, the death is usually considered accidental. Generally, all these homicides are considered nonfelonious because they are justifiable or excusable.

A **criminal homicide**, on the other hand, is the unlawful taking of another person's life. Criminal homicides are sometimes referred to as *felonious homicides* and are further divided into murder and manslaughter. **Murder** is the unlawful taking of human life *with malice aforethought,* meaning premeditation. In many jurisdictions, killing a person during the commission of a felony is also murder. Thus, an armed

homicide The intentional or negligent killing of one human being by another.

justifiable homicide The killing of another in self-defense or defense of others when danger of death or serious bodily harm exists.

excusable homicide The killing of a human being without intention and where there is no gross negligence.

criminal homicide (felonious homicide) The wrongful killing of a human being without justification or excuse in the law. Typically, there are two degrees of the offense: murder and manslaughter.

murder The unlawful killing of a human being by another with malice aforethought.

robber who shoots and kills a storekeeper who has grabbed for the robber's gun will be charged with murder. In fact, a number of jurisdictions would charge the robber's partner with murder too, even if the accomplice was waiting outside in the getaway car during the shooting. A killing incident to the commission of a felony is commonly referred to as **felony murder.**

Sometimes a criminal homicide occurs under circumstances that are not severe enough to constitute a murder, but the homicide cannot be classified as excusable or justifiable. This is the crime of **manslaughter,** and it can be voluntary or involuntary. *Voluntary manslaughter* is intentionally killing another in the sudden heat of passion caused by words or actions that provide a provocation. *Involuntary manslaughter* is accidentally killing another as a result of an act of extreme and culpable negligence. Suppose a motorist skids on an icy road and careens into another automobile, killing the other driver. Provided that the surviving driver was sober and had not violated any traffic laws, the incident would probably be ruled accidental manslaughter or involuntary manslaughter. However, if police learn that the surviving driver was intoxicated, he or she may be charged with vehicular manslaughter, a felony murder in most jurisdictions.

Most state statutes provide for varying degrees of murder, such as *first-degree* and *second-degree murder,* or "murder one" and "murder two" as television prosecutors seem so fond of labeling them. In some states, *heat-of-passion murder,* or killing motivated by some strong emotion, may also be defined in certain circumstances. The prosecuting attorney decides what charge to bring based on available evidence. Most state statutes have common elements in their definitions of murder. These include purposely, knowingly, recklessly, or negligently causing the death of another human being.

The FBI reported 16,137 people were murdered nationwide in 2004, a decrease of 2.4 percent from 2003 (FBI, 2005, p. 15). Not included in the total count for this classification are deaths caused by negligence, suicide, or accident; justifiable homicides; and attempts to murder or assaults resulting in death, which are counted as aggravated assaults. As in previous years, firearms were the weapon of choice in more than 66 percent of murders. Among the other weapons used, knives or cutting instruments were used in 13.2 percent of murders, personal weapons (such as hands, fists, or feet) in 6 percent, blunt objects (such as clubs or hammers) in 6.6 percent, and other dangerous weapons (such as poison or explosives) in the remainder. If you look again at Figure 10.2 in Chapter 10, you will see that murder is the least frequent of the index offenses. Despite its low significance statistically, murder receives the most attention from police. It is the most serious crime and is often very difficult to investigate. Murders also draw media attention, and this attention can affect what the police can and cannot do within their jurisdiction. Among the homicides identified by law enforcement agencies for the UCR in 2004, the victim-offender relationships were unknown in 44.1 percent of the cases. However, for incidents in which the relationship was known, 76.8 percent of the victims knew their killers and 23.2 percent were slain by strangers (FBI, 2005, p. 18). Furthermore, among the incidents in which the victim knew the killer, 29.8 percent were murdered by family members and 70.2 percent were killed by acquaintances. In addition, 33 percent of all female victims were killed by their husbands or boyfriends, whereas only 2.7 percent of males were slain by their wives or girlfriends (FBI, 2005, p. 23).

Murder and *Corpus Delicti*

As explained previously, *corpus delicti* is the legal term that refers to the body of the offense, or the essence of the crime. This has come to mean the basic elements of a

felony murder The killing of a person during the commission or attempted commission of a felony other than murder (e.g., during a robbery).

manslaughter The unlawful killing of another without malice. It may be voluntary, upon sudden heat of passion; involuntary, in the commission of an unlawful act; or negligent, occurring as a result of an action that could have been avoided.

crime that must be proven in court to obtain a conviction. The more literal meaning of *corpus delicti* is the actual body in a murder case, but *corpus delicti* also can be used to mean any material evidence of a crime or objective proof in a criminal case. The presentation of *corpus delicti* is necessary in a criminal case, especially a murder case, to prove beyond reasonable doubt that the defendant is guilty of the charges against him or her.

The principle of *corpus delicti* was established to protect persons from being unjustly convicted of a crime they did not commit. Historically, there have been cases in which a person was charged and convicted of murder and put to death for this crime but the individual who had allegedly been murdered miraculously reappeared after the defendant was executed. To avoid falsely convicting—and executing—an innocent person, today proof of *corpus delicti* is required to obtain a conviction of a defendant. This does not, however, mean that the corpus of an allegedly murdered victim continues to be the *corpus delicti* for murder. One does not always need to produce the body to obtain a conviction of murder. It is possible to prove the *corpus delicti* of a murder case by presenting presumptive (circumstantial) evidence that suggests the defendant's guilt *beyond reasonable doubt*. The first U.S. case in which a conviction was obtained without presentation of direct evidence (the conviction was based on circumstantial evidence) took place in 1850 in the murder trial of John Webster. This case set the precedent for subsequent defendants to be convicted of a crime without direct evidence of the crime. It is important to bear in mind that in all criminal trials the evidence must prove beyond reasonable doubt that the defendant committed the crime.

Modes of Death

As indicated in the opening paragraphs of this chapter, when police investigate a death, they must initially assess whether a crime has occurred. Next, they must determine the manner by which the deceased has died. The actual cause of death is generally determined from an autopsy, but the investigating officer can frequently deduce the likely cause of death by carefully examining the crime scene and the body. Modes of death can be generally divided into four categories: accidental death, natural causes, suicide, and criminal homicide (murder).

Accidental Deaths   A number of types of death are accidental. These may include a backyard pool drowning, an accidental fall down a flight of stairs, an unintended drug overdose, a hunting accident, and so forth.

Natural Causes   Deaths attributed to natural causes include heart attacks, strokes, various diseases, and even simply old age. It is not uncommon for an individual who dies from natural causes to have been under the care of a physician. However, in the case of a young heart attack victim, neither the deceased nor the family may have known the victim had heart problems. Although these cases may ultimately be ruled death by natural causes, it is important to carefully investigate to ensure that some external cause has not created the appearance of a heart attack.

Suicides   A variety of methods have been used to commit suicide. Shooting, poisoning, hanging, drug overdose, carbon monoxide, and wrist cutting are all commonly employed by individuals seeking to kill themselves. Police investigating the crime scene of an alleged suicide should make certain that it is a suicide and not a murder made to look like a suicide in order to throw off police.

Criminal Homicides (Murders)   Murder involves an individual intentionally killing another through any of an assortment of methods. Some of the methods

HISTORY

DR. GEORGE PARKMAN, A NOTED BOSTON PHYSICIAN during the late 1800s, owned many tenement buildings on which he collected rents; it was also well known that he would lend money to a wide assortment of people. It was his habit to go out walking each day to keep an eye on his properties and to collect the debts owed to him as they came due. On Friday, November 23, 1849, a week before Thanksgiving, he went out to see about some of his accounts—particularly one that had given him some trouble over at Harvard Medical College, a debt owed by Dr. John Webster. Parker had recently learned that the collateral Dr. Webster had put up against the $600 loan Parkman had made him had already been used as collateral in another loan.

Parkman was seen in the vicinity of the Harvard Medical school by several individuals who owed him money, but Parkman never returned home that afternoon. The Parkman family anxiously inquired into the whereabouts of George later on that day and throughout the next day. Then they contacted the police, who posted a large notice urging people to come forward with information. At the same time, John Webster was telling people his version of a meeting he'd had with Parkman on Friday afternoon. Webster claimed to have been in the Parkman's home the morning of Parkman's disappearance; he also claimed to have finally come up with the money he owed on the debt. Webster, a professor of chemistry and geology, was a short, stocky man with dark hair and glasses. He had higher social aspirations for himself and his family than he could ever afford, but he tried not to let them know that. To deceive his wife and four daughters, he had borrowed money to pay for some of their finery and a nice house, but Webster had been unable to earn that money as planned, and he continued to borrow.

Soon after Parkman's disappearance, Dr. Webster began acting nervously, and janitor Ephraim Littlefield, who worked in the building of Dr. Webster's laboratory, grew suspicious of him. Littlefield began to spy on Webster and observed him doing something by the furnace and then depositing something down his privy (a kind of indoor latrine). When Littlefield searched the depository of the privy, he found several human body parts, including a pelvis, a right thigh, and a lower left leg. He contacted the police who subsequently arrested Dr. Webster for the murder of George Parkman. The authorities were never able to find all of Parkman's body parts; they reasoned that Webster had dismembered the body and tried, unsuccessfully, to burn it. They did, however, recover additional body parts from the bottom of the furnace, including a torso and a jaw fragment with several teeth.

Because some people reported seeing Parkman on Saturday, suggesting that he may simply have left town, prosecutors questioned whether there was sufficient direct evidence to bring Webster to trial. Webster was ultimately tried for Parkman's murder, and at trial Dr. Nathan Keep, Parkman's dentist, declared that the jawbone found in the furnace with the false teeth still fitted into it was, in fact, that of George Parkman. Dr. Keep recognized his own handiwork. He had also made an impression of the jaw, which he still had, and it fit exactly the jawbone found in the furnace. The jury got to see and handle this plaster cast. This trial rested not on direct evidence against Webster but on a considerable amount of circumstantial evidence, which was sufficient to lead the jury to believe Webster was guilty beyond reasonable doubt (Schama, 1992; Thompson, 1971). Webster was convicted of the murder of Parkman and hanged for his crime on August 30, 1850.

of murder include poisoning, shooting, cutting or stabbing, drowning, clubbing, strangulation, and suffocation. Methods of investigating these categories of death are discussed in greater detail later in this chapter.

MOTIVES FOR HOMICIDE

Motive is important in the investigation of a homicide. If an underlying motive for the homicide can be determined, a suspect may be identified. Motive gives the investigation a kind of focus and helps the investigator better understand why a homicide has occurred. Let us consider some of the more common motives for homicide.

Unplanned or Spontaneous Murders

Unplanned or spontaneous murders occur quite frequently and are likely to be motivated by one or more of a variety of causes:

- Use of drugs or alcohol, resulting in a fight that turns lethal
- Reaching for a handgun or rifle during the heat of an argument
- Dispute between a boyfriend and girlfriend
- Dispute between friends over a boyfriend or girlfriend
- Disagreement over money or a business transaction
- Heat of passion when a spouse discovers his or her partner is cheating with another
- Unintentional killing during the commission of another crime, such as robbery or burglary

As each example suggests, spontaneous murders lack planning and premeditation and are highly related to opportunity. They spring from an emotional base and occur swiftly, seemingly without reason. Jealousy or emotionally charged disputes are typically at the root of spontaneous murders. Spontaneous murders have a high clearance rate because witnesses and evidence are frequently available to the investigator. The perpetrator may even be arrested at or near the scene of the murder.

Murder for Financial Gain

Murders for financial gain often occur between individuals who have a professional or contractual relationship or are linked as beneficiaries of a will or insurance policy. The financial gain may be in real wealth or in property or business holdings. For example, many small businesses have partner's wills specifying that at the death of one partner sole ownership of the business transfers to the surviving partner. In other financially motivated homicides, a person may stand to collect a sizable inheritance upon the death of another person. A common question for an investigator to ask when considering the motive in a homicide is, "Who had something to gain from this death?"

It is also important to consider that a murderer motivated by a significant amount of wealth may hire a third party to commit the crime. Frequently, the truth in such murders is brought to light only when the actual killer is apprehended and turns on his or her employer.

Unlike spontaneous homicides, murders for financial gain are carefully planned and generally meticulously carried out. The killer may go to elaborate and sometimes costly lengths to make the murder appear accidental or to arrange a viable alibi.

Sexually Motivated Murders

Sexually motivated murders, also sometimes called *lust murders,* may be planned and intentional or may occur spontaneously as a secondary aspect of a rape or another sex crime. The murder may occur before, during, or after the sexual assault. In some cases, the murder is connected to the psychological problems that motivate the person to commit the sex crime. In other cases, the murder is a way of eliminating a possible witness, or it occurs while the assailant is trying to subdue a struggling victim.

Another type of sexually motivated murder is killing a spouse to make way for another mate. This is more likely when a large estate is under the control of the murdered spouse or when a divorce might result in the loss of large amounts of money or property.

In some cases of sexually motivated murder, particularly those involving homosexuals, friends of the victim may provide important clues to the identity of the killer. The victim's neighborhood should be canvassed, as well as places the victim might have spent time (local bars, gyms, and so on). Interviews with people in these locations may provide significant information regarding who a suspect might be and where he or she might be found.

Murder for Revenge

On television detective shows, the investigator frequently asks, "Did the deceased have any enemies?" Answering this question may lead to information about the murderer in a murder for revenge. Many public figures—judges, prosecuting attorneys, politicians, and prominent businesspeople—knowingly and unknowingly make enemies. In addition, drug dealers and other criminals may cross one another and thus create enemies—sometimes numerous ones, each with a motive to murder. In some cases, the murdered victim may not be the true target of the revenge. For example, a felon angry with a judge who sent him to prison might rape and murder the judge's young daughter as a means of hurting the judge in revenge. Because the victim is not always the actual target, revenge murders are sometimes difficult to investigate.

Elimination Murders

Elimination murders are committed to remove some obstacle to a desired goal. The obstacle may be an eyewitness to another crime, a business rival, or even an opposing criminal boss. Checking on the background of the victim may provide clues to the reason for the murder. In some cases, the victim may have been eliminated because he or she was an informant or potential informant for police authorities. In such a case, how apparent the likely murderer is may depend on whether the authorities have already received information about someone from the murdered informant. However, the victim may have been providing information on a number of individuals, giving each a potential motive for murder. Although the playing field may be thus reduced, considerable investigation is required to identify which of the possible suspects is responsible.

Motiveless Murders

There are at least two forms of what might be called motiveless murders. These include stranger-to-stranger murders and mistaken identity murders. Stranger-to-stranger murders have been on the increase during the past decade. Bystanders are often killed by gang members in drive-by shootings. In some cases, the killing is a *hate crime,* and an individual is killed because of some physical or personal characteristic. For example, a homosexual man may be beaten to death by someone he meets in a bar; a Hasidic

Jew may be shot by a neo-Nazi skinhead; an African American woman may be murdered simply because she walked into a neighborhood where a Ku Klux Klan meeting was going on. Alcohol and drugs sometimes play a role in such stranger-to-stranger murders. The initiation rituals of some gangs may also contribute to these kinds of murders. Some gangs require new members to "make their bones," or murder someone, to prove their worth.

Mistaken identity murders are not especially common—except on television. However, occasionally an investigator will confront a murder that seems both senseless and without motive. A thorough examination of the victim's background may indicate that he or she had no enemies and was not worth killing for financial gain. In fact, no reason for the murder can be found. For example, a blond-haired woman is shot in the back of the head while sitting in a blue Volvo parked in the lot of a local supermarket. A background investigation reveals that the woman was happily married, had two small children, was active in civic projects, and had no apparent enemies. The case seemingly comes to a standstill. However, several weeks later, another blond-haired woman is found shot in the head in a blue Volvo outside the same supermarket. This time, however, the assailant has been seen and recognized by a supermarket employee. The police arrest the woman identified by the supermarket worker and recover the murder weapon. When arrested, the woman bursts out, "I don't care if I go to jail, as long as that bitch doesn't get my man." By interrogating the suspect, the police learn that she shot the first woman by mistake; she had not previously seen the woman she meant to kill, but she had a description of her and her car. The first murder, then, was a case of mistaken identity.

THE HOMICIDE INVESTIGATION

Although detectives handle the majority of dead-body calls, patrol officers are often called on to conduct or assist in an investigation involving a death. Therefore, all officers need at least a working knowledge of the problems and procedures involved in a death investigation.

The responding officer's first priority is to give emergency aid to the victim, if he or she is still alive, or to determine that a death has occurred. A person who is near death may appear dead to the untrained observer. Consequently, officers responding to dead-body calls should, upon arrival at the scene, examine the body. The investigator must be careful not to destroy evidence, but it is important to be sure that the person is dead rather than in need of immediate medical help. It is not advisable to rely on the opinion of a witness or bystander unless he or she happens to be a doctor, coroner, or similarly trained clinical specialist. If there is even the remote possibility that the victim may still be alive, an ambulance should be summoned. First aid should be administered by the officer until the ambulance arrives. There are a number of ways to determine whether a person is dead:

- **Appearance** In death, the face becomes pale or ashen and waxy, the lower jaw drops a bit, and the mouth may sag open. The eyes become soft to the touch, and the eyelids may be open slightly but will show no sign of movement or reflex action when touched.
- **Pupillary reaction** The pupils of a living person's eyes contract when a bright light, such as a flashlight beam, is shined into the eyes.
- **Pulse** A check for a pulse may be made on the wrist, inside the upper arm at the elbow, or under the chin at the neck.

- **Visible breathing** Note the movement of the chest or abdominal area; a mirror placed just below the nostrils may also detect breath (as a fogging of the mirror).
- **Nose** Listen or place hand at nostrils to hear or feel breathing.
- **Muscle resistance or muscle reflex** Muscle resistance and reflex are present in the body to some degree until death. Note whether limbs can be moved without resistance.
- **Cyanosis** In death, the lips become cyanotic, or bluish, as do the nail beds.

The type of investigation conducted at the scene is determined by the category of the death being investigated. The first officer responding to the death call must come to a general conclusion about the cause of death. This is important because it will dictate the type and degree of the investigation that will follow. Things that influence an officer's decision about whether a homicide has occurred include the type and amount of information furnished by the complainant and witnesses and an examination of the body. Close observation of the crime scene and body for marks of violence and other indicators, such as signs of struggle, cuts, wounds, weapons, poison, pills, blood, bruising on the body, or bullet holes, may assist the officer in drawing a conclusion. Information furnished by relatives, friends, and neighbors may permit early conclusions about the noncriminal nature of a case. For example, the person's past history of illness and absence of any signs or evidence of violence may suggest that the death was by natural causes.

Procedures in the Preliminary Investigation

The first officers arriving at the scene should observe the following priorities:

- Record the time they were notified of the death complaint.
- Record the identification information about the complainant. Include the date and the location from which the complainant called.
- En route to the scene (depending on the elapsed time between the call and the alleged death) be alert for possible fleeing suspects—people with fresh wounds, torn or bloody clothing, or any sort of furtive or evasive actions.
- Record the time of arrival at the scene and the exact location.
- Determine whether the victim is dead or severely injured. Request medical assistance if necessary. Use caution when approaching the victim to avoid disrupting or destroying possible evidence and to protect your safety in case the victim is armed.
- Determine and verify the identities of those present at the scene and anyone who left before the officers' arrival.
- Record the license plate numbers of vehicles parked near the scene so that their owners may be contacted if necessary.
- Begin brief and informal interviews of witnesses; be sure to obtain their home and business addresses and telephone numbers.
- Take immediate action to block off the crime scene to prevent contamination or destruction of evidence.

After these preliminary matters have been taken care of, the homicide investigation generally shifts its focus to other high-priority matters, which include identifying the victim, establishing the cause of death, determining the time of death, and developing a suspect.

Arrival of Investigators and Medical Examiner

When the investigators arrive at the scene, one of them will take charge of all aspects of the case. The lead investigator will coordinate and direct all investigative assignments. The head investigator should immediately take inventory of all personnel at the scene. A recap of all the information already gathered should be requested from the responding officers, and everyone at the scene should be brought up to date before continuing the investigation (Zugible & Carroll, 2005).

As in any other criminal investigation, the homicide scene must be secured and protected, photographed and sketched, and all evidence must be carefully gathered, identified, preserved, and forwarded to the lab. An accurate description of the body and all clothing worn by the victim should be recorded. (When describing a body, proceed from the head to the feet.) Observe the victim's face for injuries, blood, dirt, extraneous matter, or marks. Take color photographs of bruises or other marks on the victim's body. Note the eyes, mouth, and facial expression. Examine the victim's hands, noting whether they are clean, dirty, open, clenched, holding anything, or wearing any articles of jewelry. If the victim has been sexually molested, the medical examiner should check for pubic hairs or semen stains. Also carefully package and label the contents of wastebaskets, glasses, cups, bottles, ashtrays, and any other containers at the scene.

In addition to securing and preserving physical evidence, investigators should identify and interview possible witnesses and suspects, as well as relatives and friends of the deceased. All persons with any connection to the deceased should be asked to describe exactly what they were doing when they learned of the death. Canvassing the neighborhood may also lead to direct or hearsay information about the time of the homicide.

STATISTICS Homicides have the highest clearance rate of any index offense. According to the FBI's Uniform Crime Reports, law enforcement agencies for the nation's cities, metropolitan counties, and nonmetropolitan counties cleared 61.2 percent, 64.4 percent, and 74.2 percent, respectively, of their murder offenses in 2004 (FBI, 2005).

forensic pathology A specialized field of medicine that studies and interprets changes in body tissue and fluids in relation to criminal investigation.

All violent or suspicious deaths require the coroner or medical examiner to determine the time and precise cause of death. The determination of criminal responsibility in a death has evolved into a highly specialized field of medical science called **forensic pathology.** Most large departments have medical examiners and forensic pathologists on staff or available to assist in investigation at a death scene or death discovery scene. In other situations, the on-the-scene investigation is conducted by police investigators, who then forward all evidence with the body to the coroner's office where an autopsy is done to establish the cause and time of death and, in some instances, to identify the victim.

If possible, the homicide investigator should be present during the autopsy to observe firsthand and ask questions about the case. The pathologist or medical examiner can explain the autopsy findings as they progress. The firsthand results can then be passed on directly to others working on the case. Should the investigator have a suspected murder weapon, that weapon can be compared with wounds on the body. The officer present at an autopsy can also testify about the autopsy at a coroner's inquest, should one be conducted (Ribowsky & Shachtman, 2006).

FYI Today, there are statewide medical examiner systems, district medical examiners, county medical examiners, county coroners, and district coroners, among other arrangements. Some states, such as Texas, for example, use county or district medical examiners in metropolitan areas and justices of the peace, generally persons without a legal or medical background, to inquire into questioned deaths in rural areas. Seventeen states have mixed coroner and medical examiner systems in a variety of configurations. Nevada and Kansas have district coroners, and nine states have county coroners (Combs, Parrish, & Ing, 1992). Coroner qualifications vary widely, from no statutory qualifications in Alabama and Arkansas to qualification as a licensed physician in Kansas, Ohio, and counties in North Dakota with more than 8,000 people. Parish coroners in Louisiana must be licensed physicians "unless none will accept the office" (Combs et al., 1992). Most states using a coroner system set minimal qualifications, generally a minimum age (18–26), minimum residency (1–2 years), and occasionally, education (usually high school). Although coroners are elected to office in most jurisdictions, Nebraska designates certain office holders as coroner, such as the county attorney or sheriff. North Dakota appoints coroners through the board of county commissioners.

Identifying the Victim

Knowing who the victim is and how the victim was killed may provide clues about motive or the suspect's identity. The inability to identify a dead body greatly complicates the investigation. When investigators do not know who the victim is, it is difficult to delve into his or her background. Different types of evidence can contribute to ascertaining a deceased person's identity.

Fingerprints Fingerprint identification is the most efficient way to identify the body of a murder victim. However, this technique is effective only if the victim's prints are on file and if prints can be obtained from the corpse. If the hands or fingers have been mutilated or in other ways destroyed, investigators may not be able to use fingerprints to identify the body.

Skeletal Studies Examination of the skeleton may provide a basis for identification. This is especially true if the body has any skeletal peculiarities, such as old fractures, metal plates or pins, or evidence of certain bone diseases. Also, bones may provide clues about the victim's age, gender, and ethnicity.

Visual Inspection The victim may be recognized by someone who knows him or her, for example, a friend, relative, or coworker. However, severe trauma, incineration, or decomposition may make it impossible even for a mother to identify her own child. Visual inspection without verification has a risk of subjective error. This may occur because the person making the identification is psychologically unable to accept the death of a close friend or relative. The misidentification may occur by accident, or it may be deliberate. Visual identification combined with another method, such as fingerprint matching, is a favored method for reliable identification.

Personal Effects Sometimes a victim may be identified through his or her personal effects, such as jewelry, identification cards, or letters in pockets, a wallet, or a purse. Personal effects, however, may prove unreliable, given the easy transferability of such items. Despite their possible lack of reliability, personal effects often do provide leads to the identity of the victim.

Tattoos and Scars   Tattoos, scars, pockmarks, birthmarks, moles, and other such skin markings may be helpful in establishing a victim's identity. Alone, these markings provide only tentative or somewhat unreliable identification, but in conjunction with other, more reliable forms of identification, skin markings can lead to a positive identification.

Odontology (Dental Evidence)   Identification based on the examination of teeth, fillings, inlays, bridges, crowns, and so forth is valuable because teeth are among the most durable parts of the human body. When incineration, animals, trauma, decomposition, and insects have destroyed virtually everything else, the teeth often remain undamaged. It is unlikely that two people have identical sets of teeth. Dental evidence is legally recognized and accepted when properly presented in court.

Clothing   Articles of clothing frequently contain identification clues such as cleaner's marks, labels, initials, and similar information. Identification by clothing alone, of course, is inexact because clothing may be easily loaned, sold secondhand, or stolen. Furthermore, articles of clothing in themselves are seldom unique enough to provide a reliable basis for identification. Clothing is useful, on occasion, when searching for a missing person who is reported as wearing certain clothing.

Photographs   When other methods fail, it is not uncommon, to ask the public for help in identifying a murder victim. Photos of the victim are sometimes published in local papers or shown on local news programs. When photos are not appropriate, as in the case of disfigurement or mutilation, an artist's rendering may be substituted. Information about the identity of the victim and about the murder itself sometimes results from such public showings of the victim.

Estimating the Time of Death

It is important to establish the time of death as precisely as possible. If the time of death is too vague, it could provide enough time for the murderer to have an alibi. In some suicides, the time of death may determine whether an exclusion clause in an insurance policy can be enforced. In traffic accidents, double murders, murder-suicides, or suicide pacts, it is also important to determine the order of the deaths.

Typically, both the investigator and the medical examiner are responsible for estimating the time of death. Understanding how medical examiners estimate time of death allows the investigator to better consider the elements at the crime scene that will be relevant (Sach, 2002).

Only when a murder has witnesses can investigators pinpoint the time of death with absolute precision. In the absence of witnesses, the time of death can be estimated fairly accurately. If the death occurred within the past four days, the time of death usually can be placed within four hours of its actual occurrence. Naturally, this may vary with the factors an examiner uses and the factors available. A number of factors can be used to estimate time of death.

rigor mortis   A contracting of muscles of a body after death that disappears over time.

Rigor Mortis   Although limp immediately after death, a body stiffens as substances (mainly lactic acid) accumulate in the muscles. This stiffening is known as *rigor mortis.* Warm temperatures accelerate its appearance and disappearance, and cold slows it down. *Rigor mortis* usually begins two to four hours after death and affects the entire body in approximately six to twelve hours. *Rigor mortis* will frequently disappear in twenty-four to thirty-six hours. It disappears in about the same sequence as it appears. The early stages of *rigor mortis* can be noted in the jaw and the back of the neck, with stiffening of other muscles proceeding down the body.

Closely associated with *rigor mortis* is a condition called **cadaveric spasm**. This condition is sometimes referred to as *instantaneous rigor.* This rigidity of specific muscle groups cannot be fully explained. It typically occurs after a sudden injury to the central nervous system, but it should not be confused with *rigor mortis.* It manifests itself as a death grip, usually on a weapon, and is generally most evident in suicides. It does not disappear as *rigor mortis* does.

Livor Mortis (Postmortem Lividity) *Livor mortis,* also often called *postmortem lividity,* is a dark discoloration (usually dark blue or purplish) under the skin. It is caused by blood draining to the parts of the body nearest the ground when the heart stops beating and circulating the blood. It is especially useful to consider when determining if a body may have been moved after death. When the body has lain in the original position for several hours before being moved, *livor mortis* may be pronounced. Investigators should be careful not to confuse lividity with discoloration caused by bruises on the body. *Livor mortis* can also be useful in indicating the cause of death. For instance, in carbon monoxide poisoning, some forms of cyanide poisoning, or extremely cold conditions, *livor mortis* is not dark purple but cherry red. In potassium chlorate poisoning, lividity is light brown. Lividity usually begins within one hour after death, congeals after three or four hours, and reaches a maximum in ten to twelve hours.

Body Temperature Body temperature, though not entirely accurate alone for determining time of death, can assist in its estimation. After death, the body tends to lose heat at about 1 to 1.5 degrees per hour until it reaches room temperature. Although heat loss may be rather rapid during the first three hours after death, it levels off then, occurring more slowly until the body reaches room temperature or the temperature of its environment. Factors influencing the time required to cool the body include the difference in temperature between the body and the medium in which it is found (water, air, or soil). In addition, clothing, the victim's physical size and weight, and the weather may all affect the cooling rate.

Body Decomposition Decomposition is the breaking down of a human body due to the effects of temperature, animal and insect attack, and general putrefaction through the softening and liquefaction of tissue and the conversion of soft tissues to liquids and gases.

The actual rate at which the human body decomposes depends on a number of factors. These include air temperature, levels of moisture, the body's own bacteria and enzyme levels, and assaults by animals or insects. Early signs of putrefaction, noticeable after about twenty-four hours, are a greenish-red or blue-green coloration of the abdomen or groin. Darkening continues until the tissue color of the entire body is completely brown or black.

The rate of decomposition is influenced by the environment and the weather. The colder the temperature, the slower the decomposition; warmer temperatures

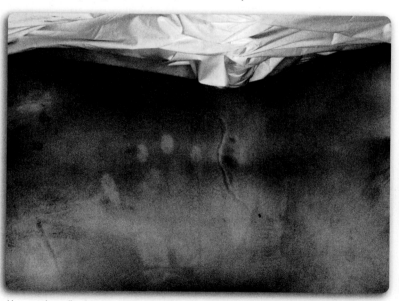

Livor mortis, or discoloration of the body where the blood has pooled internally, may be pronounced, especially if the body has lain for several hours before being moved.

cadaveric spasm A rigidity of certain muscles that usually occurs when the victim is holding something at the time of death and the hand closes tightly around the object; sometimes a sign of suicide.

livor mortis A dark discoloration of the body where blood has pooled or drained to the lowest level; also called *postmortem lividity.*

FOCUS ON TECHNOLOGY

THE BODY FARM

THE "BODY FARM" WAS THE INNOVATIVE IDEA of Dr. William Bass, a forensic anthropologist at the University of Tennessee—and it is the only location of its kind in the country. It consists of a three-acre wooded plot surrounded by a razor wire fence. A number of bodies, originating from various sources, are scattered throughout the area. Some of the cadavers had been unclaimed at the medical examiner's office, and more than 300 people have voluntarily donated their bodies to the Body Farm. The bodies are exposed to insects and the elements in a number of ways to provide insights into decomposition under varying conditions. Some of the bodies are left out in the open; others are buried in shallow graves or entombed in vaults; some are even left in cars.

Eventually, most of these bodies will end up in the university's collection of skeletons that make up a large database of body types. With a growing collection, forensic experts are charting the differences between male and female, old and young, black and white, tall and short, heavy and thin. The skeletal studies also provide a basis for computer-driven determinations of identity through facial image reconstruction. In addition to the skeletal studies, the rate of organ degeneration after death, especially the liver, is being studied. Ultimately, that should allow the time of death to be pinpointed with increasing accuracy (Bass & Jefferson, 2004).

---

increase decomposition speed. Similarly, bodies tend to decompose more rapidly in water due to large amounts of bacteria in the water and attacks by fish and other aquatic life forms.

The human body has a greater specific gravity than water, and a corpse may sink initially when placed in water. However, within three days to a week (depending on water temperature) the body will surface because of the formation of gases. Prolonged submersion in water causes the skin to wrinkle, and as liquids and gases move beneath the skin, the body will bloat and sometimes even burst.

Adipocere is a whitish gray, soapy or waxy substance that forms on the surface of the body after about six weeks. It is caused by changes in the fatty tissue and may not be seen unless there is fat in the tissue beneath the skin. When a body has been buried in damp ground or submerged in water, adipocere usually forms.

Carrion Insects   During the past several years, the role of the **forensic entomologist** has expanded, and these scientists now assist in estimating the time of death of decomposed bodies by examining the attack of the body by certain insects (Bass & Jefferson, 2004; Haskell et al., 1989; Rodriguez & Bass, 1983). Several guidelines should be followed to assist the work of the forensic entomologist. First, do not move or in other ways disturb the body. As in other crime scene investigations, take photographs of the

adipocere   A whitish-gray, soapy or waxy substance that forms on the surface of a body left for weeks in a damp location.

forensic entomologist   A person who specializes in the study of insects in relation to determining the location, time, and cause of death of a human victim.

body, including close-up photographs of the areas where insect activity is detected. The investigator should carefully describe in his or her notes the environment where the body was found (forest, bedroom, dark shed, etc.). Also, the investigator should record the temperature at the time of investigation, the relative humidity, and the general weather conditions if the body was found in an open or exposed area.

Insects must be collected from the body as soon as possible, beginning with areas of greatest decomposition, usually the face or an open wound. The goal is to collect as many different insects as possible, and at all stages of the insect's life cycle (adults, pupae, larvae, eggs). Flies typically are the first insects to attack a decomposing body. A search for fly larvae, even in the absence of other insects, may assist the investigation. Folds in the deceased's clothing and the soil directly beneath the body should be carefully examined because they frequently conceal insect larvae. If the search does not locate any evidence of hatched fly pupa cases, one may assume that the fly larvae collected represent the first cycle of an insect attack.

Other Indicators   In addition to the factors already suggested, medical examiners can draw conclusions regarding the time of death by considering the contents of the stomach. The investigator can assist the medical examiner's estimate by trying to learn what time the victim last ate. Food digestion is affected by a number of factors, and investigators should note, for example, whether vomit is found near the victim. During an autopsy, the medical examiner can ascertain to what extent items in the stomach have been digested and can infer from that about how long after a meal the death occurred.

Watches and other timepieces found near the victim may also assist the investigator in approximating the time of death. A watch or a clock in a room may be broken during a scuffle or by a stray bullet in the course of the murder. This may give an indication of the time of death. Old watches and many inexpensive timepieces will stop almost immediately when submerged in water. This, too, may offer some indication of when the body was placed in the water or killed.

When a body is found outdoors, time of death may be inferred roughly by the vegetation under and around it. If a body has remained on the ground for a long period, the decaying of vegetation underneath the body may also help in determining the time of death.

Developing a Suspect

Should a suspect be apprehended at the scene, follow procedures outlined in Chapter 2 for arresting suspects and giving *Miranda* warnings. If witnesses at the scene have provided descriptions of a suspect interview that suspect following the procedures set forth in Chapter 6. If a suspect has not been identified, it is important to try to determine a motive for the murder to point the way to a possible suspect. Here are some suggested investigative procedures for developing a case against a suspect who is in custody:

- Administer a polygraph examination if the suspect is willing and signs a waiver of legal rights.
- Have the suspect reenact the crime, and make a videotape of this reenactment.
- Take photographs of the suspect.
- Take into custody the clothing the suspect wore at the time of the homicide, and have it processed by the crime lab.
- Conduct a sobriety test, and take specimens of saliva, urine, and blood.

- Collect fingernail clippings and hair samples from the suspect.
- Examine the suspect for wounds, bite marks, or scratches.
- Take fingerprints of the suspect, and check them against available files.
- Check all telephone calls made by the suspect during the recent past, and verify the identities of people called.
- Verify all statements made by the suspect to either corroborate or disprove information given by witnesses or other sources.

TYPES OF DEATHS INVESTIGATED AND WEAPONS USED

Knowing about the most common kinds of deaths and their characteristics can greatly assist homicide investigators. Being able to recognize types of wounds and knowing what kinds of evidence to look for in certain situations can improve the chances of a successful homicide investigation. Figure 14.1 shows the various types of weapons used to commit murder in one recent year.

Natural Death

The true disposition of a dead-body call is generally not known until a preliminary investigation has been conducted. The officers receiving the call have many investigative responsibilities, particularly in unattended deaths and other types that fall under the purview of the coroner or the medical examiner's office. Teamwork with the coroner or the medical examiner's investigator at the scene of death is essential to the determination of the cause of death. Most state laws require that the death certificate include a statement not only of the cause of death but also of the mode—that is, whether the death was by natural causes, accident, suicide, or homicide. In natural deaths, the coroner or the medical examiner's office is primarily interested in establishing a cause to (1) rule out unnatural causes, (2) determine whether the death was an accident, a suicide, or a homicide, (3) eliminate dangerous conditions, and (4) determine liability.

FIGURE 14.1 Murder Circumstances by Weapon

Firearms (handguns, rifles, shotguns, others)	9,326
Knives or cutting instruments	1,866
Personal weapons (hands, fists, feet, etc.)	933
Blunt objects (clubs, hammers, etc.)	663
Strangulation	155
Explosives	1
Asphyxiation	105
Fire	114
Drowning	15
Narcotics	76
Poison	11
Other	856
Total Murders	14,121

Source: Federal Bureau of Investigation. 2005. *Crime in the United States, 2004.* Washington, DC: U.S. Government Printing Office, Table 2.9.

FOCUS ON TECHNOLOGY

COMPUTERIZED PHOTOGRAPHIC LINE-UP

TO AID IN SUSPECT IDENTIFICATION, computerized photographic line-ups can now be assembled quickly. The technician keys in the physical characteristics (reported by the victim or witnesses) that he or she wants displayed in each of several panels of composite photographs that the system will assemble. The remaining panel is a photograph of the suspect.

When approaching the location of a death call and after arriving at the scene, responding officers should be particularly alert for any unusual conditions or suspicious activities. Immediate steps must be taken to protect the scene and the property of the deceased. Nearly always, the scene of death has been disturbed, making it difficult at times to reach an early conclusion. The disturbance may have occurred in several ways. The injured victim may have been thought alive at the time of the discovery, and the scene may have been disturbed by attempts to revive or save the life of the victim. The assailant or a bystander may have moved the body for some reason. Another possibility is disturbance by early arrivals, sometimes even inexperienced police officers.

Once the officers are satisfied that the death was the result of natural causes, the following investigative duties remain:

- Notify the desk sergeant as soon as possible after verifying the validity of the complaint.
- Request any needed assistance and the coroner.
- Determine who discovered the body.
- Determine the deceased's name, race, gender, age, and marital status; the name and relationship of the next of kin; and the preference of mortuary.
- Find out who was the last person to see the deceased alive. Note when and where that happened, who else was there, and what activities occurred.
- Obtain short statements from people who witnessed the death or found the body. Establish the time of death.
- Inquire about the health history of the deceased. Also find out the actions and remarks of the deceased prior to death.

- Contact the victim's doctor if the victim was receiving treatment. Determine whether a doctor or another legally authorized health professional had attended the victim in the previous forty-eight hours.
- Check for additional injuries or other possible causes of death, even if the cause of death seems obvious.

Suicide

Suicide is intentionally killing oneself. People choose a variety of ways to end their lives, but the ten most common are hanging, taking overdoses of pharmaceutical or illegal drugs, drowning, taking poison, inhaling gases, jumping from high places, self-inflicted gunshot wounds, self-inflicted cuts or stabs, electrocution, and intentional crashes of aircraft or automobiles. The reasons, motives, and psychological intentions of suicidal people are quite complex. Self-destructive ideas or impulses that ordinarily are well controlled or mostly unconscious can be activated or released by emotional stress, physical or mental exhaustion, or alcohol- or drug-induced conditions. All of these situations intensify suicidal behavior.

Suicide is not a criminal offense, but in some jurisdictions attempted suicide is. Some jurisdictions hold an attempted suicide that kills an innocent bystander or a would-be rescuer to be murder; others, manslaughter; and still others, no crime. Some jurisdictions hold it to be murder for one person to persuade or help another to commit suicide; others make it manslaughter or a separate crime.

It is sometimes difficult to distinguish between homicide and suicide (or accidental death) by a quick examination of the crime scene. Many deaths by suicide have all the outward appearances of murder to an untrained eye. This is an important question to be answered by the responding officers. As a rule, however, self-inflicted injuries have certain fairly predictable physical features. Although the location of a wound and the manner of its occurrence are not always conclusive, they do provide a degree of probability of suicide versus homicide. For this reason, investigating officers should examine the injury and consider its manner and direction, the nature of the weapon, the presence or absence of a note, and information from any witnesses.

Suicide occurs at all socioeconomic levels; cuts across religious, racial, and political lines; and can occur among very young children and the aged. During the investigation of suicides, the officer may encounter evasion, denial, concealment, and even direct suppression of evidence. To avoid false conclusions, the investigator should try to reconstruct the true conditions of the crime scene at the time of the discovery of the body. Some of the questions an investigator should try to answer during the investigation of an apparent suicide include the following: Has anyone touched or moved the body or removed any property before the arrival of the police? If *livor mortis* has set in and the officer knows how to interpret it, does it indicate that the body has been moved? What is the temperature of the room? Has it been changed since the time of discovery? Have heaters been turned on or off? Were windows found open or closed, doors locked or unlocked? Were lights turned on or off when the discovery was made? Who turned off the automobile ignition in a carbon monoxide poisoning? Who shut off the gas on the stove (or other source) in a home gas-inhalation poisoning? What are the identities of the people present and any who left before the officers arrived?

Investigators should be cautious when investigating suspected suicide cases. Hanging victims are sometimes cut down and the knot untied (Figure 14.2), plastic bags are removed from suffocated victims, drowning victims are pulled from swimming pools, and instruments and suicide notes are sometimes removed to cover up a suicide.

FIGURE 14.2 Characteristic Bruise Patterns in Homicide and Suicide Strangulation

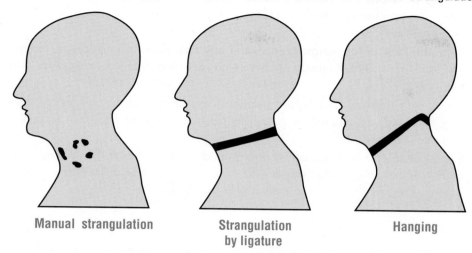

Manual strangulation   Strangulation by ligature   Hanging

Such a cover-up may be fabricated by well-meaning family members because of religious beliefs or to protect the public image of their loved one. It may also be an effort to defraud an insurance company that has a nonpayment-for-suicide clause.

Some people leave notes indicating why they killed themselves. Not all suicides, however, leave notes, letters, or even clues to their reasons for killing themselves. Only about 25 percent of all people who commit suicide leave notes. Even when notes are found, they may not conclusively show that a suicide, rather than a murder, has been committed. Nor is the absence of a note an indication that there is no suicide.

If a note is found, investigators should be careful not to handle it and should learn whether other members of the family or witnesses have already handled it. A suicide note should be handled like any other piece of physical evidence. It should be photographed and then carefully packaged in an evidence envelope bag and identified. If available, a sample of the deceased's writing should be obtained. In addition to traditional written notes, in today's technologically advanced age, investigators should not overlook the possibility of a recorded or videotaped suicide message.

Procedures in Suicide Investigations The investigation of a suicide is not nearly as complex or lengthy as the investigation of a homicide. It is recommended, however, that the following procedures be taken:

- Examine the victim. If doubt exists about the victim's being dead, call for an ambulance and administer first aid while awaiting the ambulance.

- If the victim is obviously dead, observe the scene carefully for indications of a struggle, the locations of objects in the room, the positions of chairs, the contents of ashtrays, and any weapons, pills, prescription bottles, glasses, suicide notes, and so on.

- Notify headquarters of findings at the scene and request the coroner.

- Be alert for efforts to make the victim's death appear accidental.

- Ask about the medical history, ailments, medications taken, and prescriptions (type, when filled, amount remaining, etc.).

- Examine any containers of prescription drugs and the accompanying labels. A prescription drug label should have the name of the drug and the name of the physician who issued the prescription. Generally, the name of the pharmacy is also on the label. The label should also indicate the date the prescription was filled, the number of tablets or capsules originally in the container, and the recommended dosage.

- Note the location of the medication and any indication of overdose or recent use. Also note any containers (glasses or cups) or loose tablets or capsules near the body.
- Check with relatives, friends, and neighbors. Before committing suicide, a person may make suicidal statements, give away personal items, or engage in certain other behaviors.
- Check for suicide notes (usually found quite close to the body). With handwritten notes, compare the handwriting on the note with known samples of the victim's writing. Preserve the note and turn it over to the coroner.

Poisoning

Poisoning is among the oldest methods of murder. It can be accomplished with a single lethal dose or by the accumulation of many small doses given to a victim over time. Some poisons can be administered by contact with the skin; others need to be ingested. Still others can be injected into the muscle or blood of a victim, and some may be lethal if inhaled. Some versatile poisons are lethal whether ingested, absorbed through the skin, or inhaled. Brucine, for example, is an extremely toxic chemical commonly found in pharmaceutical laboratories, as well as in many college chemistry classes. Even a very small amount, perhaps enough to cover the head of a pin, can kill a man of average height and weight.

FYI Many poisoning attempts are thwarted because the assailant uses too much poison. As a result, the victim vomits up most of the toxin before it can cause lethal damage.

toxicological screening
An examination of body tissue or fluids for poisons or other toxins.

Whenever a death is suspected to be the result of poisoning, a **toxicological screening** (an examination of tissue and body fluids for poisons) should be requested by the investigator. This will involve the collection of tissue and body fluid samples by the coroner or medical examiner's investigator, or some other authorized person. The contents of the stomach may also assist in the investigation of a suspected poisoning. It is important for the investigator to collect for analysis any drugs or drug containers that may have been used by the decedent.

A toxicological screening can sometimes reveal the presence of a toxic substance in a victim. Some drugs and poisons can be detected easily in blood, urine, or other body fluids. Others are detected only in tissue samples from the liver, kidney, or brain. Some poisons, however, such as brucine, may be missed by even highly skilled toxicologists if they are not looking specifically for that substance. Gaseous poisons and some harsh astringent fumes may be detected by an examination of lung tissue, as well as by their presence in the blood (Klaassen & Watkins, 2004).

A point to be mindful of is that many symptoms of poisoning also appear in certain diseases; however, symptoms of poisoning typically occur suddenly to a person who was previously in good health. The disease process is usually more gradual, proceeding over a period of many hours, days, or even weeks. A specific poison must be isolated and identified from tissue or body fluids before investigators can assume that the poison was taken or administered with the intention of killing the victim.

Stabbing and Cutting Wounds

Stabbing and cutting wounds differ in depth, shape, and size. Cutting, or incision, wounds are typically inflicted with a sharp edge, such as a razor or knife blade. However, any sharp flat instrument, such as the edge of a credit card, a piece of metal, or a shard of glass can produce a serious incision wound. Cutting wounds usually have even edges where the tissue has been cut. When the incision is parallel to the tissue fibers, the wound's edges lie close against one another; when the incision cuts across the fibers, the wound typically gapes open.

Incisions are made quickly by the sharp edge of an instrument, so bruises are usually not present. As a result, it is often difficult to tell whether they were made before or after death. As a general rule, incisions are deepest at the point where the cutting edge of the instrument first cut the skin. Thus, the direction of the wound can be determined by examining the cut from its deepest to shallowest points.

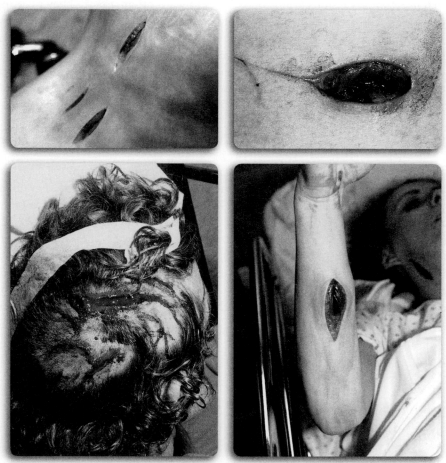

(Top Left) Cutting wounds produced by a single-edge blade; (Top Right) penetrating stab wound caused by a sharp object; (Bottom Left) lacerations on head from tire iron; (Bottom Right) defense stab wound on inside of arm.

Stabbing wounds may be produced by a knife, a knitting needle, a screwdriver, scissors, an ice pick, or any other tipped or pointed instrument. If a stab wound was produced by a sharp, flat instrument, such as a knife, it may not be possible to determine the width of the blade or instrument from the size of the external wound because the wound channel may be larger than the instrument that inflicted the damage. This is especially true for two-edged instruments, such as some throwing daggers and knives. This difference in size is due to the cutting action of the blade when it strikes the body and creates the entrance wound, as well as the cutting action when the weapon is withdrawn. If the knife is moved or turned while being withdrawn, the wound may further increase in size and develop a curved or angular surface. The wound may also exhibit characteristics related to the shape of the cutting instrument. For instance, a thick blade may produce a wedged-shaped wound, round weapons produce puncture wounds, serrated edges may produce slightly jagged edges on the surface wound, and so forth. The depth of a stab wound's channel may assist the medical examiner in determining the length of the weapon used.

Cutting wounds along the insides of a person's wrists, if deep enough to sever arteries, may result in death from loss of blood. Similarly, incisions that sever arteries in the neck of a victim will likewise cause death. Stabbing wounds typically result in death when vital organs are irreparably damaged or when arteries are severed.

defense wound Injuries on the hand or forearms of a victim who has attempted to fend off an attack.

Defense wounds result when a victim tries to ward off an attack. They may appear as stabs through the hand or cuts on the hands, fingers, or arms. Cuts on the palm or fingers may indicate that the victim sought to grab the weapon; slashes on the arm or shoulder suggest an attempt by the victim to block or shield him- or herself from a cut or stab. Investigators should carefully examine the hands, arms, and shoulders of victims to identify possible defense wounds. Bruises on the knuckles of a victim should also be noted because they may indicate that the victim struck his or her assailant.

Gunshot Wounds

Injuries and deaths resulting from gunshots are a special category of injury. The wound may result from a handgun, a rifle, or a shotgun. When a gun is fired, a number of things may affect the wound that results. These include the caliber of the weapon, the distance at which the weapon was fired, any materials the bullet traveled through before striking the victim (e.g., a wooden door or a plasterboard wall), the shape and nature of the bullet (e.g., jacketed, pellet, hollow, flat-tipped), and whether the bullet was shot directly into the victim or ricocheted off some object.

Investigators should note both the entry and exit wounds of a gunshot. This is particularly important for determining whether the gunshot was intentional, accidental,

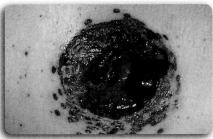
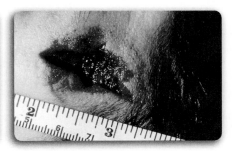

Gunshot contact wounds with muzzle imprint.

Chapter 14 Homicide **293**

or self-inflicted. Although the medical examiner will make the final determination during an autopsy, the investigator should be aware of wound characteristics to be able to determine the type of investigation to pursue.

Gunshot wounds may exhibit certain characteristic entry patterns. The size of the wound depends on the caliber of the weapon firing the bullet, although the entry wound may be somewhat smaller than the bullet because the elasticity of the skin closes the entry point slightly. Frequently, there is a gray ring around the wound. This ring may be more pronounced when the gun is fired at very close range. The discoloring results from the deposit of gunpowder on the skin and is sometimes called a **wipe ring,** or *smudging.* When a gun is fired at extremely close range, the skin around the wound may even be burned by the muzzle flash and hot gunpowder. The burn is sometimes referred to as **tattooing.**

When a gun is fired while being held against the skin of the victim, a **contact wound** results. Contact wounds generally are larger than wounds inflicted at a distance because gases discharged when the gun is fired enter the wound with the bullet. (These gases dissipate into the air when a gun is fired at a distance from the victim.) Having no place else to go but into the wound when the gun is placed against the skin, these gases burst the tissue, causing a larger entry wound. Contact wounds are typically found in suicides and in execution-type murders.

The difference between entry and exit wounds is observable. Exit wounds are generally larger than entry wounds, are likely to bleed more profusely than entry wounds, and are often irregularly shaped. The shape of the exit wound depends on the path and condition of the bullet as it passes through the victim. If the bullet has struck bone, mushroomed, or fragmented, the wound's shape will vary.

When weapons are found at the scene, they should be photographed, sketched, measured, identified, and handled only with gloved hands (see Chapter 4). Notes should be made to support the officer's actions, and the weapon should be submitted to the laboratory for examination. The trial of a homicide case often hinges on information about the weapon and the positions and types of wounds inflicted on the victim. Investigators should use extreme care when writing notes regarding these elements of a case.

Asphyxia

Death from **asphyxiation** is an extreme condition caused by a lack of oxygen and an excess of carbon dioxide in the blood. It can result from choking, suffocating, smothering, drowning, or electrocution. As previously mentioned, body discoloration occurs in all deaths. In cases of asphyxia, it is usually quite pronounced and is characteristically blue. It is particularly noticeable around the mouth and lips and finger- and toenails. In cases of asphyxiation from strangulation, one frequently finds hemorrhaging in the eyes (broken blood vessels in the white portion, which appear as red blotches, known as petechiae); this bleeding results from increased blood pressure brought on by compression of the throat or neck.

wipe ring (smudging) A gray ring around a gunshot wound resulting from the deposit of gunpowder by a gun blast at close range.

tattooing The burned skin around a gunshot wound resulting from a gun blast (muzzle flash) when fired at close range.

contact wound A wound created when a gun is fired while being held against the skin of the victim; typically found in self-inflicted wounds and in some execution-type murders.

asphyxiation Death due to a lack of oxygen and an excess of carbon dioxide in the blood.

 FYI In some cases of strangulation, skin is removed from the neck area to recover the killer's fingerprints.

Strangulation In death by strangulation, external pressure closes the airway or compresses the main arteries in the neck. Oxygen is withheld from the lungs, and the blood supply to the brain is drastically curtailed, resulting in death. When investigating a suspected strangulation, look for bloody fluids at the nose and mouth, tongue displacement, and marks on the neck indicating hands, fingers, or a ligature that may have been used to compress the throat. Also, note the scene for disturbances or signs of a struggle, and note the condition of the ground or floor beneath the body. Likewise, check the victim's fingernails for signs of skin tissue or hair or other trace evidence of the assailant. A ligature, such as a rope, strap, wire, scarf, or other pliable material, will leave horizontal marks low on the neck and show equal pressure around the neck. Manual strangulation leaves a different pattern of soft tissue damage and may occur higher on the neck (see Figure 14.2) Most strangulations are murders.

Hanging Most hangings are suicides, but some are accidental. Victims are found in sitting, standing, and lying positions. Belts, towels, bandages, wire, fabric strips, rope, and assorted other tying materials are used. Hanging does not require that the body drop or swing freely, because only pressure is required to cause death. As in strangulation, air and blood flow are restricted. In hangings, ligature marks typically start below the chin and travel up diagonally toward the ears or the top of the head. The entire noose should be removed from a hanging victim without disturbing the knot. This can be accomplished by cutting the noose and securing the ends with a cord. If the noose consists of a slipping sort of knot, the knot should be secured with a cord before the noose is cut and then secured.

Some points to consider when investigating a hanging include the following: Did the victim die as the result of the hanging, or was he or she unconscious before being placed in a hanging position? Where and how was the ligature tied? With what type of knot? Could the victim have tied the knots him- or herself? Was there a disturbance of any kind in the area? Evidence of a struggle? What paraphernalia, including the source of the ligature material, are present? Is there a suicide note and a sample of the decedent's handwriting? Did family members or someone else find a note? Did the victim provide for the possibility of "stepping back" should he or she have a change of mind or hope to be discovered? Were there any previous suicide attempts? Were there any recent changes in the behavior of the deceased? Did the deceased have any organic or terminal diseases that might have led him or her to consider suicide? Did he or she have financial problems or concerns? Did the deceased recently lose a loved one? Was the deceased trying to punish someone? Who did the victim contact just prior to death? Can it be established from *rigor* and *livor mortis* that the victim was the sole active agent of his or her own death?

Smothering Although many movies and television shows dramatically show murderers smothering their victims with a pillow, smothering is actually a fairly uncommon mode of murder. People under the influence of drugs and alcohol, invalids, the aged, and infants are much more likely to be victims of accidental smotherings. In each of these cases, the victim is likely to turn face down onto a pillow or to become tangled in blankets and, owing to an intoxicated or weakened condition, accidentally smother to death.

Smothering has murder implications when it becomes a form of infanticide. The assailant may place a hand over the mouth and nose of the child until he or she suffocates. In some cases of adult smothering, the assailant may use a plastic bag or a sheet of plastic pulled tight around the face of the victim. In such cases with adults, considerable force must be used and is likely to result in signs of a struggle, indicating that the death was not an accident.

Choking Choking involves a foreign substance or object blocking the throat and airway and generally is accidental. Small children are notorious for placing in their mouths anything that will fit. If an object is swallowed, it may tragically result in an accidental choking. In some instances, choking occurs because a person has tried to swallow too large a piece of food, has swallowed a bone, or has gasped or otherwise inhaled while swallowing.

Carbon Monoxide Poisoning Death from carbon monoxide may be an accident, a suicide, or occasionally a homicide. Carbon monoxide is an odorless, colorless gas. Sources include unvented or poorly vented gas heaters and automobile exhaust from defective muffler systems. Perhaps the most frequent source of carbon monoxide poisoning is the exhaust of a car. In a suicide, the decedent may have intentionally closed the air escapes in a garage or may have run a garden hose from the exhaust pipe into the car cabin. Carbon monoxide causes death because it combines with the hemoglobin in the blood, making it impossible for the hemoglobin to combine with life-giving oxygen. Accidental carbon monoxide poisonings have occurred when someone sat in a car in the garage while warming the engine on a cold winter morning. During the past several years, homeowners have become more aware of the dangers of accidental carbon monoxide poisoning from faulty or inadequately vented heating systems. Several companies now produce carbon monoxide alarms that sound if the concentration of the gas becomes too high in a home.

Volatile Intoxicant Sniffing Volatile intoxicants include all substances that when inhaled produce altered states of consciousness (e.g., ether, nitrous oxide, paint thinner, some glues, and gasoline). Model airplane glue (with toluene or benzene as a solvent), for example, produces a form of intoxication often accompanied by hallucinations. The glue is usually applied to a handkerchief or a piece of cloth, and the treated material is inserted in a paper bag. The bag is then placed over the mouth and nose, and the person breathes deeply of the fumes trapped in the bag; a technique sometimes referred to as *huffing*. A similar procedure is used with several other substances, including gasoline (Pranijic & Mujagic, 1998). Sniffing volatile intoxicants causes serious liver damage and can result in death after only a short period of repeated use. There are also cases of accidental death from suffocation when *sniffers* use plastic bags to inhale fumes and continue inhaling even after the oxygen is gone from the bag. Another method of intoxicant sniffing is sitting near an air-conditioning unit to sniff Freon. Freon, however, is extremely toxic, and sniffing it is often fatal.

Drug Overdoses The respiratory center of the central nervous system is depressed by certain drugs. Muscle paralysis, including paralysis of the muscles of respiration, can also occur. Narcotics and barbiturates, their effects sometimes exacerbated by alcohol, are the principal groups of drugs encountered. Other central nervous system depressants, however, may also be responsible for death by asphyxia. In general, a complete autopsy must be done in cases of suspected drug overdoses.

Autoerotic Asphyxiation In **autoerotic asphyxia,** sexual gratification is sought by near asphyxia. A rope or other ligature around the neck reduces the flow of air and oxygen to the brain, and at the same time, the individual may masturbate. Unfortunately, in some cases, unconsciousness results, and eventually total asphyxia and death. A variation of autoerotic asphyxia—or *gasping,* as it is sometimes called—may be undertaken by partners, with one partner restricting the air in the other and, theoretically, monitoring the level of consciousness (Gosink & Jumbelic, 2000; Uva, 1995).

Autoerotic asphyxia is not the most common form of death by asphyxia. However, investigators should be aware of its possibility and recognize certain of its attributes.

autoerotic asphyxiation
Seeking sexual gratification by near asphyxia.

Typically, the body of the victim is found nude or with genitalia exposed. In some cases, men are found dressed in women's underwear or clothing. There is often evidence of masturbation. There may be sexually stimulating paraphernalia, such as vibrators, sexual aids, or pornographic photos or magazines. Protective measures may have been taken, such as placing padding between the ligature and the neck to prevent marking. Mirrors, intended to allow the victim to observe the ritual, may be found near the body (Gebreth, 1996).

Drowning Death by drowning results when any liquid enters the breathing passages and prevents the access of air to the lungs. The liquid need not be water; it can be any fluid, mud, or other flowing substance. Nor is it necessary for the entire body to be immersed in the liquid. A person can drown when only the mouth and nose are under the surface. Most drownings are accidents. Simulation of drowning has to be ruled out by a medical examiner to ensure that a homicide has not been masked as a drowning after the actual murder was committed. A death by natural causes that occurs in the water must likewise be determined by an autopsy.

Vehicular Manslaughter

Many states have a statutory classification of manslaughter. In some states, special statutory rules are applied where death results from the negligent operation of a motor vehicle. Concerns about drunken and reckless driving and homicides caused by these activities have placed considerable pressure on the criminal justice system to provide harsher penalties. Since about 1983, most prosecutors in the United States have prosecuted killing caused by drunken or reckless driving as an offense greater than simple vehicular homicide. Many jurisdictions now employ the same statutes as for general murder and manslaughter (Chamelin, 2005). Investigators should be aware of the statutes for vehicular homicides, murder, and manslaughter in their jurisdictions.

Vehicular manslaughter may involve one or more cars, a collision with a pedestrian, or the death of one or more passengers. It may result from gross negligent behavior, reckless driving, or driving while under the influence of alcohol or other mind-altering substances. In addition to the activities and duties set forth earlier in this chapter for homicide investigations in general, the following should be undertaken in investigations of vehicular manslaughter cases:

* Note whether traffic control devices are present and are functioning properly. Note also whether these devices are clearly visible.
* Make notes about the weather, visibility, lighting, road conditions, obstructions, signs, signals, and markings.
* Identify the driver of the vehicle causing the fatality, and make an arrest if he or she is present.
* Note all injuries, any statements or admissions, and possible indications of intoxication or other impairment.
* Examine the suspect's car for physical evidence (e.g., fabric marks, shreds or fibers from the victim's clothing, blood, paint transfers, broken glass or lights, missing trim, or the presence of skin, hair, or stains made by the property of the victim).
* If the suspect has fled the scene, as in the case of a hit-and-run, contact the dispatcher with all available information for a local and regional broadcast.
* If a suspect has been apprehended, provide *Miranda* warnings and interview him or her if rights are waived.
* Check all information and defenses offered by the suspect to verify whether they are true.

- Conduct a field sobriety test if it appears warranted. Depending on state statutes, a blood test may also be called for.

- Locate and interview any witnesses to the incident; obtain signed statements.

- Photograph the scene as it is, before anything is touched or moved. Take pictures from different distances and angles to show intersection, streetlights, crosswalks, traffic devices, signs, skid marks, or whatever conditions exist at the scene of the incident.

- Determine the *point of impact* (POI) of the collision. This can be ascertained from debris at the location, such as broken glass and radiator water, and from skid marks and other evidence.

- Determine the *point of rest* (POR), where each vehicle came to rest after the accident, and anything to show the positions of the vehicles in the road before the collision.

- Accurately measure skid marks and their positions relative to fixed objects, measuring each skid mark separately. Link skid marks to the vehicles.

- Check conditions of the suspect's vehicle: tires (e.g., condition and wear of treads), brakes, steering, position of gearshift, emergency brake, windshield, wipers, headlights and taillights, rearview mirrors, mileage, and so on.

- Ask that the autopsy be conducted with special attention to impact patterns. This is important in reconstructing the fatal accident. Documentation of the wound pattern is likewise critical.

- Obtain a traffic accident report, and try to reconstruct the impact patterns in light of the autopsy findings, with special attention to the direction of the suspect's car and the positions of the victims.

- Conduct any other investigation deemed necessary because of the specific facts of the case.

- Complete all reports, and discuss them with the district attorney for trial purposes.

Vehicular manslaughter generally involves some type of negligent behavior.

Suspicious Circumstances

The criminal codes of many states provide for various circumstances in which a physician, funeral director, or other person shall notify the coroner's office of a death that may have occurred under suspicious circumstances. The code generally directs the coroner's office to inquire into and determine the circumstances, manner, and cause of death in the following circumstances: violent, sudden, or unusual deaths; unattended deaths; deaths in which the deceased has not been attended by a physician in the past week (or some other specified time); deaths related to or following known or suspected self-induced or criminal abortions; deaths related to known or suspected homicide, suicide, or accidental poisoning; deaths known or suspected to have resulted from or to be related to an accident or injury, either old or recent; deaths due to drowning, fire, hanging, gunshot, stabbing, cutting, exposure, starvation, alcoholism, drug addiction, or asphyxiation; deaths incident, in whole or in part, to criminal activity; deaths associated with a known or alleged rape, aggravated assault, or sodomy; deaths while in the custody of law enforcement or correctional agents; deaths known or suspected to be the result of a contagious disease that constitutes a possible health hazard to the public; deaths from occupational accidents; deaths from occupational disease or occupational safety hazards; and deaths that afford reasonable grounds to suspect that they were caused by the criminal behavior of another.

As with other deaths, the primary duty of the coroner or medical examiner is to determine the cause of death. The coroner conducts a separate investigation, usually including an autopsy performed by a qualified pathologist (a medical doctor). For the criminal investigator, the procedure for investigating these cases is substantially the same as for other types of homicides.

SUMMARY

Learning Objective 1

Investigation of deaths requires skill, care, and sensitivity. In general, deaths can be divided into four categories: natural, suicide, accidental, and homicide. The goal of classifying a death into one of these categories is to assign responsibility in both a moral sense and a legal sense.

Learning Objective 2

Homicide is the killing of one human being by another. Some homicides are premeditated; others may occur because of an accident, owing to negligence, in self-defense or in the defense of another, or as the only recourse for apprehending a dangerous fleeing felon. Even self-inflicted deaths are typically treated as homicides until the police can establish them as suicides. Homicide can be classified legally as justifiable homicide, excusable homicide, or criminal homicide, which is further divided into murder and manslaughter. State statutes further define murder and manslaughter by degrees or specific crimes.

Learning Objective 3

Some of the more common motives for homicide include unplanned or spontaneous murders, murders for financial gain, lust murders, murders for revenge, elimination murders, and motiveless murders, including stranger-to-stranger murders and cases of mistaken identity.

Learning Objective 4

When investigating a homicide, police and investigators should follow established procedures for responding to a call; protecting and preserving the crime scene; collecting, identifying, and managing evidence; interviewing and interrogating witnesses and suspects; and writing reports. Determination of criminal responsibility in a homicide has evolved into a highly specialized field of medical science known as forensic pathology. Forensic pathologists study and interpret changes in body tissues and fluids to determine such factors as time of death, circumstances of death, and scene of death.

Learning Objective 5

There are a number of ways one can determine whether a person is dead, including appearance, pupillary reaction, pulse, visible breathing, solar plexus movement, muscle resistance or muscle reflex, and cyanosis (blue color of lips and nail beds).

Learning Objective 6

A number of practices can aid in identifying a dead person, including matching fingerprints, conducting skeletal studies, making a visual inspection, searching personal effects and clothing, noting tattoos and scars, examining dental evidence, and disseminating photographs and sketches.

Learning Objective 7

Factors used to estimate time of death include postmortem changes in the body, changes in temperature, *rigor mortis* and *livor mortis,* decomposition of the body, insect infestations, and witness information, including when the victim was last seen alive. In addition, the contents of the victim's stomach and the degree of digestion of this food may assist in estimating time of death.

Learning Objective 8

Homicide investigators are called on to investigate many different types of deaths, including natural deaths, suicides, poisonings, stabbings and cuttings, gunshot wounds, asphyxia, vehicular homicides, and deaths under suspicious circumstances. Each of these types of deaths has characteristics that investigators should be trained to recognize to determine what type of weapon to seek and how to focus the investigation.

KEY TERMS

homicide 272

justifiable homicide 272

excusable homicide 272

criminal homicide (felonious homicide) 272

murder 272

felony murder 273

manslaughter 273

forensic pathology 280

rigor mortis 282

cadaveric spasm 283

livor mortis 283

adipocere 284

forensic entomologist 284

toxicological screening 290

defense wound 292

wipe ring (smudging) 293

tattooing 293

contact wound 293

asphyxiation 293

autoerotic asphyxiation 295

QUESTIONS FOR REVIEW

Learning Objective 1

1. Why are deaths classified into categories?

Learning Objective 2

2. Define *homicide, justifiable homicide, excusable homicide, criminal homicide, murder,* and *manslaughter.*

3. What is the major difference between felonious and nonfelonious homicide?

4. How would you distinguish between murder and excusable homicide?

Learning Objective 3

5. Why is it important to try to establish a motive for a homicide?

6. Why is a murder for revenge often difficult to investigate?

Learning Objective 4

7. What things should an officer be alert to when en route to a possible homicide crime scene?

8. What is the first thing an officer should do upon receipt of a call to a death scene or a possible homicide crime scene?

9. What is *forensic pathology?*

Learning Objective 5

10. How can the appearance and color of a victim assist in determining whether the victim is dead?

11. What is *cyanosis?*

Learning Objective 6

12. How might dental records assist in identifying a victim?

13. How might photographs or drawings of the victim assist in determining his or her identity?

Learning Objective 7

14. How might vegetation assist in estimating time of death?

15. How might stomach contents assist in estimating time of death?

16. How might *rigor mortis* assist in estimating time of death?

Learning Objective 8

17. How are poisons detected in a victim?

18. Briefly describe the differences between cuts (or incisions) and stab wounds.

19. What are defense wounds, and where can they be located?

20. Briefly describe the appearance of an entry wound and an exit wound caused by a bullet.

21. What are some characteristics of a contact wound?

22. What are the ten most common forms of suicide?

23. What causes death in asphyxia?

24. How is negligence involved in the charge of automobile manslaughter?

. . . .

CRITICAL THINKING EXERCISES

1. When you arrive home today, assume you are the investigating officer arriving at a death scene outside your house or apartment building. What are the first things you will do? Be sure to consider where you might locate witnesses, how you would observe and protect the scene and possible evidence, who you would notify, how identification of the victim might be made, and so forth. Write a brief paragraph recording your response. Then compare your response with others in the class. Discuss and resolve any variances.

2. Judy Jones, 14 years old, was babysitting her 10-year-old brother, Tom. They were both sitting in front of their home when a car pulled up. A man called to Judy by name and beckoned her to come over. As Judy moved toward the vehicle, the passenger door swung open. From his vantage point, Tom saw a man pointing a gun at Judy and ordering her into the car. Judy hesitated a moment, then started to move away from the car. The man fired the gun. Tom could see sparks as the bullet struck the ground near Judy's foot. Judy stopped in her tracks and moved back toward the car, crying. Tom ran into the house as the car sped off. Tom called 911 and reported what had just happened. The police arrived a few minutes later to take Tom's statement and investigate the scene. While the officers were still present, a report came in that Judy's body had been found in a nearby alley. She was naked from the waist down and had been shot once in the chest.

a. What are the next steps that the police should take?

b. Where would you expect to find clues or leads in this case?

c. What physical evidence should be sought?

d. What forensic evidence should be sought?

e. How would you investigate this case?

INVESTIGATIVE SKILL BUILDERS

Acquiring and Evaluating Information

You have arrived at the scene of a dead-body call. The location is an old, dilapidated shed behind a house in a rural area. There is no glass in the windows, and the wooden floor is rotted. In the middle of the floor is the body of a man. The victim is wearing a nice suit of clothes, but the body is badly decomposed. There is no wallet or other identification in any of the pockets. The man is wearing an expensive-looking heavy gold chain around his neck.

1. How might you estimate time of death?

2. How might you determine the identity of this victim?

3. What questions would you ask while canvassing the area?

Integrity/Honesty

You are investigating the death of a fellow officer in a freak automobile accident. The car apparently went out of control for no apparent reason and crashed into a wall, killing the officer instantly. During the course of the investigation, you learn that the officer had recently taken out a $1 million life insurance policy with double indemnity (double payment) in the case of accidental death. The policy also has a two-year suicide clause, whereby it pays nothing if death occurs by suicide in the first two years the policy is in effect. The beneficiary is his 12-year-old daughter. You also discover that the officer recently learned that his wife has had affairs with several men in the last several years and was planning to leave him. From what you have learned in your investigation, you suspect that the officer killed himself.

1. Do you file a report of suicide, knowing that this will void the officer's insurance policy?

2. Do you tell the wife what you suspect—whether or not you file a report of suicide?

15

Burglary

After completing this chapter, you will be able to:

1 Provide an overview of the crime of burglary in the United States.
2 Explain the legal elements of the crime of burglary.
3 Distinguish among the main types of burglaries.
4 Describe the trade and tools of burglars.
5 Enumerate basic procedures used in burglary investigations.
6 Discuss the special concerns of investigating safe burglaries.

FIGURE 15.1 Burglary, Number of Offenses, 2000–2004

Year	Number of Offenses	Rate per 100,000 Inhabitants
2004	2,143,456	741.0
2003	2,154,834	729.9
2002	2,151,875	741.8
2001	2,116,531	746.2
2000	2,049,946	770.4

Source: Federal Bureau of Investigation. 2005. *Crime in the United States, 2000, 2001, 2002, 2003, 2004.* Washington, DC: U.S. Government Printing Office.

THE NATURE OF BURGLARY

Burglary is the first of the four property crime index offenses to be considered in this text. The other property crime index offenses are larceny-theft, motor vehicle theft, and arson. According to the FBI's Uniform Crime Reports (FBI, 2005), more than 2 million burglaries were reported in 2004, a decrease of approximately 5 percent from the previous year (Figure 15.1). However, in 2004 law enforcement agencies only managed to clear through arrest 12.9 percent of the nation's burglaries (FBI, 2005, p. 47). Residential burglaries (65.7 percent) out-numbered nonresidential burglaries (34.7 percent) in 2004. The majority of residential burglaries (62.2 percent) occurred during the day between the hours of 6 a.m. and 6 p.m. Conversely, the majority of nonresidential burglaries (58 percent) occurred during the night between the hours of 6 p.m. and 6 a.m. (FBI, 2005, pp. 46–47).

Burglaries are among the most difficult crimes to solve. Contact between burglars and victims is infrequent, and burglaries may not be immediately discovered. For example, imagine you've just returned from a two-week vacation to find that your home has been burglarized. Although you might immediately contact the police, when did the crime actually occur? Was it earlier that day? Three days earlier? The first day you left? Because you really have no way of knowing this, it makes the case even more difficult to investigate. Victims seldom see the burglar and a time lag may interfere, so investigators must identify the *corpus delicti* (essential elements) of the crime largely through circumstantial evidence. To conduct an efficient investigation, investigators should have a solid knowledge of the legal aspects of burglary.

LEGAL ASPECTS OF THE CRIME OF BURGLARY

In common law, the offense of burglary was defined as the breaking and entering of the dwelling house of another in the nighttime, with intent to commit a felony therein. The common law sought to protect a person's habitation, and the definition of burglary was confined to dwelling houses and any buildings connected to them or included within their enclosures.

Although most state burglary statutes retain elements of the common law definition of the crime, they are less restrictive and commonly encompass entry at all times into all kinds of structures. The element of breaking originally conveyed the notion that there had to be some form of forcible entry, regardless of how slight the force. Modern-day courts have extended this interpretation. For example, if an accused broke a pane of glass to unlock a window or door, such an action would satisfy the definition of the use of some type of *force,* as would the force required to turn the handle of an unlocked door.

burglary Entering a building or structure without the consent of the person in possession of that building or structure to commit a crime therein.

Entry into the dwelling has been interpreted as the insertion of any or all of the accused's body into the dwelling. Thus, the element of entry would be satisfied if an accused extended his or her arm through a window and used a pole or stick to reach property inside a room. State burglary statutes generally hold that the crime of **burglary** consists of (1) entering or remaining in a building or occupied structure (2) without the consent of the person in possession (3) to commit a crime therein. In addition, certain state statutes classify it into first-, second-, and even third-degree burglary.

As previously indicated, most states have enacted statutes that expand the common law definition of burglary. These statutes provide criminal penalties for such behaviors as entering a dwelling without breaking, breaking and entering the dwelling house of another in the daytime (instead of at night), breaking and entering a building other than a dwelling house, and breaking and entering with intent to commit a misdemeanor (Chamelin, 2005). Crimes may be classified as *breaking and entering* rather than *burglary* to further distinguish the criminal act. Many people use the terms *burglary* and *breaking and entering* as synonyms when referring to any one of these offenses, but it is important for investigators to know the elements of the crime of burglary as defined in their respective jurisdictions.

TYPES OF BURGLARIES

residential burglary A burglary committed at a dwelling place, whether occupied or vacant.

Burglaries are generally classified as residential or commercial. **Residential burglaries** occur in buildings commonly used or suitable for habitation or in attached structures. For a crime to be a residential burglary, the building does not have to be inhabited at the time of the crime. Rental property, mobile homes, dormitory rooms, cabins, rooms rented within a house, houseboats, or any other suitable dwelling place may be burglarized. More than two-thirds of all burglaries are residential.

Most residential burglars target items of moderate value, such as televisions, stereo equipment, and jewelry, that are easily transported and "fenced" (sold for cash or drugs). Most residential burglars are not interested in confronting home dwellers, so selecting a burglary target involves locating dwellings where no one seems to be at home.

commercial burglary A burglary committed at a place of business or commerce.

Commercial burglaries occur in nonresidential buildings or structures where some form of commerce takes place. Schools, churches, ships, stores, offices, factories, warehouses, trucks, hospitals, public buildings, and so forth are all potential targets of commercial burglars. Commercial buildings in secluded or poorly lighted areas are particularly likely candidates for burglary. Frequently, commercial burglars specialize in one type of target (Hakim & Shachmurive, 1996).

In many cases, commercial burglaries are better planned than residential ones. Targets may be cased by burglars in disguise to detect security devices, to learn delivery dates of cash or merchandise, or to gain operational information from employees. Yields in commercial burglaries usually are larger than in most residential burglaries. These burglaries are also more likely to be undertaken by professionals than are most residential burglaries.

FYI According to the FBI's Crime Clock, which shows the relative frequency of occurrence of index offenses, a burglary was committed every 14.7 seconds in 2004.

THE BURGLAR—TRADE AND TOOLS

We may have a stereotype of a burglar as a person dressed in black who silently scales the outside of a building, deftly opens a window, and glides into a room to secretly gather valuable loot. Some cat burglars may fit this image, but burglars use a variety of methods of operation and come from many socioeconomic levels (O'Reilly, 1991).

Methods of Operation

The ways in which burglars operate are quite varied. Being familiar with some of the more common types of burglary operations can help in a burglary investigation. You may also be able to help a victim take precautions to prevent a reoccurrence of the crime.

During a Party The burglar loots bedrooms or other household areas where guests leave their coats, purses, or other valuables during a party; he or she may be a guest or a person who crashed the party.

Following a Telephone Call The burglar telephones a residence and, if no one answers, proceeds to the residence and knocks or rings the front doorbell. If someone answers the door, the burglar hands the resident a household sample or handbill and leaves. If no one answers, the burglar picks the lock or calls an accomplice and burglarizes the residence. Often, if a dog barks from within the residence when the burglar knocks or rings the bell, the burglar leaves.

Package Delivery The burglar feigns a package delivery. If no one answers the door, he or she picks the lock and burglarizes the premises. If someone does answer the door, the culprit asks for the addressee on the package and leaves.

Careless Residents Many burglars take advantage of the carelessness of occupants who leave doors or windows unlocked or spare keys in obvious places (e.g., under mats, over door frames, or in flowerpots) or leave ladders conspicuously laying at the side of their homes. Some burglars use accomplices to watch for the occupant returning home unexpectedly. When this occurs, the accomplice signals the inside burglar with a blast of a car horn or even with a cell phone or beeper signal.

STATISTICS According to the *Sourcebook of Criminal Justice Statistics 2004*, approximately 85 percent of burglary arrestees during 2004 were male, and 52.6 percent were under 18 years of age. Among all burglary arrestees, whites accounted for 70.9 percent, blacks for 27.2 percent, and other races for the remainder.

Tunnel or Cut-In The burglar tunnels or cuts through the roof, the ceiling, a wall, or the basement. Entry may be from above or below the premises. This method is used mostly in apartments or commercial locations.

Cat or Human Fly This burglar is an aerialist, climbing up or down the side of a building to gain entry through a window or balcony door. In some instances, the burglar will enter a target apartment or office by "stepping over" from one balcony to another.

Jimmy or Celluloid The burglar forces open doors or windows by using a metal tool, or **jimmy,** such as a tire iron, crowbar, heavy-duty screwdriver, or similar

jimmy A prying tool or instrument of any sort used to force open a door, window, or lock.

implement. Jimmying is the most common method of entry to commit a burglary. Some burglars use a small piece of celluloid plastic, such as a credit or ATM card, to open some doors by forcing the card between the doorjamb and the lock's spring bolt. Dead-bolt locks eliminate this sort of entry.

Hiding Out   The burglar enters a commercial establishment during regular business hours and then conceals him- or herself, remaining hidden until the business has closed and all employees have left. The perpetrator then steals items from the premises.

Opportunistic   The burglar drives around residential communities looking for a good target. A good target is a darkened home or a house where the intended victims seem to be away, as indicated by a pile of newspapers or by mail in the mailbox. The burglar may even check to see if air conditioners are not running during hot weather.

Smash and Grab   While an accomplice sits at the wheel of a waiting getaway car, the burglar smashes a store window, grabs jewelry or other display merchandise, and flees. Generally, this sort of burglar is a young person in need of fast cash. In February of 2006 two thieves walked into a Tiffany's, one occupied the guard by spraying pepper spray in his face while the other broke into a jewelry counter with a hammer. The pair needed just twenty-five seconds to smash a case and escape with more than $100,000 worth of items (NBC4.TV, 2006).

Research before Burglary   In this mode of burglary, the burglar researches a potential target before striking. The burglar may read the newspaper to determine which prominent people are taking trips abroad or attending social functions. The burglar may even read obituaries to find out which prominent people have died, when their funerals are being held, and, thus, when family members will be out of the house. Some burglars have accomplices in hotels, such as bellhops, clerks, or maids, who provide information about the comings and goings of wealthy guests (Cromwell & Olson, 2003).

Dishonest Workers   With access to keys and knowledge of intimate details of business and financial operations, workers may commit burglaries themselves or provide information or keys to accomplices who actually commit the burglaries.

False Report   It is not uncommon for someone trying to conceal some financial loss to report a burglary that never happened. In these cases, a careful investigation will reveal inaccuracies in the complainant's account of the theft, particularly in the method of operation, which is likely to be unlike that of actual burglars.

Tools of the Trade

The tools chosen by burglars depend on the method of entry and the type of burglary planned—a residence, a commercial enterprise, a vault, or a safe, for example. In most jurisdictions, possession of **burglary tools,** or implements obviously used to pick locks or jimmy doors or windows, is considered a separate felony offense.

Burglary tools may consist of specialized tools used by locksmiths that have few other uses. These might include various picks, master keys, and tools similar to jewelers' tools. On the other hand, burglary tools may consist of a wide variety of run-of-the-mill household tools such as screwdrivers, hammers, hacksaws, crowbars, power drills with various bits, tin snips, stiff wire, pieces of plastic, glass cutters, and flashlights. As Winona Ryder learned, even scissors can be called a burglary tool if used to disconnect a department store's sensor tag in order to steal an item of clothing (Bean, 2002). Other

burglary tools   Any assortment of tools, picks, or household items such as scissors, paperclips, or credit cards used in committing a burglary.

common items found on burglars include adhesive tape, rope, pipe wrenches, water pistols filled with noxious fluids to ward off watchdogs, chisels, punches, and even suction cups to hold and remove glass when it is cut. Many of these tools may be easily concealed and carried in briefcases, sports bags, overnight suitcases, musical instrument cases, handbags, or in belts worn under coats or clothing. Larger items may be concealed and transported in a car or a rifle case. When burglary tools are found on a suspect or in a suspect's automobile, it is advisable to ask the suspect, "Why do you have these items?" The tools may be used in a legitimate job and may not be intended for burglaries at all.

Burglars often use a variety of tools to accomplish their work.

INVESTIGATING BURGLARIES

A thorough knowledge of the methods used by burglars is essential to an effective investigation. A uniformed officer is often the first to arrive on the scene, and it is important that he or she has a basic understanding of criminal investigation and the *modus operandi* of burglars. This phase of police work should be conducted by an officer who knows both what to do and what not to do in a given situation. During the preliminary stages of a burglary investigation, the investigator should seek evidence to show the following:

1. The suspect was actually in the building.
2. The suspect was in the vicinity at the time of the burglary.
3. The suspect has loot or other property from the burglary.
4. What was the suspect's *modus operandi?*

The first element in this list is the most difficult to demonstrate. In the absence of fingerprints or palm prints, investigators should try to find traces of physical evidence on the suspect or the suspect's clothes that link the suspect to the crime scene (Eck, 1992). The physical evidence could include various materials, such as insulation and metal bits from a safe or roofing materials, plaster, concrete, mortar, brick, glass, wood splinters, paint, or tarlike substances from the scene or from the break-in of the building. Similarly, certain tools or equipment may place a suspect at a particular location. The burglar may have recently burglarized a hardware store to obtain burning equipment or may have purchased tools prior to burglarizing a safe.

Remember that some types of evidence may have latent or microscopic value. For example, in a homicide, a gun found near the body is important as the possible lethal weapon. However, a fingerprint on the weapon or on an ejected bullet casing may prove more incriminating. A drill bit found on a burglary suspect may be a good piece of evidence. But more significant may be the bits of metal clinging to the edges of the bit if they match the material of a safe that was drilled in an attempt to open it.

Precautions during the Preliminary Investigation

When responding to a burglary call, an officer should be alert for people standing around, fleeing the area, or sitting in automobiles and for suspicious-looking cars parked near the scene. Similarly, officers should be observant of lights, movements, and actions of people in the immediate area (Budd, 1999). Use of a siren en route to a burglary should be minimized or totally eliminated to avoid advertising to the burglar that the police are coming.

During the preliminary stage of a burglary investigation, there are several important procedures to follow, especially if the dispatcher has indicated that the call is for a burglary in progress. These actions include driving slower when approaching the scene to avoid squealing tires and parking the cruiser a short distance away from the call address; turning down the squelch and volume on the radio—especially on a portable radio; keeping conversations to a minimum and in hushed tones; opening and closing car doors quietly; removing and pocketing ignition keys without jangling them; and using flashlights sparingly and holding them away from the body (to avoid providing a target to a fleeing felon). If the officer is entering a dark room or building, his or her hat should be off or turned so that the brim will not interfere with vision upward. As a general rule of thumb (and depending on department policy), guns should be drawn but not cocked at this point. Officers should always consult their department policies regarding these last two points.

alarm call Notification of the police by audible or silent alarm that a crime such as a break-in has (or is) occurring.

When answering an **alarm call,** a call in response to either an audible or silent alarm, officers should search the inside of the building after the owner, proprietor, or security company representative has opened it. If K-9 units are available in the area, it is advisable to request their assistance in searching large stores or warehouses during alarm calls.

nonalarm call Notification of the police by citizen alert or direct observation that a crime such as a break-in has (or is) occurring.

When responding to **nonalarm calls,** where someone has reported the crime or where the police have discovered it, the circumstances of the case should dictate the procedure required and the decision about whether to search the premises. When there is evidence of forced entry, officers should search the premises for the burglars and determine whether they have left. As discussed in Chapter 10, never take anything or anybody encountered during the investigation for granted. That helpful occupant in the house could just as easily be the burglar. Be sure to obtain photo identification of parties found as occupants during a burglary call.

STATISTICS According to the UCR, law enforcement agencies cleared only 12.9 percent of the nation's burglary offenses in 2004.

Conducting a Burglary Investigation

For the most part, the preliminary investigation of a burglary follows the outline described in Chapter 2. This includes (1) apprehension of suspects, (2) protection of the crime scene, (3) searching for evidence, (4) determination of the method of operation, and (5) identification of witnesses, victims, and possible suspects.

diagonal deployment A method of arranging officers to both secure and observe a crime scene. Officers arrange themselves so that each can observe two sides of a building at once by placing themselves at opposing corners of the building.

Ideally, a burglary investigation should involve more than a single officer. When the first officer arrives on the scene, he or she should take an appropriate vantage point and await the arrival of backup units. When two officers arrive at the same time or when the second unit arrives, the officers should secure the premises by using a **diagonal deployment.** In this procedure, each officer places him- or herself at a corner of the building so that two sides can be observed at once. For example, one officer may watch the north and east sides while the other officer watches the south and west sides (Figure 15.2). Diagonal deployment allows two officers to cover and contain suspects until more officers arrive.

FIGURE 15.2 Diagonal Deployment

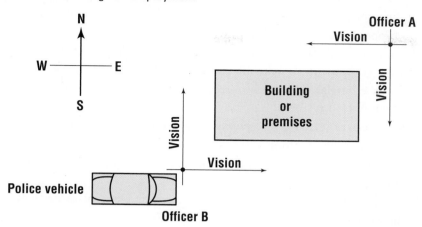

When an officer working alone must check the building immediately, he or she should first drive around the building. Circling the building allows the officer to see any obvious places where a burglar may have broken in. If driving around the building is not possible, the officer should quickly and cautiously circle the building on foot (O'Reilly, 1991).

When searching the scene of a burglary, officers should seek the manner and method of both entry and exit. The method of entry may have been by cutting a hole in the roof or wall, prying open a window or rear door, breaking a pane of glass, or even using a passkey, shim, or lock pick. Do not draw conclusions about the method of entry if you do not see one (Jacobson, Maitland, & Hough, 2003). If the entry is unknown, this should be noted in the preliminary report. The crime should be reconstructed, as much as possible, by the investigating officer. Only those facts that can be substantiated through observation of physical evidence, knowledge, or statements by witnesses or victims should be recorded.

A thorough neighborhood canvass may turn up witnesses who heard identifiable sounds, such as those of an automobile, breaking glass, barking dogs, and so forth. These sounds may assist the investigator in fixing the approximate time of the crime and may also provide other leads. The investigator should seek answers to the following questions:

- Who discovered the offense?
- Who was the last person to secure the premises?
- How did the thief reach the point of the break-in?
- Is there any indication of the thief's concealment before the burglary?
- Is the property that was taken insured? If so, for how much? When was the policy taken out?

Police must use caution when investigating burglary sites.

- Who has keys to the premises, and how accessible are those keys to others?
- Were fingerprints, palm prints, or footprints found at points of entry or exit?
- What property was taken? What is its value?
- Did the thief limit the crime to one kind of property, such as jewelry or electronic equipment, or take all kinds of valuables?
- How did the burglar gain access to secured cupboards, drawers, or dressers? Was force used? Were keys used?
- Was the burglar's search of the premises haphazard or systematic?
- Did the burglar do anything besides search for and steal property?
- Where was the stolen property usually kept by the owner? Who else knew of the property's location?
- When and where was the stolen property purchased? Does the owner have receipts?
- Are photographs of the stolen property available?
- When was the property last seen? Where and by whom?
- Who was the last person to have the stolen property before the burglary?
- Can the owner provide a complete list of all the property that was stolen?
- Can the owner identify his or her property in any way (e.g., serial numbers, identification marks, or other markings)?
- Were any checks or bank books stolen during the burglary?
- Are there any fingerprints inside or outside the premises that may need processing? If so, are they being protected?
- Does the victim suspect anyone?
- Can the victim point out any disturbed areas of the premises?
- Can the victim identify or eliminate as his or hers any items found at the scene?

When searching the scene of a burglary, officers should seek the manner of entry and exit.

Investigators should be alert for any unusual events or disturbances observed at the scene. For example, juvenile burglars frequently commit senseless acts of vandalism during burglaries. Similarly, age and other information may be inferred by the types of property stolen. For instance, when valuable jewelry is left behind but cash and stereo equipment are taken, one might infer that the burglars are youthful or at least nonprofessional (Macintrye, 2001). Similarly, investigators should carefully consider evidence showing that the burglary may be fraudulent or that the extent of the burglary may be overstated to collect inflated reimbursement from an insurance company. List all articles taken from the location, their quantity and description, and their value. Be sure to inventory all small articles, such as jewelry, coins, or other small objects that might be found on a suspect later.

If tools or implements are found, investigators *should not* attempt to make a comparison by placing an object into a suspected impression on a jimmied window or door. Doing so may contaminate or destroy evidence that might otherwise be useful later in court. The size and type of instrument used can be estimated by measuring the mark, gouge, scrape, or other injury to the door, window, or surface. The damaged area can be photographed and carefully searched for microscopic traces of physical evidence. The investigator should include in his or her notes suspected implements that may have caused the damage. For example, the investigator might write, "gouge probably caused by a 1/4-inch screwdriver" and "a 1/4-inch screwdriver was found at the premises." All evidence should be recorded and secured in the manner previously described in Chapters 3 and 4.

In some jurisdictions, the possession of burglary picks or any burglary tools is a separate crime from burglary.

Burglary Suspects and Their Apprehension

Whenever burglary suspects are apprehended, they should be immediately advised of their rights under *Miranda*. The fact that the suspect has been so advised should be recorded in the investigator's notes and report. After the *Miranda* warnings have been given, other actions the investigator should take include, but are not limited to, the following:

- Seize all of the suspect's wearing apparel, including shoes, for lab examination.
- Review each item of property found in the suspect's possession.
- Search the suspect's vehicle (obtain a search warrant or the consent of the suspect).
- Determine the names and addresses of all the suspect's friends and associates.
- Record all discovered facts and obtain the suspect's statement.
- Check the records bureau, M.O. files, bulletins, computer databases, and other sources for related or similar crimes.
- Follow up on such items as the suspect's past activities and whereabouts during questionable dates and times.
- Fingerprint and photograph the suspect, and obtain handwriting specimens (especially useful where checks or documents may have been stolen).
- Follow up on any leads that result from any of the previous actions.

If a search is to be conducted of a suspect's residence, remember that the suspect's consent and waiver or a search warrant must be obtained. Whenever a suspect voluntarily offers consent to a search of his or her premises, this consent should be recorded in writing with witnesses. Figure 15.3 illustrates a suggested waiver of search that may be prepared for the suspect to sign. Be sure that any such waiver used in your department has been reviewed and approved by the prosecutor's office.

Victims of Burglaries

Burglary is always seen as a serious crime by its victims. Although the monetary value of the items taken may not always be very high, the emotional impact it has on the victim can be long term and significant. Many people feel violated and vulnerable following a burglary, and the sensitivity of the officer investigating the crime and positive support and suggestions from the officer can frequently aid in the victim's adjustment (Victim Support

FIGURE 15.3   Waiver-of-Search Form Used by Some Agencies

I, _____ , have been informed of my constitutional right not to have a search made of my premises without a search warrant, and my right to refuse to such a search. Knowing these rights, I hereby authorize Officer(s) _____ of the _____ Police (or Sheriff's) Department, to conduct a complete search of my residence located at _____ . These officers are authorized by me to take from my residence any letters, papers, objects, and materials which they find, and which they have reasonable cause to believe may be evidence in a criminal proceeding.

   This consent to a search and this written permission is being given by me to the above-named officer(s) voluntarily and without threats or promises of any kind.

Signed: _____   Date: _____
                                                          Place: _____

Witnessed by: _____

National Office, 2005). Some practical support the investigating officer can provide includes the following:

- Assist in securing the property immediately following the incident's discovery and investigation (securing doors, windows, locks, etc.).
- Suggest how to repair or replace a lock and how to better secure the premises.
- Refer the victim to victim assistance agencies that may be able to provide financial aid for replacement of property stolen or for repairs.
- Assist victim with filling out various forms (e.g., police forms and insurance forms).
- Suggest long-term ways of better securing the premises (e.g., sensor lighting, alarms, or better locking devices).

SAFE BURGLARIES

To most people, a safe is a large metal container designed to keep articles secure from fire and burglary. In reality, not all safes provide such dual protection. Generally, safes may be divided into two classifications: (1) fire-resistant safes, or fireboxes, and (2) burglar-resistant safes, or money chests or vaults. A fire-resistant safe is resistant to fire but may provide only minimal protection from burglar attack. Such a safe is typically a thin metal shell filled with a fire-resistant material, such as vermiculite, cement, or even sawdust. Locks on fire-resistant safes are more for privacy than security and are usually not very difficult to unlock. Fire-resistant safes are typically rated for their ability to resist high temperatures for varying amounts of time.

Burglar-resistant safes, money vaults, or money chests are constructed primarily to resist unauthorized entry by burglars (Tobias, 2000). This type of safe is often made of laminated or solid steel and may have dense, heavy insulation intended to make penetration more difficult. Such safes are never *burglar proof,* but they can ward off a successful attack from a burglar for a certain amount of time. Locks on burglar-resistant safes are intended to slow entry by an unauthorized individual rather than merely to provide privacy.

Attack Methods for Opening Safes

Burglars use a number of methods to gain entry into safes. Investigators should have some understanding of these methods to more readily recognize the skill and knowledge level of the safe burglar. Such knowledge helps officers focus the investigation and accurately report the facts of the crime both to their agency and to other police agencies. Burglar-resistant safes may not provide fire protection, and fire-resistant boxes seldom provide adequate burglary protection.

Hand Manipulation Hand manipulation is all but a lost art. At one time, it involved opening a combination lock by listening to and feeling the tumblers of the lock as they fell into place. Most safes today are equipped with manipulation-proof locking systems, sometimes involving electronic locking mechanisms. Burglars, however, have found ways to electronically search for and detect the code or combination on even these locking mechanisms.

Punching In this method, the dial knob of the safe is knocked off and a punch placed on the exposed spindle behind it. The spindle is then driven backward with sufficient force to break the lockbox loose from its mountings. Once accomplished, the handle can be turned and the door opened. Some modern safes are equipped with a secondary lock that automatically engages and secures the safe if the dial is broken off. Punching is a popular technique because it requires little skill or knowledge of safe construction. An experienced burglar can complete a punch attack on a safe in just a few minutes. A disadvantage of punching is the noise made by pounding the punch to break the lockbox. Sometimes cloth or rubber is used to muffle the sound. If such materials are found, they are important pieces of evidence to try to link with a suspect.

Hauling or Carrying Away This method is most often used by inexperienced burglars or those who are not skilled enough to quickly and quietly open a safe on the premises. Experienced, professional safe burglars can open a safe in less time than it takes to haul one away. Once thieves have hauled a safe to a secluded location, they can take as much time as needed to open the safe. A similar technique is sometimes used to haul away ATM machines, so that they too can be broken into for their supply of cash on hand (Dolan, 2006).

When a safe that was hauled away is recovered, it should be photographed at the place of recovery, and the location of recovery should be treated like any other crime scene. The investigation should thoroughly seek evidence and materials that may contribute to identifying or linking a suspect to the crime. An outdoor location may provide good physical evidence, such as tire impressions.

Ripping or Peeling This method is used on fire-resistant safes because of their construction. They typically have a lightweight metal outer shell that can be peeled off the door with a bar, exposing the locking mechanism. Or the sides of the safe can be ripped off with pliers and cutting tools. The insulation material can then be chiseled or cut away and entry gained into the safe. A peel begun in several places before a successful entry suggests a less knowledgeable burglar.

Pulling or Dragging This procedure works on some older safes but is not often encountered. The burglar places a heavy metal plate with a V-shape cut out of it over and behind the dial. The plate has several heavy bolts through it. As the screws are tightened, the V plate lifts and pulls the dial and spindle out of the safe, allowing entry. This method is the opposite of punching.

Chopping   Chopping is a rather crude way to attack a safe. In this method, the safe is turned upside down, and the bottom is smashed with an ax or a sledgehammer. The smashing continues until it has produced a hole large enough to fit a hand through. The burglar then inserts his or her hand and withdraws the contents of the safe.

Torching or Burning   The oxyactylene cutting torch is one of the most effective tools used by a safe burglar. Only certain specially designed steel chests are effectively resistant to it. The small size of acetylene tanks makes this equipment easy to conceal and transport. The torch can be used to burn a hand-sized hole in the side of the safe or to burn around the hinge bolts on the door. In some safes, the burglar can use the torch to cut the locking bolt that holds the door in the locked position.

Drilling   Drilling can be a highly effective means of opening a safe, but it is time-consuming. In some cases, the burglar uses the drill to perforate the door with a series of holes placed close together. This allows the burglar to remove a piece of the door plate, exposing the lock mechanism. In other cases, the burglar drills out the safe bolt. A high-carbon drill bit the size of the bolt or larger is used. The drilling is done through the side of the safe and bores out the bolt. Even if the bolt is only partially drilled, it can be broken with a center punch and a hammer. Once the bolt has been drilled, the door will open.

Using Explosives   Even though the penalties for burglaries committed while carrying explosives are typically more severe, some safe burglars do use various explosives, including nitroglycerin, trinitrotoluene (TNT), and various plastic explosives. Burglars who use explosives usually do not work alone. They may have several helpers, each with a special task to do, or simply to serve as lookouts to avoid surprise detection. However, when the explosive charge is detonated, there is considerable noise and potential for detection.

Crime scene photograph of burglarized safe.

The explosive charge is usually placed in the dial spindle hole after the dial is removed. In some cases, when possible, safes are moved away from the wall before detonation. Doing so prevents the blast from throwing the safe backward into the wall, creating additional noise and wall vibration.

When an investigator encounters signs of the use of explosives in a safe burglary, extreme care must be exercised. Officers should not attempt to neutralize or destroy suspicious materials at the scene of safe explosions. Officers should know and follow their department's procedures regarding encountering explosives and explosive devices.

Investigating Safe Burglaries

Safe burglars usually work in groups of two or more, and they are adept at leaving few traces of their identity at the scene of the crime. Safe burglars regularly wear gloves to avoid leaving fingerprints. They time their operations with the precision of a fine watch. Safe burglars often case their jobs to obtain information about security systems, guards, possible means of entry and escape, the type and location of the safe and locking mechanisms, the habits of personnel, police patrol patterns, and activities of neighborhood residents. In many instances, however, safe burglars do leave various pieces of physical evidence: broken prying instruments, parts of screw drivers, drills, and drill bits.

While casing the targeted victim, gang members visit the establishment and observe, among other things, whether there are alarm systems on the premises. Tools that will be used during the crime are sometimes hidden in advance near or in the building. Assignments of gang members, communication equipment, lookouts, transportation, and other details are all taken into account during the planning stages of the crime.

Because safe burglars take such extensive precautions, it is unlikely that any evidence found at the scene will immediately identify a specific burglar. However, safe burglars do tend to develop a fairly consistent *modus operandi*. Establishing the M.O. can assist the investigator in developing one or more suspects. Thus, evidence at the scene can still be a critical link between suspects and the criminal activity.

Many of the suggestions already offered in this chapter with regard to burglary investigation apply to safe burglary investigation as well. These additional investigative strategies apply to safe burglaries:

- Prevent unauthorized persons from entering the location. Check the premises, inside and out, to determine the points of entry and exit and the *modus operandi*. Victims or employees may help by pointing out any disturbed areas (articles that have been moved, doors opened or closed, missing items, and so on).

- Attempt to reconstruct the activities of the burglars without disturbing possible trace evidence.

- Sketch and photograph the scene. Include the relationship of physical evidence to the safe, the safe itself, the points of entry and exit, and any damage marks.

- Collect any physical evidence at the scene, including fingerprints, palm prints, footprints, and glove prints; safe insulation material or metal fragments; broken or damaged parts from the safe; discarded or forgotten tools; broken glass, paint chips, and plaster fragments; bloodstains, clothing, and fibers; discarded candy or cigarette wrappers; and any other materials foreign to the premises.

- Interview all persons who have access to the safe or its location. Note the procedures used to secure the safe and the premises.

- Determine the make, size, weight, and serial number of the safe.

- Check areas adjacent to the premises for possible shoe prints, tire prints, or discarded items.

Once the initial investigation has been completed, the following additional investigative steps should be taken:

- Have identifiable stolen property indexed in the records bureau.

- Examine pawnshop and secondhand store records for stolen items.

- Consult personal or department M.O. files for possible leads. Send bulletins to other police agencies describing the identifiable missing items.

FOCUS ON TECHNOLOGY

NATIONAL CRIME INFORMATION CENTER

TRACING AND RECOVERING STOLEN PROPERTY is much easier using the National Crime Information Center (NCIC) operated by the FBI. Using connecting terminals throughout the United States, local, state, and federal law enforcement agencies can access the NCIC to obtain information on stolen, missing, or recovered weapons; stolen articles, vehicles, and license plates; and stolen, embezzled, or missing securities. Also available are other databases such as the Missing Persons File and the Violent Gang/Terrorist File.

- Question informants about missing property that they might have seen on the street or can be looking for.
- Investigate the whereabouts of known burglars, particularly those whose M.O.s are similar to that in the crime being investigated.

SUMMARY

Learning Objective 1

Burglary is one of the eight crimes that the FBI considers the most serious in American society, and it reports yearly statistics on burglary in its Uniform Crime Reports (UCR). In 2004, law enforcement managed to clear only 12.9 percent of all burglaries.

Learning Objective 2

State statutes precisely define what constitutes the crime of burglary in each state. Generally, these statutes have the following elements in common: Burglary consists of (1) entering a building or occupied structure (2) without the consent of the person in possession (3) to commit a crime therein.

Learning Objective 3

Burglaries can be divided into two general types: residential and commercial. More than two-thirds of all burglaries are committed against residences.

Learning Objective 4

Burglars use a variety of methods of operation, including jimmying doors, tunneling or cutting through walls and roofs, scaling buildings, smashing and grabbing, and casing or hiding out in target buildings. Burglary tools may consist of specialized lock-picking tools or run-of-the-mill household tools, such as screwdrivers, hammers, hacksaws, glass cutters, and tin snips.

Learning Objective 5

Burglary investigations generally follow the same procedures as any criminal investigation. Because some burglaries are well planned and carried out by professionals who leave few clues, a special problem for investigators is collecting physical evidence to identify a suspect and link him or her to the crime.

Learning Objective 6

Safe burglars use a variety of methods to gain entry into safes. Among these are punching, hauling, ripping or peeling, pulling or dragging, chopping, torching or burning, drilling, and explosives. Safe burglars usually work in groups of two or more and are generally adept at not leaving traces of their identities at the crime scene, thus creating a challenge for investigators.

KEY TERMS

burglary **304**

residential burglary **304**

commercial burglary **304**

jimmy **305**

burglary tools **306**

alarm call **308**

nonalarm call **308**

diagonal deployment **308**

QUESTIONS FOR REVIEW

Learning Objective 1

1. Why must investigators use largely circumstantial evidence for the *corpus delicti* of a burglary?

Learning Objective 2

2. In some states, how much force is required for the crime of breaking and entering?
3. If someone breaks a window and reaches through to steal something, has a burglary been committed? Explain.

Learning Objective 3

4. How would the burglary of a mobile home be classified?
5. If children were caught inside a school at 1:00 a.m., what might the charge be?

Learning Objective 4

6. How does a burglary occur during a party?
7. How do window smashers operate?
8. What sorts of tools are used in burglaries?

Learning Objective 5

9. What type of evidence should an investigator look for at the scene of a burglary?

10. What activities go on during the initial investigation of a burglary?

Learning Objective 6

11. What is meant by *ripping* a safe?

12. Why do some burglars use hauling as a method of safe burglary?

13. Why are safe burglars so difficult to identify and apprehend?

14. Why do some safe burglars case a location before breaking in?

CRITICAL THINKING EXERCISE

Consult local newspapers of the past five months. List all the residential and commercial burglaries reported in articles or in the "crime blotter" section. Compile a written summary, using the four activities that follow as a guide, and then compare your summary with others in the class.

1. Identify any patterns of similarity in the crimes.

2. List any property that the newspaper accounts indicate was stolen; consider whether the type of property taken suggests a pattern.

3. Which of the burglaries, if any, seem to have been committed by juveniles? Explain your answer.

4. List any evidence that the newspaper accounts report as recovered at the scene of the burglaries. Consider the significance of that evidence.

INVESTIGATIVE SKILL BUILDERS

Allocating Time

You arrive at the scene of a burglary, the apartment of a college student. After speaking with the student, you learn that she just returned from spring break and discovered that some time during the break, her apartment was burglarized. The victim has gone through the apartment and made a list of missing items. These include a stereo system valued at $250, a gold rope necklace valued at $125, an opal ring valued at $75, and an envelope containing $350 cash for next month's rent. The victim indicates that she has apartment insurance but that she is very upset about the burglary and feels very vulnerable.

1. How long should your interview with this victim take? Explain.

2. How much time should you devote to searching for evidence? Explain.

3. What should you tell the victim to make her feel less vulnerable?

Integrity/Honesty

You arrive at the scene of a commercial burglary where a safe has been ripped open and the contents stolen. While interviewing the store manager, you ask for an inventory of the stolen contents of the safe. He tells you that $1,025 in cash and credit card receipts were taken. He also tells you that his insurance has a $500 deductible, so he would like to pad the reported amount by $500 to absorb the deductible. He laughs and says, "The insurance company can better afford to lose the money than I can." What do you tell the manager he should state as the amount of money lost in the burglary?

Larceny-Theft

FIGURE 16.1 Larceny-Theft Percent Distributions in the Nation

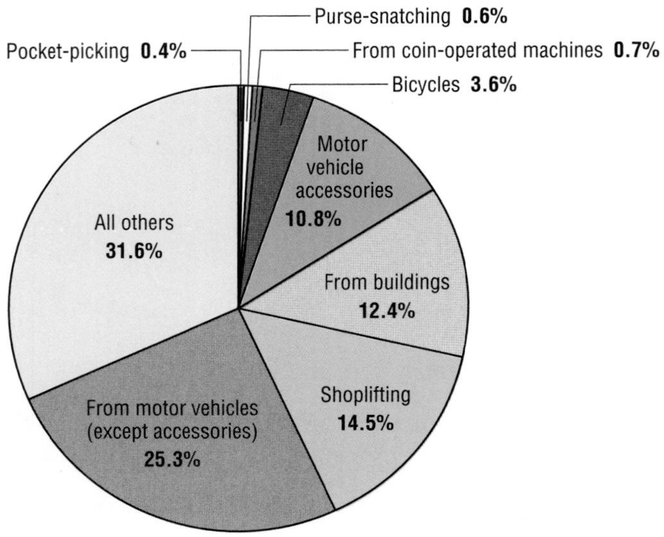

Source: Federal Bureau of Investigation. 2004. *Crime in the United States.* Washington, DC: Government Printing Office, table 2.14.

THE NATURE OF LARCENY-THEFT

Larceny-theft is the most common crime of gain and the most frequently reported of the FBI's index crimes. In 2004 larceny-theft accounted for an estimated 67.3 percent of the nation's property crimes (FBI, 2005). Thefts from motor vehicles accounted for the majority of offenses in the category of larceny-theft in 2004: 25.3 percent. Figure 16.1 shows a breakdown of larceny-theft offenses, including shoplifting, thefts from buildings, thefts of motor vehicle accessories, thefts of bicycles, thefts from coin-operated machines, purse snatching, and pocket-picking. "All other," a category that includes the less-defined larceny-theft offenses, accounted for 31.6 percent of the total.

If you look back at Figure 10.2, you will see that larceny-theft made up almost 60 percent of the index offenses reported in 2002. The items targeted in larcenies include everything imaginable, from a 20-foot-tall inflatable plastic chicken taken from a fast food chicken franchise in Sherman Oaks, California, to manhole covers in Los Angeles, California (Wallechinsky & Wallace, 2005). In addition, credit cards, checks, cash, and parts for all makes and models of automobiles are repeatedly filched. These losses frequently are paid for by consumers in the form of higher prices. During the past decade or so, even people's identities—and their associated credit and property— have been stolen.

Thieves may be young or old, male or female, rich or poor, employed or unemployed, and from any race, religion, or social status. It is difficult for an investigator to distinguish a law-abiding citizen from one with larcenous intent. It is important for investigators to learn to recognize certain techniques thieves may use, as well as to know the elements of larceny-theft as defined in their jurisdictions.

LEGAL ASPECTS OF LARCENY-THEFT

theft The taking of property without the owner's consent; a popular term for larceny.

The word *theft* describes many forms of criminal conduct and is not a common law offense. **Theft,** the taking of property without the owner's consent, is a popular name for larceny and is frequently used as a synonym for the word *larceny.*

HISTORY

IN ANCIENT ENGLAND UNDER THE SAXONS, simple larceny was originally divided into two sorts: grand larceny, in which the value of the goods stolen was above 12 pence, and petit larceny, in which the value was equal to or below that amount. The offense of grand larceny was subject to the death penalty. The distinction between petit larceny and grand larceny has been modified over time, as has the punishment for the latter.

Larceny-theft takes many forms, but state statutes defining the crime contain these five common elements:

1. the taking and
2. carrying away
3. of personal property
4. of another,
5. with the specific intent of permanently depriving the owner of his or her property.

Each of these elements is subject to slightly differing interpretations. Consequently, the actual legal definition of larceny may vary from one jurisdiction to another, depending on court decisions and interpretations.

Modern statutes, in general, retain the ancient English classification of degrees of larceny, based on a value above or below a specified amount. The values that serve as dividing lines and the penalties imposed for each degree vary considerably across the country.

Most modern statutes divide larceny into two degrees: **grand larceny** and **petty larceny.** Generally, grand larceny is considered a felony, and petty larceny is a misdemeanor. What is classified as grand larceny in one state may be classified as petty larceny in another. Some states may use the terms *grand theft* and *petty theft*. Investigators should be familiar with the statutes and the definitions of larceny-theft in their own jurisdictions. In some states, grand larceny is classified as any theft involving property valued at $100 or more; thefts of lesser value are classified as petty larcenies. In other jurisdictions, the monetary value in a grand larceny may need to exceed $300 or even $400. The estimated dollar loss attributable to property crimes (excluding arson) in 2004 was $16.1 billion. Among the individual property crimes, the dollar losses were an estimated $3.5 billion for burglary, nearly $5.1 billion for larceny-theft, and $7.6 billion for motor vehicle theft (FBI, 2005).

In spite of the childhood chant "Finders keepers, losers' weepers," keeping found property lost by its rightful owner is a form of theft. Many jurisdictions will award found property to the finder if the actual owner cannot be located after some duration of time (usually about 30 days). However, a reasonable effort must be made toward locating the rightful owner and returning the property.

larceny-theft The taking and carrying, leading, riding, or driving away the personal property of another with the specific intent of permanently depriving the owner of his or her property.

grand larceny The taking and carrying away of another's personal property with a value in excess of the cutoff amount in a given jurisdiction, with the intent of depriving the owner of it permanently; generally considered a felony.

petty larceny The taking and carrying away of another's personal property with a value below the cutoff amount in a given jurisdiction, with the intent of depriving the owner of it permanently; generally considered a misdemeanor.

TYPES OF LARCENY-THEFT

Criminal investigators may encounter many types of larceny-thefts. Figure 16.1 shows some of the main categories. We will now discuss some of the more common larcenies and the investigative techniques suggested for each.

Pickpockets and Purse Snatchers

Pickpockets may work alone or in small groups. They are particularly difficult to apprehend because the art of pocket-picking depends on stealth. A skillful pickpocket is neither seen nor detected by the victim. If, by chance, some onlooker sees the theft occur, the pickpocket may be identified. Purse snatchers are modern versions of pickpockets but tend to lack the finesse often associated with old world pickpockets. Purse snatchers frequently grab a purse by force and run, and victims of this crime may be injured by the assault. In many jurisdictions, purse snatching is classified as robbery.

Pickpockets sometimes use a bumping technique. During the bumping, they may actually lift the victim's wallet or cash from a pocket. In other situations, the pickpocket may use a razor to slit open a pocket during the bump, causing the wallet to simply fall into the pickpocket's waiting hand. Frequently, valuables are transferred to an accomplice, commonly known as a *tail,* almost as quickly as they are lifted from the victim. Then, should a victim suddenly realize the loss, the pickpocket will not have the incriminating evidence on his or her person. The pickpocket and the tail can meet later and split the take (O'Hara & O'Hara, 2003).

Traditional pickpockets are considered to be among the most skilled mechanical criminals. They use many different procedures in their work. The names for different types of pickpockets reflect their techniques:

- *Choppers* or *slitters* work crowded streets, using razor blades to cut pockets.
- *Spitters* sneeze profusely on their targets and pick their pockets while pretending to clean them off.
- *Short workers* concentrate their activities on public transportation.
- *Hugger-muggers* or *jack rollers* are prostitutes who pick the pockets of their johns after transacting their other business. Sometimes an irate accomplice will burst into the room, and in the confusion the prostitute will pick the john's pocket.
- *Toilet workers* operate in public restrooms.
- *Ticket-line operators* work ticket lines in airports, stadiums, theaters, and amusement centers.
- *Sleepers* open a purse that has been laid aside and rifle the contents.
- *Coin-droppers* intentionally drop some change on the ground and wait for someone to bend over to pick it up. The bending action exposes a wallet carried in the back pocket and makes it vulnerable for taking.

In addition, pickpockets use an assortment of innovative techniques to distract victims and mask their activities; for instance, they may take advantage of bystanders watching an ambulance pass or watching a fire, or even those watching a side walk fight—an event that may have been staged so the pickpocket could ply his or her trade.

Pickpockets are drawn to crowded settings, such as amusement parks, shopping malls, parades, concerts, sporting events, railroad and bus depots, airports, carnivals, and bars (O'Hara & O'Hara, 2003). Investigators assigned to a pickpocket detail should be alert and observant of potential suspects and victims in such situations. Recognizing known pickpockets from past experience or mug shots can greatly assist investigators. When trying to detect would-be pickpockets, be particularly aware of activities such as these:

- Individuals moving from place to place for no apparent reason
- Persons carrying jackets or coats over their arms or newspapers or magazines in their hands

- Groups of youths who huddle together, split up, and later board the same bus or train separately
- Persons who seem more interested in the people around them than in the event taking place
- People who display any unusual or unnatural behaviors
- People who sit near other people who are dozing or intoxicated when there are plenty of available seats
- Individuals who seem to be repeatedly dropping change or keys as they may be intentionally creating a distraction conducive to pickpocketing

Shoplifters

Shoplifting accounts for nearly 30 percent of all retail losses in the United States each year. In 2004 shoplifting represented 14.5 percent of all larceny-theft offenses reported in the FBI's Uniform Crime Reports. Shoplifters may be amateurs or professionals; they may be young or old. They are not always apprehended (Christman & Sennewald, 2006), and even when apprehended, they are not always prosecuted. Stores may not prosecute because of fear of losing a good customer, the cost of the court case, fear of being embarrassed in court, or the hope that a simple reprimand will solve the problem.

Shoplifting, taking goods from a retail establishment without paying for them, generally occurs while the person is posing as a customer. Such thievery can be distinguished from the theft of goods from warehouses, factories, and offices by employees, usually referred to as **employee pilfering** (Wyman, 1999). Shoplifting occurs for a number of reasons, not all of which involve monetary gain.

The amateur often steals on the impulse of the moment or on a dare. In many instances, a young amateur shoplifter does not even need the stolen item. This sort of amateur shoplifts as a challenge, simply to show he or she can, to gain status in a group, or even to relieve boredom (Klemke, 1992). Some amateurs shoplift simply because the opportunity presents itself. Even some otherwise law-abiding citizens may succumb to an overwhelming urge to "get something for nothing" when they believe no one is watching and no one will be the wiser (Shulman, 2003).

The *modus operandi* of most amateurs is fairly predictable. It usually involves an attempt to conceal merchandise in a shopping bag, purse, pocket, backpack, coat, or under clothing. In some instances, amateurs may simply wear a garment out of the store, either concealing it under their own clothes or leaving their own clothes behind. Switching a price tag or sticker from an inexpensive item with one from an expensive item is another common technique amateurs use (even professionals use this one). Another technique is to place small items in the pockets of garments being purchased or in boxes or packages of items being purchased. If an extra item is detected at the checkout, the thief simply feigns ignorance of how it might have gotten there.

When people think of shoplifting, they tend to think of clothing and other dry goods, jewelry, and expensive luxury items, but a common target of shoplifters is meat from supermarkets. Cigarettes, baby laxatives (used in the cutting of drugs), alcohol, and an assortment of other grocery items also are regularly shoplifted.

Professional shoplifters tend to be more imaginative than amateurs, and their motive is money or profit. They are also trained in shoplifting techniques. Their crimes are premeditated, executed with care and stealth, and often assisted by special devices and accomplices. Professional shoplifters carry special containers with trapdoors into which merchandise can be quickly slipped. These **booster devices** frequently look like

shoplifting The taking of goods from a retail establishment without paying for them, while posing as a customer.

employee pilfering The theft of goods from warehouses, factories, retail businesses, and offices by employees.

booster device A container, generally a box, with a spring-loaded trap door, allowing the professional shoplifter to conceal stolen goods very quickly.

Professional shoplifters use a variety of devices to conceal stolen merchandise.

common packages of merchandise, and during the holidays they may be gift wrapped (Klemke, 1992). Specially designed clothing, such as booster skirts, booster coats, and booster bloomers, feature concealed pockets for hiding stolen merchandise. In addition, professionals may wear special harnesses and belts and carry hooks with retractable springs.

Some professionals work in teams. They may even work with accomplices who are employed by the store. One such team effort might involve a version of *tag switching*. The accomplice is usually a cashier who does not question a $5 price tag on a $500 camera or does not ring up all of the items that the other thief has placed on the counter. In another version, one or more accomplices create a disturbance or commotion to distract store personnel while other members of the team grab merchandise and escape with it.

An accomplice or accomplices may feign a medical emergency or a domestic argument, or a group may create a general commotion as a cover for the thefts.

Drug addicts are often crime-prone persons because they must constantly seek the means to support their habit. Shoplifting is a means of obtaining items to sell to support their addiction. Caught in a desperate situation, drug addicts are capable of using violence to escape apprehension. Others may use burglary or more predatory crimes, such as mugging or robbery, for drug money, but shoplift food. The addict shoplifting for his or her habit will usually "shop" for merchandise with high ticket prices. Such a theft allows the addict to recover more profit when he or she sells the item to a **fence,** a dealer in stolen goods, or to a pawnbroker.

fence Slang term for a professional receiver, concealer, and disburser of stolen property.

Kleptomania is an irresistible urge to steal—sometimes as a result of an emotional condition. In some cases, kleptomania is a sexually motivated behavior (see Chapter 12). The defense of kleptomania is frequently used for any excessive, repetitive, and apparently unreasonable stealing. Shoplifting caused by kleptomania represents a relatively small percentage of larceny-theft cases. True kleptomaniacs have a serious psychological problem and should be provided with therapy.

During the early 1960s Mary Owen Cameron (1964) conducted what has become a classic study on shoplifting. Cameron found that about 10 percent of all shoplifting was accomplished by professionals who obtained their income through shoplifting goods and fencing them. Cameron identified these individuals as *boosters* or *heels*; amateurs, or *snitches,* actually commit the majority of instances of shoplifting events and tend to steal items for their own use.

The enormous economic losses sustained from the chronic problem of shoplifting have forced retailers to turn to private security firms and mechanical security devices. Undercover security agents, hidden surveillance cameras, and various electronic tags on products are commonly used to deter and detect shoplifting. Local police agencies, as a rule, are called to the scene of a shoplifting *after* the shoplifter has been apprehended. Criminal investigators, however, may be called on to investigate professional shoplifters or shoplifting teams. This is particularly true when merchants realize they have been struck repeatedly for sizable amounts.

Shoplifting suspects can usually be detected by careful observation. Their strategies, like those of pickpockets, depend on smooth, quick movements, concealment, various types of distractions, and stealth. Persons wearing outerwear inappropriate to the season or carrying objects that could conceal merchandise should be suspect.

Not all pawnshops intentionally buy or sell stolen property, but some are not very cautious about verifying ownership of property pawned at the shop.

People holding objects while scanning the store or nervously glancing around should also be monitored.

STATISTICS In 2004, 28 percent of larceny-theft arrests were of persons under 18 years of age, and 72 percent of the arrestees were 18 or older (FBI, 2005).

FRAUD

Fraud is misrepresentation, trickery, or deception with criminal intent to deprive someone of his or her property. Criminal intent is called *mens rea* in criminal law. Fraud is a less serious crime than larceny-theft or burglary, but it has great economic impact. There are many types of fraud, some of which are more characteristic of business crimes and organized crime. It is the concept that one can get something for nothing. This discussion is limited to some of the more common forms of fraud that fall into the category of larceny by fraud or deception. Note that fraud differs from larceny-theft in that deceit, not stealth, is used to obtain others' property and goods illegally.

fraud Misrepresentation, trickery, or deception with criminal intent to deprive someone of his or her property.

Credit Card Fraud

The enormous availability and use of credit cards has moved this type of fraud to the forefront during recent years. Banks, department stores, furniture stores, jewelry stores, and gasoline companies all issue and honor credit cards (Montague, 2004). In the 1990s, gasoline credit cards, which once permitted only purchases of service station products and repairs, became more general charge cards. Although one could continue to use the card at the issuing service station, one could also use it as one would any general, bank-issued credit card.

The use of stolen, forged, or unauthorized credit cards or credit card numbers has become a huge illegal business (Montague, 2004). Companies issuing credit cards are often in states other than the one where the card customer resides, and dollar limits on most cards are usually several hundreds or thousands of dollars. Several years ago, it became a felony to forge, resell, or use a stolen or unauthorized credit card.

Thieves obtain credit cards and credit card numbers by theft—either from the mail or from the card's owner—by fraudulent application to the issuing company, by counterfeiting, or by obtaining the digitized information, including PIN (Personalized Identification Number) information, surreptitiously when the owner uses his or her credit card (using devices known as *reader/collectors* when the owner swipes his or her credit card to use it). Newly issued credit cards stolen from the mail were once highly sought because they had not been reported stolen or lost and the thief could actually place his or her own signature on the card. To combat this, many issuing companies now require an "activation" telephone call before the card will be accepted by any store. During the activation call, the company requires the caller to know certain security information. This may include the maiden name or birth date of a parent, the card owner's Social Security number, a code number appearing on the old credit card, or some similar secret information.

Theft of credit card numbers has significantly increased during merchandise transactions handled over the Internet. In addition, a number of scams begin with a telephone call from someone identifying him- or herself as a security agent with MasterCard or Visa and end with you telling this individual your security code (the code on the back of the credit card). The script runs something like this:

> "Hello, this is Jonathan Powel, and I'm calling from the security and fraud department of Visa. My Badge number is 14589. Your Visa card has been flagged for an unusual purchase pattern, and I am calling to verify whether you actually have made these purchases. The purchases were made on your Merchant Bank Visa. Did you purchase an Electric Guitar for $462.57, from Bananas.com online?"
>
> "No," replies the card owner.
>
> The caller continues, "Then we will need to issue a credit to your account. We have noticed a number of recent purchases on your account ranging from $200 to $450, but always just under $500, a pattern that flags most credit cards for investigation. Before you receive your next statement, we will send you a new credit card and credit your account for the questionable purchases. We will be sending that card to (gives the card owner's address), is that correct?"
>
> The card owner confirms the address.
>
> The caller continues, "I will be initiating a full fraud investigation. If you have any questions, please call the 800 number listed on your card; that number is 1-800-VISA, and ask for Security. You will need to refer to the following control number. Do you have something to write it down on?"
>
> The card owner says, "Yes."
>
> "Good, the number is (a six digit number is given)." The caller then says, "I will need to verify that you still do have possession of your card. Please turn over the card, so you are looking at its back. Please read me that seven-digit number to verify that you do actually still have possession of the card." [The last three digits of this series are the security code needed to make purchases on most Internet sites.]
>
> The card owner dutifully recites the number, which includes the security code.
>
> The caller confirms that these are the correct numbers needed to verify that the card is still in the owner's possession, thanks the card owner, and hangs up.

FOCUS ON TECHNOLOGY

HOW IDENTITY THEFT CREDIT CARD SCAMS WORK

STARTING IN 2003, many people across the country began receiving telephone calls in which the caller identified him- or herself as someone working for the security and fraud department for either MasterCard or Visa. The purpose of the call is to get the card owner to provide the security code.

This scam artist has already obtained the card owner's card number and street address, but lacks the three-digit verification code on its back. Perhaps the caller obtained the information through use of a reader/collector when the card owner made a purchase somewhere. The reader/collector would have taken the information from the magnetic strip on the back of the card as the card owner swiped it during the purchase transaction. Or the thief may have taken a statement from the card owner's mail. Once the thief obtains the security code from the card owner, a series of purchases will be made rapidly via the Internet before the owner gets the next month's statement and can figure out that he or she has been scammed.

In reality, neither MasterCard nor Visa will ever call and ask for the security information on the back of your credit card.

The thief now has all the information needed to use the card owner's credit card to make purchases over the Internet.

Check Fraud

Forging checks and writing bad checks are different statutory violations in most jurisdictions. A bad check is one that a person tries to cash when he or she has insufficient funds in the bank to cover the draft. Everyone at some time or another accidentally writes an overdraft on a checking account. This is usually corrected by the recipient's redepositing the check when there are sufficient funds. Or the recipient may ask the issuer to buy the bad check back with cash, a process sometimes referred to as *bad check reconciliation* (Sennewald & Tsukayama, 2001). However, the occasional overdrawn account is distinguishable from persistently and knowingly writing checks with not sufficient funds (NSF). It is likewise distinguishable from opening a new checking account with a small deposit and proceeding to **hang paper** (write bad checks) all over town exceeding the amount of the deposit in the account.

hang paper Knowingly and intentionally writing bad checks; slang expression.

FOCUS ON TECHNOLOGY

NATIONAL FRAUDULENT CHECK FILE

INVESTIGATING CHECK FRAUD is difficult because professional bad check passers operate in a city for a short time and then move to another city or state. The FBI's National Fraudulent Check File (NFCF) makes it easier to identify such persons, their patterns of travel, and their techniques. The NFCF also maintains a database of information about check writing standards (Wade & Trozzi, 2003).

Check forgery comes in two forms: forgery of the signature on the front of the check, or forgery of the payee's name on the reverse of the check, as the endorsement. In addition, it may involve the use of forged or stolen identification to convince the victim that the false signature is real. The checks may be stolen from an individual (personal checks) or a business (commercial checks) or may be third-party checks such as payroll checks (LaBonte, 2006; McCaghy & Cernkovick, 1987). Blank checks are often obtained in burglaries or from stolen purses and wallets.

Forgery Signatures Forgery of the signature on the front of a check is usually a fairly easy crime to accomplish if the thief is not too greedy. Typically, the signature need not even be very close to that of the real account owner because most banks will not bother to verify the signature on a check received from a merchant unless it is for a large amount. Most bad signature checks are not negotiated at a bank, however, but through the purchase at stores of large ticket items that can easily be fenced (such as televisions, stereos, and computers). Banks typically only check signatures if there is a protest by the account owner (LaBonte, 2006).

Endorsement Fraud Forging the endorsement on the back of a check generally involves some degree of *identity theft* (discussed in detail later in this chapter) and negotiating a check written to someone else. Endorsement frauds are more commonly committed at a bank than in a merchant's store. The checks are usually valid and have been taken from the payee's home, purse, or wallet. The thief must have some form of fraudulent identification to show the bank in order to negotiate the check (LaBonte, 2006).

Counterfeit Checks Among the fastest growing sources of fraudulent checks are those derived from counterfeited checks. Counterfeit checks can be created using desktop computer software or by making exact copies on sophisticated scanner-printers. Desktop publishing software permits the check counterfeiter to create checks with individualized and sequenced numbers—just as one might have in a real check book—as well as the necessary series of numbers on the bottom of the check that include the bank branch, account number, and routing information. When a counterfeiter is done, the "bad check" will look very real. Frequently, check counterfeiters will include magnetic ink character recognition (MICR) line characters, so that the bank's check reader will not detect the fraud (LaBonte, 2006).

Counterfeiting Money

Police usually become involved with counterfeit money when a retailer, private citizen, or bank brings to their attention that someone has passed what appear to be fake bills. The Secret Service provides the public with information on how to identify counterfeit money online at http://www.ustreas.gov/usss/money_detect.shtml. Information includes how to identify both counterfeit bills and coins. When an individual identifies a counterfeit bill, the individual is asked to turn this bill in at any local bank along with a downloadable "Counterfeit Report" from the Secret Service website (Figure 16.2).

Historically, the most common denominations for counterfeit bills have been $10, $20, and $50. However, there have been instances where counterfeiters have produced $5 and even $1 bills in an attempt to fly under the radar, so to speak, since these bills are less likely to be suspected of being counterfeit. At one time, counterfeit bills required a master artist/engraver, who could design the simulated bills and create plates that were then used in the printing process to produce authentic-looking fake money. The paper used for making money has long intentionally included various elements intended to deter counterfeiting, such as red and blue fibers imbedded in the paper itself, and special colored inks are used to print the money. Nonetheless, counterfeiters have also long worked to outwit the government by bleaching one dollar bills and using this authentic paper to print higher denomination bills (such as $50 or $100 denominations).

Due to the advances in computer and scanner-printer technology, there have been changes in counterfeiting. Desk-top counterfeiting, as it may be called, involves scanning $20, $50, or $100 bills, and printing them using a color printer; making potential counterfeiters out of even the most nonartistic of criminals. The reproductions are not clever redrawn images but perfect replicas of real currency. By adding some desktop publishing software to the equation, even the serial numbers of the bills can be altered to create a series of bills rather than hundreds of bills with the same serial number (Associated Press, 2006).

In their efforts to make it more difficult to counterfeit U.S. currency, the Federal Reserve, the Department of the Treasury, and the U.S. Secret Service continue to improve currency designs. Since 1996 new currency designs have included a number of security features intended both to make counterfeiting more difficult and to improve counterfeit detection by merchants, banks, and even the average citizen. These features include the following:

- **Color-shifting ink** When the numeral in the lower right corner on the face of a note is tilted by moving the note up and down, the color-shifting ink should change color from copper to green. If it doesn't, it is a counterfeit.
- **Watermarks** If a new note is held up to the light, a watermark, or faint image, should be visible that is similar to the larger portrait of the president in the center of the bill. The watermark is part of the paper itself, and it can be seen from

FIGURE 16.2 Secret Service Counterfeit Report Form

United States Secret Service

Counterfeit Note Report

INSTRUCTIONS TO BANK:
1. Prepare two copies of this form for each suspected counterfeit note.
2. Submit copies of completed form with each suspected counterfeit note to your LOCAL SECRET SERVICE OFFICE.
3. If desired, an additional copy of this form should be prepared and retained for your records.

This form is not subject to the requirements of P.L. 96–511 "Paperwork Reduction Act of 1980." 44 USC, Chapter 35, Section 3518 (c)(1)(A) states that, "...this chapter [Chapter 35] does not apply to the collection of information ... during the conduct of a Federal criminal investigation... "

FROM: (Indicate Bank's Name and Mailing Address (include Zip Code)

DO NOT WRITE IN THIS SPACE

Telephone Number of Bank (include area code) _____

Point-of-Contact (include extension and e-mail address, if applicable) _____

Classification Number _____

FOLD HERE

IMPORTANT NOTICE

FOLD HERE

Bank tellers and persons surrendering the note should date and initial each counterfeit note with pen and ink in the border areas of the note for identification. If the person surrendering the note knows from whom he/she received it, or has a description of the passer, or his/her auto, or any other information, TELEPHONE the local Secret Service office IMMEDIATELY and hold the note. (The telephone number of your local Secret Service office can be found in the front cover of your telephone directory.) Otherwise, if no information is available, please mail the note to our local office on the day it is received.

DESCRIPTION OF COUNTERFEIT NOTE OR RAISED NOTE (for raised note give serial number only)

DENOMINATION	FEDERAL RESERVE BANK *(Series 1996 — Letter/Number)*		CHECK LETTER/QUADRANT NO.
CHECK LETTER/FACE PLATE NO.	BACK PLATE NO.	SERIES	SERIAL NUMBER

COUNTERFEIT NOTE RECEIVED FROM

NAME OF CUSTOMER/BUSINESS	DATE OF DEPOSIT
CUSTOMER'S HOME ADDRESS	CUSTOMER'S HOME PHONE A/C
	CUSTOMER'S BUSINESS PHONE A/C
NAME OF PERSON SURRENDERING AND INITIALING NOTE	NAME OF TELLER RECEIVING AND INITIALING NOTE

INFORMATION ABOUT COUNTERFEIT NOTE

DOES THE CUSTOMER HAVE ANY INFORMATION AS TO THE SOURCE OF THE COUNTERFEIT?	☐ YES ☐ NO
WAS THERE ANY SUSPICIOUS ACTIVITY?	☐ YES ☐ NO
IS THIS A NON-CUSTOMER?	☐ YES ☐ NO

REMARKS:

DISPOSITION (For Secret Service Use Only)

☐ Genuine note and SSF 1604 returned to bank (Receipt No. _____)   ☐ Acknowledgement of Receipt returned to bank

☐ Other (Specify)

UNITED STATES SECRET SERVICE   PLEASE SUBMIT TO THE LOCAL SECRET SERVICE JURISDICTIONAL FIELD OFFICE   SSF 1604 (03/2003)
(Previous Editions may not be used.)

---

both sides of the note. It cannot be bleached out, so bleaching a $5 note to print a $50 or a $100 note will result in a mismatched watermark and presidential portrait on the bill.

- **Security thread** When a new note is held up to the light, a vertical thread or plastic strip should be visible along the edge of the presidential portrait in the middle of the bill. This strip has been embedded in the paper, is visible from either side of the note, and will glow when the bill is held under an ultraviolet light source. (U.S. Secret Service, 2006a)

Overall, counterfeiting of U.S. currency remains at comparatively low levels. About one percent of all counterfeit currency in the world is U.S. currency, but most of it originates outside of the United States (U.S. Secret Service, 2006b). In 2006, the U.S. government announced that it would be redesigning the $5 note to update and improve security features on the bill. The change in the $5 note came after changes had already been made in the $20 note (in 2003), the $50 note (in 2004), and the $10 note (in early 2006). The Treasury's plans include following the release of the new $5 note with a newly designed $100 in 2008 or 2009 (U.S. Secret Service, 2006b).

Confidence Games

A confidence game, also sometimes known as a *bunco,* is obtaining money or property by a trick, swindle, or device that takes advantage of the victim's confidence in the swindler. Con artists prosper only because of the fundamental dishonesty of their victims. The old adage "you can't cheat an honest man" resounds as an accurate statement when considering confidence games (Hyde & Zanetti, 2002). The con usually involves a get-rich-quick scheme where the con man first inspires rapport, trust, and a firm belief in his integrity. Second, the con man tempts the victim with some tale or plan, which draws nearly irresistible forces of excitement and cupidity on the part of the victim (also known as *the mark*). Third, the con man will allege that the victim will make large sums of money by means of some deal that is clearly not entirely legal or honest—but because of this, it is described to the victim as "a sure thing." As the victim's greed for large and easy profits is fanned into a hot fire of desire, the mark will place his or her scruples aside and put his or her money into the con (Hyde & Zanetti, 2002).

Con artists tend to use one of two basic approaches: either taking the victim for whatever money he or she has at the time (the *short con*) or setting up the mark for higher stakes that require considerable planning and execution (the *long con*). Most confidence games have three basic ingredients:

1. Finding a likely victim (*locating a mark*), which means identifying someone with money to fleece.

2. Enticing the mark by making an offer (*the spiel*) that sounds like getting something for nothing, appeals to superstition, or appeals to some aspect of vulnerable human nature (*baiting and setting the hook*).

3. Getting the victim to give up his or her money (*reeling in the mark*).

The confidence artist's business is to stimulate the interest and greed of the victim until his or her reason, judgment, and logic is overwhelmed. Bunco operators are excellent high-pressure salespeople, good actors, congenial people, and experts in psychology and human nature. The basic philosophy of confidence games is that there is larceny in everyone's heart, and some people are able to bring that quality out in others.

Bank Examiner Swindle

The bank examiner swindle is a fairly sophisticated con game. It may involve three or more people working in concert to swindle a victim. This con requires some background research. The thieves must learn the mark's name, address, phone number, bank, and latest banking transaction. The con artist contacts the *mark,* usually by telephone, and identifies him- or herself as a federal bank examiner. The phony bank examiner will then *bait the hook* by offering *the spiel,* saying that there has been a computer malfunction and that he or she needs to verify the latest transaction and the bank balance of the mark's account. After learning the balance, the caller indicates that there is a discrepancy between the mark's records and the bank's. Next, the phony bank examiner explains that he or she is investigating a dishonest teller at the bank who may be tampering with accounts. Now the caller asks for the mark's assistance in catching the dishonest teller—playing on human nature and the desire of many people to play spy or undercover detective. This phase of the con is sometimes referred to as *setting the hook.*

When the victim agrees to help, he or she is asked to go to the bank and withdraw an amount just short of the actual account balance. The mark is told that he or she will be protected at all times by a federal agent, who will watch the withdrawal and make sure the mark returns home safely. After returning home, the mark is visited by a member of the con team. It may be the person who originally called on the telephone or another member. He or she explains that things went exactly as planned and it is now necessary to take the money that was withdrawn into custody as evidence. This end of the game is referred to as *reeling in the mark.*

The con artist will usually write out an official-looking receipt for the money. In some cases, he or she may even promise to redeposit the money in the bank for the mark and may provide the victim with a fake deposit slip. The "agent" will tell the victim that the entire matter must be kept strictly confidential and is not to be discussed with anyone. The victim may even be promised a reward for participating in the investigation. It may take several days or weeks for the mark to learn that he or she has actually been swindled.

Pigeon Drop   The pigeon drop bunco is typically operated by two people. It is said to be among the oldest swindles on record. The first bunco operator is usually neatly dressed and gifted, or practiced, at persuasion. Upon sighting the potential victim—the pigeon—Operator 1 will "find" a previously planted wallet or envelope so that the victim can see the operator picking it up. The con artist next opens the wallet or envelope and expresses surprise at the contents (all within view and earshot of the pigeon). The bunco operator then looks up to find the victim watching and asks whether the victim saw him or her pick up the wallet or envelope. The victim naturally says "Yes." The operator then tells the victim that the wallet contains a large sum of money and shows the contents briefly.

The contents are either counterfeit bills or some genuine bills mixed with fake currency totaling several thousand dollars. At about this time, Operator 2 happens along, posing as a disinterested bystander. When consulted, Operator 2 suggests that either of the two original parties might have found the envelope. Therefore, they should split the found money—provided they cannot find the actual owner during the next 24 hours. Operator 2 will further suggest that each of the parties put up a specified sum of money as security and to show good faith.

When the victim produces the good-faith money, Operator 1 places it in an envelope and shows it to Operator 2. Using sleight of hand, Operator 2 switches the envelope with an identical one filled with worthless paper slips. The pigeon is allowed to hold both the wallet or original envelope and the second envelope. The three agree to meet at a specified place in 24 hours, and they depart. However, the swindlers go home with the pigeon's money, and the victim goes home with worthless clippings (Adkins, 1975).

Carnival Buncos   Carnival buncos refer loosely to several different swindles involving crooked games of chance. Some of the more common ones that investigators might encounter follow.

In three-card monte, the bunco operator uses three playing cards: for example, an ace and two picture cards. The con man coaxes an onlooker into betting that he or

Even legitimate carnival games of chance require one to play and win many times before being awarded a large prize.

she can tell which of the three is a specified card. The cards are turned face down and quickly moved around. Then the bystander makes his or her selection. Initially, the bystander wins, and usually he or she is a **shill,** an accomplice of the bunco operator. As the shill continues to bet and win, other onlookers begin to think that this is really an easy win. However, as soon as one of them makes a bet, the bunco operator uses sleight of hand to remove the specified card from the table or inverted box. Thus, it is impossible to choose the correct card.

shill A slang term for a secret coconspirator or accomplice in a confidence game.

The switch is made so quickly that no one watching is the wiser. However, in a matter of just a few minutes, a skilled bunco operator can make several hundred dollars (depending on the size of bets). In some cases, the mark is actually permitted to win one or two times, to lull him or her into a false sense of confidence. The bunco operator may even persuade the mark to place a much larger bet to try to win back his or her money. Naturally, when the mark places a larger bet, he or she will lose.

The shell game works like three-card monte, but instead of cards the bunco operator uses walnut shells, soda caps, small Dixie cups, or similar objects. The bunco operator places a pea or a small ball of some sort under one of the shells. Then, working on a table or an inverted box, the operator quickly slides the caps around the surface. The challenge in this game is to locate the pea (or ball). By the time the operator asks, "Under which cap is the little ball?" he or she has already palmed it. It is, therefore, not under any of the caps or shells. After showing the mark that the ball is not where he or she thought it was, the bunco operator quickly replaces the ball under another cap while revealing it to onlookers. It appears that the person making the wager simply guessed wrong.

Some carnival games of chance are run dishonestly. They may take each victim for only a small amount of money but produce huge overall profits. The standard practice in these crooked games is to entice a customer to try the game—sometimes for free. Part of the lure is big, expensive prizes on display in the game booth. The customer may find the game quite easy when trying it for free and will try it again for money. After winning the game, the customer receives a tiny cheap, prize that was shelved out of sight under the counter. The carnival worker then explains that to get a big prize you must win many times and trade your prize for a larger one each time your win. Thus, it could be quite expensive to actually win a big prize. Variations on this basic scheme involve rigged games with weighted bottles, under- or overinflated balls and balloons, dull darts, misfiring rifles, and so forth.

Insurance Fraud

Fraud contributes significantly to Americans' insurance costs each year. Phony accident schemes, faked burglaries, exaggerated injuries, and false medical charges all contribute to millions of dollars in losses for insurance companies. For example, someone may intentionally walk in front of a car and make it appear that he or she has been hit or injured. Someone else may claim to have fallen on another's property or in a store. A person may have his or her own car stolen simply to receive the insurance money. A person who reports a burglary may not actually have been visited by a burglar. Some physicians even submit duplicate bills to insurance companies, order unnecessary tests, or upgrade the service bill for treatment not actually rendered (Garcia, 1992). Sometimes insurance swindlers enlist the aid of crooked lawyers and waste hours of court time suing others or insurance companies. At the end of 2004, the Coalition Against Insurance Fraud reported that auto insurance fraud amounts to approximately $14 billion in false claims a year. A ground-breaking study by the Insurance Research Council in 1996 found that one-third of all bodily injury claims for auto accidents contained some amount of fraud. In this study, most of the 33 out of 100 bodily injury claims identified as fraudulent included "padding" or "build-up"—exaggeration of injuries based on actual accidents (Insurance Information Institute, 2006).

Suspicious claims, even though they may eventually be paid, are usually investigated by insurance companies. In some instances, insurance investigators may need help from law enforcement investigators as well. The nature and scope of the investigation varies. In some cases, insurance investigators may keep a suspected insurance scam artist under surveillance for days or weeks. In other cases, a quick interview with the alleged victim may reveal false statements or deception.

Consumer and Business Fraud

Many financial and business schemes are perfectly legitimate. However, a number of them are exploitive and prey on the same human weaknesses as the traditional confidence artist. Let's look at some common consumer and business frauds.

Bait and Switch   In a typical bait and switch, advertised bargain merchandise lures, or baits, a customer into the store. Once there, the consumer is told that the store had only a single unit of that sale item and it has been sold. However, the salesperson will be happy to sell the customer a more expensive version of the item. The salesperson will even try to convince the consumer he or she is better off with the more expensive item.

Look-Alike or Sound-Alike Products   Sellers offer inferior products with names that sound like or are packaged like better-quality or higher-priced items.

Misrepresentation or False Advertising   Such frauds involve misrepresentation of product performance, warranty, quality, or the cost of credit. For example, a better product than the one actually for sale is pictured in the advertisement. Or there is a false or misleading promise in the text. For instance, sometimes beef

HISTORY

IN 1963 AUDITORS AT THE ALLIED CRUDE VEGETABLE OIL REFINING CORPORATION discovered a salad oil scam that Anthony De Angelis had been pulling off to extend the company's inventory of salad oil. De Angelis filled many of the company's oil vats with water, and through a system of underground pipes connecting the phony oil vats, pumped in a layer of oil to float on the water. For nearly ten years banks loaned hundreds of millions of dollars to De Angelis to finance worldwide salad oil deals. By the time the auditors discovered the fraud, De Angelis had already sold $175 million of bogus salad oil.

"on the hoof" is advertised for perhaps $1.99 a pound for all cuts. These deals usually require that the consumer buy full sides of beef. Of course, beef on the hoof means a live cow weighed before butchering—including the weight of the head, hide, legs, and hooves. In effect, a buyer may pay several hundred dollars for inedible cow parts. The actual cost of the edible beef received, then, may be $4 or $5 a pound.

Service Swindles   The basic M.O. for such frauds is to repair a home appliance or an automobile when repairs are not needed or to overcharge for repairs. An alternative is to charge for repairs never undertaken or parts never used or to offer home repairs at what appear to be rock-bottom prices but to never actually complete them.

Misrepresentation of Warranty   Such frauds are intentional failures to provide a consumer with facts about a product's warranty provisions and exclusions. For example, some computer warranties are "carry-in only." This means that any repair must be made at a service location, not in the consumer's home. Furthermore, the responsibility and expense for getting the computer to the service location, whether by hand or by mail, is the consumer's.

FYI   Every year, tens of thousands of people are victims of investment scams. One very popular come-on in 1991 involved Operation Desert Storm. Con operators used patriotism in their spiel to convince victims to invest in phony oil and gas leases. Some 3,500 investors put a total of $50 million into these investments, relying on the promoters' claims that the war would drive up oil prices. The operation was a Ponzi scheme; that is, the early investors were paid with money raised from later investors. The wells were either plugged or not owned by the company making the offer. The scheme collapsed when the supply of new investors dried up.

Telemarketing and Mail Fraud

Telemarketing fraud and other types of fraud using the telephone have increased in recent years, especially as crimes against the elderly (Sharpe, 2004). In one such scam, a telemarketer offers enormous savings for purchasing some high-priced item or dream vacation by credit card. The actual scam is to have the victim tell the caller his or her credit card number. Since no product will ever be delivered, it is easy to offer a sewing machine or jewelry for just a few dollars. Once the caller acquires the victim's credit card number, he or she then uses the account number to make illegal purchases. Other common telemarketing frauds include the following:

- **Prize offers.** Prize offers are one of the most popular telephone scams. These scammers tell you that you have been awarded a prize—that it is not a contest, but a promotion. To qualify to receive the prize, you have to do something. Generally, you will have to buy something, attend a sales presentation, or even give out your credit card number to win. Legitimate contests do not require you to purchase a product to qualify for a prize. Legitimate time-share offers may indicate you have been awarded some prize or even a shopping mall gift certificate; reputable time-share offers will tell you, upon request, that the sales presentation you must attend to qualify will run about 90 minutes and which company is sponsoring the time-share. If the caller is unable or unwilling to provide this information, be wary. If a deal sounds too good to be true, it probably is.

- **Travel packages.** Be leery of free or low-cost travel packages. Frequently these vacations have hidden costs, or require nonrefundable deposits—even if you never use the travel package. As well, many of these offers have so many black-out days, or limited availability, that you will never be able to book the trip—again, forfeiting any deposit that has been made.

- **Investments.** People lose millions of dollars each year to "get rich quick" schemes that promise high returns with little or no risk. These can include gemstones, rare coins, oil and gas leases, precious metals, art, and other "investment opportunities." As a rule, these are worthless. If you are interested making such an investment, you would be wise to do so through a reputable broker.

- **Charities.** Con artists often label phony charities with names that sound like better-known, reputable organizations. Always ask for their information in writing. You can also check them out with watchdog groups suchas the Better Business Bureau or the state Attorney General. Even legitimate charities can sometimes have dishonest private charitable collection companies working for them. Many pay the telephone solicitor based on the number of donations they obtain, so another tricky scam is to call previous donors several times a year in hopes they do not recall already having donated for the year.

- **Recovery scams.** If you fall victim to one or another of the scams described here, you may be called again by someone promising to get the lost money back. Report such calls to the police, and be careful not to lose more money to this scam. This is a common practice of the thieves, who already know the victim is somewhat gullible and vulnerable. Even law enforcement officials cannot guarantee that they can recover money lost in a scam.

Similar scams operate through the mail. In some cases, potential victims receive notices that they have been "awarded" a prize. Prizes are described as portable sewing machines, expensive-sounding 35-mm cameras, and so forth. The accompanying letter explains that this is not a contest prize but a promotional incentive award. All the victim needs to do is send a small amount of money, usually $3 to $10, to cover postage and handling for the award to be delivered. The portable sewing machine turns out to be a cheap, handheld, toy-like mending device, and the 35-mm camera is a plastic fixed-lens device worth about a dollar. Victims have reported sending hundreds of dollars over time, convinced that they are actually going to receive an expensive product, such as a new car, television, cash, or trips.

FIGURE 16.3 Chain Letter pyramid

Number of Mailings	Number of Participants
1	6
2	36
3	216
4	1,296
5	7,776
6	46,656
7	279,936
8	1,679,616
9	10,077,696
10	60,466,176
11	362,797,056
12	2,176,782,336
13	13,060,694,016

Source: United States Postal Service, Publication 256.

Ponzi Schemes Named for Carlo Ponzi, who bilked thousands of Bostonians of their money, Ponzi, or pyramid, schemes offer prospective investors weekly or monthly returns on their investments. Initial investors—the top of the pyramid—do receive the promised return at first. As word spreads, more investors contribute, and additional layers of the pyramid are added (Walsh, 2003). The con artist uses the new investors' money to pay the interest on the older ones'. However, eventually, the interest payments exceed the new capital, and the swindler flees with the remaining investment cash.

Chain Letters Chain letters are another type of pyramid scheme and are often illegal. Any chain letter that requires payment of money or something of value is a violation of federal mail fraud laws. People lose hundreds of dollars every year in chain letter schemes. Earlier investors in the pyramid may receive considerable money or items of value. However, as successive layers are heaped on the pyramid pile, fewer and fewer participants actually receive the promised items. Figure 16.3 shows how a typical chain letter scheme works. Initially, six people are asked to each send a letter to six other people, each of whom must then send letters to six more people, and so on. The letter asks that a specified amount of money be sent to someone farther up the chain. But, as Figure 16.3 shows, the geometric progression of participants will quickly exceed the population of the United States—and even that of the world.

Of course, not all solicitations made through the mail or over the telephone are scams. It is exactly this fact that allows confidence artists to remain successful in these swindles. Other common mail and telephone frauds involve bunco operators masquerading as doctors, lawyers, real estate agents, stock brokers, art dealers, salespeople, parcel delivery agents, and many other service representatives. These various scams usually involve the three basic ingredients of a con game discussed earlier in the chapter.

Identity Theft

During the course of a busy day, people write checks at the grocery store or other merchant shops and charge their coffee at Starbucks, their movie tickets at theaters, their dinner at a restaurant, or even rent a car. Some people may apply for a credit card or membership in a health club or gym, check their bank balance online, or read their e-mail messages. When people do these things, chances are that they do not give their actions a second thought; these are simply the everyday transactions of life. But an identity thief does carefully think about these types of transactions and how best to obtain someone's identification information from such transactions. **Identity theft** occurs when someone uses another person's personal information without that person's permission to commit fraud or other crimes.

Identity theft is very serious, and it is one of the fastest growing crimes in the world. Approximately 11.8 million Americans (one in twenty adults) had been victimized by identity theft by April 2003 (Star Systems, 2003). Credit card numbers, driver's license numbers, Social Security numbers, date of birth, and other personal identification can net criminals thousands of dollars in a very short period of time.

Incidents of identify theft continue to increase dramatically, according to an independent nationwide survey of consumers released by electronic commerce and payments leader First Data Corp. (NYSE: FDC). The survey found that 6.8 percent of adults had been victimized by identity theft, and a striking 43.4 percent of adults had received a *phishing* contact. Further, the study indicates that as many as 54 million Americans have been the victims of ID-related fraud (Star Systems, 2005).

Phishing is a growing form of attempted identity theft in which consumers are contacted via bogus e-mail messages that try to lure them into providing personal information such as their Social Security number or financial account information. Phishers (those perpetrating the fraud) may send e-mail notes purporting to come from banks or other financial institutions, credit card companies, retailers, government agencies, or other entities with which consumers are likely to have a relationship.

People whose identities have been stolen can spend months or years and thousands of dollars attempting to clarify the situation and cleaning up the mess the thieves have made of their good name and credit record. In the meantime, victims of identity theft may lose job opportunities, be refused loans for education, housing, or cars, and even get arrested for crimes they didn't commit. Humiliation, anger, and frustration are among the feelings victims experience as they navigate the process of rescuing their identity.

One of the leading forms of identity theft involves credit card frauds. There are two major forms of credit card fraud involving identity theft: account takeovers and application frauds.

Account Takeover An account takeover occurs when a thief acquires someone's existing credit account information and purchases products and services using either the actual credit card, a counterfeit credit card with the same number, or simply the account number and expiration date. Victims learn of account takeovers when they receive their monthly account statement; so a thief may have up to thirty days to use the account before the owner realizes he or she has been victimized.

Application Fraud Application fraud, or what some experts call *true name fraud,* involves a thief using someone's Social Security number or other identifying information to open new accounts in the victim's name. Victims are not likely to learn of application fraud for some time because the monthly account statements are mailed to an address used by the imposter.

The Federal Trade Commission created a list of the various ways identity thieves typically obtain information about their victims, as well as how these thieves use the information once they obtain it. Figure 16.4 lists this information.

identity theft Using another person's personal information without that person's permission to commit fraud or other crimes.

phishing A growing form of attempted identity theft in which consumers are contacted via bogus e-mail messages that try to lure them into providing personal information such as their Social Security number or financial account information.

FIGURE 16.4 How Identity Thefts Work

How identity thieves get your personal information:

- They get information from businesses or other institutions by:
  - stealing records or information while they're on the job
  - bribing an employee who has access to these records
  - hacking these records
  - conning information out of employees
- They may steal your mail, including bank and credit card statements, credit card offers, new checks, and tax information.
- They may rummage through your trash, the trash of businesses, or public trash dumps in a practice known as "dumpster diving."
- They may get your credit reports by abusing their employer's authorized access to them, or by posing as a landlord, employer, or someone else who may have a legal right to access your report.
- They may steal your credit or debit card numbers by capturing the information in a data storage device in a practice known as "skimming." They may swipe your card for an actual purchase, or attach the device to an ATM machine where you may enter or swipe your card.
- They may steal your wallet or purse.
- They may complete a "change of address form" to divert your mail to another location.
- They may steal personal information they find in your home.
- They may steal personal information from you through e-mail or phone by posing as legitimate companies and claiming that you have a problem with your account. This practice is known as *phishing* online, or pretexting by phone.

How identity thieves use your personal information:

- They may call your credit card issuer to change the billing address on your credit card account. The imposter then runs up charges on your account. Because your bills are being sent to a different address, it may be some time before you realize there is a problem.
- They may open new credit card accounts in your name. When they use the credit cards and don't pay the bills, the delinquent accounts are reported on your credit report.
- They may establish phone or wireless service in your name.
- They may open a bank account in your name and write bad checks on that account.
- They may counterfeit checks or credit or debit cards, or authorize electronic transfers in your name, and drain your bank account.
- They may file for bankruptcy under your name to avoid paying debts they've incurred under your name, or to avoid eviction.
- They may buy a car by taking out an auto loan in your name.
- They may get identification such as a driver's license issued with their picture, in your name.
- They may get a job or file fraudulent tax returns in your name.
- They may give your name to the police during an arrest. If they don't show up for their court date, a warrant for arrest is issued in your name.

Source: Federal Trade Commission. 2005. *Take Charge: Fighting Back against Identity Theft.* Washington, DC: U.S. Government Printing Office. Also available online at www.ftc.gov/bcp/conline/pubs/credit/idtheft.htm

In response to the growing problem of identity theft, Congress has enacted the Identity Theft and Assumption Deterrence Act. As a result of this act, identity theft—stealing another person's identity for economic gain—is now a federal crime, punishable with up to twenty-five years in prison if convicted of the offense. This act also provides a means for victims of identity theft to seek restitution for losses and expenditures related to resolving the problems that resulted from the identity theft.

Investigating Fraud

Investigating cases of fraud presents challenges to the criminal investigator. Generally there is no crime scene that can be searched for traces of evidence or indications of the offender's *modus operandi*. Information about the crime must come from the victim and witnesses and from any documents or forms used or created by the person committing the fraud.

Investigating any type of check fraud, for example, requires obtaining full details about all checks written and all transactions involved. The check or checks become the main piece of evidence and should be examined and handled like any piece of evidence that is being sent to the lab. In addition, the names of all bank employees involved in the transaction should be obtained. Interviews with bank personnel may provide a description of the bad check passer, an address from the identification he or she used, an indication of whether he or she had a vehicle, and a description of the vehicle, if any.

For any crime of fraud, investigators should obtain the following information:

- Description of the offense
- Description of the victim
- Description of the suspect
- Documentary and physical evidence
- *Corpus delicti* of the offense

RECEIVING STOLEN PROPERTY

From television and movie police dramas, most people have heard the expression "possession of stolen property" used to describe a criminal offense. More accurately, the crime referred to by that phrase should be "receiving or concealing stolen property." Although statutes vary across the nation, they rarely, if ever, classify mere possession of stolen property as a crime. The reason for this is quite simple. Possession is a fairly weak act and is difficult to justify as a crime in the absence of *mens rea,* or criminal intent. On the other hand, the phrase "receiving and concealing" carries with it the inference that one had possession of stolen property with knowledge that it was stolen. Receiving and concealing further implies that there may have been intentional and overt attempts to prevent discovery of the stolen property. These two elements—(1) receiving, buying, or concealing stolen or illegally obtained goods and (2) knowing the goods to be stolen or illegally obtained—constitute the offense of receiving stolen goods.

Fence is the popular name for a go-between who knowingly receives and disposes of stolen property. A fence buys stolen goods from a thief and sells them to others for a profit. Naturally, the amount of money the fence pays the thief is substantially less than the value of the item, and less than he or she expects to resell the item for (Warr, Blumstein & Farrington, 2002).

A fencing operation may be small and simple or large and complex. It may consist of one person who buys stolen property from thieves and sells it from the trunk of his or her car. Or it may be a network of fine art and antique dealers communicating by computer networks. In some cases, a thief works with a fence almost on a consignment basis. In other words, the fence may already have a buyer for a specific item and may arrange for a thief to steal the item. A prearranged price may even be set between fence and thief. In other cases, the thief simply brings anything he or she steals to the fence, hoping a purchase price can be arranged.

Periodically, police agencies establish fencing **sting operations.** Police officers set up a location, such as a store or small warehouse, and go into business as fences. When they have obtained enough evidence on a number of thieves, they obtain arrest warrants and capture the felons. Fencing sting operations often recover a wide variety of products and merchandise, including televisions, radios, credit cards, guns, computers, payroll checks, and savings bonds.

The role of the fence should not be underestimated. The fence is a crucial element in larceny. Without fences and other receivers and concealers of stolen goods, thefts and various larcenies would not be profitable to the perpetrators. The objective in most thefts of merchandise is not the item itself; rather, it is the money that can be obtained for the item.

sting operation An undercover operation set up by law enforcement personnel to catch, or "sting," offenders committing a crime; often used to collect evidence against thieves.

Investigating Fences and Other Receivers of Stolen Property

Investigators should maintain contact with the local business community. They should periodically speak to business groups and remind those in attendance to be careful when a supplier offers too good a deal. When investigating possible fences, criminal investigators should pursue the following investigative activities:

- Establish proof that the property was stolen.
- Determine when the property was received by the accused.
- Review records concerning the method of payment, the amount, place of payment, receipts, and so forth.
- Establish the circumstances of the receipt of the property: from whom, to whom, and when the property was exchanged.
- Identify where the property was found, and find out if and how it was concealed.
- Gather evidence that the accused knew the property was stolen.
- Obtain a description of the property, an estimate of its value, and the name and address of the owner.
- Obtain the identity of the person from whom the fence purchased the property.
- Determine the purchase price.
- Gather evidence of hiding, concealing, or destroying identification marks.
- Establish the failure to maintain proper records.
- Observe the conduct of the accused and any statements made when informed that the property was stolen.

Ways of Preventing Fencing

It has been long established that one way to inhibit fencing is to place identification numbers on products. Not only does this inhibit fences, it also reduces the kinds of items a burglar or thief is likely to steal. When individuals or businesses cannot positively identify their stolen merchandise, it becomes all the more difficult for prosecutors to obtain a conviction of a fence or a thief.

Many manufacturers do make the effort to stencil or stamp identification numbers on their products. However, these precautions are to no avail if the consumer fails to record or register these numbers. Many local police agencies sponsor identification programs. These frequently involve lending an electric etching device to members of the community so that they can etch an identification number on their home appliances, televisions, stereos, and so on. These numbers can be registered with the police and can be used to identify items should they be stolen.

. . . .

SUMMARY

Learning Objective 1

Larceny-theft is one of eight crimes that the FBI considers the most serious crimes in American society, and it reports yearly statistics on larceny-theft in the Uniform Crime Reports. In 2004, larceny-theft made up almost 67.3 percent of the nation's property crimes.

Learning Objective 2

State statutes define what constitutes the crime of larceny-theft in each state. Generally, these statutes have the following elements in common: larceny-theft consists of (1) the taking and (2) carrying away (3) of personal property (4) of another (5) with the specific intent of permanently depriving the owner of his or her property. States may have degrees of larceny, such as *grand larceny* (sometimes called *grand theft*) and *petty larceny* (sometimes called *petty theft*). The definitions and penalties for these offenses vary among the states.

Learning Objective 3

The most common types of larceny-theft offenses include thefts from motor vehicles, shoplifting, thefts from buildings, thefts of motor vehicle accessories, thefts from coin-operated machines, purse snatching, and pocket-picking. Most larceny-theft cases are solved through experience—working many cases—and by a basic understanding of the motivation for the offenses and of the techniques that both amateurs and professionals often use.

Learning Objective 4

Fraud is depriving someone of his or her property by using misrepresentation, trickery, or deception. It is related to larceny-theft because it is larceny or theft by deception. Fraud can take many forms, including but not limited to the following: credit card fraud, check fraud, confidence games, insurance fraud, consumer and business fraud, and telemarketing and mail fraud.

Learning Objective 5

In most states, receiving, buying, or concealing stolen or illegally obtained goods and knowing the goods to be stolen or illegally obtained constitutes the offense of receiving stolen goods or property. *Fence* is the popular term for a go-between who knowingly receives and disposes of stolen goods. Without fences and other receivers of stolen goods, larceny-theft would not be profitable to perpetrators.

Learning Objective 6

Identity theft is among the fastest growing crimes in the United States today. It is estimated that one in every twenty Americans has fallen victim to identity theft. People whose identities have been stolen can spend months or years and thousands of dollars attempting to clarify the situation and cleaning up the mess the thieves have made of their good name and credit record. The Identity Theft and Assumption Deterrence Act has made stealing another person's identity for economic gain a federal crime, punishable with up to twenty-five years in prison.

KEY TERMS

theft 320

larceny-theft 321

grand larceny 321

petty larceny 321

shoplifting 323

employee pilfering 323

booster device 323

fence 324

fraud 325

hang paper 327

shill 333

identity theft 338

phishing 338

sting operation 341

QUESTIONS FOR REVIEW

Learning Objective 1

1. What is the significance of larceny-theft among the crime index offenses?

Learning Objective 2

2. Define *larceny-theft.*

3. Distinguish between *theft* and *larceny.*

Learning Objective 3

4. What are four *pickpocket* techniques?

5. Why do some jurisdictions classify purse snatching as robbery rather than larceny?

6. Why do crowded places attract pickpockets?

7. Why should officers be alert to people sitting next to other people who have fallen asleep?

8. What kinds of things should an investigator look for when attempting to apprehend pickpockets?

9. What is a *booster device?*

10. What are some differences between a professional shoplifter and an amateur?

11. What are some investigative techniques for detecting potential shoplifters?

Learning Objective 4

12. What are three basic elements of *fraud?*

13. Explain what is involved in a *pigeon drop.*

14. How does a *bank examiner scam* work?

Learning Objective 5

15. Why is it difficult to prove a criminal case for possession of stolen goods alone?

16. What is meant by the term *fence?*

Learning Objective 6

17. What is meant by *identity theft?*

18. What are some of the ways identity thieves use stolen personal information?

CRITICAL THINKING EXERCISE

Divide into three groups. Then, as assigned by your instructor, complete one of the following projects.

1. Research newspapers and magazines to locate published accounts from recent years that describe at least three of the types of fraud discussed in the chapter. Assemble and organize the facts of each case according to the five categories listed in the section titled Investigating Fraud. Present the cases to the class, informing them how the frauds were perpetrated, investigated, and prosecuted.

2. Contact at least two supermarkets and two department stores to determine their procedures for handling bad checks received from customers. Ascertain if and when the stores involve police, collection agencies, or other organizations. Assemble the information into an oral report to the class on the scope of the problem of check fraud in your community.

3. Contact friends, family members, and classmates, or rely on your own experiences to gather three to five personal accounts of telephone or mail solicitations for an awarded prize or other telemarketing fraud. Ascertain the come-ons and what the awardees had to do to gain the prize. Determine if anyone paid a required handling fee or delivery charge for such an award and what the results were. Assemble the completed stories and present them to the class. Discuss what courses of action persons can take when they receive such solicitations.

INVESTIGATIVE SKILL BUILDERS

Servicing Clients and Customers

You arrive at the scene of a disturbance inside a specialty store that sells televisions, radios, and other electronic items. As you walk in, you can hear a man's voice shouting, "Fraud! Crook! You're a swindler." The proprietor at the counter tells you he wants the customer to leave, but he will not. The customer is a man in his seventies who is disgruntled about a clock radio he purchased from the store. The man shouts, "The damn clock won't work. It doesn't do half the things the salesman told me it would do. I want my money back."

The proprietor tells you that the man does not have his receipt and that there are no cash refunds without a receipt. The proprietor points to a sign behind the counter that reads, "No cash refunds without a valid receipt." The customer is visibly upset. He tells you that he has never had any sort of problem like this when dealing with one of the large department stores. He tells you, "That man behind the counter sold me this clock just two days ago, and he knows it." You ask the proprietor if that is true. He tells you that he does remember selling the clock to the man but that rules are rules, and he will not take the clock back. As a police officer, what actions, if any, should you take?

Integrity/Honesty

You are a veteran police officer. Your 15-year-old daughter comes home and tells you that she has just gotten a great job that pays $9 an hour. You ask what she is doing, and she tells you that she is making telephone calls to people to inform them that they have been given prize awards. You are confused by her response and, after some additional questions, learn that she is working in a boiler-room-style telephone bank for what sounds like a telemarketing scam.

Her job is to call people and inform them that they have been selected to receive a special vacation trip to Hawaii. It is an all-expenses-paid trip, including airfare and hotel accommodations. All the person has to do is send in a refundable $300 deposit to hold the spot. You call a friend on the bunco unit of your department and learn that there are several complaints against this company concerning not refunding the deposits and that an undercover investigation is under way.

1. Do you volunteer your daughter's services to assist in the undercover operation?
2. Do you mention to your friend that your daughter is working for this suspected fraudulent telemarketer?
3. Do you allow your daughter to continue working for the company or risk blowing the undercover operation by forbidding her to do so?

17

Motor Vehicle Theft

After completing this chapter, you will be able to:

1   Provide an overview of the crime of motor vehicle theft in the United States.
2   List some of the common types of motor vehicle theft.
3   Explain the legal aspects of the crime of motor vehicle theft.
4   Discuss some useful techniques for motor vehicle theft investigators.
5   Describe motor vehicle thefts other than automobile theft.
6   Specify certain activities intended to prevent motor vehicle theft.

THE NATURE OF MOTOR VEHICLE THEFT

Thefts *from* motor vehicles are included under larceny-theft in the official crime data of the FBI (see Chapter 16). **Motor vehicle theft** is a separate category of serious property crime and is itself one of the eight index offenses. The Uniform Crime Report defines it as "the theft or attempted theft of a motor vehicle." Included in this category are thefts of automobiles, trucks, buses, motorcycles, construction and farm machinery, aircraft, and recreational vehicles such as boats and snowmobiles. The number of motor vehicle thefts was estimated at 1,237,114 in 2004. This figure is approximately the same as motor vehicle thefts in 2005 (FBI, 2005, 2006). Based on law enforcement agency reports, the UCR estimated the combined value of motor vehicles stolen nationwide in 2004 at approximately $7.6 billion, and law enforcement agencies in the United States, collectively, cleared 13 percent of motor vehicle theft offenses (FBI, 2005).

motor vehicle theft The theft or attempted theft of any type of motorized vehicle.

Automobile theft has traditionally been considered a problem for larger American cities. However, the theft of and from automobiles is a significant problem in most cities, regardless of size. According to a National Insurance Crime Bureau (NICB) study released in May 2006, six of the top ten U.S. metropolitan areas for vehicle theft in 2005 were in California (Figure 17.1).

The NICB also reported that the 1995 Honda Civic was the most stolen vehicle in 2004. Motor vehicle thieves continue to target imports over domestic brands. Many vehicles on the top ten list (Figure 17.2) are ten to seventeen model years old. These cars have been consistent top sellers for many years, and some of their parts are interchangeable. Thieves dismantle them for their components. The NICB compiles its list using National Crime Information Center data, which is based on police reports.

The Certified Collateral Corporation (CCC) bases its report on insurance claims, counting total losses (stolen and not recovered or declared a complete loss by insurance companies) of each particular model from more than 350 property/casualty insurers in North America and calculating the theft rate based on registrations. According to CCC Information Services, the 2001 BMW M Roadster was the most frequently stolen vehicle in 2005. Figure 17.3 lists of the top twenty-five kinds of vehicle stolen during 2005.

Methods used to steal cars and frauds connected with stolen and missing cars have become increasingly diverse and complex. Cars have been stolen from every conceivable place: homes, shopping malls, main streets, side streets, parking lots and garages, and even right off the sales floors of dealerships. These thefts cost owners time and money.

FIGURE 17.1 Motor Vehicle Thefts: Top Ten U.S. Metropolitan Areas, 2005

Rank	Metropolitan Statistical Area	Vehicles Stolen	Rate[1]
1	Modesto, CA	7,071	1,418.80
2	Las Vegas/Paradise, NV	22,465	1,360.90
3	Stockton, CA	7,586	1,167.30
4	Phoenix/Mesa/Scottsdale, AZ	41,000	1,103.50
5	Visalia/Porterville, CA	4,257	1,060.20
6	Seattle/Tacoma/Bellevue, WA	33,494	1,057.60
7	Sacramento/Arden-Arcade/Roseville, CA	20,268	1,005.00
8	San Diego/Carlsbad/San Marcos, CA	28,845	983.90
9	Fresno, CA	8,478	978.11
10	Yakima, WA	2,212	965.54

[1]Ranked by the rate of vehicle thefts reported per 100,000 people, based on the 2000 Census.
Source: National Insurance Crime Bureau (2006).

FIGURE 17.2 Most Frequently Stolen Passenger Vehicles, 2004

Rank	Year	Make	Model
1	1995	Honda	Civic
2	1989	Toyota	Camry
3	1991	Honda	Accord
4	1994	Dodge	Caravan
5	1994	Chevrolet	Full Size C/K 1500 Pickup
6	1997	Ford	F150 Series
7	2003	Dodge	Ram Pickup
8	1990	Acura	Integra
9	1988	Toyota	Pickup
10	1991	Nissan	Sentra

Source: National Insurance Crime Bureau (2006).

FIGURE 17.3 Most Frequently Stolen Passenger Vehicles, 2005

Rank	Year	Make	Model
1	2001	BMW	M Roadster
2	1998	Acura	Integra
3	2004	Mercury	Marauder
4	1999	Acura	Integra
5	1995	Acura	Integra
6	2002	Audi	S4
7	1996	Acura	Integra
8	1997	Acura	Integra
9	2001	Acura	Integra
10	2000	Jaguar	XJR
11	1994	Acura	Integra
12	2005	Suzuki	Aerio
13	2004	Suzuki	Aerio
14	1998	Land Rover	Range Rover
15	1998	Jaguar	XJR
16	2003	Mercury	Marauder
17	2000	Acura	Integra
18	2002	Cadillac	Escalade
19	2000	Audi	A8
20	2000	Audi	S4
21	1993	Mercedes-Benz	600
22	1995	Land Rover	Range Rover
23	2005	Cadillac	Escalade
24	2000	Honda	Civic
25	2001	Audi	S4

Source: CCC Information Services, Inc. (2006).

They also cost the U.S. automobile insurance industry huge sums of money and numbers of personnel hours each year.

TYPES OF MOTOR VEHICLE THEFT

Motor vehicle thefts are generally classified by the thief's motive for stealing a vehicle. There are numerous motives for stealing vehicles. For the most part, though, these motives may be divided into five major categories: joyriding; transportation; to commit another crime; fraud; and stripping, chopping, and resale.

Joyriding

Teenagers who steal a car simply to drive around and then abandon it account for most **joyriding.** According to the UCR, nationwide juveniles were responsible for 16.4 percent of all cleared motor vehicle thefts in 2004 (FBI 2005). Joyriders sometimes work alone, sometimes in small groups. According to teens, their basic motives include getting a free ride, having fun and excitement racing down streets as sport, impressing peers or completing a gang initiation, relieving boredom, and getting a rush. Youthful thieves keep a vehicle for a relatively short time and generally abandon it once it runs out of gas, is immobilized in a wreck, or when they tire of the ride (Carpenter, Glassner, Johnson, & Loughlin, 1988; Garabedian & Gibbons, 2005; Glassner, Berg, Ksander, & Johnson, 1988). Joyriding typically is not done out of malice but simply for something to do (Sanders, 2005). Joyriders look for easy targets, such as vehicles in which the owner has left keys in the ignition or in a magnetic key box in the wheel well. Because joyriding is a crime of opportunity, it often occurs where juveniles congregate. Several vehicle thefts near such a location may establish a pattern and provide important clues to investigators. In some states, joyriding is a separate offense from motor vehicle theft. A good investigator should know the law in his or her jurisdiction.

> **joyriding** The temporary taking of a motor vehicle without the intent of permanently depriving the owner of the vehicle; generally undertaken by juveniles.

Transportation

Hitchhikers, transients, and runaways who steal cars for transportation are sometimes lumped together with joyriders. There are, however, several distinguishing characteristics. First, the objective of a theft for transportation is usually a specific ride from one point to another, not aimlessly driving around for the fun of it. Furthermore, offenders who steal cars for transportation are generally older than joyriders. Finally, a vehicle stolen for transportation is usually kept longer and driven farther before being abandoned than a car taken for a joyride.

To Commit Another Crime

Some offenders steal a car to use as transportation when committing another crime. The robbery of a bank, an armored car, or a supermarket almost always involves the use of a getaway car that has been stolen. Sometimes one stolen car is driven to a second one, or to a legally owned car, to make it more difficult for the police to find the thieves. Other crimes that commonly include the use of a stolen vehicle include kidnapping, burglary, assassination, and murder for hire (Maxfield & Clarke, 2004).

A stolen vehicle used to commit a crime is nearly 200 times more likely to end up in a crash than one driven by a noncriminal. This accident probability is so high for several reasons. First, being chased at high speeds increases the likelihood of an accident. Second, the criminal may be unfamiliar with the roads and road conditions. And third, the driver of the stolen vehicle may be unfamiliar with its operation or unable to handle it under various conditions.

The obvious reason a criminal uses a stolen vehicle to commit another crime is to avoid being detected and identified by witnesses or the police. The criminal is likely to steal the vehicle just before committing the other crime. Doing so provides a short period during which the theft has not been discovered and the vehicle has not been reported as stolen. In some cases, license plates stolen from one vehicle are transferred to another stolen car. With these techniques, the thief hopes to prolong the time before the police can identify the vehicle he or she is driving as stolen.

Fraud

Some fraudulent thefts are actually perpetrated by the owner of the vehicle or someone acting on behalf of the owner. In some cases, an owner or someone acting as the owner's agent drives the vehicle far from the owner's home and burns it or dumps it in a lake or ravine. The owner then files a claim for the "stolen vehicle" with his or her insurer. Sometimes an owner drives the vehicle to an area of town known for gangs of strippers, who dismantle and sell parts of cars. After waiting a short time, the owner reports that the car has been stolen. When the police finally locate it—if they do—it is likely to be a skeleton of a car, stripped of anything of value. The reason for these fraudulent thefts is usually to acquire money from the insurance company or to obtain a replacement vehicle (Maxfield & Clarke, 2004).

Another fraud commonly associated with automobile thefts is the *VIN clone* or **salvage switch.** In this crime, the criminal acquires title to a late model car by legitimate means. For example, he or she may buy a wreck at a junkyard for a couple of hundred dollars. The offender then disposes of the wreck as salvage or scrap metal but retains the license plates, registration, title, and various engine and chassis identification number plates. Next, the criminal finds and steals a vehicle of the same make and model as the wreck and replaces the various identification numbers and license plates on the stolen car with those retained from the salvaged wreck. The thief now appears to have all the correct identification plates and ownership documents for the stolen car, which he or she will sell to an unsuspecting buyer.

With the increase in Internet auctions, many people have begun to purchase their family vehicles through such sites. The vast majority of online car deals go through without a hitch, but a number of scams have specifically targeted Internet auto shoppers. Many of the con artists work their deception from Eastern Bloc countries or African countries such as Nigeria.

The scam begins with an individual bidding on a reputable auction website such as Yahoo.com Auto Auction or e-Bay Auto Auction. After a period of time has elapsed, the would-be car buyer receives an e-mail identifying the buyer as the highest bidder and stating that the vehicle is his or hers. However, if the victim checks (which frequently is not done), the buyer is likely to notice that his or her name is not indicated as the highest bidder on the auction website. The con artist has merely captured the victim's e-mail address and contacted him or her directly about a car that actually existed (as shown on the auction website) but was being sold by an unsuspecting third party to an actual high bidder.

Typically, an escrow account is used when buying a car online. This provides an impartial middleman—an agency that holds the money securely until the vehicle is shipped to the new owner. However, con men use escrow sites with legitimate-sounding names, such as "safe-purchases.com," which are really bank accounts controlled by the criminals. Once the funds are transferred into this so-called escrow account, the money is withdrawn, the account closed, and for all intents and purposes the paper trail is erased.

There are several other common vehicle frauds:

- **Airbag fraud.** After an accident, the airbag is intentionally replaced with a nonoperational, fake or defective bag without the car owner knowing it. One out of every twenty-five previously deployed airbags is replaced with either a dummy or a nonworking airbag unit, costing insurance companies and consumers an average of $50 million a year.

salvage switch Switching vehicle identification number plates from wrecked vehicles to stolen cars of the same make and model.

- **Odometer rollbacks.** Unscrupulous individuals in private sales and dishonest used car dealers illegally turn back the odometer on a car with high mileage, making it appear that the car has low mileage. Each case of odometer fraud costs consumers more than $2,300. Digital odometers are rolled back in a matter of seconds by equipment that can be purchased over the Internet.

- **VIN cloning or salvage switching.** By taking the VIN plate from a junked vehicle the thief has legally purchased and attaching it to a stolen vehicle of the same make, color, and model, a car thief is able to make the stolen vehicle appear legal (he or she will have a legal title for the VIN plate. More than 1.5 million vehicles are stolen in the United States each year. Of these, 225,000 have their vehicle identification numbers switched to conceal their identity and are sold to unknowing consumers.

- **Curbstoning.** Sales of used cars by an individual fall under different legal rulings than those sold by a licensed dealer. An estimated 60 to 90 percent of vehicles sold in classified ads, or at the curb, are sold by unlicensed dealers posing as private sellers.

Stripping, Chopping, and Resale

Stripping, chopping, and reselling stolen cars have one commonality: all are techniques professional thieves use to profit from the theft of a vehicle.

Stripping Some vehicles are stolen for the purpose of **stripping** them of valuable parts and accessories for resale or for sale to wrecking yards, used car lots, and auto repair shops. Tires, wheel covers, transmissions, motors, wheels, airbags, radios, CB radios, CD players, and even car telephones are attractive to thieves because they

stripping Illegally removing parts and accessories from motor vehicles to use or sell them.

Some owners burn their cars or arrange to have someone burn them to fraudulently collect payments from their auto insurers.

generally do not have any identifying numbers and thus are easy to dispose of. In some cases, the thief hunts for a particular make and model of vehicle. If the keys are in the car, it is quickly driven away. If not, the ignition wires are short-circuited to start the engine. In some cases, thieves boldly drive up with a tow truck, hook up the target vehicle, and drive away with it in tow. Once mobile, the stolen vehicle is taken to a secluded area or a garage and stripped of all desirable parts. When the thieves are finished with the carcass, the chassis and unwanted parts are abandoned.

chop shop A place for chopping, or dismantling, stolen motor vehicles into parts and accessories that cannot be easily identified, which are then resold.

chopping The dismantling of stolen motor vehicles into parts and accessories for use or sale.

Chopping A **chop shop** is a place where stolen vehicles are taken for **chopping** or dismantling into parts or accessories that cannot be easily identified, which are resold to repair shops or private citizens. Chop shops often operate out of auto repair shops or wrecking yards that appear to be legitimate businesses: Stolen vehicles can be quickly chopped, or cut up with torches, and the parts stored without likely detection. As Figures 17.2 and 17.3 illustrate, it is not always brand new vehicles that are stolen. Older models whose parts are interchangeable are gold mines for criminals to chop or strip and sell. Although stripping gangs and chop shops are similar, there are several distinctions. For example, chop shops can remove identifying numbers from the motor and other similarly identified items in the car. Furthermore, they frequently handle a greater volume of stolen cars because those that have not yet been chopped can be concealed on the premises. Finally, because the front business is often a repair or salvage yard, parts can quickly become inventory. In some cases, chop shops take special orders and direct a thief to acquire a particular make and model of car to obtain a certain vehicle part.

Resale Rather than steal a vehicle for stripping or chopping, some professional thieves steal cars to resell them. In some cases, car thieves actually steal a specific type of car on request from a would-be customer. Others specialize in stealing only certain types of cars. Like other car thieves, they may take a car whose owner has neglectfully left the key in the ignition or clipped to the visor. Alternatively, a resale thief may enter a used car dealership, pose as a potential buyer, and arrange to test drive a vehicle. Once the thief leaves the lot, he or she does not return with the auto. Similarly, this sort of thief may answer an unsuspecting car seller's ad in the newspaper. As with the car dealer, the thief arranges to test drive the car and simply never returns it. Cars may also be stolen by transacting a sale with a bad check.

Few vehicles stolen by professional resale thieves are ever recovered. These thieves are specialists, capable of obtaining not only cars but false or forged papers for these stolen vehicles. The resale thief may repaint, recover seats, repair any body damage, and match identification numbers to false documents before selling the car to an individual, to a dealer, or at a public auction.

Vehicles manufactured in the United States are very popular in other countries. Mexico and several South and Central American countries regularly receive stolen and altered U.S. vehicles for resale. Many Hondas and Toyotas are stolen because thieves have found they can file key blanks to fit a number of locks on different 1990s models of those brands, making it possible to unlock the cars and drive them away (Bishop, 2006). Furthering the potential of exporting stolen vehicles for resale is the fact that other countries have few effective controls over vehicles crossing their borders. This form of stolen vehicle liquidation has become so popular that in some Caribbean countries as many as 20 percent of all vehicles on the roads were stolen and shipped from the United States (Beckman & Daly, 1990).

FYI A stolen American vehicle often nets double its original price overseas. There, the theft is often erroneously seen as a victimless crime because American cars are usually covered by insurance.

LEGAL ASPECTS OF THE CRIME OF MOTOR VEHICLE THEFT

Motor vehicle theft is a form of larceny because it is the taking and driving away of a motor vehicle from the owner or possessor with the intent of permanently depriving him or her of it. The law of motor vehicle theft is not well developed. This situation exists despite the importance of motor vehicles in modern society and the large losses suffered each year due to stolen vehicles.

Prosecution for motor vehicle theft varies among the states. In some states, thieves are charged with "grand theft auto." In others, they are prosecuted for "unauthorized use of a motor vehicle" rather than for motor vehicle theft. To combat motor vehicle theft, states have enacted a variety of laws that require stiffer penalties for motor-vehicle-related crimes. For example, in some states persons who commit the crimes of robbery, burglary, aggravated or sexual assault, eluding police, kidnapping, or manslaughter with a stolen car face longer prison terms than those specified for any of those crimes committed without using a stolen car. In other states juveniles face mandatory penalties for the first offense in a motor-vehicle-related crime, such as joyriding.

INVESTIGATING MOTOR VEHICLE THEFT

Once the police receive notification of a vehicle theft, they respond to the complainant, obtain all pertinent information, and write a formal report (see Chapter 9). It is the investigating officer's job to verify all the information obtained about the theft. The investigating officer must also verify that a theft has taken place. In some cases a report of a stolen automobile will turn out to be nothing more than the owner's misplacing it in a large shopping mall parking lot or garage. In other cases, what starts as a stolen car report may later turn out to be the unauthorized use of the vehicle by a family member. In still other stolen vehicle cases, investigators may determine that the car has been lawfully repossessed because the owner fell behind on payments. Cars are also reported stolen when they have been involved in hit-and-run accidents or other crimes (Beckman & Daly, 1990).

Having accurate information in the theft report does not ensure that the vehicle will be recovered. However, having inaccurate information increases the likelihood that it will not be recovered. You should not take for granted that the person reporting the theft knows the correct license plate number and vehicle identification number (VIN). Check the registration to ensure accuracy. Completeness and accuracy in reporting theft data are essential both to the investigation and to the protection of fellow officers in the field who will be looking for the stolen car. The responding officer should give the dispatcher the following information about the stolen vehicle:

- Make and model of the vehicle
- Year of the vehicle
- Color or colors of the vehicle
- Name, address, and telephone number of the owner

- License plate number and state that issued it
- Vehicle identification number (VIN)
- Location and time of the theft
- Any distinctive characteristics, special equipment, or damage

Answers to the following questions are also useful in a motor vehicle theft investigation:

- Who was the last person to use the vehicle? If not the owner, what was that person's relationship to the owner?
- Were keys left in the ignition or concealed in a location outside the vehicle?
- Had the vehicle been left unlocked?
- Had the vehicle been left with windows up or down?
- Has the owner kept up with payments on the vehicle?
- Is the owner in financial difficulty?
- Were there any items of merchandise or equipment or any valuables in the cabin, glove box, or trunk?
- Was the registration, insurance card, or owner's title in the vehicle?

When investigating stolen vehicles, it is important to remember that the market for stolen cars changes to meet demand. It is not always the most expensive or best-looking cars that are stolen. Nor do thieves choose autos to steal for the ease or difficulty of taking them. Thefts are based on the ease of selling the stolen vehicles or their parts. As a car gets older, demand for its parts grows, especially if there are large numbers of that model of vehicle on the road. Figure 17.4 lists the top twenty-five types of vehicles stolen in 2004 and 2005. Seven of the top ten cars stolen in 2004 were also in the top ten in 2005 (and number eleven in 2004 moved up to number nine in the 2005 listing).

Identifying a Stolen Vehicle

Even when a vehicle that matches the make, model, year, and color of a stolen vehicle has been recovered, it may not be the stolen vehicle. To ensure that the right vehicle has been found, the investigator relies on identification numbers affixed to or inscribed on various parts of the car. The most important of these is the **vehicle identification number (VIN).** The VIN is the primary nonduplicated, serialized number assigned by the manufacturer to each vehicle made. This number specifically identifies the motor vehicle.

American automobile manufacturers first began using VINs as the primary means of identifying a vehicle in 1954. Unfortunately, VINs were not uniformly positioned in vehicles. Nor, for that matter, was there a consistent way of attaching the metal plate containing the VIN to the vehicle. The VIN plate might be in the glove box on some models, on the dashboard on others, and even on a doorpost on other models. Similarly, it might be attached by spot welding, screws, rivets, or some sort of plastic fasteners. Because of these inconsistencies, removing or altering a VIN plate was not difficult.

In 1968 VIN plates on all domestic vehicles and most imports began to be uniformly placed on the left side (driver's side) of the dashboard. In this position, the VIN is clearly visible through the windshield of the car. In 1981 the auto industry adopted a standardized seventeen-character VIN for all automobiles manufactured or

vehicle identification number (VIN) A non-duplicated, serialized number assigned by a motor vehicle manufacturer (of autos especially) to each vehicle made.

FIGURE 17.4 Comparison of Top Twenty-Five Vehicles Stolen in 2004 and 2005

	Stolen in 2004				Stolen in 2005		
Rank	Year	Make	Model	Rank	Year	Make	Model
1	1999	Acura	Integra	1	2001	BMW	M Roadster
2	2002	BMW	M Roadster	2	1998	Acura	Integra
3	1998	Acura	Integra	3	2004	Mercury	Marauder
4	1991	GMC	V2500	4	1999	Acura	Integra
5	2002	Audi	S4	5	1995	Acura	Integra
6	1996	Acura	Integra	6	2002	Audi	S4
7	1995	Acura	Integra	7	1996	Acura	Integra
8	2004	Mercury	Marauder	8	1997	Acura	Integra
9	1997	Acura	Integra	9	2001	Acura	Integra
10	1992	Mercedes-Benz	600	10	2000	Jaguar	XJR
11	2001	Acura	Integra	11	1994	Acura	Integra
12	1989	Chevrolet	R25	12	2005	Suzuki	Aerio
13	1993	Cadillac	Fleetwood	13	2004	Suzuki	Aerio
14	1994	Acura	Integra	14	1998	Land Rover	Range Rover
15	1996	Lexus	GS	15	1998	Jaguar	XJR
16	2000	Acura	Integra	16	2003	Mercury	Marauder
17	1999	Mercedes-Benz	CL	17	2000	Acura	Integra
18	1996	Lexus	SC	18	2002	Cadillac	Escalade
19	2004	Cadillac	Escalade	19	2000	Audi	A8
20	1996	BMW	750	20	2000	Audi	S4
21	1998	Land Rover	Range Rover	21	1993	Mercedes-Benz	600
22	1994	Audi	Cabriolet	22	1995	Land Rover	Range Rover
23	2001	BMW	M Roadster	23	2005	Cadillac	Escalade
24	2003	Cadillac	Escalade	24	2000	Honda	Civic
25	2000	Honda	Civic	25	2001	Audi	S4

Source: CCC Information Services, Inc. (2006).

sold in the United States. Before this standardization, VINs varied from eleven to thirteen characters. The first ten characters of the standardized VIN identify the country of origin, manufacturer, make, restraint system, model, body style, engine type, year, and assembly plant. The eleventh is a mathematically computed check digit to verify all of the other characters in the VIN. The last six characters are the sequential production number of the vehicle. Contemporary VIN characters represent auto characteristics as follows:

Character Number	Identifies
1	Country in which the vehicle was manufactured
2	Manufacturer
3	Vehicle type or manufacturing division
4–8	Vehicle features such as body style, engine type, model, and series
9	VIN accuracy as check digit
10	Model year
11	Assembly plant for the vehicle
12–17	Sequence of the vehicle for production as it rolled off the manufacturer's assembly line

A VIN plate contains a seventeen-digit number assigned by the vehicle manufacturer and is generally located on the driver's side of the dashboard.

In 1984 the federal government enacted the Motor Vehicle Theft Law Enforcement Act. The law is an effort to thwart stripping, chopping, and resale of stolen vehicles. It requires manufacturers to put additional identification numbers on up to fourteen major automobile parts on certain lines of autos. The parts requiring additional identification are those generally sought by chop shops: engines, transmissions, all doors, hoods, bumpers, front fenders, trunk lids, rear quarter panels, and deck lids, tailgates, or hatchbacks (if present). The car lines requiring additional identification numbers are those designated as high-theft lines. The numbers match the seventeen-character VIN used on the vehicle and must be inscribed on the part or printed on an attached label. The labels must be attached in such a manner that their removal will create significant damage to the part or leave a visible trace of the label. The law carries a fine of $10,000 or five years' imprisonment or both for removal, intentional destruction, or tampering with an identification number on a vehicle or vehicle part.

When verifying a suspected stolen automobile's VIN, and investigator should look for signs indicating that the metal plate has been changed or disturbed. It is virtually impossible to remove the VIN plate and attach it to another vehicle without leaving some telltale sign. One should make sure that the plate is affixed firmly to the vehicle. An authentic VIN plate should fit snugly in place.

Recognizing a Stolen Vehicle

With experience on the street, an investigator develops an instinct or sixth sense about stolen cars. There are no foolproof means of recognizing a stolen vehicle, however, a number of visible and compelling signs should make an officer suspicious about a vehicle (Hawkins, 1984):

- New license on an old vehicle or an old license on a new one
- Missing plates from either the front or the rear of the vehicle
- Mismatched plates (in jurisdictions where front and rear plates are required)
- Commercial plates on a passenger car or noncommercial plates on a truck
- Misaligned numerals or letters on the license plate
- Broken or missing glass in windows
- Damage to doors or trunks near locks
- Punched-out locks
- Vehicles operated without lights at night
- Vehicles standing at the side of the road with missing parts
- Vehicles standing at the side of a road with doors left open
- Vehicles with what appear to be bullet holes in the glass or body
- Vehicles parked with the engines left running
- Vehicles abandoned on streets or in parking lots for several days

In addition to these visible indicators of a possible stolen car, some observable driver behaviors or characteristics should make an officer suspicious (Hawkins, 1984):

- Appearing nervous or perspiring on a cool day or evening
- Making repeated attempts to move away from the police cruiser

- Driving in an erratic way (making many lane changes, speeding and slowing up, and so forth)
- Leaving a service station without paying
- Driving in a reckless or overtly careless way
- Refusing to stop for minor traffic infractions
- Being young (perhaps appearing under the legal driving age for the jurisdiction)

If a police officer stops a car that he or she suspects has been stolen, the officer should be cautiously observant in questioning the driver and any occupants of the car. Consider whether the driver is being too polite or cooperative and observe any other occupants for nervous or evasive behavior. The officer should observe whether the driver knows where various documents are or needs to search for them—if they can be produced at all. If the driver's license and car registration are produced, these documents should be examined carefully. Have there been any alterations? Can the driver answer questions about his or her age, address, or weight correctly? Are answers given without hesitation? Are there any discrepancies, such as a difference between the address on the driver's license and that on the registration? Was the driver's license issued by the same state as the car's license plate? Finally, the officer should have the driver sign his or her name and compare the sample signature with the signature on the license. If the officer sees any tools in the car that might be used to break into or start a car, the driver should be asked to produce the car's keys.

Vehicles with nonmatching front and rear license plates or plates that have obviously been altered are common indicators of a stolen vehicle.

Thieves gain entry to and start vehicles using a number of different methods. Becoming familiar with these techniques will help an investigator recognize potential or actual thieves by observing certain behaviors or seeing car theft tools. Joyriding teens look for an easy target—an unlocked car, keys dangling from an ignition, or a spare key in a magnetic box attached to the inside of a wheel well. Youths looking for a ride may feel around the wheel wells of cars parked on the street or in a lot until they find such a spare key. If the objective is stripping or chopping the vehicle, thieves in a tow truck may simply whisk the vehicle away.

Like joyriders, strippers, choppers, and resellers appreciate an easy target but resort to a variety of tools when forced entry is necessary. Some thieves make a crude entry by using a screwdriver, a prybar, or a wire clothes hanger. Other car thieves use a thin but sturdy length of metal known in the trade as a **slim Jim.** This device slides between the window glass and the door frame and is used to unlock the door. Even remote-operated security systems can be breached. Thieves vary the frequency on a remote locking device until they gain entry to the car. When all else fails, the thief breaks a window to gain entry. Once inside the car, the thief starts the engine by hot-wiring or short-circuiting the ignition system. In some cases, inserting a screwdriver into the ignition breaks the lock housing and exposes the starter wires. Some car thieves use a slide hammer, commonly used to pull dents out of fenders and auto bodies. Forcing the end of the hammer into the ignition allows the lock to be quickly removed and exposes the ignition wires. Professional thieves may have illegally obtained master keys for various automobiles and simply insert the master key to unlock the car and start the ignition. A skilled car thief can gain entry to a locked car and start the engine in less than sixty seconds.

slim Jim A tool consisting of a sturdy length of metal used by auto and truck thieves to unlock doors.

When a car is stopped as a possible stolen vehicle or a stolen vehicle is recovered, the police often check the owner's registration at the state motor vehicle bureau. Police also use state driver's license bureaus to try to match the vehicle registration with the driver. Sometimes further checks are required. One valuable source of vehicle theft information is the FBI's National Crime Information Center (NCIC). Vehicle theft investigators can query the NCIC files to learn about stolen vehicles, vehicles wanted in connection with felonies, stolen parts and accessories, stolen license plates, and drivers' criminal records.

Another resource for vehicle theft investigators is the National Insurance Crime Bureau (NICB). The NICB is a nonprofit organization, not a government agency, that gathers and distributes information about motor vehicle theft. It also helps educate law enforcement officers in investigative techniques of vehicle identification, fraud, and theft. The NICB maintains computerized databases that investigators can query to obtain information and leads. Among these databases are a theft file, a salvage file, an export file, and an impound file. Each year the NICB publishes and distributes to police agencies a manual for identifying automobiles. This manual contains a summary of motor vehicle laws of the states, federal motor vehicle marking standards, information on vehicle identification numbers, and information on domestic and imported vehicles. Every five years the NICB publishes a similar manual for commercial vehicles and off-road equipment.

Examining Stolen Vehicles for Evidence

The immediate area where a car is recovered becomes the crime scene. On stripped car recoveries, note the location of the vehicle (on the street, in an alley, in a vacant lot, and so forth) and the direction in which the vehicle was pointing when discovered. Search the area immediately surrounding the vehicle for possible physical evidence or other identifying information that may lead to the thief. In addition, check for any oil or transmission fluid trails indicating the path of travel. Carefully process any property left in the abandoned vehicle. Although the items may belong to the car's owner, they may also belong to the thief. Avoid contaminating any source of possible latent fingerprints (steering wheel, door handles, mirrors, seat adjustment knobs, radio buttons, dashboard, steering column, and so on).

Searching a Stolen Vehicle

After processing the vehicle for latent fingerprints, thoroughly search the vehicle for any trace evidence that might suggest the identity or whereabouts of a suspect. In some cases, as when cars are recovered after being used in a kidnapping or homicide, only crime lab technicians should search the vehicle. When searching a vehicle, never discount anything. Small scraps of paper, burned matches, cigarette butts in ashtrays, supermarket receipts, and so forth may provide useful information for locating a suspect or prosecuting a defendant once apprehended. As with any crime scene, keep accurate notes concerning any physical evidence that is found. Searches of stolen vehicles have produced evidence of narcotics on floor mats, bloodstains on upholstery, and fiber from kidnapping victims' clothing in trunks. Additionally, evidence recovered in the search may lead to the solution of other crimes.

If the investigator knows that a vehicle has been involved in other crimes involving narcotics, stolen jewelry, money, or other small articles of value, he or she should be sure to search areas of the vehicle that could easily conceal such items. Searches should be made inside the air cleaner or oil filter; under or behind the dashboard panel; behind the engine compartment cowling; and inside doors, tires, body panels, and exhaust systems. In short, any area of the vehicle that may conceal or might have been used to conceal stolen items should be examined.

Disposing of Recovered Vehicles

If a stolen vehicle is to be processed for fingerprints, searched for possible evidence, or examined by a forensic technician, it is **impounded.** Taking the vehicle into legal custody ensures that no unauthorized persons enter or touch the vehicle or any of its contents. If you are the investigating officer when a vehicle is impounded, take an inventory of the car's contents. The officer on the scene should be sure the tow truck driver signs the inventory at the scene. The officer should also check to be sure the vehicle is secured at the impound lot or garage. An impounded vehicle cannot be released without an official impound release form indicating that it is no longer required as evidence. If the vehicle is not required as evidence in some other crime, it is stored. A stored vehicle can be released by the storage garage or lot attendant to the owner or the owner's agent.

impound To take into legal custody.

Whenever a stolen vehicle is recovered, the investigating officer should notify the registered owner. Notification should include telling the owner where the vehicle was recovered and what its current condition and disposition are. If the vehicle is drivable and only being stored, the owner should be informed where it is and how to secure its release. If the vehicle is material evidence in another crime and has been impounded, the owner should be informed of this. The owner also should get some idea of when he or she will be able to retrieve the car.

The officer's final report on the vehicle theft should include information pertinent to the vehicle's use in any other criminal activity or case. Notification of the vehicle's recovery should be made, and noted in the report, to all other interested or involved agencies.

INVESTIGATING OTHER MOTOR VEHICLE THEFTS

Trucks, buses, motorcycles, construction and farm machinery, aircraft, and recreational vehicles such as boats and snowmobiles all fall within the category of motor vehicles. Investigating thefts of such vehicles is similar to investigating auto thefts. Manufacturers and sellers can provide useful information regarding the location of identifying numbers and possible outlets for stolen parts. We will now take a closer look at investigating the theft of one of these types of motor vehicles—motorcycles.

During the past ten or fifteen years, the theft of motorcycles has been increasing along with their popularity. Motorcycles can be stolen easily and dismantled with considerable speed and ease. Because of the motorcycle's relatively small size and weight, it can be quickly lifted onto the back of a truck or into a van and transported away. As with automobiles, the ignition system of a motorcycle is no match for a skilled cycle thief. Also, VINs on motorcycles are not as difficult to remove or alter as on automobiles. Motorcycle VINs are inscribed on fewer parts and can actually be stamped over or altered with relative success.

Motorcycles are typically stolen for stripping or resale. Investigating a motorcycle theft is generally similar to investigating an automobile theft. One of the most effective tools an officer can use to combat motorcycle theft is knowledge. Become familiar with local traffic and safety laws relating to motorcycle operation and equipment requirements. Good local and state traffic regulation and law enforcement help. Current computerized databases

allow officers to determine the status of a motorcycle, the rider's right to possession of the vehicle, proper registration, licensing, and identification of the rider and owner.

There are several problems in recovering and identifying stolen motorcycles. First, more than seventy different brands of motorcycles are sold in the United States. As with pre-1968 automobiles, many of these manufacturers have used different numbering systems and locations for identifying the vehicle. Second, motorcycles frequently are registered by the engine number rather than the frame number. Because the identification number does not include a model number, several motorcycles may actually be registered with the same identification number. In addition, many people fail to register off-road bikes or dirt bikes. When these vehicles are stolen, it is almost impossible to identify them, even when they are recovered. A third problem is that several motorcycles have parts that can be used interchangeably year after year. Parts can be changed and exchanged, making it difficult to locate a cycle's parts once the cycle has been dismantled and distributed.

Today motorcycle VINs are usually die-stamped into the frame of the motorcycle, although the location may vary among manufacturers. The VIN can also be found, on most models, on the left and right sides of the headstock, or engine cradle. Finally, most manufacturers also die-stamp a serial number on the engine case itself.

PREVENTING MOTOR VEHICLE THEFT

Generally, the theft of a vehicle requires two things—a desire on the part of a thief and an opportunity, sometimes inadvertently provided by the owner. Limit the opportunities, and one can expect a corresponding reduction in thefts. In other words, an unlocked car with the key in the ignition is a more likely target for a thief than one with the doors locked and no keys present. A car left with the engine running so that the driver can run into a convenience store, "just for a minute," becomes a probable candidate for being stolen (Stern, 1990).

To decrease the opportunity for theft, a number of car manufacturers have installed devices reminding drivers to secure their vehicles. Some of these buzz when keys are left in the ignition or doors are left unlocked as the driver exits the vehicle. Others actually sound a mechanical voice, telling the driver, "Your keys are in the ignition."

Automobile security systems are among the many devices motor vehicle owners have installed to prevent motor vehicle theft.

Some vehicles have automatic systems that can be programmed to lock the doors whenever they are closed.

FYI Police in New York City were among the first to use a decal identification program to deter motor vehicle theft. Their program, called Combat Auto Theft (CAT), proved highly successful. During the first three years of the program's operation, 37,326 vehicles were registered but only 67 of those displaying the CAT decal were stolen (Hildreth, 1990).

In addition, a number of manufacturers now sell vehicles with various antitheft devices, such as alarms and engine and fuel cutoff devices. Aftermarket devices (those not originally installed by the manufacturer) are also available for older or lower-priced vehicles. These include the boot, a device installed under a front tire to prevent the vehicle from being moved; and the collar, a device to deter penetration of the steering column. Recently, some businesses have been selling official-looking decals for vehicles. These decals suggest that the car is equipped with some sort of alarm or antitheft device. In reality, the car is equipped with a decal. Similarly, a small black box (about the size of a package of cigarettes) with battery-operated red and green lights can be secured to the dashboard. It resembles several aftermarket alarm systems, and when switched on the red light slowly blinks, suggesting that an actual alarm is armed.

Each year numerous law enforcement agencies try to reduce the number of vehicle thefts in their jurisdictions. Some have succeeded simply by educating vehicle owners who reside in the area. They educate people about the importance of locking their cars. Likewise, they stress keeping windows rolled up in a parked vehicle and not leaving keys in the ignition, on the visor, or in hiding places on the outside of the vehicle. Others have increased patrols in high vehicle theft areas to reduce crime. In some jurisdictions, officers use tips and informants to discover body shops where vehicles are being stripped and chopped. Some officers routinely visit and inspect local salvage yards for stolen vehicle parts (Stern, 1990).

Some jurisdictions have set up decal alert programs. To take part in such a prevention program, owners register their vehicles with their local law enforcement agency. An owner agrees to let officers stop the car and question the driver without probable cause if the car is seen on the street during certain hours (such as 1:00 a.m. to 5:00 a.m.). A decal issued by the law enforcement agency identifies the vehicle as registered in the program. Some cities have achieved great success with such programs, having only 0.1 percent of registered autos seized by car thieves.

Many jurisdictions and agencies employ technology to make recovery of stolen vehicles easier. Their hope is to reduce thefts by deterring thieves who will most certainly be captured if they steal a car. A number of jurisdictions rely on computer networks of the FBI, state, and local police to identify and find stolen vehicles. Some have begun using a revolutionary system for tracking down stolen vehicles and thieves. A small transceiver that acts as a homing device is installed on a vehicle. Each transceiver has its own unique, registered code. If the vehicle is stolen, the owner alerts police, and the homing device is activated. A tracking device in a police car picks up the signal, allowing officers to monitor, track, and recover the stolen vehicle.

SUMMARY

Learning Objective 1

Motor vehicle theft is one of eight crimes that the FBI considers the most serious in American society, and the FBI reports yearly statistics on motor vehicle theft in its Uniform Crime Reports (UCR). In 2004 the number of motor vehicle thefts was estimated at 1,237,114; this figure is approximately the same as that of motor vehicle thefts in 2005.

Learning Objective 2

Motor vehicle theft is generally classified by the thief's motive for taking a vehicle. These motives include joyriding, transportation, to commit another crime, fraud, and stripping, chopping, and resale.

Learning Objective 3

State statutes vary in their treatment of motor vehicle theft. In some states, thieves may be charged with "grand theft auto," and in others the charge may be "unauthorized use of a motor vehicle." States have enacted a variety of laws that require stiffer penalties for motor vehicle–related crimes.

Learning Objective 4

The motor vehicle theft investigator's first job is to determine if a theft has taken place and then to gather and report complete and accurate information regarding the theft. Investigators rely on numbers (especially the vehicle identification number [VIN]) inscribed on the vehicle to identify stolen vehicles. Using their powers of observation and experience, officers can recognize possible stolen vehicles by certain telltale signs on the vehicle as well as by the behavior of the driver and passengers. When a stolen vehicle is recovered, a thorough search must be made both inside and outside the vehicle to gather and preserve evidence, and the owner must be informed of the vehicle's disposition.

Learning Objective 5

In addition to automobiles, motor vehicle thefts can include trucks, buses, motorcycles, construction and farm machinery, aircraft, and recreational vehicles such as boats and snowmobiles. Investigating these thefts is similar to investigating auto thefts. Manufacturers and sellers can provide useful information regarding type and location of identification numbers, which can vary widely for these types of motor vehicles.

Learning Objective 6

Law enforcement agencies, manufacturers, and various organizations and associations have devised a variety of activities and products to prevent motor vehicle theft. These include educating the public, increasing patrols and inspections, installing mechanical and electronic antitheft devices, and setting up police–citizen prevention programs.

KEY TERMS

motor vehicle theft **347**

joyriding **349**

salvage switch **350**

stripping **351**

chop shop **352**

chopping **352**

vehicle identification number (VIN) **354**

slim Jim **357**

impound **359**

QUESTIONS FOR REVIEW

Learning Objective 1

1. What category of motor vehicle makes up the largest part of all motor vehicle thefts?

Learning Objective 2

2. Into what five major categories can automobile thefts be divided?

3. How might juveniles and professional car thieves differ in their operations?

4. What is meant by *joyriding*?

5. Why might a criminal steal a car before committing a kidnapping?

6. Why might a person burn or hire someone to burn his or her own vehicle?

7. What is meant by a *chop shop* and a *salvage switch*?

8. Why are many stolen U.S. cars resold overseas?

Learning Objective 3

9. Why do charges for stealing motor vehicles vary among the states?

Learning Objective 4

10. List five things that are important to include in a motor vehicle theft report.

11. What are five things to be suspicious of when looking for stolen vehicles?

12. What is a VIN, what is its purpose, and where is it located on most automobiles?

13. How might the information in an automobile theft report be useful for recovering the stolen vehicle?

14. Why should the area immediately surrounding a recovered stolen vehicle be considered a crime scene?

15. Where might an investigator look for latent fingerprints in a recovered stolen car?

Learning Objective 5

16. Why are motorcycles somewhat easy to steal and dispose of?

17. What are some of the factors contributing to the problems in recovering motorcycles?

Learning Objective 6

18. What are some of the measures being taken to deter or apprehend car thieves?

CRITICAL THINKING EXERCISES

1. Bob Jones parked his 1998 Acura Integra in front of his home on Long Island, New York, at around 6:00 p.m. At about 12:00 a.m. Mr. Jones happened to look out his window and immediately noticed that his car was gone. He telephoned the police, who arrived about ten minutes later. You are the responding police officer.

a. What questions should you ask?

b. What information should you record in your field notes?

c. What actions should you take after the initial interview?

2. Contact the local police in your area. Gather data that will enable you to profile motor vehicle theft trends in your area during the past ten years. Use the various types of motor vehicles described in the chapter. Also attempt to classify the thefts according to the five categories outlined in the chapter. Create visuals to illustrate the data, and write a brief summary of your findings.

· ·

INVESTIGATIVE SKILL BUILDERS

Teaching Others

You are an experienced patrol officer. You have been asked to take a rookie on patrol with you and to teach the rookie how to spot suspicious and possibly stolen vehicles.

1. What are the most important things to tell the rookie to look for?

2. What will you tell the rookie to look for regarding drivers?

Integrity/Honesty

Your personal car needs tires, so you go to a local tire store. You have been dealing with this tire store for years and know the owner pretty well. He knows you are a police officer. He tells you that the tires for your car cost $70 each and that you need four. He also tells you that because you are such a steady customer, he has a special deal for you. He explains that he bought an odd lot of these tires from some guy in a truck and that he can sell them to you for $35 a tire. He assures you that these are the same kind of tires as the $70 ones.

1. Do you have any questions for the store owner?

2. Should you look a gift horse in the mouth or simply buy the tires?

Arson and Bombing Investigations

After completing this chapter, you will be able to:

1 Provide an overview of the crime of arson in the United States.
2 Explain the legal elements of the crime of arson.
3 List some common motives for arson.
4 Describe types of evidence that help arson investigators determine that a specific fire occurred and was deliberately set.
5 Provide an overview of bombing incidents in the United States.
6 List the most common kinds of bombs police agencies deal with.
7 Describe some investigative techniques used in bombing incidents.
8 Explain what a *suicide bomber* is.

FIGURE 18.1 Arson by Type of Property

Property Classification	Number of Offenses	Percent Distribution[1]
Total	63,215	100.0
Total structure	28,202	44.6
Single occupancy residential	12,758	20.2
Other residential	4,773	7.6
Storage	1,902	3.0
Industrial/manufacturing	207	0.5
Other commercial	2,700	4.3
Community/public	3,246	5.1
Other structure	2,536	4.0
Total mobile	19,088	30.2
Motor vehicles	18,070	28.6
Other mobile	10,118	1.6
Other	15,925	21.8

[1]Because of rounding, percentages may not add to total.

Source: Federal Bureau of Investigation. 2005. *Crime in the United States, 2004.* Washington, DC: U.S. Government Printing Office, table 2.31.

THE CRIME OF ARSON

Arson is the last of the index offenses that this text will consider. It is one of the most frightening crimes because it involves the destruction of both property and, potentially, human lives. Estimates of total property loss each year for all arsons range from $1.5 billion to $5 billion. Even more disturbing are the approximately 800 to 1,000 deaths related to arson each year.

Since 1979, the FBI has included arson as a Part I index offense in the Uniform Crime Report (UCR). Only fires determined through investigation to have been willfully or maliciously set are classified by the FBI as arsons. Fires of suspicious or unknown origin are excluded. In 2004 a total of 63,215 arson offenses were reported, a decrease of 6.4 percent from the prior year. Responding agencies provided detailed information on the type of structure, and Figure 18.1 shows this breakdown.

Detection and investigation of arson cases are extremely difficult. One problem is confusion over jurisdiction. Since arson involves fire, one might think it is the province of the fire department and not the police department. In reality, either the police department or the fire department could reasonably claim jurisdiction. Unfortunately, in most areas neither department on its own has sufficient resources to investigate this crime as thoroughly as other types of crimes are investigated. Arson investigators from police and fire departments need to cooperate and pool resources to provide the attention required to apprehend arsonists (Daeid, 2004).

LEGAL ELEMENTS OF THE CRIME OF ARSON

arson Malicious and intentional or fraudulent burning of buildings or property.

Arson is a combination crime against persons and property. Under common law, arson was defined as the malicious, willful burning of another's house or building. Although some states retain this definition, others have expanded it. Despite variations from state to state, **arson** is generally defined as the malicious and intentional or fraudulent burning of buildings or property. In most jurisdictions, arson broadly covers the burning of all kinds of buildings and structures, as well as crops, forests, farm equipment, and personal property such as boats, cars, or other vehicles. Arson also includes the willful burning of one's own property with the intention of defrauding an insurance company (Ford, 2005). As with other crimes that derive from common law, *mens rea* is an important element of the crime of arson: Proof of intent must show that the act was done voluntarily, knowingly, and purposely.

Some jurisdictions categorize an arson as aggravated or simple. In addition to elements of intentional burning of buildings or property, **aggravated arson** usually includes knowingly creating an imminent danger to human life or a risk of great bodily harm to others. **Simple arson** is the intentional burning of property without creating an imminent risk or threat to human life. In most jurisdictions, aggravated arson is a felony. When a death occurs as a result of arson, the charge may include felonious murder (first-degree murder) as well. In some states, the crime of arson is divided into first, second, third, and fourth degrees. Many jurisdictions have enacted statutes with more severe punishments for burning schools and other public buildings than for general arson.

In addition to aggravated and simple arson, most jurisdictions include a lesser crime known as attempted arson. The elements of **attempted arson** include demonstrating intent to set a fire and some overt act toward actually setting the fire. For example, pouring gasoline on piles of boxes in a building's basement, but being interrupted before lighting a match, could be interpreted as attempted arson. Having several cans of gasoline stored in a well-ventilated garage could not be interpreted as attempted arson. However, having several cans of gasoline or kerosene in a poorly ventilated shed or garage that ignites and causes a fire, or leaving embers smoldering in a camp fire that later results in a forest fire, can be considered "negligent." **Negligent fires** are fires that occur or become uncontrollable as a consequence of culpable negligent behavior resulting in damage or injury to property or people.

MOTIVES FOR ARSON

Motive is *not* an element of the crime of arson—nor of any other crime for that matter. A conviction can be obtained even when the prosecutor is unable to show any motive for the acts of the accused. However, when motive can be shown, it helps a prosecutor's case. Motive provides a compelling explanation for the court or the jury, helping them understand why the accused committed the crime. There can be many motives for arson. For example, a fraud fire may be started to destroy property in order to collect insurance money, as a means of preventing serious financial loss, to terminate an unprofitable lease, or for other reasons that bring the arsonist or his employer financial gain (Bouquard, 2004). An arsonist may be the proprietor or operator of a business who has a potential monetary gain from insurance as a result of a fire. Or he or she may be a person totally unrelated to the fire victim, perhaps an insurance adjuster or contractor seeking additional work. An alarming number of fires have been set by firefighters or security officers, who seek recognition for their heroism in fighting the blaze or even saving a life during the fire they actually started.

One researcher suggested that arsonists use fire as a tool and divided their motives into two broad categories: rational and irrational (Krzeszowski, 1993). *Rational motives* include goals such as revenge or profit. *Irrational motives* typically are not goals and are related to uncontrollable urges or various mental disorders. As you read through

aggravated arson
Malicious and intentional or fraudulent burning of buildings or property and knowingly creating an imminent danger to human life or a risk of great bodily harm to others.

simple arson   Malicious and intentional or fraudulent burning of buildings or property that does not create an imminent risk or threat to human life.

attempted arson   The demonstrated intent to set a fire coupled with some overt act toward actually setting the fire.

negligent fires   Fires that occur or become uncontrollable as a consequence of culpable negligent behavior, resulting in damage or injury to property or people.

the following list of common motives uncovered in arson investigations, see if you can classify them as rational or irrational:

- Revenge, spite, or jealousy
- Profit, insurance fraud
- Sabotage of a competitor's business
- Terrorism, intimidation, or extortion
- Destruction of evidence of a crime
- Concealment of evidence
- Vanity, to fulfill a hero fantasy
- Securing employment as a guard
- Ensuring selection as a volunteer firefighter
- Landlord-tenant disputes or breaking a lease
- Destruction of records
- Vandalism
- Pyromania
- Fascination with fire
- Other mental disorders
- Suicide

Fire Classifications

Fires, somewhat like homicides, may be classified in a number of ways. The major classifications for fires are natural, accidental, criminal, suspicious, or of unknown origins. Fires classified as *criminal* are typically referred to as arson (Almirall & Furton, 2004).

Natural Fires   A natural fire includes those used to burn leaves or refuge or fires set in a campfire or other type of safety ring or burning area.

Accidental Fires   Accidental fires may occur from a number of causes including faulty wiring, overheating appliances, inproprerly stored combustable liquids or soiled rags, children playing with matches, firecrackers, or stove top burners. It is not uncommon for arsonists to try to make their intentionally set fires appear as if they were accidental.

Criminal or Incendiary Fires   Criminal fires, or arsons, involve fires set intentionally and maliciously in an effort to destroy property, buildings, or other structures or to conceal evidence of another crime. Investigators must demonstrate that the fire was not an accident or of natural causes.

Suspicious Fires   A suspicious fire appears on the surface to have elements of arson, but it may not be demonstrated (at least not immediately) as being intentional (arson). Such fires may occur shortly after a merchant has taken out a large insurance policy or "coincidentally" in a building where some other crime such as a robbery or murder has just occurred. Investigation may ultimately reveal sufficient evidence to relabel a suspicious fire as *arson*.

Unknown Origin Fires   Fires with unknown origins are those in which there is no apparent evidence of the cause. It is impossible to determine whether these fires are accidental, natural, or criminal.

INVESTIGATING ARSON

Once a fire is out, the investigator must determine where and how the fire started: Was the fire from accidental or natural origins, or was it intentionally set (Deltaan, 2002; Fitch and Porter, 1997)? Initially, the investigator looks for accidental or natural causes. In some fires, no evidence can be found that clearly indicates the fire was accidental (such as an electrical short, a cigarette dropped on a bed, or faulty heating devices) or natural (such as evidence of a lightning strike or spontaneous combustion). In these cases, the fire may be ruled suspicious or of unknown origin. When any fire-setting device, igniter, or **accelerant** (fire booster) is found near the site, the fire may be classified as an **incendiary fire** (Bouquard, 2004). Such evidence is an indication of arson.

Investigating arson differs from investigating crimes previously discussed in this textbook. First among the differences is the unavoidable problem of being unable to secure the crime scene immediately. The determination that the crime of arson has occurred happens either during the fire or after it has been extinguished. During the course of fighting the fire, fire, police, or medical personnel may walk through the crime scene, obliterating evidence of the crime. Subsequently, official personnel examining the origins and causes of the fire may disturb or destroy evidence. Evidence also may be destroyed by the flames themselves.

Typically, investigators begin their investigation of suspected arson by examining the outside of a structure. They look for external causes of a burn or any means of entering the building to set the fire. As with any crime scene, photographs and notes are taken as the investigator examines the exterior of the structure.

Since arson does not have an immediate *corpus delicti*, it is the responsibility of the investigator to show that a specific fire occurred and was deliberately set (DeHaan, 2002; Redsickler, 2007). Toward this end, the investigator must seek both direct and circumstantial evidence. The first step after securing the scene is to determine the origin of the burn. Understanding the nature of fire can assist an investigator in determining its point of origin (Siegel & Houck, 2006).

The **fire triangle** is composed of the three basic elements needed for a fire: air or oxygen, fuel, and heat. One or more of these elements is usually present in abnormal amounts in the area of an arson. Extra *air* or *oxygen* may result from opened vents, windows, and doors or from openings cut in walls or ceilings. Oxygen may also be found in various compounds, such as nitrates, at the arson site. *Fuel* in disproportionate amounts may be observed as stacks of rags, paper, boxes, or other flammable materials piled up at the scene or brought to it. Sparks, flames, chemical reaction, and compression may each cause enough *heat* to ignite a fire (Angle et al., 2001). Disproportionate heat may result from accelerants, such as lighter fluid, paint thinner, or gasoline, added to the fire after it was ignited.

Direct ignition is simply setting a fire by applying matches or another flame. Direct ignition is the most basic cause of all fires (Siegel & Hock, 2006). Gasoline, kerosene, paint thinner, lighter fluid, or other combustible chemicals and materials may be thrown or spread over the part of the structure to be burned. These will cause a more rapid spread of flames and a more complete combustion of the affected area. The fire is immediate and is ignited directly by the arsonist.

Delayed ignition, in contrast, involves the use of some sort of mechanical, chemical, or other timing device. This may be as simple as a cigarette placed in a matchbook or as complex as a radio-activated electronic ignition set off by a telephone call. Delayed ignition is intended to give an arsonist time to escape or to establish an alibi during

accelerant A booster such as gasoline, kerosene, or paint thinner added to a fire to speed its progress.

incendiary fire A fire in which a fire-setting device, an igniter, or an accelerant is found.

fire triangle The three basic elements for a fire: oxygen, fuel, and heat.

direct ignition Setting a fire by directly applying a flame.

delayed ignition Setting a fire indirectly by means of a mechanical, chemical, or other timing device.

the time of the fire (Norman, 2006; Quintiere, 1997). Some delayed-ignition devices, or portions of them, are not entirely destroyed by a fire. The arson investigator should be careful to scrutinize all suspect areas for incendiary materials, equipment, devices, or other means of fire starting.

The crime of arson is generally committed under cover of darkness, at a time, and in a manner calculated to divert suspicion. Only the arsonist or those acting with him or her are usually present at the scene. The perpetrator hopes that the fire will destroy any incriminating evidence he or she may leave behind. Arsons are difficult to solve, in part because a timing device can detonate and ignite a fire hours or days later, when the arsonist is miles from the site. This means that the arsonist can set the stage and trigger for a fire and then have an "airtight alibi" for the time of the fire. Naturally, the alibi may be weakened if the prosecution can show that the fire was started with a time-delay device of some sort.

STATISTICS Overall, according to the UCR, in 2004 law enforcement agencies cleared 17.1 percent of arson offenses by arrest or exceptional means. Also during 2004, clearances of juveniles for the offense of arson were proportionally higher than for any other crime; 42.7 percent of arson clearances nationwide involved only juveniles.

Burn Patterns

The point of origin (place of ignition) and cause of a fire must be determined as soon as possible in an arson investigation. Burn patterns show the effects of burning or partial burning during the fire. These patterns are important elements in determining the point of origin, the spread of the fire, the temperature, the duration, and the presence of accelerants (Lentini, 2006). Frequently these patterns provide clues to where the fire was ignited. The type of fire, access to oxygen, accelerants, and duration of the burn all affect burn patterns.

V Pattern Many of us are already familiar with different burn patterns from various activities in life, but we are unaware that we have observed them. For example, if you have ever had a roaring fire in your fireplace, you are familiar with the V-shaped burn pattern left on the back wall of the fireplace. When a fire is unobstructed and has an upward draft, flames tend to fan up and outward, creating a V- or cone-shaped burn pattern similar to the sooty residue left on fireplace back walls. Strong side drafts may distort the cone shape, but when the V pattern can be established, the point of the V usually leads to the source of the fuel in the fire.

Alligatoring Anyone who has sat by a campfire may recall seeing a blistering that resembled scales on the burning logs. This scalelike pattern, or **alligatoring,** is common on charred wood. Larger, rolling scales or blisters indicate rapid, intense heat; small, flat alligatoring results from low-intensity heat over a long period of time (National Fire Protection Association, 1995).

alligatoring A scalelike burn pattern on wood. Large scales indicate rapid, intense heat; small, flat scales indicate low-intensity heat over a long period of time.

Pour or Spill This pattern appears as a boundary between burned and unburned material. It is caused by pouring some type of liquid accelerant on a floor or surface and then igniting it. For example, imagine you spilled a can of gasoline on the floor of your living room. The gasoline would run out, forming a spill across the floor. If you ignited the gasoline, the burning pattern would immediately follow the spill pattern. Discovering a pour burn pattern is fairly good evidence that an arson has taken place.

Depth of Charring   Charring, the dark blackening of burned wood, can indicate the intensity of the heat, the duration of a burn, and the point of origin. One can reasonably expect that the longer a fire burns a piece of wood, the deeper the charring will be. Thus, tracing lightly charred materials to materials with the deepest charring leads to the fire's point of origin. When investigators discover charring of significant depth, it is reasonable to search that area for further evidence of ignition. Finally, the relative depth of charring can provide clues as to how the fire was ventilated, spread, or accelerated. Remember, though, that charring can vary, depending on the type of wood, its moisture content, the use of an accelerant, and the effectiveness of firefighters' efforts in that area of the structure.

Arson investigators sift through the rubble of a fire to determine if it may be classified as an incendiary fire.

Crazing   Irregular cracks and lines in glass and ceramic materials produced by rapid, intense heat are known as **crazing.** Crazing into small sections suggests that the item was near the point of origin, and the intense heat may have been caused by an accelerant. Larger segments indicate that the item was some distance away from the point of origin (Gardner, 2005).

crazing   Irregular cracks and lines in glass and ceramic materials caused by rapid, intense heat.

Spalling   The chipping, crumbling, or breaking off of cement or masonry by rapid, intense heat is called **spalling.** The fragments may look slightly discolored or chalky (Avillo, 2002; Canfield, 1984). This discoloration, coupled with the presence of certain odors, may indicate the use of an accelerant and probable arson.

spalling   Chipping, crumbling, or flaking of cement or masonry caused by rapid, intense heat.

Smoke   If witnesses saw a fire begin, the color of smoke could indicate the material used to start the blaze. Black smoke, for example, indicates that the material may have contained petroleum. White smoke generally indicates that some vegetation, such as straw or dried leaves, was burned. Once the entire structure has begun to burn, it may be difficult to discern from the smoke what materials are burning.

Arson Indicators

Evidence of an accelerant found at the point of origin of a fire is a primary form of physical evidence of an arson fire (Icove & DeHaan, 2003). As we have seen, burn patterns found at the scene may lead an investigator to suspect arson. Additionally, other evidence may lead an arson investigator to recognize a fire as arson.

Multiple Points of Origin   Many arsonists set several fires in a building in widely separated areas to ensure better combustion and more complete destruction.

Odors   Gasoline (the most common accelerant), kerosene, paint thinner, and other flammable liquids have distinctive odors. If used as accelerants, they sometimes leave recognizable odors even after the flames have been extinguished.

CAREERS FOCUS

ARSON AND FIRE INVESTIGATORS

PART DETECTIVE AND PART SCIENTIST, engineer, and law enforcer, the fire investigator has a combination of skills and knowledge bases rolled into one. It is the fire investigator who must examine a fire scene to determine and document the origin and cause of a fire. If found to be of suspicious origins, the fire investigator must establish what caused the fire and be able to bring expert and authoritative testimony to the courtroom when a suspect has been found and taken to trial.

Although many people use the terms "fire investigator" and "arson investigator" interchangeably, they are not one and the same. Technically, an arson investigator will try to determine who is responsible for setting a fire; a fire investigator will attempt to determine the cause and origin of a fire. However, fire investigators frequently are also arson investigators. In some jurisdictions arson investigators may be police officers or ATF agents who do not have the background to perform a fire investigation—an area that is becoming increasingly grounded in the science and engineering of fire behavior—and they will work with a fire investigator. The job of fire investigation is complex, challenging, and requires someone trained in the area of fire engineering.

It is not uncommon for a fire investigator to have a background in mechanical, electrical, civil, and even chemical engineering. Their work frequently has them looking at something that was destroyed, and they need to have the skill to put it back together again either in a theoretical manner or physically to determine the origin and cause of the fire. Technical training plays a role in understanding the behavior of the fire and how it attacked the structure one is investigating, whether it be an appliance, piece of equipment, or a building. This technical aspect of the job requires knowledge of building construction and materials and the effects of fire on those materials. Evidence preservation methods, the effects of fire suppression, fire behavior, and burn patterns are also important technical aspects. Search techniques must also be learned so that fire cause evidence and ignition sources are preserved during the investigation.

Although fire investigators do not all have a law enforcement background, many do. In some states fire investigators are fire marshals who are also full-powered police officers (some fire marshals are fire service personnel who have received police training and are sworn as "peace officers"). In other jurisdictions, local fire marshals may be members of the local fire department or work under the municipal government. They may receive some basic training on code enforcement and origin and cause but have no law enforcement powers at all! Because fire investigators must follow due process of law in matters such as collecting evidence, search and seizure, interrogation, and court testimony, police or criminal justice training is extremely helpful.

Speed and Spread of Fire   The speed at which a fire spreads after its initial discovery may suggest arson. Fires that seem to spread extremely rapidly and engulf major portions of a building or structure very quickly may be considered suspicious.

Holes in Walls or Floors   Arsonists sometimes chop holes in walls or floors to expose raw wood or to improve the draft for the fire. They may cut holes through ceilings and floors to make the fire travel faster between upper and lower floors.

trailer   A material (rope or rags soaked in accelerant, shredded paper, gunpowder, fluid accelerant, and so on) used to spread a fire.

Alarm Tampering   Destroyed or disabled alarms or sprinkler systems indicate the possibility of arson. In addition, timing devices may be set, or **trailers** (paper, rags, or rope soaked in accelerants) may be ignited to bypass or disable alarm or security systems.

Intensity of Heat   The fact that the heat generated by the fire was particularly intense may be a clue that flammable liquids or compounds were added to the burning materials. Likewise, difficulty in putting out the fire may indicate the presence of an accelerant.

A trailer (left side of photograph) was used to spread the fire to this barn.

Cooperation among Arson Investigators

Different agencies, often with joint jurisdiction, investigate suspicious fires. In some larger cities, a suspicious fire may be investigated by special units from the fire and police departments. In other cities and in unincorporated townships, a suspicious fire may be investigated by the state fire marshal, the state police, the sheriff's department, local fire investigators, or perhaps local town or borough police officers. In addition, insurance investigators may investigate a suspicious fire involving a large claim or a recently written policy (Redsickler, 2007).

As a general rule of thumb, it is the fire department's role to determine the nature and origin of the burning. Lack of trained personnel is a major problem in arson investigations. U.S. firefighters have traditionally been volunteers. In fact, nearly 80 percent of all firefighters in the United States are volunteers (Angle et al., 2001; Redsickler, 2007). All fire companies require some level of training before allowing anyone to help fight a fire. However, a firefighter's training is typically in survival (for the safety of victims and fellow firefighters) and in managing and extinguishing fires. Little specific training is given in how to investigate causes of fires. Many jurisdictions, therefore, depend heavily on state fire marshals, working in concert with local police agencies, to investigate suspicious fires. The fire marshal's role, however, is generally limited to determining the cause and the point of origin of a suspicious fire. The local police agency follows through on further criminal investigation of the arson. Figure 18.2 shows the basic steps that an arson investigation should follow.

In some jurisdictions, the fire department uses its expertise to investigate suspicious fires. Experienced firefighters have basic knowledge about how fires start, spread, and accelerate. To give this responsibility to the police would be a duplication of effort. Furthermore, fire personnel—including the fire marshal—have certain legal authority that police do not. For example, to determine the cause of a fire, fire personnel may enter the fire scene without a search warrant. Furthermore, firefighters may help police agencies by identifying people who regularly seem to be on the scene of suspicious fires. The following suspicious persons and circumstances should be taken into account in an arson investigation:

- Presence of familiar faces watching the fire (faces observed at other fires)
- Persons showing undue or excessive interest in the fire

FIGURE 18.2 Steps in an Arson Investigation

```
┌──────────────┐                      ┌──────────────┐      ┌──────────────┐
│  Prosecute.  │                      │ A fire is    │ ───▶ │ Secure the   │
└──────────────┘                      │ discovered.  │      │ fire scene.  │
       ▲                              └──────────────┘      └──────────────┘
       │                                                           │
┌──────────────────┐                                               ▼
│ Arrest a suspect.│                                    ┌──────────────────────┐
│ 1. Write report. │                                    │ Determine the        │
│ 2. Prepare case. │                                    │ nature of the fire.  │
└──────────────────┘                                    │ 1. Natural           │
       ▲                                                │ 2. Accidental        │
       │                                                │ 3. Suspicious        │
       │                                                │ 4. Criminal          │
       │                                                │ 5. Unknown origins   │
┌────────────────────────┐  ┌──────────────────┐        └──────────────────────┘
│ Conduct the criminal   │  │ Search for       │                   │
│ arson investigation.   │  │ evidence         │                   ▼
│ 1. Seek physical       │◀─│ of arson.        │◀─ ┌──────────────────────┐
│    evidence.           │  │ 1. Incendiaries  │   │ Locate the fire's     │
│ 2. Gather latent       │  │ 2. Odors         │   │ point of origin.      │
│    prints.             │  │ 3. Unusual events│   │ 1. Burn patterns      │
│ 3. Interview witnesses.│  └──────────────────┘   │ 2. Other indicators   │
│ 4. Locate suspects.    │                         └──────────────────────┘
└────────────────────────┘
```

- Overly helpful or solicitous people
- Person who discovers the fire and seeks recognition as a hero
- People with evidence of accelerants on their hands, clothing, shoes, and so on
- Type and amount of merchandise destroyed in a retail store fire
- Unusual circumstances, such as removal of specific pieces of furniture or art or items of sentimental value (diplomas, birth or marriage certificates, pets, and so on) prior to the fire
- Tracks, footprints, fingerprints, or other physical evidence foreign to the scene
- Receptacles (cans, jars, and so on) containing residue of accelerants or possible latent fingerprints
- Timing devices or fragments of timing devices

As in any criminal investigation, witnesses can provide a wealth of information that may lead to suspects and an arrest. Information investigators may obtain from witnesses in the area include the following:

- Time of the fire and general weather conditions
- What attracted the witnesses' attention to the fire
- Location at which the fire was burning when first observed
- Color of the smoke when the fire began
- Intensity of flames and speed of spreading
- Any unusual odors detected
- Possible observation of multiple fires in different locations
- Any explosions heard prior to discovery of the fire
- Observation of anyone fleeing the scene
- Vehicles seen parked at or leaving the scene around the time of the fire
- Information about the owner or tenants of the burned structure

CRIMINAL BOMBING

Bombing incidents, like arson incidents, destroy property and take innocent lives. Bombers include anarchists, racists, militants, religious zealots, hate mongers, criminals, and the mentally impaired. Especially fearsome is the random horror generated by improvised explosive devices detonated from remote sites. The FBI and the Bureau of Alcohol, Tobacco, and Firearms (ATF) gather and coordinate information on bombings reported by state and local public safety agencies (Department of Justice, 2000). According to the ATF, a **bombing** is any incident in which a device constructed with criminal intent and using high explosives, low explosives, or blasting agents explodes. Bombing incidents are generally divided into explosive bombings and incendiary bombings (Figure 18.3). Criminal bombing incidents decreased in the United States in 1995, but more people were injured or killed than in the previous year. Property damage from bombing incidents also increased. These increases are the result of the injuries, deaths, and property damage from the bombing of the Murrah Federal Building in Oklahoma City on April 19, 1995.

bombing An incident in which a device constructed with criminal intent and using high explosives, low explosives, or blasting agents explodes.

FIGURE 18.3 Bombings by Type of Incident and Device, Property Damage, and Outcome of Incident

	Total Actual and Attempted Bombings	Actual		Attempted		Property Damage (Dollar Value)	Persons Injured	Deaths
		Explosive	Incendiary	Explosive	Incendiary			
1980	1,249	742	336	99	72	$12,562,257	160	34
1981	1,142	637	315	92	98	67,082,456[a]	133[a]	30
1982	795	485	194	77	39	7,202,848	99	16
1983	687	442	127	77	41	6,342,652	100	12
1984	803	518	127	118	40	5,618,581	112	6
1985	847	575	102	113	57	6,352,000	144	28
1986	858	580	129	101	48	3,405,000	185	14
1987	848	600	104	102	42	4,201,000	107	21
1988	977[b]	593	156	161	40	2,257,000	145	20
1989	1,208[c]	641	203	243	91	5,000,000	202	11
1990	1,582	931	267	254	130	9,600,000	222	27
1991	2,499	1,551	423	395	130	6,440,000	230	29
1992	2,989	1,911	582	384	112	12,500,000	349	26
1993	2,980	1,880	538	375	187	518,000,000[d]	1,323[e]	49
1994	3,163	1,916	545	522	180	7,500,000	308	31
1995	2,577	1,562	406	417	192	105,000,000[f]	744[g]	193[g]
1996	2,573	1,457	427	504	185	5,000,000	236	23
1997	2,217	1,212	378	473	154	9,000,000	204	18
1998	2,300[h]	1,225	307	488	142	6,000,000	160	16
1999	1,797	970	223	378	114	2,000,000	114	9

[a]Includes major bombing incidents resulting in an unusually high number of personal injuries and deaths or substantial damage to property.
[b]Includes 27 incidents involving combination devices.
[c]Includes 30 incidents involving combination devices.
[d]Includes $510 million damage done to the World Trade Center by a bomb on February 26, 1993.
[e]Includes 1,042 persons injured in the World Trade Center bombing.
[f]Includes $100 million damage in the Oklahoma City bombing on April 19, 1995.
[g]Includes 518 people injured and 168 people killed in the Oklahoma City bombing.
[h]Includes 63 incidents involving combination devices.

Source: U.S. Department of Justice, Bureau of Justice Statistics. 2005. *Sourcebook of Criminal Justice Statistics.* Washington, DC: U.S. Government Printing Office, table 3.170.

The main functions of any police agency in a bombing incident are to protect human life and property, remove the bomb menace, if possible, and investigate and apprehend the bombers or threateners (Stewart, 2006). Explosives is a highly specialized field, and disposing of explosives is equally specialized. This chapter offers some general information on explosives and some suggested procedures for dealing with bombing incidents. However, individuals who have not been specifically trained in explosive materials should never try to disarm a suspected bomb.

Explosives

It is important for an arson investigator to understand the fire triangle. It is equally important for a bombing investigator to understand what constitutes an explosive. An **explosive** is any material that produces a rapid, violent reaction when subjected to heat or a strong blow or shock. During the reaction, the explosive gives off large amounts of gases at high pressure. Explosives may be solids, liquids, or gases. All explosives consist of a fuel, an oxidizer (a substance that supplies the oxygen to make the fuel burn), and a detonator—a device that ignites or sets off the reaction (Akhavan, 2004). Generally speaking, there are four types of explosives.

explosive Any material that produces a rapid, violent reaction when subjected to heat or a strong blow or shock.

Primary Explosives These explosives are extremely sensitive to heat. Even a spark of static electricity can cause them to explode. They must be handled in small quantities and are used chiefly as detonators to set off other explosions.

High Explosives Among materials classified as **high explosives,** the rate of change to a gas is very rapid. That is, the material detonates, or explodes, very rapidly. Liquids and solids change to hot gases that expand with a huge blast of heat and pressure. Included in this category are nitroglycerin, TNT, RDX, and various grades of plastic explosives (Crippin, 2006). High explosives are relatively stable. They explode only upon the shock of a blasting cap to which a fuse is attached, a detonating cord, or an electric detonator. Such explosives tend to have a shattering effect. There is a great deal of fragmenting near the detonation point and less fragmenting farther away. The velocity of high explosives ranges from 3,200 to 27,000 feet per second.

high explosive An explosive material in which the rate of change to a gas is very rapid; explodes only upon the shock of a blasting cap, a detonation cord, or an electric detonator; includes nitroglycerin, TNT, RDX, and plastic explosives.

Low Explosives Among **low explosives,** the rate of change to a gas is quite slow. They deflagrate, or burn rapidly, rather than explode. The most common types of low explosives are black powder and smokeless powder, used to propel ammunition from a gun (Akhavan, 2004; Crippin, 2006). Similarly, dust or grain explosions, gas explosions, certain chemical and fertilizer combinations, and volatile vapor explosions are examples of low explosion. Low explosions must be ignited by heat, friction, or a spark. They do not require the shock of a blasting cap or other explosive ignition.

low explosive An explosive material in which the rate of change to a gas is quite slow; the material deflagrates, or burns rapidly, rather than exploding; includes black powder, smokeless powder, and fertilizers.

Low explosives should not be regarded as low in hazard; nor should their destructive potential be underestimated. Some of these substances have been used in the most devastating blasts in history. The Oklahoma City bombing in April of 1995, for example, resulted from the explosion of a truck filled with fertilizer, detonated in front of the Murrah Building. The blast destroyed more than one-third of the structure and killed more than 100 people, including 13 children in a day care center (*Oklahoma Today,* 2005). Low explosives are frequently used in blasting operations. They have a pushing rather than a shattering effect, and a twisting and tearing type of deformation. Velocities of low explosives range from 1,200 to 3,200 feet per second.

Blasting Agents These explosives are the safest and least expensive. They are widely used in industry to shatter rock in excavation and mining. Common blasting agents include dynamite and mixtures of ammonium and fuel oil.

Explosive Accessories

When searching the site of a bombing, an investigator must try to find evidence of the mechanism used to detonate the bomb. A bomber may use the simplest of methods—a flame from a fuse—or a sophisticated remote timing device. Knowing some of the kinds of accessories bombers use can help you know what kinds of things to look for when you investigate a bombing incident.

Many agencies use specially trained dogs to search for evidence after an explosion.

Blasting Caps Blasting caps are used to set off, or ignite, high explosives. They contain small amounts of a sensitive, powerful primary explosive. The blasting cap, when ignited, detonates the larger concentration of explosives. Two types of blasting caps are common: electric and nonelectric. Electric blasting caps, as their name implies, are used where there is a source of electricity. Under certain circumstances, radio waves emitted by a transmitter can detonate an electric blasting cap. Occasionally, caps are connected to lighting circuits. When the lights are turned on, the bomb explodes. Nonelectric blasting caps detonate from the spurt of flame provided by a burning fuse or another flame- or spark-producing device (Crippin, 2006).

Safety Fuses Safety fuses convey a flame through a medium at a continuous and uniform rate to a nonelectric blasting cap. As their name implies, they allow the person lighting the fuse to seek safety before the blast (Crippin, 2006). In some cases, these fuses may be used for direct firing of a charge, as in the case of blasting powder. Safety fuses often consist of a fine core of special black powder enclosed in and protected by various coverings and waterproofing materials. The speed at which most domestic fuses burn is 30 or 40 seconds per foot. Pressure, degree of confinement, temperature, and moisture all influence the rate of burning of a fuse. Many safety fuses cannot be extinguished by water or by tamping with a foot. If necessary to save a life, and as a last resort, pull the fuse out or cut the fuse ahead of the burning.

Detonation Cords Detonation cords are round, flexible cords, similar in appearance to safety fuses. The explosive core of a detonation cord is protected by a sheath of various textiles, waterproofing materials, or plastics. Various coloring and textile patterns differentiate the particular strengths and types of detonation cords. They are used in various ways to detonate high explosives in the same manner as blasting caps (Crippin, 2006).

Electric Squibs Electric squibs also are known as electric matches. Their function is like that of an electric blasting cap. They may be used to ignite black powder or vaporous gases. The squib provides a spurt of flame or sparks similar to that provided by a burning fuse.

TYPES OF BOMBS

Police must deal with many types of explosive and incendiary devices. Homemade bombs are the kinds of devices police agencies are most familiar with. These range from crude boxes filled with blasting powder or sticks of dynamite to sophisticated radio-detonated devices of plastic or chemical explosives (Fisher, 2004). The list of materials and chemicals—some commonly found in the home—that can be used to make homemade bombs is unlimited. Contrary to popular opinion, neither commercial explosives nor blasting caps are necessary to construct highly effective bombs. Nor, for that matter, are particularly high levels of knowledge or education required. Considerable literature—some underground and some openly available in stores, libraries, and on the Internet—provide information on explosives and bomb construction. A trip to the local hardware and grocery store can provide the raw materials for a devastating bomb.

Pipe Bombs

Black powder or smokeless powder is frequently used to load pipe bombs, one of the most common types of bombs police encounter (Tomajczyk, 1999). A pipe bomb

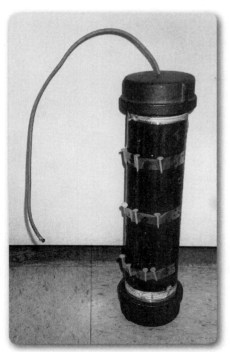

Pipe bombs are common because the materials to make them are easy to get and the bombs are relatively simple to put together.

consists of a short piece of pipe, capped at both ends. A small hole is drilled either in one of the capped ends or in the side of the pipe to insert the fuse. The pipe is filled with the powder and sometimes a stick of dynamite to shatter the pipe. Spikes can be wired to the outside of the pipe to increase the shrapnel effect of the bomb. These devices are often ignited by a safety fuse, perhaps with matches and a cigarette taped to the end of the fuse. The safety fuse transmits the flame to the low explosive inside the pipe. When ignited, the low explosive inside the pipe explodes. The gases produced are under pressure and result in a blast and fragmentation of the pipe (Beveridge, 1998).

Potato guns have grown popular among some youths. A potato gun is usually made from a length of PVC tubing large enough to snugly hold an average-sized raw potato at one end. The other end of the pipe is sealed. A small opening is cut in the side of the pipe to insert a vaporous gas, frequently from an aerosol can of hair spray. Through another small opening on the sealed end of the pipe, a sparking device or an electric match (gas grill starters are sometimes used) is inserted. In some cases, a fuse may be used. All openings around the sparking device are sealed with tape or putty. When the sparking device is engaged, the spark ignites the fumes trapped in the pipe, causing an explosion. This explosion propels the potato with significant force, sometimes for more than 500 yards. In addition to the damage that may be caused by such a projectile, these devices sometimes explode like pipe bombs.

FIGURE 18.4 Mail Bomb Incidents Investigated by the U.S. Postal Inspection Service, 1995–2004

Fiscal Year	Incidents	Explosions	Injuries	Deaths
1995	20	11	8	2
1996	12	1	1	0
1997	18	1	1	0
1998	7	3	3	1
1999	6	2	0	0
2000	7	4	2	0
2001	3	3	2	1
2002	0	0	0	0
2003	2	1	0	0
2004	26	6	4	0

Source: U.S. Department of Justice, Bureau of Justice Statistics. 2005. *Sourcebook of Criminal Justice Stastics.* Washington, DC: U.S. Government Printing Office, table 4.00001.

Firebombs

Some bombs are created to induce burning. The crudest of these is the Molotov cocktail. This device is a bottle filled with a flammable liquid, usually gasoline. A saturated fuse of cloth or other thick wicking is inserted into the bottle. The fuse is ignited and the bomb quickly thrown at the target. Some firecrackers can create a similar result (Tomajczyk, 1999).

Letter and Package Bombs

Letter and package bombs are not common but are particularly disturbing when they do occur. Figure 18.4 shows the number of mailed bombs investigated by the U.S. Postal Inspection Service between 1995 and 2004; a total of 100 incidents of mail bombings occurred during this ten year period. Mail bombs can be sent from a location in New York City to one in Fairbanks, Alaska, and provide little or no warning to the victim. They may be addressed to a particular position in a company (such as President, Chairperson, or Director of Advertising) or to a public official (such as Attorney General, Police Chief, or Mayor). Sometimes a mail bomb is addressed to a specific person. Letter bombs are often indistinguishable from other mailed letters. Envelopes are of the usual size and color, with names and addresses in the correct places. The envelope may have a return address, which may be fictitious. Letter bombs vary from about 1/8 inch to 5/16 inch in thickness, and they usually weigh less than 5 ounces (Fischer & Janoski, 2000). Typically, a letter bomb is triggered by a pressure-release mechanism. Opening the letter releases a floating, cocked firing pin—a rod through the center of the envelope—which detonates the explosives in the envelope.

Package bombs vary widely in size, weight, shape, and the color of the wrappings. They may arrive disguised as gifts, equipment, books, or other objects. Package bombs may also be sent with some form of special handling: by certified or registered mail or even by overnight express (Fischer & Janoski, 2000). Some package bombs operate like letter bombs, with pressure-release mechanisms. Others contain a spring detonating device, held under tension by the package's sealing tape or string. When the package is opened and the tape or string cut, the spring is released and detonates the bomb. Some package bombs are rigged with a triggering device in the cover or hinge. Opening the unwrapped box triggers the explosion. In some package bombs, a mercury switch is used as the triggering device. Shaking, tipping, or inverting the package causes the mercury to flow, completing an electric circuit and detonating the bomb.

FYI First-class letters and parcels are protected against search and seizure under the Fourth Amendment to the Constitution and, therefore, cannot be opened without a search warrant. If there is probable cause to believe that the contents of a first-class letter or parcel violate federal law, postal inspectors can get a search warrant to open the letter or parcel. Other classes of mail do not contain private correspondence and may therefore be opened without a warrant.

Whenever a letter or package is suspected of containing a possible explosive device, the area should be evacuated and the police department and the Postal Inspection Service notified immediately. Postal inspectors collaborate with federal, state, and local authorities in investigating actual and threatened mail bombs. It is impossible for postal employees to screen all letters and packages for explosive devices. However, mail bombs have certain similarities that have repeatedly shown up (Figure 18.5). Knowledge of the characteristics of suspect parcels may help prevent a tragedy.

FIGURE 18.5 Letter and Package Bomb Indicators

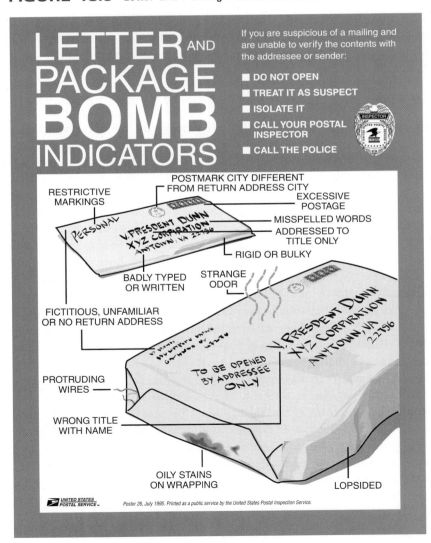

Booby Trap Bombs

Some criminals use bombs as booby traps. The explosion warns the criminal that intruders are near and slows their entry, allowing an escape. The blast may also panic the intruder, scaring him or her away. The explosion may even injure or kill anyone coming near the scene. Detonation of a booby trap bomb may be manual, remote, or timed, or the bomb may be set off by the victim through a hidden trip wire, pressure spring, or plate. Booby trap bombs may be placed in fields and woods surrounding an area of illegal activity (such as illegal drug crops), or they may be attached to windows or doors of a building or residence (as by a militant antigovernment organization). The only limit on the placement of a booby trap bomb is the bomber's imagination. As well, booby trap bombs are sometimes used as secondary devices at a bombing to attack law enforcement and rescure workers with a second unexpected bomb blast (Tomajczyk, 1999).

INVESTIGATING BOMBING INCIDENTS

Actions taken in bombing incidents are controlled by the characteristics of the actual or suspected bomb. Figure 18.6 shows bomb threat cards developed by the FBI to gather information in bomb threat investigations. Operating procedures generally should take into account the various skill levels of personnel involved in a bomb incident response.

FIGURE 18.6 Bomb Threat Cards

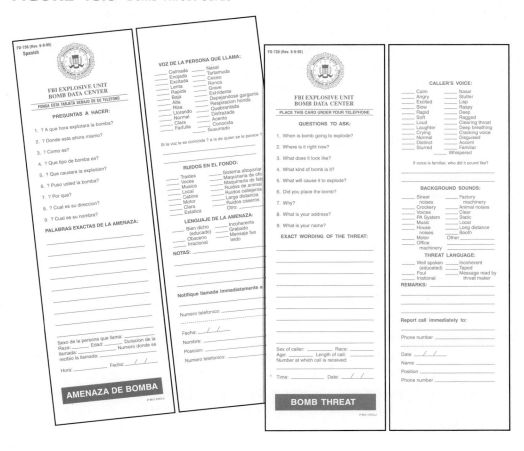

Searching for Bombs

Bomb searches are typically conducted by two-person teams. Although there are various ways to search an area for a bomb, the search should always be a systematic effort. In other words, searchers should move carefully from one room to another from the top of a structure to the bottom, or from the bottom to the top. Bomb searches should not be undertaken haphazardly (Thurman, 2006).

When a search team first enters an area where a bomb may be, the team should stop and stand silently for a moment. Bombs are often equipped with clockwork timing devices, the sound of which may offer a clue to the explosive's location. The team can then search the room systematically, using a grid pattern (see Chapter 3). Although a bomb search may be undertaken by local police officers, their task ends upon location of the device. Untrained officers should make no effort to move, remove, or in any way jar a suspicious object.

Disposing of an Unexploded Bomb

When an unexploded bomb or explosive device is located, the police officer's first consideration should be to protect human life and property. This means moving people away from the suspected bomb area, not moving the suspected bomb away from the people (Vince & Sherlock, 2005). The officer should take these steps to both protect and secure the area and aid in the investigation of the attempted bombing:

- Immediately notify qualified bomb disposal personnel, who can evaluate the suspected bomb and take necessary actions.
- Clear the danger area of all occupants to ensure as much safety as possible. A simple ruse, such as a possible gas leak, may be used as an excuse to evacuate a building without causing panic from fear of a bomb.
- Create a *clear zone* with a perimeter at least 300 feet from the explosive device, and establish a guard to prevent reentry.
- Alert fire department, rescue, and medical emergency units.
- Protect and preserve the scene so that all possible physical evidence can be obtained.
- Note whether the package or object is ticking or making any other audible noise.
- Without touching the object, observe whether it appears to be attached to anything or fastened down. Notify the bomb disposal team about these observations.
- If deemed advisable, remove any flammable materials from the immediate area of the suspected bomb to reduce injury or damage should an explosion occur.
- Shut off power, gas, and fuel lines leading into the danger area if the type of bomb warrants this action. Such action could prevent additional explosions that might add to the damage.
- Set up surveillance of the crowd of spectators to identify possible suspects.
- Photograph or videotape the crowd to possibly reveal familiar faces that have appeared at other bombing sites.
- Interview the person who discovered the suspected bomb. Likewise, interview anyone else at the scene at the time regarding the possible identity of the bomber.

FOCUS ON TECHNOLOGY

BOMB DISPOSAL ROBOT

REMOTE-CONTROLLED BOMB disposal robots can safely remove explosive devices and save lives.

- Canvass the neighborhood immediately around the bomb location. Question individuals about any unknown or suspicious persons they may have seen in the area or possible leads to a suspect's automobile or location.
- Notify the proper agencies when the danger has been declared over.
- Carefully preserve the bomb after it has been disarmed or dismantled and examined for fingerprints or the source of component parts.

Investigating an Exploded Bomb

The primary objectives of an investigation following the explosion of a bomb are to (1) establish the nature of the bomb, (2) discover the method of ignition, and (3) obtain any other evidence that may assist in identification and apprehension of the person or persons responsible.

The scene of an explosion should be carefully searched to ensure that a secondary bomb has not been set as an entrapment device. Once it has been determined that there is no danger from a second device, and any buildings or structures involved have been declared safe, a thorough search of the scene should be undertaken to locate the seat of the blast. The **seat of the blast** is the location where the explosive detonated; this location

seat of the blast The primary location where an explosive has detonated.

is typically easy to locate because the explosion will leave a large crater (Trimm, 2005). The search should begin at the crater and spiral outward in ever-increasing circles around the crater (Thurman, 2006; Trimm, 2005). Investigators should carefully sift through dirt and debris looking for bits of metal or pieces of explosive wrapping that may contain date-shift codes traceable to the manufacturer of the explosives.

During this search for forensic evidence, the first half inch of soil or debris from the seat of the blast should be collected for analysis. Any objects in close proximity to the blast should also be collected. Soft materials often attract explosive residue and under analysis may assist in determining what type of explosives were used (Stewart, 2006). Large immovable objects can be wiped with a cotton swab moistened with acetone to collect trace evidence of explosives (Trimm, 2005).

A number of investigative procedures must be considered prior to and during a search for evidence at an explosion crime scene, including the following:

- Assess the need for immediate response to the scene by explosives specialists.
- Control the scene, including supervision, organization, communications, and coordination of rescue efforts if warranted.
- Determine the degree of urgency (e.g., need for medical assistance, ambulances, the fire department, and other essential personnel) upon arrival at the scene based on immediately known facts, visible conditions, and other elements.
- Determine whether power, gas, and fuel lines should be shut off.
- Clear the danger area of all occupants, and establish a secure perimeter to protect the crime scene from all unauthorized people. Allow only essential personnel into the area.
- Carefully remove flammable materials from the area to prevent any further damage.
- Photograph or videotape both the interior and the exterior of the structure once it is declared safe.
- As in any crime scene, photograph, collect, and document any physical evidence found at the scene. This may include evidence of forced entry, fragments of the bomb itself, portions of the detonating device, or any other relevant evidence.
- As with unexploded bombs, photograph or videotape the crowd gathered at the scene. Interview witnesses and victims, and canvass the areas immediately around the explosion.
- Note cars in the vicinity of the explosion, and record their license numbers. Identify the owners, and interview them as potential witnesses or suspects.
- Search and screen the bombing debris to obtain evidence of the type of container used and the mode of ignition, as well as fragments of components, such as batteries, wire, clockworks, and packaging materials.
- Pay special attention to recovering residue deposits to identify the materials used to create the explosion.
- If a plant or business is the victim of a bombing, consider recently dismissed or irate employees as possible suspects.
- Trace any identified materials found at the scene to their supply sources for possible leads to the identification of the bomber.
- If suspects develop during the investigation, consider relevant factors such as evidence of motive, plan, design or scheme, ability and opportunity, possession of means, fabrication, destruction and suppression of evidence, phony alibis, false statements, and other indications of possible guilt.

- Check local mental institutions for possible bombing suspects.
- Consider previous bombing cases to determine whether they might contribute to the solution of the case under investigation.
- If persons were injured or killed in the explosion, establish their identities and properly notify their next of kin as quickly as possible. Identifying victims may provide a possible reason for the bombing and lead to potential suspects or other valuable investigative information.

SUICIDE BOMBINGS

Suicide bombers have become today's weapon of choice for a number of terrorist organizations (terrorisim is more fully examined in Chapter 22). An act that was once considered surprising, terrible, and horrific has now become the stuff of almost daily television news programs (Zedalis, 2006). September 11, 2001, represented a watershed event in U.S. history, including for law enforcement and investigation. On that day, nineteen members of the Al Qaeda terrorist organization engaged in strategic-level suicide bombings against the United States. By the day's end, the World Trade Center towers in New York City were nothing more than twisted heaps of glass, steel and concrete; one section of the Pentagon had been devastated; and the tattered remains of the final hijacked plane were spread across a field in Pennsylvania. Approximately 3,000 Americans died in the attacks, and the disruptive aftermath struck a serious blow to the nation's economy, air travel, and the average Amercian's sense of personal security (IACP, 2005a).

Suicide bombers are the most feared weapons in the arsenal of modern-day political activists. Unlike the bombing campaigns of the Irish Revolutionary Army (IRA) during the 1970s and 1980s, there is no telephone warning in modern suicide bombing attacks—the act itself and its resultant chaos announce the attack. Some suicide bomber attacks have been successful against military targets, but most are carried out against civilians and must be investigated by both federal and local police agencies.

Suicide bombing has been described as a kind of blurring of crime and war (IACP, 2005a). Modern suicide bombing is often credited with having begun in Lebanon during the 1980s. The Shi'ia Amal group, which had links with Herzbolah (sometimes written as *Hizballa* and literally meaning "the party of God"), introduced a new tactic in Beirut in 1983: a series of well-planned truck suicide bombings (Poland, 2005). Suicide bombings frequently have the apperance of a war-like act rather than a criminal one, but law enforcement is faced with the task and challenge of preventing such actions and of conducting investigations after a bombing has occurred. Law enforcement personnel need to know how to recognize potential suicide bombers and what to do when one is identified.

What Is a Suicide Bomber?

The Institute for Counter-Terrorism (ICT) defines suicide bombing as an "operational method in which the very act of the attack is dependent upon the death of the perpetrator. The terrorist is fully aware that if he/she does not kill him/herself, the planned attack will not be implemented" (Zedalis, 2005, p.2). *Suicide bomber* is an intentionally emotionally laden term; groups using this tactic want to make martyrs of the perpetrators. Not long after the September 11 disaster, many in law enforcement and political circles began using the term *homicide bomber* in an effort to emphasize the criminal homicides that were being perpetrated and to de-emphasize the individuals as martyrs for their cause (Ehrenfeld, 2005; Eversole & Barr, 2003).

suicide bomber An individual who, using either a vehicle, aircraft, or a self-contained explosive device on his or her person or carried by this individual, detonates the device among a group of people or crashes the vehicle or aircraft into a building, structure, or populated area.

A **suicide bomber** is an individual who, using either a vehicle, aircraft, or a self-contained explosive device on his or her person or carried by this individual, detonates the device among a group of people or crashes the vehicle or aircraft into a building, structure, or populated area. In an effort to aid law enforcement in identifying potential suicide bombers, the International Association of Police Chiefs (2005a, p.5) have developed the following profile for suicide bombers:

- An individual wearing heavy clothing, regardless of the season or weather. Long coats or skirts may be used to conceal explosive belts or other devices.

- An unusual gait, especially a robotic walk. This may indicate someone forcing or willing him- or herself to go through with a suicide bombing mission.

- Tunnel vision. The bomber often fixates on the target and as a result will look straight ahead. The bomber may also show signs of irritability, sweating, tics, or other nervous behavioral manifestations.

- The appearance of being drugged, including enlarged pupils, a fixed stare, or erratic behaviors.

- Bags or backpacks (used to carry explosives, nails, and other shrapnel). The bomber typically holds his or her bag or backpack tightly, sometimes gingerly, and may even refuse to be separated from it.

- A fresh shave, noticeable because of lighter skin where a beard has been removed. A male with a fresh shave and lighter skin on the lower portion of his face may be a religious zealot who has just shaved his beard in an effort not to draw attention and to blend in better with other people in the area.

- A hand in the pocket or tightly gripping something (such as a telephone or MP-3 player). The bomber could be holding a detonator or a trigger for an explosive device. Such triggers may be concealed in other types of devices to avoid being detected.

- Evasive or furtive movements. It may seem obvious but it should not be overlooked that anyone who avoids eye contact, evades security cameras and security or law enforcement officers, or who appears to be surreptitiously conducting surveillance of a potential target may be a bomber.

Suicide Boming Incident Response

Suicide bombings may be carried out by a lone bomber or several bombers. If a suspected suicide bomber is identified in some location, law enforcement should take a series of actions. The response to a suspected suicide bomber includes the following (adapted from IAPC, 2005b):

- **Immediate notification.** The responding officer should immediately contact his or her supervisor or watch commander to bring in the necessary bomb response squad, tactical team, airborne law enforcement, and possible hazmat resources. The local field office of the Federal Bureau of Investigation and the operational area multiagency counterterrorism network, such as the Terrorism Early Warning (TEW) Group, should also be notified.

- **Containment of the bomber.** The officer should not allow the suicide bomber to move toward masses of people. The officer should establish a security perimeter and quickly, and as quietly as possible, evacuate endangered citizens.

- **Maintain standoff distance.** The old adage "If you can see the bomber, the bomber can see you" applies here. But the responding officer should also bear in mind that the bomb is mobile. The officer should seek appropriate cover, being mindful of blast concussion, rebound, and shrapnel should the device be detonated. Except in extreme situations, the responding officer should not get close to a suspected bomber. When a bomber cannot reach a desired target, he or she may detonate to avoid capture. Even if the bomber wants to surrender, or is wounded or dead, the officer should remain at a standoff distance until the bomb squad arrives and takes over.

- **Define the circumstances when lethal force is justified.** Lethal force is justified if the suspect represents a significant threat of death or serious injury to an officer or others. Officers should be aware that the threat of death or serious injury need not be imminent with suicide bombers, as is sometimes noted in police use of force policies. This point is very important in any deadly force encounter, but even more so when dealing with explosive devices capable of widespread death and destruction. When officers have a reasonable basis to believe that the suspect has the capacity to detonate a bomb, they need not wait until a suicide bomber makes a move or takes other action potentially sufficient to carry out the bombing. The *threat* of such use is, in most instances, sufficient justification to employ deadly force.

- **If lethal force is used, aim for the head.** Police officers are trained and instructed to fire at the *center of body mass* (the torso) when using lethal force, but suicide bombers are an exception. Using this tactic with bombers is inappropriate for two reasons. First, it may only wound the bomber, and a wounded bomber may still detonate the device. (Suicide bombers do not generally wear body armor, but it has been known to happen.) Second, if a round fired by the officer strikes the explosive device, it may cause detonation. Hence, if lethal force is necessary, all shots should be directed at the bomber's head. An accurately placed head shot should kill the bomber before he or she has time to detonate the device.

- **Radio frequency suppression and predetonation.** Jamming devices can block the signals of cell phone and command-detonated systems. These jamming devices create an electronic barrier around an explosive device that stops radio signals and cell phone calls from detonating it.

Should the bomber detonate the device, investigation of the bomb site should follow the strategies and procedures described earlier in this chapter regarding investigating bomb sites.

SUMMARY

Learning Objective 1

Arson is one of the crimes that the FBI considers the most serious in American society, and it reports yearly statistics on arson in the Uniform Crime Report (UCR). In 2004 there were 63,215 arson offenses reported to law enforcement agencies.

Learning Objective 2

State statutes define what constitutes the crime of arson in each state. Generally, these statutes define arson as the malicious and intentional or fraudulent burning of buildings or property. Some jurisdictions categorize an arson as aggravated or simple. In most jurisdictions, aggravated arson is a felony. In some states, arson is divided into first, second, third, and fourth degrees. In addition, many jurisdictions have enacted statutes with more severe punishments for burning schools and other public buildings than for general arson.

Learning Objective 3

Motives for arson can be classified as rational or irrational. Rational motives are goal oriented and include revenge, profit from fraud, sabotage, and intimidation. Irrational motives lack direction and include such things as pyromania and vandalism.

Learning Objective 4

Arson is difficult to investigate because valuable evidence is often destroyed in the fire. Investigators study burn patterns to help them determine the point of origin, the spread of the fire, the temperature, the duration, and the presence of accelerants. In addition, certain indicators may lead an investigator to suspect arson. These indicators include multiple points of origin, odors of accelerants, the speed and spread of the fire, holes in walls or floors, alarm tampering, and the intensity of the fire.

Learning Objective 5

Bombing incidents generally are divided into explosive bombings and incendiary bombings. In 1999 actual and attempted explosive bombings made up 81 percent of bombing incidents. Four types of explosives are used in making bombs: primary, low, high, and blasting agents.

Learning Objective 6

Homemade bombs are the kinds of devices that most police agencies deal with. Such bombs include pipe bombs, firebombs, letter and package bombs, and booby trap bombs.

Learning Objective 7

The main functions of any police or safety service agency in a bombing incident are to protect human life and property, remove the bomb menace, and investigate and apprehend the bomber. Like arson, a bombing incident is difficult to investigate because valuable evidence is destroyed in the blast. As in any other crime, the bombing site must be preserved, evidence collected and identified, witnesses and suspects interviewed, and reports and follow-up investigations completed.

Learning Objective 8

Suicide bombers have become the weapon of choice for a number of terrorist organizations. Suicide bombers are difficult to recognize and difficult to stop once identified. Nonetheless, procedures to be followed if a suicide bomber is detected have been developed to maintain as much safety for the public as possible.

KEY TERMS

arson **366**

aggravated arson **367**

simple arson **367**

attempted arson **367**

negligent fires **367**

accelerant **369**

incendiary fire **369**

fire triangle **369**

direct ignition **369**

delayed ignition **369**

alligatoring **370**

crazing **371**

spalling **371**

trailer **372**

bombing **375**

explosive **376**

high explosive **376**

low explosive **376**

seat of the blast **383**

suicide bomber **386**

QUESTIONS FOR REVIEW

Learning Objective 1

1. How does the FBI classify arson?

Learning Objective 2

2. What is the *corpus delicti* of arson?
3. What type of crime is arson in most states?

Learning Objective 3

4. What are four motives for arson?

Learning Objective 4

5. What kinds of evidence may commonly be found at the scene of an arson?
6. What significance does a fire's point of origin have for an arson investigation?
7. What is the relationship between fire and police departments in arson investigations?
8. What factors make arsons difficult to investigate?
9. What can charring of wood indicate about a fire?
10. What conditions cause a V-shaped burn pattern?

Learning Objective 5

11. Define *bombing, high explosive,* and *low explosive.*
12. Is TNT a high or low explosive?
13. How is a safety fuse used?
14. What is an electric squib?

Learning Objective 6

15. Name four types of bombs that a bomb squad would deal with.
16. Why are letter and package bombs so difficult to detect?
17. Why should an officer not touch a suspected bomb found in a building?

Learning Objective 7

18. What is the prime function of the police in bomb matters?
19. What are some actions an officer should perform upon discovering an unexploded bomb?

Learning Objective 8

20. What is the first thing an officer should do if he or she discovers a suicide bomber?
21. If lethal force is used, why should an officer only take a head shot?

CRITICAL THINKING EXERCISES

Divide into two groups, and as assigned by your instructor, complete one of the following activities. Write a group report to present to the entire class.

1. Survey local or regional newspapers to identify news stories about arson or bombing incidents that have occurred in your area or state in the last twelve months. If you have to go back further than twelve months to find stories, do so. Assume that your group is a task force set up to investigate local or state arson and bombing incidents. What investigative leads can the group draw from the information provided?

2. Find your state's statutes defining arson and bombing or bomb threatening. Create a chart of the text of the statutes. Then determine who in your community is responsible for investigating arson and bombing incidents and who is responsible for disposing of unexploded bombs.

. . . .

INVESTIGATIVE SKILL BUILDERS

Interpreting and Communicating Information

You are an officer working dispatch in a medium-sized urban police department. At 11:30 a.m., you receive a telephone call from a man who says, "You have thirty minutes before a bomb goes off at one of the elementary schools in the city. You get to guess which one." There are seven elementary schools in your city and only six officers on duty during this shift.

1. Who do you call at each school?
2. What do you tell the person at each school?
3. Who else will you notify?

Integrity/Honesty

You are a member of the fire marshal's team investigating a possible arson at a shoe store. As you look around, you see the store manager showing an expensive pair of boots, spared by the flames, to the assistant manager, who is tallying the store's losses for the insurance report. You think you hear one of them say, "I'm sure we can add these boots to the losses." What actions, if any, should you take?

9

Organized Crime

After completing this chapter, you will be able to:

1 Provide an overview of organized crime.
2 Discuss some of the major organized crime groups.
3 Describe some techniques useful in investigating organized crime groups.
4 List some major laws enacted to combat organized crime.
5 Discuss the future of organized crime.

WHAT IS ORGANIZED CRIME?

The term *organized crime* conjures up images of large men in dark suits, secret rituals, meetings of family members, and gangland killings. This stereotype has commonly been applied to a sophisticated crime organization called the *Mafia* or *La Cosa Nostra* (LCN). The Mafia was made infamous during the 1960s by revelations offered by mobster Joseph Valachi (Maas, 1968) and in the 1970s by such popular films as *The Godfather* and *The Valachi Papers* (Martens & Cunningham-Niederer, 1985). The terms "the mob" and "the mafia" no longer refer only to groups such as the Mafia or the LCN but today are synonyms for organized crime groups generally. Organized crime groups are usually bound by ethnic ties, and they engage in supplying illegal goods and services as a business (Blok, 2001). These goods and services include, but are not limited to, illegal gambling, drug trafficking, loan-sharking, money laundering, credit card fraud, and extortion. Even legitimate businesses are taken over by organized crime groups and used to launder illegal income. Federal agencies estimate that Italian organized crime groups maintain approximately 25,000 members and 250,000 affiliates worldwide. There are more than 3,000 members and affiliates in the United States scattered mostly throughout the major cities in the Northeast, the Midwest, California, and the South (FBI, 2005).

The definition and understanding of what constitutes organized crime varies. The President's Commission on Organized Crime (1983) defined it as "a continuing, structured collectivity of persons who utilize criminality, violence, and a willingness to corrupt in order to gain and maintain power and profit." The FBI (1993) has defined organized crime as "a continuing criminal conspiracy, having an organized structure, fed by fear and corruption and motivated by greed." In this textbook, I define **organized crime** as a highly structured, disciplined, self-perpetuating association of people, usually bound by ethnic ties, who conspire to commit crimes for profit and use fear and corruption to protect their activities from criminal prosecution. Most organized crime groups share several basic goals:

- Continuation and propagation of the group
- Undying loyalty among members
- Financial gain
- Power and influence beyond the limits of the group

Organized crime groups are shrouded in secrecy, wield enormous power, and have fabulous wealth. They may engage in legal enterprises as well as illegal ones, and they frequently use force and intimidation, even murder, to further their goals. Organized crime groups are distorted parallels of career paths and management structures in legitimate business. In other words, organized crime groups operate like business enterprises (Lunde, 2004).

Organized crime groups like the Mafia have a formal pyramid structure similar to that of many corporations. At the top is the leader, or *don.* Below the don are upper-level henchmen and *counselors,* who correspond to upper-level managers in legitimate business structures. Next in the pyramid are lower-level *lieutenants,* who resemble middle managers or supervisors. At the bottom are *soldiers* and *button men,* who do the day-to-day grunt work and correspond to line workers in typical businesses. Groups like the Colombian drug cartels have a decentralized structure (Smithson, 2003). They resemble an association of small groups operating under a board of directors composed of the leaders, one from each group. As part of their *corporate* expansion, they have become partners with Mexican drug cartels who are responsible for as much as two-thirds of all cocaine sales in the United States (Smithson, 2003).

organized crime A highly structured, disciplined, self-perpetuating association of people, usually bound by ethnic ties, who conspire to commit crimes for profit and use fear and corruption to protect their activities from criminal prosecution.

ORGANIZED CRIME GROUPS

Many organized crime groups are offshoots of ethnic gangs that formed out of a need for association, protection, and defense against political, economic, and social isolation. They generally began as small territorial groups involved in petty crime within their own underclass neighborhoods. Individual members formed associations and committed crimes for personal success. Preying on their own communities, they used theft, extortion, gambling, and prostitution as sources of income. As their wealth grew, some groups obtained power, status, and political influence. Successful groups developed an organizational structure as their enterprises grew, and over time they extended beyond their territories. Even as they expanded, they retained their ethnic characteristics.

Several major organized crime groups operate in the United States today. Although these groups are organized along ethnic lines, they make up a tiny fraction of their communities. Most members of immigrant and ethnic communities in the United States are hardworking, law-abiding citizens who are as outraged by the violence these groups generate as anyone else. In addition, they are often the victims, preyed upon by gang members from their own ethnic communities.

John, *"the dapper Don"* Gotti, was also called the *Teflon Don* because he managed to avoid prosecution for many years while maintaining a highly profitable organized criminal enterprise.

FYI Organized crime leaders often acquire distinctive nicknames. After beginning his career as a not very successful burglar in the late 1960s, John Gotti turned to hijacking trucks. His career took an upswing, as did his appearance. Gotti began wearing fine, expensive suits and soon was nicknamed *Dapper Don*. Gotti expanded to gambling, loan-sharking, and drug trafficking. Several charges for crimes, including murder, were brought against Gotti in the 1980s. The charges did not stick, giving rise to another nickname—the *Teflon Don*. One of his underbosses turned state's evidence against him, in the 1990s, and Gotti was convicted of murder in 1993 and sentenced to life in prison without parole. Gotti died on June 10, 2002, at the age of 61, having served eleven years of his life sentence.

La Cosa Nostra (LCN)

La Cosa Nostra is the best-known organized crime group operating in the United States today. The origins of the LCN and of other contemporary Italian organized crime groups, such as the Sicilian Mafia and the Camorra, can be traced to cultural patterns unique to southern Italy and the island of Sicily. Throughout its history, Sicily was ruled by foreigners or outsiders. The Mafia developed as an alternative to these weak outsider governments. Small companies of armed Sicilians, mostly criminals, took the law into their own hands. Wealthy landowners in southern Italy hired armies of these Sicilians as caretakers to oversee and protect their property because the government was too weak to maintain order (Dileva, 2006). These caretakers developed into tight-knit organizations and began collecting tribute, or "protection," from the peasants. The landowners also used the Mafia to put down peasant revolts. Based on their relationship with the landowners and the growth of their power, these groups came to regard themselves as "men of honor" and developed a set of rituals, including a code of silence regarding their activities. The

Charles (Lucky) Luciano, who conceived the name and idea of *La Cosa Nostra* for the new American Mafia, is led into court in Manhattan in 1936 for sentencing in a prostitution case.

groups became known as *families* and were usually associated with the landowner to whom they were attached (Raab, 2005).

Mass Italian immigration to the United States began in 1870 and continued well into the first half of the twentieth century. About 80 percent of the immigrants were from Italy's impoverished rural south, with about 25 percent from Sicily alone. The first groups came to New York City, the gateway to America. Soon they spread to other large cities across the United States (Dickie, 2004). Italian gangs formed and began committing many of the same crimes they had committed in Italy. The gangs preyed mainly on their own communities, taking advantage of the immigrants' fear of the Mafia. Most gangs operated under a single leader, fought to guard their territory, and had little, if any, connection with other gangs.

Prohibition (1920–1933) served as the catalyst for the growth of the gangs as well as for uniting opposing ethnic factions. Seeking to improve their profits from bootlegging, gang leaders and groups cooperated to increase the distribution of illegal alcohol in the metropolitan areas the gangs controlled. The Capone gang in Chicago is an example of the power and influence that Italian gangs developed during Prohibition. Al Capone and the members of his gang started as local hoods and rose to become wealthy gangsters who controlled politics as well as crime in Chicago. When Capone was tried for federal tax evasion in 1931, his gang's gross annual income was estimated at $70 million.

When the Great Depression hit in 1929, the Mafia was rolling in money from illegal alcohol. Desperate business owners accepted loans at outlandish interest rates. When the debtors fell behind, their businesses were taken over to repay the loans. In some cases, the Mafia would slowly buy into a legitimate business until it had gained a controlling interest. As the wealth and influence of the Mafia grew, it expanded into other criminal enterprises, such as labor racketeering, narcotics, murder, gambling, loan-sharking, pornography, and extortion.

As the ethnic Italian organized crime groups gained power and influence, friction developed among them. There were several bloody turf wars, ending with a meeting of Mafia bosses in New York in 1931. At this meeting, official codes for governing criminal groups of Mafia origin were set up. Here, also, the groups took on the collective name La Cosa Nostra (LCN) and divided the new American Mafia into families, each with its own sphere of influence. A few months later a commission was set up to assign territories, settle disputes, and exercise internal discipline. The commission was originally composed of the five New York families and Al Capone from Chicago. Later it was expanded to include bosses from other families across the country, establishing the bureaucratic structure for which the Mafia is known.

During the remainder of the 1930s, World War II, and the postwar years, LCN consolidated its power and succeeded the Irish, Jewish, German, and other ethnic organized crime groups as the most powerful criminal organization in the United States (FBI, 1993, 2005).

Hispanic Crime Groups

In the early 1970s cocaine was a drug for well-to-do jet-setters and show business types. Ghetto kids were not yet making fast money selling it on street corners. That began to change as Colombian drug rings organized to increase and control production and distribution of the white powder. Throughout the 1970s, the smugglers gathered power in the cocaine trade, setting up cartels centered around various tight-knit families to control the movement of cocaine into the United States. Of the twenty or so cartels, the most prominent came to be those based in the cities of Medellin and Cali (Smithson, 2003; Youngers & Rosin, 2005).

The cocaine wars began in south Florida in the late 1970s when the Colombians took the drug trade away from Cuban gangs, and it spread to Hispanic neighborhoods in places like New York City, Brooklyn, and Hartford, where Dominican and Puerto Rican gangs had small-time drug operations. The Colombians were more willing to deal with Cubans, Dominicans, and Puerto Ricans than with American blacks, and Hispanic gangs became middlemen between the Colombian importers and the black street gangs that sell drugs on the street.

In December 1993 Pablo Escobar, the head of the Medellin cartel, was killed by Colombian antidrug forces. The Cali cartel was able to take over most of the Medellin cartel's market in cocaine trafficking. Like the Chinese triads, the Cali cartel has a superior global network to move raw

Colombian drug lord Pablo Escobar, killed at age 44 by U.S.-backed Colombian antidrug forces, was an early prototype of the new international gangster.

materials and finished products. The Cali cartel, which was thought to be the largest supplier of cocaine to the United States and Europe, began to fall apart by the end of 1999. By the dawn of the new millennium, the Cali cartel no longer dominated the cocaine market. Law enforcement efforts against the Medellin and Cali cartels had effectively segmented and decentralized the drug trade out of Colombia, making it extremely difficult to control (Chepesiuk, 2005; Smithson, 2003). A number of veteran drug traffickers who had been operating under the auspice of the Cali cartel quickly rose in power in their own right, and by 2002 much of the cocaine trafficking in Colombia was centered in the northern Valle del Causa region, of which Cali is the capital city. Cocaine traffickers in that region began to operate independently of each other and passed the major responsibilities for smuggling and wholesaling on to drug trafficking syndicates in Mexico. Among the new drug organizations that arose in the region were the Henao-Montoya syndicate, the Montoya-Sanchez organization, and the Urdinola-Graijles network (Chepesiuk, 2005; Smithson, 2003). In 2005 several high-ranking leaders of the Montoya-Sanchez organization were arrested and indicted on drug charges. Juan Carlos Montoya Sanchez and Carlos Felipe Tor Sanchez both plead guilty to conspiring to import cocaine into the United States (U.S. Department of Justice, 2005).

Jamaican Posses

The posses, named after the vigilante groups in the cheap European Westerns popular in Jamaica, rose out of shanty towns to political power by aligning themselves with the major political parties on the island. The gang chiefs, known as "community leaders," became champions of the poor, pressuring the political parties controlling the government to distribute welfare to those in need. Rival parties hired gangs of thugs to influence elections. Gang members exported cocaine and marijuana to the United States to buy guns for political warfare.

Jamaican street gangs or posses originally began forming during the 1970s, chiefly around Kingston, Jamaica. Members tended to come from the same general neighborhood as other members of that posse, with several notable exceptions. For example, the Rat posse was composed entirely of members who had killed a Jamaican police officer; Hotsteppers posse members had all escaped from a Jamaican prison and had all been convicted of a capital crime; and the Shower posse was so named because of their practice of raining a shower of bullets on their victims (Connors et al., 1997).

In the 1980 election the political warfare grew especially ugly. Hundreds of Jamaicans died when gang members working for rival factions fired on political rallies and even police stations. Though put in power by gang warfare, the new prime minister tried to rein in the gangs. He unleashed the corrupt Jamaican police on the gangs, which had served their purpose and were now a nuisance (Schatzberg & Kelly, 1997).

By 1984 many posse members had fled to New York City and Miami where their flair for violence gave them an advantage over local drug dealers. Posses soon expanded to other cities, including Brooklyn, Philadelphia, Boston, Rochester, Washington, Houston, Dallas, Denver, Detroit, and Los Angeles. The posses' drive to control the crack trade in the 1980s was bloodier than the gang killings of Prohibition days. Posses murdered more than 1,400 people in less than five years (Kleinknecht, 1996). According to some sources, between 1985 and 1992 more than 4,000 U.S. homicides were attributed to Jamaican posses (Connors et al., 1997).

Today law enforcement officials regard Jamaican posse crack houses and firearms operations as more sophisticated than the operations of any of their contemporary organized criminal competitors. The Jamaican posses strive for an organizational structure similar to that of the Mafia (Connors et al., 1997). Many of the middle- and high-level positions in Jamaican posses are filled by criminal fugitives from Jamaica. Lower-level positions are recruited directly from the ranks of urban African Americans. Because of pressure by law enforcement and Immigration and Customs Enforcement (ICE) officials, the overall structure of posses is not as stable as the structure of some other organized crime groups.

In addition to being motivated by profits from gunrunning and drug trafficking, Jamaican posses were originally politically motivated. Considerable money from their U.S. criminal enterprises was sent to Jamaican-based posses to buy local elections on the island. Some wealthy U.S.-based posse members retire to Jamaica and live the life of local "dons." Like other organized crime groups in the United States, local posses have begun buying legitimate businesses with profits from their criminal activity.

Asian Crime Groups

Asian crime groups in the United States consist of groups organized by criminals predominantly from East and Southeast Asia. Members of these groups are of Chinese, Korean, Japanese, Thai, Filipino, Cambodian, Laotian, and Vietnamese descent. However, new Asian criminal enterprises have been emerging as domestic and international threats in the new millennium (Smithson, 2003). These groups include members from the South Pacific Island nations as well as groups from Southwest Asia such as Pakistan, India, Afghanistan, Nepal, and Iran. In the United States, Asian criminal enterprises have been identified in more than fifty metropolitan areas, but they are most prevalent in Boston, Chicago, Honolulu, Las Vegas, Los Angeles, New Orleans, New York, Newark, Philadelphia, Portland, San Francisco, Seattle, and Washington, D.C. (Frank, 2003).

Asian crime groups can be categorized as *traditional* or *nontraditional.* Traditional Asian crime groups include the Chinese triads based in Hong Kong, Taiwan, and Macau as well as the Japanese Yakuza or Boryokudan. Nontraditional criminal enterprises include groups such as Chinese criminally influenced tongs, triad affiliates, and other ethnic Asian street gangs in the United States and other countries with sizable Asian communities.

In general, the criminal conduct engaged in by Asian crime groups in the United States includes traditional racketeering activities normally associated with organized crime, such as extortion, murder, kidnapping, illegal gambling, prostitution, and loan-sharking, and also international organized crime problems such as alien smuggling, heroin and methamphetamine drug trafficking, financial frauds such as illegal credit cards, theft of automobiles and computer chips, counterfeiting computer and clothing products, and money laundering (FBI, 2006).

Triads   The triads are the oldest of the organized crime groups, having come into being in the late 1600s. China was invaded by the Manchus, a tribe from Mongolia who set up the Ching dynasty, which began in 1644 and lasted until 1911. The Manchus had an iron grip on northern China, but in the south they faced continual rebellion. Secret societies sprang up all over southern China. At first their main goal was to overthrow the Ching and restore native Chinese rulers to the throne. As the societies gained the support of the peasants, they also worked to aid the people while still opposing the government. Members of the societies were bound together by an intricate system of secret rituals, oaths, passwords, ceremonial dress, hand signals, and ceremonial intermingling of blood; some of these rituals are still in use today (Ter Haar, 2000).

By the mid-1800s, after several failed uprisings, the Manchus had the triads on the run. Some fled to Hong Kong, where there were already triad societies, and to North America, where they organized triad groups in Canada and the United States. The British gave the societies the name *triads* because their flags and banners were triangular. Faced with a lack of operating funds, the triads became involved in opium smuggling, extortion, and prostitution. Soon the triads were a distinctly criminal organization with less involvement in social and political activities, and this remains true today.

Hong Kong is the center of the diverse triad organizations, and groups operate in China, Taiwan, Canada, the United States, and other countries with large Chinatowns that triad members can infiltrate and prey on. Some major triad groups are the 14K, the Wo Group, the Big Four, the Chiu Chow, and the Kung Lok. Under such umbrella groups are networks of triads that work with Chinese street gangs. Triads run drugs, smuggle illegal aliens, make counterfeit currency and credit cards, commit fraud and forgery, and conduct the traditional organized crime activities. Many senior triad members have fronts as legitimate businessmen but continue to operate illegal enterprises (Kleinknecht, 1996). Today, triads operating in the United States have begun shifting their criminal activities to credit card frauds and human trafficking. Both are extremely profitable but are less risky for criminal gang members than drug smuggling (Castells, 2000; Sardijin, 2006).

Tongs   Tongs began as benevolent societies set up along family or business lines in major American cities with large Chinese populations. The term *tong* means "meeting hall" or "meeting place" in Chinese. Tongs can trace their beginnings to Chinese triads,

When U.S. officials seize vessels, they often find illegal aliens. Chinese organized crime groups have smuggled tens of thousands of illegal Chinese aliens into the United States.

are organized along similar lines, and sometimes communicate with each other. During the middle of the nineteenth century, a significant number of Chinese immigrated to the United States. They were lured by advertisements promising high pay and quick fortunes in California and New York. Males were especially welcome to build the railroads and work the mines. Business owners and families of Chinese origin helped the newcomers find jobs, housing, and medical care. In time, they formed their own organizations to provide welfare services, set up rules and regulations, care for the needy, and act as a liaison with the outside, where the newly arrived immigrants were regarded with suspicion by American laborers (McIllwain, 2004).

When the California gold rush was over, anti-Chinese sentiment drove out many of the immigrants, who headed east, founding Chinatowns in Chicago, New York, Boston, Philadelphia, and other cities. Chinatowns were divided into districts according to Chinese surnames, and the newly arrived could register with the appropriate tong. Criminal activities such as gambling and prostitution became lucrative businesses and fell under tong control. As the tongs grew, they vied for control of territories and rackets. Legitimate and respectable businessmen joined the tongs just to protect their families and businesses. In 1913 a peace agreement among rival associations stopped the bloody warfare. The vice-related activities seemed to disappear, and the tongs seemed to become socially conscious organizations dedicated to bettering the Chinese community.

The mid-1960s brought a change in the image of Chinatowns throughout the United States. The Immigration and Naturalization Act of 1965 allowed Chinese immigration at the same level as that of other preferred nations. Chinese immigration, which had been averaging a little more than 100 people a year, suddenly exceeded 20,000 a year. The nation's Chinatowns, already hemmed in geographically, had a hard time absorbing the newcomers. These Chinese immigrants were very different from those of the nineteenth century who had been descendants of farmers with a tradition of hard work and humility. Many of the newcomers were from the slums of Hong Kong where triad-linked street gangs were the law and Chinese traditions had long been lost.

FYI The term *racket,* as applied to crime, supposedly comes from old-time New York political fund-raising gatherings. They were called rackets because of the noise the attendees made. Later, gangs put on their own rackets, for which merchants and other business owners were forced to buy tickets. The term came to be applied to any enterprise activity resulting in illegal income.

The new Chinese immigrants found that life in the United States was not easy. For people who could not speak English, the only jobs were in garment sweatshops or in restaurants, waiting tables. Chinese youth found it especially hard. Their inability to speak English made them poor students in big-city school systems, where they were often put into classes with much younger students. The most insecure coped with these problems by banding together in gangs.

The gangs engaged in robbery, extortion, and other crimes to support themselves and soon were staking out territories. Fearing that the gangs would intrude on their underground gambling and other vice activities, the tongs hired rival gangs to protect their interests. Soon gang wars were raging in San Francisco, New York City, and Toronto. While Chinese gangsters were killing off each other, more level-headed Chinese gangsters were setting up a national Chinese crime syndicate. Taking their cue from the Mafia, these groups hid behind legitimate businesses to launder money from their illegal gambling, extortion, and heroin smuggling. The **money laundering** took many forms, from investing in real estate to having groups of "mules" use cash to buy luxury items to export.

Tongs are involved in many Chinese community functions that help Asian businesses operate, yet many of them are fronts for the criminal operations of organized Chinese crime syndicates. Despite their continued involvement in illegal gambling, extortion, prostitution, and smuggling illegal aliens, drug trafficking is the preferred enterprise for Chinese organized crime syndicates (Kleinknecht, 1996).

money laundering Investing illegally obtained money into businesses and real estate operated and maintained within the law.

Yakuza The Yakuza had their origins in the customs and traditions of the samurai warrior class of ancient Japan. The samurai were known for their extreme loyalty and discipline. By the 1700s, Yakuza gangs had appeared. They were set up in families, reflecting the Japanese tradition of a strong-willed "father" leader who demanded blind obedience from his "children." They capitalized on the traditions of samurai honor and courage while committing crimes and were considered Robin Hoods. In the late 1800s they moved into the cities, recruiting members from the ghettos. The social and political upheaval that followed World War II provided the perfect setting for the Yakuza to take over the black market in Japan and to expand their criminal activities.

As Japanese people and businesses moved West in postwar years, so did the Yakuza (Kaplan & Dubro, 2003).

The Yakuza control Japan's casinos, brothels, white-slave trade, nightclubs, entertainment industry, gunrunning, loan-sharking, drug trafficking, and money laundering. They also practice a unique form of corporate extortion called *sokaiya*. Yakuza members show up at a Japanese corporation and demand a huge payoff. If refused, they threaten to spread damaging rumors about the business. Or Yakuza members may threaten to turn up at a stockholder meeting to spill company secrets, to raise questions about company management, or to create a scene—throw furniture, shout and scream, even slap the chairman of the board. Because the Japanese are so anxious to save face and not be publicly shamed, corporations generally pay up.

The Yakuza are entrenched in Honolulu, San Francisco, Los Angeles, Paris, London, Rotterdam, São Paolo, and other cities worldwide, where they operate in conjunction with other Asian crime groups and with the LCN. Yakuza groups run drugs and arms, launder money, and blackmail Japanese corporations around the world, even trying their luck with American corporations. Some Yakuza are identifiable by their distinctive markings—elaborate body tattoos and missing finger joints, detached in secret rituals to show loyalty (House Committee on Foreign Affairs, 1994; Kleinknecht, 1996).

Viet Ching At the close of the Vietnam War in the late 1970s, Vietnamese immigrants began immigrating to other countries. Throughout the 1980s, many of these immigrants came to the United States. Among these immigrants were many who were of Chinese ancestry, more commonly referred to as Viet Ching. In the United States a number of Viet Ching formed small associations or gangs and preyed upon Asian communities. Like tongs, these gangs soon were offering protection to local Asian merchants and the drug trade.

Other immigrants from Vietnam included former members of the Vietnamese armed forces and criminals. Many of these men banded together once they arrived in the United States and formed vicious, strong-arm gangs. Like other Asian immigrant criminals, these Vietnamese gangs preyed largely on Asian, and mostly Vietnamese, communities. They were soon involved in the full range of rackets, murder, arson, extortion, and drug trafficking (Kelly, 2000).

Asian street gangs, as well as other street gangs, use marks, scars, and tattoos (indicators) to show other members as well as nonmembers that they are "down for the gang" and involved in criminal activity. These indicators can be intimidating to the victims as well as the general public.

These indicators are important to law enforcement because they can provide an indication that the individual being questioned or interviewed is a gang member. While the public frequently associates certain tattoos with gangs (for example an M for the Mexican Mob), a common identifier found on many Asian and especially Vietnamese gang members are patterns of cigarette burns. Cigarette burns will not identify the subject as a member of a particular gang; however, it can help one to recognize that the individual is likely in some Asian gang.

These burn marks may be found in groups of two or more, by themselves or in the form of a design. They are usually found on the back of the hand or on the forearm. The cigarette burn mark is made by pressing a lit cigarette against the skin for a period of time, leaving a circular mark or dot. Some gang members may burn their upper forearm in an attempt to hide it from parents and law enforcement (Walker, 2007).

Russian Mafia

The emergence of the Russian Mafia was one of the major developments in transnational organized crime in the 1990s (Varese, 2005). Life in the Soviet Union equipped many Russian and East European gangsters with skills suited to the scams they have pulled off in the United States and elsewhere in the West. Soviet citizens had to negotiate their way through the vast Communist bureaucracy, with its endless flow of documents, to get a job, to buy a car, to travel, to get medical care—to do just about everything. To survive, criminals had to learn how to get around the constraints of this totalitarian system. Their tools were bribery, forgery, and counterfeiting. They also had to evade the Soviet police and the dreaded KGB, whose favorite interrogation techniques were beating and torture. Ordinary Soviets often used the talents of gangsters to get what they needed; they referred to these outlaws as *mafia,* and the name stuck.

The Russian Mafia's roots are not in Italy (where the Italian Mafia originated) but in the Soviet political system before the fall of the Communist Party when power was exercised through criminality, violence, and intimidation (Varese, 2005). Some experts on the Russian Mafia maintain that to some extent the Russian Mafia has replaced the Communist Party by providing "order" in Russia and throughout a number of formerly Eastern bloc countries (Varese, 2005). In fact, the Russian Mafia is often viewed as having originally emerged as an alliance between criminals and former Communists in the state bureaucracy, including former members of the KGB (the Russian secret police), many of whom started out as strong-arm men for the new Mafia (Varese, 2005).

The breakup of the Soviet Union in 1991 brought Russian and Eastern European gangsters out of the underground. They took advantage of the political chaos in all the former republics to invade every area of life. After they had the fifteen former Soviet republics under control, they turned their enterprise skills to Western Europe and North America, particularly the United States.

Agents lead Russian Mafia crime boss Vyacheslav Ivanov from the FBI office in New York City after his arrest on extortion charges in 1995.

Russian and East European gangs were operating in North America well before the breakup of the Soviet Union, mostly in New York, Los Angeles, and Toronto. Some smaller groups could be found in Chicago, Boston, Wilmington, Phoenix, San Francisco, and other smaller cities. With the breakup of the Soviet Union and the increased freedom of travel, thousands of Russian gangsters flooded the United States. They hooked up with established Russian and East European gangsters who knew the language, the U.S. system of law, and the way the system worked. Soon, many had their own criminal networks and were demanding more and more of the criminal pie. This loose-knit collection of gangsters calls itself the *Organizatsiya,* or organization. They deal in drugs, extortion, kidnapping, bank fraud, counterfeiting, contraband exports, contract murder, and trafficking in dangerous weapons and components. They are forging working relationships with other ethnic organized crime groups, especially the Italian Mafia (Kleinknecht, 1996).

Street Gangs

During the late 1950s and early 1960s, youthful street gangs were a problem only in several large American cities. In the beginning, these gangs chiefly fought one another, committed petty crimes, and pulled off small-time extortions. Today street gangs are involved in murder, drug trafficking, and a host of other serious crimes, all connected to the drug trade. Drug gangs from the nation's largest cities have expanded into medium-sized and small cities where there is less competition for drug trade and where they can maximize profits in the drug market (Katz & Webb, 2006).

The most expansive and best organized of these street gangs are the Crips and the Bloods—the African American street gangs of Los Angeles. These gangs have grown into national organizations that send recruiters into prospective territories (even rural areas) to organize affiliated gang sets. These federations provide an extensive network for the gangs' illegal enterprises, including the manufacture and distribution of crack cocaine, murder for hire, extortion, and the sale of illegal firearms. Identifying the gang federation a member belongs to is not hard. Since the gangs emerged after the Watts riot in 1965, the Crips have worn blue colors and the Bloods have worn red. Blood gangs can go under any name; Crips gangs usually have the name of the federation in their title (Katz & Webb, 2006; Smithson, 2003; Spergel, 1993).

The number of street gangs that law enforcement officers must deal with is mind-boggling. Today, virtually every city in the United States with a population of more than 250,000 reports a serious gang problem. Gangs are also prevalent in small and medium-sized cities as well. For instance, 87 percent of cities with populations between 100,000 and 249,999 and 27 percent of cities with populations of 2,500 to 49,000 report having an active youth gang problems in their city (Katz & Webb, 2006).

Outlaw Motorcycle Gangs

During the 1940s, as American soldiers returned from World War II, free-living motorcycle gangs began to form. Veterans established these clubs, organizing them as paramilitary groups. These early gangs were emulated by more youthful motorcycle enthusiasts and romanticized by movies of the 1950s and 1960s.

Typically, the organizational structure of the outlaw motorcycle gang involves a number of local chapters and a "Mother Club," which supervises the local chapters. Each local chapter has a Mother Club adviser who, in effect, exercises direct supervision over the membership. The Mother Club adviser is largely responsible for appointing members to the various positions of responsibility in the gang. As the overseer, the Mother Club establishes and enforces policy for the organization, schedules mandatory trips or *runs,* and has final authority over most club matters (Mather, 2004).

By the mid 1980s there were approximately 1,000 motorcycle gangs operating in the United States. Among these, the most influential are Hell's Angels, Outlaws, Pagans, Warlocks, Mongols, Breeds, and the Bandidos. Hell's Angels are the most well known and the best organized of the groups, with chapters in the United States, Canada, Britain, Germany, France, Brazil, Russia, Japan, and other countries. Outlaw motorcycle gangs are engaged in numerous criminal enterprises, the most frequent and most lucrative of which are drug and illegal firearms trafficking (Davis 1982).

Due to serious interdiction efforts by law enforcement during the 1990s, coupled with the diminished demand for methamphetamine and its cheaper production from Mexican sources, outlaw motorcycle gangs are generally considered an organized crime force in decline. However, if these groups are able to adapt to the new conditions facing them, they may once again become a force within

Outlaw motorcycle gangs have chapters in many countries.

the narcotics marketplace. It has been suggested in some law enforcement circles that one way outlaw motorcycle gangs could accomplish this adaptation would be through the production and distribution of the new methamphetamine derivative, *ice.* Ice is an extremely addictive designer drug that has become popular, especially on the West Coast, and has been steadily making its way east through parties and raves. On the East Coast, the Atlantic City casino environment represents an already established market for ice. Since the outlaw motorcycle gangs previously established themselves as a dominant force in the manufacture and distribution of methamphetamine, the transition to producing and distributing ice is certainly possible (Sher & Marsden, 2006; Smithson, 2003).

INVESTIGATING ORGANIZED CRIME

For many years, federal, state, and local law enforcement officials investigated and prosecuted individual members of organized crime groups for crimes such as extortion, fraud, drug trafficking, or murder. The convicted felon went to prison, but someone else in the organization was always standing by ready to carry on in the member's absence, and the criminal enterprise continued. Minimum sentences for specific crimes allowed convicted felons to return quickly to the crime organization with enhanced stature for having served the sentence and maintained silence about the organization. Furthermore, incarcerating one individual failed to remove the organization's profit from criminal activity. Another aspect of organized crime that protected it from effective prosecution was its corruption of judges, lawyers, politicians, law enforcement officials, financial institutions, and businesses.

FOCUS ON TECHNOLOGY

COMPUTERIZED CRIME MAPPING (GEOGRAPHIC PROFILING)

ADVANCES IN COMPUTER-AIDED DISPATCHING SYSTEMS and mapping software programs have made it easier for law enforcement officers to spot crime patterns in neighborhoods and devise creative strategies for fighting them. Video screens display neighborhood diagrams using multicolored dots, ovals, and other symbols to plot everything from shooting locations to drug markets. See Chapter 5 for a more complete examination of this technique.

Enterprise Theory of Investigation

enterprise theory of investigation An approach to criminal investigation that targets entire crime organizations instead of individual criminals within them.

Since the early 1980s, law enforcement agencies investigating organized crime have relied on the **enterprise theory of investigation** (ETI). In an ETI investigation, an entire crime organization is targeted under the Racketeer Influenced and Corrupt Organizations Act, commonly known as RICO. Passed by Congress in 1970, RICO allows a single prosecution of an entire multidefendant organized crime group for all its diverse criminal activities. The crimes do not have to be linked by the same perpetrator or a common criminal conspiracy. Thus prosecutors can include years of criminal acts in a sweeping racketeering indictment. Prosecutors have used RICO effectively against established, highly structured organized crime groups like LCN. Many states also have enacted their own RICO statutes.

General Provisions of the RICO Statute   The RICO statute is broader than other criminal statutes we have discussed. It does not create individual offenses but defines a pattern of offenses for which an individual or an entity can be prosecuted. The RICO statute starts out by listing the federal and state crimes that may form the basis of a RICO offense. These include such crimes as gambling, bribery, dealing in obscene matter, dealing in narcotics or other dangerous drugs, mail fraud, witness tampering, and obstruction of justice.

predicate crime A crime that is a basis of a violation of the RICO statute.

The crimes outlined in RICO are referred to as **predicate crimes** because they constitute a predicate, or basis, for a violation of the statute. The RICO statute requires a *pattern* of racketeering activity. That is, a violator must have committed at least *two predicate offenses* within a ten-year period, one of which took place after RICO became effective. Persons convicted of RICO violations are subject to fines and imprisonment. They are also subject to punishment for the individual predicate crimes of which they are convicted. All fines are added together, and jail terms must be served consecutively, not concurrently.

forfeiture The loss of money or property to the state as a criminal sanction.

Additional Provisions of the RICO Statute   The RICO statute recognized the profit motive of organized crime and the need to remove the source of the profit. In addition to the fines levied for RICO violations, the statute provides for **forfeiture** of assets acquired directly or indirectly from racketeering activity. In addition, persons or entities who have had their well-being, their property, or their reputations damaged by the RICO violations can bring a civil action against the violators and sue for damages. Another civil provision of the RICO statute allows the government to obtain an **injunction** to keep members of an organized crime group from controlling a legitimate enterprise, such as a labor union, and using its funds for illegal activities.

Investigative Techniques

Investigating and prosecuting organized crime requires effective legal tools as well as effective investigative strategies. A successful investigation depends to a large extent on maintaining the secrecy of the investigation as much as possible. Some investigative tools, such as electronic surveillance, can generally be used without disclosing even the existence of an investigation. Other useful tools, such as grand jury subpoenas and search warrants, however, may reveal law enforcement's interest in a particular person, group, or place. A carefully coordinated investigative strategy can minimize the extent to which use of these tools impedes an ongoing investigation (Nardini, 2006).

One very effective technique for investigating organized crime has been creation of organized crime task forces. Task forces combine resources and personnel from federal, state, and local law enforcement and regulatory agencies to investigate and prosecute organized crime. Some federal agencies that play an important role in investigating organized crime on the national level are the FBI, the U.S. Postal Service, the Secret Service, the Department of Labor, the Securities and Exchange Commission, and the Internal Revenue Service. State attorneys general, district attorneys, and county and city prosecutors can assist law enforcement authorities in investigating organized crime groups that violate state and local laws. Financial analysis, electronic surveillance, informants, undercover operations, pressure from citizens' groups and commissions, and computerized communications and analysis are all tools in the battle against organized crime (Albanese, 1995).

STATISTICS Organized crime earns annual profits estimated at more than $1 trillion worldwide. An estimated $1 billion in crime profits is wire-transferred through financial markets every day.

Financial analysis refers to locating and following a financial paper trail. Identifying sources of revenue for large and frequent bank deposits can sometimes lead investigators to organized crime organizations. The Internal Revenue Service (IRS) plays a key role in this part of an investigation. Existing IRS codes and regulations provide a means for law enforcement to investigate and analyze the net worth, tax payments (or failure to pay taxes), and general expenditures of an organization.

Electronic surveillance includes the use of wiretaps, concealed video- and audiotaping, and an assortment of other covert strategies. Many investigators regard electronic surveillance as one of the most popular methods of gathering evidence against notorious mobsters. Similarly, **informers,** existing members of criminal syndicates who provide information leading to indictments, and evidence and testimony during trials, are a viable weapon against organized crime. Historically, **undercover operations** and infiltrations have been effective—albeit dangerous—in combating organized criminal activities. Citizens' commissions have been successful at bringing public attention and pressure to bear against organized crime groups (Albanese, 1995; Albanese & Pursley, 1993).

injunction A court order prohibiting a party from a specific course of action or ordering a party to perform some action.

informer A member of an organized crime group who provides information and testimony for law enforcement investigations and prosecutions.

undercover operation An investigative police operation designed to secretly uncover evidence against an individual or an organized criminal group.

Computer-assisted communications and analysis during investigations has proven invaluable. Computers provide a means of unraveling the intricate fake companies used by many criminal organizations to conceal and launder their ill-gotten money. Sophisticated databases used by the FBI and the IRS give investigators a way to analyze paper trails and coordinate their efforts with other agencies. Furthermore, with advances in electronic banking and money transfers, computers are likely to play a significant role in both laundering and concealing the profits of organized criminal groups. Consequently, investigators will need strong computer skills to compete.

Laws to Combat Organized Crime

To defend against the onslaught of organized crime in the United States, law enforcement agencies have had to develop creative legal strategies. The laws that have had the greatest impact in this regard are discussed next.

> **FYI** A 1996 investigation by the National Association of Securities Dealers, Inc. and the FBI revealed that organized crime groups have moved into Wall Street, establishing a network of stock promoters, securities dealers, and boiler rooms that sell stock nationwide using hard-sell tactics (Business Week, December 1996). The transactions involve small-capitalization stocks for which promoters quickly drive up the price. Then they get out of the market, leaving buyers with overpriced stocks that they can sell only at a loss. Other securities dealers and traders are said to pay extortion money to organized crime as "just another cost of doing business" on Wall Street.

The Hobbs Act The Hobbs Act is an antiracketeering act that became law during the 1940s. It has been used to crack down on any activity that interferes with interstate commerce.

The Controlled Substance Act of 1970 The Comprehensive Drug Abuse and Control Act of 1970, popularly called the Controlled Substance Act, created a coordinated and codified system of drug control that classified all narcotics and dangerous drugs. Another objective was to create a closed regulatory system for the legitimate handling of controlled drugs by physicians, pharmacists, and those involved in the manufacture of pharmaceuticals. The system required legitimate handlers to register with designated state agencies, maintain records, and make biennial inventories of all controlled drugs in stock.

absolute immunity A guarantee that, as long as a witness complies with the court and testifies, the testimony cannot be used against him or her in any criminal action.

recalcitrant witness A witness who refuses to testify in a criminal proceeding, even after being offered immunity.

The Organized Crime Control Act of 1970 The central purpose of this act was to fight organized crime by strengthening legal tools. It provided much stiffer penalties for violations and extended the ways evidence could be gathered. To encourage witness participation, three things were done. First, **absolute immunity,** a guarantee that the witness would not be prosecuted for any involvement, could be offered. With absolute immunity, as long as a witness complies with the court and testifies, the testimony cannot be used against him or her in any criminal action. Second, any witness who refused to testify, even with immunity, could be labeled a **recalcitrant witness.** Recalcitrant witnesses could be confined until they chose to testify. The incarceration, however, could not exceed the length of the court proceeding or the full term of the grand jury, including all extensions. Third, protection was given to witnesses whose lives would be threatened as result of their testifying. The act also stiffened perjury penalties (Chamelin, 2005).

The Bank Secrecy Act of 1970 This act addressed money laundering, including a requirement that banks report any transaction of $10,000 or more. Similarly, a bank must report if $10,000 or more leaves or enters the country. Furthermore, citizens must report on their annual tax returns any foreign bank accounts they have (Abadinsky, 2006).

The Comprehensive Crime Control Act of 1984 This act was another attempt to squelch drug and organized crime activities. In addition to reforms in bail and sentencing, it expanded forfeiture authority and provided amendments intended to aid in the investigation of money laundering.

The Money Laundering Control Act of 1986 Like the Bank Secrecy Act of 1970, this act addressed money laundering. It made money laundering a federal offense. The law made it illegal to cause a domestic financial institution to fail to report transactions of $10,000 or more. This prohibition includes attempts to have financial institutions make false statements by providing them with incorrect or misleading information.

The Anti-Drug Abuse Act of 1986 This law greatly expanded federal, state, and local drug abuse control efforts. It created mandatory sentences for certain drug-related crimes and made it a crime to involve juveniles in drug distribution or sales. In addition, the law made it illegal to distribute drugs within 1,000 feet of a school.

The Anti-Drug Abuse Act of 1988 This act was a complement to the Anti-Drug Abuse Act of 1986. It established a cabinet-level position intended to ease and make more effective federal drug enforcement activities. The position is popularly known as the drug czar. In addition to increasing penalties for a number of drug offenses, the law also created mandatory sentences for certain drug-related crimes involving children.

Asset Seizure and Forfeiture Laws The intent of forfeiture is to remove the financial rewards of criminal activity. For example, once a drug smuggler is arrested at the airport, the government may seize the private airplane used to fly the drugs in as well as the trafficker's home, cars, and restaurant—all bought with drug proceeds. Upon conviction, the drug smuggler loses ownership of these items. Both the Comprehensive Crime Control Act of 1984 and the Anti-Drug Abuse Act of 1986 extended law enforcement's authority to seize profits and property resulting from drug trafficking. In addition, these acts provided a legal means for seizing cash connected with money laundering activities. Proceeds from forfeitures are funneled back into the fight against crime. Seized boats are sometimes given to law enforcement agencies that need them. Funds from forfeiture are also used to purchase needed equipment.

Conspiracy Laws Simply defined, a **conspiracy** is an agreement between two or more parties to commit an unlawful act by unlawful means. Usually, someone who plans to commit a crime may withdraw from the plan before the act is committed. This is not the case, however, for conspiracy. Once an agreement has been struck, the parties involved are co-conspirators, and withdrawal will not allow them to escape the charge of conspiracy.

conspiracy A crime in which two or more parties are in concert in a criminal purpose.

THE FUTURE OF ORGANIZED CRIME

Patterns in organized crime suggest that the traditional, bureaucratic, organized crime *family* is on the decline. Years of cooperative investigations by federal and state authorities in many large cities have weakened the Mafia considerably. These investigations, however, may not be the only explanation. Another reason may be that Mafia family heads have been so successful at educating their offspring that the children are not interested in entering the family "business." As these family heads grow older and step—or are pushed—into retirement, no younger immediate family members have been tutored in the business and are ready to step in. Instead, some families have had to reach down the bureaucratic structure and elevate lower-level lieutenants who apparently lack the strength and leadership of the old dons (Finckenauer, 2008).

Finally, other criminal organizations are seeking control over criminal activities once controlled by the Mafia. These groups, such as the Chinese triads, Jamaican posses, and Colombian cartels, are more ruthless, violent, and brutal than today's *mafiosi*.

The future of investigation of criminal organizations is likely to remain in the area of money laundering and misuses of electronic transfers of funds between financial institutions (Albanese, 1995). Unfortunately, investigators will probably trace human carnage along the same route as they trace the paper and electronic trail to the organizational leaders.

SUMMARY

Learning Objective 1

Organized crime is a highly structured, disciplined, self-perpetuating association of people, usually bound by ethnic ties, who conspire to commit crimes for profit and use fear and corruption to protect their activities from criminal prosecution. Organized crime activities include, but are not limited to, illegal gambling, drug trafficking, loan-sharking, money laundering, credit card fraud, extortion, and murder for hire.

Learning Objective 2

Numerous organized crime groups have emerged in America's cities, neighborhoods, and rural areas. These groups are generally identified by their ethnic origins. These major crime organizations involve, but are not limited to, Chinese, Japanese, African American, Jamaican, Hispanic, Italian, and Russian criminal enterprises.

Learning Objective 3

Since the early 1980s, law enforcement agencies investigating organized crime have relied on the enterprise theory of investigation. Under the Racketeer Influenced and Corrupt Organizations Act (RICO), entire crime organizations can be prosecuted for all their diverse criminal activities. In addition, investigators use a variety of techniques to enhance investigation and prosecution of organized crime groups, including task forces, asset forfeiture, informants, undercover operations, and computer-assisted communications and analysis.

Learning Objective 4

A number of laws have been passed to assist in the investigation and prosecution of organized crime groups. Among these laws are the Controlled Substance Act of 1970, the Organized Crime Control Act of 1970 (especially the RICO Act provision), the Bank Secrecy Act of 1970, the Comprehensive Crime Control Act of 1984, the Money Laundering Control Act of 1986, the Anti-Drug Abuse Act of 1986, the Anti-Drug Abuse Act of 1988, and various asset seizure, forfeiture, and conspiracy laws.

Learning Objective 5

The future of the United States in regard to organized crime is not promising. The traditional bureaucratic organization of the Mafia is on the decline. In its place is an array of loosely defined organizations from a host of different ethnic groups. These organizations are more ruthless and more creative in devising and perpetrating scams and rackets on the American public.

KEY TERMS

organized crime **392**

money laundering **399**

enterprise theory of investigation **404**

predicate crime **404**

forfeiture **404**

injunction **405**

informer **405**

undercover operation **405**

absolute immunity **406**

recalcitrant witness **406**

conspiracy **407**

QUESTIONS FOR REVIEW

Learning Objective 1

1. Where do many Americans get their ideas and images about who is involved in organized crime?

Learning Objective 2

2. How did many organized crime groups originate?

3. What goals do organized crime groups have in common?

4. What is another name for the American Mafia?

5. How did the Colombian cartels originate?

6. How are Jamaican posses political?

7. With what ethnic organized crime groups are tongs, triads, and Yakuza associated?

8. Why are organized youthful street gangs so difficult for law enforcement to investigate?

9. How did outlaw motorcycle gangs originate?

Learning Objective 3

10. How have federal asset forfeiture laws assisted law enforcement in its pursuit of organized criminals?

11. What does RICO stand for, and how does it assist in curbing organized crime?

Learning Objective 4

12. Why can an individual not avoid a *conspiracy* charge by backing out of the crime at the last moment?

13. What effects did the Comprehensive Crime Control Act of 1984 have on organized crime investigations?

14. How might computers assist investigations of organized criminal groups?

Learning Objective 5

15. How would you characterize the future of organized crime groups in the United States?

CRITICAL THINKING EXERCISES

1. You have just been appointed head of a task force to combat organized crime in your local community. What will be your first goal? What legal means might you use to reach this goal?

2. You are an undercover officer assigned to infiltrate an organized crime group in your local community. What are some things you might try in your effort to infiltrate this group? What safety precautions might you take?

INVESTIGATIVE SKILL BUILDERS

Participating as a Member of a Team

Divide the class into three groups, and have each group designate two representatives to meet with either a prosecutor from your state attorney's office or a member of your local police department. At this meeting, the representatives should discuss the kinds of techniques and strategies used to investigate and prosecute organized crime in your community. Have them bring this information back to the group. Using this information and information obtained by group members at the library, prepare a report on strategies for handling organized crime.

Integrity/Honesty

You are the newly elected sheriff of a rural community. You are highly qualified for the position, having served as an investigator for the sheriff's department in a larger community for four years and as chief investigator for five years. You also have a master's degree in criminal justice. During your campaign for sheriff, you made the usual promises to uphold the law and enforce it fairly and impartially. You promised to run the sheriff's office ethically and in a professional manner. As with all campaigns, you had a number of campaign supporters. Some contributed money or services; others helped with posters and leaflets. Shortly after you were elected, several of the larger contributors came to you and asked if you might have any deputy sheriff's positions for their friends or relatives. You had half expected something like this and, as long as the applicants were qualified, had no trouble hiring several.

Several months later you make an impressive drug bust. A major drug trafficking ring has been operating in your jurisdiction, and you manage to capture the leader. The man is in his late twenties but has already developed a reputation as a key player in an organized drug syndicate. Along with $100,000 in cash, you find a kilo of uncut heroin. The day after the bust, you receive a visit from one of your largest contributors. He tells you that you need to lose the evidence in the drug case and let the suspect go. You are shocked and a little angry that he would even suggest such an action. He tells you that the man you arrested provided the money for your campaign. The man you are talking with was only a front.

1. What should you tell this contributor?
2. What options, if any, do you have?

White-Collar Crime

After completing this chapter, you will be able to:

1 Explain what is meant by white-collar crime.
2 List some types of white-collar crime.
3 Describe some challenges of investigating white-collar crime.
4 Describe various categories of computer crime.
5 Explain some considerations in investigating computer crime.

WHAT IS WHITE-COLLAR CRIME?

white-collar crime A non-violent crime committed by an individual or a corporation that is a breach of trust, confidence, or duty.

Typically, **white-collar crime** is business-related or occupational crime. Edwin Sutherland, a noted social scientist, is often credited with having coined the term in a 1939 address to the American Sociological Society. In this address, and in later writings, Sutherland (1949) defined white-collar crime as "a crime committed by a person of respectability and high social status in the course of his occupation." During the 1980s, a special report issued by the Bureau of Justice Statistics (1987) defined white-collar crime as "nonviolent crime for financial gain committed by deception."

Gary Gordon (1996) suggested that changes in the nature of white-collar crime are so profound that law enforcement must begin thinking about white-collar and economic crimes somewhat differently:

> Technology has changed the landscape of white collar crime negating the traditional Sutherland definition of respected persons whose status in the organization provides them the opportunity to commit crime. Technology-based crimes and frauds involving computers, credit-cards, cellular phones and other means of telecommunications, require a reassessment of the present definitions of white collar and economic crimes. (p. 143)

This perspective is embraced in the exploration of white-collar crimes detailed in this chapter. In 2003 the FBI defined white-collar crime as follows:

> White-collar crimes are categorized by deceit, concealment, or violation of trust and are not dependent on the application or threat of physical force or violence. Such acts are committed by individuals and organizations to obtain money, property, or services, to avoid the payment or loss of money or services, or to secure a personal or business advantage.

Taken together, these definitions cover virtually every aspect of white-collar crime. In fact, even certain variations of traditional frauds and larcenies, discussed in Chapter 16, may fit the definition of a white-collar crime. Regardless of definition, white-collar crimes cost society billions of dollars each year; estimates range from $40 billion to $200 billion (Roberts & Mann, 2005).

Many people think of traditionally associated crimes such as embezzlement, industrial espionage, insider trading, bribery and extortion, tax evasion, and various corporate crimes when they hear the phrase *white-collar crime*. Yet white-collar crime is actually a much more complicated and varied assortment of offenses that includes various frauds, such as those associated with auto repairs, charities, land sales, identity thefts, and promotional and telemarketing scams. Because of technological changes, white-collar crimes have further expanded to include crimes committed in cyber space and on the Internet (Wall, 2006). In addition, white-collar crime includes virtually any occupation-related law violation, even what some may call mundane office crimes such as stealing pencils, reams of paper, or rubberbands. White-collar crimes also include public health statute violations, price-fixing, violations of food standards or quality, adulteration of drugs and illegal drug diversion by pharmacists, physicians, and other health professionals, and environmental statute violations (Gaines, Ball, & Shichor, 2001; Wall, 2006).

Most people, including some law enforcement agencies, tend to believe that white-collar crimes are some sort of sophisticated theft. Embezzlement, for example, is usually committed without violence and often involves an intricate plan resulting in more monetary gain than the typical burglary or robbery. Few fully understand that the consequences of white-collar crimes can include serious injury and deaths. For example, each year thousands of people die from the long-term effects of illegal toxic waste dumping. It is estimated that 100,000 deaths each year occur as a result of deliberate industrial or job-related safety violations, and unknown hundreds of people are made ill or die from diluted or out-of-date medications sold to unsuspecting patients. Emphysema and lung cancer deaths also occur each year because of the long-term effects of industrial and automotive pollution (Wall, 2006).

The enforcement of laws concerning white-collar offenses differs from traditional law enforcement. In more traditional street crimes, people are victimized directly or with some degree of immediacy, and the police are summoned to investigate the crime. When a crime occurs before the police become involved, the police are in a reactive posture. In white-collar crimes, however, victims are frequently unaware of a crime until long after it has occurred. Therefore, law enforcement and regulatory agencies need to strike a more proactive posture. They must attempt to investigate cases and educate potential victims simply from suspicious circumstances.

Historically, law enforcement has virtually ignored many aspects of white-collar crime. Convicted offenders have typically gotten off with a fine and a slap on the wrist by the courts, and jail time was seldom associated with white-collar crimes. During the past decade, white-collar crimes have become of greater concern to Americans. With the media popularizing such cases as stock manipulations, concealment of savings-and-loan insolvency, and insider trading by figures such as Ivan Boesky and Michael Milken, Americans have begun to take notice (Simpson, 2002). Even middle America has grown concerned in the face of such white-collar criminals as television evangelist Jim Bakker, who was convicted of overselling lodging guarantees, called "lifetime memberships," at his Heritage USA religious retreat. In all, Bakker used his television pulpit to defraud $3.7 million from his television congregation. The public was taken by surprise in 1995 when Nicholas William Leeson brought down Barings, one of the most solvent and well-respected financial institutions in the world. In a few short months, Leeson allegedly lost more than $1 billion of company money on bad speculative investments (Pedersen et al., 1995).

Perhaps the greatest example of a white-collar violation of trust arose when the Enron scam was exposed in 2002.

Perhaps the greatest example of a white-collar violation of a position of trust arose in 2002 when news broke about the Enron scam: The Federal Energy Regulatory Commission (FERC) released internal documents revealing how Enron had created phantom shortages in California's unregulated electricity market to fleece ratepayers of an estimated $20 billion during the 2001 energy crisis. Following long trials, former Enron executives Kenneth Lay and Jeffrey Skilling were found guilty of fraud and conspiracy (Schoen, 2006).

IDENTIFYING WHITE-COLLAR CRIMES

White-collar crimes represent a varied range of activities and behaviors. Persons may act alone or in concert when committing white-collar crimes, and the victims of white-collar crimes may be individuals, corporations, or the general public. White-collar crimes fall into three major categories: occupational crimes, corporate crimes, and individual crimes.

occupational crime The use of one's occupation to illegally obtain personal gain.

Occupational crimes include all offenses committed by individuals in the course of their occupation and by employees against their employers (Friedrichs, 2002). For example, when a physician bills Medicaid for tests he or she never actually ran on a patient, this physician is guilty of an occupational crime—a white-collar crime. Similarly, a checkout person who steals cash from the register at a supermarket is guilty of embezzlement or theft from his or her employer.

corporate crime Any activity that is undertaken by a corporation for its benefit but which violates the law.

Corporate crimes involve "the offenses committed by corporate officials for the corporation and the offenses of the corporation itself" (Clinard & Quinney, 1973, p. 172). When a corporation dumps industrial waste into a river or in other ways violates various environmental laws, it is guilty of corporate crimes. During the past several years, sanctions for such crimes have increased. There has also been an increase in green cops, or environmental protection investigators. Green cops are charged with investigating, and on occasion arresting, corporate executives responsible for environmental crimes.

individual crimes Individuals acting on their own behalf or with others to defraud the public.

The third category, **individual crimes,** involves individuals acting on their own behalf or in concert with several others to defraud the public through such activities as telemarketing scams, Internet auction frauds, and auto repair or insurance frauds (Shover & Hochstetler, 2006). Given the increased access to and use of the Internet for product purchases, banking, and paying bills, this area of crime has become an enormous problem for the public and for law enforcement agencies across the nation; it is frequently combined with identity theft.

Categories of White-Collar Crime

Herbert Edelhertz (1970) divided white-collar crimes into four distinct categories: ad hoc violations, abuses of trust, collateral business crimes, and con games.

Ad Hoc Violations Ad hoc violations are illegal activities committed by individuals for personal gain or profit. Tax evasion or various welfare and social service frauds, such as selling food stamps for cash, are ad hoc violations.

Abuses of Trust Abuses of trust include any misuse of authority or malfeasance or public corruption committed by an individual in a place of trust in an organization or government. Abuses of trust include embezzlement, graft, bribery, and bestowal of jobs or privileges on those who do not deserve them. Nicholas Leeson's manipulation of purchase orders to cover his failing investments of Barings funds is a further illustration of abuse of trust.

Collateral Business Crimes   Collateral business crimes encompass any prohibited activities by which organizations intend to further the business interests of a company. Falsifying odometer readings on used cars, attempting to conceal environmental crimes, or using uncalibrated gasoline pumps or weighted scales are collateral business crimes.

Con Games   Confidence games, or con games, discussed in Chapter 16, involve a variety of activities designed to swindle people out of their money or property. These may include fraudulent gold mine sales, sales of phony vacations, and other promises of "something for nothing" that never materialize.

Elements of White-Collar Crimes

In later writings, Edelhertz offered five basic elements of white-collar crimes: intent, disguise of purpose, reliance on the victim's ignorance, voluntary assistance from the victim, and concealment (Edelhertz et al., 1977).

Intent   In white-collar crimes, intent is the offender's awareness that the activities are wrong or illegal. It does not matter whether the offender knows the specific statutes violated. What is important is that the offender realizes that his or her actions are deceiving the victim in some way.

Disguise of Purpose   Disguise of purpose refers to the offender's conduct while carrying out the scheme. In common street crimes, a wrongful intent is usually followed by some overt and observable action. For example, a bank robbery is planned (intent), and then the robber enters the bank, brandishes a weapon, and declares a robbery. White-collar crimes are seldom that overt. More often, white-collar criminals try to create a facade of normalcy and legitimacy behind which their actual purpose is hidden. For example, a loan officer in a bank may file a fictitious loan application, complete with an applicant name, address, job location, credit references, and every other element required for a loan. Thus the facade of a real loan application has been created. When the loan officer grants the loan, he or she simply keeps the funds. When the funds are not repaid, the loan officer may say that the applicant has defaulted, again creating a facade of normalcy—even against the prying eyes of a bank examiner.

STATISTICS   In 2005 the National White Collar Crime Center (NW3C) surveyed 1,600 U.S. households. The NW3C found that nearly one in every two households reported having experienced at least one form of white-collar crime victimization during the preceding year. Furthermore, nearly two-thirds of the sample reported having experienced a white-collar crime at some point in their lifetime (Kane & Wall, 2006).

Reliance on the Victim's Ignorance   Reliance on the victim's ignorance literally means that the victim is unable to see that he or she is being deceived. For example, returning to the loan officer illustration, it is likely that the offender is confident that his or her fabricated application will be undetectable by other bank personnel and even outside accountants.

Voluntary Assistance from the Victim   Some sort of voluntary assistance from the victim is typically required because not every step in most white-collar crimes is completely under the control of the criminal. Most white-collar crimes involve duping or inducing the victim to voluntarily become involved in the crime. Voluntary assistance may refer to actions on the part of the victim who is to be defrauded of money or property. Alternatively, voluntary assistance may come from a kind of intermediate victim. For example, the dishonest loan officer may initially require the assistance of a bank cashier or teller (the intermediate victim) to complete the processing of the phony loan and receive the money from the bank (the true victim).

Concealment   Concealment to cover up their criminal activities is the goal of all white-collar criminals. For example, the loan officer hopes nobody will ever learn that several of the loans he or she authorized were fake. In the back of the loan officer's mind, he or she may even plan to repay the loan before anyone discovers the phony application.

An example of concealment may be drawn from the savings-and-loan scandals, which began receiving significant media coverage in about 1989. In 1990 the Government Accounting Office estimated that it would cost at least $325 billion to bail out the insolvent thrifts, or savings and loans, and that it could cost as much as $500 billion over the next thirty or forty years (Johnston, 1990). A considerable number of charges were leveled against various fraudulent savings and loan institutions, and many of these charges were for attempts to *cover up* fraudulent behavior or to conceal the institution's insolvency. Of the alleged 179 violations of criminal law reported during the General Accounting Office's 1989 examination of savings and loans, 42 violations were for concealment activities (General Accounting Office, 1989).

Law enforcement agencies have many methods of detecting various white-collar crimes. These involve examination of the financial or personal histories of suspected individuals or surveillance of these individuals' activities. If a complainant has summoned the police, the investigation may include such techniques as examining bank and credit records, tax returns, criminal histories, mailing records, box number accounts, using inside informants, and tracing computer IP addresses. Some of these activities can be undertaken immediately by the investigator. Others, such as searches, undercover investigation, electronic surveillance, and computer tracing require official authorization, including warrants.

TYPES OF WHITE-COLLAR CRIME

It is impossible to cover all types of white-collar crimes here (see Figure 20.1). This section focuses on some representative types of white-collar crime.

Embezzlement and Employee Thefts

embezzlement The misappropriation or misapplication of money or property entrusted to one's care, custody, or control.

Embezzlement is usually thought of as a theft committed by an individual against his or her employer. Typically, this sort of white-collar crime involves the use of one's position in a business or organization to steal company funds or company property for personal use, gain, or profit (Crumbley, 2003). Perhaps when you think of embezzlement, you envision a corporate administrator or a bank executive running off to the Bahamas with the company's or bank's money. To be sure, people in fairly high positions have embezzled large sums of money. For example, Rochelle D. Graham, the former CEO of the Zoe Life Enrichment Foundation embezzled $400,000 in state and federal funds between 2002 and 2003. Graham's company received a $438,000 grant from the Pennsylvania Department of Community and Economic Development in 2001. The money was intended for helping up to 200 low-income families through a two-year savings program called the Self-Sufficiency Project. Savings from the program were to be matched by state and federal money. Although 45 families had applied for funding, none received any funds. Instead, Graham had transferred the grant money

FIGURE 20.1 Types of White-Collar Crime

- Employee theft (embezzlement and pilferage)
- Cargo theft
- Health care fraud
- Auto repair fraud
- Consumer or personal fraud
- Insurance fraud
- Charities fraud
- Corporate tax fraud
- Personal income tax frauds
- Computer-related or other high-tech crimes
- Internet frauds (including phishing, fake auctions, Nigerian letters, and fake lotteries)
- Check fraud or counterfeiting
- Telecommunications fraud (including cellular phone and ATM frauds)
- Credit, debit, charge, or bank card fraud (and other identity frauds)
- Corporate financial crime
- Money laundering
- Savings and loan or stockbrokerage crime
- Mortgage loan fraud
- Coupon and rebate fraud
- Illegal toxic waste dumping
- Arson for profit

---

to a common Zoe account, and at her initial hearing it was learned that she had spent approximately $107,000 on hotels and travel, $200,000 on miscellaneous business expenses, had given $65,000 to her ex-husband, and had also made checks to herself for over $54,000 (Doody, 2004).

Not all embezzlement or organizational theft occurs at the top. Theft by employees may occur at all levels of a business or company. In addition to money, thefts may include products sold or distributed by the organization and materials and equipment used by the organization. Truck drivers may cut deals with loading dock receiving clerks to steal cartons of products and split the profits. Retail clerks may steal garments by placing them under their own clothing or concealing them in a variety of other ways. Shoe managers may steal cash by juggling the books or falsifying records during storewide markdowns. Factory workers may steal an assortment of products or equipment by putting them out with the trash and returning later to recover the stolen items. In short, there are virtually no limits to the ways employees can embezzle or steal from their employers.

Industrial Espionage

Another fairly common form of white-collar crime is **industrial espionage.** This type of white-collar criminal activity may include industrial spies who infiltrate a company by posing as workers. It may also include computer experts who breach even sophisticated computer security systems to gain entry to corporate computer systems (Vacca, 2005). Once in the company's computer, files and records can be looted, altered, or destroyed. Besides high-tech industries, other large companies are subject to industrial spying. Toy companies are in constant competition to produce toys that capture the largest shares of the industry market. Advance information about a forthcoming toy can give a competitor the opportunity to knock off a similar, competing toy. This has long been true for the garment industry as well, where designers carefully guard their new designs until they are publicly shown.

industrial espionage Espionage work undertaken in corporate and industrial areas to keep up with or surpass competitors.

The problem of industrial espionage had become so severe that in 1996 the Industrial Espionage Act was passed, making the theft of trade secrets a federal crime. A number of individual states already had legislation regarding this crime, but this was the first federal act intended to combat the problem. The act laid down very stiff penalties for violations, including fines as high as $10 million and prison sentences of up to fifteen years, all at the discretion of the presiding judge (Murphy, 2005).

In industrial espionage cases, investigators should carefully consider the complainant/victim as a possible suspect. Complainant/victims of industrial espionage sometimes have ulterior motives for reporting or staging a crime. For example, a fashion designer may have his or her designs insured and may be seeking to defraud the insurance company. Investigators should inquire about the possibility of insured losses in all cases of industrial espionage.

Insider Trading

insider trading An employee's or manager's use of information gained in the course of his or her job and not generally available to the public to benefit from fluctuations in the stock market.

Insider trading in stocks and bonds has also become a serious criminal problem. Insider trading typically involves a corporate executive with direct knowledge or market-sensitive information about a tradeable stock who uses this information for personal gain. The information may involve advance knowledge of a corporate takeover, information about financial problems faced by a corporation, or any other confidential information that might affect stock sales.

In recent years federal courts have expanded the scope of insider trading to include people working in many kinds of financial institutions, such as banks and savings and loans, who abuse confidential information on pending corporate actions. The abuse may be employees' using the information for their own gain or sharing it with others, who use it for their gain. These practices violate federal trade codes.

In 2004 Martha Stewart served five months in prison and five months in home confinement for conspiracy, perjury, making a false statement, and obstruction of justice stemming from her involvement in an insider-trader crime.

Consider the case of Martha Stewart. In 2001 Martha Stewart sold almost 4,000 shares of ImClone Systems after being tipped that former ImClone CEO Sam Waksal, a friend of Stewart's, was trying to dump his own shares in the company. Prosecutors had stated that Stewart and Peter Bacanovic (her stockbroker at the time) then tried to cover up the reason for the trade. Peter Bacanovic, 41, was later found guilty of conspiracy, perjury, making a false statement, and obstruction of justice. Martha Stewart herself was found guilty of obstructing justice

HISTORY

FOR TWENTY-THREE YEARS, the fugitive American financier Robert Vesco lived in opulent self-imposed exile, first in Costa Rica, then in the Bahamas, and finally in Cuba. Vesco was charged in 1972 with stealing $224 million from Investors Overseas Services, Ltd., a Swiss-based mutual fund. Using his investors' money, he traipsed around in the tropics, eluding law enforcement officials by paying off politicians and government leaders. Hoping to foster good-will with the United States, the Cuban government announced in June 1995 that Vesco would be extradited (Chua-Eoan, 1996). In August 1996, however, a court in Havana handed down a sentence of thirteen years in prison for Vesco's role in a shady investment deal. Vesco had misled foreign investors by making them believe that a plant-based drug known as TX was being produced in Cuba, but it was not (Fletcher, 1996).

because of her refusal to answer questions about the insider trade; she was sentenced to ten months of incarceration, five to be served in prison and five under house arrest (CNN/Money, 2004; Steinhaus, 2004).

The problem for law enforcement investigations involves distinguishing a good stock tip from insider information. Many stockbrokers call their clients with tips on stocks they have been watching and believe will soon go up in value or split. Such information, when consistently accurate, gives brokerage houses a good reputation. However, a tip from a source who has confidential information about a company or its financial standing may be a criminal act.

Bribery, Kickbacks, and Payoffs

Bribery, kickbacks, and payoffs may occur between individuals, businesses, and government agencies and representatives in both the private and the public sectors (Miller & Cross, 2005). Typically, this sort of white-collar crime involves at least one person in a position of authority. It may be a government official, such as a police officer or administrator, a town council member, the mayor, or a member of the governor's staff. Or it may be a business official, such as a buyer for a department store, a contractor, or even a security guard.

Although similar in nature, bribes, kickbacks, and payoffs are not identical. A **bribe** is the payment of cash, goods, or services to someone in exchange for a special service, product, or behavior. Bribes are sometimes confused with extortion. The difference is in who initiates the arrangement. If someone in a position of authority or control demands money, goods, or services from another party in exchange for something, the crime is extortion. On the other hand, if one party asks another to use a position of authority or control to the first party's advantage, in exchange for money, goods, or services, it is a bribe.

Kickbacks involve an agreement between two or more parties that one of them will pay money in exchange for receiving a contract or job. For example, a contractor may arrange with a city manager to receive a large city building contract in exchange for paying the city manager a large sum of money. The city manager may in turn owe a kickback to others, such as city council members who agreed to give the contractor the contract. Or a home health care company may pay kickbacks to physicians in return for referrals to its services.

A **payoff** is receiving compensation or money from an individual in exchange for some favor. In some ways, it is similar to a bribe. Payoffs can occur in any industry.

bribe The payment of cash, goods, or services to someone in exchange for some special service, product, or behavior.

kickback The payment back of a portion of the purchase price to the buyer or a public official by the seller to induce a purchase or to improperly influence future purchases.

payoff Receiving compensation or money from an individual in exchange for some favor.

payola A payment to a disc jockey for a favor such as promoting a favorite recording.

In the late 1990s, for example, there were allegations that the music industry was using payoffs to get selected videos on the air. These allegations were reminiscent of the **payola** scandals of the 1950s and 1960s, in which disc jockeys got payoffs to play certain records while excluding others.

Tax Evasion

Perhaps the most common form of white-collar criminality is tax cheating or tax evasion. Many average American citizens do it by underreporting their income, claiming false deductions, inflating the amount of charitable contributions, smuggle goods or assets, or undertaking some other type of deception (James, 2002). In some cases, underreported income may simply be an error. In other cases, it is a deliberate attempt to avoid paying tax. The opportunity for tax evasion varies across socioeconomic strata, but it occurs nonetheless. An important element of tax fraud is *willfulness*. Tax evasion is enormously difficult to prove and successfully prosecute. Furthermore, it is difficult to discern between careless or unintentional underreporting of income and willful tax evasion. The IRS estimated that the overall gross tax gap—the difference between what taxpayers should have paid and what they actually underpaid—for tax year 2001 was $345 billion. IRS enforcement activities, coupled with other late payments, recovered about $55 billion of the tax gap, leaving a net tax gap of $290 billion in 2001 (Internal Revenue Service, 2006a).

FYI Tax return preparer fraud generally involves the preparation and filing of false income tax returns by preparers who claim inflated personal or business expenses, false deductions, unallowable credits, or excessive exemptions on returns prepared for their clients. Preparers may also manipulate income figures to obtain tax credits, such as the Earned Income Tax Credit, fraudulently. In some situations, the client (taxpayer) may not have knowledge of the false expenses, deductions, exemptions, or credits shown on his or her tax return. However, when the IRS detects the false return, the taxpayer—not the return preparer—must pay the additional taxes and interest and may be subject to penalties (Internal Revenue Service, 2006b).

Corporate Crime

Corporate crimes are crimes committed for the benefit of a legitimate business organization or enterprise. Corporate crime may take many forms, including price fixing, bribery, and kickbacks (discussed previously), tax evasion or other tax violations, assorted frauds, environmental crimes or concealments, and a variety of other criminal activities. Corporate and occupational crimes are sometimes confused. If a corporate official violates the law acting for the corporation, it is usually deemed a corporate crime. If the corporate official gains personally from the commission of a crime against the corporation, as in the case of embezzlement of corporate funds, it is an occupational crime (Yeager & Clinard, 2006).

Since the beginning of the nineteenth century, certain business practices have been defined in the law as illegal. These include restraint of trade, deceptive advertising practices, misrepresentations and frauds against banks, sales of phony stocks and securities, dangerous or faulty manufacturing of foods and drugs, environmental pollution, and the unlawful use of patents and trademarks.

During the latter portion of the nineteenth century, public concern grew concerning the development of corporate monopolies. These monopolies threatened to eliminate free trade and competition in U.S. markets. In an effort to protect free enterprise in America, a number of federal regulations were enacted. Among the earliest was the Sherman Antitrust Act (1890). This legislation made it illegal to restrain trade and forbade the formation of monopolies. In addition, it made price fixing—collusion between large corporations to set artificially high, rather than competitive, prices—a felony, with a maximum corporate fine of $1 million. The legislation further provides for the levying of private treble-damage suits by victims of price fixing. In other words, a company injured by price fixing could receive three times the actual losses it incurred (Brownlee, 2004).

For the most part, like many aspects of white-collar criminality, corporate violations are policed by various regulatory agencies. The Federal Trade Commission, established in 1914, is responsible for examining many corporate trade practices. In all, more than fifty federal regulatory agencies have varying degrees of police power over corporate violations of law. Regulatory agencies can impose a variety of sanctions on errant corporations: fines, recalls, decrees and unilateral orders of compliance, injunctions, financial penalties, and even jail time for CEOs and other corporate leaders.

INVESTIGATING WHITE-COLLAR CRIME

White-collar crimes encompass a wide variety of offenses and are generally very difficult to prevent—let alone detect. When detected, some white-collar crimes are not reported to the police but are handled unofficially by the corporate victim, or the employer of the white-collar criminal. In other cases, white-collar criminality is detected and investigated.

On the federal level, detection of white-collar crimes is left chiefly to administrative departments and regulatory agencies. In determining whether to pursue criminal or civil violations, these agencies typically consider the seriousness of the offense, the intentions of the offender, and the offender's prior record. The Department of Justice receives any evidence of criminal activity, and, if necessary, the FBI may be asked to conduct an investigation. Some federal agencies have their own investigative branches. For example, both the IRS and the U.S. Postal Service have investigative/enforcement branches. Federal investigations of many white-collar crimes are reactive, coming only after a complaint has been filed with the agency.

The investigation of white-collar crimes requires patience, imagination, the willingness to ask for help from other agencies, and increasingly sophisticated computer and technology skills (Sharp, 1994). Advances in technology have increased the need for investigators to improve their knowledge of computers and accounting, and many federal law enforcement agencies require 12 to 17 credits in accounting for entry-level agent positions.

At the state and local levels, the investigation of white-collar crimes is often messy, lengthy, and inefficient. Jurisdictional disputes may arise between the state attorney general and local prosecutors, and a lack of technical expertise among investigators may further hamper investigations (Sharp, 1994). However, local investigators working in concert with local prosecutors can successfully pursue and prosecute white-collar criminals (Benson, Cullen, & Maakestad, 1990; Sharp, 1994). Unfortunately, many prosecutors do not regard white-collar criminal activity as a serious problem. Benson, Cullen, and Maakestad (1990) found that white-collar crimes were more likely to be prosecuted at the local level if substantial harm had resulted and no other agencies were willing to take action. Provisions of the RICO statute (see Chapter 19) are sometimes used in prosecuting white-collar crimes.

Frequently, white-collar crime investigation and law enforcement is left in the hands of the corporations themselves. Many large corporations spend millions of dollars each year on internal audits and investigations that uncover employees guilty of white-collar offenses.

Law enforcement agencies across the nation have begun to recognize how widespread white-collar crime has become. In some jurisdictions, local, state, and federal law enforcement agencies and prosecutors' offices have teamed together to detect and apprehend white-collar criminals. By joining together, the agencies increase their personnel power, share resources, and find experts with the technological or other skills needed for a specific investigation.

Computer and Cyber Crime

When computers first began emerging in the 1940s, most were complex, large (sometimes filling an entire room), and difficult, if not impossible, for the average person to operate. Computer engineers used complex languages such as Fortran to create operational programs. Even when computers were used in business settings, few corporate managers had the skills to use the cumbersome and complex machines themselves.

With the advances in menu- and icon-driven user-friendly programs today, computer use has become commonplace. The general population has grown more computer literate during the past decade, and that includes both honest, law-abiding citizens and dishonest, criminal ones. It is not surprising, then, that with the explosion in the amount of computer equipment available to the public and the number of people who know how to use it, computer-related crimes are increasing (Johnson, 2006).

cyber crime Crimes committed on the Internet using the computer as either a tool or a targeted victim.

Some people have begun referring to computer-related crime as *cyber crime* and to the people who perpetrate it as *cyber criminals.* **Cyber crimes** are crimes committed on the Internet using the computer as either a tool or a targeted victim. It is difficult to classify these crimes into distinct groups because computer-related crimes evolve on a daily basis. However, all cyber crimes involve both the computer and the person behind it as victims—it just depends on which of the two is the main target (Aghatise, 2006). There are many varieties of cyber crime; some are directed at the computer itself, such as viruses and computer hijack takeovers, whereas others are directed at the computer user and may include phishing, lotteries, fake auctions, Nigerian letters, and an assortment of other scams.

With the increase in computer-related crimes, investigators need to have a working understanding of common computer-crime terms. Figure 20.2 lists some common computer-crime-related terms and their meanings.

For many types of computer crimes, all one needs is a personal computer (PC) equipped with a modem, the right software, and the desire to commit a crime. Regardless of security programs and passwords designed to limit access via telephone, large corporate and government computer systems are still vulnerable to intrusion and tampering.

Computers operated by the U.S. Department of Defense, various defense contractors, utility companies, universities, hospitals, research institutes, banks, and an assortment of Fortune 500 companies have all been invaded by hackers. Sometimes the hackers are teenagers who want to get in simply to show that they actually did it. Sometimes, however, the invasions have more sinister purposes. They may be part of a government or industrial espionage plan or simply act as a criminal means of shutting down a computer network.

In April 1999 David L. Smith of Aberdeen Township, New Jersey, was arrested for creating and releasing "Melissa," a computer virus designed to mail itself to the first fifty addresses listed in the address book of Microsoft Outlook, an e-mail software application for PCs. The virus was allegedly named after a lap dancer Smith once

FIGURE 20.2 Common Terms Related to Computer Crimes

Antivirus program	A program designed to detect a *computer virus* that has attached itself to a program on a disk or hard drive. Most antivirus programs contain a subprogram intended to *cure* the program by removing the virus.
Backdoor	A glitch in a computer system that permits someone entry without the proper code or password. Sometimes such entry can be made by gaining entry to an unsecured segment of a program and opening a window between the unsecured and secured segments.
Browsing	Unauthorized examination of someone else's data after unlawful entry into another's computer files.
Cookies	Small text files stored on computers while the user is browsing the Internet. These little pieces of data store information such as the user's e-mail identification, passwords, and history of pages on the Internet the user has visited.
Computer-supported crime	This phrase covers the use of computers by criminals for communication and document or data storage. These activities might not be illegal in and of themselves, but they are often invaluable in the investigation of actual crimes.
Computer virus	A program designed to attach itself to some other program and to attack and destroy the program. Sometimes, viruses are designed to *ride* one program into a system and then to attack and destroy data or memory in the computer's main drive. Some viruses are simply obnoxious rather than really destructive; they may cause a computer to automatically shut down or to show disks as blank even when the data are still present.
Cyber crime	A variety of specific crimes dealing with computers and networks (such as hacking) and the facilitation of traditional crime through the use of computers (child pornography, hate crimes, and telemarketing and Internet fraud).
Data diddling	A procedure sometimes used by insiders to place false information into a computer, as in placing a false name on a payroll or paying a fraudulent bill.
Denial of service attacks	Computer hackers flood a company's website or server with too much computer traffic, forcing the company's computer network to shut down until the attack can be brought under control.
Encryption	Any procedure used in cryptography to convert plain text into cipher text to prevent anyone but the intended recipient from reading the data.
Firewalls	Software programs designed to keep private networks and individual computers separate from the Internet. These programs control access into and out of the computer or network and can screen and track attempts to enter.
Fraud	As it relates to computer crimes, fraud represents any use of trickery, deception, or falsification involving computers to obtain money, services, or property.
Hacking	Illegal entry into a computer system, usually through trial and error or done systematically by using a random-digit program, a modem, and an automatic caller.
Hidden text	Many computer systems include an option to protect information from the casual user—or infiltrator—by hiding it. A cursory examination of the stored files may not reveal hidden files, directories, or partitions to the untrained viewer.
Impersonation	In computer-related crimes, the unauthorized use of someone's identity, code, or password. It is sometimes associated with calling card or voice-mail frauds as well.

FIGURE 20.2 (*Continued*)

Masquerading	Like *impersonation,* an unauthorized use of someone else's identity, code, or password.
Nigerian letter	This scam operates as follows: the target receives an unsolicited fax, email, or letter, often concerning Nigeria or another African nation, containing either a money laundering or other illegal proposal. The *bait* is the lure of fictional millions of dollars described in the letter. The goal is to get you to come up with money for the expenses required to transfer those millions to you. These letters are often called *419 letters,* which refers to the Nigerian statute that makes this activity illegal there.
Phishing	This scam involves sending an e-mail to a user falsely claiming to be an established legitimate business enterprise (a bank, or PayPal is often used, complete with appropriate letterheads and logos) in an attempt to scam the user into surrendering private information that will be used for identity theft.
Phreaking	Telephone hacking.
Picks	These are programs designed to break through or bypass security locks and safeguards intended to prevent unauthorized duplication of software.
Program piracy	Unauthorized copying of commercial programs.
Salami slice	Establishing an unauthorized account in a company's or bank's computerized records. At regular intervals small amounts, perhaps only fractions of a cent, are placed in the unauthorized account. Sometimes these transfers go unnoticed for long periods because the amounts are covered by rounding figures. These pennies and fractions of pennies can eventually amount to many hundreds of thousands of dollars.
Superzapping	The use of repair, diagnosis, or maintenance programs to sidestep antitheft programs on a corporate computer system. Although some manipulation of the program may be necessary, once inside the *superzapper* is soon able to control the system's operations.
Trapdoor	A phenomenon similar to a *backdoor.* Usually, however, trapdoors are intentionally left by a computer programmer so that he or she can gain entry, no matter what antitheft or security measures may be added later.
Trashing	Taking information from discarded printouts, computer disks, or tapes. This can sometimes uncover important information and may occur in government or industrial espionage cases.
Trojan horse	A hidden program that may lay dormant until a particular program is called up or a particular time or date occurs in the computer clock and calendar. When the Trojan horse program awakens, it may contain a computer virus or run specific program tasks or data manipulations.
Volatile memory	Memory that loses its content when the power is turned off or lost.

encountered in Florida. Although this virus might appear at first to be nothing but a nuisance, in reality it was a serious attack. Melissa first surfaced in March of 1999 after being released to an Internet newsgroup in a Microsoft Word document containing a list of pornographic websites. When the recipient opened the e-mail, enticed by the promise of pornographic access, Melissa was launched into the unsuspecting user's computer. Corporate e-mail sites around the globe were soon bombarded and overwhelmed by e-mails. Even high-tech giants such as Microsoft, Intel, and Lucent Technologies, along with many university websites, were forced to shut down Internet access until they could get a handle on the situation (Emigh, 2004).

Cyber crime encompasses any criminal act dealing with computers and networks (called hacking), and traditional crimes conducted through the Internet. Hate crimes, telemarketing and Internet fraud, identity theft, and credit card account thefts are considered to be cyber crimes when the illegal activities are committed through the use of a computer and the Internet. A National Institute of Justice report outlined five distinct categories of computer crime (Conley & McEwen 1990):

- Internal computer crimes
- Telecommunications crimes
- Computer manipulation crimes
- Support of criminal enterprises
- Hardware or software thefts

Internal Computer Crimes

This category of crime includes any alteration of an existing computer program that causes it to operate in a manner other than that for which it was designed. This includes changes in programs that result in sudden losses or deletion of data, lockouts of legitimate users, deterioration of memory sectors, and so forth. These sorts of problems are caused by what are generically called **computer viruses.** Computer viruses literally attach themselves to some other program when that program is placed in a contaminated computer. Usually, viruses are transferred from one computer to another when a user shares programs on disks or signs on to a computer bulletin board. If an infected computer is discovered soon after a virus has attached itself, it can be *cured* with any of a number of commercial *antivirus* programs. Unfortunately, if the virus is discovered too late, it can ruin the data and memory sectors of a computer's hard drive.

computer virus A computer program, usually hidden within another computer program, that inserts itself into programs and applications and destroys data or halts execution of existing programs.

Telecommunications Crimes

Telecommunications crimes involve illegal access to or use of computer systems over telephone lines. They may involve the use of a random-digit program to determine a valid access code for a computer system or the misuse of toll-free numbers, calling card numbers, and voice-mail systems. In addition, telecommunications crimes include the misuse of computer bulletin boards or the creation of underground bulletin boards to carry out criminal activities. These may include sale or solicitation of child pornography, drugs, or stolen property, or even murder for hire. During recent years, terrorists have begun to use bulletin boards to send and receive messages and to provide members with information about law enforcement activities. For example, after the tragic bombing at the 1996 Summer Olympic Games, many Americans were shocked to learn that instructions for constructing a pipe bomb were readily available on a number of computer bulletin boards.

FYI Cryptography, the technology that scrambles messages and data so that eavesdroppers or snoopers cannot read them, was for many years the province of military and intelligence agencies. About thirty years ago, however, cryptography was combined with computer technology to provide encryption software. The public now had an inexpensive shield of privacy for electronic data. This capability has spawned a debate regarding the privacy of electronic data. On one side are private computer users who maintain their right to protect and safeguard their computer files from intrusion. On the other side are law enforcement agencies who maintain their right to protect society from abuses that might be hidden in encrypted data.

Superhacker Kevin Mitnick was arrested by the FBI in 1995 after a two-year cat-and-mouse game in which he breached computer networks nationwide to steal thousands of computer files and credit card numbers.

Computer Manipulation Crimes

These types of crimes involve changing data or creating records in a system for the specific purpose of advancing some other crime. For example, in 1994 the chief administrator of a large Pennsylvania hospital wrote false bills to the hospital and then authorized them to be paid. The bills were entered into the hospital's computer information system and went undetected for four years until a routine audit uncovered them as fraudulent.

Support of Criminal Enterprises

Computer programs are an aid not only to legitimate businesses but to illegal ones as well. For instance, criminals can use computer-based account ledgers to keep track of their drug business or the profits and expenses of an auto theft ring. Computers may even be used by criminals to maintain information or to simulate a planned crime.

With the additional technology of color laser printers and various graphics programs, computers can be used to create counterfeit concert, theater, and sporting event tickets, certificates of authenticity, stocks, and even money. As computer and printing technology expands, so do the possibilities of illegal behaviors.

Hardware and Software Thefts

The theft of computers, monitors, and other hardware devices seems rather uncomplicated. Theft of software, however, has a number of more subtle shades of ambiguity. Software piracy is a serious problem because it is relatively easy to accomplish. It involves the unauthorized duplication and distribution of software programs. Software companies lose millions of dollars a year to this type of crime. Some software companies have put safeguards, or locks, on their programs, which are intended to prevent unauthorized duplication, but these efforts are not always successful. It is a simple task to obtain a **pick program** designed to bypass the security measures intended to prevent duplication. Adding to the problems related to this type of crime are the attitudes of many consumers of commercial programs. Many do not recognize the problems caused by making a duplicate program for a friend. Others do not believe it is a crime if no fee is charged for the duplicate program. Still others rationalize that the high cost of programs entitles them to make copies. Especially worrisome are illegal **hackers** who gain access to or enter others' computer systems to steal secrets or money.

pick program A computer program designed to bypass security measures against duplication of electronic files.

hacker A person proficient at using or programming a computer and who is capable of infiltrating other computer systems.

INVESTIGATING COMPUTER CRIME

As technology advances, so do the ways criminals adapt to these innovations. In 1998 the National Institute of Justice (NIJ), in partnership with the National Cybercrime Training Partnership (NCTP) and the Office of Law Enforcement Standards (OLES), began development of a possible resource to be used in an effort to combat electronic crime. The coalition produced a series of documents directed at assisting law enforcement agencies in their efforts to thwart cyber criminals. As these documents indicate, law enforcement's response to electronic devices and the evidence these devices produce requires officers, investigators, forensic examiners, and police administrators to all play interrelated roles (NIJ, 2001).

When police or investigators are working with electronic devices, they must recognize the fragile nature of electronic evidence and the principles and procedures necessary for the safe collection and preservation of such evidence. Whenever dealing with electronic evidence, there is the potential to alter, damage, or even destroy this evidence, and all actions used to secure electronic evidence are likely to be closely scrutinized by the courts. Law enforcement agencies must have procedures in effect that promote effective *electronic crime scene investigations.* Frequently, a particular case under investigation will require a higher degree of expertise, training, or equipment than a local police department may have at its immediate disposal. Administrators must have a plan of action to respond to such cases (NIJ, 2001).

When a report of a computer crime is received by a police agency, the department's report policy is initially followed. The investigator assigned to the case interviews the complainant to determine whether a crime has been committed. Once it is determined that a crime has been committed, and what the crime is, the usual investigative procedures continue to offer an investigator guidelines.

Other people or employees may provide information regarding the crime or possible suspects. Investigation of computer crimes is similar to investigation of other internal organization crimes. It typically begins at the lowest levels of employees and continues to the highest levels of administration. Investigators should remember that *any* of the people interviewed could be in collusion with one another to commit the crime. Caution should be used when trying to eliminate possible suspects.

A special audit or a repair order may have brought the crime to the attention of the authorities, as in traditional embezzlement cases. Borrowing from such cases, investigators should determine which employees might have had access to or reasons to be involved with computer operations related to the computer crime.

Because evidence in computer crime investigations may be electronic records, which are easily lost or destroyed in error, it is critical that investigators move cautiously. The general principles of investigation for computer crimes are similar to those for other crimes. However, if an investigator is not conversant with computer *lingo* or comfortable with and knowledgeable about computer hardware, he or she should seek the assistance of a computer specialist. In fact, investigators may have to become *cybercops* and carry laptop computers along with their badges and weapons.

The Latent Nature of Electronic Evidence

Electronic evidence includes all information and data of investigative value that may be stored on or transmitted by an electronic device. Thus electronic evidence is latent evidence in the same sense that fingerprints are latent evidence. In their natural state, one may not be able to *see* what is contained in the physical object (the device) that holds the evidence. Equipment and software programs may be necessary to make the evidence visible, in the same way that powders or chemical may be necessary to make latent fingerprints at a crime scene visible to the eye. However, in addition to the actual evidence, testimony may also be required to explain the examination and collection process of the electronic evidence.

What Is Electronic Evidence?

electronic evidence
Latent evidence in the form of information stored on computers on hard drives in user-created files that may be useful in a criminal investigation.

Electronic evidence may include information stored on computers on hard drives in user-created files such as:

- Address books
- Audio/video files
- Calendars
- Database files
- Document or text files
- E-mail files
- Image/graphic files
- Internet bookmarks/favorites files
- Spreadsheet files

Computers, and several other electronic devices, contain memory that requires continuous power to maintain the information, such as AC power or a battery. Data can easily be lost by disconnecting these devices from their power sources. Investigators must use caution when examining and collecting evidence from these devices, as some cyber criminals have created booby-traps and password protection sequences that will destroy evidence if the computer is tampered with or after a series of incorrect passwords are tried.

Electronic evidence can also be collected from peripheral devices such as external or removable memory storage devices, Zip cards, disks, flash drives, and streaming tapes, which are used to store or move data. These memory and storage devices also must be handled cautiously. Digital cameras, handheld PDAs, telephones, and similar devices frequently have a removable memory card or stick containing information or data that may provide evidence in a criminal matter (Vacca, 2005).

Problems Investigators May Face

The lack of clear and unambiguous definitions of computer crimes is a problem for law enforcement agencies. Furthermore, several categories of computer crime may overlap, creating a potential problem in determining charges. Finally, computer illiteracy and computer fears in police departments hinder some investigations and prosecutions.

To resolve some of these problems, criminal investigators should become more familiar with computers, computer jargon, and methods of computer crime. Investigators should begin to develop contacts and resources they can turn to when faced with various computer crime problems. Clearly, computer crimes will become more prevalent in the future.

FYI The FBI can provide a Computer Analysis and Response Team (CART) to assist departments conducting investigations involving computers. The CART program is staffed with experienced computer professionals who are well equipped with hardware and software that enable them to recover information stored in computer systems.

FOCUS ON TECHNOLOGY

SEIZING A DOS- OR WINDOWS-BASED COMPUTER

1. Never touch the keyboard. If the computer is off, leave it that way.

2. If the computer is on, without touching anything, photograph the entire area, including cable and connector hookups and what appears on the screen.

3. Carefully remove any disks in any of the disk drives and tag, secure, and record them as evidence.

4. If the computer is on, disconnect the plug from the wall to turn it off. Do not use the On/Off switch.

5. Place a virus-free bootable disk in each disk drive, re-plug the computer into the wall receptacle, and turn on the computer.

6. Using a utility program on the bootable disk, park the hard drive head in a neutral position so that data will not be damaged in transport. Do not use the machine's Park command. Remove the bootable disks.

7. Place a blank disk in each of the disk drives and seal each with evidence tape.

8. Turn off the computer and remove the plug from the wall. Remove all the connecting cables, taking care to label how they are connected to the computer.

9. Take into custody anything in the area related to the computer. This may include disks; peripheral equipment such as keyboard, a mouse, or an external CD-ROM drive; printouts; and discarded items in the wastebasket. Keep disks away from magnetic fields.

10. Thoroughly inspect the area around the screen and keyboard before moving the computer. Look for labels, tags, or notes containing number series or terms that may be passwords or cryptographic keywords. Collect all such items as evidence.

After the initial investigation and report, officers should develop a plan for the continued investigation of the crime. Although the investigation may deviate from this plan along the way, guidelines will assist officers in their follow-up investigation. The plan should include the names and telephone numbers of computer consultants if any are to be used in the investigation. It should indicate the nature of the crime, any persons suspected of being part of the crime, the type of hardware or software involved, any witnesses, the personnel needs of the investigation, and an estimate of how long the investigation may take. The nature of the crime should include whether it is a local, state, or federal law violation. The appropriate prosecuting attorney should be contacted and his or her aid solicited if needed.

Whenever an officer finds a computer involved in a crime and must seize it, he or she should follow certain guidelines (Noblett, 1992). These guidelines are presented in the Focus on Technology feature.

CAREERS FOCUS

CORPORATE INVESTIGATOR

CORPORATE INVESTIGATORS WORK for companies other than investigative firms. Generally they are private investigators who work for large corporations and report to a corporate chain of command. They conduct internal or external investigations. External investigations can consist of preventing criminal schemes, thefts of company assets, and fraudulent deliveries of products by suppliers. Investigators may also investigate the business practices of a company's competitors or check out an executive candidate or a prospective overseas partner. In internal investigations, they may ensure that expense accounts are not abused and apprehend employees who are stealing (Smith, Grabosky, & Urbas, 2004).

Corporate investigators generally specialize in some aspect of business. Investigators who specialize in finance, for example, may be hired to investigate the financial standing of companies or individuals. They generally develop confidential financial profiles of individuals or companies who may be parties to large financial transactions. An asset search is a common type of procedure in such an investigation. Computers are an integral part of a corporate investigator's work. They allow investigators to affordably gather massive amounts of information in a short period of time. Investigators can access dozens of online databases containing financial records, motor vehicle registrations, credit reports, association memberships, and other information.

Many corporate investigators enter from the military or law enforcement jobs and apply their experience as law enforcement officers, military police, or government agents. Most corporate investigators must have a bachelor's degree, preferably in a business-related field. Some corporate investigators have master's of business administration or law degrees, and others are certified public accountants. The hiring process may require a criminal history check, a personal interview, an ethics interview, a practical test, verification of education claims, and license review. Investigators hired by larger companies may receive formal training from their employers on business practices, management structure, and various finance-related topics.

When investigating a computer crime in a large organization, it is sometimes necessary to develop an undercover operation. It is essential that the officers participating in this operation actually have the computer knowledge they need to remain undercover. Sending in officers who cannot blend with others in the organization is equivalent to sending them in wearing blue police uniforms. Furthermore, having those computer skills will permit the officers to recognize evidence when they find it.

The process of conducting interviews and interrogations in a computer case is essentially the same as in any other investigation. The rights of the suspect during searches or seizures of evidence are also the same.

Among the major problems in investigating computer crimes is the need to determine whether the crime was committed by someone within the organization or by someone outside it. It is important to determine exactly what the crime is. Given ambiguities in the classification of computer crimes, a victim within the organization may have to determine whether it would better serve justice to handle the crime internally or through the criminal justice system.

Finally, a serious problem facing the investigation of computer crimes is the reluctance of some victims to prosecute a computer felon. Many large corporations, financial organizations, and even government agencies fail to report such crimes or fail to pursue prosecution of offenders, often fearing negative publicity. A large corporation may not want it known that a hacker was able to bypass its computer security strategies and gain entry. A financial organization, such as a bank, may be even more reluctant to have its depositors learn that someone broke through and *diddled* (altered or in some way manipulated) depositor accounts.

SUMMARY

Learning Objective 1

White-collar crimes are nonviolent crimes committed by individuals and corporations that are a breach of trust, confidence, or duty. The basic elements of a white-collar crime are intent, disguise of purpose, reliance on the victim's ignorance, voluntary assistance from the victim, and concealment.

Learning Objective 2

A variety of crimes can be considered white-collar crimes. Among these are embezzlement and employee thefts; industrial espionage; insider trading; bribery, kickbacks, and payoffs; tax evasion; and corporate crime.

Learning Objective 3

White-collar crimes are generally very difficult to prevent, let alone detect. Even when they are detected, they may not be reported to law enforcement officials. Some are handled unofficially by the corporate victim or the employer of the white-collar criminal. In other cases, white-collar crime is investigated by law enforcement agencies.

Learning Objective 4

Computer crime is a crime committed with or against computers. It can include internal computer crimes, telecommunications crimes, computer manipulation crimes, support of criminal enterprises, and hardware and software thefts.

Learning Objective 5

Because evidence in computer crimes can be easily lost or destroyed, it is critical that investigators move cautiously. The general principles of investigating computer crimes are similar to those for other crimes.

KEY TERMS

white-collar crime 412

occupational crime 414

corporate crime 414

individual crimes 414

embezzlement 416

industrial espionage 417

insider trading 418

bribe 419

kickback 419

payoff 419

payola 420

cyber crime 422

computer virus 425

pick program 426

hacker 426

electronic evidence 428

QUESTIONS FOR REVIEW

Learning Objective 1

1. Define *white-collar crime*.
2. Name the four categories into which Edelhertz divided white-collar crime.
3. What are Edelhertz's five basic elements of white-collar crime?

Learning Objective 2

4. What is meant by *embezzlement*?

5. How might an employee steal from his or her employer?

6. What is *industrial espionage*?

7. Why might a dress manufacturer commit industrial espionage?

8. How does insider trading operate?

9. Why is insider trading a crime?

10. What is the difference between *bribery* and *extortion*?

11. What is meant by the term *payoff*?

12. What are three examples of corporate crime?

Learning Objective 3

13. Why should local, state, and federal investigations of white-collar crimes be team efforts?

14. Why are many white-collar criminals never prosecuted?

Learning Objective 4

15. What is meant by telecommunications crimes?

16. What is meant by computer manipulation crimes?

Learning Objective 5

17. Why are computer crimes difficult to investigate?

18. Why are computer crimes increasing?

CRITICAL THINKING EXERCISES

1. Using the following checklist, consider how secure the computer system is in your college or university. You will need to contact the computer support center at your school to answer some of these questions. Once these questions have been answered, develop a plan for improving the security of the system.

    a. Is someone in charge of security for the system?

    b. Are there measures to protect all users' output?

    c. Are codes or passwords used to limit access to the system?

    d. Are there any provisions for securely destroying (for instance, shredding or incinerating) output that is not picked up by users?

    e. Have there been any unauthorized uses of the computer system in the past ten years?

    f. Has the system ever contracted a virus?

    g. What safeguards have been taken against viruses?

    h. Are errors made by staff members at the computer support center categorized by type or frequency?

    i. What sanctions are imposed on staff when repeated errors are made?

2. Using newsmagazines or newspapers in your library, locate four different instances of white-collar crime (not four stories about the same crime). After reading these stories, answer the following questions about each:

    a. What type of white-collar crime is discussed?

    b. How was the crime detected?

    c. What agencies were involved in the investigation?

    d. What sanctions, if any, were discussed or imposed?

INVESTIGATIVE SKILL BUILDERS

Using Reasoning

You are a criminal investigator in a medium-sized rural community. One of the larger chain department stores in your town has contacted you about employee pilferage. You meet with the store's security manager, John Gilligan, who explains the problem.

Mr. Gilligan tells you that in the past week he has found high-cost price tags in the garbage and a number of low-cost items without tags on the shelf. He reasons that someone has been switching tags and buying expensive items for low prices. He believes that it is an employee because he found the tags in the backroom garbage bin. He has totaled the tags he found, and they amount to $7,857.

1. Is Mr. Gilligan correct in reasoning that the theft is being undertaken by an employee or employees?
2. How might you determine which employee or employees are involved?
3. How might the thieves make a monetary profit on this theft?

Honesty/Integrity

You are filling out your income tax forms for the year. You remember that you attended the Academy of Criminal Justice Sciences national meeting. Because this meeting relates to your position as chief of police in a medium-sized department, expenses for it are tax deductible. You have an envelope with all your receipts for airfare, hotel, conference registration, and food. The receipts total $845. You also have a statement from your department indicating it reimbursed you $600 for this trip. Should you deduct the full amount of receipted expenses? Explain your answer.

Narcotics and Dangerous Drugs

After completing this chapter, you will be able to:

1 Offer definitions of narcotics and dangerous drugs.
2 Identify and describe some common types of dangerous drugs.
3 List and discuss other dangerous drugs.
4 Discuss legal aspects of narcotics and dangerous drugs.
5 Specify some procedures related to illicit drug investigations.

NARCOTICS

At one time, the term *narcotic* referred to a variety of substances inducing altered states of consciousness and derived from distillations of the opium poppy plant (*Papavar somniferum*). In today's common and inconsistent parlance, the term **narcotic** is used for any drug that produces a stupor, insensibility, or sleep (DEA, 2005). As a consequence, narcotics could include substances ranging from alcohol to heroin to crack cocaine.

> **narcotic** Any drug that produces a stupor, insensibility, or sleep.

Some individuals define narcotics as those substances that bind at opiate receptors (cellular membrane proteins activated by substances like heroin or morphine); others refer to any illicit substance as a narcotic. In a legal context, narcotic refers to opium, opium derivatives, and their semisynthetic substitutes (DEA, 2005). Cocaine and coca leaves, which are also classified as narcotics in the Controlled Substances Act (CSA), neither bind at opiate receptors nor produce morphinelike effects. They are discussed later in this chapter when examining stimulants. For the purposes of this text, the term *narcotic* refers to drugs that produce morphinelike effects.

In law enforcement circles the term *narcotic* may be used as a euphemism to designate any drug that is allegedly dangerous, is heavily abused, or has a high potential for abuse. Marijuana, cocaine, PCP, amphetamines, and barbiturates, along with heroin and other opium derivatives have all been considered in narcotics regulations.

Properly defined, narcotics include only the natural derivatives of *Papavar somniferum,* having both analgesic and sedative properties, and any synthetic derivatives or compounds of similar pharmacological structure and action (Fredrickson & Siljander, 2004; Ksir, Oakely, & Hart, 2005).

The range of drugs accurately labeled *narcotics* can be limited to two specific categories:

1. *Natural narcotics* (compounds derived directly from *Papavar somniferum*): opium, morphine, and heroin.
2. *Synthetic narcotics* (compounds possessing similar pharmacological structures and properties): Dilaudid, Percodan, codeine, methadone, Demerol, Darvon, Talwin.

Taken together as a group, natural and synthetic narcotics differ widely in their uses, effects, and addiction potential. Any substance that is derived directly or indirectly from opium is classified as an **opiate.** Addiction to opiates is an actual physical dependence. It is augmented by the development of a tolerance requiring larger and larger amounts of the substance to avoid withdrawal symptoms. Manufacturers and distributors of medicinal opiates are stringently controlled by the federal government through laws designed to keep these products available only for legitimate medical use. Those who distribute these drugs are registered and monitored by federal authorities and must comply with specific record-keeping and drug security requirements.

> **opiate** Any of the narcotic drugs produced from the opium poppy.

Narcotic Drug Abuse

The abuse of narcotic drugs dates back to ancient times, and their use today is still a serious problem. The appeal of morphinelike drugs lies in their ability to reduce sensitivity to both psychological and physical stimuli and to produce a state of euphoria. These drugs dull fear, tension, and anxiety. A person under the influence of morphinelike narcotics is usually lethargic and indifferent to his or her environment and personal circumstances. Chronic use leads to both physical and psychological dependence. Tolerance develops, and ever-increasing doses are needed to achieve the desired effect. As the need for the drug increases, the addict's activities become increasingly drug-centered. Drug-suppressed desire for food and growing cravings for the drugs frequently result in protein deficiencies in chronic narcotic abusers (Walsh & Schwartz-Bloom, 2004).

When deprived of morphine or heroin, the addict usually experiences the first withdrawal symptoms shortly before the time of the next scheduled dose, or *fix*. **Withdrawal symptoms** can include nausea, sweating, chills, physical shaking, diarrhea, constant yawning, insomnia, fatigue, restlessness, anxiety, irritability, muscle aches and pains, and stomach cramping (Goldberg, 2006). Complaints of cramping and vomiting and demands for the drug increase in intensity and peak 36 to 72 hours after the last fix. Less severe symptoms, such as watery eyes, runny nose, yawning, and perspiration, tend to appear about 8 to 12 hours after the last dose. Thereafter, the addict may fall into a restless sleep.

The longer the addicted person is without drugs, the greater and more violent his or her withdrawal becomes. Restlessness becomes irritability and insomnia. Individuals may experience gooseflesh, chills, tremors, and violent muscular contractions. These withdrawal symptoms typically reach their peak 48 to 72 hours after the last fix. The addict becomes weak, depressed, nauseated, and cramped. Vomiting, stomach cramps, and diarrhea are common. Heart rate and blood pressure become elevated. Chills alternating with flushes and excessive sweating are also common symptoms at this point of withdrawal. Pain in the bones and muscles of the back and extremities occurs, as do muscle spasms and kicking movements—perhaps the source of the expression "kicking the habit." The withdrawal discomfort at this point is so severe that many addicts become suicidal. The withdrawal runs its course, and most residual symptoms disappear in about 7 to 10 days (Goldberg, 2006). How long it will be before physiological and psychological equilibrium returns is unpredictable. Fear of withdrawal symptoms drives addicts to lie, cheat, steal, and turn to prostitution to obtain money to purchase their next dose of drugs. Figure 21.1 shows the effects of some illegal drugs.

Categories of Drugs

Narcotics and various other controlled substances vary in their effects on people. For the most part, drugs can be divided into four major categories based on their manifest effects: narcotics, depressants, stimulants, and hallucinogens. Two additional categories account for cannabis and inhalants (Lyman, 2002).

Narcotics Narcotics are drugs with a depressant effect on the central nervous system. Euphoria and a general feeling of warmth and well-being are frequently associated with their use. Narcotics are used to relieve pain and induce sleep. Prolonged use of narcotics results in both psychological and physiological dependence. Also, tolerance to dose level occurs over prolonged use, requiring the user to increase the dosage to obtain the same effects (Goode, 2004). Physical dependence is an involuntary effect of prolonged use of narcotics; this condition is evidenced by withdrawal symptoms once the addicted individual stops using the drug.

Depressants **Depressants** or **sedatives** are used to allay irritation or nervousness. These drug compounds, commonly referred to as *barbiturates* and *tranquilizers,* can create a lethargic and sleepy feeling in the user but may also produce a general feeling of calm and well-being. Drugs such as Seconal, Valium, Nembutal, and others are sometimes prescribed for legitimate reasons, but because of their addictive quality their users sometimes become hooked. When sedatives are used over long periods, the user may develop a tolerance and require larger doses to produce the same sense of relaxation. Both psychological and physiological dependence may result from

---

withdrawal symptoms
Symptoms that appear shortly after a drug addict misses a scheduled dose, or *fix;* may include nausea, sweating, chills, physical shaking, diarrhea, constant yawning, insomnia, fatigue, restlessness, anxiety, irritability, muscle aches and pains, and stomach cramping.

depressant or sedative
Any drug used to allay irritation or nervousness; creates lethargy in the user but may also produce a general feeling of calm and well-being.

FIGURE 21.1   Some Effects of Illegal Drugs

Drug Type	Short-Term Effects Desired	Other	Duration of Acute Effects	DEA View of Risk of Dependence
Heroin	• Euphoria • Pain reduction	• Respiratory depression • Nausea • Drowsiness	• 3 to 6 hours	• Physical: high • Psychological: high
Cocaine	• Excitement • Euphoria • Increased alertness, wakefulness	• Increased blood pressure • Increased respiratory rate • Nausea • Cold sweats • Twitching • Headache	• 1 to 2 hours	• Physical: possible • Psychological: high
Crack cocaine	• Same as cocaine • More rapid high than cocaine	• Same as cocaine	• About 5 minutes	• Same as cocaine
Marijuana	• Euphoria • Relaxation	• Accelerated heartbeat • Impairment of perception, judgment, fine motor skills, and memory	• 2 to 4 hours	• Physical: unknown • Psychological: moderate
Amphetamines	• Euphoria • Excitement • Increased alertness, wakefulness	• Increased blood pressure • Increased pulse rate • Insomnia • Loss of appetite	• 2 to 4 hours	• Physical: possible • Psychological: high
LSD	• Illusions and hallucinations • Excitement • Euphoria	• Poor perception of time and distance • Acute anxiety, restlessness, sleeplessness • Sometimes depression	• 8 to 12 hours	• Physical: none • Psychological: unknown

Sources: NIDA, "Heroin," *NIDA capsules,* August 1986; DEA, *Drugs of abuse,* 2005; G. R. Gay, "Clinical management of acute and chronic cocaine poisoning: Concepts, components and configuration," *Annals of emergency medicine* (1982) 11(10):562–572 as cited in NIDA, Dale D. Chitwood, "Patterns and consequences of cocaine use," in *Cocaine use in America: Epidemiologic and clinical perspectives,* Nicholas J. Kozel and Edgar H. Adams, eds., NIDA research monograph 61, 1985; NIDA, James A. Inciardi, "Crack-cocaine in Miami," in *The epidemiology of cocaine use and abuse,* Susan Schober and Charles Schade, eds., NIDA research monograph 110, 1991; and NIDA, "Marijuana," *NIDA capsules,* August 1986.

prolonged use. An individual under the influence of some depressants may appear to be intoxicated; that is, their coordination, speech, and thought processes may be slowed or impaired (Ksir, Oakley & Hart, 2005).

stimulant A drug with a stimulating effect on the central nervous system, causing wakefulness and alertness while masking symptoms of fatigue.

Stimulants **Stimulants** are drugs or other substances that increase the activity of tissues (such as the central nervous system), thereby affecting the physiological processes of the body. Commonly referred to in the vernacular as *uppers,* stimulants may remove inhibitions and produce a feeling of zest and excitement. When injected or smoked, these drugs cause intense feelings of euphoria (Kuhn, Swartzwelder, & Wilson, 2003). Tolerance to stimulants can develop through abuse; most authorities, however, suggest that physical dependence does not develop, although psychological dependence is not uncommon among abusers. The abuse of methamphetamine, a powerful stimulant, has become a very serious problem in the United States. First identified by law enforcement during the 1960s, this powerful amphetamine, sometimes referred to simply as *meth* or *crank,* can be used through snorting, injection, or smoking (Siegel & Houck, 2006). Injection remains the most effective way to deliver the drug, but smokable methamphetamine, better known as *ice,* has the same chemical properties as common methamphetamine. To make smoking possible, meth is distilled into a rocklike form. Smoking ice is extremely addictive. Estimates of drug use among U.S. citizens based on self-report surveys, such as the National Household Survey on Drug Use, indicate that more than 13 million Americans have used methamphetamine at least once in the previous year (Feucht, 2006).

Much of the methamphetamine used in the United States today comes from abroad, but some is manufactured in the United States. In 1999 U.S. law enforcement agencies seized evidence from 7,438 clandestine meth labs. By 2004 that number had more than doubled, to 17,170. More astonishing is the increase in the number of lab seizures in eastern states, where meth labs had been virtually nonexistent just five or six years ago (Feucht, 2006).

FYI By 2004 law enforcement efforts to curb methamphetamine labs appeared to be successful. Before the glow of success had a chance to set in, however, international drug cartels began distributing an even purer form of the drug known as *ice*—a highly addictive smokable version. In their continuing efforts to inhibit domestic production of ice, many states have developed laws prohibiting the open sale of *precursor drugs*—legal medicines containing pseudophedrine and ephedrine that can be used to produce methamphetamine. These once openly over-the-counter drugs are now housed in secure areas of the drug store or behind the pharmacy counter, and many states limit the quantity of cold medications one can buy each day and month and require customers to show proof of identity and sign a log of purchasers (Associated Press, 2005; Huus, 2006).

hallucinogen A drug causing changes in sensory perception to create mind-altering hallucinations and loss of an accurate sense of time and space.

Hallucinogens **Hallucinogens** are substances capable of altering perceptions and producing hallucinations. Hallucinogens may produce the perception of heightened senses and visualization of vivid colors. They may also produce exaggerated feelings of fear or terror, or visions of monsters or terrifying imagined situations. Repeated or extensive use of hallucinogens may produce psychological dependence, and hallucinogens have been known to produce *flashbacks,* or hallucinogenic images and states of mind, even months after use has ended. Hallucinogens can be found in nature or produced in a laboratory, even a makeshift *kitchen laboratory.* Among the commonly abused drugs included in this category are lysergic acid diethylamide (LSD), Psilocybin and Psilocin (from Aztec mushrooms, sometimes referred to as *magic mushrooms* or *shrooms*), mescaline (from peyote cactus plants), phencyclidine (PCP), marijuana, and nutmeg and mace (Myristicin). Drugs other than those classified as hallucinogens—such as amphetamines and cocaine—can also produce illusions and delusion in users (Walsh & Schwartz-Bloom, 2004).

Cannabis (*Cannabis sativa*) Although sometimes considered a mild hallucinogen, cannabis should actually be put in its own category (*Cannabis sativa*). Cannabis is among the most commonly abused drugs, and it grows in almost all parts of the world. At one time, cannabis was a leading U.S. cash crop—second only to cotton. It was used to produce hemp rope and linens and other textiles. Although illegal, cannabis cultivation is once again becoming important in some areas of the United States. The northwest United States is the regional capital of indoor marijuana cultivation. Drug-related cannabis products include marijuana, hashish, and hash oil. Tetrahydrocannabinol, more commonly referred to as THIC, is the primary psychoactive element in cannabis and cannabis-related products (Booth, 2004).

Inhalants Substances that cause perceptible changes in brain function through inhalation are classified as **inhalants.** These inhalants can be further classified into four categories:

- Aerosols
- Gases
- Solvents
- Nitrites

> **inhalants** Substances that cause perceptible changes in brain function through inhalation.

A wide variety of substances are abused as inhalants, frequently because they are both inexpensive and fairly accessible. Commonly used inhalants include model airplane glue, colored markers, industrial and household cleaning chemicals, gasoline, paint, nitrites (poppers, snappers, and rush), and nitrous oxide. Individuals of all ages may abuse inhalants, but their use is particularly prevalent among adolescents and preadolescents (Falvo, 2005).

TYPES OF NARCOTICS

Most people take drugs for the effects they produce. As we saw earlier, the effects may be mood changes, excitement, sedation, relaxation, pleasure, stimulation, or pain reduction. Most illegal drugs are consumed for their mind-altering effects.

Opium

There were no legal restrictions on the importation or use of opium until the early 1900s. In the United States, the unrestricted availability of opium, the influx of opium-smoking immigrants from East Asia, and the invention of the hypodermic needle contributed to the more severe variety of compulsive drug abuse seen at the turn of the twentieth century. In those days, medicines often contained opium without any warning label. Today, state, federal, and international laws govern the production and distribution of narcotic substances (Musto, 2002).

Although opium is used in the form of paregoric to treat diarrhea, most opium imported into the United States is broken down into its alkaloid constituents. These alkaloids are divided into two distinct chemical classes, phenanthrenes and isoquinolines.

The principal phenanthrenes are morphine, codeine, and thebaine; the isoquinolines have no significant central nervous system effects and are not regulated under the Controlled Substances Act.

Heroin

Heroin (diacetylmorphine) was originally synthesized from morphine in 1874, and at that time it was believed to be a cure for morphine addiction. Heroin is a central nervous system depressant that also relieves pain. Tolerance for this drug builds up faster than for any other opiate. Consequently, the danger of drug dependency is considerably greater. Heroin has come to be considered by many as the most dangerous and enslaving drug on the drug scene (Lyman, 2002). Heroin was first controlled by the Harrison Act of 1914, a law enacted because of concerns over a growing use and abuse of opium in the United States, especially among middle-class women who purchased an over-the-counter remedy better known as laudanum (tincture of opium). Heroin is an odorless crystalline white powder. In the United States, heroin is frequently sold in glassine packets, sometimes called *decks,* or in capsules, referred to as *caps.* The darker the heroin's color, the more impurities it contains. Heroin is the chief opiate abused in the United States and many other countries. Generally, heroin is injected.

FYI Although opium is no longer widely abused in the United States, its byproducts are. Morphine is made from opium, and heroin is made from morphine. The three drugs have similar effects. However, heroin is the strongest, and opium is the least powerful.

By the time heroin reaches its market of users on the street, it has usually been diluted, or *cut* or *stepped on,* considerably. Heroin reaching the United States ranges from 20 to 80 percent pure. Deaths from heroin overdoses are not uncommon. Sometimes death occurs because the user is unaware that the drug is more pure and potent than on previous occasions. Investigators should also be aware that addicts may be murdered for a variety of reasons by being given a hot shot of heroin, or a nearly pure concentration of heroin. In some situations, addicts die because of an allergic or toxic reaction to materials used by the dealer to dilute the heroin. Powdered milk, sugar, and quinine are commonly used to cut heroin, but talcum powder has been used on occasion, with lethal results. Talcum powder is inert and cannot be absorbed by the human body. When injected intravenously with heroin, it travels the arterial system until it eventually forms blockages. Depending on their location, these blockages may cause loss of limbs or death.

Heroin remains a serious narcotic addiction in the United States. Studies in the 1990s estimated that as many as 750,000 Americans were addicted to this drug ("Heroin Comes Back," 1990). A 2004 report from the Drug Abuse Awareness Network (DAWN) indicated that from 2001 to 2002 drug-abuse-related emergency room visits involving narcotic analgesics (typically heroin, morphine, and similar opiates) increased from 90,232 to 108,320; the trend from 1995 to 2002 indicated an increase of more than 153 percent (DAWN, 2004). An even larger number of people may be controlled, occasional users not actually addicted to heroin (Zinberg, 1995). The 1980s were marked by a surge in the use by addicts of crack cocaine. The 1990s and the new millennium, however, show an alarming resurgence in heroin's popularity among addicted Americans.

Heroin is not well absorbed if taken orally. Users, therefore, usually administer the drug by intravenous injection. In the United States, some addicts combine cocaine with heroin, snorting, injecting, or even smoking the combination. In other countries, notably England, "chasing the dragon," or smoking the fumes of heroin oil, has been popular since the 1970s (Schuckit, 1995).

After processing, heroin is packaged and sold by the kilo (about 2.2 pounds). The initial purchaser of pure heroin expects to cut it at least three times before further sale. In other words, the wholesale distributor will dilute each kilo of heroin purchased to 6.6 pounds. Principal distributors may pay $25,000 to $30,000 or more for a single kilo of nearly pure heroin. Price variations occur due to market fluctuations caused by federal drug enforcement efforts and varying levels of cooperation with the governments of countries where poppies are grown or heroin laboratories are hidden.

STATISTICS According to the Drug Enforcement Administration 2005 report, *Drugs of Abuse,* by 2002 approximately 3.7 million Americans reported using heroin at least once in their lifetime.

Wholesale distributors sell the cut heroin to middle-level traffickers at prices ranging from about $10,000 to $20,000 a pound. This middle-level trafficker will also dilute the heroin and will sell the product to dealers at prices ranging from about $500 to $1,000 per ounce. The price variation at this stage is generally related to how adulterated the heroin has already become.

Pure heroin is rarely sold on the street. A *bag* (slang for a small unit of heroin sold on the street) currently contains about 30 to 50 milligrams of powder, only a portion of which is heroin. The remainder could be sugar, starch, acetaminophen, procaine, benzocaine, quinine, or any of numerous cutting agents for heroin. Traditionally, the purity of heroin in a bag ranged from 1 percent to 10 percent. More recently, heroin purity has ranged from 10 percent to 70 percent. Black tar heroin is often sold in chunks weighing about an ounce. Its purity is generally less than South American heroin, and it is most frequently smoked or dissolved, diluted, and injected (DEA, 2005).

Dealers again cut the heroin and put it into smaller bags for street sale. Decks and caps are prevalent methods of packaging for street sales. These packages may be sold by street dealers who work for the dealer or work for themselves after purchasing the packages from the dealer. By the time the addict purchases the heroin from the street dealer, it has been reduced to about 4 to 10 percent of its original potency. The profit potential along most of heroin's distribution process is enormous. The original kilo of heroin, with all the adulterations at each level, may have been stepped on 20 or 30 times. This has produced a total of 44 to 66 pounds of heroin at the street level. At a price of $50 a gram, the total return on the original kilo soars to more than $1.5 million.

Criminal investigators should be aware that many heroin addicts are predatory criminals. During the sequence of buying and selling at the street level, drug peddlers may be hijacked, robbed, or ripped off. This may result in violence, additional crimes, and, in some cases, homicides. Addicts also become involved in a variety of other criminal activities to obtain money to maintain their habit and avoid the onslaught of withdrawal.

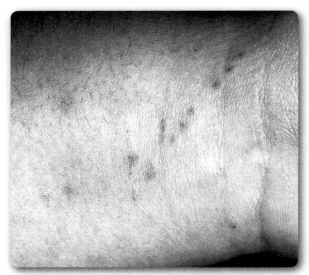

The scarring patterns that result from collapsed veins on a heroin user are commonly called tracks.

Because heroin is chiefly injected intravenously, needle marks or tracks may be observed on an addict's body. Investigators should be aware that these tracks may be observed in a variety of places on the body but are most often in places that are easy to reach. Veins in the elbow folds, along the forearms, on the backs of the hands, and on the legs are the most common. However, repeated injection of a vein results in its eventual collapse, resulting in the scarring referred to as *tracks.*

On some addicts who attempt to conceal their addiction, injection marks may be found between the toes or under the tongue. Tracks indicate previous use of the drugs; they do not usually indicate recent use. Recent use can sometimes be detected by finding a series of small scabs, which usually last about a week to ten days. These scabs are due to small localized infections brought about by unsterilized injection outfits, generally unclean conditions when injecting the heroin, and various impurities in the drug itself.

Cocaine

Cocaine, the most potent stimulant of natural origin, is extracted from the leaves of the coca plant (*Erythroxylum coca*), which is indigenous to the Andean highlands of South America. Natives in this region chew or brew coca leaves into a tea for refreshment and to relieve fatigue, similar to the customs of chewing tobacco and drinking tea or coffee (Gootenberg, 1999).

Cocaine is a white, odorless, crystalline powder resembling snow, Epsom salts, or camphor. As an analgesic, it has been largely supplanted by synthetic drugs. Its medical applications are now mainly restricted to operations of the ear, eye, nose, and throat. Its medical use was popular because it constricted the blood vessels and limited bleeding in anesthetized areas.

Illicit cocaine is typically adulterated to about half its total volume with various sugars and local anesthetics. Amphetamines and other drugs with stimulant properties may also be used. As with heroin, the cost of the drug and the potential for enormous profits increase the likelihood of cutting the drug at various levels along the distribution process. The major source of cocaine in the United States is South America.

The effects of cocaine include stimulation of the central nervous system and increases in heart rate, blood pressure, and body temperature. Because of its central nervous system effects, the drug is habit-forming. The pleasure effects of cocaine are mixed with mild hallucinations. A commonly reported hallucination is that of insects crawling on the skin. Cocaine remains a serious danger because it can produce paranoia and anxiety, and an overdose can result in death.

Cocaine has a fairly fast effect. When inhaled through the nose, it goes to the back of the nasal cavity, combines with mucus, and drips down the back of the throat. The nose and upper gum become numb and then the high begins (Goode, 2004). If the drug is mainlined, or taken intravenously, all of the infections associated with heroin use can occur, including abscesses and hepatitis. Some heroin addicts combine heroin and cocaine in one injection. This has been called a *speedball.* The effects of the two drugs are directly opposite, and the body is seriously abused by their combined use—sometimes to the point of death.

HISTORY

DURING THE LATE NINETEENTH AND EARLY TWENTIETH CENTURIES, cocaine was widely used in various tonics, elixirs, and patented medicines. The coca leaves were deemed so safe that in 1885 they were added to a concoction of carbonated water and extracts taken from the kola nut and sold under the name Coca-Cola. As the dangers of cocaine became more apparent, the coca leaves were removed from the drink's ingredients, and a non-narcotic version remained on the market.

Freebasing Cocaine   Freebasing cocaine involves separating the base of cocaine from its hydrochloride powder. Cocaine is dissolved in a solution of distilled water and calcium carbonate or lactose. The mixture is stirred or shaken to completely dissolve the cocaine. Next, several drops of ether are added to the solution, and the mixture is shaken again. The cocaine is attracted to the ether, while the other additives and impurities are attracted to the calcium carbonate or lactose solution (Lyman, 2002).

The newly formed ether-cocaine solution separates from the larger solution in a manner similar to oil separating from water. The ether-cocaine solution rises to the surface. By using an eyedropper, one can suction off the ether-cocaine solution and place it in a container to allow the moisture and ether to evaporate. The resultant crystals are smoked and produce a more potent high, because the concentration of base cocaine is much greater now that it has been freebased. The evaporation process may occur naturally or may be accelerated by adding heat. However, since ether is an extremely flammable and volatile chemical, heating the ether-cocaine solution can be dangerous.

Crack Cocaine   Crack cocaine, contrary to popular belief, is neither *freebase cocaine* nor *purified cocaine*. As Inciardi and McElrath (2004) pointed out, some of the confusion about what crack cocaine is results from the different ways the word *freebase* is used. As a noun, *freebase* refers to a drug, a cocaine product converted to the base state from cocaine hydrochloride after adulterants have been chemically removed. Crack cocaine, however, is converted to the base state without removing the adulterants. As a verb of action, *freebase* means to inhale vapors of cocaine base, of which crack is but one form. Finally, crack cocaine is anything but pure. When crack is processed, the baking soda used in the process remains as a salt and actually reduces the overall purity of the cocaine product. Crack gets its name, in fact, from the cracking sound that the residue of baking soda often makes when heated.

Crack cocaine can easily be produced in a dealer's kitchen. The process involves mixing cocaine, water, and baking powder. This solution is slowly heated until all the moisture has evaporated. The remaining *cookie* of combined cocaine and baking powder is then broken into small pieces, which are placed in small containers or wrapped in plastic wrap and sold for as little as $5 or $10. These bits, or *rocks,* as they are commonly called, are placed into pipes and ignited, and the cocaine fumes are inhaled. Crack cocaine is substantially less expensive than powdered cocaine, creating a much wider, and unfortunately more youthful, market for the drug.

Crack cocaine, like freebase cocaine, is a concentrate of the base cocaine, so it is considerably more potent than powdered cocaine. The DEA estimates that 75 percent of those who try crack cocaine will become addicted with as few as three uses. Moreover, they estimate that as many as half of all people who try crack may become addicted after only a single use (Constantine, 1990). Crack cocaine has maintained its popularity with users because it produces a high similar to but much more intense than that of powdered cocaine (Knowles, 1996).

> **FYI** Coca plants are harvested from two to six times each year. The leaves are soaked with solutions to chemically extract coca paste. This paste, or crude cocaine, is then shipped to illegal laboratories in various countries, including the United States, for processing into cocaine.

Morphine

Morphine is the principal alkaloid of opium. It was discovered in 1806 by F. W. A. Serturner. Morphine is converted from crude opium by a fairly simple process of boiling and filtering. Opium is placed in water and heated until it breaks down into a liquid. Next, chemicals are added to the solution to filter out impurities. This results in a chemical separation of the morphine base from the original opium-and-water solution. Because morphine is a condensed extract of opium, it is significantly more potent. It is usually estimated to be three times stronger than opium.

In its natural state, morphine is not readily soluble in water. Therefore, it is treated with sulfuric acid. The resultant, morphine sulfate, is quite soluble and is the most common form used. Morphine is white and comes in three main forms: powder, cubes, and $\frac{1}{8}$- and $\frac{1}{2}$-grain tablets. The texture is very light, similar to that of chalk dust. Peddlers adulterate the powder with milk sugar, cutting the potency considerably. The drug is taken orally or intravenously. Most addicts prefer intravenous injections because the effects are more immediate and pronounced. The improvised hypodermic "outfit" is the same as that used to inject heroin.

Thebaine

Thebaine, a minor constituent of opium, is controlled in Schedule II of the CSA as well as under international law. Although chemically similar to both morphine and codeine, thebaine produces stimulatory rather than depressant effects. Thebaine is not used therapeutically but is converted into a variety of substances including oxycodone, oxymorphone, nalbuphine, naloxone, naltrexone, and buprenorphine (DEA, 2005).

Codeine

The alkaloid codeine can be found in crude opium in concentrations from 0.7 percent to about 2.5 percent. It was identified in 1832 when discovered as an impurity in a batch of morphine. Codeine is commonly found in a variety of legally controlled medical preparations sold in the United States. It is the least addictive of the opium derivatives and very similar in appearance to morphine (a white crystalline powder). The narcotic is used illicitly in the same manner as morphine and heroin. Codeine is commonly found in combination with aspirin, Tylenol, and various cough syrups, and it is occasionally used by addicts deprived of their regular source of heroin (DEA, 2005). Its primary effects include dulled perception, straying attention, and a general lack of awareness of surroundings. When withdrawal symptoms do occur, they are usually less severe than from more potent drugs, such as heroin or morphine. Abusers generally obtain codeine by stealing it from drugstores or feigning illness to acquire prescriptions for medications that contain codeine.

Percodan

Percodan (oxycodone, dihydrohydroxycodeinone) is extremely important in medicine as an analgesic (painkiller). The addictive potential of dihydrohydroxycodeinone, the narcotic ingredient of Percodan, is somewhere between morphine and codeine, but the drug is much closer to morphine in its effects. Percodan and codeine are taken orally by some addicts when heroin is not available. Addicts may also dissolve Percodan tablets in water, filter out the insoluble binders, and inject the active drug intravenously.

Methadone

In response to a shortage of morphine during World War II, German chemists synthesized methadone. Although chemically unlike morphine or heroin, it produces many of the same effects and can be administered orally or by injection. Methadone does not produce the euphoric high sought by heroin users, but a similar tolerance and dependency does occur. Withdrawal symptoms develop more slowly and are less severe than in withdrawal from morphine or heroine, but methadone withdrawal symptoms may be more prolonged. Methadone was introduced in the United States in 1947 as an analgesic. Commercially, it has been distributed under such names as Dolophine Hydrochloride, Amidone, and Methadone.

Since the 1960s, methadone has been widely used in the detoxification of heroin addicts and in methadone maintenance programs. Methadone treatment maintains an addict's physical and mental dependency on a drug but is intended to keep the user away from the criminal behavior necessary to support a heroin habit. Unfortunately, many heroin addicts who miss the euphoric sensation revert to heroin abuse.

OTHER DANGEROUS DRUGS

To be truly prepared to undertake the duties of a criminal investigator, it is important to understand certain dangerous drugs other than narcotics. Identifying drug offenders requires a broad understanding of a number of the most common drugs of abuse in the United States.

Stimulants

Drugs classified as stimulants directly stimulate the central nervous system, producing excitation, a feeling of alertness, and sometimes a temporary rise in blood pressure and respiration. A typical abuse cycle may begin with the lawful use of a stimulant for some legitimate reason. After using the drug for a while, the individual begins to depend on its effects. In addition to cocaine, commonly abused stimulants include nicotine, caffeine, amphetamines, phenmetrazine, and methylphenidate.

Tolerance to stimulants occurs quickly, and abusers may require larger doses to obtain comparable results. When taking large doses of stimulants, the abuser may need to take depressants (discussed next) to get to sleep. This cycle of uppers and downers puts enormous stress on the body. Symptoms of chronic stimulant abuse include grinding the teeth, touching or picking at the face, rapid speech patterns, confusion, and—in some cases—paranoia. As tolerance increases, the possibility of a toxic overdose increases.

Depressants (Sedatives and Hypnotics)

The barbiturates, made from barbituric acid, constitute the largest group of sedatives. Their effects are opposite from those of stimulants. They are the most frequently prescribed drugs to induce sleep and to reduce daytime tension and anxiety. They are known as hypnotics and are commonly referred to as sleeping pills. Because of their sedative effect, they are also called *downers* by drug users. People can legally buy and use these drugs only with a doctor's prescription. However, abusers sometimes feign sleep problems to obtain prescriptions. This group of drugs depresses the central nervous system and relieves anxiety. Barbiturates are valuable when used properly but extremely dangerous when abused.

Repeated use of barbiturates can be addicting. Signs of physical dependence appear with doses well above therapeutic levels. Withdrawal from barbiturates is especially dangerous and is characterized by convulsions and delirium. Chronic use produces slurred speech, staggering, loss of balance, and irritability. Overdoses of barbiturates, particularly in conjunction with alcohol, result in unconsciousness and death.

Barbiturates are often diverted from legitimate channels. Popular brand-name depressants bear trademarks or other identifying symbols. Their trade names are usually recognizable by the ending "al," for example, Seconal, Nembutal, Amytal, and Luminal. Individual barbiturates are distinguished from one another by the colors of the gelatin capsules in which they are packed. Frequently, barbiturates are nicknamed on the streets by their capsule colors. Seconal capsules, for example, are sometimes referred to as *reds* because of their red color, Nembutal capsules are sometimes called *yellows,* and so forth.

Glutethimide (Doriden)   Glutethimide, when introduced in 1954, was incorrectly believed to be a nonaddictive barbiturate substitute. The sedative effects of this drug begin approximately thirty minutes after its ingestion. Its effects, however, may last as long as eight hours. Since the effects of the drug can last so long, it is difficult to treat or reverse an overdose. Recently, glutethimide has been illicitly used with codeine tablets to give a heroinlike effect. Street names for this potentially lethal combination include *dors and 4s* and *Ds and Cs.*

Methaqualone   Methaqualone is chemically different from barbiturates and unrelated to glutethimide. It does, however, have similar sedative-hypnotic effects (drowsiness, motor/speech dysfunctions, and so forth). Although it does not have as strong a knockout effect as barbiturates, it does produce a "drunken" intoxication, and its effects can be dangerously increased by combination with alcohol (Akers, 1992). Originally, methaqualone was mistakenly thought to be safe and nonaddictive and to have aphrodisiac qualities. Actually, it has caused many cases of serious poisoning and has also been implicated in highway accidents and hazardous driving. Large doses cause coma and may be accompanied by thrashing or convulsions. Methaqualone has been marketed in the United States under various brand names, such as Quaalude, Parest, Optimil, Somnafac, and Sopor.

Tranquilizers

Tranquilizers were originally developed as medical aids to psychotherapy for mental patients. Larger doses and more potent tranquilizers continue to be used in this manner. The benzodiazepines (Valium and Librium), however, are more often prescribed by physicians for general anxiety and as antidepressants (Akers, 1992). Although tranquilizers are not usually part of illicit drug traffic, they are sometimes diverted from the prescription industry, pharmacies, hospitals, and even family medicine chests, for sale on the streets. Even when not diverted to the illicit drug market, tranquilizers are sometimes seriously abused as prescription drugs, and strong dependence on them can become a serious problem.

In the mid-1990s a new tranquilizer surfaced. This drug, commonly called the *rape drug* or *ruffys,* is actually a powerful Valiumlike drug called Ruhibnol. The drug is slipped into the drinks of unsuspecting young women at parties and in bars. The drug quickly causes the victim to feel slightly dizzy and often nauseated. The would-be rapist then helps the young woman home, where she soon falls into what physicians sometimes refer to as a *twilight state.* In a twilight state, a person is neither fully asleep nor fully awake. During this period, however, the victim is helpless to ward off a sexual assault and often remembers the attack only as a dream.

Hallucinogens

Hallucinogens, also referred to as psychedelics or consciousness-expanding drugs, are capable of distorting perception of objective reality. Alterations of time and space perception, illusions, hallucinations, and delusions may be either mild or overwhelming, depending on the dose. The effects experienced after taking hallucinogens are not related solely to the drug. They are also modified by the emotional state, mental attitude, and environment of the user. The results of taking hallucinogens are quite variable. One might experience a very pleasurable high, see bright and beautiful colors, hear music and sounds as never before, and feel calm and relaxed. On the other hand, one might just as easily have a "bad trip," during which one might see frightening monsters or believe one was being attacked. The most commonly abused hallucinogens are LSD 25 (lysergic acid diethylamide) and PCP (phencyclidine).

LSD 25 (Lysergic Acid Diethylamide)   Dr. Albert Hofmann, a biochemist at Sandoz Laboratories in Basel, Switzerland, first synthesized LSD in 1938 from a dark purple fungus named *ergot.* On an April afternnon in 1943, Dr. Hofmann accidentally inhaled an infinitesimal amount of the new compound. He recognized its perception-altering properties and repeated his intake a few days later to confirm his findings (Cohen, 1964).

Since then, LSD has become known as one of the most powerful drugs abused on the drug scene. An average dose of LSD is a tiny speck, perhaps 30 or 40 micrograms, or about the amount one could place on the tip of a pin. The effects of LSD may last eight to twelve hours. Users may place the LSD on a cube of sugar, on a blotter, or in food or drinks. Inmates have been known to receive letters that have had their corners dipped in LSD. By sucking a corner, the inmate ingests the drug. Along with mental and perceptual effects, the user may have dilated pupils, a flushed face, chills, and perhaps a rise in temperature and heart rate. Like other hallucinogens, LSD does not produce physical dependence and is not considered addictive, although many users regularly use it.

PCP (Phencyclidine)   Phencyclidine, or as it is commonly called, PCP, was originally produced as an animal tranquilizer and anesthetic. It affects a number of different neurotransmitters and may function as a stimulant, a depressant, or an analgesic. An extremely powerful drug, PCP can produce irrational and disoriented reactions, hallucinations, feelings of invulnerability, speech difficulty, and frightening death feelings. High doses may produce psychosis, convulsions, coma, and death. The actual effects of PCP are sometimes influenced by the user's expectations and emotional state.

In the drug vernacular, PCP is referred to as *angel dust* or simply *dust*. It dissolves readily in water and, as a street drug, may be both adulterated and misrepresented as something it is not. PCP is often misrepresented as THC, the psychoactive ingredient in marijuana. It has also been sold as LSD or other hallucinogens.

The prevailing patterns of street-level abuse are oral ingestion of the drug, alone or in combination with other drugs, and smoking the drug after it has been sprinkled on parsley, marijuana, or tobacco—in the vernacular, after these items have been "dusted."

Reported experiences of the effects of phencyclidine seem so unpleasant that one wonders how PCP has become so popular. In low doses, the experience usually proceeds in three stages: changes in body image, sometimes accompanied by feelings of depersonalization; perceptual distortions, infrequently evidenced as visual or auditory hallucinations; and feelings of apathy or estrangement. The experience often includes drowsiness, inability to verbalize, and feelings of emptiness, weightlessness, or "nothingness." Reports of difficulty in thinking, poor concentration, and preoccupation with death are common. Common signs of PCP use include flushing, profuse sweating, involuntary eye movements, loss of muscle control, nausea, and vomiting. In addition, people under the influence of PCP are sometimes irrational in their behavior and very violent, and they seem to have extraordinary strength (DEA, 2005). Users of PCP feel the effects about two to five minutes after smoking a small amount. When PCP is taken orally, the onset of effects takes somewhat longer. The high, once begun, may continue for 4 to 6 hours, but the user may not feel normal for 24 to 48 hours.

Other Hallucinogens   In addition to LSD 25 and PCP, a large number of synthetic and natural hallucinogens present problems of varying degrees to law enforcement. These include mescaline (peyote), psilocybin and psilocyn (*magic mushrooms*), and dimethyltryptamine (DMT).

Mescaline   Mescaline, which is derived from the buttons of the peyote cactus—literally cut and dried slices that look like buttons—has been used for centuries by various Southwestern Native American tribes and Indians of Central America in religious rites. Generally ground into a powder, peyote is taken orally (White, 2003). Because of its bitter taste, the drug is often ingested with tea, coffee, milk, orange juice, or some other beverage. Mescaline is available on the illicit market as a crystalline powder, in capsules, or as a liquid in ampules or vials. A dose of 350 to 500 milligrams of mescaline produces illusions and hallucinations for 5 to 12 hours. Like LSD, mescaline is not likely to produce physical dependence but may result in psychological dependence.

Psilocybin and Psilocyn   Also derived from plants, psilocybin and psilocyn are obtained from *Psilocybe* mushrooms, generally grown in Mexico. The hallucinogens in fungi such as mushrooms are based on an indole-amine nucleus. In the genus *Psilocybe* there are approximately 140 species; among these are 80 known to contain hallucinogens (White, 2003). Like mescaline, they have been used in Indian rites for centuries. During the 1960s, they were discovered by hippies interested in so-called mind-expanding drugs and were nicknamed *magic mushrooms* or *shrooms*. Their effects are similar to those of mescaline, except that a smaller dose, 4 to 8 milligrams, is ample to produce hallucinatory effects for about 6 hours. In addition to the actual mushrooms, psilocybin and psilocyn are available in crystalline, powdered, or liquid form (Schuckit, 2000). Again, these drugs do not produce physical dependency, although chronic users have been known to develop a tolerance to them.

Dimethyltryptamine (DMT) Dimethyltryptamine (DMT) is a short-acting hallucinogen found in the seeds of certain plants native to the West Indies and parts of South America. The powdered seeds have been used for centuries as a snuff, called *cohoba,* in religious ceremonies to produce a state of mind that the Haitian natives claimed enabled them to communicate with their gods. Chemists in illegal labs have also produced DMT synthetically. The drug is not taken orally. Rather, its vapor is inhaled from the smoke given off by burning the ground seeds or powder mixed with tobacco, parsley leaves, or marijuana. The drug can also be injected. The effects of a single dose of 60 to 150 milligrams last only 45 to 60 minutes and are mainly hallucinations. The drug may cause psychological dependence, but it has not been proved to cause any physical dependence.

Marijuana (Cannabis)

Marijuana is a dried plant material obtained from the Indian hemp plant *Cannabis sativa.* It has limited medical use in the United States, and that use remains largely experimental rather than approved. In addition to use of the plants in the production of rope, linens, and bags, the sterilized seeds of marijuana are occasionally used commercially in various bird seed mixtures. Marijuana grows as a shrublike plant 4 to 20 feet tall. In full bloom, the plant's leaves are a dark green, similar to the hue of evergreen trees, on the outside and a lighter green on the undersurface. The leaves of the plant have 5 to 11 leaflets or fingers (always an odd number). These leaflets are 2 to 6 inches long, slender, and pointed almost equally at both ends, with sawlike edges and pronounced ridges running from the center diagonally to the edges. The green plant has a slightly mintlike odor, is sticky to the touch, and is covered with fine hairs that are barely visible to the naked eye.

The female of the species contains an abundant amount of delta-9-tetrahydrocannabinol (THC), which is the actual narcotic element of marijuana. Marijuana varies in strength, depending on where it is grown, whether it is wild or cultivated, whether it is smoked or eaten, and which portion of the plant is used (leaves, seeds, stems, or resin).

For use as a drug, the leaves and flowering tops (buds) of the plant are dried in indirect heat. They are packaged in compressed bricks similar to miniature bales of hay. The bricks may be square or slightly oblong in shape and weigh 1 kilo (about 2.2 pounds). The bulk price for a kilo may range from $1,500 to more than $2,500, depending on several factors, including the quality of the marijuana, the type of marijuana it is, its source (for instance, Colombia, Mexico, or domestic), and the part of the country where it is to be sold. The marijuana will be subdivided during the distribution process, reaching street sales at weights of about an ounce or less. At current street prices, a single ounce of high-quality marijuana may cost as much as $350.

There are several ways of using marijuana. The most prevalent method in the United States is to smoke it, usually as a cigarette. In the past, marijuana cigarettes have been called *reefers, joints, sticks, jays, weed, Mary Jane,* or *numbers.* The most common terms for marijuana today include *grass* and *pot,* although some of the terms from earlier times remain. Marijuana may also be smoked in ordinary pipes or water pipes, or in special marijuana pipes called *bongs.* Occasionally, users may make a tea from the twigs or ground seeds, or marijuana may simply be added to various foods and eaten.

The immediate effects of marijuana on the smoker are best described as a kind of intoxication, or high. The overall effect is that of a mild depressant, resulting in drowsiness, reduced nervous system activity, and slowed reaction time. With higher THC content, the effects may be more dramatic, including sensory distortion. Marijuana is not physically addicting, and there is no withdrawal if one suddenly stops using the drug. However, considerable psychological dependence is possible from prolonged use of marijuana.

There is growing medical evidence that marijuana can relieve certain types of pain, nausea, vomiting and other symptoms caused by such illnesses as multiple sclerosis, cancer, and AIDS—or by the harsh drugs sometimes used to treat them. And it can do so with remarkable safety. Indeed, marijuana is less toxic than many of the drugs physicians prescribe every day as standard remedies (Joy, Watson, & Benson, 1999). As of May 2002, five states with official registration programs reported a total of more than 3,400 patients, ranging from a high of 79 patients per 100,000 population in Oregon to a low of 3 per 100,000 in Colorado. California, which lacks a statewide registration system, has the highest concentration of patients, estimated at 30,000, or 89 per 100,000 (Gieringer, 2003). In response to this situation, DEA agents have raided and shut down medical marijuana providers in several states, backed by a 2001 U.S. Supreme Court ruling affirming that federal drug laws take precedence over state laws and barring doctors from prescribing illegal drugs. Opposition in defiance of the DEA tactics has risen, especially in California cities such as Santa Cruz and San Francisco. According to Zimmerman, Crumpacker, and Bayer (1998):

> The political issues surrounding marijuana use have prevented cancer doctors from coming to a consensus regarding the use of marijuana to control nausea and vomiting from chemotherapy. Nonetheless many patients, doctors, and nurses commonly speak of the unwritten and unspoken acceptance of marijuana use by those receiving cancer chemotherapy. (p. 42)

Because the use of medical marijuana is such a hot button issue, it is important for investigators to have a clear understanding of their state's laws and their agency's policy with regard to the use and distribution of this drug for medical purposes.

FYI Since 1996, eleven states have legalized medical marijuana use: Alaska, Arizona, California, Colorado, Hawaii, Maine, Nevada, Oregon, Rhode Island, Vermont, and Washington. Eight of the ten did so through the initiative process; Hawaii's law was enacted by the legislature and signed by the governor in 2000; Vermont's was enacted by the legislature and passed into law without the governor's signature in May 2004; and Rhode Island's was enacted overriding the governor's veto in January 2006.

Hashish Hashish, or *hash,* consists of the THC-rich resin scraped from the leaves and buds of the marijuana plant. The resin is dried and compressed into small blocks. The color of hash typically ranges from brownish tan to dark brown. Hash is cut into small cubes and sold by weight. Because of the high concentration of resin, hashish is often five or six times as potent as marijuana leaves. Hash is usually smoked in pipes, although it, too, can be used in foods.

Hash Oil Hash oil is a dark, amber-brown, syrupy concentrate of resin produced by a process of repeated extractions. Samples of hash oil have been found to contain as much as 60 percent THC. A drop or two of this oil on a cigarette is easily equal in psychoactive effect to smoking an entire marijuana cigarette. Hash oil may also be smoked by placing a small amount in a glass pipe and heating the oil until it fumes. These fumes can then be inhaled by the smoker.

Nutmeg and Mace

Nutmeg, under usual circumstances, is used without hallucinogenic effects in many food preparations; but if used in sufficient quantity, nutmeg can induce visual and auditory hallucinations. The effects distort time and space and create a sense of detachment from reality (Goldberg, 2006). Nutmeg is made from the seeds of the Myristica tree, and mace comes from the fruit of the same tree. Nutmeg is chewed or snuffed with tobacco. Nutmeg and mace are capable of producing an effect if one to two teaspoons are consumed, but it can take as long as 5 hours to feel any effects. Nutmeg and mace never became very popular hallucinogens because of their rather unpleasant side effects, which include nausea, sever headaches, vomiting, tachycardia, and sensory distortion—followed by an extremely bad hangover (Goldberg, 2006). Nonetheless, when prison inmates can get hold of nutmeg, they do use it as a hallucinogen. It is banned as contraband in most prison kitchens.

Kava

Kava, also known as *ava, awa, sakau, tonga,* and *yaona,* derives from the root of a South Seas black pepper plant, *Piper methysticum,* which is found in Polynesia, Melanesia, and Micronesia. The root is dried, ground, and made into a tea. Immigrants from Tonga have occasionally clashed with legal authorities after drinking Kava tea and driving. Kava drinking is a social and ceremonial ritual that has been around for thousands of years in the South Pacific (Renteln, 2004). Kava drinking is also fairly common among South Pacific immigrant groups residing in the United States, and it has begun to become somewhat popular among others in America, even to the opening of Kava bars. Kava is a central nervous system depressant and analgesic that causes drowsiness, and in the United States, it is commonly sold as a natural remedy for anxiety and insomnia. Those who drink Kava tend to describe feeling very relaxed. Police see Kava's negative impact on the roadways; there have been a number of arrests and convictions for driving under the influence in California and Utah. Law enforcement views Kava as a serious problem because the effects include putting some people to sleep as well as slowing motor and reflex responsiveness (Swarbrick, 2004).

Designer Drugs

Designer drugs are so called because they are created in the laboratory by adding or taking away something in an existing drug's chemical composition. Because the new substance no longer has the same composition as the original, it may escape federal regulation until its danger is recognized and it is added to the schedule of controlled substances.

designer drug Substance produced in clandestine laboratories by adding or taking away something in an existing drug's chemical composition.

The practice was first observed in the 1960s when it was used on a small number of tranquilizers. However, during the 1980s and 1990s, the trend in designer drugs was more toward producing synthetic narcotics—for example, a synthetic heroin that is up to 1,000 times more potent than natural heroin. Designer drugs have also included analogs such as MDMA, or ecstasy, which combines an amphetaminelike rush with a hallucinatory experience, and nexus, which combines the hallucinogens DMT and 2c-B.

Ice Along similar lines to the designer drugs is smokable methamphetamine, or *ice.* Ice is a freebase form of methamphetamine (speed) and is called by many street names, including *L.A. glass, hot ice, super ice,* and *L.A. ice.* Typically, ice is smoked in a glass pipe or a cigarette. Ice may be nearly clear and look like a piece of cracked ice taken from the freezer. In this case, the ice was produced with a water base and will burn quickly. Some ice has a yellowish tint. Such ice is oil-based and tends to burn slower and longer

Police now take no chances when they raid illegal drug labs and protect themselves from dangerous chemicals when gathering evidence.

than water-based ice. The high received from smoking ice generally lasts 8 to 30 hours, as compared with a crack high of 8 to 20 minutes (Goldberg, 2006; Pennell, 1990).

Ice is much cheaper to make than crack cocaine and is both deadlier and more addictive than crack. The physiological effects of smoking ice include a rapid heartbeat, increased blood pressure, extreme energy, sleeplessness, euphoria, and possible seizures that can occur as soon as 6 seconds after one puff of ice. Pupils of the eyes contract, and smokers sometimes spike fevers as high as 106 degrees, causing brain damage. Extended use of ice can be fatal.

Ecstasy (MDMA) MDMA (methylenedioxymethamphetamine) is a synthetic, psychoactive drug chemically similar to the stimulant methamphetamine and the hallucinogen mescaline. Common street names for MDMA include ecstasy, Adam, XTC, hug, beans, and love drug. MDMA acts as both a stimulant and a psychedelic, producing an energizing effect as well as distortions in time and perception and enhanced enjoyment from tactile experiences. MDMA exerts its primary effects in the brain on neurons that use the chemical serotonin to communicate with other neurons. The serotonin system plays an important role in regulating mood, aggression, sexual activity, sleep, and sensitivity to pain (NIDA, 2006).

The use of MDMA can interfere with the body's ability to regulate temperature. The specific effects on an individual can be somewhat unpredictable, and occasionally this can lead to a sharp increase in body temperature (hyperthermia) resulting in liver, kidney, and cardiovascular system failure, and death.

Because ecstasy is considered a *party drug,* it is often taken by people who do not know exactly what is in the drug, and other drugs chemically similar to MDMA, such as MDA (methylenedioxyamphetamine, the parent drug of MDMA) and PMA (para-methoxyamphetamine, associated with fatalities in the United States and Australia) are sometimes sold as ecstasy. These drugs can be neurotoxic or create additional health risks to the user. Furthermore, ecstasy tablets may contain other substances in addition to MDMA, such as ephedrine (a stimulant), dextromethorphan (DXM, a cough suppressant that has PCP-like effects at high doses), ketamine (an anesthetic used mostly by veterinarians that also has PCP-like effects), caffeine, cocaine, and methamphetamine. The combination of MDMA with one or more of these drugs may be inherently dangerous, but users might also combine them with substances such as marijuana and alcohol, putting themselves at further risk (NIDA, 2006).

The recreational use of MDMA has been on a fairly steady rise during the past twenty years. In fact, the rate of ecstasy use has increased even in the face of reductions in the use of other substances (Yudko, Hall, & McPherson, 2003). Users frequently have a false sense of safety when taking ecstasy because it lacks the obvious negative effects of other amphetamine-type drugs.

Inhalants

Though not generally considered part of the illicit drug trade, inhalants have been a serious problem for many law enforcement agencies. A number of common household solvents, cleaners, and aerosols have been used primarily by teenagers to obtain a high. Other materials used frequently by juveniles include gasoline, paint, and freon. Vials of amyl or butyl nitrite have become a commonly abused inhalant among some homosexuals who believe it produces an extended orgasm (Goode, 2004). In addition, some contemporary youths inhale freon from air conditioners to obtain a high—often with deadly results.

LEGAL ASPECTS

Federal and state laws define drug offenses. Specific drug laws and penalties vary between levels of government and from one jurisdiction to another. Drug investigators should be aware of their local community ordinances as well as state and federal drug laws.

Categories of Drug Offenses

Generally, drug offenses fall into three categories: possession, distribution, and manufacturing of dangerous or illicit drugs.

Possession **Possession** or use laws prohibit having a controlled drug on one's person or under one's control, as in one's car or house. Most states prohibit possession of a controlled substance in other than expressly permitted circumstances, such as when prescribed by a doctor. Some states also separately prohibit drug use or being under the influence of a controlled substance. Specific provisions and levels of proof to differentiate simple possession from possession with intent to sell vary among the states with such laws (Miller, 2005).

possession A drug offense that consists of having a controlled drug on one's person or under one's control such as in the house or vehicle.

Distribution The charge of **distribution** may be imposed on an individual for any exchange of illegal drugs between two or more parties. Generally, distribution offenses include sale, trade, gifts, and delivery of unlawful drugs, regardless of whether one stands to profit. Typically, the charge of distribution of a drug is considered more serious than mere possession.

distribution Selling, trading, giving, or delivering illicit drugs, regardless of whether one stands to profit from the transaction.

Manufacturing **Manufacturing** offenses include any activity to cultivate, harvest, process, produce, or manufacture illegal drugs. Some drugs, such as LSD 25, PCP, and methamphetamine, can be produced by amateur chemists in illegal labs. Similarly, cocaine is processed from coca paste in illegal laboratories, and crack cocaine is processed in kitchen labs. Marijuana, in contrast, requires no special processing and is used in its natural state as an agricultural crop.

manufacturing Any activity to cultivate, harvest, produce, process, or manufacture illegal drugs.

The Controlled Substance Act

The Controlled Substance Act (CSA), Title II of the federal Comprehensive Drug Abuse Prevention and Control Act of 1970, requires federal law enforcement agencies to control the abuse of narcotics and other dangerous drugs and chemical substances. Since its enactment, many states have used the CSA as a model for their own laws. The CSA is intended to place certain controls on a variety of drugs and chemical substances. Also, the CSA provides criteria for determining whether a substance should be controlled. Finally, the CSA provides procedures for bringing a substance under control.

In its criteria for controlled-substance inclusion, the CSA uses five categories, called schedules (Figure 21.2). A drug's placement on one schedule or another is determined by its medical use, potential for abuse, and likelihood for causing dependence. The Department of Health and Human Services and the DEA may add to, delete from, or change the schedule of controlled substances. The major role played by the DEA is to determine whether a substance has the potential for serious abuse. When the DEA determines that a drug or chemical should be classified as a **controlled substance,** it also determines on which schedule the item should be listed.

controlled substance A drug or substance whose use and possession are regulated under the Controlled Substance Act.

Federal Anti-Drug-Abuse Legislation

Major initiatives against drug abuse were undertaken on the federal level in the 1980s (Figure 21.3). The first half of the decade emphasized legislation to reduce the supply

FIGURE 21.2 Federal Schedules of Controlled Substances

Federal law schedules drugs according to their effects, medical use, and potential for abuse.

DEA Schedule	Abuse Potential	Examples of Drugs Covered	Some of the Effects	Medical Use
I	Highest	Heroin, LSD, hashish, marijuana, methaqualone, designer drugs, barbiturates, hallucinogens	Unpredictable effects, severe psychological or physical dependence, or death	Limited medical use; some legal for limited research use only
II	High	Morphine, PCP, codeine, cocaine, methadone, Demerol, benzedrine, Dexedrine, Methylphenidate, Oxycodone, Amphetamine, Methamphetamines	May lead to severe psychological or physical dependence	Accepted use with restrictions
III	Medium	Codeine with aspirin or Tylenol, some amphetamines, anabolic steroids	May lead to moderate or low physical dependence or high psychological dependence	Accepted use
IV	Low	Darvon, Talwin, phenobarbital, Equanil, Miltown, Librium, diazepam	May lead to limited physical or psychological dependence	Accepted use
V	Lowest	Over-the-counter or prescription compounds with codeine, Lomotil, Robitussin A-C	May lead to limited physical or psychological dependence	Accepted use

Source: Adapted from DEA, *Drugs of Abuse,* 2005.

FIGURE 21.3 Major Federal Anti-Drug-Abuse Legislation

The 1984 Crime Control Act

- Expanded criminal and civil asset forfeiture laws.
- Amended the Bail Reform Act to target pretrial detention of defendants accused of serious drug offenses.
- Established a determinate sentencing system.
- Increased federal criminal penalties for drug offenses.

The 1986 Anti-Drug-Abuse Act

- Budgeted money for prevention and treatment programs, giving the programs a larger share of federal drug control funds than previously.
- Restored mandatory prison sentences for large-scale distribution of marijuana.
- Imposed new sanctions on money laundering.
- Added controlled substances' analogs (designer drugs) to the drug schedule.
- Created a drug law enforcement grant program to assist state and local efforts.
- Contained various provisions designed to strengthen international drug control efforts.

The 1988 Anti-Drug-Abuse Act

- Increased penalties for offenses related to drug trafficking, created new federal offenses and regulatory requirements, and changed criminal procedures.
- Altered the organization and coordination of federal anti-drug efforts.
- Increased treatment and prevention efforts aimed at reduction of drug demand.
- Endorsed the use of sanctions aimed at drug users to reduce the demand for drugs.
- Targeted for reduction drug production abroad and international trafficking in drugs.

The Crime Control Act of 1990

- Doubled the appropriations authorized for drug law enforcement grants to states and localities.
- Expanded drug control and education programs aimed at the nation's schools.
- Expanded specific drug enforcement assistance to rural states.
- Expanded regulation of precursor chemicals used in the manufacture of illegal drugs.
- Provided additional measures aimed at seizure and forfeiture of drug trafficker assets.
- Sanctioned anabolic steroids under the Controlled Substances Act.
- Included provisions on international money laundering, rural drug enforcement, drug-free school zones, drug paraphernalia, and drug enforcement grants.

The Reducing Americans' Vulnerability to Ecstasy Act (RAVE) of 2003

- Amended the crack house statute (Sec. 416 of the Controlled Substance Act) to more directly target the promoters of "raves" where drugs such as MDMA (ecstasy) are widely used.
- Directed the sentencing commission to review and consider stiffening federal sentencing guidelines with respect to offenses involving the club drug gamma hydroxybutyric (GHB), the so-called date rape drug.
- Authorized funding to DEA for drug education efforts directed at youth, their parents, and others about "club drugs."

Source: U.S. Department of Justice, Bureau of Justice Statistics, 1992, *Drugs, Crime, and the Justice System,* Washington, DC: Government Printing Office; Mark Eddy, 2003, "War on Drugs: Legislation in the 108th Congress and Related Developments," *Issue Brief for Congress.* Washington, DC: U.S. Government Printing Office, IB10113.

of illegal drugs. This effort included aggressive internal enforcement of drug laws through drug and asset seizures and cutting off supplies. The second half increased spending for prevention and treatment. The legislation also focused on any use of illegal drugs and on individual users.

INVESTIGATING ILLEGAL DRUG CASES

Illicit drug cases generally involve the same basic investigative practices applied to other criminal violations. However, the nature of this type of case requires some specialized investigative approaches and skills.

Illicit drug cases require special knowledge and familiarity with narcotics and other dangerous drugs and their applicable laws. Because of the increasing menace of drug abuse, and the violence that has become commonly associated with the drug trade, drug suppression has become a primary mission of many law enforcement agencies. As suggested in Chapter 19, organizations specializing in drug importation and distribution have used violence to protect their markets in the United States. The dollar amounts involved in the drug trade are so enormous that human life has been made to seem insignificant by contrast. Therefore, extreme caution must be taken by officers involved in any drug investigation.

Drug investigations may include open investigations, undercover field investigations, and even stings. During an undercover investigation, an officer may assume the role of a drug buyer or dealer to gather evidence against drug distributors. Drug investigations typically involve several stages, which begin when information reaches the police about the possibility of drug activity (Lyman, 2002). During the preliminary stages of the investigation, officers must verify that the information is correct and that illicit drug activity is occurring or has occurred. Considerable care is required during this stage of the investigation because sources of information are not always reliable. Information may be verified through the use of standard surveillance techniques (see Chapter 8). In addition, street test kits that identify certain drugs are available to help an officer determine probable cause for arrests. Once it has been established that unlawful drug activity has occurred, the investigation can proceed along a number of lines, including undercover operations and the use of informants.

> **FYI** Federal, state, and local agencies share responsibility for enforcing drug laws. According to the FBI, state and local authorities made an estimated 1.6 million arrests for drug violations in 2003 (Eddy, 2003).

Undercover Drug Operations

The term *undercover* has been used as a generic label for decoy work, sting operations, and police intelligence-gathering efforts (Marx, 1980, 1989). According to George Miller (1987), there are two types of undercover work: light cover and deep cover. Both types are useful in drug investigations. **Light cover** drug investigations involve donning various costumes and assuming roles during a regular shift of duty. Having donned these disguises, officers spend time on the streets gathering information about drug deals and dealers. They may even attempt to set up narcotics purchases, or *buys*. At the end of that day's shift, they return to the police station, change out of their disguises, and go home.

light cover An undercover police operation that extends only as long as the officer's tour of duty.

Deep cover, on the other hand, involves an officer entirely submerging him- or herself in the role of an underworld figure. To a large measure, the officer becomes the person he or she pretends to be. The duration of a deep cover operation may be several days, weeks, or months. The officer's primary responsibility during a deep cover drug operation is to locate key figures in the drug distribution network and collect incriminating evidence against them.

During light cover operations, officers may operate in teams, with an ample number of backup officers observing the undercover officer's activities, ready to move in to assist. In deep cover operations, however, the greatest protection for the officer is secrecy. Deep cover officers often do not report even to superiors at regular intervals. Instead, they sporadically contact a superior or supervisor to advise them of the progress of their assignment. Undercover drug investigators face many risks, including increased use of automatic weapons by drug dealers, increased violence by foreign nationals involved in drug trafficking, handling informants whose allegiance may be confused, and the lure of big-money deals (Lyman, 1990; Pogrebin & Poole, 2003). In addition, undercover officers may have to feign friendships with criminals or even commit crimes to maintain their cover.

deep cover An undercover operation that may extend for a long period of time, during which the officer totally assumes another identity.

Informants and Other Aids

The use of informants to obtain information, leads, or evidence in police work is common practice. In drug cases, informants may also be useful for arranging introductions to drug dealers or distributors. The use of informants should be undertaken cautiously. Informants may lead investigators to information and arrests. However, especially given the enormous profits being made in the illegal drug trade, an unreliable informant could just as easily lead an investigator into a trap.

When conducting drug buys, whether working with an informant or using other methods, officers should keep the following things in mind:

- Learn to recognize the characteristic behavior of illicit drug users and the physical symptoms resulting from the use of narcotics and dangerous drugs.
- Become familiar with the paraphernalia used in preparation and use of illicit drugs: hypodermic needles, pipes, bongs, beakers, ampules, vials, and so forth.
- Learn street jargon relating to narcotics and other dangerous drugs.
- Learn to recognize the telltale marks and punctures on the arms and bodies of drug users; such conditions or appearance are indicative of illicit drug use.
- Avoid conducting buys inside private residences, garages, or other enclosed structures. Besides reducing the backup and arrest team's ability to get to you quickly, making buys in such places may also cause the loss of evidence.
- Always maintain control over the buy situation. Tell the suspect how the deal will be set up, where it will occur, when parties will meet, and so forth. It may be wiser to lose the arrest than to allow yourself to be compromised by letting the suspect set the rules and a trap.
- Do not flash buy money in crowded areas. While you may be concentrating on a potential drug arrest, other offenders may be seeking mugging victims.
- Be sure to turn off the overhead dome light in your vehicle before going to a buy location. When the light goes on as you open the door, you become an illuminated target.
- Be certain that everyone on the backup team knows the signal to come in.

- Attempt to arrange the arrests after the deal has been completed, rather than during the actual buy. This will allow you to leave the scene and move away from potential danger.

Probable Cause and Searches

Drug investigators must have a clear understanding of the laws regarding illicit drugs, particularly search and seizure laws. In addition, officers must understand the legal elements of probable cause for search and arrest. Specific criteria for establishing probable cause vary slightly from one jurisdiction to the next. There are, however, a number of broad general guidelines to follow. Courts have generally held that **probable cause,** also called *reasonable suspicion,* means that the officer has a reasonable, good faith belief in the legality of the action he or she is about to take (Gaines & Kappeler, 2005). Probable cause can also be understood as occurring when a person of average intelligence and foresight (ordinary prudence) is led to believe that a crime has been committed (Berg, 1992). In other words, probable cause may exist even when there is some doubt. But for the arrest to be lawful, more than a mere suspicion that a crime has been committed is necessary.

Whenever possible, the best way for an officer to search a person, vehicle, or premises is with a search warrant issued by a magistrate. Such a warrant means that a magistrate has received information from a sworn affiant that probable cause exists to believe that the fruits or instrumentation of a crime are possessed by an individual or are present at a particular location.

There is no special trick to effectively searching persons, property, premises, or vehicles. Illicit drugs may be found in a variety of places or containers. The predominant rule in all searches is to be extremely methodical and thorough. In all instances, the officer must be certain that the search has been undertaken lawfully. This means (1) there is valid, willing, voluntary consent, offered either orally or in writing (the courts will review consent searches to make sure the consent was freely and clearly given and without duress or coercion), (2) there is a search warrant (obtained by demonstrating probable cause to a magistrate or judge), or (3) the search is incidental to an arrest and is limited to the area under the offender's *immediate control. Under immediate control* typically means approximately within arm's reach. If the officer desires a more extensive search, a warrant is required.

Searches of Persons Searches of persons can occur for several reasons. First, officers may search for weapons in the interest of self-protection. These *stop-and-frisks,* or *Terry-stops,* derive their name from the case of *Terry v. Ohio* (1968). This case involved a trio of suspects who were stopped and searched while apparently casing a store for robbery. The officer, Detective McFadden, did, in fact, find that two of the three men were carrying pistols. Both Terry and one of his associates were arrested and convicted on concealed weapons charges. Terry appealed on the grounds that the search was illegal and the evidence of the gun should have been suppressed at trial.

The Supreme Court did not agree with Terry. Instead, the high court ruled that police have the authority to detain a person briefly for questioning even without probable cause if they have reason to believe the person may have been involved in a crime. This detention does not constitute an arrest; however, the officer is entitled to frisk or pat down the individual to ensure the officer's personal safety.

A second type of search of a person, usually incidental to an arrest, is made to check for both weapons and other contraband. Officers should be aware that suspects

probable cause
Reasonable grounds to believe that a person should be arrested or searched or that a person's property should be searched or seized.

DEA SPECIAL AGENT

THE DRUG ENFORCEMENT ADMINISTRATION (DEA) is responsible for enforcing laws concerning all narcotic drugs. It controls the registration provisions of federal drug laws, combats illegal drug traffic, and regulates distribution of dangerous drugs. The agency also determines the quantities of narcotics permitted in the United States for medical purposes.

The initial requirements are U.S. citizenship, availability for assignments in the United States and at foreign posts of duty, and being between the ages of 21 and 36. All applicants must also pass vision and hearing tests, be in excellent physical condition, and have a valid driver's license. A DEA special agent candidate must have a four-year college degree, and professional experience in law enforcement or the military is preferred. Like FBI special agent candidates, DEA special agent candidates must complete a polygraph examination, drug abuse screening, psychological suitability assessment, and an exhaustive background investigation. Those successfully completing the requirements go through a training period and pass a physical fitness test to be appointed DEA special agents.

Agents may conduct complex criminal investigations, carry out surveillance of criminals, and infiltrate illegal drug organizations. They may work closely with confidential sources of information to collect evidence leading to the seizure of assets gained from the sale of illegal drugs. Being a DEA special agent is a difficult and dangerous job. At one time or another, agents will work undercover, and their duties will take them throughout the world.

---

have been known to conceal illicit drugs on or in various parts of their bodies and clothing. Searches of the body include hair, ears, mouth (under the tongue), body cavities, groin area, tape on the body, soles of the feet, and between toes. Other areas that should be searched are hats and hatbands, hat linings, coats or jackets, ties, belts, socks, and shoes (soles and heels). In some cases, a drug smuggler may ingest balloons or condoms filled with narcotics. The acid in the suspect's stomach will eventually cause the balloon to deteriorate, releasing the drug and likely killing the smuggler. When this is suspected, it is important that the smuggler be convinced to regurgitate the balloons as quickly as possible. Although most balloons may be successfully passed, drug couriers frequently die when drugs in balloons rush into their system after stomach acids have dissolved the containers.

Searches of Vehicles   The question of the scope of a lawful search that follows an arrest is of particular concern with respect to automobiles. Discussion of vehicle searches frequently begins with consideration of *Carrol v. United States* (1925). In this case, the Supreme Court established clear distinctions among searches of people, vehicles, and premises. Basically, the Court held that a warrantless search of a vehicle was legitimate, provided the officer had probable cause to believe the vehicle contained evidence or contraband.

The scope of a vehicular search can be better understood by following the rationale set forth in *Chimel v. California* (1969). In the *Chimel* case, officers arrested a man without a warrant. While holding the man in one room of his home, the police proceeded to search the entire three-bedroom house, including, the garage, attic, and workshop. The Supreme Court held that searches incidental to arrest are limited to the area within the arrestee's immediate control, or that area within which he or she might reach a weapon.

As applied to the search of a car, courts have repeatedly held that if probable cause has been established, vehicles can be searched without warrants because vehicles can be quickly moved out of the jurisdiction where the warrant would be sought and applicable. However, the scope of these searches was originally limited to the cabin and immediate reach of the occupants (*South Dakota v. Opperman, 1976*).

In 1991 the Supreme Court further extended the scope of searches with respect to automobiles. A general rule for determining the scope of a motorist's consent to a search of his or her car was established. Also, the Court simplified the rules concerning warrantless searches of vehicles and of containers found inside a car. The Court declared that a person's general consent to a search of the interior of an automobile justifies a search of any closed container found inside that vehicle that might reasonably hold objects of the search. Therefore, an officer, once he or she receives general consent to search a car, does not need to ask permission to look inside each closed container (*Florida v. Jimeno, 1991*).

The Court's decisions do not alter the rule that a search of a vehicle incident to an arrest must bear a reasonable relation to the particular arrest. For example, in arresting for a traffic violation, the officer cannot conduct an incidental search because no fruits, instrumentalities, or contraband are usually connected with traffic violations. If, however, during the course of a lawful traffic stop, the officer observes contraband, weapons, burglary tools, or other illegal items in plain sight, the situation changes. Once observed, the items may be seized, and probable cause may be established for a more extensive search of the vehicle, including its trunk or other areas of concealment.

Officers of the U.S. and Haitian coast guards stand watch over drugs seized from a Colombian sailboat near Port-au-Prince in March of 1997.

There are three main areas related to searching a vehicle without benefit of a warrant. These include a stop, question, and frisk of an operator; a search of a motor vehicle incident to a lawful arrest; and under certain exigent circumstances (Stering, 2005).

Stop, Question, and Frisk   A motor vehicle can be stopped, and its operator and occupants frisked as a type of protective search (effectively like a *Terry-stop*). Such frisks are intended to determine whether a subject is armed for the safety of the officer. The search is confined to the areas of the automobile from which a suspect might gain access to a weapon; the search is typically limited to the passenger compartment, within approximately an arm's length from where the occupant or driver had been seated. However, under certain circumstances, such as when an operator or occupant is outside of the vehicle, or standing at an open truck, the trunk falls under the *immediate area* rule, and it too can be searched.

Search of a Vehicle Incident to an Arrest   If an operator or a subject riding in the vehicle is arrested, a search incident to this lawful arrest may be undertaken. Searches incident to an arrest are generally limited to the area where the operator or passenger could have conceivably reached for a weapon while in the car, or reached for and destroyed possible evidence. When an arrest has been made, it is sometimes prudent to impound the vehicle and have it towed into police custody, where it can safely wait for a warrant to be obtained.

Exigent Circumstances   Exigent circumstances are emergency situations in which a reasonable person is led to believe that entry (or other relevant prompt action) is necessary to prevent physical harm to an officer or other person(s), the destruction of relevant evidence, the escape of a suspect, or some other consequence that will impede lawful police actions. When exigent circumstances arise in a vehicle stop, such as concern that moving the vehicle will result in the loss or destruction of evidence, an immediate search of the vehicle is permissible.

Vehicles are often used to transport and conceal narcotics and dangerous drugs. A variety of places within, outside, under, and as part of the vehicle have been used to conceal contraband. Illicit drugs have been found in the ashtrays, in the glove compartment, in the steering column, in compartments concealed in or under the dashboard, beneath the seats, in the car's upholstery, in door panels, in the engine compartment, in the hollows of tires, in a specially constructed gas tank with a false bottom or compartment, on the undercarriage (welded, taped, or tied), in bumpers, under fenders, and in other places limited only by the imagination and patience of the officer.

Searches of Premises   When conducting a lawful search of a premises, search sections or rooms in a systematic, thorough manner. Tools and equipment that may be useful in searching include a camera, a measuring tape, screwdrivers, wrenches (for plumbing traps), a light (flashlight or portable floodlight), an extension cord, a shovel, and a metal rod for probing flower beds or places indicating soil disturbances. The searchers should look into, around, under, and through all objects, containers, materials, and places of possible concealment. A recorder should be appointed to take notes of any evidence found during a search. If drugs are found, ask the suspect (if present) what they are, get an admission of ownership, and keep notes of exact conversations. Both the searcher and the recorder should mark any found evidence. The officer finding the evidence should keep it until turning it over to the crime laboratory for technical examination and identification. The name of the manager or landlord of the residence should be obtained for report purposes.

FOCUS ON TECHNOLOGY

LASER RANGEFINDER

INVESTIGATORS USE A HIGH-ACCURACY LASER UNIT to measure the inside of trailers and containers without unloading them. It is then easy to compare the inside and outside dimensions of suspect containers to locate hidden compartments that might contain illegal drugs. By not having to unload cargo to take measurements, more inspections can be conducted.

Drugs have been secreted in a number of places. Suggested places to search for illicit drugs include the following:

- Bathroom medicine cabinets (pill bottles labeled *aspirin* may not actually contain aspirin)
- Hampers of dirty clothes (check individual articles of clothing)
- The undersides of washbowls
- Under the toilet lid
- Inside the toilet tank and in the float ball
- The cardboard tube of the toilet paper roll
- Lipstick tubes and other cosmetic containers
- Baby powder containers, toothpaste tubes, shaving cream cans, and so on
- Tissue boxes
- Face cream (object may be submerged) or hollowed-out bars of soap
- Behind wall and light fixtures, in air ducts, in doorjambs, and in the hollow of doors
- Areas behind blinds and under floor coverings

Other places include the kitchen and food storage areas. Illicit drugs may be concealed in various foods: tea, coffee, flour, sugar, chips, beans, grains, and others. Drugs may be concealed in kitchen appliances or taped to their backs or bottoms. Cabinets, sinks, and even garbage disposals should all be examined as possible places of concealment. Searches of bedrooms, the living room, and other parts of the house should include closets, clothing, furniture, wall hangings, televisions and radios, and areas beneath rugs and carpeting and behind loose moldings, as well as in bedposts, mattresses, pillows. Stuffed toys and in and under playpens, baby cribs, dressers, changing tables, and in containers hung from windows should also be searched. Any object may be a potential place of concealment of drugs, and none should be overlooked. Basements, areas beneath houses, porches, stairs, attics, and garages are also used to conceal contraband. When searching the grounds around premises, it is important to look for indications of recently disturbed shrubs or earth. It may also be helpful to locate well-traveled paths or areas leading to air vents or other hiding places evidenced by obvious foot traffic impressions.

Investigators should also be mindful of booby traps (see Chapter 18). Particularly where drugs are concerned, it is not uncommon for criminals to place explosive charges in unexpected places. When an unsuspecting officer moves an object, turns a switch, or even walks in the wrong place, the explosive may be detonated. For example, it is not difficult to remove the glass bulb from a light bulb and fill it with a small quantity of gasoline. If the base is replaced on the bulb and carefully sealed with silicon (to prevent the gasoline from seeping), a simple explosive has been made. When the bulb is placed in a socket and switched on, the gasoline will ignite and explode.

Arrest Situations

When patrol officers witness what they believe may be a drug buy, they may not want to immediately make an arrest. Instead, it may be more fruitful to obtain as complete a description as possible of both parties and any vehicles involved. There is no urgency in making the arrest because it is very likely that the drug buyer and seller will continue to meet and conduct business over time. If the buy is observed and the officer has probable cause, he or she does have the legal authority to make a drug arrest. In many cases, however, it is more prudent to simply observe and gather information. Whenever drug arrests are planned or made, certain procedures should be followed:

- Use sufficient personnel to handle the arrest safely.
- In addition to arrest warrants, have a search warrant if possible; be mindful of the legal limits of the search.
- Brief all participating officers on the part each is to play during the arrest and the search.
- Move quickly and simultaneously on all locations.
- If circumstances justify it, use force to enter a premises and locate the suspects quickly. It takes only seconds to flush evidence down the toilet or otherwise destroy evidence.
- As soon as a suspect is in custody, handcuff his or her hands behind the back; advise the suspect of legal rights; conduct the search; if necessary, call in a doctor for an internal body search.
- If available, use drug-sniffing dogs to search the premises.
- If a suspect has needle marks, photograph them.
- Check names, addresses, and telephone numbers found in a suspect's effects for investigative leads about associates and possible meeting places.
- Request crime laboratory analysis of all materials and substances believed to be or contain drugs.
- Consider blood and urine tests of suspects where advisable.

SUMMARY

Learning Objective 1

The term *narcotic* is used to describe any drug that produces a stupor, insensibility, or sleep. It includes in its meaning substances ranging from alcohol to heroin or crack cocaine. In the legal sense, a narcotic is any drug that is allegedly dangerous, is heavily abused, or has a high potential for abuse.

Learning Objective 2

Most people take drugs for the effects they produce. Most illegal drugs are consumed for their mind-altering effects. Among these drugs are heroin, cocaine, morphine, codeine, Percodan, and methadone.

Learning Objective 3

In addition to narcotics, other dangerous drugs that are among the most commonly abused drugs in the United States include stimulants, depressants, hallucinogens, marijuana, designer drugs, and inhalants.

Learning Objective 4

Federal, state, and local laws define drug offenses. Specific drug laws and penalties vary, but offenses generally fall into these three categories: possession, distribution, and manufacturing of dangerous or illicit drugs.

Learning Objective 5

Investigating illicit drug cases generally involves the same basic practices as investigating other crimes. However, the nature of drug cases requires special approaches and skills. These specialties include knowledge of drugs, their effects, and applicable laws; undercover drug operations; use of informants; and understanding of search and seizure laws.

KEY TERMS

narcotic **435**	hallucinogen **438**	manufacturing **453**
opiate **435**	inhalants **439**	controlled substance **454**
withdrawal symptoms **436**	designer drug **451**	light cover **456**
depressant or sedative **436**	possession **453**	deep cover **457**
stimulant **438**	distribution **453**	probable cause **458**

QUESTIONS FOR REVIEW

Learning Objective 1

1. Define *narcotic.*
2. What are the four major categories of drugs?
3. From what plant do *opiates* derive?

Learning Objective 2

4. How do heroin addicts obtain their drugs?

5. Which is considered stronger, morphine or heroin?

6. What category of drug is cocaine?

7. What is freebasing?

8. How is crack cocaine different from run-of-the-mill powder cocaine?

9. What are the contents of a speedball?

10. From what is codeine derived?

11. How do addicts administer Percodan?

12. How is methadone used to treat heroin addicts?

Learning Objective 3

13. What are the physical effects of the use of stimulants?

14. What kind of drug are sleeping pills?

15. How are different types of barbiturates distinguished?

16. Which hallucinogens are most frequently abused?

17. Describe the effects of drugs from the category *hallucinogens*.

18. How might cannabis be useful to medical science?

19. What does hash oil look like?

20. What is a designer drug?

21. What are some of the dangers of the drug called ice?

Learning Objective 4

22. What are the three primary parts of the Controlled Substance Act?

23. What is meant by the crime of *manufacturing* drugs?

Learning Objective 5

24. What are the main differences between *light cover* and *deep cover* drug investigations?

. . . .

CRITICAL THINKING EXERCISE

Divide into two groups to present a debate on the question, "Should drugs be legalized?" One group should gather data and prepare arguments to give this answer: "Yes, legalizing drugs would solve the drug problem." The other group should prepare to give this answer: "No, legalizing drugs would be dangerous."

. . . .

INVESTIGATIVE SKILL BUILDERS

Participating as a Member of a Team

Divide into three or four teams of about seven or eight members. Identify a team leader in each group. Next, assign one or two members of each team to contact the local police chief, state's attorney, and mayor. The team members should ask each official how he or she would stand on a bill in the state legislature that would make growing marijuana for personal use legal. Have the team representatives learn as much of each figure's viewpoint as possible. Finally, each group should produce a report that includes team members' views about the legalization of marijuana in light of the viewpoints offered by the chief, the state's attorney, and the mayor.

Integrity/Honesty

You are an off-duty police officer attending a college football game. In front of you are four reasonably well-dressed college-age men. Their behavior is fairly appropriate for the setting of a football game. However, at halftime you notice that one of the men has taken a reasonably large *joint* (marijuana cigarette) out of his pocket and is lighting it. The men pass the joint to one another. At one point, one of the men notices that you are watching. He smiles as he turns to you and asks, "Would you like a toke?"

1. How do you respond to the offer?
2. Do you identify yourself as a police officer?
3. Do you make any arrests? Explain.

Terrorism and Cyber Predators

CHAPTER OBJECTIVES

After completing this chapter, you will be able to:

1. Describe the nature of terrorism.
2. Provide an overview of terrorism in the United States.
3. Discuss some of the major domestic terrorist groups in the United States.
4. Identify some of the major international terrorist groups.
5. Describe some antiterrorist activities.
6. Discuss the role of local law enforcement with regard to terrorism.
7. Explain what is meant by *cyber predators*.
8. Discuss the nature of those who use child pornography.
9. Detail the implications of cyber predators for local law enforcement.

TERRORISM IN PERSPECTIVE

Law enforcement investigators deal with a wide assortment of crimes, criminal types, and violent interpersonal behaviors. Some crimes have a political motivation, including those categorized as *terrorism.*

From a law enforcement perspective, *terrorism* is a rather elusive term. It is laden with emotions and in most law enforcement communities conjures images of bombs and threats of violence, kidnapping, and murder. The public reaction is similarly negative, involving an uneasiness about personal safety. When terrorist acts fall within certain guidelines, the FBI may act in concert with local agencies. This chapter considers some of the key points concerning investigations of terrorist acts, but many facets of terrorist behavior are beyond the scope of a single chapter.

The word *terrorism* was first popularized during the French Revolution, and it is indeed ironic that it had a decidedly positive connotation then. The *regime de la terreur,* from which the English word derives, was intended as a system for establishing order during a period of turmoil and upheaval following the revolutionary actions of 1789 (Hoffman, 2006). In modern times, however, terrorism has come to be understood somewhat differently.

terrorism The unlawful use or threat of violence against persons and property to further political, social, or religious objectives. It is generally intended to intimidate or coerce a government, individuals, or groups to modify their behavior.

The U.S. Department of Defense (2007) defines **terrorism** as "the calculated use of unlawful violence or threat of unlawful violence to inculcate fear; intended to coerce or to intimidate governments or societies in the pursuit of goals that are generally political, religious, or ideological." Within this definition are three key elements: violence, fear, and intimidation.

The Terrorism Research Center (www.terrorism.com) cautions that "One man's terrorist is another man's freedom fighter," but it offers this definition for terrorism: "The use of force or violence against persons or property in violation of the criminal laws of the United States for purposes of intimidation, coercion, or ransom." Similarly, the FBI defines terrorism as follows:

"Terrorism is the unlawful use of force or violence against persons or property to intimidate or coerce a government, the civilian population, or any segment thereof, in furtherance of political or social objectives" (28 Code of *Federal Regulations,* Section 0.85).

Terrorism is defined in U.S. Code, Title 18, ¶ 2331 as:

(A) Violent acts or acts dangerous to human life that are a violation of the criminal laws of the United States or of any State, or that would be a criminal violation if committed within the jurisdiction of the United States or any other State;
(B) [that] appear to be intended
  (i) to intimidate or coerce a civilian population
  (ii) to influence the policy of a government by intimidation or coercion; or
  (iii) to affect the conduct of a government by mass destruction, assassination, or kidnapping.

Motives for Terrorism

Terrorism is often described in terms of pure emotionalism or *fanaticism,* but its instrumental or strategic dimensions should not be overlooked. Terrorists have many different reasons or motives for their acts. Many politically motivated terrorists, whether they are of the left or the right, want to bring down an existing government or regime. Many religious terrorists want to attack those who they see as attacking, challenging, or in some manner interfering with their religion. Others want publicity for their cause. Prior to 2001, it was generally believed that almost all suicide terrorists had had at least one relative or close friend killed, maimed, or abused by an enemy (Anti-Defamation League,

2002; Kushner, 1996). Today, many suicide bombers are recruited for other reasons, including promises of martyrdom and rewards after death.

There are also fairly pragmatic, or strategic, reasons terrorists use extreme violence to further their cause. Frequently, terrorists groups are fairly small and could never defeat a professional army or strong government in a head-on battle or war. Instead, these bands of individuals resort to high-profile acts of violence to influence some specific large audience that otherwise might not be motivated to respond to their cause (Martin, 2003). Terrorists often act based on one or more of these basic motives:

1. Strong moral convictions
2. Simplified definitions for good and evil
3. A desire to find a utopia
4. Code of self-sacrifice

Moral convictions are a powerful motivating element for terrorists. Terrorists hold an unambiguous certainty about the righteousness of their cause or movement; to them there are no areas of gray. They consider their goals and objectives to be principled and beyond reproach; consequently, any methods employed are absolutely justified. Along with this sense of moral conviction, terrorists hold a clear and unequivocal belief that they have been morally wronged by some group or government. This powerful evil stands against them, their beliefs, their families' welfare, the religious tenets they adhere to, and the government they support. Regardless of how noble they believe their cause is, the actions of terrorists constitute a variety of serious crimes.

Some efforts have been made to equate terrorists with other types of traditional violent criminals (see, for example, LaFree, 2005). In some situations, a terrorist's action may not be a political instrument but an end in itself, the result of an uncontrollable compulsion or psychopathology. From this perspective, terrorists do what they do because of their emotional problems. Their self-destructive behaviors combined with difficulties they have with authorities and perhaps even dysfunctional or improper parenting are at the root of their actions (Jurgensmeyer, 2000).

Today few law enforcement agencies find any similarity between run-of the-mill violent criminals and political terrorists. Many people who commit violent crimes are compelled to do so because of some emotional disturbance or mental deficiency. Others may be motivated by revenge, profit, hatred, or the need to silence witnesses or associates. Political terrorists, however, cannot be neatly placed in one of these categories. Political terrorists are motivated by their philosophical (sometimes religious) and ideological beliefs. They are zealots willing to sacrifice their own lives or the lives of others for the cause they believe in.

Terrorism and Criminal Charges

Criminal charges that can be levied with regard to acts of terrorism include treason, sedition, sabotage, and espionage. More traditional categories of crime such as kidnapping, murder, attempted murder, conspiracy, or making terroristic threats may also be involved. In addition, a series of crimes related to terrorism can be found in the U.S. Criminal Code (2003), Title 18, Chapter 113:

1. Use of certain weapons of mass destruction (¶ 2332a)
2. Acts of terrorism transcending national boundaries (¶ 2332b)
3. Harboring or concealing terrorists (¶ 2339a)
4. Providing material support to terrorists (¶ 2339b)

5. Providing material support or resources to designated foreign terrorist organizations (¶ 2339b)

Although alleged terrorists can be charged with a variety of crimes, the majority of cases brought by the U.S. government against suspected terrorists since September 11, 2001, have been for "providing material support to terrorists and/or terrorist organizations" (Roth, 2003). Interestingly, these laws were originally established in 1996, shortly after the bombing in Oklahoma City, in the Antiterrorism and Effective Death Penalty Act (AEDPA) but were slightly amended to increase the penalties after September 11, 2001, in the USA Patriot Act (**U**niting and **S**trengthening **A**merica by **P**roviding **A**ppropriate **T**ools **R**equired to **I**ntercept and **O**bstruct **T**errorism). The original act, which has been revised twice, ran over 300 pages in length and was passed only six weeks after the attack occurring on September 11. Much of the act deals with criminal procedures (surveillance, wiretapping, and intelligence gathering by law enforcement), information sharing, search and seizure, interrogation, and detention of suspects. A more detailed discussion of the Patriot Act, and its implications for law enforcement, is offered later in this chapter.

Categories of Terrorism

In general, terrorism falls into one of two categories: domestic terrorism or international terrorism. Typically, **domestic terrorism** involves any threat or use of violence by an individual or group of individuals operating entirely within the borders of the United States or its territories without involvement of foreign direction.

International terrorism involve violent acts or dangers brought against people or property that are criminal in nature and are intended to intimidate or coerce a civilian population or otherwise affect the conduct of a government by intimidation, assassination, or kidnapping. To qualify as an international terrorist act, it must occur outside

domestic terrorism An unlawful violent act directed at elements of the U.S. government or population by groups or individuals who are based and operate entirely within the United States and Puerto Rico without foreign direction.

international terrorism Violent acts or dangers brought against people or property; intended to intimidate or coerce a civilian population or otherwise affect the conduct of a government by intimidation, assassination, or kidnapping. It must occur outside the borders of the United States or otherwise transcend national boundaries.

Eight people died and 4,700 were injured in the March 1995 nerve gas attack by terrorists in a Tokyo subway.

the borders of the United States, or otherwise transcend national boundaries in terms of the means by which the act occurs, the persons they intend to coerce or intimidate, or the location from which the perpetrator operates or seeks asylum (Murphy & Plotkin, 2003).

International terrorism, then, is any terrorist act against the United States or U.S. concerns that is foreign based or is directed by countries or groups sponsored by countries outside of the United States. The FBI divides international terrorism into three subcategories: (1) foreign state sponsors using terrorism as a tool of foreign policy, such as Iraq, Libya, and Afghanistan; (2) formalized terrorist groups such as the Lebanese Hezbollah, the Egyptian al-Gamm'a al-Islamiyya, the Palestinian Hamas, and bin Laden's Al Qaeda; and (3) loosely affiliated international radical extremists who have a variety of identities and travel freely in the United States unknown to law enforcement or the government.

TERRORISM IN THE UNITED STATES

Until recently, many Americans did not view political terrorism as a serious threat to safety in the United States. Naturally, they were aware of such political acts of terrorism as the 1972 murders of Israeli athletes during the Olympic games in Munich; the Americans seized in 1979 in the U.S. embassy in Iran and held for more than a year; the 1981 assassination of Egyptian President Anwar Sadat; the 1983 terrorist attacks on U.S. Marines in Beirut, Lebanon, which left 241 military personnel dead; the terrorist-caused crash of Korea Air Lines Flight 858 in 1987, which left 115 passengers and crew members dead; and the terrorist bombing attack on Christmas 1988 that caused Pan American Flight 103 to crash in Lockerbie, Scotland, killing 270 people. In many of these and other terrorist assaults, American lives were lost, yet Americans felt safe sleeping in their homes at night and walking through their shopping malls during the day.

In 1993 Americans were shaken awake to the perils of political terrorism with the bombing of the World Trade Center in New York City (Painton, 1993). But even this wake-up call soon fit neatly into the comfortable contours of foreign political terrorism—after all, the suspects in the case were all from the Middle East. Furthermore, anti-American terrorism had persistently occurred in other nations, and an attack on American soil was viewed by many as inevitable. For many Americans, the realization that they, too, were vulnerable to such violence came in April of 1995 with the bombing of the Alfred P. Murrah Federal Building in Oklahoma City. In that blast 168 men, women, and children perished, but Americans soon became complacent, believing that "terrorism is someone else's problem—not America's." On September 11, 2001, every American became aware of exactly how vulnerable U.S. citizens are. Two airplanes crashed into the World Trade Center buildings in New York City, causing a catastrophic fire and the ultimate collapse of both buildings into huge piles of rubble,

On Sept 11, 2001 two planes crashed into the Twin Towers of the World Trade Center New York City. 2,595 people in these buildings were killed along with the 157 people who were in the aircraft were also killed.

killing 2,595 people as they burned and collapsed as well as 157 people who had been aboard the airplanes. Elsewhere on that fateful day another airplane crashed into the side of the Pentagon in Washington, D.C., and a fourth plane—alleged to be heading toward the White House—crashed in a field in Pennsylvania, brought down by passengers trying to abort the hijackers' plans. This incident received enormous media coverage—it was the most devastating incident of terrorism in history. It changed the way the United States viewed terrorism and terrorists; had a domino effect on legislation having to do with privacy, interrogation, search and seizure, and immigration; caused a major alteration in the structure of federal law enforcement agencies; and led to creation of a new overarching federal agency named Homeland Security.

Legal Expansions Created by the Patriot Act

The Patriot Act (USAPA) created a series of new laws and made changes in more than fifteen existing statutes. The purpose of the first Patriot Act was to quickly provide broad new powers to domestic law enforcement agencies and international intelligence agencies in an effort to provide the tools necessary to fight terrorism, to expand the definition of terrorist activities, and to change sanctions for violent terrorism, which had taken on a new sense of violence and danger following the September 11 incident.

It is impossible to discuss all of the provisions of the Patriot Act in the confines of this chapter, but a few of the more important elements with regard to law enforcement and investigation are highlighted. Among its provisions, USAPA expanded four important instruments of surveillance: namely, wiretapping, search warrants, pen/trap orders (installing devices that record telephone calls), and subpoenas. Congress had previously passed the Foreign Intelligence Surveillance Act (FISA), which allowed the government to expand its domestic intelligence operations. The USAPA provided greater authority to the FBI to more effectively monitor telephone, Internet, and computer records without first demonstrating to the courts that these instruments were being used by a suspect to advance terrorist criminal activities.

Under current legislation, law enforcement agencies can serve a single wiretap or pen/trap order on any person regardless of whether this individual or entity is named in a court order. Prior to enactment of Patriot Act I, telephone companies could be ordered to install pen/trap devices on their networks that would monitor calls coming in to and out from a subject under surveillance. The USAPA extended this monitoring activity to include the Internet. As a result, law enforcement agencies can now obtain e-mail addresses of individuals with whom a subject under surveillance communicates, as well as track websites visited by this subject. It is now possible to require an Internet service provider (ISP) to install a device that records e-mail and other electronic communications so investigators can look for communications initiated or received by a subject under surveillance. As a consequence of the USAPA, law enforcement agencies no longer need to show a court that the information or communications are relevant to a specific criminal investigation, nor do they have to report where the order was served or what information was obtained as a result of the tracking.

Patriot Act I also permitted law enforcement agencies to monitor cable operations and to obtain access to cable operators' records and systems. This opened the door for law enforcement to obtain information on telephone and Internet actions transmitted through cable systems. Prior to the of USAPA, cable companies were required to notify cable customers in advance that records were being requested, even when the cable customer was the subject of a criminal investigation. Information can now be secured about people with whom the cable customer communicates, the content of these communications, and their cable subscription records.

Furthermore, Patriot Act I expanded the general definition of terrorism, as understood by law enforcement agencies, to enable the government to more closely monitor those individuals suspected of *harboring* and giving *material support* to terrorists. It further increased the authority of the attorney general to detain and deport noncitizens with little or no judicial review. The attorney general was empowered to certify that he or she has *reasonable grounds to believe* that a given noncitizen is a danger to national security and therefore is eligible for deportation.

These new statutes and the elasticity added to a number of existing statutes are seen in many law enforcement circles as a boon granted to them and an aid in their efforts to curb violent criminal acts such as terrorism. However, these same changes have been viewed through troubled eyes by civil libertarians, who believe that the Patriot Act has eroded—and in some cases eliminated—civil rights. They are particularly troubled by elements of the act that permit the government (or agents of the government such as police) to share information from grand jury proceedings and from criminal wiretaps with intelligence agencies. The First Amendment protections of American citizens—such as what they watch on television in the privacy of their own homes—may be violated by provisions in the USAPA. Effectively, the concerns center on the possibility that law enforcement investigations may not be limited to actual terrorist threats but may encompass a much wider range of activities and investigative interests of the police (Halperin, 2001).

Further controversy arose in 2003 when it was revealed that Patriot Act II included all of the previous enactments along with a few new wrinkles such as the US-VISIT program, in which foreign visitors and immigrants are fingerprinted and photographed upon entry to the United States. Citizens of twenty-seven European and other U.S.-allied countries are exempt from this provision. Currently, the Patriot Act provisions remain in force, and the fervor of concern over the provisions empowering police agencies with increased abilities both to spy on American citizens and to take away their civil rights seems to have quieted down quite a bit.

The ACLU is among those concerned about the potential of the Patriot Acts to erode civil liberties. In 2003 the ACLU drafted a memo detailing their concerns that the acts diminish personal privacy by removing checks on government power, Figure 22.1 lists these concerns.

Section 1001 of the USA Patriot Act, Public Law 107-56, directs the Office of the Inspector General (OIG) of the U.S. Department of Justice (DOJ) to undertake a series of actions related to claims of civil rights or civil liberties violations that may be alleged to have been committed by employees of various agencies that make up the DOJ—including various agencies under the auspice of the Office of Homeland Security. In 2006 the OIG reported that during the period between July 1, 2005, and December 31, 2005, the Office of the Inspector General processed 701 complaints, which had been received chiefly through e-mails or the U.S. Postal Service. Of these complaints, 570 did not fall under the jurisdiction of the OIG, or they simply did not warrant any further investigation. Slightly over half of these complaints (315) involved allegations against agencies and entities outside of the Department of Justice, including other federal agencies, local governments, or private businesses. The remaining 255 complaints raised allegations that on their face did not warrant any

FIGURE 22.1   Erosion of Civil Liberties Due to Provisions of the Patriot Acts

- Making it easier for the government to initiate surveillance and wiretapping of U.S. citizens under the authority of the shadowy, top-secret Foreign Intelligence Surveillance Court. (Sections 101, 102, and 107)
- Permitting the government, under certain circumstances, to bypass the Foreign Intelligence Surveillance Court altogether and conduct warrantless wiretaps and searches. (Sections 103 and 104)
- Sheltering federal agents engaged in illegal surveillance without a court order from criminal prosecution if they are following orders of high Executive Branch officials. (Section 106)
- Creating a new category of "domestic security surveillance" that permits electronic eavesdropping of entirely domestic activity under looser standards than are provided for ordinary criminal surveillance under Title III. (Section 122)
- Using an overbroad definition of terrorism that could cover some protest tactics such as those used by Operation Rescue or protesters at Vieques Island, Puerto Rico, as a new predicate for criminal wiretapping and other electronic surveillance. (Sections 120 and 121)
- Providing for general surveillance orders covering multiple functions of high-tech devices, and by further expanding pen register and trap and trace authority for intelligence surveillance of United States citizens and lawful permanent residents. (Sections 107 and 124)
- Creating a new, separate crime of using encryption technology that could add five years to any sentence for crimes committed with a computer. (Section 404)
- Expanding nationwide search warrants so they do not have to meet even the broad definition of terrorism in the USA PATRIOT Act. (Section 125)
- Giving the government secret access to credit reports without consent and without judicial process. (Section 126)
- Enhancing the government's ability to obtain sensitive information without prior judicial approval by creating administrative subpoenas and providing new penalties for failure to comply with written demands for records. (Sections 128 and 129)
- Allowing sampling and cataloging of innocent Americans' genetic information without court order and without consent. (Sections 301–306)
- Permitting, without any connection to antiterrorism efforts, sensitive personal information about U.S. citizens to be shared with local and state law enforcement. (Section 311)
- Terminating court-approved limits on police spying, which were initially put in place to prevent McCarthy-style law enforcement persecution based on political or religious affiliation. (Section 312)
- Permitting searches, wiretaps, and surveillance of United States citizens on behalf of foreign governments—including dictatorships and human rights abusers—in the absence of Senate-approved treaties. (Sections 321 and 322)

Source: American Civil Liberties Union. 2003. Interested Persons Memo: Section-by-Section Analysis of Justice Department draft "Domestic Security Enhancement Act of 2003," also known as "PATRIOT Act II." Retrieved from www.aclu.org/safefree/general/17203leg20030214.html

investigation. For example, in one complaint an FBI agent was alleged to have pumped chemical substances into the complainant's home; another allegation was that the complainant had been given some sort of memory loss substance; and a third example is the allegation that the complainant's face had somehow been physically altered to change his appearance.

Of the 131 remaining complaints that did have to do with DOJ employees or components, 123 raised management issues and were referred to the appropriate DOJ component for handling. Examples of these included inmates' allegations about the general conditions of the federal prisons, and complaints that the FBI had not initiated an investigation into a particular complainant's allegations. None of the 701 complaints processed during the report's time period specifically alleged any misconduct by DOJ employees relating to the use of a provision in the Patriot Act. Thus, despite the concern that there would be abuses, to date law enforcement agencies seemingly have used the provisions of the Patriot Act largely as they were intended.

HISTORY

THROUGHOUT THE 1970s, police confronted such terroristic acts as the bombing of the Army recruitment office on White Hall Street in New York City, for which the then-notorious student activist group the Weathermen claimed responsibility; the bombing of Hearst's Castle in southern California, believed to be the work of the Symbionese Liberation Army; and assorted robberies, bombings, and other crimes alleged to have been committed by the Black Panthers. During the 1980s, the United Freedom Front claimed responsibility for ten bombings of corporate and military targets in the New York City area, and police dealt with various domestic right-wing groups, such as the white supremacist group the Covenant, the Sword, and the Arm of the Lord (Ross & Gurr, 1989). The truth is, the history of America is checkered with accounts of terrorist tactics used by assorted hate groups such as the Ku Klux Klan and various neo-Nazi and white supremacists.

DOMESTIC TERRORIST GROUPS

The face of domestic terrorism began to change in the mid-1990s. There was a decline in traditional left-wing extremism and an increase in activities among extremists associated with right-wing groups and special-interest organizations. Figure 22.2 provides a twenty-one year tally of terrorist-related incidents in the United States. The full list of groups involved in domestic terrorism is beyond the scope of this textbook, so this discussion is limited to some of the major categories of current terrorist groups and their basic characteristics.

Left-Wing Groups

These groups advocate liberal, often radical, measures to effect change in the established political order. During the 1960s and 1970s, left-wing groups formed to protest the war in Vietnam or as centers of action in the Black Power movement. Groups disillusioned with the federal government's involvement in the war in Vietnam and civil rights policies at home wreaked havoc. Arson, bombings, demonstrations, and violence of all types became commonplace. Student-based groups such as Students for a Democratic Society (SDS) and more militant splinter organizations like the Weather Underground Organization (WUO) used terrorist acts to make their voices heard.

This same era also witnessed the growth of the militant, anti-white Black Panther movement and groups such as the Black Liberation Army (BLA). As the United States wound down its involvement in Vietnam in the early 1970s, terrorist attacks from residual groups focused on symbols of American imperialism and what many of these groups saw as the capitalist exploitation of Third World nations. The new targets became financial institutions, banks, corporate offices, and military facilities.

Left-wing terrorism has declined in recent years. This decline may be due to the arrest of many leftist group leaders during the 1980s and the rejection of communism as a viable economic and political system by many national governments in the 1990s. Among current groups with a left-wing orientation are the African

FIGURE 22.2   Terrorism in the United States by Group, 1980–2001

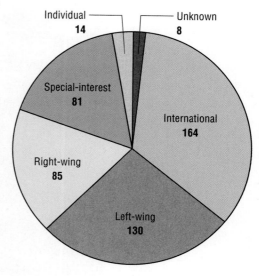

FBI, 2004. *Terrorism 2000/2001*. Oklahoma City, Oklahoma: National Memorial Institute for the Prevention of Terrorism.

National Ujammu, Ansaru Allah Community, United Freedom Front, and Dar-U1 Movement. Although Puerto Rico voted to remain a U.S. commonwealth in 1993, extremist groups such as the Armed Forces of National Liberation (FALN) and the Macheteros are still willing to plan and conduct terrorist acts to draw attention to their desire for independence.

Right-Wing Groups

Of recent concern to law enforcement officials are the activities of right-wing terrorist groups. Right-wing groups are conservative, favoring traditional views and values. They distrust government activism and oppose sudden changes in the established order. Terrorist groups characterized as right-wing are generally conservative, racist, antigovernment, survivalist, and promote advancement of the white race. Some espouse fundamentalist Christian beliefs. Among these are the Ku Klux Klan, Posse Comitatus, the Aryan Nation, neo-Nazis and skinheads, and citizen militias and patriot groups.

During the 1970s and 1980s, law enforcement agencies became aware of a network of right-wing groups operating in the United States. These groups maintained a steady stream of racist, antifederalist, and conservative religious beliefs and rhetoric. Law enforcement officials were already familiar with the right-wing activities of the Ku Klux Klan and the American Nazi Party, but the new groups were far more radical. Many of them maintained paramilitary **survivalist training** to be prepared to protect themselves from agents of the federal government. Many groups and individual members of such groups stockpiled automatic weapons, explosives, and even hand-fired missiles.

During the late 1980s and early 1990s, terrorist incidents were witnessed at abortion clinics across the United States, as were incidents involving self-styled patriot groups, which often endorsed defying federal regulations and law. In addition, the Unabomber, whose bombs had killed three people and injured twenty-three over an eighteen-year period, had again become active during the 1990s. In April 1996, federal

survivalist training A type of training in which separatist groups practice guerrilla warfare tactics to prepare to protect themselves from law enforcement officials or other agents of the government.

A common element of citizen militia training is instruction in shooting a weapon.

HISTORY

APRIL 19, THE DATE OF THE BOMBING of the Murrah Building in Oklahoma City in 1995, has significance for members of militia and patriot groups. On April 19, 1775, the Battle of Lexington began. It was the first battle of the Revolutionary War. On April 19, 1993, the siege of the Branch Davidian compound by federal agents at Waco, Texas, ended. When Timothy McVeigh rented the Ryder truck used in the Oklahoma City bombing, he used a forged driver's license whose date of issue was April 19, 1993. And on April 19, 1995, Richard Wayne Snell, a member of a white supremacist group, was executed for the murders of a Jewish business owner and a black police officer.

agents seized Theodore Kaczynski, a former college professor, as the suspect in the Unabomber case. Beginning in 1994 and escalating in 1996, a rash of mysterious fires assailed black churches across the South. Various **hate groups** have been investigated in those arson cases (Dickey, 1996).

hate group A group antagonistic toward various minority groups in the United States.

Members of radical right-wing groups do not regard themselves as terrorists. Rather, they style themselves as "patriots," "tax protesters," "citizen militias," and "constitutionalists." They believe that the country is headed toward disaster and that they must be ready to fight to protect their inalienable rights. During recent years, they have become more outspoken against the federal government, expressing their belief that it has become too invasive and restrictive.

The militia movement is the youngest of the major right-wing antigovernment movements in the United States (the sovereign citizen movement and the tax protest movement are the two others), and it has seared itself into the American consciousness as virtually no other fringe movement has. The publicity given to militia groups in the wake of the Oklahoma City bombing in 1995, when the militia movement was erroneously linked to that tragedy, made them into a household name (Snow, 2002).

The most militant of the right-wing groups are citizen militias and patriot groups, which continue to attract supporters. They dress in combat fatigues, carry assault weapons, and participate in paramilitary maneuvers and guerrilla training. Formal militia groups have been reported in at least twenty-two states. Membership estimates for each state vary, but they range from as few as fifty to as many as several thousand. The larger organizations are located in the Midwest and West, with notable groups in Michigan, Montana, Idaho, Texas, Arizona, Alabama, Mississippi, Georgia, Pennsylvania, and Ohio.

One antigovernment, antitax group based in Montana, calling itself the Freemen, held law enforcement officers at bay for nearly three months in 1996. On March 25 federal agents arrived with warrants for the arrest of several people at a ranch that had been lost in a tax foreclosure. Members of the group had been charged with defrauding banks and other companies of $1.8 million and with holding seminars for 800 people on how to conduct fraud. The indicted persons refused to surrender to the authorities. On March 28 several members were charged with threatening local law enforcement officials. During the three-month standoff, a number of occupants, including some minors, came out of the complex without incident. The remaining holdouts came out on June 13. When they appeared in court the next day, some were defiant, denying that the court had any jurisdiction over them.

Extremist right-wing groups feed on fear and spread paranoia. Many militia members believe that the U.S. government is part of a conspiracy to create a "new world order," and they resent the involvement of the United Nations in international affairs.

According to believers, in this new order, existing international boundaries will be dissolved, the United States will be overtaken by armies of the one-world government, and the world will be ruled by the United Nations. Many believe that signs on the interstate are actually coded to provide directions for invading armies.

Other militia supporters believe that the federal government is either too powerful or simply illegal. Their antigovernment stance has resulted from the changing political environment of civil rights legislation, environmental legislation, and gun-control legislation and from clashes between militia members and law enforcement officials. Many are so fed up with the federal government that they are ready to take up arms to overthrow it (Merkl & Weinberg, 2003).

Those who are arming themselves against the day United Nations tanks roll across the nation's heartland to establish the one-world government may number as many as 100,000. If you add all the people in as many as forty states who accept the patriot rhetoric about a sinister and conspiratorial out-of-control federal government, businesses put out of business by environmental regulations, and all the unemployed who blame their plight on federal policies, that number may rise to 12 million.

One extremist fringe religious movement uniting many of the white supremacist groups calls itself the Christian Identity Movement. Members of this group maintain a steady stream of anti-Semitic, white racist, fundamentalist Christian, and antifederalist rhetoric and beliefs. Right-wing groups in this movement are bound together by a shared hostility against Jews and nonwhites. They believe Jews have taken control of the economic structure of the United States and have put a stranglehold on the purse strings of white Christian Americans (Roth, 2002). This conspiracy theory has led believers of the movement to advocate the overthrow of the federal government. Other believers resent educational and job opportunities federally mandated for nonwhites, which they think should go to white Christian Americans. Moreover, followers believe that nonwhites are destroying America by making it racially unpure.

Another idea popular among the Christian Identity Movement is the origin of the *pre-Adamite,* or how nonwhite individuals came to be. One notion argues that the "beasts of the field" in Genesis were actually the nonwhite races. These so-called beasts of the field were in place to serve as slave laborers for Adam's race—that is, for white people. Another popular notion is that the *millennial kingdom* will only be achieved after the battle between Aryan people and the forces of Satan (the Jews and nonwhites) has been fought and won. Such a battle would cleanse the earth of all others and set the stage for the millennium (Lamy, 1996).

In the theology of the Christian Identity Movement, the federal government is compared to the evil forces in the book of Revelations. Thus the federal government and its agents (law enforcement officers) are viewed as the servants of Satan that must be destroyed. In fact, the U.S. government is frequently referred to as a seven-headed dragon, with the ATF, FBI, IRS, EPA, and other federal agencies serving as the heads that feed the dragon. The World Bank and the United Nations are described as supporting a New (Zionist) World Order, which is being imposed on the righteous Aryan people (Watson, 2002).

FYI One product of the militia movement is common law courts. These courts—which have no legitimate authority—consist of self-appointed judges and juries who sometimes issue fraudulent indictments and warrants.

Special-Interest Groups

These groups seek resolution of specific issues rather than widespread political changes. Examples include groups that espouse terrorism to promote environmental issues or animal rights, such as the Animal Liberation Front (ALF), Up the IRS, and the Earth Night Action Group. Also included in this category are extremist antiabortion groups who attack abortion clinics and their personnel. The causes these groups promote may not be criminal, but the means—violence and destruction—they use to attain their goals are. They differ from traditional law-abiding special-interest groups in their use of criminal activity and violence to achieve their goals.

INTERNATIONAL TERRORISM

International Terrorist Groups in the United States

The United States has long been resented in some countries around the world. Critics of the U.S. government say it has supported dictators who helped American companies operating in their countries or who shared America's dislike of the Soviet Union. With the dismantling of the USSR, the United States became the world's only superpower and thus a target of much of the world's bitterness and frustration. Americans were frequent targets of terrorism, but most incidents took place overseas. Most Americans felt little threat at home from international terrorism until the Al-Qaeda attacks in 2001. Americans realized then that the United States was still unpopular among other nations and that foreign terrorists could now operate within the once-safe boundaries of the fifty states.

Foreign terrorists view the United States as a priority target, an attractive refuge from prosecution, and a staging area for obtaining funds and support for their activities. America's open society makes it possible for terrorists and their supporters to live in and travel freely throughout the nation. A number of international terrorist groups whose allegiance stems from their ethnic ancestry in the Middle East operate in the United States. Many of these groups oppose Jewish organizations in the United States or are antagonized by U.S. support of Israel.

Terrorist Groups with International Agendas

Formal terrorist groups such as the extremist Egyptian Al-Gama'at Al-Islamiyya, the militant Islamic Hezbollah (also called the Party of God and the Islamic Jihad), the Palestinian terrorists Hamas (Islamic Resistance Movement), Al-Aqsa Martyrs' Brigade, the Palestinian Islamic Jihad, and, of course, Al-Qaeda are believed to be conducting criminal activities as well as military-style training in the United States and in other countries in support of their groups' objectives. In addition to these formal groups, loosely affiliated individuals and groups also view the United States as both a target and a staging area. They take advantage of the advanced technology available in the United States, travel undetected, and manage to get around U.S. laws. Investigation of international terrorist groups usually requires communication and cooperation with INTERPOL and the law enforcement agencies of other countries. Let's consider who these terrorist groups are, and what their origins have been.

Al-Gama'at Al-Islamiyya (IG) Egypt's largest militant group, active since the late 1970s, appears to be loosely organized. It has an external wing with supporters in several countries worldwide. The group issued a ceasefire in March 1999, but its spiritual leader, Shaykh Umar Abd al-Rahman—sentenced to life in prison in

January 1996 for his involvement in the World Trade Center bombing of 1993 and incarcerated in the United States—rescinded his support for the ceasefire in June 2000. The IG has not conducted an attack inside Egypt since August 1998. Senior members signed Osama bin Laden's fatwa in February 1998 calling for attacks against the United States (U.S. Department of State, 2004).

Hezbollah Hezbollah is a Lebanese umbrella organization of radical Islamic Shi'ite groups and organizations. It opposes the West, seeks to create a Muslim fundamentalist state modeled on Iran, and is a bitter foe of Israel. Hezbollah, whose name means "party of God," is a terrorist group believed responsible for nearly 200 attacks since 1982 that have killed more than 800 people. Sheikh Mohammed Hussein Fadlallah is the group's spiritual leader, and Imad Fayez Mugniyah is the key planner of Hezbollah's worldwide terrorist operations (Byers, 2003).

White (2006, p. 168) claims that Hezbollah participated in the Al-Aqsa intifada (uprising) and that its international branch may well be the most effective terrorist network in the world. While Hezbollah is part of the jihadist network, its origins are rooted in the struggle for a Palestinian state (Byers, 2003). Hezbollah has, however, forged alliances with non-jihadist groups (White, 2006).

Hamas Hamas (a word meaning courage and bravery) is the largest and most influential Palestinian militant movement. Hamas is also the Arabic acronym for the Islamic Resistance Movement (*Harakat al-Muqawamah al-Islamiyya*). It was founded in 1987 and opposed the 1993 Peace Accords between Israel and the Palestinian Liberation Organization (PLO). In 1998 Hamas claimed that Palestine was an Islamic homeland that could never be surrendered to non-Muslims and that waging a holy war to return control of Palestine to Palestinian Muslims was their religious duty (Pedahzur, 2005).

In January 2006 Hamas won the Palestinian Authority's (PA) general legislative elections, defeating Fatah, the party of the PA's president, Mahmoud Abbas, and setting the stage for a power struggle. Since attaining power, Hamas has continued its refusal to recognize the state of Israel, leading to crippling economic sanctions. Hamas maintained a ceasefire brokered in March 2005 until June 9, 2006, when it ended the truce after reports that errant Israeli shells killed several civilians on a Gaza beach. The Israeli Defense Forces later denied responsibility for the deaths.

The Al-Aqsa Martyrs' Brigade The al-Aqsa Martyrs' Brigade (Kata'ib Shuhada' al-Aqsa) emerged from Yasser Arafat's Fatah faction of the PLO in 2001 and was fiercely loyal to Arafat and the Palestinian Authority. The group acted with the help of senior officers of other elements of the Palestinian Authority's armed entities, the Tanzim and Force 17 (all of which reported to Yasser Arafat when he was president to the PLO), who provided illegal weapons, training, and intelligence to help carry out their attacks. The brigade works in complete secrecy and is probably composed of a few hundred men operating in loosely connected cells.

The al-Aqsa Martyrs' Brigade organized some of the most gruesome terrorist attacks in Israel, especially during the escalation of violence in 2001 and 2002. In that period, the al-Aqsa Martyrs' Brigade increased the level of its cooperation with other terrorist organizations, including Hamas and Islamic Jihad; in addition, they began using women as suicide bombers (Martin, 2004). A number of bombings and shootings were perpetrated by the al-Aqsa Martyrs' Brigade individually or in partnership with other terrorist groups.

Palestinian Islamic Jihad (PIJ) The Palestinian Islamic Jihad (*Harakat al-Jihad al-Islami al-Filastini*) was founded in 1979–80 by Palestinian students in Egypt who had split from the Palestinian Muslim Brotherhood in the Gaza Strip. The founders were highly influenced by the Islamic revolution in Iran, on one hand, and the radicalization and militancy of Egyptian Islamic student organizations, on the other. The PIJ Fathi Shqaqi faction has in recent years become the most prominent Palestinian terrorist group to adopt the Islamic Jihad ideology. It views Israel, the *Zionist Jewish entity,* as the main enemy of the Muslim Brothers and the first target for destruction. It calls for an Islamic armed struggle and strives for the liberation of all of Palestine. This is to be accomplished by guerilla groups, led by a revolutionary vanguard, which carry out terrorist attacks aimed at weakening Israel. Its militants see themselves as those who lay the groundwork for the day when the great Islamic Arabic army will be able to destroy Israel in a military confrontation (White, 2006).

Al-Qaeda Al-Qaeda is an international terrorist network led by Osama bin Laden. It seeks to rid Muslim countries of what it sees as the profane influence of the West and replace their governments with fundamentalist Islamic regimes. Al-Qaeda had its origins in the uprising against the Soviet occupation of Afghanistan in 1979. Thousands of volunteers from around the Middle East came to Afghanistan as mujahideen, warriors fighting to defend fellow Muslims. In the mid-1980s, Osama bin Laden became the prime financier for an organization that recruited Muslims from mosques around the world. Al-Qaeda evolved from the Maktab al-Khadamat (Office of Services, MAK), a Mujahid organization fighting to establish an Islamic state during the Soviet war in Afghanistan in the 1980s. These "Afghan Arab" mujahideen, which numbered in the thousands, were crucial in defeating Soviet forces.

After the Soviets withdrew from Afghanistan, bin Laden returned to his native Saudi Arabia. He founded an organization to help veterans of the Afghan war, many of whom went on to fight elsewhere (including Bosnia) and who comprise the basis of Al-Qaeda. The Iraqi invasion of Kuwait in 1990 had put the Saudi Arabian ruling House of Saud at risk both from internal dissent and the perceived possibility of further Iraqi expansionism. In the face of a seemingly massive Iraqi military presence, Saudi Arabia's own forces although well armed were outnumbered. Bin Laden offered the services of his mujahideen to King Fahd to protect Saudi Arabia from the Iraqi army. After some deliberation the Saudi monarch refused bin Laden's offer and instead opted to allow the United States and allied forces to deploy on his territory. Bin Laden considered this a treacherous deed. He believed that the presence of foreign troops in the "land of the two mosques" (Mecca and Medina) profaned sacred soil. After speaking publicly against the Saudi government for harboring U.S. troops, he was quickly forced into exile to Sudan and his Saudi citizenship was revoked.

Al-Qaeda has targeted U.S. and other Western interests as well as Jewish targets and Muslim governments it sees as corrupt or impious—above all, the Saudi monarchy. Al-Qaeda linked attacks include the following:

- March 2004 bomb attacks on Madrid commuter trains, which killed nearly 200 people and left more than 1,800 injured
- May 2003 car bomb attacks on three residential compounds in Riyadh, Saudi Arabia
- November 2002 car bomb attack and a failed attempt to shoot down an Israeli jetliner with shoulder-fired missiles, both in Mombasa, Kenya
- October 2002 attack on a French tanker off the coast of Yemen

- Several spring 2002 bombings in Pakistan
- April 2002 explosion of a fuel tanker outside a synagogue in Tunisia
- September 11, 2001, hijacking attacks on the World Trade Center and the Pentagon
- October 2000 USS *Cole* bombing
- August 1998 bombings of the U.S. embassies in Nairobi, Kenya, and Dar es Salaam, Tanzania

Al-Qaeda is suspected of carrying out or directing sympathetic groups to carry out the May 2003 suicide attacks on Western interests in Casablanca, Morocco; the October 2002 nightclub bombing in Bali, Indonesia; and the 1993 World Trade Center bombing. On July 13, 2006, a man claiming to be a spokesperson for Al-Qaeda called a local news agency in Srinagar to announce the arrival of the group in Kashmir. The alleged Al-Qaeda spokesman said the blasts were a "consequence of Indian oppression and suppression of minorities, particularly Muslims." There have been reports that Al-Qaeda had infiltrated into the valley during the past few years, particularly once the United States went after it in Afghanistan and Pakistan after the 9/11 attacks. It has additionally been claimed that links have been found between Al-Qaeda and terror groups like Lashkar-e-Toiba (LeT) of Pakistan (Ahmad & Joshi, 2006).

The New Terrorism

U.S. law enforcement, security, and intelligence systems have only recently begun to come to terms with the nature of modern terrorist groups of the new millennium such as Al-Qaeda. These modern groups differ significantly from those of the old Cold War days of the latter part of the twentieth century (Hoffman, 2006). One central difference is their objectives: Cold War terrorist groups had specific and attainable goals, mostly political in nature—release of political prisoners, cash ransoms, and so forth. Al-Qaeda goes beyond these attainable politically charged goals into what may be referred to as *transcendental* goals, effectively a vision formed by religious belief.

Many modern terrorist motives are also new. Terrorist groups such as Al-Qaeda have international objectives, and globalization has allowed these groups to facilitate other terrorist groups on a worldwide level. Rather than a terrorist group using terrorism to foster change in a single society or focus on a specific government, terrorism has gone international to support global causes with Western countries serving as primary targets (Hoffman, 2006). Terrorist attacks have become increasingly more sophisticated, larger, and more catastrophic, and they have the deliberate intention of inflicting mass casualties on civilians and noncombatants.

This new millennium terrorism has a much greater potential to cause harm to Americans and to require the intervention of police agencies at the local, municipal, and county levels as well as at the federal level of investigation. Terrorists are likely to increase their use of advanced information technologies for offensive and defensive purposes and to support their organizational structure (Arquilla, Ronfeldt, & Zanini, 2006). Consequently, police agencies need to increase their understanding of computer technology, cyberspace, and cyber crimes that might be used to financially support terrorist activities.

The American Response to Terrorism

In an effort to thwart terrorist activity and attacks on U.S. targets, the United States government has revamped the mission and structure of a number of federal law enforcement agencies and created some new ones to coordinate counterterrorism activities.

The National Strategy for Homeland Security and the Homeland Security Act of 2002 created the Department of Homeland Security (DHS). The overall mission of the DHS is articulated on their website as follows:

> We will lead the unified national effort to secure America. We will prevent and deter terrorist attacks and protect against and respond to threats and hazards to the nation. We will ensure safe and secure borders, welcome lawful immigrants and visitors, and promote the free-flow of commerce. (DHS, 2007)

Currently, the DHS coordinates the activities of more than 180,000 employees and is charged with overseeing these seven strategic goals:

- **Creating awareness.** Identify and understand threats, assess vulnerabilities, determine potential impacts, and disseminate timely information to our homeland security partners and the American public.
- **Prevention.** Detect, deter, and mitigate threats to our homeland.
- **Providing protection.** Safeguard the people of the United States and their freedoms, critical infrastructure, property, and the economy of our nation from acts of terrorism, natural disasters, or other emergencies.
- **Developing appropriate responses.** Lead, manage, and coordinate the national response to acts of terrorism, natural disasters, or other emergencies.
- **Recovery.** Lead national, state, local, and private-sector efforts to restore services and rebuild communities after acts of terrorism, natural disasters, or other emergencies.
- **Service.** Serve the public effectively by facilitating lawful trade, travel, and immigration.
- **Organizational excellence.** Value our most important resource, our people. Create a culture that promotes a common identity, innovation, mutual respect, accountability, and teamwork to achieve efficiencies, effectiveness, and operational synergies.

To accomplish these goals, DHS has established four directorates: Border and Transportation Security, Emergency Preparedness and Response, Science and Technology, and Information Analysis and Infrastructure Protection.

Border and Transportation Security   BTS is responsible for maintaining the security of the nation's borders and transportation systems. It brought together a number of major border security and transportation operations under one roof, including the following:

- U.S. Customs Service (Treasury)
- Immigration and Naturalization Service (part) (Justice)
- Federal Protective Service
- Transportation Security Administration (Transportation)
- Federal Law Enforcement Training Center (Treasury)
- Animal and Plant Health Inspection Service (part) (Agriculture)
- Office for Domestic Preparedness (Justice)

Emergency Preparedness and Response   EPR oversees domestic disaster preparedness training and coordinates government disaster response. This directorate seeks to ensure that the United States is prepared for, and able to recover from, both terrorist attacks and natural disasters. It brings these agencies together:

- Federal Emergency Management Agency (FEMA)
- Strategic National Stockpile and the National Disaster Medical System (HHS)

- Nuclear Incident Response Team (Energy)
- Domestic Emergency Support Teams (Justice)
- National Domestic Preparedness Office (FBI)

Science and Technology This directorate utilizes all available scientific and technological advantages to best secure the homeland, including preparing for and responding to the full range of terrorist threats involving weapons of mass destruction. The following assets have become part of this effort:

- CBRN Countermeasures Programs (Energy)
- Environmental Measurements Laboratory (Energy)
- National BW Defense Analysis Center (Defense)
- Plum Island Animal Disease Center (Agriculture)

Information Analysis and Infrastructure Protection This directorate analyzes intelligence and information from other agencies (including the CIA, FBI, DIA, and NSA) involving threats to homeland security and evaluates vulnerabilities in the nation's infrastructure. This directorate brings these agencies together:

- Federal Computer Incident Response Center (GSA)
- National Communications System (Defense)
- National Infrastructure Protection Center (FBI)
- Energy Security and Assurance Program (Energy)

The Secret Service and the Coast Guard are also housed under the auspice of the Department of Homeland Security but remain intact and report directly to the secretary. In addition, the INS adjudications and benefits programs report directly to the deputy secretary at the U.S. Citizenship and Immigration Services.

In addition, two completely new agencies were created with the goal of combating terrorism. The first is the National Counterterrorism Center (NCTC), which has been staffed with terrorism specialists from the CIA, FBI, and the Pentagon; the Privacy and Civil Liberties Board; and the National Counterproliferation Center. This agency provides analysis services, integrating all intelligence pertaining to terrorism and counterterrorism acquired from other agencies and focusing solely on domestic counterterrorism information.

The second agency is the office of the Director of National Intelligence (DNI), which is charged with coordinating data obtained from the nation's primary intelligence-gathering agencies, synthesizing this information, and serving as the principle intelligence adviser to the president and to the statutory intelligence adviser to the National Security Council.

ANTITERRORISM ACTIVITIES

The United States government is tireless in its efforts to gather counterintelligence, applying this *intelligence model* to terrorist activities rather than the more traditional *criminal justice model.* The intelligence model considers terrorist activity as threats to the security of the state rather than as traditional criminal acts (Bhoumik, 2005). Consequently, rather than seeking to deter criminal behavior through threats of arrest and punishment, the goal is to secure information that can be used to prevent the terrorist act. **Counterintelligence** involves obtaining information about potential terrorist activities while they are still being planned. Federal agencies, as well as several

counterintelligence
Gathering political and military information about foreign countries and institutions to prevent terrorist actions.

state and large urban police agencies, compile intelligence on people and groups they believe have serious potential for future criminal involvement in terrorist activities.

It seems reasonably clear today that the U.S. law enforcement community has gotten a somewhat late start in the counterintelligence game. For example, the FBI came under almost scathing attacks for its perceived lack of intelligence and mishandling of suspected individuals following the attack on the World Trade Center in September 2001. In a memorandum written by FBI Special Agent Robert Wright Jr. ninety-one days *before* the September 11 terrorist attacks, he warned that Americans would die as a result of the bureau's failure to adequately pursue investigations of terrorists living in the country. Special Agent Wright had led a four-year investigation into terrorist money laundering in the United States, and his June 9, 2001, Mission Statement memo warned that "The FBI has proven for the past decade it cannot identify and prevent acts of terrorism against the United States and its citizens at home and abroad." He continued, "Even worse, there is virtually no effort on the part of the FBI's International Terrorism Unit to neutralize known and suspected international terrorists living in the United States" (Johnson, 2002). Furthermore, even though the Central Intelligence Agency (CIA) suspected that Khalid al-Midhar and Nawaf Alhzmi had ties to Al-Qaeda in March 2000, the agency did not share this information with the FBI or other agencies until three weeks before the attacks occurred. It is little wonder than many citizens were unhappy with the level of intelligence efforts undertaken by U.S. government agencies.

A large portion of the problem was the low priority that federal law enforcement had previously given terrorism. In the summer of 2001, only 6 percent of FBI agents were assigned to counterintelligence activities. Ironically, on September 10, 2001, the Department of Justice proposed to cut $65 million from a counterterrorism program that provided local and state law enforcement agencies with training and equipment. That same day, the Department of Justice also refused to support a request made by the FBI for $58 million to hire 400 new employees, including individuals who would specifically be used to combat terrorism (Johnston & Natta, 2002).

The pendulum, however, has now swung the other way. The federal government spent nearly $50 billion to fight domestic terrorism in 2005, with $3 billion going directly to the FBI and the Department of Justice (Congressional Budget Office, 2005). In a further effort to combat terrorism, the FBI has increased the number of agents assigned to investigate terrorism from 535 to more than 3,000.

Counterintelligence involves gathering information from a number of sources and sharing that information. The Department of Homeland Security was, in part, established in an effort to streamline and make more effective this information generation and sharing process. Counterintelligence information may be obtained through snitches and paid informers or offered voluntarily by disillusioned former group members. It may include information gathered in undercover operations in which officers infiltrate suspect groups or from various forms of surveillance. Investigators from various agencies can use the information gathered to plan specific operations, to assess the actual threat presented by a specific individual or group, and to share with other agencies in the area.

The major differences between investigating an act of criminal terrorism and a conventional crime are the extensive use of intelligence and the attempt to prevent the terrorist action from occurring. Many terrorist groups operating in the United States today are large and fairly well organized, operating across state lines and over large areas. Records held by various levels of law enforcement on the activities of these groups may represent the raw data needed to apprehend offenders, but strong communication links and coordination between various law enforcement organizations and agencies are necessary to effectively utilize this information.

CAREERS FOCUS

FOREIGN SERVICE SPECIAL AGENT

SPECIAL AGENTS OF THE BUREAU OF DIPLOMATIC SECURITY are responsible for the security of Foreign Service personnel and property and sensitive information throughout the world. They are also responsible for protecting the Secretary of State, certain foreign dignitaries during their visits to the United States, and others designated by the Secretary of State. Major job responsibilities include protective services, criminal investigations, background checks, managing security programs for Foreign Service posts, and administrative, training, and liaison functions. The Foreign Service is part of the U.S. Department of State.

Applicants must be citizens of the United States, must be at least 21 and not more than 37 at the time of their appointment, must have at least a bachelor's degree from an accredited college or university, and must have one year of specialized experience. Although not a requirement, foreign language ability is desirable. Applicants should have a valid U.S. driver's license and be able to pass a defensive driving course during initial training.

Candidates must be willing to travel to a variety of overseas posts, many of which are remote and unhealthful or have limited medical support. Applicants must meet rigorous medical fitness standards and must undergo a thorough background investigation to determine their eligibility for a security clearance and their suitability for appointment to the Foreign Service. Agent candidates must be willing to carry firearms and must qualify with firearms during initial training and periodically thereafter. Applicants must be fit for strenuous physical exertion and be able to pass periodic physical fitness tests. Candidates must successfully complete all aspects of the training program. After a probationary period not to exceed four years, the special agent becomes a permanent employee.

Initial salary at appointment will normally be at Foreign Service grade FP-6, step 3. Exceptions may be made to increase the number of steps based on such factors as a master's degree in a related field (such as criminal justice), a law degree, or other directly related specialized experience. However, maximum salary is limited to the grade that the candidate is qualified for at the time of appointment. No appointments are made above the FP-6, step 14 level ($ 51,788 base pay).

LOCAL POLICE AND TERRORISM

Once an act of terrorism is detected and police are notified, a patrol unit from the local police is likely to be dispatched and arrive first on the scene. As in any arrival to a crime scene, officers must be alert and cautious as they arrive and exit their vehicles. The crime scene should be immediately secured, and witnesses, victims, and possible suspects should be identified as quickly as possible. The arriving officers should advise headquarters of the situation and any additional personnel or services required. In turn, headquarters should contact their *terrorism liaison officer*. Originating shortly after September 11, 2001, many municipal and county police agencies, along with fire and health agencies across the country, began to designate an officer who became part of a larger network of police terrorism liaisons. This provided a mechanism for agencies to channel and exchange information to and from state level regional intelligence centers (Baca, 2006).

Once the officer on the scene makes an assessment that terrorists are involved, or that an act of terrorism has occurred, the officer should notify headquarters. If hostages are involved, the department's hostage negotiator (if one is available) should be contacted. If the local agency does not have the necessary specialists, the state and federal agency offices in the area should be immediately consulted. Although some larger police agencies may have specialists in incendiary and explosive devices, most smaller agencies do not. Similarly, many smaller agencies do not have specialists in dealing with terrorists or conducting hostage or terrorist negotiations. It is important for local agencies to recognize their own limitations and to seek appropriate assistance.

Chapter 22 Terrorism and Cyber Predators **487**

As in other criminal cases, crimes of terrorism require careful and accurate record keeping. The record should begin with the first notification of the police. This may often be a threat of violence or notification of a kidnapping, with demands from the kidnapper. The activities investigators should undertake include the following:

- Record the time and date the threat was received, who received the threat, and how it was received.

- Indicate the character of the threat (e.g., bombings, arson, kidnapping, or murder).

- Identify the target and time of the terrorist threat.

- Determine what prompted the threat.

- Determine any organizational ties of the threat maker.

- Record any telephone conversations, and examine the tape for background noises and telltale characteristics of the threat maker.

- If the threat is written, avoid handling the document with ungloved hands. Determine who has already handled the document, and secure samples of their fingerprints. Have the document examined by the forensic lab to identify possible fingerprints or other identifying marks.

- If the threat was in person, question the reporting individual and obtain a description of the threat maker.

When officers arrive at the scene of terrorist activity, they may not immediately realize that it is not a conventional crime. For example, a bank robbery may be an attempt to obtain money for a radical political group's efforts; hence, in a broad sense this is a terrorist activity. The arriving officers are likely to see the event as merely another bank robbery, and it is appropriate to work the scene as one would any other robbery. However, once it is determined that the crime may be classified as an act of political terrorism, the proper officers or agencies should be notified. Some large departments may have officers assigned to a **crisis negotiation team,** specialists in defusing potentially dangerous situations, but smaller departments may need to contact state-level enforcement or the local office of Homeland Security and the FBI.

crisis negotiation team A group of specialists trained to defuse potentially dangerous situations.

Suspect Background Information

As suggested earlier, terrorist investigations rely heavily on intelligence data and on cooperation among a number of agencies. These efforts frequently produce a large amount of data requiring considerable personnel hours and computer-assisted analysis. Some of the information likely to emerge from this analysis are various potential suspects.

FYI Any fraud relating to application for or use of a U.S. visa or passport can result in a ten-year prison term and a $50,000 fine. If the fraud is related to terrorism, it can result in a twenty-year prison term and a $250,000 fine. In 2005 Diplomatic Security of the U.S. Department of State investigated 3,564 new cases of passport and visa fraud and made 583 arrests.

History demonstrates that persons involved in terrorism often have previous law violations. Careful attention should be given to examining various records and the background characteristics of potential suspects. Information sources that may prove helpful in locating suspects or obtaining evidence of criminal involvement are discussed

FOCUS ON TECHNOLOGY

TRACE EXPLOSIVES DETECTOR

AN EXPLOSIVES TRACE DETECTION SYSTEM TRAPS TRACES of vapors or particles given off or left behind by explosives. These trapped samples are evaporated and drawn into the detection system where they are analyzed. This process takes less than three seconds, and an audible alarm and screen display indicate the presence of explosives. These devices are frequently portable (handheld) and provide comprehensive explosive detection capabilities. Devices can trace both particulates and vapors, allowing for noninvasive searches of luggage, mail, vehicles, documents, and containers. Many of these devices are capable of detecting even minute traces of C-4, TNT, dynamite, PETN, Semtex, EGDN, DMNB, RDX, and nitroglycerine.

An explosives trace detection system traps traces of vapors or particles given off or left behind by explosives. These trapped samples are evaporated and drawn into the detection system where they are analyzed. An audible alarm and screen display indicate the presence of explosives.

in Chapter 8. These sources include *modus operandi* files, arrest records, employment records, motor vehicle records, and utility records. With the extension to searches and seizures provided by the Patriot Act, telephone and cable records and, in some situations, wiretaps or Internet tracking may also provide useful information.

Physical Evidence

One of the most important elements of terrorist-related investigations is collection and preservation of physical evidence. In both the 1993 New York City World Trade Center bombing and the 1995 bombing of the Murrah Federal Building in Oklahoma City, it was physical evidence that led investigators to suspects. In the first case, a fragment of a truck axle led ATF investigators first to a rental agency and then to a suspect. Similarly, wreckage from the rented truck used to house the fertilizer/explosives in the Oklahoma bombing case led investigators to arrest Timothy McVeigh as the prime suspect and later to locate Terry Nichols as a co-conspirator and Michael Fortier as a prosecution witness.

The search for physical evidence in terrorism cases should extend from the physical crime scene to surrounding areas and to locations where a suspect may have conducted surveillance or concealed him- or herself before or during an incident (such

A twisted piece of truck axle found near the Oklahoma City bombing site gave investigators a vital first clue in the investigation that led to a verdict of guilty against Timothy McVeigh on June 2, 1997.

as an arson or bombing). Because terrorist activities frequently involve more than one person, it may be important to establish each co-conspirator's activities and whereabouts during the terrorist event through physical evidence.

Procedures for appropriate collection of evidence are covered in Chapter 4. However, it should be noted that during terrorist investigations, items that may seem unrelated to the crime may prove critical later in the case. A can of Coke may ultimately lead to a suspect if investigators trace the manufacturer's identification code and locate the town, and even the store, where the can was purchased. By examining minute debris and the detonating device left by the bomb that brought down Pan American Flight 103 over Lockerbie, Scotland, authorities were able to identify the most likely suspects.

In addition to items that may have been touched or accidentally left by the terrorists, materials used in bombs or devices may offer clues. Parts of these contrivances may be traced to their sources—often right to the retail level. When a series of bombings or arsons have occurred, materials found at the scenes may be linked to show a common origin. Many establishments maintain records of their transactions, and locating the retailer of an item used by a terrorist can help to identify a suspect.

CYBER CRIMES

As discussed in Chapter 20, a considerable amount of crime has begun to emerge either on the Internet or through use of a computer. Identity thefts, phishing expeditions, fake lotteries, Nigerian letter scams, and a host of other con games and consumer frauds have been and will continue to be perpetrated over the Internet. The problem for law enforcement has been that they must apply traditional laws intended to protect people from physical harms or to protect their physical property to crimes committed in cyberspace. This has resulted in the evolution of some cyber-based laws. In an effort to combat movie piracy, the Motion Picture Association of America (MPAA) filed suit against individual consumers who downloaded or shared films over peer-to-peer (P2P) networks (*MPAA v. The People,* 2004). This suit followed Napster's unsuccessful battle with A&M Records concerning the unlawful downloading of MP3 recordings (*A&M Records v. Napster,* 2001). These legal cases have arisen due to the popularity of the Internet and users' ability to easily transfer electronic audio and visual media (Jewkes, 2007). Another evolving law centers on pornography, in particular, child pornography on the Internet. Congress enacted the Child Pornography Prevention Act of 1996

(CPPA) in an effort to battle the sexual exploitation of children. But the bill was very broadly drawn and did not anticipate advances in technology that might lead this act to encroach on the First Amendment rights of free speech. Most people would agree that the use of real children in the production of sexually explicit videos or photographs is an obvious and glaring exploitation of children. The question, however, has arisen whether the government has the right to criminalize the production or possession of *virtual* child pornography in which no child is actually used in the production of pornography and the images have been completely created from fiction (Cisneros, 2002). In *Ashcroft v. The Free Speech Coalition* (2002), the U.S. Supreme Court held that the government may not criminalize such action because the production of virtual child pornography does not sexually abuse an actual child. Nonetheless, the sexual exploitation of children has become a serious problem. Exploitation is often initiated through Internet contacts, and it is investigated by local police agencies.

Cyber Predators

cyber predator Individuals, usually men, who use the Internet to hunt for victims to take advantage of—especially children, preteens, and teens who may be manipulated or seduced into meeting and engaging in sexual activity.

Every day millions of kids spend time in Internet chat rooms, talking to strangers. Many children don't realize is that some of the surfers chatting with them may be sexual predators. **Cyber predators** are individuals, usually men, who use the Internet to hunt for victims to take advantage of—especially children, preteens, and teens, who may be manipulated or seduced into meeting and engaging in sexual activity. The Internet has become a favorite place for pedophiles who hide under the anonymous cloak of a chat name. According to Arnold Bell (2004), an FBI expert on child protection, approximately six out of every ten children who use the Internet have received an e-mail or instant message from a perfect stranger—and more than half have written back! One in thirty-three children has been aggressively solicited to meet their *cyber friend* in person, and approximately one in four children between the ages of 10 and 17 has been exposed to unwanted sexual material online. More than 45 million children used the Internet in 2002, and pedophiles run more than 20,000 websites and prowl thousands of chat rooms (Collins, 2004).

The Internet has presented people with a wonderful outlet and gateway to new worlds; it has also presented the law enforcement community with an assortment of serious problems, which include an alarming number of situations involving explicit chat discussions, solicitations, and graphic images of online activities that victimize minors. Officers encounter troubling images and dialogue during undercover operations and in other investigative of efforts, such as computer forensic examinations targeted at locating missing children (Bowker & Gray, 2005).

Because computers provide anonymity, they create electronic shadows on the Internet that permit cyber predators to lurk and hide. Concealed in the privacy of their own homes, pedophiles can use the Internet to anonymously and simultaneously prepare numerous children for future molestations. Furthermore, with merely the click of a mouse, child pornographers can easily distribute their wares to anyone seeking to purchase such materials—including other offenders or even juveniles (Bowker & Gray, 2005).

Cyber sex offenders who target young people use computers for purposes that may include viewing, storing, producing, sending, and receiving child pornography; contacting, grooming, and enticing juveniles for victimization; and communicating with (and, thus, helping to validate) each other. Upon apprehension, these individuals often attempt to justify their actions. Law enforcement officers must learn to identify and understand such offenders to effectively diffuse their defenses and lay the groundwork for a successful prosecution. Figure 22.3 details the various ways child pornography may be distributed on the Internet.

FIGURE 22.3 Distribution Methods for Pornography on the Internet

Method	Use
Web pages and websites	There are websites specifically devoted to child pornography images; in some cases these images may be embedded with other more generic pornographic images. There is debate about whether real child pornography is readily available on the Web through a conventional search using standard keywords. The vigilance of Internet security providers and police tracking and closing down actual child pornography sites has limited these sites. One is more likely to find *legal* pornography sites with images of adults purporting to be minors or sites monitored by police *sting* operations seeking to capture pedophiles.
Web cam	Images of abuse may be broadcast in real time. In these live broadcasts, viewers are sometimes permitted to make online requests for particular sexual activities to be carried out on the victim—for a fee.
E-mail	E-mail attachments are sometimes used by professional distributors of child pornography, but more frequently they are used to share images among users or are sent to a potential victim as part of the grooming/seduction process. This method is considered risky by experienced users because of the danger in unwittingly sending e-mails to undercover police posing as pedophiles or as potential victims.
E-groups	Specific child pornography e-groups permit members to receive and share pornographic images and exchange information about new sites. Some of these groups appear on reputable servers and are swiftly shut down when they are detected. However, the use of code names or camouflaging child pornography images among legal adult pornography prolong their existence.
Newsgroups	Specific child pornography newsgroups provide members with a forum in which to discuss their sexual interests in children and to post child pornography. This is one of the major methods of distributing child pornography. Some child pornography newsgroups are well known to both users and authorities (for example, the *abpep-t* or alternative binaries picture erotica preteen group). Most commercial servers block access to such sites. Some servers do provide access to them, but the user runs the risk of having his or her identity captured either by the credit card payments required for access or the record kept by the server of the user's IP address. However, a computer-savvy user can access these groups using techniques that hide his or her identity by concealing the user's true IP address.
Bulletin board systems (BBS)	Bulletin boards may be used legally to host discussions that provide advice to seekers of child pornography, including the URLs of child pornography sites and even ratings of these sites. These bulletin boards may be monitored by system administrators to exclude bogus or irrelevant postings, such as those by vigilantes.
Chat rooms	Chat rooms may be used to exchange child pornography and to locate potential victims. Chat rooms may be password-protected. Open chat rooms are typically avoided by seasoned child pornographers because they are often infiltrated by undercover police.
Peer-to-peer (P2P) networks	P2P networks facilitate file sharing among child pornography users. These networks permit closed group discussions and allow members to trade images with a lower degree of risk than in an open chat room.

Source: Adapted from Wortley and Smallbone (2006), pp. 10–11.

As Figure 22.3 illustrates, there are an assortment of ways those interested in child pornography can contact and discuss this interest with others with similar views, as well as methods by which to share, sell, or otherwise distribute child pornography images. These include child pornography websites, live real-time web-cam sites, E-mail and E-groups, bulletin board postings, open chat rooms, and P2P networks. One might reasonably ask, "Who are these users of child pornography?"

Profiles of Child Pornography Users

One U.S. study found that the typical person arrested for child pornography offenses was a Caucasian male age 26 or older (Wolak, Kimberly, & Finkelhor, 2003). Furthermore, the majority (97 percent) of these offenders acted alone and more than two-thirds of them (67 percent) did possess child pornography. Sadly, beyond these tangential elements there is no single prototype of Internet child pornography users, and there is no easy way for law enforcement agencies investigating these criminals to recognize an offender. In fact, having a preconceived notion about who, or what type of person, might be a child sex offender can be damaging to a police investigation (Simon, 2000; Wortley & Smallbone, 2006).

According to Wortley and Smallbone (2006) "users of internet child pornography are not necessarily involved in hands-on sexual abuse of children" (pp. 13–14). For example, it is not known how many people access child pornography on the Internet without ever physically abusing a child. Before Internet access became wide spread, between one-fifth and one-third of those arrested for possession of child pornography were also involved in actual abuse of children (Dobson, 2003, Wellard, 2001). The Internet makes it easy for people who may never have actively sought out traditional forms of child pornography to satisfy their curiosity online, and this may encourage casual users. What we do know about users of child pornography is that they come from all walks of life and show few warning signs of this proclivity toward child pornography. In fact, users of child pornography on the Internet are more than likely to be in a relationship, to be employed, to have an above average IQ, to be college educated, and to not have a criminal record (Blundell, Sherry, Burke, & Sowerbutts, 2002).

Wolak, Mitchell and Fikelhor (2003) established that sex crimes against minors comprise a varied and diverse range of offenses including sexual assaults, illegal use of the Internet to transmit sexual material, solicitation of minors, and the possession, distribution, and production of child pornography. They categorize these crimes into three major groups based on common elements that challenge law enforcement investigations. These categories are Internet crimes against identified victims, Internet solicitations to undercover law enforcement, and Internet child pornography (Figure 22.4).

Internet Crime against Identified Victims   This is the only category that includes victims of Internet-related crimes who have been identified and contacted during the criminal investigation. The types of cases that might fall into this category include completed and attempted sex crimes (both forcible and nonforcible), production of child pornography, and illegal Internet solicitations. In the Wolak, Mitchell, and Finkelhor (2003) study, about 40 percent of arrests were for this category of crime.

Within this broad category are two subcategories: Internet-initiated and family or prior acquaintance offenses. The most publicized identified victim cases include those where offenders lured their victims to a meeting after first meeting online,

FIGURE 22.4   Categories of Internet Sex Crimes against Children

Internet Crimes against Identified Victims	Internet Solicitations to Undercover Law Enforcement	Internet Child Pornography
Crimes with identified victims including production of child pornography.	Undercover law enforcement investigators posed as minors; excludes crimes involving identified victims.	Possession/distribution/trade of child pornography only; excludes crime where child pornography was produced.

Internet-Initiated

Offender used the Internet to initiate a relationship with the victim.

Family or Prior Acquaintance

Offender was a family member or prior acquaintance of the victim.

and then seduced this child victim. About half of the cases investigated in the Wolak, Mitchell and Finkelhor (2003) study were designated Internet-initiated; the other half were by family and prior acquaintances. This has important implications for police investigations: Police should be mindful that not all Internet sex crimes against minors originate through offenders trolling for victims in chat rooms or other online venues.

Internet Solicitations to Undercover Law Enforcement   A second distinct set of sex crimes against minors found in the Wolak, Mitchell and Finkelhor (2003) study involved arrests for Internet solicitations to undercover law enforcement officers. These types of arrests are sometimes referred to as *proactive* cases because law enforcement officers pose as minors, typically 13 to 15 years of age, in chat rooms and on Internet personal profiles and wait to be contacted by offenders seeking underaged victims. About 25 percent of the study subjects were classified as Internet solicitations to undercover law enforcement.

Internet Child Pornography   A third set of crimes identified in the Wolak, Mitchell, and Finkelhor (2003) study included offenders who used the Internet to possess, distribute, and trade child pornography. These offenders did not produce child pornography themselves or offend in any other Internet-related way against identified victims or solicit any undercover investigator posing as a minor on the Internet. Over a third (36 percent) of all of the cases examined fell into this category.

Internet child pornography is unlike most crimes local police departments handle. Local citizens may access child pornography images that were produced and stored in another city or on another continent. Alternatively, they may produce or distribute images that are downloaded by people thousands of miles away. An investigation that begins in one police district will almost certainly cross jurisdictional boundaries. Therefore, most of the major investigations of Internet child pornography have involved cooperation among jurisdictions, often at an international level.

The Internet provides an avenue for other types of child sexual abuses as well. For example, it provides a means for networking among child abuse predators, facilitating a virtual subculture of pedophiles who are able to share information, tactics, support for each other's beliefs, and even abused children (O'Connell, 2001). The Internet can be used to seek out, groom, and even seduce child victims. Pedophiles may enter children's or teens' chat rooms using false profiles, assume identities as children, and establish relationships with potential victims, including arranging meetings.

The Internet can be used by sexual predators for cyberstalking and sexually harassing children (Donnerstein, 2002). **Cyberstalking** involves sending threatening or sexually explicit messages to children via e-mail (Milhorn, 2005). The Internet can also be used to plan or promote child sexual tourism. **Sexual tourism** involves traveling—both in the United States and in foreign countries—for the expressed purpose of locating children with whom to engage in sexual activity and sexual abuse (Edelson & Bergen, 2001). Similar to sexual tourism, the Internet can and has been used to facilitate trafficking in children, a variation on the "mail-order bride" scheme in which the *commodities* being sold or traded are not adult brides but children (Sanderson, 2005).

cyberstalking Using the Internet to track and repeatedly contact people, especially children. Transmitting threatening or sexually explicit messages via e-mail to children.

sexual tourism Traveling—both in the United States and in foreign countries—for the expressed purpose of locating children with whom to engage in sexual activity, sexual abuse, or sexual exploitation.

FYI It has been estimated that more than 2 million children are enslaved in the global commercial sex trade. Many of these children are either sold into prostitution to pay off family debts or forcibly recruited on the street to work in brothels, where they are required to have sex with as many as thirty men each day. Some prostituted children are just 5 years old.

Implications for Law Enforcement

The greatest problem facing law enforcement may well be that a large segment of the teen and preteen population of the United States are willing to voluntarily enter into sexual relationships with adults they meet online. New legislation can assist in the prosecution of individuals who sexually exploit children via the Internet, but these sexual predators do not fit into any neat and consistent profile, do not always coerce or force themselves on children they convince to meet with them, and are not from any consistent socioeconomic or ethnic groups. Thus combating child sexual cyber predators is a difficult problem for law enforcement agencies.

What, then, might be viable strategies for local law enforcement agencies to use in combating cyber predators? First, agencies should acquire technical knowledge and expertise concerning the use of the Internet (chat rooms, P2P networks, bulletin boards, blogs, and so forth). Departments should begin to develop specialized Internet units, or cooperate among several local agencies to develop such a unit, that investigate Internet crimes (Wortley & Smallbone, 2006). Local agencies need to establish linkages with other agencies and jurisdictions to share information and coordinate activities. Local agencies also need to prioritize their efforts. The volume of Internet crime, pornography, and cyber predator activity is enormous, and police agencies need to concentrate their resources and energy on the most serious offenses and offenders in their area, particularly incidents that involve the abuse of children (Jewkes & Andrews, 2005).

SUMMARY

Learning Objective 1

Terrorism is the unlawful use or threat of violence against persons and property to further political or social objectives. It is generally intended to intimidate or coerce a government, individuals, or groups to modify their behavior or policies.

Learning Objective 2

Until recently, many Americans did not view terrorism as a serious threat. The realization that they were vulnerable to the violence of political terrorism first came with the bombing of the Murrah Federal Building in Oklahoma City in April 1995. However, Americans soon once again became complacent. On September 11, 2001, every American finally woke up to exactly how vulnerable to terrorism we are at home.

Learning Objective 3

Domestic terrorist groups operating in the United States can be classified as left-wing, right-wing, or special-interest groups. These groups are often disillusioned with government policies and seek changes to the established order through terrorist acts.

Learning Objective 4

International terrorist groups may be based in the United States or in foreign countries. They may live and travel throughout the United States while receiving support and funding from foreign-based groups antagonistic to Americans and to U.S. government policies.

Learning Objective 5

Federal and state governments use a variety of strategies to combat terrorism. One of the most important is counterintelligence, gathering data on people and groups that have a serious potential for future terrorist activities.

Learning Objective 6

Local police officials are generally the first to respond to a terrorist incident. The same investigative precautions and procedures that apply to any crime apply to a terrorist incident. One of the most important elements of investigating a terrorist-related event is the collection and preservation of physical evidence.

Learning Objective 7

Cyber predators use the Internet to locate potential child victims and frequently lure them into meeting with them to engage in sexual activity. Sometimes this sexual activity is consensual, but at other times is forcible. Because it is between an adult and a minor, it is always rape (either forcible rape or statutory).

Learning Objective 8

Users of child pornography do not fit neatly into any category or type of individual. The Internet makes it easy for people who may never have actively sought out traditional forms of child pornography to satisfy their curiosity online, and this may encourage casual users. Users of child pornography may come from all walks of life and show few warning signs of this proclivity toward child pornography.

Learning Objective 9

The most viable strategies for local law enforcement agencies to use in combating cyber predators include acquiring technical knowledge and expertise concerning the use of the Internet, developing specialized Internet units, and cooperating with other agencies to develop information on Internet crimes.

KEY TERMS

terrorism **468**

domestic terrorism **470**

international terrorism **470**

survivalist training **476**

hate group **477**

counterintelligence **484**

crisis negotiation team **487**

cyber predator **490**

cyberstalking **494**

sexual tourism **494**

QUESTIONS FOR REVIEW

Learning Objective 1

1. What is *terrorism*?

Learning Objective 2

2. Why have Americans believed they were invulnerable to terrorist attacks?

3. What events finally made Americans realize exactly how vulnerable to terrorist attacks they are at home?

Learning Objective 3

4. Why has left-wing terrorism declined in the United States in recent years?

5. What do many right-wing militia groups have in common?

6. How are special-interest terrorist groups different from political terrorists?

Learning Objective 4

7. Why do international terrorists target the United States?

8. List three well-known international terrorist groups.

9. What is meant by the *new terrorism*?

Learning Objective 5

10. What is the major difference between investigating conventional criminals and investigating political terrorists?

Learning Objective 6

11. In what ways are investigations of terrorism similar to those of organized crime groups?

12. How are crime scenes handled by patrol units that arrive at a terrorist event?

13. How is physical evidence important to an investigation of terrorist activity?

14. How can even minute bits of physical evidence be helpful in a terrorist bombing case?

Learning Objective 7

15. How might a cyber predator lure a 14-year-old girl into a meeting with him?

16. What are some of the techniques used by cyber predators?

Learning Objective 8

17. How might a child pornographer be located?

18. What are some typical characteristics of a child pornography user?

Learning Objective 9

19. What can a local police agency do to try and reduce cyber crimes in their jurisdiction?

CRITICAL THINKING EXERCISES

1. You are working dispatch, and a phone call comes in reporting a bomb threat.
   a. What will you need to do?
   b. What questions will you ask the caller?

2. Using a variety of resources, write a paper examining the policies and arguments of a political activist group. The group may be an animal rights group, an environmental preservation group, a right- or left-wing group, or a separatist group. If the group has a history of using terrorist tactics, be sure to document them. The report should be at least five pages long and should clearly present the group's ideological stance and political orientation.

INVESTIGATIVE SKILL BUILDERS

Working with Cultural Diversity

You have just begun work as an investigator for a larger city police department. Your partner is of Asian decent, but you are not sure exactly what her ethnicity is. You and your partner are called to a section of town known locally as Little Vietnam, where a robbery has taken place. When you arrive, another Asian officer is already interviewing the proprietor in Vietnamese. You repeatedly hear the term *Viet Chin* mentioned by the storekeeper. You are aware that this is a fairly organized gang of men of Vietnamese decent who have been terrorizing local merchants for protection money. Your partner looks at you and asks, "I don't suppose you speak Vietnamese, do you?" You reply, "No."

1. Should you ask your partner at this point what her ethnicity is?

2. Should you ever ask your partner what her ethnicity is?

3. Should you have answered her question with, "No, I don't, but don't you?"

Integrity/Honesty

You and a partner have been called to the scene of a terrorist hostage situation. A terrorist has taken a kindergarten class hostage, along with its teacher. There are twenty-six children in the class. Originally, the terrorist was demanding the release of political prisoners named on a list he provided to the hostage negotiation team already on the scene. The terrorist has also demanded a helicopter and $2 million in cash. The terrorist has threatened to kill a child every fifteen minutes until his demands are met. To show he means business, he sends the teacher out and shoots her in the back as she walks toward the police. Fifteen minutes later, he sends out a small boy, whom he also shoots in the back. The SWAT team moves in and manages to apprehend the terrorist. You and your partner take the terrorist into custody and are asked to transport him to headquarters.

After your partner has driven several blocks from the crowds and ambulances, he turns into an alley and stops the car. Before you can even ask what he is doing, he has gotten out of the driver's seat and is in the backseat with the terrorist. He immediately begins beating the hand-cuffed man with his nightstick.

1. What is your immediate response?
2. What actions will you take when you get to headquarters?

GLOSSARY

Numbers in parentheses indicate the chapter in which the term is introduced.

ABC surveillance A three-officer foot surveillance in which Officer A follows the subject and in turn is followed by Officer B. The third surveillant, Officer C, normally walks on the other side of the street parallel to subject. (8)

absolute immunity A guarantee that, as long as a witness complies with the court and testifies, the testimony cannot be used against him or her in any criminal action. (19)

accelerant A booster such as gasoline, kerosene, or paint thinner added to a fire to speed its progress. (18)

action stereotyping Misreading common or stereotypic behaviors and interactions of people at or near a crime scene who may actually be the offenders. (10)

adhesive-tape technique A method of collecting microscopic evidence in which transparent tape is used to cover an area to which physical evidence such as fibers may be present. When the tape is pulled off, the evidence adheres to the sticky surface of the tape. (4)

adipocere A whitish-gray, soapy or waxy substance that forms on the surface of a body left for weeks in a damp location. (14)

administrative law The body of law created by administrative agencies in the form of rules, regulations, orders, and decisions, sometimes with criminal penalties for violations. (1)

admission A voluntary statement by the accused person containing information and facts about a crime but falling short of a full confession. (6)

affected terms Words or phrases that convey negative judgments or carry negative or pejorative attitudes about something. (9)

affected words Words that have negative connotations in certain contexts in a given culture. (6)

aggravated arson Malicious and intentional or fraudulent burning of buildings or property and knowingly creating an imminent danger to human life or a risk of great bodily harm to others. (18)

aggravated (felonious) assault An unlawful attack on another person with the intention of causing severe bodily harm. (11)

alarm call Notification of the police by audible or silent alarm that a crime such as a break-in has (or is) occurring. (15)

alcoholic robber A person who robs to sustain an addiction to alcohol or who attributes criminal actions to the influence of alcohol. (10)

alibi A defense offered by a suspect or defendant that attempts to prove that he or she was elsewhere at the time of the crime in question. (6)

alleles Individual differences in base pairs in a DNA sequence. (4)

alligatoring A scalelike burn pattern on wood. Large scales indicate rapid, intense heat; small, flat scales indicate low-intensity heat over a long period of time. (18)

anatomical dolls Dolls or puppets with sex-appropriate genitalia, used in interviews with suspected child victims of sexual abuse or assault. (12)

apprehension The act of seizing or arresting a criminal offender. (5)

arrest report A report that documents the circumstances of the arrest or detention of individuals by the police. (9)

arson Malicious and intentional or fraudulent burning of buildings or property. (18)

asphyxiation Death due to a lack of oxygen and an excess of carbon dioxide in the blood. (14)

assault An unlawful attempt or threat to commit a physical injury to another through the use of force. (11)

attempted arson The demonstrated intent to set a fire coupled with some overt act toward actually setting the fire. (18)

autoerotic asphyxiation Seeking sexual gratification by near asphyxia. (14)

aware hearing A technique of listening and literally hearing what is being said without interrupting the speaker. (6)

base pair Two of four varieties of nucleic acid found on each rung of the DNA ladder. (4)

baseline method A sketching method that takes measurements along and from a single reference line, called a baseline, which can be established by using a length of string, a chalk line, or some convenient means. (3)

battered child syndrome The group of injuries suffered by physically abused children. (11)

battery Once used commonly to refer to actually carrying out the threat of physical harm in an assault; today most jurisdictions use the terms synonymously and call the crime *assault*. (11)

behavioral analysis interview A nonaccusatory interview designed to identify whether a person is telling the truth or withholding information. (6)

blackmail The unlawful demand of money or property under threat to do bodily harm, to injure property, to accuse of a crime, or to expose disgraceful defects; commonly included under extortion statutes. (13)

bloodstains Dried spills or drops of blood at the crime scene. (4)

blood-typing Method of classifying blood into four major groups: A, B, AB, and O. Another factor, called *Rh factor*, also helps determine a person's blood type, which is positive or negative for the Rh factor. (4)

bombing An incident in which a device constructed with criminal intent and using high explosives, low explosives, or blasting agents explodes. (18)

booster device A container, generally a box, with a spring-loaded trap door, allowing the professional shoplifter to conceal stolen goods very quickly. (16)

bore The opening in the barrel of a gun or rifle. (4)

bribe The payment of cash, goods, or services to someone in exchange for some special service, product, or behavior. (20)

bulb The rounded area at the end joint of every finger and thumb. (7)

burglary Entering a building or structure without the consent of the person in possession of that building or structure to commit a crime therein. (15)

burglary tools Any assortment of tools, picks, or household items such as scissors, paperclips, or credit cards used in committing a burglary. (15)

cadaveric spasm A rigidity of certain muscles that usually occurs when the victim is holding something at the time of death and the hand closes tightly around the object; sometimes a sign of suicide. (14)

carjacking Robbery of a car with the driver and or occupants still in it. (10)

cartridge The casing that holds the bullet (projectile), gunpowder, and primer together as a single unit. (4)

case law The sum total of all reported cases that interpret previous decisions, statutes, regulations, and constitutional provisions that then become part of a nation's or a state's common law. (1)

chain of command A supervisory hierarchy; levels of personnel from the top to the bottom providing span of control and regulated communications channels. (2)

chain of custody Proof of the possession of evidence from the moment it is found until the moment it is offered in evidence at court. (2)

child abuse Physical harm, including sexual abuse, or emotional harm inflicted on children. (11)

child molesting Broad term encompassing any behavior motivated by an unnatural sexual interest in minor children. (12)

chop shop A place for chopping, or dismantling, stolen motor vehicles into parts and accessories that cannot be easily identified, which are then resold. (17)

chopping The dismantling of stolen motor vehicles into parts and accessories for use or sale. (17)

circumstantial evidence Evidence of other facts from which deductions can be drawn to show indirectly the facts to be proven. (2)

citizen's arrest An arrest by a private individual, as contrasted with a police officer, permitted under certain circumstances for a felony or for a misdemeanor amounting to a breach of the peace. (11)

classification A method of organizing fingerprints based on particular characteristics. (7)

clear cases To solve criminal cases by arresting, charging a suspect with a crime, and turning the case over to the courts for prosecution. (10)

close surveillance Surveillance conducted while remaining very close in proximity to the subject. (8)

CODIS A computer network combining a database of several indexes of DNA profiles obtained from criminal offenders, crime scenes, and unidentified persons. (4)

cognitive interview An interviewing technique that helps victims or witnesses mentally put themselves at the crime scene to gather information about the crime. (6)

commercial burglary A burglary committed at a place of business or commerce. (15)

commercial robbery Robbery of a commercial location such as a bank, service station, restaurant, or other commercial enterprise. (10)

common law Principles and rules of action based on usage and custom in ancient England and incorporated into colonial American laws and subsequent state statutes. (1)

comparison description A physical description in which a victim or witness notes similarities and differences between the suspect and another person, whose characteristics are known. (2)

compass point method A sketching method that requires a protractor or some method of measuring angles between two lines. One point is selected as the origin, and a line extended from the origin becomes an axis from which angles can be measured. (3)

competency The quality of evidence, or its fitness to be presented, to assist in determining questions of fact; a requirement for admissibility in court; also used to describe a witness as legally fit and qualified to give testimony. (2)

complacency Lack of care resulting from having grown accustomed to a given pattern of events or behavior; taking for granted certain events and circumstances. (11)

complainant An individual who seeks satisfaction or action for an injury or for damages sustained. It may be the victim of a crime or someone acting on behalf of the victim. (6)

complaint A formal allegation by which a legal action is commenced against a party; a request for police action in some matter. (6)

complaint or incident report A police report written to document events surrounding misdemeanor and miscellaneous incidents. (9)

composite description A description obtained by compiling separate, slightly varying descriptions into a whole. (2)

computer virus A computer program, usually hidden within another computer program, that inserts itself into programs and applications and destroys data or halts execution of existing programs. (20)

concentric fractures Irregular, but concentric circular crack patterns in the broken glass around the point of impact. (4)

conchoidal fractures Provides information about the direction of the force that broke the glass because glass breaks first on the side opposite to the force applied to it. (4)

confession A voluntary statement—written, oral, or recorded—by an accused person, admitting participating in or commission of a criminal act. (6)

conspiracy A crime in which two or more parties are in concert in a criminal purpose. (19)

contact wound A wound created when a gun is fired while being held against the skin of the victim; typically found in self-inflicted wounds and in some execution-type murders. (14)

contributing to the delinquency of a minor An act or omission that contributes to making or tends to make a child delinquent. (12)

controlled substance A drug or substance whose use and possession are regulated under the Controlled Substance Act. (21)

convicted offender index Contains DNA profiles of individuals convicted of felony sex offenses and other violent crimes. (4)

convoy Following a subject using multiple surveillants in tandem. (8)

cop speak Specialized vocabulary, or jargon, used by police. (8)

corporate crime Any activity that is undertaken by a corporation for its benefit but which violates the law. (20)

corpus delicti All the material facts showing that a crime has been committed; Latin for "body of the crime." (2)

counterintelligence Gathering political and military information about foreign countries and institutions to prevent terrorist actions. (22)

crazing Irregular cracks and lines in glass and ceramic materials caused by rapid, intense heat. (18)

crime An offense against the public at large, proclaimed in a law and punishable by a governing body. (1)

crime index A collection of statistics in the FBI's Uniform Crime Reports on the number of murder, rape, robbery, assault, burglary, larceny-theft, motor vehicle theft, and arson crimes reported in a calendar year. (10)

criminal homicide (felonious homicide) The wrongful killing of a human being without justification or excuse in the law. Typically, there are two degrees of the offense: murder and manslaughter. (14)

criminal investigation The lawful search for people and things to reconstruct the circumstances of an illegal act, apprehend or determine the guilty party, and aid in the state's prosecution of the offender. (1)

criminal jackets Official police records of criminals. (8)

criminal law The body of law that for the purpose of preventing harm to society defines what behavior is criminal and prescribes the punishment to be imposed for such behavior. (1)

criminalist (or forensic specialist) A person specifically trained to collect evidence and to make scientific tests and assessments of various types of physical evidence. (3)

crisis negotiation team A group of specialists trained to defuse potentially dangerous situations. (22)

cross projection method A sketching method in which the ceiling appears to open up like the lid of a hinged box, with the four walls opening outward. Measurements are then indicated from a point on the floor to the wall. (3)

cults Religious or quasi-religious groups sometimes considered extreme, with followers who sometimes act in an unconventional manner. (5)

custody Loss of the liberty to leave the presence of a law enforcement officer, regardless of whether one has been told specifically, "You are under arrest." (2)

cyber crime Crimes committed on the Internet using the computer as either a tool or a targeted victim. (20)

cyber predator Individuals, usually men, who use the Internet to hunt for victims to take advantage of—especially children, preteens, and teens who may be manipulated or seduced into meeting and engaging in sexual activity. (22)

cyberstalking Using the Internet to track and repeatedly contact people, especially children. Transmitting threatening or sexually explicit messages via e-mail to children. (22)

dactylography The scientific study of fingerprints as a means of identification. (7)

date rape Forced sexual intercourse that occurs between friends or acquaintances or while a couple is on a date; also called *acquaintance rape.* (12)

deductive reasoning Drawing conclusions from logically related events or observations. (1)

deep cover An undercover operation that may extend for a long period of time, during which the officer totally assumes another identity. (21)

defendant In criminal law, the person who is accused of a crime. (1)

defense wound Injuries on the hand or forearms of a victim who has attempted to fend off an attack. (14)

delayed ignition Setting a fire indirectly by means of a mechanical, chemical, or other timing device. (18)

depressant or sedative Any drug used to allay irritation or nervousness; creates lethargy in the user but may also produce a general feeling of calm and well-being. (21)

designer drug Substance produced in clandestine laboratories by adding or taking away something in an existing drug's chemical composition. (21)

diagonal deployment A method of arranging officers to both secure and observe a crime scene. Officers arrange themselves so that each can observe two sides of a building at once by placing themselves at opposing corners of the building. (15)

direct ignition Setting a fire by directly applying a flame. (18)

distribution Selling, trading, giving, or delivering illicit drugs, regardless of whether one stands to profit from the transaction. (21)

DNA fingerprinting In its simplest form, this involves taking a specimen, slicing it into fragments, radiating these fragments, and exposing them to X-ray film. The resulting line patterns on the film are the DNA fingerprints. (4)

DNA profiling A process where DNA is extracted from biological evidence samples collected at a crime scene and compared with samples taken from the victim and suspects. The DNA samples are analyzed and compared to determine whether they have a common origin. (4)

domestic assault Any type of battery that occurs between individuals who are related or between individuals and their significant others. (11)

domestic terrorism An unlawful violent act directed at elements of the U.S. government or population by groups or individuals who are based and operate entirely within the United States and Puerto Rico without foreign direction. (22)

domestic violence statutes Laws that outlaw physical violence against any family member; responding officers serve as the complainant in domestic assault situations under certain circumstances. (11)

drug-addicted robber A person who robs others to sustain an addiction to some type of illegal drug. (10)

due process of law The rights of people suspected of or charged with crimes, prescribed by the U.S. Constitution, state constitutions, and federal and state statutes. (1)

dying declaration A statement given by a victim at a crime scene, in anticipation of death. It is admissible as evidence in court. (2)

electronic evidence Latent evidence in the form of information stored on computers on hard drives in user-created files that may be useful in a criminal investigation. (20)

elimination print   Fingerprints taken of all persons whose prints are likely to be found at a crime scene but who have a lawful reason to have been there and are not suspects. (7)

embezzlement   The misappropriation or misapplication of money or property entrusted to one's care, custody, or control. (20)

employee pilfering   The theft of goods from warehouses, factories, retail businesses, and offices by employees. (16)

enterprise theory of investigation   An approach to criminal investigation that targets entire crime organizations instead of individual criminals within them. (19)

evidence   Any item that helps to establish the facts of a related criminal case. It may be found at the scene of the crime or on the victim or taken from the suspect or the suspect's environment. (3)

evidence report   A report written about the evidence found at a crime scene; usually an evidence inventory is attached as part of the report. (9)

exclusionary rule   The rule that evidence obtained in violation of constitutional guarantees against unlawful search and seizure cannot be used at trial. (2)

excusable homicide   The killing of a human being without intention and where there is no gross negligence. (14)

explosive   Any material that produces a rapid, violent reaction when subjected to heat or a strong blow or shock. (18)

extortion   Obtaining money or property from another by wrongful use of actual or threatened force, violence, or under color of official right; refers to such acts by public officials. (13)

facial recognition systems   Computer-based security systems that are able to automatically detect and identify human faces. (8)

felony   A relatively serious criminal offense punishable by death or by imprisonment for more than a year in a state or federal prison. (1)

felony murder   The killing of a person during the commission or attempted commission of a felony other than murder (e.g., during a robbery). (14)

felony report   A police record created to document the events surrounding a felony. (9)

fence   Slang term for a professional receiver, concealer, and disburser of stolen property. (16)

fingerprint   An impression created by the friction ridges on a person's fingers, palms, or feet. (7)

fire triangle   The three basic elements for a fire: oxygen, fuel, and heat. (18)

fixed, or stationary, surveillance   Close watch on a subject or object from a single location and vantage point, such as a building or vehicle. (8)

follow-up or supplemental report   A report written during the secondary level of criminal investigation, indicating any actions or information obtained after the initial report was written. (9)

forcible rape   Sexual intercourse against a person's will by use or threat of force. (12)

forensic entomologist   A person who specializes in the study of insects in relation to determining the location, time, and cause of death of a human victim. (14)

forensic index   Contains DNA profiles created from various crime scene evidence. (4)

forensic pathology   A specialized field of medicine that studies and interprets changes in body tissue and fluids in relation to criminal investigation. (14)

forensic science   The application of science to law, and the use of science and technology to determine the value of evidence. (3)

forfeiture   The loss of money or property to the state as a criminal sanction. (19)

form section   A boxed section of a police report form designed for fill-in and check-off informational items. (9)

fraud   Misrepresentation, trickery, or deception with criminal intent to deprive someone of his or her property. (16)

friction ridges   Minute raised lines on the surface of fingertips, palms, and heels of feet. (7)

genome   The full complement of an individual's DNA. (4)

geographic profiling   A computer-assisted investigative method that uses locations of a series of crimes to determine the most likely area where an offender may be found. (5)

grand larceny   The taking and carrying away of another's personal property with a value in excess of the cutoff amount in a given jurisdiction, with the intent of depriving the owner of it permanently; generally considered a felony. (16)

grid search pattern   A search pattern that consists of two strip searches, the second perpendicular to the first. It allows the area to be viewed from two angles. (3)

hacker   A person proficient at using or programming a computer and who is capable of infiltrating other computer systems. (20)

hallucinogen   A drug causing changes in sensory perception to create mind-altering hallucinations and loss of an accurate sense of time and space. (21)

hang paper   Knowingly and intentionally writing bad checks; slang expression. (16)

hate group   A group antagonistic toward various minority groups in the United States. (22)

high explosive   An explosive material in which the rate of change to a gas is very rapid; explodes only upon the shock of a blasting cap, a detonation cord, or an electric detonator; includes nitroglycerin, TNT, RDX, and plastic explosives. (18)

homicide   The intentional or negligent killing of one human being by another. (14)

hostage   An innocent person held captive by one who threatens to kill or harm the person if his or her demands are not met and who uses the person's safety to negotiate for money, property, or escape. (13)

hostage negotiator   An individual specially trained to deal with persons holding hostages. (13)

hot pursuit   Crossing jurisdictional lines during an ongoing chase of a suspect. (2)

identification   A process in which physical characteristics and qualities are used to definitely know or recognize a person. (5)

identity theft   Using another person's personal information without that person's permission to commit fraud or other crimes. (16)

impound   To take into legal custody. (17)

incendiary fire   A fire in which a fire-setting device, an igniter, or an accelerant is found. (18)

incest Sexual acts, usually intercourse, between persons who are so closely related that their marriage is illegal or forbidden by custom. (12)

indecent exposure Exhibiting the private parts of one's body in a lewd or indecent manner to the sight of others in a public place. (12)

index offense One of the eight crimes (murder, rape, robbery, assault, burglary, larceny-theft, motor vehicle theft, and arson) that the FBI considers the most serious and that are combined to create the crime index. (10)

individual crimes Individuals acting on their own behalf or with others to defraud the public. (20)

inductive reasoning Making inferences from apparently separate observations or pieces of evidence. (1)

industrial espionage Espionage work undertaken in corporate and industrial areas to keep up with or surpass competitors. (20)

informer A member of an organized crime group who provides information and testimony for law enforcement investigations and prosecutions. (19)

inhalants Substances that cause perceptible changes in brain function through inhalation. (21)

injunction A court order prohibiting a party from a specific course of action or ordering a party to perform some action. (19)

insider trading An employee's or manager's use of information gained in the course of his or her job and not generally available to the public to benefit from fluctuations in the stock market. (20)

integrated automated fingerprint identification system (IAFIS) A computer system maintained by the FBI that uses a mathematically created image identifying up to 250 characteristics of each print; this is the largest centralized biometric database in the world. (7)

international terrorism Violent acts or dangers brought against people or property; intended to intimidate or coerce a civilian population or otherwise affect the conduct of a government by intimidation, assassination, or kidnapping. It must occur outside the borders of the United States or otherwise transcend national boundaries. (22)

interrogation Questioning to obtain information from persons suspected of being directly or indirectly involved in a crime. (6)

interview Questioning to obtain information regarding a person's knowledge about a crime, suspect, or event. (6)

intrafamily violence Any type of violent behavior directed toward a family member. (11)

invisible print A latent print not visible without some form of developing. (7)

jimmy A prying tool or instrument of any sort used to force open a door, window, or lock. (15)

joyriding The temporary taking of a motor vehicle without the intent of permanently depriving the owner of the vehicle; generally undertaken by juveniles. (17)

justifiable homicide The killing of another in self-defense or defense of others when danger of death or serious bodily harm exists. (14)

kickback The payment back of a portion of the purchase price to the buyer or a public official by the seller to induce a purchase or to improperly influence future purchases. (20)

kidnapping Taking another person from one location to another against that person's will using force or coercion. (13)

larceny-theft The taking and carrying, leading, riding, or driving away the personal property of another with the specific intent of permanently depriving the owner of his or her property. (16)

latent print An impression transferred to a surface by sweat, oil, dirt, blood, or some other substance on the ridges of the fingers; it may be visible or invisible. (7)

leading surveillance Type of mobile surveillance where the surveillant walks ahead of the subject. (8)

lewd and lascivious behavior with a child Touching any part of a child to arousal with a child appealing to or gratifying the sexual desires of either the child or the perpetrating adult. (12)

light cover An undercover police operation that extends only as long as the officer's tour of duty. (21)

Lindbergh law Federal antikidnapping legislation passed in 1932. (13)

line of communication A channel for communicating with another person. (13)

livor mortis A dark discoloration of the body where blood has pooled or drained to the lowest level; also called *postmortem lividity*. (14)

low explosive An explosive material in which the rate of change to a gas is quite slow; the material deflagrates, or burns rapidly, rather than exploding; includes black powder, smokeless powder, and fertilizers. (18)

manslaughter The unlawful killing of another without malice. It may be voluntary, upon sudden heat of passion; involuntary, in the commission of an unlawful act; or negligent, occurring as a result of an action that could have been avoided. (14)

manufactured fibers Comprised of two subgroups: regenerated and synthetic fibers. Regenerated fibers are made from natural materials processed from the cellulose in cotton and wood pulp. Synthetic fibers are produced entirely from chemicals. (4)

manufacturing Any activity to cultivate, harvest, produce, process, or manufacture illegal drugs. (21)

materiality The importance of evidence in influencing the court's opinion because of its connection with the issue; a requirement for admissibility in court. (2)

megapixels Refers to picture image resolution. A mega equals 1 million. Pixels are the smallest unit of brightness and color; more pixels means sharper, clearer, and better images. (3)

Miranda warning A cautionary statement to suspects in police custody, advising them of their rights to remain silent and to have an attorney present during interrogation. (2)

misdemeanor A less serious crime that is generally punishable by a prison sentence of not more than one year in a county or city jail. (1)

modus operandi (M.O.) The method of operation that a criminal uses to commit a crime; Latin term for "mode of operation." (5)

money laundering Investing illegally obtained money into businesses and real estate operated and maintained within the law. (19)

motive A wrongdoer's reason(s) for committing a crime. (5)

motor vehicle theft The theft or attempted theft of any type of motorized vehicle. (17)

moving surveillance   The observation of a subject while moving on foot, in a vehicle, or in an aircraft. (8)

Munchausen syndrome by proxy   A parenting disorder in which parents or caregivers, usually the mother, fabricate symptoms in their children to gain attention. (11)

murder   The unlawful killing of a human being by another with malice aforethought. (14)

mutual consent   Willing participation by both parties in sexual acts. (12)

narcotic   Any drug that produces a stupor, insensibility, or sleep. (21)

narrative section   A lined or blank section of a police report form designed for detailed descriptions and accounts of events. (9)

naturally occurring fibers   Derived from various vegetative and animal sources and used in manufacturing cords, ropes, linens, and clothing. (4)

negligent fires   Fires that occur or become uncontrollable as a consequence of culpable negligent behavior, resulting in damage or injury to property or people. (18)

nonalarm call   Notification of the police by citizen alert or direct observation that a crime such as a break-in has (or is) occurring. (15)

occupational crime   The use of one's occupation to illegally obtain personal gain. (20)

opiate   Any of the narcotic drugs produced from the opium poppy. (21)

opportunistic robber   A person who steals small amounts of property or cash whenever the opportunity presents itself. (10)

organized crime   A highly structured, disciplined, self-perpetuating association of people, usually bound by ethnic ties, who conspire to commit crimes for profit and use fear and corruption to protect their activities from criminal prosecution. (19)

payoff   Receiving compensation or money from an individual in exchange for some favor. (20)

payola   A payment to a disc jockey for a favor such as promoting a favorite recording. (20)

pedophile   An adult who is sexually attracted to children or performs sexual acts with children; usually a man with a female victim. (12)

penal code   A collection of state statutes that define criminal offenses and specify corresponding fines and punishments. (1)

perimeter box surveillance   A vehicle surveillance technique that allows surveillants to maintain coverage even if the subject suddenly turns at an intersection. (8)

persuasion   Motivating and convincing a person to offer information or to comply with a request. (6)

petty larceny   The taking and carrying away of another's personal property with a value below the cutoff amount in a given jurisdiction, with the intent of depriving the owner of it permanently; generally considered a misdemeanor. (16)

phishing   A growing form of attempted identity theft in which consumers are contacted via bogus e-mail messages that try to lure them into providing personal information such as their Social Security number or financial account information. (16)

physical stereotyping   A misconception that a criminal is a certain type of person. (10)

pick program   A computer program designed to bypass security measures against duplication of electronic files. (20)

pie (or wheel) search pattern   A search pattern in which the area is divided into pie-shaped sections, usually six in number. Each section is then searched, usually by a variation of the strip search. (3)

plastic print   A type of visible print formed when substances such as butter, grease, wax, peanut butter, and so forth that have a plastic-like texture are touched. (7)

polygraph   A mechanical device that permits an assessment of deception associated with stress as manifested in physiological data. (6)

possession   A drug offense that consists of having a controlled drug on one's person or under one's control such as in the house or vehicle. (21)

precedent   A decision in a court case that furnishes an example or authority for deciding subsequent cases in which identical or similar facts are presented. (1)

predicate crime   A crime that is a basis of a violation of the RICO statute. (19)

preliminary investigation   Fact-gathering activities that take place at the scene of a crime immediately after the crime has been reported to or discovered by police officers. (2)

***prima facie* evidence**   Evidence good and sufficient on its surface to establish a given fact or chain of facts, if not rebutted or contradicted, to be proof of the fact; Latin for "on the surface." (2)

probable cause   Reasonable grounds to believe that a person should be arrested or searched or that a person's property should be searched or seized. (21)

procedural law   The body of law that prescribes the manner or method by which rights and responsibilities may be exercised and enforced. (1)

professional robber   A person who has incorporated robbery into a lifestyle and who robs as a means of economic support. (10)

property report   A specific report directed toward documenting property taken or damaged during a crime. (9)

prosecutor   Name given to the government as the party that accuses a person of a crime. (1)

psychological profiling   A method of suspect identification that seeks to identify an individual's mental, emotional, and personality characteristics as manifested in things done or left behind at the crime scene. (5)

radial fractures   Cracks that start at the center of the point of impact where an object strikes a pane of glass and radiate outward, creating a slightly star-shaped pattern. (4)

ransom   Money, property, or other consideration paid or demanded in exchange for the release of a kidnapping victim. (13)

rape   An act of sexual intercourse, or penetration of the victim's vagina, without consent from the victim and against the victim's will by force, coercion, or duress. (12)

rape kit   An evidence kit typically housed in hospital emergency rooms and used to secure physical evidence specimens in rape cases. (12)

rapport   A relationship of mutual trust and emotional affinity that develops between an interviewer or interrogator and the person being interviewed or interrogated. (6)

reagents Chemicals used to detect or test for the presence of blood or other substances. (4)

recalcitrant witness A witness who refuses to testify in a criminal proceeding, even after being offered immunity. (19)

rectangular-coordinates method A sketching method that involves measuring the distance of an object from two fixed lines at right angles to each other. It is often used to locate an object in a room. (3)

relevancy The applicability of evidence in determining the truth or falsity of the issue being tried; a requirement for admissibility in court. (2)

repression The act of suppressing or preventing an action from taking place. (5)

residential burglary A burglary committed at a dwelling place, whether occupied or vacant. (15)

residential robbery A robbery in which the target is a person in a private residence, hotel or motel room, trailer or mobile home, or other attached areas of a residence. (10)

response time The lag time between a crime being reported and the arrival of police at the crime scene. (10)

restraining order Court order requiring a person to do or refrain from doing a particular thing. (11)

rigor mortis A contracting of muscles of a body after death that disappears over time. (14)

robbery The unlawful taking or attempted taking of another's personal property in his or her immediate possession and against his or her will by force or the threat of force. (10)

rules of evidence Rules of court that govern the admissibility of evidence at trials and hearings. (2)

salvage switch Switching vehicle identification number plates from wrecked vehicles to stolen cars of the same make and model. (17)

seat of the blast The primary location where an explosive has detonated. (18)

sex crime Any of an assortment of criminal violations related to sexual conduct. (12)

sexist language Insensitive, politically incorrect language used in reference to gender or gender issues, occupations, and the like. (9)

sexual seduction Sexual intercourse, or other illegal sexual acts, between an adult and a willing minor child. (12)

sexual tourism Traveling—both in the United States and in foreign countries—for the expressed purpose of locating children with whom to engage in sexual activity, sexual abuse, or sexual exploitation. (22)

shill A slang term for a secret coconspirator or accomplice in a confidence game. (16)

shoplifting The taking of goods from a retail establishment without paying for them, while posing as a customer. (16)

short tandem repeat (STR) loci A standard battery of 13 core loci, each containing a short sequence of DNA, that differ among individuals and can be used for identification. (4)

simple arson Malicious and intentional or fraudulent burning of buildings or property that does not create an imminent risk or threat to human life. (18)

simple assault Intentionally causing fear in a person of immediate bodily harm or death. (11)

situational stereotyping False or mistaken conclusions from the manifest appearance of certain situations. (10)

slim Jim A tool consisting of a sturdy length of metal used by auto and truck thieves to unlock doors. (17)

spalling Chipping, crumbling, or flaking of cement or masonry caused by rapid, intense heat. (18)

spiral search pattern A search pattern typically used in outdoor areas and normally launched by a single person. He or she begins at the outermost corner and walks in a decreasing spiral toward a central point. (3)

stalking Intentionally and repeatedly following, attempting to contact, harassing, or intimidating another person. (11)

standard of comparison A model, measure, or object with which evidence is compared to determine whether both came from the same source. (3)

statutory law The body of laws passed by legislative bodies, including the U.S. Congress, state legislatures, and local governing bodies. (1)

statutory rape Sexual intercourse with a minor, with or without the minor's consent. (12)

stimulant A drug with a stimulating effect on the central nervous system, causing wakefulness and alertness while masking symptoms of fatigue. (21)

sting operation An undercover operation set up by law enforcement personnel to catch, or "sting," offenders committing a crime; often used to collect evidence against thieves. (16)

street robbery Any of an assortment of robberies that occur in street settings. (10)

striations Marks and lines or scratches on the sides of a bullet made as the bullet passes through the rifled bore of a weapon. (4)

stripping Illegally removing parts and accessories from motor vehicles to use or sell them. (17)

strip search pattern A search pattern in which the space to be searched is divided into a series of lanes. One or more searchers proceed up and down the lane, continuing until the area has been completely searched. (3)

substantive law The body of law that creates, defines, and regulates rights and defines crime and its penalties. (1)

suicide bomber An individuals who, using either a vehicle, aircraft, or a self-contained explosive device on his or her person or carried by this individual, detonates the device among a group of people or crashes the vehicle or aircraft into a building, structure, or populated area. (18)

surveillance The secret observation of people, groups, places, vehicles, and things over a prolonged period in an effort to gather information about a crime or criminal behavior. (8)

survivalist training A type of training in which separatist groups practice guerrilla warfare tactics to prepare to protect themselves from law enforcement officials or other agents of the government. (22)

synopsis A summary or abstract of a larger body of writing, such as a police report. (9)

tagging Writing a word, initials, or a symbol on a wall to identify an individual or group such as a gang. (5)

tattooing The burned skin around a gunshot wound resulting from a gun blast (muzzle flash) when fired at close range. (14)

ten-print card A card or form onto which fingerprints and other personal data are transferred and filed for future retrieval. (7)

terrorism The unlawful use or threat of violence against persons and property to further political, social, or religious objectives. It is generally intended to intimidate or coerce a government, individuals, or groups to modify their behavior. (22)

theft The taking of property without the owner's consent; a popular term for larceny. (16)

third degree The use or threat of physical, mental, or emotional cruelty, or water or food deprivation, to obtain a confession. (6)

toxicological screening An examination of body tissue or fluids for poisons or other toxins. (14)

trademark A distinctive characteristic by which a criminal becomes known. (5)

traffic collision report A report that contains all the facts about the accident. (9)

trailer A material (rope or rags soaked in accelerant, shredded paper, gunpowder, fluid accelerant, and so on) used to spread a fire. (18)

triangulation method A sketching method that requires measuring the distance of an object along a straight line from two widely separated, fixed reference points. (3)

undercover operation An investigative police operation designed to secretly uncover evidence against an individual or an organized criminal group. (19)

vehicle-driver robbery Robbery of an object of value in or attached to a vehicle or from the driver of the vehicle. (10)

vehicle identification number (VIN) A non-duplicated, serialized number assigned by a motor vehicle manufacturer (of autos especially) to each vehicle made. (17)

visible print A fingerprint found at a crime scene that is immediately visible to the naked eye. (7)

white-collar crime A non-violent crime committed by an individual or a corporation that is a breach of trust, confidence, or duty. (20)

wipe ring (smudging) A gray ring around a gunshot wound resulting from the deposit of gunpowder by a gun blast at close range. (14)

withdrawal symptoms Symptoms that appear shortly after a drug addict misses a scheduled dose, or *fix;* may include nausea, sweating, chills, physical shaking, diarrhea, constant yawning, insomnia, fatigue, restlessness, anxiety, irritability, muscle aches and pains, and stomach cramping. (21)

zone search pattern A search pattern in which the area is divided into four quadrants, each of which is then examined with one of the other patterns. (3)

REFERENCES

Chapter 1

Ablow, Keith. 2005. *Inside the mind of Scott Peterson.* New York: St. Martins Press.

Atkinson, William W. 2005. *Reasoning: Inductive, deductive, & fallacious.* Whitefish, MT: Kessinger.

Crier, Catherine. 2005. A *deadly game: The untold story of the Scott Peterson investigation.* New York: HarperCollins.

King, Gary. 2001. *Murder in Hollywood: The secret life & mysterious death of Bonny Lee Bakley.* New York: St. Martin's Press.

Rush, George. 2004. *The dictionary of criminal justice* (6th ed.). Gilford, CT: Dushkin/McGraw-Hill.

Sutherland, Edwin, and Donald Cressey. 1974. *Criminology* (9th ed.). Philadelphia, PA: Lippincott.

Sweetingham, Lisa. 2005. Actor Robert Blake acquitted of his wife's murder. Retrieved from http://www.courttv.com/trials/blake/031605_verdict_ctv.html

Chapter 2

Berg, Bruce L. 1999. *Policing in modern society.* Boston, MA: Butterworth/Heinemann.

Best, Arthur. 2004. *Evidence: Examples & explanations* (5th ed.). New York: Aspen.

Biggs, Michael. 2003. *Just the facts: Investigative report writing* (2nd ed.). Upper Saddle River, NJ: Prentice-Hall.

Brown, Michael F. 2003. *Criminal investigation, law, & practice* (2nd ed.). Austin, TX: Thomas Investigative Publications, Inc.

Davis, Joseph N. 2004. *Painless police report writing.* Upper Saddle River, NJ: Pearson/Prentice-Hall.

Emanuel, Steven. 2004. *Evidence.* New York: Aspen.

Gardner, R. 2005. *Practical crime scene processing and investigation.* Boca Raton, FL: CRC Press.

Greenwood, Peter, Jan Chaiken, Joan Petersilia, et al. 1975. *The criminal investigation process: Observations and analysis.* Los Angeles, CA: The RAND Corporation.

Federal Bureau of Investigation. 2004. *Handbook of forensic services 2003.* Washington, DC: U.S. Government Printing Office.

Lepore, Michael. 2004. The 1991 Rodney King police brutality case & the LA riots. Retrieved from http://www.Crimsombird.com/history/RodneyKing.htm

Miranda v. Arizona. 384 US 436, 444 (1966).

Morris, Norval. 1959. Corpus delicti and circumstantial evidence. *Law Quarterly Review* 68:391–396.

Mueller, Christopher B., and Laird C. Kirkpatrick. 2004. *Evidence under the rules: Text, cases, & problems* (5th ed.). New York: Aspen.

National Institute of Justice. 2000. *Crime scene investigation: A guide for law enforcement. Series: Research report.* Technical Working Group on Crime Scene Investigation, National Institute of Justice. Washington, DC: U.S. Government Printing Office.

Ogle, Robert R. 2007. *Crime scene investigation and reconstruction* (2nd ed.). Upper Saddle River, NJ: Prentice-Hall.

Peak, Kenneth J. 2006. *Policing America: Methods, issues, challenges* (5th ed.). Upper Saddle River, NJ: Prentice-Hall.

Perkins, Rollin M. 1962. The corpus delicti of murder. *Virginia Law Review* 48:173–195.

Roberg, Roy R. 2005. *Police & society* (3rd ed.). Los Angeles, CA: Roxbury.

Spelman, W. G., and D. K. Brown. 1981. *Calling the police: A replication of the citizen reporting component of the Kansas City Response Time Analysis.* Washington, DC: Police Foundation.

Uniform Crime Report. 2005. *Crimes in the United States 2004.* Washington, DC: Federal Bureau of Investigations.

Weston, Paul B., and Charles A. Lushbaugh. 2006. *Criminal investigation* (10th ed.). Upper Saddle River, NJ: Pearson/Prentice-Hall.

Yeschke, Charles. 2002. *The art of investigative interviewing* (2nd ed.). Boston, MA: Butterworth/Heinemann.

Chapter 3

Fisher, Barry. 2004. *Techniques of crime scene investigation* (7th ed.). Boca Raton, FL: CRC Press.

Gardner, Ross M. 2005. *Practical crime scene processing and investigation.* Baco Raton, FL: CRC Press.

Geberth, Vernon J. 2006. *Practical homicide investigation* (4th ed.). Boca Raton, FL: CRC Press.

Genge, Ngaire. 2002. *The forensic casebook: The science of crime scene investigation.* New York: Ballantine.

Giard, James. 2007. *Criminalistics: Forensic science and crime.* Boston, MA: Jones and Bartlett.

Lee, Henry C., Timothy Palmbach, and Marilyn T. Miller. 2001. *Henry Lee's crime scene handbook.* New York: Academic Press.

National Institute of Justice. 2004. *Crime scene investigation: A reference for law enforcement.* Technical Working Group on Crime Scene Investigation, National Institute of Justice. Washington, DC: U.S. Government Printing Office.

Ogle, Robert R., Jr. 2004. *Crime scene investigation and reconstruction.* Upper Saddle River, NJ: Prentice-Hall.

Robinson, Edward M. 2006. *Crime scene photography.* New York: Academic Press.

Saferstein, Richard. 2003. *Criminalistics: An introduction to forensic science* (8th ed.). Upper Saddle River, NJ: Prentice-Hall.

Smith, Jeff. 2003. Instant photography for crime scene investigators. *Law & Order* 51(11):56–59.

Staggs, Steven. 1997. *Crime scene & evidence photographer's guide.* Wildomar, CA: Staggs.

Vince, Joseph. 2005. *Evidence collection.* Boston, MA: Jones and Bartlett.

Weston, Paul B., and Charles A. Lushbaugh. 2006. *Criminal investigation: Basic perspectives* (10th ed.). Upper Saddle River, NJ: Prentice-Hall.

Worrall, John L. 2005. *Criminal evidence: An introduction.* Los Angeles, CA: Roxbury.

Chapter 4

Baucher, Elizabeth. 2005. *Document analysis.* Broommall, PA: Mason Crest.

Bennett, Trevor, and Katy Halloway. 2005. The association between multiple drug misuse and crime. *International Journal of Offender Therapy and Comparative Criminology* 49(1):63–81.

Brewster, F., J. Thorpe, G. Gettinby, and B. Caddy. 1985. The retention of glass particles in woven fabrics. *Journal of Forensic Science* 30(3):798–805.

Butler, John M. 2005. *Forensic DNA typing* (2nd ed.). New York: Academic Press.

Butler, John M., and Christopher H. Becker. 2001. *Improved analysis of DNA short tandem repeats with time-of-flight mass spectrometry.*

Washington, DC: U.S. Department of Justice, U.S. Government Printing Office.

Caddy, Brian. 2001. *Forensic examination of glass & paint: Analysis & interpretation.* Boca Raton, FL: CRC Press.

DePresca, John. 1997. Handling crime scene evidence. *Law & Order* (August): 75–79.

Fierro, M. I. 1993. Identification of human remains. In *Medicolegal investigations of death,* W. U. Spitz, ed. Springfiled, IL: Charles C. Thomas.

Goddard, Calvin. 1930. The Valentine Day massacre: A study in ammunition-tracing. *American Journal of Police Science* 1:60–78.

Goldstein, Ira. 1992. Drugs and homicide: Questions for the future. *CESAR Reports, Center for Substance Abuse Research* 2(1):3.

Greenfeld, Lawrence A. 1998. *Alcohol and crime: An analysis on national data on the prevalence of alcohol involvement in crime.* National Symposium on Alcohol Abuse and Crime. Washington, DC: U.S. Department of Justice, U.S. Government Printing Office.

Hatcher, Julian S. 1998. *Textbook of firearms investigation, identification, and evidence.* Richmond, IN: Palladium Press.

Helmer, William J., and Arthur J. Bilek. 2004. *The St. Valentine's Day massacre: The untold story of the gangland bloodbath that brought down Al Capone.* Nashville, TN: Cumberland House.

Hunter, William. 2005. *DNA analysis.* Bloomall, PA: Mason Crest.

James, Stuart H., and Jon J. Nordby. 2005. *Forensic science* (2nd ed.). Boca Raton, FL: CRC Press.

James, Stuart H., and William G. Eckert. 1998. *Interpretation of bloodstain evidence at crime scenes.* Boca Raton, FL: CRC Press.

Josefi, Maria. 1995. *Handbook of forensic science.* Washington, DC: Department of Justice, Federal Bureau of Investigation.

Landsteiner, Karl. 1947. *The specificity of serological reactions.* Boston, MA: Harvard University Press.

Moenssen, A. A., F. E. Inbau, and J. E. Starrs. 1986. *Scientific evidence in criminal cases* (3rd ed.). New York: Foundation Press.

Mokrzycki, Gregg M. 1999. Advances in document examination: The Video Spectral Comparator 2000. *Forensic Science Communication* 1(3). Retrieved from http://www.fbi.gov/hq/lab/fsc/backissu/oct1999/mokrzyck.htm

Ogle, Robert R., Jr. 2004. *Crime scene investigation and reconstruction.* Upper Saddle River, NJ: Prentice-Hall.

Robertson, James. 1992. *Forensic examination of fibers.* Westergate, West Sussex: Ellis Horwood, Ltd.

Rudin, Norah, and Keith Iman. 2001. *Introduction to forensic DNA analysis* (2nd ed.). Boca Raton, FL: CRC Press.

Saferstein, Richard E. 1993. *Forensic science handbook III.* Upper Saddle River, NJ: Prentice-Hall.

Saferstein, Richard E. 2002. *Forensic science handbook I* (2nd ed.) Upper Saddle River, NJ: Prentice-Hall.

Saferstein, Richard E. 2003. *Criminalistics: An introduction to forensic science* (8th ed.). Upper Saddle River, NJ: Prentice-Hall.

Scientific Working Group for Material Analysis. 2005a. Initial examination of glass. *Forensic Science Communications* 7(1). Retrieved from http://www.fbi.gov/hq/lab/fsc/backissu/jan2005/standards/2005standards6.htm

Scientific Working Group for Material Analysis. 2005b. Glass fractures. *Forensic Science Communications* 7(1). Retrieved from http://www2.fbi.gov/hq/lab/fsc/backissu/jan2005/standards/2005standards7.htm

Steadman, G. 2002. Survey of DNA crime labs. *BJS Bulletin,* NCJ 191191.

Williams, Robin, and P. Johnson. 2005. Inclusiveness/effectiveness and intrusiveness: Issues in developing uses of DNA profiling in support of criminal investigations. *Journal of Law, Medicine, and Ethics* 33(3): 545–558.

Chapter 5

Bumgarner, J. (2004). *Profiling and criminal justice in America.* Santa Barbara, CA: ABC-CLIO.

Bureau of Criminal Identification and Investigation. 1964. *Modus operandi and crime reporting manual.* Sacramento, CA: State of California,

Department of Justice, Division of Criminal Law and Enforcement.

Calohan, George H., and Lori Jareo. 2001. *My search for "the Son of Sam."* Lincoln, NE: Writers Club Press.

Chaiken, Jan M., and M. R. Chaiken. 1982. *Varieties of criminal behavior.* Santa Monica, CA: RAND.

Douglas, John E., and Alan Burgess. 1986. Criminal profiling: A viable investigative tool against violent crime. *FBI Law Enforcement Bulletin* (December): 11–12.

Federal Bureau of Investigation 2005. *Crimes in the United States, 2004.* Washington, DC: U.S. Government Printing Office.

Gaines, Larry K., and Victor E. Kappeler. 2003. *Policing in America* (4th ed.). Cincinnati, OH: Anderson.

Geberth, V. 1996. *Practical homicide investigation.* Boca Raton, FL: CRC Press.

Girod, Robert J., Sr. 2004. *Profiling the criminal mind: Behavioral science and criminal investigative analysis.* Lincoln, NE: iUniverse, Inc.

Godwin, Maurice. 1996. *Mapping human predators: The geographic behavior of fifty-four American serial killers.* Paper presented at the 1st International Conference on GeoComputation, University of Leeds, UK, September.

Godwin, Maurice. 2004. *Tracker: Hunting down serial killers.* New York: Thunder's Mouth Press.

Harris, D. 2002. *Profiles in injustice.* New York: New Press.

Holmes, R., and S. Holmes. 2002. *Profiling violent crime: An investigative tool,* (3rd ed.). Thousand Oaks, CA: Sage.

Langer, W. 1978. *The mind of Adolf Hitler.* New York: World Publishing.

Rossmo, Kim. 2000. *Geographic profiling.* Boca Raton, FL: CRC Press.

Weiss, Jim, and Mickey Davis. 2004. Geographic profiling finds serial criminals. *Law & Order* 52 (12):31, 34–38.

Chapter 6

Abrams, S. 1991. The directed lie control question. *Polygraph* 20(1):26–32.

Berg, Bruce L. 2007. *Qualitative research methods for the social sciences* (6th ed.). Allyn & Bacon.

Boetig, Brian Parsi. 2005. Reducing a guilty suspect's resistance to confessing: Applying criminological theory to interrogation theme development. *FBI Law Enforcement Bulletin* 74(8):13–22.

Buckley, Joseph P. 2005. *Essentials of the Reid technique: Criminal interrogations and confessions.* Sudbury, MA: Jones & Bartlett.

Bull, Ray H. 1988. What is the lie-detection test? In *The polygraph: Tests, lies, truth and science,* Geoffrey Davies, ed. Beverly Hill, CA: Sage, 1–10.

Collett, Peter. 2004. *The book of tells.* New York: Bantam Books.

Elley, N. 2001. To tell the truth. *Psychology Today* 34(5):88.

Fisher, R. P., and M. L. McCauley. 1995. Information retrieval: Interviewing witnesses. In *Psychology and policing,* N. Brewer and C. Wilson, eds. Hillsdale, NJ: Erlbaum, 81–99.

Geiselman, Edward R., Ronald P. Fisher, David S. Raymond, Lynn M. Jurkevich, and Monica L. Warhaftig. 1987. Enhancing eyewitness memory: Refining the cognitive interview. *Journal of Police Science and Administration* 15(4):292–295.

Geiselman, R., and R. Fisher. 1997. Ten years of cognitive interviewing. In *Intersections in basic and applied memory research,* D. Payne and F. Conrad, eds. Mahwah, NJ: Lawrence Erlbaum, 291–310.

Gordon, Nathan J., and William L. Fleisher. 2006. *Effective interviewing and interrogation techniques* (2nd ed.). New York: Academic Press.

Graham, Michael. 2004. *Cleary and Graham's handbook of Illinois evidence* (8th ed.). New York: Aspen.

Hollien, Harry. 1990. *The acoustics of crime: The new science of forensic phonetics.* New York: Plenum Press.

Holmes, Warren D. 1995. Interrogation. *Polygraph* 24(4):241.

Inbau, Fred E., John E. Reid, and Joseph P. Buckley. 2004. *Criminal interrogation and confessions* (4th ed.). Sudbury, MA: Jones and Bartlett.

In re Gault. 387 U.S. 1 (1967).

McCloud, Douglas G. 1991. A survey of polygraph utilization. *Law & Order* (September):123–124.

Miranda v. Arizona. 384 U.S. 436, 86 S.Ct. 1602, 16 L.Ed. 2d 694 (1966).

Milne, Rebecca, and Ray Bull. 1999. *Investigative interviewing, psychology, and practice.* Chicago IL: John Wiley & Sons.

Moore, Mark H., V. Petric, and Anthony A. Braga. 2003. *The Polygraph and lie detection.* Washington, DC: National Academics Press.

Moran v. Burbine. 475 U.S. 412, 426 (1986).

Morgan, J. B. 1990. *The police function and the investigation of crime.* Brookfield, VT: Avebury.

Napier, Michael R., and Susan H. Adams. 2002. Criminal confessions overcoming the challenges. *FBI Law Enforcement Bulletin* 71(11):9–18.

Napier, Michael R., and Susan H. Adams. 1998. Magic words to obtain confessions. *FBI Law Enforcement Bulletin* 67(10):11–19.

Navarro, Joe, and John R. Schafer. 2001. Detecting deception. *FBI Law Enforcement Bulletin* 70(7):9–13.

Palmiotto, Michael J. 1995. *Criminal investigation.* Chicago, IL: Nelson-Hall.

Paladin Manual. 1991. *Interrogation: Techniques and tricks to secure evidence.* Boulder, CO: Paladin Press.

Rafky, D. M., and R. C. Sussman. 1985. Polygraphic reliability and validity: Individual components and stress of issues in criminal tests. *Journal of Police Science and Administration* 13(4):280–296.

Richardson, Jerry. 2000. *Magic of rapport.* Capitola, CA: Meta.

Sullivan, John F. 2007. *Gatekeeper: Memories of a CIA polygraph examiner.* Dulles, VA: Potomac Books.

Rosenthal, A. M. 1999. *Thirty-eight witnesses: The Kitty Genovese case.* Berkeley, CA: University of Calif. Press.

Yeschke, Charles L. 2002. *The art of investigative interviewing* (2nd ed.). Boston, MA: Butterworth-Heinemann.

Wainwright, Loudon. 1964. A very special murderer. *Life Magazine* (July 3): 21.

Walters, Stan B. 2002. *Principles of kinesic interview and interrogation.* Boca Raton, FL: CRC Press.

Wasby, Stephen L. 1970. *The impact of the United States Court: Some perspectives.* Homewood, IL: Dorsey.

Zulawski, David E. 2001. *Practical aspects of interview and interrogation* (2nd ed.). Boca Raton, FL: CRC Press.

Chapter 7

Almong, Joseph, and Amnon Gabay. 1986. A modified super glue technique. *Journal of Forensic Science* 31(1):250–253.

Ashbaugh, David R. 1999. *Quantitative-qualitative friction ridge analysis: An introduction to basic and advanced ridgeology.* Boca Raton, FL: CRC Press.

Buracker, Carroll, and William Stover. 1984. Automated fingerprint identification—regional application of technology. *FBI Law Enforcement Bulletin,* 1–5.

Burker, Tod W. 1992. Laser fingerprinting: Technology of the 1990s. *Law & Order* (August):75–76.

CBS News Online. 2002. Sniper ties to suspicious Ala. camp? Retrieved April 7, 2006, from http://www.cbsnews.com/stories/2002/10/24/national/main526805.shtml

Champod, Christophe, Chris J. Lennard, Pierre Margot, and Milutin Stoilovic. 2004. *Fingerprints and other ridge skin impressions.* Boco Raton, FL: CRC Press.

CNN.com. 2002. Prosecutor: Juvenile's fingerprints only ones on sniper rifle. Retrieved April 7, 2006, from http://archives.cnn.com/2002/LAW/11/08/sniper.case/index.html

Collins, Clarence G. 2001. *Fingerprint science.* Belmont, CA: Wadsworth.

Commonwealth v. Albright. 101 Pa. Sup. Ct. 317 (1931).

Digital prints at Union Bank. 2002. *American Banker,* 167(225):18.

Elmer-DeWitt, Phillip. 1985. Take a byte out of crime. *Time* (October 14):96.

Federal Bureau of Investigation. 1984. *The science of fingerprints.* Washington, DC: U.S. Government Printing Office.

Federal Bureau of Investigation. 2000. Unsolved case fingerprint matching. *FBI Law Enforcement Bulletin* 69(3):12–13.

Fisher, Barry. 2003. *Techniques of crime scene investigation* (7th ed.). Boca Raton, FL: CRC Press.

Futrell, Ross. 1996. Hidden evidence: Latent prints on human skin. *FBI Law Enforcement Bulletin* 58(4):21–24.

Guo, Y. C., and L. P. Xing. 1992. Visualizing method for fingerprint on skin by impression on a polyethylene terepthalate (PET) semirigid sheet. *Journal of Forensic Science* 37(2):4–12.

Jones, Gary W. 2000. *Introduction to fingerprint comparison.* Wildomar, CA: Staggs.

Lamble v. State. 96 N.J.L. 231:114 A. 346 (1921).

Lee, Henry C. 2001. *Advances in fingerprint technology* (2nd ed.). Boca Raton, FL: CRC Press.

Lewis, L. A., R. W. Smithwick, G. L. Devault, B. Bolinger, and S. A. Lewis, 2001. Processes involved in the development of latent fingerprints using cyanocrylate fuming technique. *Journal of Forensic Science* 46(2):69–74.

Maltoni, Davide, Dario Maio, Anil K. Jain, and Salil Prabhakar. 2005. *Handbook of fingerprint recognition.* New York: Springer.

McDougall, Paul. 2006. Army tries fingerprint matching to catch Iraq insurgents: Soldiers are carrying field kits they can use to collect digital fingerprints and other physical evidence from battle sites. *Information Week.* Retrieved from http://www.informationweek.com/showArticle.jhtml?articleID=179103427

People v. Jennings. 252 III. 534: 96 N.E. 1077 (1911).

Safferstein, Richard. 2003. *Criminalistics: An introduction to forensic science.* Upper Saddle River, NJ: Prentice-Hall.

Schmerber v. California. 384 U.S. 757, 763–764 (1966).

Silver, Jonathan D. 2003. City neighborhoods, more city police training to do fingerprinting to solve car thefts. *Pittsburgh Post Gazette.* Retrieved April 6, 2006, from http://www.post-gazette.com/neigh_city/20030612printsc3.asp

State v. Ceriello. 86 N.J.L. 309; A. 812 (1915).

State v. Connors. 87 N.J.L. 419; 94A 812 (1915).

Trozzi, Timothy A., Rebecca L. Schwartz, and Mitchell L. Hollars. 2000. *Processing guide for developing latent prints.* Washington, DC: U.S. Department of Justice, Federal Bureau of Investigation.

Willett, Edward. 1997. Fingerprints. *Science Columns.* Retrieved from http://www.edwardwillett.com/Columns/fingerprints.htm

Xinhua New Agency. 2004. US starts taking digital photos, fingerprints of foreign air travelers. COMTEX News Network, Inc. (January 5).

Chapter 8

ACLU Fact Sheet. 2002. ACLU opposes use of face recognition software in airports due to ineffectiveness and privacy concerns. Retrieved from http://www.aclu.org/privacy/gen/15100res20020221.html

ACLU Fact Sheet. 2003. ACLU fact sheet on Patriot Act II (3/28/2003): Justice Department contemplates more sweeping powers. Retrieved from http://www.aclu.org/safefree/general/17383leg20030328.html

Acm IV Security Services. 1993. *Secrets of surveillance: A professional's guide to tailing subjects by vehicle, foot, airplane, and public transportation.* Boulder, CO: Paladin Press.

Adams, Thomas, F. 2007. *Police field operations* (7th ed.). Upper Saddle River, NJ: Prentice Hall.

Brookes, Paul. 2001. *Electronic surveillance* (2nd ed.). Burlington, MA: Newnes.

Etzioni, Amital. 2004. *How patriotic is the Patriot Act?* New York: Routledge.

Feder, Barney, J. 2004. Technology strains to find menace in the crowd. *New York Times* (May 31):5.

Florida v. Riley. 488 U.S. 445 (1989).

Jenkins, Peter. 2003. *Advanced surveillance: The complete manual of surveillance training.* Keighley, UK: Intel.

Katz v. United States, 389 U.S. 347 (1967).

McKeown, Kevin, and Dave Stern. 2000. *Our secrets are my business.* New York: Penguin Putnam.

Monmonie, Mark. 2003. *Spying with maps: Surveillance technologies & the future of privacy.* Chicago: University of Chicago Press.

Podesta, John. 2002. USA Patriot Act: The good, the bad, and the sunset. *Human Rights Magazine.* Retrieved from http://www.abanet.org/irr/hr/winter02/podesta.html

Siljander Raymond, and Darin D. Fredrickson. 2003. *A guide for uniformed & plainclothes personnel.* Springfield, IL: Charles C Thomas.

Staples, William. 2000. *Everyday surveillance.* Lanham, MD: Rowman & Littlefield.

United States v. Causby, 328 U.S. 256 (1946).

United States v. Knotts, 460 U.S. 276 (1983).

Chapter 9

Brown, Jerrold G., and Clarice R. Cox. 1998. *Report writing for criminal justice professionals* (2nd ed.). Cincinnati, OH: Anderson.

CNN.com, 2003. New police cars have voice recognition. Retrieved from http://www.cnn.com/2003/TECH/ptech/10/27/futuristic.cruiser.ap/index.html

Frazee, Barbara, and Joseph N. Davis. 2004. *Painless police report writing: An English guide for criminal justice professionals* (2nd ed.). Upper Saddle River, NJ: Prentice-Hall.

Gastil, J. 1998. Generic pronouns and sexist language: The oxymoronic character of masculine generics. *Sex Roles* 23:629–641.

Godwin, Paul A. 1993. Painless report writing. *Law & Order.* 41(2): 38–42.

Goodman, Debbie J. 2007. *Report it in writing* (4th ed.). Upper Saddle River, NJ: Prentice-Hall.

Guffrey, Jame E. 2004. *Report writing fundamentals for police and correctional officers.* Upper Saddle River, NJ: Prentice-Hall.

Hess, John, and Christopher Thaiss. 1998. *Writing for law enforcement.* New York: Longman.

Hess, Karen M., and Henry M. Wrobleski. 2002. *For the record: Report writing in law enforcement* (5th ed.). Bloomington, IN: Innovative Systems.

Lester, Mark, and Larry Beason. 2004. *The McGraw-Hill handbook of English grammar and usage.* New York: McGraw-Hill.

Manning, Margie. 2000. $150,000 dictation system lets police call in reports. *St. Louis Business Journal* (February): 14.

Meier, Nicholas, and R. J. Adams. 1999. *Plain English for cops.* Durham, NC: Carolina Academic Press.

National Highway Traffic Safety Administration. 2004. Traffic safety facts. Retrieved from http://www-nrd.nhtsa.dot.gov/pdf/nrd30/ncsa/TSF2004/809911.pdf

National Highway Traffic Safety Administration. 2006. NHTSA, Virginia Tech Transportation Institute release findings of breakthrough research on real-world driver behavior, distraction and crash factors. Washington, DC: Author.

Pailca, Sam. 2003. *Office of professional accountability: Annual report.* Seattle, WA: Seattle Police Department, Washington State.

Pasquale, Dan. 2006. Report writing tune-up. *Police Magazine* (April): 23.

Routledge, Devaillis. 2000. *The new police report manual* (2nd ed.). Belmont. CA: Wadsworth.

Rupp, Kelly Rogers. 2004. *Police writing: A guide to the essentials.* Upper Saddle River, NJ: Prentice-Hall.

Swift, Kate, and Casey Miller. 2001. *The handbook of nonsexist writing.* Lincoln, NE: iUniverse.

Chapter 10

Baker, Jerry W., and Carl P. Florez. 1980. Robbery response. *The Police Chief* 47(10):46–47.

Bureau of Justice Statistics. 2005. Criminal victimization in the United States, 2003, statistical tables. Washington, D.C.: US Department of Justice, USGPO, (NCJ 207811) table 107, p. 125.

Collins, Randall. 2005. *Interaction ritual chains.* Princeton, NJ: Princeton University Press.

Conklin, John. 1972. *Robbery and the criminal justice system.* New York: Lippincott.

Digital technology catches bank robbers. 2004. *Organized Crime Digest* (October 14).

Dunlap, R. W. 1997. *Asian home invasion robbery.* Paper presented to the 19th International Asian Organized Crime Conference, Orlando, Florida, April.

Federal Bureau of Investigation. 2005a. *Crime in the United States, 2004.* Washington, DC: U.S. Government Printing Office, Table 1.

Federal Bureau of Investigation. 2005b. *Crime in the United States, 2002.* Washington, DC: U.S. Government Printing Office, Table 19.

Goffman, Irving. 1982. *Interaction rituals.* New York: Pantheon Books.

Guerette, R. T., and R. V. Clarke. 2003. Product life cycles and crime: Automated teller machines and robbery. *Security Journal* 16(1):7–18.

Holt, T., and J. Spencer. 2005. A little yellow box: The targeting of automatic teller machines as a strategy in reducing street robbery. *Crime Prevention and Community Safety* 7(2):15–28.

Hurley, J. T. 1995. Violent crime hits home: Home invasion robbery. *FBI Law Enforcement Bulletin* 64(6):9–13.

Jacobs, Bruce A., Volkan, Topalli, and Richard Wright. 2003. Carjacking, streetlife, and offender motivation. *British Journal of Criminology* 43(4):673–688.

Karlberg, Jennifer C., and Doris J. James. 2005. *Substance dependence, abuse, & treatment of jail inmates, 2002.* Bureau of Justice Statistics, Special Report NCJ 209588. Washington, DC: U.S. Government Printing Office.

Klaus, Patsy. 2004. *Carjacking, 1993–2002.* Bureau of Justice Statistics Crime Data Brief. Washington, DC: U.S. Government Printing Office.

Kellerman, A. L., L., Westphal, L., Fischer, and B. Harvard. 1995. Weapon involved in home invasion crimes. *Journal of the American Medical Association* 273(22):1759–1762.

Martin, Gill. 2000. *Commercial robbery.* Leicester, UK: Perpetuity Press.

Navarro, Mireya. 1995. Miami tourism gaines as crime rate drops. *New York Times* (Travel Advisory Section, June 21):1.

Scott, Michael S. 2003. *Robbery at automated teller machines.* Center for Problem Oriented Policing. Washington, DC: Department of Justice COP Response Center.

Uris, Leon. 1983. *Topaz.* New York: Bantam Books.

Chapter 11

Blackman, Ann, Wendy Coe, Scott Norvell, Elizabeth Rudulph, Andrea Sachs, and Richard Woodbury. 1994. When violence hits home. *Time* (July 4):18–25.

Booth, Cathy, Jeanne McDowell, and Janice C. Simpson. 1993. Till death do us part. *Time* (January 18):38–45.

California penal code. 2006. Belmont, CA: Thompson/West.

Connor, Greg. 1990. Domestic disputes: A model pro-arrest policy. *Law & Order* (February):66–67.

Criminal vicitmization, 2004. 2004. U.S. Department of Justice, Bureau of Justice Statistics (NCJ 210674). Washington, DC: U.S. Government Printing Office.

Crosson-Tower, Cynthia. 2005. *Understanding child abuse and neglect* (6th ed.). Boston, MA: Allyn & Bacon.

Federal Bureau of Investigation. 2005. *Crime in the United States, 2004.* Washington, DC: U.S. Government Printing Office.

Geberth, Vernon J. 1992. Stalkers. *Law & Order* (October):138–143.

Geberth, Vernon J. 1994. Munchausen syndrome by proxy (MSBP). *Law & Order* (August):95–97.

Hanon, K. 1991. Child abuse: Muchausen's syndrome by proxy. *FBI Law Enforcment Bulletin* (December):8–11.

Hayward-Brown, Helen. 2004. Munchausen syndrome by proxy. *Judicial Officers Bulletin* 16(5):33–34, 40.

Hoffman, James. 2005. *Stalkers & Stalking.* master's thesis, Department of Criminal Justice, California State University Long Beach, Long Beach, California.

Jackson, James G. 1996. Ending the cycle. *The Police Chief* 63(2): 33–34.

Langan, Patrick A., and Christopher A. Innes. 1986. *Preventing domestic violence against women.* Bureau of Justice Statistics Special Report. Washington, DC: Department of Justice.

Lasher, Louisa J., and Mary S. Sheridan. 2004. *Muchausen by proxy: Identification, intervention, and case management.* Binghamton, NY: Haworth Press.

Layton, Charles. 2002. The information squeeze. *American Journalism Review* (September). Retrieved from http://www.ajr.org/Article.asp?id=2617

Meloy, J. R. 1999. Stalking: An old behavior, a new crime. *The Psychiatric Clinics of North America* 22:85–99.

Palacios, Norma. 2006. *Domestic violence and self-esteem.* Masters Thesis, Department of Criminal Justice, California State University Long Beach, Long Beach, California.

Payne, Brian K. 2005. *Crime and elder abuse: An integrated perspective.* Springfield, IL: Charles C Thomas.

Police Foundation. 1977. *Domestic violence and the police: Studies in Detroit and Kansas City.* Washington, DC: Author.

Rennison, Callie Marie. 2003. *Intimate partner violence 1993–2001.* Bureau of Crime Statistics Crime Data Brief. Washington, DC: U.S. Department of Justice, Office of Justice Programs.

Roberts, Albert R., and Karel Kurst-Swanger. 2002. Police response to battered women: Past, present, and future. In *Handbook of domestic violence intervention strategies: Policies, programs & legal remedies,* Albert R. Roberts and Marjory Fields, eds. New York: Oxford University Press, 127–146.

Sherman, Lawrence W., and Richard A. Berk. 1984. The specific deterrent effects of arrest for domestic Assault. *American Sociological Review* 49(4):261–272.

Sourcebook. 2004. *Sourcebook of criminal justice statistics on line.* Table 3.163.2004. Retrieved from http://www.albany.edu/sourcebook/pdf/t31632004.pdf.

Stalking fact sheet. 2005. National Center for Victims of Crime, Stalking Resource Center. Retrieved from http://www.ncvc.org/src/AGP.Net/Components/DocumentViewer/Download.aspxnz?DocumentID=40616

Tjaden, Patricia, and Nancy Thoennes. 1998. *Stalking in America: Findings from the National Violence Against Women Survey.* Research in Brief (April). U.S. Department of Justice, Office of Justice Programs, National Institute of Justice Centers for Disease Control and Prevention. Washington, DC: U.S. Government Printing Office.

Tjaden Patricia, and Nancy Thoennes. 2000. *Extent, nature, and consequences of intimate partner violence: Findings from the National Violence Against Women Survey.* Washington, DC: U.S. Department of Justice (NCJ 181867).

Tucker, J. T. 1993. The effectiveness of Florida Stalking Statutes Section 784,048. *Florida Law Review* 45(4):609–707.

Zona, M. A., K. K. Sharma, and J. Lane. 1993. A comparative study of erotomanic and obsessional subjects in a forensic sample. *Journal of Forensic Sciences* 38(4):894–903.

Chapter 12

American Psychiatric Association. 2000. *Diagnostic and statistical manual of mental disorders* (4th ed., *text revision*). Arlington, VA: Author.

Bower, Bruce. 1991. Sex abuse: Direct approach may aid Recall. *Science News* 140(16):245.

Brochman, Sue. 1991. Silent victims: Bringing male rape out of the closet. *The Advocate* 582 (July 30): 38–43.

Bureau of Justice Statistics. 2005. *Criminal victimization in the United States, 2003, statistical tables.* U.S. Department of Justice, Office of Justice Programs, NCJ 207811. Washington, DC: U.S. Government Printing Office.

Carney, Thomas P. 2003. *Practical investigation of sex crimes: A strategic and operational approach.* Boca Raton, FL: CRC Press.

Courtois, Christine A. 1996. *Healing the incest wound: Adult survivors in therapy.* New York: Norton.

Erickson, Eric. 1963. *Childhood and society* (2nd ed.). New York: Norton.

Fontana-Rosa, J. C. 2001. Legal competency in a case of pedophilia: Advertising on the Internet. *International Journal of Offender Therapy and Comparative Criminology* 45(1):118–128.

Gullo, David. 1994. Child abuse: Interviewing possible victims. *FBI Law Enforcement Bulletin* 63(1):19–22.

Hickey, Eric W. 2006. *Sex crimes and paraphilia.* Upper Saddle River, NJ: Prentice-Hall.

Jampole, Lois, and Kathie M. Weber. 1987. An assessment of the behavior of sexually abused and nonsexually abused children with anatomically correct dolls. *Child Abuse and Neglect.* 11(2):9–12.

Keppel, Robert, D., and Richard Walter. 1999. Profiling killers: A revised classification model for understanding murder. *International Journal of Offender Therapy and Comparative Criminology* 43(4):417–439.

Litton, Shay. 2006. Characteristics of child molesters. In *Sex Crimes and Paraphilia,* Eric W. Hickey, ed. Upper Saddle River, NJ: Prentice-Hall, p. 319–328.

Lynch, Raymond, and Michael Bussiculo. 1991. A law enforcement officer's guide to interviewing child sex abuse victims. *Law & Order* (May):90–94.

Meadows, Susannah. 2006. Lacrosse scandal: The Duke accuser—new credibility questions. *Newsweek* (June 19): 8.

Murray, J. B. 2000. Psychological profile of pedophiles and child molesters. *Journal of Psychology* 134(2):211–224.

New saliva kit for crime scene and rape kit analysis. *Journal of Clinical Engineering* 31(2):75.

Office for Victims of Crime. 2000. *First response to victims of crime: A handbook for law enforcement officers.* U.S. Department of Justice Office of Justice Programs, NCJ 176971. Washington, DC: U.S. Government Printing Office.

Overton, W. C., D. Burns, and J. Atkins. 1994. Child sexual abuse investigation. *Law & Order* (July):97–100.

Rosenberg, Howard. 2005. Let TV go to the circus: The public wants and deserves to see Jacko's trial. *Broadcasting & Cable* 135(10):50.

Salfati, C. Gabrielle, and Alicia L. Bateman. 2005. Serial homicide: An investigation of behavioral consistency. *Journal of Investigative Psychology and Offender Profiling* 2(2):221–244.

Showalter, Elaine. 2005. Is Jacko our Wilde man? *LA Times* (June 12, Local Section):1.

Tobin, Pnina, and Levinson Kessner. 2002. *Keeping kids safe: A child sexual abuse prevention manual.* Alameda, CA: Hunter House Inc.

Wilson, Sandy, and S. L. Bolton. 2000. *Daddy's apprentice: Incest, corruption, and betrayal—a survivor's story.* Boston, MA: Writer's Showcase Press.

Zulawski, David E. 2001. *Practical aspects of interview and interrogation* (2nd ed.). Boca Raton, FL: CRC Press.

Chapter 13

Associated Press. 2006. Al-Qaida-linked group claims GIs' abduction. Associated Press (June 19).

Chamelin, Neil C. 2005. *Criminal law for police officers* (9th ed.). Englewood Cliffs, NJ: Prentice-Hall.

Chrabot, Toni Marie, and Winnie D. Miller. 2004. Kidnapping investigations: Enhancing the flow of information. *FBI Law Enforcement Bulletin* 73(7):12–16.

CourtTV. 2002. Police: Gunman kidnaps Utah girl. Retrieved from http://www.courttv.com/archive/news/2002/0605/abduct_ap.html

Haberman, Maggie, and Jeane MacIntosh. 2003. *Held captive: The kidnapping and rescue of Elizabeth Smart.* New York: Avon.

Hoff, Patricia. 2000. *Parental kidnapping: Prevention and remedies.* Washington, DC: American Bar Association, Center on Children and the Law.

Johnson, Kevin, and Toni Locy. 2004. Low pay squeezes FBI agents—and perhaps U.S. security. *USA Today* (April 5):1.

Kirn, Walter. 2002. Invasion of the baby snatchers. *Time International* (August 18):64.

Messick, Hank, and Burt Goldblatt. 1974. *Kidnapping: The illustrated history.* New York: Dial.

United States Code. 1970. Title 18, Secs. 873, 875–877.

Whitcomb, Christopher. 2002. *Cold zero: Inside the FBI hostage rescue team.* Clayton, Australia: Warner Books.

Chapter 14

Bass, William, and Jon Jefferson. 2004. *Death's acre: Inside the legendary forensic lab the Body Farm where the dead do tell tales.* Berkeley, CA: Berkeley Trade.

Chamelin, Neil C. 2005. *Criminal law for police officers* (9th ed.), Englewood Cliffs, NJ: Prentice-Hall.

Combs, D. L., R. Gibson Parrish, and Roy Ing. 1992. *Death investigation in the United States and Canada.* Atlanta, GA: U.S. Department of Health and Human Services, Public Health Service, Centers for Disease Control.

Federal Bureau of Investigation. 2005. *Crime in the United States, 2004.* Washington, DC: U.S. Government Printing Office.

Gebreth, Vernon J. 1996. *Practical homicide investigations: Tactics, procedures and forensic techniques* (3rd ed.). Boca Raton, FL: CRC Press.

Gosink, P. D., and M. I. Jumbelic. 2000. Autoerotic asphyxiation in a female. *American Journal of Forensic Medical Pathology* 21(2):114–118.

Haskell, N. H., David G. McShaffrey, D. A. Hawley, R. E. Williams, and J. E. Pless. 1989. Use of aquatic insects in determining submersion interval. *Journal of Forensic Science* 34(3): 622–623.

Klaassen, Curtis D., and John B. Watkins. 2004. *Casarett and Doull's essentials of toxicology.* Boston, MA: McGraw-Hill.

Pranijic, N., and H. Mujagic. 1998. Gasoline sniffing and lead toxicity in workers at gasoline stations. *Journal of Occupational and Environmental Medicine* 40(11):1024.

Ribowsky, Shiya, and Tom Shachtman. 2006. *Dead center: Behind the scenes at the world's largest medical examiner's office.* New York: Regan Books.

Rodriguez, W. C., and C. Bass. 1983. Determination of time of death by means of carrion insects. Paper presented at the annual meeting of the American Academy of Forensic Sciences, February 15–19, Cincinnati, Ohio.

Sach, Jessica Snyder. 2002. *Nature, forensics, and the struggle to pinpoint time of death.* Jackson, TN: Perseus Books Group.

Schama, Simon. 1992. *Dead certainties: Unwarranted speculations.* New York: Vintage Books.

Uva, J. 1995. Autoerotic asphyxiation in the United States. *Journal of Forensic Sciences* 40:570–583.

Thompson, Helen. 1971. *Murder at Harvard.* New York: Houghton Mifflin.

Zugible, Frederick, and David L. Carroll. 2005. *Dissecting death: Secrets of a medical examiner.* New York: Broadway Publishing.

Chapter 15

Bean, Matt. 2002. Guards: Ryder cut tags off merchandise and then hid them. *CourtTV News.* Retrieved from http://www.courttv.com/archive/trials/ryder/103002_ctv.html

Budd, T. 1999. *Burglary of domestic dwellings.* London: Home Office.

Chamelin, Neil C. 2005. *Criminal law for police officers* (9th ed.). Englewood Cliffs, NJ: Prentice-Hall.

Cromwell, Paul F., and James. N. Olson. 2003. *Breaking and entering: Burglars on burglary.* Belmont, CA: Wadsworth.

Dolan, Matthew. 2006. Thieves turn down ATMs, caring them open or carrying them away. *Baltimore Sun.* Retrieved from http://www.securityinfowatch.com/article/article.jsp?siteSection=339&id=8717

Eck, John E. 1992. *Solving crimes: The investigation of burglary and robbery.* New York: Police Executive Research Forum. Washington, DC: National Institute of Justice, United States Department of Justice.

Federal Bureau of Investigation. 2005. *Crime in the United States, 2004.* Washington, DC: U.S. Government Printing Office.

Hakim, Simon, and Yochanan Shachmurive. 1996. Spatial and temporal patterns of commercial burglaries: The evidence examined. *American Journal of Economics and Sociology* (October):1–16.

Jacobson, Jessica, Lee Maitland, and Mike Hough. 2003. *The reducing burglary initiative: Investigating burglary.* London, UK: Home Office Research Study 264.

Macintrye, Stuart Dunlop. 2001. *Burglary decision making.* Ph.D. dissertation. Faculty of Arts, School of Criminal Justice, Griffith University.

NBC4.TV. 2006. Break-in at Tiffany: Thief smashes jewelry case with hammer. Retrieved from http://www.nbc4.tv/news/6891061/detail.

html?subid=10101581.

O'Reilly, Harry T. 1991. *Practical burglary investigation.* Huntsville, TX: OICJ Publications.

Tobias, Marc Weber. 2000. *Locks, safes and security: An international police reference.* Springfield, IL: Charles C Thomas.

Victim Support National Office. 2005. *Investigating the practical support needs of burglary victims.* London: Author.

Chapter 16

Associated Press. 2006. Secret Service investigating counterfeiting scheme. Retrieved from http://cbs2chicago.com/topstories/local_story_212085956.html

Adkins, Ottie. 1975. Crimes against the elderly. *Police Chief* 42(1):40.

Cameron, Mary Owen. 1964. *The booster and the snitch.* New York: Free Press.

Christman, John H., and Charles A. Sennewald. 2006. *Shoplifting: Managing the problem.* Alexandria, VI: ASIS International.

Federal Bureau of Investigation. 2005. *Crime in the United States, 2004.* Washington, DC: Department of Justice, U.S. Government Printing Office.

Garcia, James L. 1992. Health insurance fraud: A growing problem, *USA Today* 120(2562):29–30.

Hyde, Stephen, and Gene Zanetti. 2002. *Players: Con men, hustlers, gamblers and scam artists.* New York: Thunder's Mouth Press.

Insurance Information Institute. 2006. Insurance fraud. Retrieved from http://www.iii.org/media/hottopics/insurance/fraud/

Klemke, Lloyd. 1992. *The sociology of shoplifters: Boosters and snitches Today.* Westport, CT: Praeger.

LaBonte, Jay. 2006. *The truth about check fraud.* Morrisville, NC: Lulu Press.

McCaghy, C. H., and S. A. Cernkovick. 1987. *Crime in American society.* New York: Macmillan.

Montague, David A. 2004. *Fraud prevention techniques for credit card fraud.* Victoria, CA: Trafford.

O'Hara, Charles E., and Gregory L. O'Hara. 2003. *Fundamentals of criminal investigation* (7th ed.). Springfield. IL: Charles C Thomas.

Sennewald, Charles A., and John Tsukayama. 2001. *The process of investigation.* Woburn, MA: Butterworth-Heinemann.

Sharpe, Charles. 2004. *Frauds against the elderly.* Jefferson, NC: McFarland.

Shulman, Terrence Daryl. 2003. *Something for nothing: Shoplifting addiction and recovery.* Harverford, PA: Infinity.

Star Systems. 2003. New survey shows consumers willing to do their part, eager for use of existing solutions. Retrieved from http://www.star.com/?go=press.ShowSingleRelease&id= 80.

Star Systems. 2005. New identity theft survey reveals latest count of victims, need for greater protection. Retrieved from http://www.star.com/?go=press.ShowSingleRelease&id=111.

U.S. Secret Service. 2006a, Counterfeit Deterrence. *Fact Sheet: The New Color of Money.* Washington, DC: The U.S. Secret Service Office of Public Affairs.

U.S. Secret Service. 2006b. The US Treasury, Federal Reserve and US Secret Service Announce the Redesign of the $5 Note. *Fact Sheet: The New Color of Money.* Washington, DC: U.S. Secret Service Office of Public Affairs.

Wade, Collen, and Yvette E. Trozzi, 2003. *Handbook of forensic services.* Quantico, VI: FBI Laboratory Publication, Federal Bureau of Investigation.

Wallechinsky, David, and Amy Wallace. 2005. *The new book of lists: The original compendium of curious information.* New York: Canongate Books U.S.

Walsh, James. 2003. *You can't cheat an honest man* (2nd ed.). Aberdeen, WA: Silver Lake.

Warr, Mark, Alfred Blumstein, and David Farrington. 2002. *Companions in crime: The social aspects of criminal conduct.* New York: Cambridge University Press.

Wyman, J. Robert. 1999. *Loss prevention and the small business: The security professional's guide to asset protection strategies.* Woburn, MA: Butterworth-Heinemann.

Chapter 17

Beckman, Mary E., and Michael R. Daly. 1990. Motor vehicle theft investigations: Emerging international trends. *FBI Law Enforcement Bulletin* 59(9):16.

Bishop, Bill. 2006. No brakes on car theft in county. *The Register–Guardian* (Eugene, OR). May 28:A1.

Carpenter, Cheryl, Barry Glassner, Bruce Johnson, and Julia Loughlin. 1988. *Kids, drugs, and crime.* Lexington, MA: D. C. Heath, 187–208.

CCC Information Services, Inc. 2006. Retrieved from http://www.cccis.com/IndexAction.do

Federal Bureau of Investigation. 2005. *Crime in the United States, 2004.* Washington, DC: Department of Justice, U.S. Government Printing Office.

Federal Bureau of Investigation. 2006. Preliminary crime statistics for 2005. Press Release. Washington, DC: Department of Justice.

Garabedian, Peter, and Don C. Gibbons. 2005. *Becoming delinquent: Young offenders & the correctional process.* New Brunswick: Aldine Transaction.

Glassner, Barry, Bruce L. Berg, Margret Ksander, and Bruce Johnson. 1988. The deterrence effect of juvenile versus adult jurisdiction. *Social Problems.* 31(2):219–221.

Hawkins, Nancy E. 1984. Recognizing stolen vehicles. *The National Centurion* 2(6):32.

Hildreth, Reed. 1990. The CAT program. *Law & Order* (May):92–93.

Maxfield, Michael G., and R. V. G. Clarke. (Eds.). 2004. *Understanding and preventing car theft.* Crime Prevention Studies, vol. 17. Monsey, NY: Criminal Justice Press, Willow Tree Press.

National Insurance Crime Bureau. 2006. Vehicle theft fraud: Taking an age-old crime to the next level. Retrieved from www.nicb.org/cps/rde/xbrc/SID-4031FED9A-8DE73B5/nicb VEHICLE-THEF-FRAUD.pdf

Sanders, Bill. 2005. *Youth culture & youth culture in the inner city.* New York: Routledge.

Stern, G. M. 1990. Effective strategies to minimize auto thefts and break-ins. *Law & Order* (July): 65–66.

Chapter 18

Akhavan, Jacqueline. 2004. *The chemistry of explosives.* Cambridge, UK: The Royal Society of Chemistry.

Almirall, Jose E., and Kenneth G. Furton. 2004. *Analysis and interpretation of fire scene evidence.* Boca Raton, FL: CRC Press.

Angle, James, Michael Gala, William Lombardo, Craig Maciuba, and David S. Harlow. 2001. *Firefighting strategies and tactics.* Albany, NY: Delmar.

Avillo, Anthony. 2002. *Fireground strategies.* Tulsa, OK: Pennwell.

Beveridge, Alexander. 1998. *Explosions.* Bristol, PA: Taylor and Francis.

Bouquard, Thomas J. 2004. *Arson investigation: The step-by-step procedures.* Srpingfield, IL: Charles C Thomas.

Canfield, D. V. 1984. Causes of spalling of concrete at elevated temperatures. *Fire and Arson Investigator* 34 (June):324–331.

Crippin, James B. 2006. *Explosives and chemcial weapons identification.* Boca Raton, FL: CRC Press.

Daeid, Niamh Nic. 2004. *Fire investigation.* Boca Raton, FL: CRC Press.

DeHaan, John D. 2002. *Kirk's fire investigation,* (4th ed.). Saddle River, NJ: Prentice-Hall.

Department of Justice. 2000. *A guide for explosion and bombing scene investigation.* Washington, DC: National Institute of Justice, U.S. Government Printing Office.

Ehrenfeld, Rachel. 2005. *Funding evil: how terrorism is financed—and how to stop it.* Chicago, IL: Bonus Books.

Eversole, John M., and Robert C. Barr (eds.). 2003. *The fire chief's handbook* (6th ed.). Tulsa, OK: Pennwell.

Fischer, Robert, and Richard J. Janoski. 2000. *Loss prevention and security applications for contemporary problems.* Woburn, MA: Butterworth-Heinemann.

Fisher, Barry A. J. 2004. *Techniques of crime scene investigation.* Boca Raton, FL: CRC Press.

Fitch, Richard D., and Edward A. Porter. 1997. *Accidental or incendiary?* Springfield, IL: Charles C Thomas.

Ford, Jean Otto. 2005. *Explosives and arson investigation.* Broomall, PA: Mason Crest.

Gardner, Ross, M. 2005. *Practical crime scene processing and investigation.* Boca Raton, FL: CRC Press.

International Association of Chiefs of Police. 2005a. Suicide (homicide) bombers: Part I. *Training key number 581.* Alexandria, VA: Author.

International Association of Chiefs of Police. 2005b. Suicide (homicide) bombers: Part II. *Training key number 582.* Alexandria, VA: Author.

Icove, David J., and John D. DeHaan. 2003. *Forensic fire scene reconstruction.* Saddle River, NJ: Prentice-Hall.

Krzeszowski, Frank E. 1993. What sets off an arsonist. *Security Management* (January): 42–47.

Lentini, John J. 2006. *Scientific protocols for fire investigation.* Boca Raton, FL: CRC Press.

National Fire Protection Association. 1995. Fire patterns. Sections 921–925. Boston, MA: Author.

Norman, John. 2006. *Fire officer's handbook of tactics.* Saddle Brook, NJ: Penn Well.

Oklahoma Today. 2005. *The official record of the Oklahoma City bombing.* Norman, OK: University of Oklahoma Press.

Poland, James M. 2005. *Understanding terrorism.* Upper Saddle River, NJ: Prentice-Hall.

Quintiere, James G. 1997. *Principles of fire behavior.* Albany, NY: Delmar.

Redsickler, David R. 2007. *Practical fire and arson investigation* (3rd ed.). Boca Raton, FL: CRC Press.

Siegel, Jay A., and Max M. Houck. 2006. *Fundamentals of forensic science.* Burlington, MA: Elsevier Academic Press.

Stewart, Gail. 2006. *Crime scene investigations: Bombings.* Chicago, IL: Lucent Books.

Thurman, James T. 2006. *Practical bomb scene investigation.* Boca Raton, FL: CRC Press.

Tomajczyk, Stephen F. 1999. *Bomb squads.* Osceola, WI: MBI.

Trimm, Harold H. 2005. *Barron's forensics the easy way.* Hauppauge, NY: Barron's Educational Series.

Vince, Joseph J. and William E. Sherlock. 2005. *Evidence collection.* Boston, MA: Jones & Bartlett.

Zedalis, Debra D. 2006. *Female suicide bombs.* Jefferson, NC: Mcfarland.

Chapter 19

Abadinsky, Howard. 2006. *Organized crime* (8th ed.). Belmont CA: Wadsworth.

Albanese, Jay. 1995. *Organized crime in America* (3rd ed.). Cincinnati, OH: Anderson.

Albanese, Jay, and Robert D. Pursley. 1993. *Crime in America: Some existing and emerging issues.* Englewood Cliffs, NJ: Prentice-Hall.

Blok, A. 2001. *Honour and violence.* Malden, MA: Blackwell.

Castells, Manuel. 2000. *End of millennium.* Malden, MA: Blackwell.

Chamelin, Neil C. 2005. *Criminal law for police officers* (9th ed.). Englewood Cliffs, NJ: Prentice-Hall.

Chepesiuk, Ron. 2005. *Drug lords: The rise and fall of the Cali cartel.* Lancashire, UK: Milo Books Limited.

Connors, Edward, Barbara Websterm, Newl Miller, Claire Johnson, Elizabeth Fraser, and Bill Falcon. 1997. *Urban street gang enforcement.* Collingdale, PA: Diane.

Davis, James. 1982. *Street gangs: Youth, biker and prison gangs.* Dubuque, IA: Kendall/Hunt.

Dickie, J. 2004. *Cosa Nostra: A history of the Sicilian Mafia.* New York: Palgrave Macmillan.

Dileva, Anthony. 2006. *La Cosa Nostra: A historical look at the Mafia's influence on American organized crime.* Unpublished thesis. Department of Criminal Justice, California State University, Long Beach.

Federal Bureau of Investigation. 1993. *An introduction to organized crime in the United States.* Organized Crime/Drug Branch, Criminal Investigative Division (July). Washington, DC: U.S. Government Printing Office.

Federal Bureau of Investigation. 2005. Italian organized crime. Retrieved from www.fbi.gov/hq/cid/orgcrime/lcn/ioc.htm

Federal Bureau of Investigation. 2006. Asian criminal enterprises. Retrieved from www.fbi.gov/hq/cid/orgcrime/aace/asiancrim.htm

Finckenauer, James. 2008. *Organized crime in America* (2nd ed. rev.). Belmont, CA: Wadsworth.

Frank, Marcus. 2003. *Asian criminal enterprises.* Paper presented at the 25th International Asian Organized Crime Conference, Boston, MA (May 25–30).

House Committee on Foreign Affairs. 1994. *The threat of international organized crime: Hearing before the Subcommittee on International Security, International Organizations and Human Rights.* Washington, DC: U.S. Government Printing Office.

Kaplan, David E., and Alec Dubro. 2003. *Yakuza: Japan's criminal underworld.* Berkeley, CA: University of California Press.

Katz, Charles M., and Vincent J. Webb. 2006. *Policing gangs in America.* New York: Cambridge University Press.

Kelly, Robert J. 2000. *Encyclopedia of organized crime in the U.S.: From Capone's Chicago to the new urban underworld.* Westport, CT: Greenwood Press.

Kleinknecht, William. 1996. *The new ethnic mobs.* New York: Free Press.

Lunde, P. 2004. *Organized crime: An inside guide to the world's most successful industry.* New York: DK Publishing.

Maas, Peter. 1968. *The Valachi Papers.* New York: Bantam.

Martens, Frederick, and Michael Cunningham-Niederer. 1985. Media magic, Mafia mania. *Federal Probation* 49:60–68.

Mather, Chris. 2004. *Crime school: True crime meets the world of business and finance.* Buffalo, NY: Firefly Books.

McIllwain, Jeffery Scott. 2004. *Organized crime in Chinatown: Race and racketeering in New York City, 1890–1910.* Jefferson, NC: McFarland.

Nardini, William J. 2006. Investigating and prosecuting organized crime in the United States. *Journal of International Criminal Justice* 4(3):528–538.

President's Commission on Organized Crime. 1983. *America's habit.* Washington, DC: U.S. Government Printing Office.

Raab, S. 2005. *Five families: The rise, decline, and resurgence of America's most powerful mafia empires.* New York: St. Martin Press.

Sardijin, M. R. J. 2006. *Chinese human smuggling in transit.* Devon, UK: William Publishing.

Schatzberg, Rufus, and Robert J. Kelly. 1997. *African American organized crime.* New Brunswick, NJ: Rutgers University Press.

Sher, Julian, and William Marsden. 2006. *Angels of death: Inside the biker gang's crime empire.* New York: Carroll and Graf.

Smithson, Michael W. 2003. *Encyclopedia of murder and violent crime.* Thousand Oaks, CA: Sage.

Spergel, Irving. 1993. *Gang suppression and intervention.* Darby, PA: Diane.

Ter Haar, B. J. 2000. *The ritual and mythology of the Chinese triad: Creating an identity.* Leiden, The Netherlands: Koninklijke Brill N.V.

Varese, Frederico. 2005. *The Russian mafia: Private protection in a new market economy.* New York: Oxford University Press.

Walker, Robert. 2007. Asian gang members marks, scars and tatoos. *Gangs or us.* Retrieved March 17, 2007, from www.gangsorus.com/asianmarks.htm

U.S. Department of Justice. 2005. High-ranking Colombian drug traffickers plead guilty to cocaine charges. Press Release. Retrieved from www.usdoj.gov/usao/fls/PressRelease/051118-01.html

Youngers, Coletta A., and Eileen Rosin. 2005. *Drugs and democracy in Latin America: The impact of U.S. policy.* Boulder, CO: Lynn Rienner.

Chapter 20

Aghatise, Joseph. 2006. Cybercrime definition. Computer Crime Research Center. Retrieved from www.crime-research.org/articles/joseph06

Benson, Michael, Francis Cullen, and William Maakestad. 1990. Local prosecutors and corporate Crime. *Crime and Delinquency* 36:356–372.

Brownlee, W. Elliot. 2004. *Federal taxation in America: A short history* (2nd ed.). New York: Cambridge University Press.

Bureau of Justice Statistics. 1987. *Federal offenses and offenders: White collar crime, a special report.* Washington, DC: Department of Justice, U.S. Government Printing Office.

Chua-Eoan, Howard. 1996. The predator's fall. *Time* 145(25):36–38.

Clinard, Marshal, and Richard Quinney. 1973. *Criminal behavior systems: A typology.* New York: Holt, Rinehart & Winston.

CNN/Money. 2004. Stewart convicted on all charges. Retrieved from http://money.cnn.com/2004/03/05/news/companies/martha_verdict/

Conley, C. H., and J. T. McEwen. 1990. Computer crime. *NIJ Reports* 218:2–7.

Crumbley, D. Larry. 2003. *Forensic and investigative accounting.* Chicago, IL: CCH Incorporated.

Doody, Angela. 2004. Former CEO faces criminal charges. *Central Penn Business Journal* (October 22). Retrieved from www.allbusiness.com/specialty-businesses/non-profit-businesses/1168060-1.html

Edelhertz, Herbert. 1970. *The nature, impact and prosecution of white collar crime.* Washington, DC: National Institute of Law Enforcement and Criminal Justice.

Edelhertz, Herbert, et al. 1977. *The investigation of white collar crime: A manual for law enforcement agencies.* Washington, DC: National Institute of Justice.

Emigh, Jacqueline. 2004. Cyber-crime can have real-world ramifications. Access and Control & Security Systems (January). Retrieved from www.stat.harris.com/news/media/Article_Cyber_Crime_1_04.pdf#search=%22cyber%20crimes%20listed%22

Federal Bureau of Investigation, 2003. White collar crime. *Facts and figures.* Washington, DC: Department of Justice, U.S. Government Printing Office.

Fletcher, Pascal. 1996. Cuban court gives Vesco 13 years. *USA Today* (August 27):5A.

Friedrichs, David O. 2002. Occupational crime, occupational deviance, and workplace crime: Sorting out the difference. *Criminal Justice* 2(3):243–256.

General Accounting Office. 1989. *Thrift failures: Costly failures resulted from regulatory violations and unsafe practices.* Report to Congress. Washington, DC: General Accounting Office, T-AFMD-89-4, June.

Gordon, Gary G. 1996. White collar/economic crimes: Breaking out of the white collar paradigm. *Proceedings of the academic workshop on definitional dilemma: Can and should there be a universal definition of white-collar crime.* National White Collar Crime Center and West Virginia University, June 20–22.

Heller, Gary. 2004. *White holler crime:* Club fed and the federal courthouse. Oakland, CA: Red Anvil Press.

Internal Revenue Service. 2006a. IRS updates tax gap estimates. Compliance and Enforcement, IR-2006-28, February 14). Retrieved from www.irs.gov/newsroom/article/0,,id=154496,00.html

Internal Revenue Service. 2006b. Tax return preparer fraud. Fact Sheet (February 16). Retrieved from http://www.irs.gov/newsroom/article/0,,id=153948,00.html

James, Simon R. 2002. *Taxation.* New York: Routledge.

Johnson, Thomas A. 2006. *Forensic computer crime investigation.* Boca Raton, FL: CRC Press.

Johnston, O. 1990. Government Accounting Office says S&L cost could rise to $500 billion. *Los Angeles Times* (April 7):1, 28.

Kane, John, and April D. Wall. 2006. *The national public survey on white collar crime.* Fairmont, WV: National White Collar Crime Center.

Miller, Roger LeRoy, and Frank B. Cross. 2005. *The legal and e-commerce environment.* Mason, OH: West Legal Studies in Business.

Murphy, Christopher. 2005. *Competitive intelligence: Gathering, analyzing, and putting it to work.* Burlington, VT: Gower.

National Institute of Justice. 2001. *Electronic crime scene investigation: A guide for first responders.* Washington, DC: U.S. Government Printing Office.

Noblett, Michael G. 1992. Computer analysis and response team (CART): The microcomputer as evidence. *Crime Laboratory Digest* 19(1):10–15.

Pedersen, Daniel, William Underhill, Marc Levenson, Tony Clifton, Melissa Roberts, Steven Strasser, and Peter McKillop. 1995. Busted! *Newsweek* (March 13):37–47.

Roberts, Barry S., and Robert A. Mann. 2005. *Smith and Robertson's business law.* Mason, OH: West Legal Studies in Business.

Schoen, John W. 2006. Corporate fraud alive and well in U.S. Retrieved from www.msnbc.msn.com/id/12762573/

Sharp, Arthur G. 1994. White-collar crime: More resources needed to combat growing trend. *Law & Order* 42(7):91–96.

Shover, Neal, and Andrew Hochstetler. 2006. *Choosing white-collar crime.* New York: Cambridge University Press.

Simpson, Sally. 2002. *Corporate crime, law, and social control.* New York: Cambridge University Press.

Smith, Russell G., Peter N. Grabosky, and Gregor Urbas. 2004. *Cyber criminals on trial.* New York: Cambridge University Press.

Steinhaus, Rochelle. 2004. Judge sentences Stewart to prison, but grants stay pending appeal. CourtTVnews (July 16). Retrieved from www.courttv.com/trials/stewart/071604_ctv.html

Sutherland, Edwin. 1949. *White collar crime.* New York: Dryden Press.

Vacca, John R. 2005. *Computer forensics: Computer crime scene investigation.* Hingham, MA: Charles River Media, Inc.

Wall, David S. 2006. *Crime and the Internet.* New York: Routledge.

Yeager, Peter, and Marshall Clinard. 2006. *Corporate crime.* New Brunswick, NJ: Transaction.

Chapter 21

Akers, Ronald L. 1992. *Drugs, alcohol, and society.* Belmont, CA: Wadsworth.

Associated Press. 2005. Congress poised to pass anti-meth Law. Retrieved from www.msnbc.msn.com/id/10405933/

Berg, Bruce L. 1992. *Law enforcement: An introduction to police in society,* Boston, MA: Allyn & Bacon.

Booth, Martin. 2004. *Cannabis: A history.* New York: Picador.

Carrol v. United States. 267 U.S. 132 (1925).

Chimel v. California. 395 U.S. 752 (1969).

Cohen, Sidney. 1964. *The beyond within.* New York: Atheneum.

Constantine, Thomas A. 1990. Drug wars. *The Police Chief* 57(5):37.

DAWN, 2004. Narcotic analgesics, 2002 update. *The DAWN Report.* Washington, DC: U.S. Department of Health & Human Services, U.S. Government Printing Office.

Drug Enforcement Administration. 2005. *Drugs of abuse.* Washington, DC: U.S. Department of Justice, U.S. Government Printing Office.

Eddy, Mark. 2003. War on drugs: Legislation in the 108th Congress and related developments. *Issue Brief for Congress.* Washington, DC: U.S. Government Printing Office, IB10113.

Falvo, Donna R. 2005. *Medical and psychosocial aspects of chronic illness and disability.* Sudbury, MA: Jones and Bartlett.

Feucht, Thomas E. 2006. Research on drugs and crime in the U.S. Paper presented at the 4th annual China–U.S. Symposium on Criminal Justice, Shanghai, China, October.

Florida v. Jimeno. 59 L.W. 4471 (May 23, 1991).

Fredrickson, Darin D., and Raymond P. Siljander. 2004. *Street drug investigation: A practical guide for plainclothes and uniformed personnel.* Springfield, Il: Charles C Thomas.

Gaines, Larry K., and Victor, E. Kappeler. 2005. *Policing in America* (5th ed.). Cincinnati, OH: Anderson.

Gieringer, Dale H. 2003. The acceptance of medical marijuana in the U.S. *Journal of Cannabis Therapeutics* 3(1):53–65.

Goldberg, Raymond. 2006. *Drugs across the spectrum.* Belmont CA: Thompson/Wadsworth.

Goode, Eric. 2004. *Drugs in American society.* Boston, MA: McGraw-Hill.

Gootenberg, Paul. 1999. *Cocaine.* New York: Routledge.

Heroin comes back. 1990. *Time* (February 19):63.

Huus, Kari. 2006. "Crystal cartels alter face of U.S. meth epidemic. Retrieved from www.msnbc.msn.com/id/14817871/

Inciardi, James, and Karen McElrath (eds.). 2004. *The American drug scene* (4th ed.). Los Angeles, CA: Roxbury.

Joy, Janet E., Stanley Watson Jr., and John A. Benson Jr. 1999. *Marijuana and medicine.* Washington, DC: National Academy Press.

Knowles, James Gordon. 1996. Dealing crack cocaine. *FBI Law Enforcement Bulletin* 65(7):1–7.

Ksir, Charles, Ray Oakley, and Carl L. Hart. 2005. *Drugs, society, and human behavior* (11th ed.). Boston, MA: McGraw-Hill.

Kuhn, Cynthia Swartzwelder, and Wilkie Wilson. 2003. *Buzzed: The straight facts about the most used and abused drugs from alcohol to ecstasy.* New York: W. W. Norton.

Lyman, Michael D. 1990. Minimizing danger in drug enforcement. *Law & Order* (September):143–147.

Lyman, Michael D. 2002. *Practical drug enforcement.* Boca Raton, FL: CRC Press.

Marx, Gary T. 1980. The new undercover police work. *Urban Life* (8):399–446.

Marx, Gary T. 1989. *Undercover: Police surveillance in America.* Berkeley, CA: University of California Press.

Miller, George I. 1987. Observations of police undercover work. *Criminology* 25:27–46.

Miller, Gary. 2005. *Drugs and the law: Detection, recognition and investigation* (3rd ed.). New York: Gould.

Musto, David. 2002. *Drugs in America: A historical reader.* New York: New York University Press.

National Institutes of Health. 2006. NIDA infofacts: MDMA (ecstasy). Washington, DC: U.S. Department of Health and Human Services, U.S. Government Printing Office.

Pennell, Susan. 1990. Ice: DUF interview results from san Diego. *NIJ Reports: Research in Action* (September):12–13.

Pogrebin, Mark, and Eric D. Poole. 2003. Vice isn't nice: A look at the effects of working undercover. In *Qualitative approaches to criminal justice: Perspectives from the field,* Mark Pogrebin (ed.). Thousand Oaks, CA: Sage.

Renteln, Alison Dundes. 2004. *The culture of defense.* New York: Oxford University Press.

Schuckit, Marc A. 1995. Chasing the dragon. In *The American drug scene,* James Inciardi and Karen McElrath (eds.). Los Angeles, CA: Roxbury.

Schuckit, Marc A. 2000. *Drugs and alcohol abuse: A clinical goal to diagnosis and treatment.* New York: Springer Science.

Siegel, Jay A., and Max M. Houck. 2006. *Fundamentals of forensic science.* Burlington, MA: Elsevier Academic Press.

South Dakota v. Opperman. 428 U.S. 364 (1976).

Stering, Robert. 2005. *Police officer's handbook: An introductory guide.* Sudbury, MA: Jones and Bartlett.

Swarbrick, James. 2004. *Encyclopedia of pharmaceutical technology* (2nd ed.). Boca Raton, FL: CRC Press.

Terry v. Ohio. 392 U.S. 1 (1968).

Walsh, Carol T., and Rochelle D. Schwartz-Bloom. 2004. *Levine's pharmacology: Drug actions and reactions* (7th ed.). New York: Taylor and Francis.

White, P. C. 2003. *Crime scene to court: The essentials of forensic science.* London, UK: Royal Society of Chemistry Press.

Yudko, Errol, Harold V. Hall, and Sandra B. McPherson. 2003. *Methamphetamine use: Clinical and forensic aspects.* Boca Raton, FL: CRC Press.

Zimmerman, Bill, Nancy Crumpacker, and Rick Bayer. 1998. *Is marijuana the right medicine for you?* New Canaan, CT: Keats.

Zinberg, Norman E. 1995. Nonaddictive opiate use. In *The American drug scene,* James Inciardi and Karen McElrath (eds.). Los Angeles, CA: Roxbury.

Chapter 22

A&M Records v. Napster. 239 F.3d 1004, 9th Cir. (2001).

Ahmad, Rashid, and Arun Joshi. 2006. Al-Qaeda drops bombshell, says has network in J&K. *Hindustan Times* (July 13):1.

Arquilla, John, David Ronfeldt, and Michele Zanini. 2006. In *Terrorism and counterterrorism,* Russell D. Howard and Reid L. Sawyer (eds.) Dubuque, IA: McGraw-Hill, pp. 107–129.

Ashcroft v. The Free Speech Coalition. 122 S. Ct. 1389 (2002).

Anti-Defamation League. 2002. *Countering suicide terrorism.* New York: Author.

Baca, Leroy D. 2006. Senate Committee on Homeland Security and Governmental Affairs. Testimony, of Leroy D. Baca, Sheriff, Los Angeles County (September 12). Retrieved from http://hsgac.senate.gov/_files/091206Baca.pdf

Bell, Arnold. 2004. Internet safety for the wired generation. Retrieved from www.fbi.gov/page2/sept04/cac090104.htm

Bhoumik, Arunabha. 2005. Democratic responses to terrorism: A comparative study of the United States, Israel, and India. *Denver Journal of International Law and Policy* (Spring):285.

Blundell, B., M. Sherry, A. Burke, and S. Sowerbutts. 2002. Child pornography and the Internet: Accessibility and policing. *Australian Police Journal* 56(1):59–65.

Bowker, Arthur, and Michael Gray. 2005. The cybersex offender and children. *FBI Law Enforcement Bulletin* 4(3):12–17.

Byers, Anne. 2003. *Lebanon's Hezbollah.* New York: Rosen.

Cisneros, Dannielle. 2002. 'Virtual child' pornography on the Internet: A 'virtual victim'? *Law & Technology Review* (19):1.

Collins, Geneva. 2004. Protecting children from online predators. *Community Links* (August):3–4.

Congressional Budget Office. 2005. *Federal funding for Homeland Security: An update* (July 20). Washington, DC: Author.

Department of Homeland Security. 2006. History: Who became part of the department? Retrieved from http://www.dhs.gov/xabout/history/editorial_0133.shtm

Department of Homeland Security. 2007. Strategic plan. Retrieved from www.dhs.gov/xabout/strategicplan/index.shtm

Dickey, Christopher. 1996. Terrorism: Target America. *Newsweek* (July 8):22–25.

Dobson, A. 2003. Caught in the net. *Care and Health* (February 13):609.

Donnerstein, E. 2002. The Internet. In *Children, adolescents and the media,* V. C. Strasburger and B. J. Wilson (eds.). Thousand Oaks, CA: Sage.

Edelson, Jeffrey L., and Raquel Kennedy Bergen. 2001. *Sourcebook on violence against women.* Thousand Oaks, CA: Sage.

Halperin, Morton. 2001. Less secure, less free: Striking terror at civil liberty. *The American Prospect* 12 (November 19):10–13.

Hoffman, Bruce. 2006. Defining terrorism. In *Terrorism and counterterrorism,* Russell D. Howard and Reid L. Sawyer (eds.). Dubuque, IA: McGraw-Hill, pp. 3–23.

Jewkes, Yvonne. 2007. *Crime online.* Cullomptom, Devon, UK: Willan Publishing.

Jewkes, Yvonne, and C. Andrews. 2005. Policing the filth: The problems of investigating online child pornography in England and Wales. *Policing and Society* 15:42–62.

Johnson, Jeff. 2002. Tearful FBI agent apologizes to Sept. 11 families and victims. Retrieved from www.cnsnews.com/ViewNation.asp?Page=/Nation/archive/200205/NAT20020530d.html

Johnston, David, and Van Natta Jr. 2002. Wary of risk, slow to adapt, FBI stumbles in terror war. *New York Times* (June 2), Section 1, p. 24.

Jurgensmeyer, Mark. 2000. *Terror in the mind of God.* Berkeley, CA: University of California Press.

Kushner, H. 1996. Suicide bombers: Business as usual. *Studies in Conflict and Terrorism* 19:329–338.

LaFree, Gary. 2005. *Setting a criminological agenda for the study of terrorism and homeland security.* Paper presented at the 14th World Congress of Criminology. Philadelphia, PA.

Lamy, Philip. 1996. *Millennium rage.* New York: Plenum Press.

Martin, Augustus. 2003. *Understanding terrorism: Challenges, perspectives, and issues.* Thousand Oaks, CA: Sage.

Martin, Augustus. 2004. *The new era of terrorism: Selected readings.* Thousand Oaks, CA: Sage.

Merkl, Peter H., and Leonard Weinberg. 2003. *Right-wing extremism in the twenty-first century.* Portland, OR: Frank Cass.

Milhorn, Thomas. 2005. *Crime: Computer viruses to twin towers.* Boca Raton, FL: Universal.

MPAA v. The People. C 04-04862 WHA (2004).

Murphy, Gerald R., and Martha R. Plotkin. 2003. *Protecting your community from terrorism: Strategies for local law enforcement, Vol. 1: Local-federal partnerships.* Washington, DC: Community Oriented Policing Services and Police Executive Research Forum.

O'Connell, Rachel. 2001. Pedophiles networking on the Internet. In *Child abuse on the Internet: Ending the silence,* Carlos Arnaldo (ed.). New York: Berghahn Books, pp. 65–80.

Office of the Inspector General. 2006. *Report to Congress on implementation of section 1001 of the USA PATRIOT Act.* Washington, DC: U.S. Department of Justice, U.S. Government Printing Office.

Painton, Priscilla. 1993. Who could have done it? *Time* (March 8):33.

Pedahzur, Ami. 2005. *Suicide terrorism.* Malden, MA: Polity Press.

Ross, Jeffrey Ian, and Ted R. Gurr. 1989. Why terrorism subsides: A comparative study of Canada and the United States. *Journal of Comparative Politics* 21:405–420.

Roth, Siobahn. 2003. Material support law: Weapon in the war on terror. *Legal Times* (May 9).

Roth, Stephen. 2002. *Anti-Semitism worldwide.* Lincoln, NE: University of Nebraska Press.

Sanderson, Christiane. 2005. *The Seduction of children: Empowering parents and teachers to protect children from child sexual abuse.* Philadelphia, PA: Jessica Kingsley.

Simon, L. 2000. An examination of the assumptions of specialization, mental disorder, and dangerousness in sex offenders. *Behavioral Science and the Law* 18:275–308.

Snow, Robert L. 2002. *Terrorist among us: The militia threat.* Cambridge, MA: Perseus.

U.S. Department of Defense. 2007. What is terrorism? Retrieved March 19, 2007, from http://www.Terrorism-research.com.

U.S. Department of State. 2004. *Patterns of global terrorism 2003.* Washington, DC: U.S. Government Printing Office.

Watson, Dale L. 2002. Executive Assistant Director, Counterterrorism and Counter Intelligence, FBI, "Statement for the Record on the Terrorist Threat Confronting the United States, made before the Senate Select Committee on Intelligence." February 6.

Wellard, S. 2001. Cause and effect. *Community Care* (March 15):26–27.

White, Jonathan R. 2006. *Terrorism and homeland security.* Belmont, CA: Wadsworth.

Wolak Janis, Kimberly Mitchell, and David Finkelhor. 2003. *Internet sex crimes against minors: The response of law enforcement.* Durham, NH: National Center for Missing and Exploited Children.

Wortley, Richard, and Stephen Smallbone. 2006. *Child pornography on the Internet.* Washington, DC: U.S. Department of Justice Office of Community Oriented Policing Services. Problem Oriented Guides for Police, Problem-Specific Guides Series No. 41.

PHOTO CREDITS

INDEX